# *POLITICAL PARTIES AND CIVIC ACTION GROUPS*

**The Greenwood Encyclopedia of American Institutions**

Each work in the *Encyclopedia* is designed to provide concise histories of major voluntary groups and nonprofit organizations that have played significant roles in American civic, cultural, political, and economic life from the colonial era to the present. Previously published:

1. *Labor Unions*
Gary M Fink, Editor-in-Chief

2. *Social Service Organizations*
Peter Romanofsky, Editor-in-Chief

3. *Fraternal Organizations*
Alvin J. Schmidt

The Greenwood Encyclopedia of American Institutions

# Political Parties and Civic Action Groups

EDWARD L. SCHAPSMEIER AND
FREDERICK H. SCHAPSMEIER

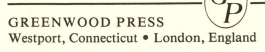

GREENWOOD PRESS
Westport, Connecticut • London, England

**Library of Congress Cataloging in Publication Data**

Schapsmeier, Edward L
  Political parties and civic action groups.

  (The Greenwood encyclopedia of American institutions)
  Bibliography:  p.
  Includes index.
  1.  Political parties—United States—Handbooks,
manuals, etc.  2.  Political clubs—United States
—Handbooks, manuals, etc.  I.  Schapsmeier,
Frederick H., joint author.  II.  Title.  III.  Series:
Greenwood encyclopedia of American institutions.
JK2260.S36        324.273                    80-1714
ISBN 0-313-21442-5 (lib. bdg.)

Library of Congress Catalog Card Number: 80-1714
ISBN: 0-313-21442-5

First published in 1981

Greenwood Press
A division of Congressional Information Service, Inc.
88 Post Road West, Westport, Connecticut 06881

Printed in the United States of America

10 9 8 7 6 5 4 3 2

TO MARY, ANDREW, SANDRA, AND WILLIAM
WITH LOVE AND AFFECTION

# CONTENTS

*Tables*                                                        xxvii

*Consultants*                                                    xxix

*Preface*                                                        xxxi

**A** _____

Action Committee to Increase Opportunities for Negroes            3
Action on Smoking and Health                                      3
AFL-CIO Committee on Political Education. See Committee on
    Political Education                        4
AFL-Labor's League for Political Education: See Labor's League
    for Political Education                     4
Afro-American Party                                               4
Albany Regency                                                    4
Alianza Federal de Mercedes                                       5
Alianza Hispano-Americano                                         6
Alimony Unlimited: See Committee for Fair Divorce and
    Alimony Laws                               7
All American Council                                              7
Alliance for Displaced Homemakers                                 8
Alternative Candidate Task Force for 1968                         9
America First Committee                                          10
America First Party: See Constitution Party                      11
American Agriculture Movement                                    11
American Agri-Women                                              13
American and Foreign Anti-Slavery Society                        13
American Anti-Slavery Society                                    14
American Anti-Vivisection Society                                15
American Assembly                                                16

American Association for the United Nations: See United Nations
   Association of the United States of America    16
American Association of Retired Persons    16
American Association of University Women    17
American Association on Indian Affairs: See Association on American
   Indian Affairs    18
American Automobile Association    18
American Bar Association    19
American Beat Consensus    20
American Bimetallic League    21
American Civil Liberties Union    21
American Coalition of Patriotic Societies    23
American Colonization Society    24
American Commonwealth Political Federation    25
American Conservative Union    26
American Council of Christian Churches    27
American Council of Young Political Leaders    28
American Council on Alcohol Problems: See Anti-Saloon League
   of America    28
American Country Life Association    28
American Equal Rights Association    30
American Farm Bureau Federation    30
American Federation of Labor Committee on Political Education:
   See Committee on Political Education    32
American Federation of Labor-Congress of Industrial
   Organization Political Action Committee: See Political
   Action Committee    32
American First Party: See Christian Nationalist Party    32
American Independent Party    32
American Indian Defense Association: See Association on American
   Indian Affairs    36
American Indian Movement    36
American Indo-China Veterans Legion    37
American Institute of International Affairs: See Council on
   Foreign Relations    38
American Labor Party    38
American League against War and Fascism    39
American League for Peace and Democracy: See American League
   against War and Fascism    40
American League to Abolish Capital Punishment    40
American Legion    41
American Legislators Association: See Council of State
   Governments    43
American Liberty League    43

American Library Association 44
American Medical Political Action Committee 45
American Municipal Association: See National League of Cities 46
American National Party 46
American Nazi Party: See National Socialist White People's Party 47
American Negro Labor Congress: See National Negro Congress 47
American Parole Association: See National Council on Crime and
    Delinquency 47
American Party (1856): See Know-Nothing Party 47
American Party (1968): See American Independent Party 47
American Peace Society 47
American Protective Association 48
American Protective Tariff League: See Trade Relations Council
    of the United States 49
American Republican Party: See American Independent Party 49
American Security Council 49
American Society for Public Administration 50
American Society for the Prevention of Cruelty to Animals 51
American Society of Sanitary Engineering 51
American Union against Militarism 52
American Vegetarian Party 53
American Veterans Committee 54
American Veterans of Foreign Service: See Veterans of Foreign Wars
    of the United States 54
American Veterans of World War II-Korea-Vietnam: See AMVETS 54
American Woman Suffrage Association 54
American Workers Party: See Conference for Progressive
    Labor Action 55
Americans for Constitutional Action 55
Americans for Democratic Action 56
Americans for Energy Independence 58
Americans for Indian Opportunity 59
Amnesty International 60
AMVETS 61
Anarchist Federation 62
Anti-Defamation League of the B'nai B'rith 63
Anti-Enlistment League: See War Resisters League 64
Anti-Federalist Party 64
Anti-Imperialist League 65
Anti-Masonic Party 66
Anti-Monopoly Party 67
Anti-Saloon League of America 67
Armed Forces of Puerto Rican National Liberation: See Fuerzas
    Armádas de Liberacíon Nacional Puertorriqueña 69

Army of the Philippines, Cuba, and Puerto Rico: See Veterans of
  Foreign Wars of the United States                                69
Association against the Prohibition Amendment                      69
Association for Humane Abortion: See Association for the Study
  of Abortion                                                     71
Association for the Study of Abortion                             71
Association on American Indian Affairs                            72


**B**

Bipartisan Congressional Clearinghouse                            73
Birch Society, John: See John Birch Society                       73
Black Congressional Caucus                                        73
Black Panther Party                                               74
Black Panthers: See Black Panther Party                          76
Black Political Convention: See National Black Political Assembly 76
Blind Federation: See National Federation of the Blind           76
Bonus Army                                                        76
Bonus Expeditionary Force: See Bonus Army                        77
Bonus Marchers: See Bonus Army                                   77
Breckinridge Democrats: See National Democratic Party            77
Brookings Institution                                            77
Bull Moose Party: See Progressive Party (1912)                   78
Bull Moosers: See Progressive Party (1912)                       79
Business and Professional Women's Clubs, Inc., The Federation
  of: See National Federation of Business and Professional
  Women's Clubs                                                   79
Business-Industry Political Action Committee                     79
Byrd Machine                                                     79


**C**

Carnegie Endowment for International Peace                        81
Catholic War Veterans of the United States of America            82
Catholic Workers Movement                                        82
Center for Community Change                                       84
Center for the Study of Responsive Law: See Public Interest
  Research Group                                                  84
Cermak Machine: See Democratic Central Committee of
  Cook County                                                    84
Chamber of Commerce of the United States                         84
Chicago Boss System: See Democratic Central Committee of
  Cook County                                                    86

Christian American Patriots: See Christian Party    86
Christian Anti-Communism Crusade    86
Christian Crusade    88
Christian Freedom Foundation    89
Christian Front    89
Christian Nationalist Crusade: See Christian Nationalist Party    90
Christian Nationalist Party    90
Christian Party    91
Church of God Party: See Theocratic Party    92
Church Peace Union: See Council on Religion and International
   Affairs    92
CIO-Political Action Committee: See Political Action Committee    92
Citizens Committee for the Right to Keep and Bear Arms    92
Citizens Conference on State Legislatures    93
Citizens' Councils of America    94
Citizen's Party    96
City Managers' Association: See International City Management
   Association    96
Coalition for a Democratic Majority    97
Coalition for Human Needs and Budget Priorities    98
Commission on Interracial Cooperation: See Southern
   Regional Council    98
Committee for a Free China: See Committee of One Million    98
Committee for Economic Development    99
Committee for Fair Divorce and Alimony Laws    100
Committee for Nonviolent Action    100
Committee for the Nation to Rebuild Prices and Purchasing Power    101
Committee for the New Majority    102
Committee of Americans for the Canal Treaties    102
Committee of One Million    103
Committee on Conservative Alternatives: See American
   Conservative Union    105
Committee on Militarism in Education    105
Committee on Political Education    105
Committee to Defend America by Aiding the Allies    107
Committee to Support Moderate Republicans: See Republicans
   for Progress    108
Committees of Correspondence    108
Committees of Safety: See Committees of Correspondence    108
Common Cause    108
Commongood Party: See People's Party (1971)    110
Commonweal of Christ: See Coxey's Army    110
Communist Labor Party: See Communist Party of the United
   States of America    110

Communist Party of America: See Communist Party of the
    United States of America    110
Communist Party of the United States (Marxist-Leninist): See
    Communist Party of the United States of America    110
Communist Party of the United States of America    110
Communist Party, U.S.A.: See Communist Party of the United
    States of America    116
Communist Political Association: See Communist Party of the
    United States of America    116
Conference for Progressive Political Action    116
Congress of Industrial Organization-Political Action Committee:
    See Political Action Committee    117
Congress of Racial Equality    117
Congress on Population and Environment: See Council on
    Population and Environment    118
Conservative Caucus, The    118
Conservative Party    120
Conservative Party of New York: See Conservative Party    121
Conservative Union: See American Conservative Union    121
Constitution Parties of the United States: See Constitution Party    121
Constitution Party    121
Constitutional Union Party    123
Consumer Federation of America    124
Continental Association    124
Cook County Machine: See Democratic Central Committee of
    Cook County    125
CORE: See Congress of Racial Equality    125
Council of Energy Resources Tribes    125
Council of State Governments    125
Council on Foreign Relations    126
Council on Population and Environment    127
Country Life Association: See American Country Life
    Association    128
Country People's Caucus: See People's Party (1971)    128
Country People's Party: See People's Party (1971)    128
Cox Machine    128
Coxey's Army    128
Crazies    129
Crump Machine    130

# D

Daley Machine: See Democratic Central Committee of
    Cook County    133

Democratic Advisory Council 133
Democratic (Breckinridge Faction) Party: See National
   Democratic Party 134
Democratic Central Committee of Cook County 134
Democratic National Committee 136
Democratic Party 137
Democratic-Republican Party 158
Democratic Study Group 160
Democrats: See Democratic Party 160
Deutschamerikanische Volksbund: See German-American Bund 161
Dirty Shirt Party: See Workingmen's Party 161
Disabled American Veterans 161
Disabled Veterans of the World War: See Disabled American
   Veterans 162
Dixiecrat Party: See States' Rights Party 162
Du Bois Clubs of America: See W. E. B. Du Bois Clubs of America 162

# E

Education for Democracy 163
Emergency Peace Campaign 163
End Poverty in California 164
Equal Rights Democrats: See Equal Rights (Locofoco) Party 164
Equal Rights (Locofoco) Party 164
Equal Rights Party (1872) 165
Equal Rights Party (1884) 165
Essex Junto 166

# F

Fair Campaign Practices Committee 168
Fair Play for Cuba Committee 168
Farm Bureau: See American Farm Bureau Federation 169
Farmer-Labor Party 169
Farmer's Educational and Cooperative Union of America: See
   National Farmers Union 170
Farmers Holiday Association 170
Farmers Union: See National Farmers Union 170
Federalist Party 170
Federalists: See Federalist Party 172

Federation of American Zionists: See Zionist Organization
  of America                                                            172
Fellowship of Reconciliation                                           172
Fight for Freedom                                                      173
Filipino American Political Association                                173
Foreign Policy Association                                             174
Fraternal Order of Police                                              175
Free Democracy of the United States: See Free Soil Party               177
Free Democratic Party: See Free Soil Party                             177
Free Libertarian Party: See Libertarian Party                          178
Free Soil Party                                                        178
Free Speech League                                                     179
Freedom and Peace Party                                                179
Freedom Center International                                           180
Freedom Democrats: See Mississippi Freedom Democratic Party            180
Freedom Now Party                                                      180
Freedoms Foundation at Valley Forge                                    180
Free-State Party                                                       183
Friends of the Earth: See League of Conservation Voters                183
Friends Peace Committee                                                184
Fuerzas Armádas de Liberacíon Nacional Puertorriqueña                  184

## G

German-American Bund                                                   187
Gold Bugs: See National Democratic Party                               188
Gold Democrats: See National Democratic Party                          188
GOP: See Republican Party                                              188
Governors' Conference: See National Governors' Conference              188
Grand Army of the Republic                                             188
Grand Old Party: See Republican Party                                  189
Grange: See National Grange                                            189
Gray Panthers                                                          189
Green Cross: See National Safety Council                               190
Greenback Independent Party: See Greenback Party                       190
Greenback Nationalist Party: See Greenback Party                       190
Greenback Party                                                        190
Greenback-Labor and National Party: See Greenback Party                192
Greenback-Labor Party: See Greenback Party                             192

## H

Hartford Convention: See Essex Junto                                   193
Home Prohibition Party: See Prohibition Party                          193

Human Rights Party: See People's Party (1971)                    193

## I

Immigration Restriction League                                   194
Independence League: See Independence Party                      195
Independence Party                                               195
Independent Citizens Committee for the Arts, Sciences and
   Professions                                    196
Independent (Greenback) Party: See Greenback Party               197
Independent National Party: See Greenback Party                  197
Independent Party: See Greenback Party                           197
Independent Progressive Party                                    197
Independent Republican Party                                     198
Independent Republicans: See Mugwumps                            198
Indian Rights Association                                        198
Industrial Workers of the World: See Anarchist Federation        199
Institute for Democratic Education. See Anti-Defamation League
   of the B'nai B'rith                            199
Institute for Government Research: See Brookings Institution     199
Institute for Policy Studies: See National Conference of Alternative
   State and Local Public Policies                199
Institute of Medicine: See National Academy of Sciences         199
Intercollegiate Socialist Society of America: See League for
   Industrial Democracy                           199
International City Management Association                         199
International City Managers' Association: See International City
   Management Association                         200
International Congress of Women: See Women's International
   League for Peace and Freedom                    200
International Downtown Executives Association                     200
International Working People's Association                        201
Invisible Empire of the Knights of the Ku Klux Klan: See
   Ku Klux Klan                                    202
IWW: See Anarchist Federation                                    202

## J

Jeffersonian Democrats: See Democratic-Republican Party          203
Jeffersonian Republicans: See Democratic-Republican Party        203
Jewish Defense League                                            203
Jewish Socialist Verband of America                              205
Jobless Party                                                    205

John Birch Society                                                         206
Join Hands                                                                 208


**K** _____

Keep America Out of War Congress                                           210
Kelly-Nash Machine: See Democratic Central Committee
  of Cook County                                                 210
Knights of Columbus                                                        210
Knights of the Golden Circle                                               211
Knights of the White Camelia                                               213
Know-Nothing Party                                                         214
Ku Klux Klan                                                               216


**L** _____

La Raza Unida Party                                                        220
Labor Party: See Farmer-Labor Party                                        221
Labor Reform Party: See National Labor Reform Party                        221
Labor's League for Political Education                                     221
Land Labor Clubs: See Single Tax Movement                                  222
League for Independent Political Action                                    222
League for Industrial Democracy                                            223
League of Conservation Voters                                              225
League of Nations Association: See Foreign Policy Association              226
League of United Southerners                                               226
League of Women Voters of the United States                                226
League to Enforce Peace                                                    227
Liberal Party                                                              228
Liberal Republican Party                                                   229
Liberal Union, The: See People's Party (1971)                              230
Libertarian League: See Anarchist Federation                               230
Libertarian Party                                                          230
Liberty League: See American Liberty League                                232
Liberty Lobby                                                              232
Liberty Party (1839)                                                       233
Liberty Party (1932)                                                       234
Liberty Union: See People's Party (1971)                                   235
Locofoco Party: See Equal Rights (Locofoco) Party                          235
Lowndes County Freedom Organization                                        235
Loyal Democrats of Mississippi                                             235

# M

Marine Corps League                                                              237
Mayors Conference: See United States Conference of Mayors                        238
Mexican-American Political Association                                           238
Midwestern Governors Conference                                                 239
Minutemen: See Patriotic Party                                                  239
Mississippi Freedom Democratic Party                                            239
Mississippi Valley Association: See Water Resources Congress                    240
Mobilization Committee to End the War in Vietnam                                240
Moral Majority                                                                  241
Morality in Media                                                               243
Movement for a New Congress                                                     244
Mugwumps                                                                        245

# N

Nader's Raiders: See Public Interest Research Group                             246
National Academy of Sciences                                                    246
National Afro-American Council: See National Afro-American League               247
National Afro-American League                                                   247
National Alliance of Businessmen                                                248
National American Woman Suffrage Association                                    249
National Association for the Advancement of Colored People                      250
National Association Knights of the Ku Klux Klan: See Ku Klux Klan              252
National Association of Broadcasters                                            252
National Association of Manufacturers                                           252
National Association of Probation Officers: See National Council
     on Crime and Delinquency                                                   254
National Association on Indian Affairs: See Association on
     American Indian Affairs                                                    254
National Black Political Assembly                                               254
National Center for Voluntary Action                                            255
National Christian Association                                                  256
National Christian Democratic Party                                            257
National Citizens Political Action Committee                                    257
National Civic Federation                                                       258
National Civil Service League                                                   259
National Civil Service Reform League: See National Civil
     Service League                                                             260
National Committee for a Sane Nuclear Policy, The: See SANE:
     A Citizens' Organization for a Sane World                                  260
National Committee for an Effective Congress                                    261

National Committee for Citizens in Education 261
National Committee for Support of the Public Schools: See National
    Committee for Citizens in Education 262
National Committee of Inquiry 262
National Committee on the Cause and Cure of War 263
National Committee to Free America from Jewish Domination:
    See National Socialist White People's Party 263
National Conference for a New Politics 263
National Conference of Alternative State and Local Public
    Policies 264
National Conference of Christians and Jews 265
National Conference of Concerned Democrats 266
National Conference of State Legislative Leaders 267
National Conference of State Legislatures 267
National Congress of Parents and Teachers 268
National Constitutional Party: See Constitutional Union Party 270
National Council for Historic Site and Buildings: See National
    Trust for Historic Preservation 270
National Council for Industrial Safety: See National Safety Council 270
National Council for Prevention of War 270
National Council for the Limitation of Armaments: See National
    Council for Prevention of War 271
National Council of Senior Citizens 271
National Council of Senior Citizens for Health Care under Social
    Security: See National Council of Senior Citizens 272
National Council of Women of the United States 272
National Council on Crime and Delinquency 273
National Democratic Party (1860) 275
National Democratic Party (1896) 276
National Democratic Party of Alabama 277
National Education Association: See National Education
    Association-Political Action Committee 278
National Education Association-Political Action Committee 278
National Emergency Committee 281
National Equal Rights League 282
National Farm Women's Forum: See American Agri-Women 283
National Farmers Organization 283
National Farmers Union 284
National Federation of Business and Professional Women's Clubs 285
National Federation of Republican Women 287
National Federation of the Blind 287
National Governors' Conference 288

National Grange                                                                290
National (Greenback) Party: See Greenback Party                                292
National Greenback-Labor Party: See Greenback Party                            292
National Gun Control Center                                                    292
National Hamiltonian Party                                                     292
National Housing Conference                                                    293
National Labor Reform Party                                                    294
National League of Cities                                                      295
National Legislative Conference                                                295
National Liberty Party                                                         296
National Municipal League                                                      296
National Negro Congress                                                        298
National Order of Women Legislators                                           299
National Organization for the Reform of Marijuana Laws                         300
National Organization for Women                                                300
National Party                                                                 303
National Planning Association                                                  303
National Probation Association: See National Council on Crime
   and Delinquency                                              305
National Progressive Republican League                                         305
National Progressives of America                                              306
National Republican Congressional Committee                                    307
National Republican Heritage Groups Council                                    308
National Republican Party                                                      308
National Research Council: See National Academy of Sciences                    310
National Rifle Association: See National Rifle Association
   of America                                                   310
National Rifle Association of America                                          310
National Right to Life Committee                                               312
National Right to Work Committee                                               314
National Rivers and Harbors Congress: See Water
   Resources Congress                                           315
National Safety Council                                                        315
National Security League                                                       316
National Silver Party: See Silver Republican Party                             317
National Silver Republican Party: See Silver Republican Party                  317
National Silver Republicans: See Silver Republican Party                       317
National Small Business Association                                            317
National Socialist White People's Party                                        318
National Society of State Legislators                                          319
National Society of the Army of the Philippines: See Veterans of
   Foreign Wars of the United States                            320

National States' Rights Party                                          320
National Student Association                                           321
National Student Lobby                                                 323
National Taxpayers Union                                               324
National Teachers' Association                                         324
National Tenants Organization                                         324
National Trust for Historic Preservation                              325
National Union for Social Justice                                     326
National Union Party                                                   327
National Union Republican Party: See National Union Party             328
National Woman Suffrage Association                                    328
National Woman's Christian Temperance Union: See Woman's
  Christian Temperance Union                                          329
National Woman's Party                                                 329
National Women's Political Caucus                                      330
National Youth Alliance                                                331
National Party of Puerto Rico: See Fuerzas Armádas de Liberacion
  Nacíonal Puertorriqueña                                             332
Nationalities Division of the Democratic National Committee: See
  All American Council                                                332
National-Wide Committee on Import-Export Policy                       332
Native American Party: See Know-Nothing Party                         333
Navy League of the United States                                      334
Nazi Party: See National Socialist White People's Party               335
New American Party: See People's Party (1971)                         335
New Party: See People's Party (1971)                                  335
Niagara Movement                                                       335
No Party: See People's Party                                           336
Non-Partisan Committee for Peace through Revision of the
  Neutrality Act                                                      336
Nonpartisan League                                                     337
Nonviolent Action Against Nuclear Weapons: See Committee
  for Nonviolent Action                                               338
Northern Irish Aid Committee                                           338

# O

Old Age Revolving Pensions, Ltd.: See Townsend Plan
  National Lobby                                                      340
Order of the Star-Spangled Banner: See Know-Nothing Party             340
Order of United Americans: See Know-Nothing Party                     340

Organization of Afro-American Unity 340
Other Americans, Inc.: See Society of Separationists 341

# P

Pacifica Foundation: See War Resisters League 342
Paralyzed Veterans of America 342
Patriotic Party 343
Patrons of Husbandry: See National Grange 344
Peace and Freedom Party 344
Pendergast Machine 344
People United to Save Humanity 346
People's Party (1823) 347
People's Party (1891): See Populist Party 348
People's Party (1971) 348
People's Peace Prosperity Party 350
Polish National Alliance 350
Political Action Committee 351
Political Rights Defense Fund: See Young Socialist Alliance 354
Poor Man's Party 354
Poor People's Campaign 354
Popular Front: See Communist Party of the United States
  of America 355
Populist Party 355
Progressive Alliance 357
Progressive Citizens of America 358
Progressive Labor Party 359
Progressive Party (1912) 361
Progressive Party (1924) 363
Progressive Party (1948) 364
Prohibition Party 366
Protect America's Children 370
PTA: See National Congress of Parents and Teachers 370
Public Citizens, Inc.: See Public Interest Research Group 370
Public Interest Research Group 370
PUSH: See People United to Save Humanity 372

# Q

Quay Machine 373

# R

Radical Republicans                                                        375
Referendum '70                                                            376
Republican Congressional Committee: See National Republican
    Congressional Committee                           377
Republican Governors Association                                          377
Republican National Committee                                             377
Republican Party                                                          378
Republicans: See Republican Party                                        398
Republicans for Progress                                                  398
Resurgence Youth Movement: See Anarchist Federation                      399
Revolutionary Youth Movement: See Students for a Democratic
    Society                                           399
Right to Life Committee: See National Right to Life Committee            399
Right to Work Committee: See National Right to Work Committee            399
Ripon Society                                                            399
Rural American Women, Inc.                                               400

# S

SANE: A Citizens' Organization for a Sane World                          402
Save Our Children: See Protect America's Children                        404
Senior Citizens: See National Council of Senior Citizens                404
Share Our Wealth Movement                                               404
Sierra Club                                                              404
Silver Republican Party                                                  406
Silver Republicans: See Silver Republican Party                         406
Silver Shirts: See Christian Party                                      406
Single Tax Clubs: See Single Tax Movement                               406
Single Tax Movement                                                     406
Social Democracy of America: See Social Democratic Party
    of America                                       407
Social Democratic Federation                                            407
Social Democratic Party of America                                      408
Social Democratic Workingmen's Party: See Socialist Labor Party         408
Socialist Labor Party                                                   408
Socialist Party of America                                              413
Socialist Party-Democratic Socialist Federation: See Socialist
    Party of America                                 420
Socialist Workers Party                                                 421
Society for the Prevention of Cruelty to Animals: See American
    Society for the Prevention of Cruelty to Animals  424
Society of Christian Socialists                                         424

Society of Saint Tammany: See Tammany Hall 424
Society of Separationists 424
Society of Tammany: See Tammany Hall 425
Sons of Liberty 425
Sound Money Democrats: See National Democratic Party 426
South Carolina Colored Democratic Party: See South Carolina
    Progressive Democratic Party 426
South Carolina Progressive Democratic Party 426
Southeastern Governors' Conference: See Southern Governors'
    Conference 427
Southern Christian Leadership Conference 427
Southern Governors' Conference 430
Southern Regional Council 431
States' Rights Party 432
Statesman Party. See Prohibition Party 433
Straight-Out Democratic Party 434
Student Committee for the Loyalty Oath: See Young Americans
    for Freedom 434
Student Coordinating Committee: See Student Nonviolent
    Coordinating Committee 434
Student League for Industrial Democracy: See Students for a
    Democratic Society 434
Student Nonviolent Coordination Committee 434
Students for a Democratic Society 436
Support Your Local Police Committee: See John Birch Society 440

T

Tammy Hall 441
Tax Cut Party 442
Television Broadcasters Association: See National Association
    of Broadcasters 443
Theocratic Party 443
Townsend Clubs: See Townsend Plan National Lobby 443
Townsend Clubs of America: See Townsend Plan National Lobby 443
Townsend National Insurance Plan, Inc.: See Townsend Plan
    National Lobby 443
Townsend National Recovery Plan, Inc.: See Townsend Plan
    National Lobby 443
Townsend Plan: See Townsend Plan National Lobby 443
Townsend Plan, Inc. See Townsend Plan National Lobby 443
Townsend Plan National Lobby 443
Trade Relations Council of the United States 445

Trilateral Commission, The                                                     446
Tweed Ring: See Tammany Hall                                                   447

# U

Union Labor Party                                                              448
Union League                                                                   449
Union Party                                                                    450
United Citizens' Party                                                         451
United Communist Party: See Communist Party of the United
  States of America                                                           452
United Farmers Educational League                                             452
United Klans of American Knights of the Ku Klux Klan: See
  Ku Klux Klan                                                                453
United Labor Party                                                            453
United Nations Association of the United States of America                    454
United State Committee for the United Nations: See United
  Nations Association of the United States of America                         455
United States Committee to Aid the National Liberation Front
  of South Vietnam                                                            455
United States Conference of Mayors                                            456
United States National Student Association: See National
  Student Association                                                         457
Universal Negro Improvement Association                                       457
Universal Party                                                               458
Urban Coalition Action Council of New York: See Common Cause                  458

# V

Veterans of Foreign Wars of the United States                                 459
VFW: See Veterans of Foreign Wars of the United States                       460
Voter Education Project                                                       460

# W

War Resisters League                                                          462
Water Resources Association: See Water Resources Congress                     463
Water Resources Congress                                                      463
Weather Underground: See Weatherman                                           464
Weatherman                                                                    464
Weatherpeople: See Weatherman                                                 466
W. E. B. Du Bois Clubs of America                                             466
Western Governors' Conference                                                 467
Whig Party                                                                    468

White Citizens Councils: See Citizens' Councils of America          471
William Allen White Committee: See Committee to Defend America
   by Aiding the Allies                                             471
Wisconsin Progressive Party                                         471
Wobblies: See Anarchist Federation                                  472
Woman's Christian Temperance Union                                  472
Woman's Peace Party                                                 473
Women's International League for Peace and Freedom                  474
Women's Militia: See Weatherman                                     476
Women's National Democratic Club                                    476
Women's National Republican Club                                    476
Women's Organization for National Prohibition Reform               477
Workers (Communist) Party of America: See Communist Party
   of the United States of America                                478
Workers Party of America: See Communist Party of the United
   States of America                                              478
Workingmen's Party                                                  478
World Federalists                                                   479

## Y

Young Americans for Freedom                                         480
Young Communist League                                              481
Young Democratic Clubs of America: See Young Democrats
   of America                                                     483
Young Democrats of America                                          483
Young People's Socialist League                                     484
Young Progressives of America                                       486
Young Republican National Federation                                486
Young Socialist Alliance                                            487
YRs: See Young Republican National Federation                       488

## Z

Zionist Organization of America                                     489

*Appendix 1: Listing of Organizations by Primary Function*          491

Agricultural and Rural Organizations                                491
Associations and Societies                                          491
Business Groups                                                     492
Civic Improvement Organizations                                     493
Civil Rights Groups                                                 493

Committees and Congresses                                    494
Conferences and Clubs                                       495
Councils, Institutes, and Foundations                       496
Educational Organizations                                   496
Federations and Leagues                                     497
Foreign Affairs Groups                                      498
Good Government Groups                                      499
Humanitarian Organizations                                  499
Labor Parties and Organizations                             500
Lobbies                                                      500
Minority Parties and Organizations                          502
Patriotic Parties and Societies                             503
Peace Groups                                                 503
Political and Organizational Movements                      504
Political Machines, Caucuses, and Coalitions                505
Political Parties                                            506
Professional Organizations                                  508
Reform Groups                                                508
Religious Groups and Associations                           509
Special Interest Groups                                      510
Veterans' Organizations                                      511
Women's Groups                                               512
Youth Groups                                                 512


*Appendix 2: Chronology*                                     515
*Glossary*                                                   529
*Index*                                                      539

# TABLES

1. American Independent Party Presidential Candidates and Votes,
   1968-1976                                                                35

2. Communist Party of the United States (CPUSA) Presidential
   Candidates and Votes, 1924-1980                                         115

3. Constitution Party Presidential Candidates and Votes,
   1952-1964                                                               122

4. Democratic Party Presidential Candidates and Votes, 1828-1980     157

5. Free Soil Party Presidential Candidates and Votes, 1848-1852      179

6. Greenback Party Presidential Candidates and Votes, 1876-1888      191

7. Populist Party Presidential Candidates and Votes, 1892-1908       356

8. Prohibition Party Presidential Candidates and Votes,
   1872-1980                                                               367

9. Republican Party Presidential Candidates and Votes, 1856-1980     380

10. Socialist Labor Party Presidential Candidates and Votes,
    1892-1976                                                              409

11. Socialist Party of America Presidential Candidates and Votes,
    1904-1980                                                              414

12. Socialist Workers Party Presidential Candidates and Votes,
    1948-1980                                                              422

13. Whig Party Presidential Candidates and Votes, 1836-1856          469

# CONSULTANTS

Howard Ball, Professor of Political Science, Mississippi State University

Jack S. Blocker, Jr., Professor of History, Huron College

Maria J. Falco, Dean, College of Arts and Science, Loyola University

Charles Gotsch, Professor of Social Sciences and Humanities, Columbia-Green Community College

Bernard K. Johnpoll, Professor of Political Science, State University of New York at Albany

# PREFACE

Americans best demonstrate the fact they are truly a nation of joiners through political action. Organized protest invariably takes the form of collective action. Individual activists seek to fulfill their role as concerned citizens by becoming a member of a political organization—be it a party or civic action group. In his classic *Democracy in America* (1835), Alexis de Toqueville cogently observed, "In no country in the world has the principle of association been more successfully used, or applied to a greater multitude of objects, than in America." These words are just as true now as when they were written.

Political organizations existed in the United States even before nationhood. Sometimes they were structured, often they were informal, and frequently they were what we would now call factions. The American Revolution gave impetus to collective political action, and the process of formulating and ratifying the U.S. Constitution gave birth to the first formal political parties. The Constitution does not specifically mention or recognize the existence of political parties, but the Bill of Rights did protect such organizations by guaranteeing the right of association and petition. In unequivocal terms the First Amendment declares, "Congress shall make no law . . . abridging the freedom of speech, or of the press; or the right of the people to assemble, and to petition the Government for a redress of grievances."

Subsequently organized groups have come into existence in this nation for a myriad of purposes and to agitate for every conceivable cause. Depending upon one's viewpoint, these many organizations may be adjudged noble or ignoble; radical or reactionary; conservative or liberal; beneficial or harmful. At times it has been suggested that too much freedom exists for ideologues, extremists, and dissenters. Also criticized are those one-issue groups that eschew compromise. Activists who protest do promote political turmoil, but the prohibition of protest would be a dangerous blow to the body politic. It was James Madison, one of the nation's Founding Fathers, who counseled in Number 10 of *The Federalist* (1787), "But it could not be less folly to abolish liberty, which is essential to political life, because it nourishes action, than it would be to wish the annihilation of air, . . . because it imparts to fire its destructive agency."

It is truly amazing how many political organizations have existed or now exist in the United States. Issues, ideas, and ideologies are the prime progenitors of political associations, whether they take the form of parties or civic action groups. Some want to transform, others to reform, and yet others to retain the status quo. Their very existence, no matter how short-lived and whether they are positive or negative in outlook, does testify to the viability of democracy in America.

Since it was impossible to chronicle the histories of all of the political organizations that ever existed in the United States, some basis for selection had to be established. First, the political party or civic action group had to have a formal existence or possess a recognizable semblance of organizational structure. This criterion excludes some desultory movements and formless associations. It would, however, include some political machines or entities despite their seemingly informal nature and unschematic pattern of organization. Second, an organization, whether originally intended or not, had to be involved in activities with political implications, such as lobbying, promoting good citizenship, soliciting votes, improving living standards, molding public opinion, pressuring some governmental body, or in some manner trying to influence the direction of domestic or foreign policy. Finally, organizations had to have historical significance or relevance to the national political scene. Thus some purely local- or state-oriented political groups may be omitted not because they are unimportant but because they had no impact on the national scene. On the other hand, some may be included because they did indeed influence national politics.

The application of these overall criteria was easy in some instances and difficult in others because some organizations were organized originally for nonpolitical purposes but later became active in politics. These types of organizations, by whatever designation they wish to use (associations, clubs, committees, foundations, societies, and so forth) and for whatever reasons they were formed (educational, fraternal, or religious), later got involved in political activity while not formally acknowledging this fact. Thus by the very nature of the situation, our definition of political parties and civic action groups was broadly defined in terms of identifying organizations for inclusion in this book. In some instances we were forced to select a representative or model organization, since the plethora of groups made it impossible to include them all. Interpretations relative to the historical significance of a given organization were based on historical data as understood by the authors.

All entries in *Political Parties and Civic Action Groups* are listed alphabetically. A series of special appendices is included in the back of the book, which groups entries under special headings. To aid in finding related organizations, there are cross-references within the texts of some entries. These are designated by an asterisk (*). Yet another source of locating material is the General Index. Here entries are again listed, but in variant forms based on key words in the title. This index also contains names and topics referred to in the text that are not included as entries. This volume also contains a Glossary, which defines technical terms and political terminology.

Our thanks go to those who served as consultants, to those organizations supplying historical data, and to the librarians of many institutions for their generous assistance. And last, but not least, we are grateful for the assistance given by Alberta Carr.

May 1980

Edward L. Schapsmeier
Bloomington, Indiana

Frederick H. Schapsmeier
Oshkosh, Wisconsin

# POLITICAL PARTIES AND CIVIC ACTION GROUPS

# A

**ACTION COMMITTEE TO INCREASE OPPORTUNITIES FOR NEGROES (ACTION).** Founded in 1964 in St. Louis, Missouri, by Percy Green, a former chairman of the Employment Committee of the Congress on Racial Equality* (CORE), to promote equal employment for blacks. As its head, Green worked with other members of CORE to initiate an equal-opportunity campaign in the city of St. Louis. The first targets of ACTION's activity were Southwestern Bell Telephone Company, Union Electric Company, and the Jefferson Bank.

In order to encourage compliance, ACTION members picketed these firms and called upon blacks to boycott businesses refusing to hire blacks. Affirmative-action programs were ultimately inaugurated throughout St. Louis, with much of the success of these programs due to the activity of ACTION. Membership in ACTION was never more than one hundred, but its formation served as a prototype for other such organizations in cities throughout the United States. ACTION gradually dissolved after attaining its objectives, and by 1968 it was no longer in existence. Its political influence had a positive stimulus upon federal affirmative-action programs.

For further information, see Ernest Patterson, *Black City Politics* (1974).

**ACTION ON SMOKING AND HEALTH (ASH).** Founded in 1967 at Washington, D.C., by John F. Banzhaf III, who currently serves as executive director, for the purpose of promoting the rights of nonsmokers. Membership is comprised of some fifty doctors, lawyers, and educators who believe that the public should be protected from the health hazard inherent in cigarettes.

ASH initiated its anti-smoking campaign by petitioning the Federal Communications Commission for equal time to counteract the pro-smoking content of cigarette commercials. It played a leading role in securing legislation that, in 1971, banned all cigarette commercials on radio and television. ASH was also instrumental in securing federal regulations that required tobacco companies to print a health warning on each pack.

ASH was successful in getting the Civil Aeronautics Board to order airlines to provide no-smoking areas for passengers not wanting to be seated among smokers. The organization works for the enactment of state laws or local ordinances forbidding smoking in public facilities, such as elevators, buses, and restaurants. ASH has initiated lawsuits designed to require tobacco companies to compensate smokers who have lung cancer or other illnesses ostensibly caused from smoking cigarettes. Although small in numbers, ASH has been very instrumental in securing greater legal protection for non-smokers.

Current national headquarters is located in Washington, D.C. A small staff issues press releases and publishes a quarterly, *Smoking and Health Newsletter*.

**AFL-CIO COMMITTEE ON POLITICAL EDUCATION.** See Committee on Political Education.

**AFL-LABOR'S LEAGUE FOR POLITICAL EDUCATION.** See Labor's League for Political Education.

**AFRO-AMERICAN PARTY (AAP).** Founded in 1960 in the state of Alabama by the Reverend Clennon King for the purpose of promoting black participation in politics. Because of the long-standing white supremacy and segregationist practices of the Democratic Party* in the South, the AAP sought to establish itself as a viable alternative for black voters.

In 1960 the name of Reverend King appeared on the Alabama ballot as a presidential candidate, along with Reginald Carter as his vice-presidential running mate. Local candidates also ran under the AAP label. The presidential ticket drew 1,485 popular votes. No candidates were elected to any office. Due to its poor showing, subsequent civil-rights legislation, and efforts by Democrats to win a black following, the AAP became defunct by 1964. Its appearance did serve to spur efforts by southern Democrats to attract the votes of blacks. Similar black parties in other states served the same purpose.

For further information, see Hanes Walton, Jr., *Black Political Parties* (1972).

**ALBANY REGENCY (AR).** Founded in 1820 at Albany, New York, by Martin Van Buren, who was elected president in 1836, as a radical faction of the Democratic-Republican Party* to gain statewide control over the party. Given its name by the *Albany Daily Advertiser*, the AR constituted a political machine that dominated New York politics and even influenced the outcome of national elections. In addition to Van Buren, who won election to the U.S. Senate in 1820, other leaders of the AR included William Marcy,

Silas Wright, John A. Dix, Azariah C. Flagg, Benjamin F. Butler, and Edwin Croswell.

The AR utilized the spoils system (patronage), legislative caucus, and party newspapers to win elections and implement its policies. In 1821 the AR controlled New York's constitutional convention and consequently eliminated most property restrictions relative to voting (except regarding the free Negro, who was not enfranchised). The AR helped form a Virginia-New York alliance by its political union with the Richmond Junto, another political machine, to ensure the nomination and election of Andrew Jackson as president in both 1828 and 1832. The AR was also instrumental in securing the presidency for Martin Van Buren in 1836. AR activities during the Jacksonian era contributed to the formation of what became the modern Democratic Party.*

The AR was weakened by a rift between two factions within the Democratic Party: the Barnburners and the Hunkers. The former were loyal followers of Van Buren who desired to see the ex-president nominated once again for the presidency. The latter had opposed Van Buren's independent treasury system of 1840 and hence were opposed to his renomination as the Democrats' presidential candidate. This powerful state political machine, the first of its kind, disintegrated and was finally destroyed when Martin Van Buren accepted the presidential nomination of the Free Soil Party* in 1848.

The national significance of the AR was the coalition of northern political machines and southern slaveholders within the Democratic Party from the Jackson administration to the Buchanan administration based on the consensus of party loyalty to the Democracy, or Democratic Party. This coalition allowed the Democracy to dominate national politics from 1824 to 1856, give tacit approval to slavery, expand the spoils system, emphasize states' rights, and eventually create the conditions resulting in civil war.

For further information, see Robert V. Remeni, *Martin Van Buren and the Making of the Democratic Party* (1959).

**ALIANZA FEDERAL DE MERCEDES (AFDM).** Founded in 1964 by Reis López Tijerina in the state of New Mexico for the purpose of regaining lands ostensibly taken illegally from Latinos by the U.S. government. Known also as the Alianza de Pueblos Libres, the AFDM combined militant action to regain land lost in the Mexican cession of 1845 with a demand for civil rights and better living standards for Mexican-Americans living in the Southwest.

Tijerina proposed the establishment of an independent country on lands formerly belonging to Mexico and now part of the United States. Under its new constitution, this newly created nation would give preference to Chicanos, abolish private property, create tribunals to determine land policy, and negotiate repurchase of this territory by the U.S. government.

The money received in this second sale was to be distributed to the five million heirs of the original Mexican land-grant holders. Petitions to this effect were addressed to the governor of New Mexico and President Lyndon B. Johnson. A demonstration march was also staged, going from Albuquerque to Sante Fe. Those participating were small in number and representative of the most radical element within the Hispanic community living in New Mexico.

In 1966 Tijerina and his small band of AFDM followers sought unsuccessfully to take over a portion of a national forest. Again in 1967 an armed band of AFDM members led by Tijerina seized and occupied the small town of Tierra Amarilla in New Mexico, the county seat in a sparsely settled northern portion of the state. Violence ensued when state police and national guard troops sought to evict them. Tijerina was subsequently arrested, tried, and convicted of assaulting a federal officer and of being responsible for the destruction of government property. When he was sentenced to prison in 1969, the AFDM began to decline. From its high point in 1967, with perhaps a thousand followers, membership declined to a mere handful of revolutionary guerrillas who still resist the authority of the state of New Mexico and the government of the United States.

Although the AFDM became moribund as an organization, it left a legacy that resulted in greater political activity and protests by Mexican-Americans. Recognizing that violence was self-destructive, Hispanic leaders realized they must work within the American political system to gain social and economic benefits for their people. Likewise, Anglo political leaders in states with heavy Chicano populations became aware of the need to bring these people into the major parties and respond to their legitimate demands for equal treatment. The greater awareness of the need to become active politically led, not only to the formation of the La Raza Unida Party,* but to an increased involvement in the two major parties.

For further information, see Elizabeth S. Martinez and Enriqueta Y. Vasquez, *Viva La Raza: The Struggle of the Mexican-American People* (1976).

**ALIANZA HISPANO-AMERICANO (AHA).** Founded in 1894 at Los Angeles, California, by a group of Mexican-Americans for the purpose of promoting the "social, economic, and fraternal" progress of Chicanos. The AHA was organized as a fraternal lodge with a ritual resembling that of the Scottish Rite of Freemasonry. AHA members, once numbering seventy-five thousand, were provided with insurance and opportunities for fellowship.

Aside from its fraternal aspect, the AHA sought to upgrade urban life for Latinos, fought against discrimination, awarded scholarships to encourage higher education for young Mexican-Americans, and established women's auxiliaries throughout California and the Southwest. In 1960 one of its leaders, J. Carlos McCormick, organized Viva Kennedy Clubs to help gain

Hispanic votes for Democratic presidential candidate John F. Kennedy. The AHA has called for full civil rights for Mexican-Americans and full employment without job discrimination.

In recent years the AHA has become less political in its orientation, even changing its name to Alianza. The latter, along with a marked decline in activism, was done to disassociate the organization from the civil rights violence during the Vietnam era. The Alianza represented middle-class Mexican-Americans who desired to support law and order as well as social assimilation into Anglo society. Its primary purpose in the 1970s was to serve as a fraternal benefit insurance society. At present national headquarters is located in Tucson, Arizona. Current secretary-treasurer is Beatriz Yslas.

For more information, see Beatrice Griffith, *American Me* (1946).

**ALIMONY UNLIMITED.** See Committee for Fair Divorce and Alimony Laws.

**ALL AMERICAN COUNCIL (AAC).** Founded in 1932 at Washington, D.C., by the Democratic National Committee* (DNC) for the purpose of gaining the votes of ethnic groups in America for the presidential election of that year. Its first chairman was Senator Theodore F. Green (D-R.I.). Current chairman is the former mayor of New York City, Robert F. Wagner. The AAC based its appeal to ethnic groups on the basis that the Democratic Party* could alleviate the economic hardships caused by the Great Depression and that its presidential candidate, Governor Franklin D. Roosevelt of New York, understood their plight since he knew the problems associated with an urban-industrial society. Incumbent President Herbert C. Hoover was portrayed as neither comprehending nor caring about the difficulties encountered by ethnic minorities. The AAC was highly successful in 1932; Roosevelt captured the bulk of the ethnic vote throughout the United States.

The AAC grew out of the Nationalities Division of the DNC, as established in 1932, and was renamed the AAC in 1964. It is made up of 23 ethnic divisions representing 210 congressional districts throughout the nation. The AAC canvasses for the votes of ethnic groups in a variety of ways. Among them are the use of poltical advertisements in some 450 foreign-language newspapers published in the United States, representing thirty-four different languages; preparing radio and television programs aimed specifically at special ethnic populations; seeking out and ascertaining ethnic concerns relative to domestic issues; researching to discover how U.S. foreign policy affects the former homelands of immigrants and hyphenate Americans; and providing the DNC with national-origin breakdowns pertaining to voting patterns in congressional districts throughout the country.

A variety of programs of the Democratic Party—among them the New Deal of Franklin D. Roosevelt, the Fair Deal of Harry S. Truman, the New Frontier of John F. Kennedy, and the Great Society of Lyndon B. Johnson—have had great appeal to ethnic voters living in metropolitan centers.

Generally ethnic voters have also supported the anti-Communist stand of these presidents, since many such groups represent peoples whose relatives live behind the Iron Curtain in Communist satellite countries. This voting bloc collectively supports President Jimmy Carter's stand on human rights as a means to force the Soviet Union to liberalize its control over Eastern Europe.

On the other hand, some ethnic groups have been alienated by the Carter administration's foreign policy as it related to Cuba, Israel, and Taiwan. Cuban exiles oppose normalization of diplomatic relations with Fidel Castro's government, American Jews dislike what they believe to be a pro-Arab stand by the United States, and pro-Taiwan Chinese claim that American treaty commitments are being abandoned.

Despite these negative aspects, the Democrats have been very successful since 1932 in garnering the vast majority of the ethnic vote in the United States. Their emphasis upon civil rights and the broadening of economic opportunities consistently has had great appeal to ethnic voting blocs.

**ALLIANCE FOR DISPLACED HOMEMAKERS (ADH).** Founded in 1975 at Oakland, California, by Laurie Shields and Tish Sommers for the purpose of promoting employment for older ex-housewives. Shields is a widow and former marketing specialist, and Sommers heads the Task Force on Older Women of the National Organization for Women* (NOW). ADH's first activity was to lobby for passage of a measure in California to establish a pilot training program for displaced homemakers seeking gainful employment. Eligible for participation in this job training program would be mature women who were divorced or who had been abandoned by their husbands and were without practicable means of support. This type of woman had never developed either professional or vocational skills and sought state-sponsored special programs to enable her to develop these skills.

In 1976 the ADH succeeded in influencing the California state legislature to establish a six-month pilot program in Alameda County for retraining former housewives. The emphasis was upon teaching vocational job skills so that women who were previously untrained or who possessed obsolete skills might be prepared to enter the job market rather than seek welfare assistance. This program did much to provide a means for earning a livelihood for women whose previous talents were housekeeping and the raising of children.

Membership in ADH is relatively small, with locals in Arizona, California, Maryland, Minnesota, New Jersey, and Pennsylvania. Plans for the future include organizing ADH locals in all of the states. Where local organizations exist, lobbying continues to establish training programs based on the California model. Financial and organizational assistance in this endeavor has been provided by NOW and other women's organizations.

**ALTERNATIVE CANDIDATE TASK FORCE FOR 1968 (ACT-68).** Founded in 1967 at Washington, D.C., by Sam Brown, a former president of the National Student Association,* for the purpose of promoting a national "dump Johnson" movement. Although membership was relatively small, consisting mostly of college students, it was resolute in its determination to prevent Lyndon B. Johnson from being renominated by the Democratic Party* as its 1968 presidential candidate.

Key leaders in ACT-68, in addition to Brown, included Clint Deveaux, a former student body president at the State University of New York at Buffalo; David Hawk, a student at the Union Theological Seminary; Stephen Cohen, a student at the Harvard Law School; Cindy Samuels, a student at Smith College; Marge Sklencar, a student body president at Mundelein College; and Sue Hester, a recent graduate of Wheaton College. Despite a small membership on the campuses of several dozen colleges and universities, ACT-68 had considerable success in arousing student opposition to President Johnson and his administration's Vietnam policy.

Although ACT-68 had little influence with important party officials within the Democratic Party, it found its opportunity to oppose President Johnson's renomination when Senator Eugene McCarthy (D-Minn.) entered the New Hampshire presidential primary as an anti-Vietnam war candidate. ACT-68 mobilized hundreds of students to go to New Hampshire in order to campaign for Senator McCarthy as an alternative to Lyndon Johnson. In the "Clean for Gene Children's Crusade" for McCarthy, Brown became known as "chief kid." This activity helped Senator McCarthy to poll 28,791 votes, only 230 fewer than President Johnson received. As a result of this poor showing, Lyndon Johnson withdrew from the presidential race.

When Senator McCarthy continued his quest for the Democratic presidential nomination, Sam Brown became one of his campaign directors. Even after the Democratic National Convention rejected McCarthy as its presidential nominee, choosing Hubert H. Humphrey instead, Brown and others in ACT-68 remained loyal to the Minnesotan of their first choice. The repercussion of this decision may have been to draw enough of the college student vote away from Senator Humphrey to ensure his defeat by Richard M. Nixon, the presidential nominee of the Republican Party.*

In 1972 Brown was elected state treasurer of Colorado on a platform opposing the 1976 winter Olympic games as detrimental to the Colorado environment. In January 1977 Brown was appointed by President Carter to the directorship of the federal agency ACTION, which comprises the Peace Corps, Volunteers in Service to America (VISTA), and several programs for senior citizens.

As a member of the 1976 Democratic Party Platform Committee, Brown was instrumental in achieving amnesty for military evaders and deserters.

For further information, see Sidney Hyman, *Youth in Politics, Expectations and Realities* (1972).

**AMERICA FIRST COMMITTEE (AFC).** Founded in 1940 at Chicago by General Robert E. Wood, the president of Sears, Roebuck and Company, and a group of noninterventionists, for the purpose of keeping the United States out of World War II. Wood, who previously had been on the War Resources Board of World War I, served as the first acting chairman. The AFC, which existed from September 21, 1940, until December 7, 1941 (Pearl Harbor), was originally known as the Emergency Committee to Defend America First. Its origins stemmed from an informal organization started by R. Douglas Stuart, Jr., while a student at Yale University. Both Wood and Stuart were members of the AFC's seven-member executive board, which also included Hanford MacNider, former national commander of the American Legion*; General Thomas S. Hammond, president of Whiting Corporation; William H. Regnery, president of Western Shade Cloth Company; Clay Judson, a Chicago lawyer; and Jay C. Hormel, president of Hormel Meat Packing Company.

Soon after its formation, the AFC became the most important organization to oppose President Franklin D. Roosevelt's interventionist policies prior to the attack on Pearl Harbor. The AFC represented isolationists, pacifists, left-wing anti-war activists, and those who believed that U.S. entry into World War I was a mistake that should not be repeated. Important members of the AFC included: aviator hero Charles A. Lindbergh (its most prominent spokesman), John T. Flynn, Chester Bowles, Alice Roosevelt Longworth, General Hugh S. Johnson, Robert Young, Lillian Gish, and the Reverend John A. O'Brien. The following U.S. senators were also members: Henry Cabot Lodge (R-Mass.), Arthur Capper (R-Kans.), Gerald P. Nye (R-N.D.), Burton K. Wheeler (D-Mont.), Robert M. La Follette, Jr. (R-Wis.), and Arthur M. Vandenberg (R-Mich.).

Two events sparked the formation of the AFC: the Destroyer-Bases Agreement with Great Britain and passage of the Selective Training and Service Act of 1940. The former transferred fifty U.S. destroyers to Britain in exchange for ninety-nine-year leases on air and naval bases in Antigua, the Bahamas, Bermuda, British Guiana, Jamaica, St. Lucia, and Trinidad. The latter, known also as the Burke-Wadsworth bill, initiated conscription in order to enlarge the nation's armed forces. The AFC vehemently opposed a whole host of preparedness measures taken by FDR, including repeal or modification of the Neutrality Act of 1935, extension of the U.S. security zone and naval patrol areas into the North Atlantic, enactment of the Lend-Lease Act of 1941, the U.S.-Danish agreement relative to the American defense of Greenland, President Roosevelt's declaration on June 16, 1941, of an unlimited emergency, the U.S.-Iceland agreement whereby U.S. forces took up occupation duties, the Atlantic Charter (which indicated a U.S.-British alliance), Roosevelt's "shoot-on-sight" order to the U.S. Navy regarding German and Italian vessels entering American coastal waters, and the eighteen-month extension of the Selective Training and Service Act.

At the peak of its success the AFC had hundreds of thousands of members in over 450 local units throughout the United States. Public rallies were conducted, radio time was purchased, and advertisements were placed in newspapers. The AFC's impact on public opinion was great but not sufficient to prevent President Roosevelt from developing a defense program and pursuing an interventionist foreign policy. The AFC was attacked vociferously by pro-administration backers and such organizations as the Committee to Defend America by Aiding the Allies.* Some extremist statements made by spokespeople for the AFC brought charges that it was pro-Nazi and fascist-oriented. These allegations gained currency when Charles A. Lindberg made certain remarks that could be interpreted as being both anti-Semitic and pro-German. The AFC's reputation was besmirched even further in 1944, even though it was no longer in existence, when Gerald L. K. Smith used "America First" as his party label in running for the presidency. The phrase "America First" originally was used by President Calvin Coolidge in his 1924 inaugural address as a description of his noninterventionist foreign policy. Smith, dubbed by many as a demogogue, attracted only 1,780 votes.

The AFC represented the isolationist views of millions of Americans, but it could not persuade the majority that Nazi Germany posed no threat to the United States if it conquered Britain and the Soviet Union. The attack by the Japanese on Pearl Harbor brought an immediate end to the AFC.

For further information, see Wayne S. Cole, *America First: The Battle against Intervention, 1940–1941* (1953).

**AMERICA FIRST PARTY.** See Constitution Party.

**AMERICAN AGRICULTURE MOVEMENT (AAM).** Founded in 1977 at Springfield, Colorado, by Eugene and Derral Schroder, Alvin Jenkins, and Jerry Wright for the purposes of publicizing the economic plight of the nation's farmers. Eugene Schroder, a veterinarian, and his brother Derral, who owns and operates an eight-thousand acre farm, are considered the prime movers in starting the AAM. Jenkins and Wright are also farmers with large holdings in eastern Colorado.

Although the AAM has hundreds of locals in rural areas throughout the nation, it has no specific national headquarters and no formal officers. A national convention was held June 5-6, 1978, in Washington, D.C., where Don Patterson, a farmer, and Congressman Richard Nolan (D-Minn.) served as spokesmen for the AAM. At this time representatives of AAM met with President Jimmy Carter to press for raising of the parity ratio to 100 percent. Such a measure would ensure farmers the cost of production plus a profit on the raising of livestock and grains, as well as dairying. The Carter administration opposed such legislation as being inflationary.

One of the first acts of protest initiated by the AAM was to call a strike set for December 14, 1977. The 7.8 million persons living on farms in the United States were asked to cease selling livestock, grains, and other commodities and were enjoined not to buy farm machinery or any other items to be used on their farms. This strike, or holding action, was supported by the National Farmers Union* but was not successful. Farmers were also asked not to plant any crops in the spring of 1978 but most ignored this request too.

Perhaps the most successful form of protest employed by the AAM has been the tractorcade. Long lines of tractors driven by farmers, with banners flying, drove through the streets to publicize their grievances. Such tractorcades were held throughout the nation, including Washington, D.C., and Plains, Georgia. Farmers complained that their cost of production (cost of seed, fertilizer, herbicides, fuel, and taxes) was so high that they could not make a profit despite long hours in the field. They criticized the U.S. Department of Agriculture and the American Farm Bureau Federation* for not championing federal legislation to provide economic assistance to hard-pressed farmers. Accompanying the tractorcades were picketing and lobbying of state and federal officials.

Some six hundred locals in forty states initiated protests to dramatize the plights of American farmers. Congress did raise target prices (guaranteed minimums) on farm commodities in 1977 but too far below the 100 percent parity level. Because farmers constitute less than 4 percent of the national population, it was difficult for the AAM to dissuade the Carter administration from pursuing a cheap food policy. Secretary of Agriculture Bob Bergland sought to raise the level of farm income by increasing U.S. exports of agricultural commodities. This policy was reversed in part when President Carter ordered an embargo on the sale of American farm commodities to the Soviet Union to protest the latter's invasion of Afghanistan. Members of the AAM, who number in the thousands, contend that, unless price supports are increased drastically, more farmers will be forced out of business. How big the AAM will grow depends upon the extent of continuing hard times for rural America.

In 1980 Marvin Meek of Plainview, Texas, the national chairman of AAM, was chosen to be a delegate at the Democratic National Convention. He worked to promote a dump Carter movement. Meek and others in the AAM felt President Jimmy Carter had not done enough for farmers during the course of his administration. Although the AAM made no official endorsement of a presidential candidate, most within the organization supported Republican Ronald Reagan.

**AMERICAN AGRI-WOMEN (AAW).** Founded in 1974 at Milwaukee, Wisconsin, by the delegates of the National Farm Women's Forum for the purpose of promoting a better understanding by urbanites of the problems confronting farmers. Sharon Steffens of Grand Rapids, Michigan, was elected president and still serves in that capacity. Membership in the AAW is about one thousand, representing farmers' wives from all of the major agricultural regions of the United States.

In order to influence public opinion, particularly among the big-city population, the AAW has initiated educational projects seeking to enlighten the general public as to the economic problems confronting agriculture. Using printed materials, forums, and advertising through various media, the AAW seeks to explain that high food prices should not be blamed on farmers because farm income in fact has steadily declined. It also opposes consumer food boycotts, explaining that this type of action interrupts the level of agricultural production and thus usually leads to even higher prices.

In conjunction with the American Agriculture Movement* the AAW informs political candidates of the difficulties faced by farm families, holds local rallies, and sends representatives to testify before congressional committees on pending legislation affecting farmers. With current national headquarters in Milwaukee, the AAW cooperates with such other organizations as the Cotton Wives, CowBelles, Porkettes, and Wheathearts. At a time when the farm population has declined to 3.6 percent of the national population, the AAW finds it increasingly difficult to convince urban Americans that farmers also are the victims of inflation and high costs of production.

**AMERICAN AND FOREIGN ANTI-SLAVERY SOCIETY (AFAS).** Founded in 1840 at New York City by James G. Birney, Wendell Phillips, the Tappan brothers (Arthur and Lewis), and Theodore Dwight Weld for the purpose of promoting the abolition of slavery. This organization was formed by those seeking to end the institution of slavery but who disagreed with the more militant tactics of the American Anti-Slavery Society.*

The AFAS sought to bring about the emancipation of slaves by moral suasion, legal action, and political agitation and through international cooperation to stop the slave trade. Although its membership was relatively small, its influence among Christian churches did much to arouse the conscience of millions of Americans. Because it did not resort to violence or verbal abuse, it attracted many prominent Americans to the anti-slavey cause who previously had been repulsed by the radical stance of some abolitionists. The work of the AFAS did much to prepare public opinion for eventual emancipation and the termination of slavery.

Because the major political parties of the time—the Democratic* and Whig* parties—tended to straddle the issue of slavery, AFAS adherents did much to promote the founding of the Liberty Party* (LP) in 1839 as an anti-slavery party. James G. Birney served as the LP's first presidential candidate. Running under the LP banner again in 1844, Birney drew enough votes away from Whig candidate Henry Clay in New York to ensure the election of the Democratic Party's nominee, James K. Polk, to the presidency.

When the LP became defunct, the AFAS shifted its support to the Free Soil Party* and finally to the Republican Party.* The impact of the AFAS was significant in preparing public opinion for the time when the issue of slavery had to be dealt with as an election issue. In this sense it utilized the democratic process even though Abraham Lincoln's election as president in 1860 precipitated the Civil War.

For more information, see Dwight L. Dumond, *Antislavery: The Crusade for Freedom in America* (1961).

**AMERICAN ANTI-SLAVERY SOCIETY (AAS).** Founded in 1833 at Philadelphia by William Lloyd Garrison and other anti-slavery advocates for the purpose of promoting the abolition of slavery in the United States. Garrison, who founded the New England Anti-Slavery society in 1832 and initiated publication of the *Liberator* in 1831, was the prime mover of the AAS and its president from 1841 until 1863. Garrison disdained the emigration approach of the American Colonization Society* and indicated that in his fight for total and immediate emancipation of all slaves he would abide by the following code: "I am in earnest—I will not equivocate—I will not excuse—I will not retreat a single inch—and I will be heard."

By 1840 the AAS had grown to an affiliated membership of some two hundred thousand. But in this year a split took place among abolitionists when the American and Foreign Anti-Slavery Society* was formed by those in disagreement with the outspoken views and aggressive tactics of the strong-willed Garrison. Garrison alienated moderates and church leaders with his militancy, uncompromising stand, and extremist statements. Garrison courted many libel suits and was often in danger of physical harm because of his intemperate language. Because the Bible and the U.S. Constitution were used to defend the institution of slavery, he denounced both documents, as well as those who used Christianity and constitutional law to prove that slaves were property and inferior. His pacifism and advocacy of women's equality (while participating in the abolitionist movement) also were very unpopular in an era when women lacked the suffrage.

Because Garrison scorned the political process and even advocated peaceful dissolution of the Union, his following gradually dissipated, leaving only the more militant as followers. His intemperate speech may have inflamed passions unduly, but it did bring public attention to the evils of slavery. Often in the South, moderate anti-slavery advocates like Theodore Weld and Free-Soilers like Abraham Lincoln were unfairly identified as Garrison-type abolitionists. Thus although Garrison did help to crystallize northern public opinion against slavery, he also made it more difficult to work out a peaceful and gradual solution. The AAS dissolved in 1865 when it became apparent that the Union was the victor in the Civil War and the emancipation of slaves was a reality.

For more information, see John L. Thomas, *The Liberator: William Lloyd Garrison* (1963).

**AMERICAN ANTI-VIVISECTION SOCIETY (AA-VS).** Founded in 1883 at Philadelphia by a group of animal lovers for the purpose of preventing the use of animals for vivisectional experiments. Prime movers included Robert Ryerss, a Quaker who operated the Infirmary for Dumb Animals; Henry Flanders, who served as AA-VS's first president; and Dr. Thomas G. Norton, a physician. Others among the founders included Protestant clergymen, a Catholic priest, and several prominent socialites of Philadelphia.

Although membership in the AA-VS has never been large, currently totaling about fifteen thousand, the organization has been noted for its zeal in attempting to end the practice of using animals of any kind for medical and scientific experiments. It lobbies on the national, state, and local levels to secure laws forbidding the use of animals for any type of experiment where they suffer bodily harm. Although it has not succeeded in securing total legal bans on such practices, AA-VS has achieved some success in securing legislation that regulates more closely the use of animals for experimentation. The AA-VS is opposed by the medical profession and the scientific community, but it has used educational and mail campaigns and has succeeded in modifying clinical practices to eliminate any factor of cruelty or inhumane treatment relative to the use of animals for research purposes.

In 1926 the AA-VS sponsored the first International Anti-Vivisection Convention (now held annually) to bolster its efforts to outlaw vivisection everywhere in the world. In 1965 the AA-VS succeeded in getting some governors and mayors to proclaim October 4 as World Day for Animals. Currently Owen B. Hunt serves as president of the AA-VS. Its official journal is the monthly publication *A-V*.

**AMERICAN ASSEMBLY (AA).** Founded in 1950 at New York City by Dwight D. Eisenhower, then president of Columbia University, for the purpose of bringing together leaders in business, labor, education, government, and the professions so that they might serve as an ad hoc national public-affairs forum. Assemblies or meetings were called at least annually (usually more often) to discuss significant issues related to domestic or foreign issues. Conclusions reached by the assemblies, or discussion sessions, were frequently published as reports in book form. As such they were often far in advance of public opinion but served to focus attention upon important issues and thus were instrumental in initiating changes relative to the government's policies in both domestic and foreign affairs.

One influential publication arising out of an assembly forum was *International Stability and Progress* (1957). It proposed that the United States extend diplomatic recognition to the People's Republic of China and conclude a trade pact with that nation. In 1960 President Eisenhower asked the AA to assist his newly appointed Commission on National Goals. The results, published as *Goals for Americans* (1960), contained many proposals that later were incorporated into New Frontier and Great Society programs. Other published reports of the AA include *The Population Dilemma* (1963), urging implementation of birth control programs all over the world; *United States Monetary Policy* (1964), suggesting revenue sharing; *The Courts, the Public, and the Law Explosion* (1965), introducing the concept of no-fault automobile insurance; *Ombudsmen for American Government?* (1967), calling attention to the possible use in the United States of the Scandinavian office of ombudsman; and *The Health of Americans* (1970), proposing among other things the repeal of existing anti-abortion laws.

The precise impact of AA reports on public opinion would be difficult to ascertain, but they did certainly initiate many proposals now accepted or adopted. The activities of AA are funded by grants and contributions from corporations, foundations, and individuals. Its current president is Clifford C. Nelson, with Courtney C. Brown serving as chairman. Although its permanent headquarters is located at Columbia University, AA meetings are frequently convened in cities other than New York and sometimes they are held in foreign countries.

**AMERICAN ASSOCIATION FOR THE UNITED NATIONS.** See United Nations Association of the United States of America.

**AMERICAN ASSOCIATION OF RETIRED PERSONS (AARP).** Founded in 1958 at Long Beach, California, by a group of senior citizens for the purpose of promoting a better life for those who have or are about to retire from active employment. Membership, which now totals nearly five million, is open to everyone over fifty-five years of age. For their annual dues, members receive information and services of value to older people. These include medical, life, and automobile insurance; discounts on prescription and nonprescription drugs; special rates on travel tours; adult educational programs; driver training; and assistance in finding temporary or part-time work.

The AARP provides counseling for the aged and those about to retire, and supplies information about recreational and social activities geared to the lifestyle of older persons. The AARP monitors federal and state legislation relating to the aged and lobbies for laws beneficial to those who live on fixed pensions. Representatives of the AARP have testified before congressional committees, in cooperation with the National Association of Older Americans and the Gray Panthers,* to have Social Security benefits increase, modify mandatory retirement laws, and eliminate discrimination against the elderly. The influence of the AARP on Congress has been significant because of the political power of senior citizens at the polls.

The AARP operates a pharmacy, a travel service, and the Institute of Lifetime Learning, all of which have offices in major cities throughout the United States. Present national headquarters is located in Washington, D.C. Current executive director is Bernard E. Nash. The AARP is affiliated with the National Retired Teachers Association. Official AARP publications are the bimonthly *Modern Maturity* and a monthly newsletter, *AARP News Bulletin*.

For more information, see Henry J. Pratt, *The Gray Lobby* (1977).

**AMERICAN ASSOCIATION OF UNIVERSITY WOMEN (AAUW).** Founded in 1882 at Boston by Marion Talbot of Boston University and Ellen H. Richards of Vassar College for the purpose of promoting higher education among women. Originally formed as the Association of Collegiate Alumnae (ACA), its membership consisted of sixty-five women representing eight colleges and universities. In 1921 the ACA merged with the Southern Association of College Women to form the AAUW. Its constitution was amended in 1957 to broaden AAUW's objectives to include developing a "program to enable college women to continue their intellectual growth, to further the advancement of women, and to discharge the special responsibilities to society of those who have enjoyed the advantages of higher education."

Over the years the AAUW has endorsed those endeavors aimed at broadening the role of women in American society. These have included support for woman suffrage, equal pay for equal work, full coverage of women under the provisions of the Fair Labor Standards Act, election of women to political offices, appointment of women to diplomatic posts and public offices, and ratification of the equal rights amendment to the U.S. Constitution. It has striven to secure congressional legislation to eliminate job discrimination on the basis of sex and to achieve compliance with affirmative-action laws so as to increase the number of females on the staffs of educational institutions.

On the international scene, the AAUW endorsed American entry into the League of Nations, the World Court, and the United Nations. The AAUW is an affiliate of the International Federation of University Women and seeks to promote higher education among females throughout the world.

The AAUW has the following standing committees: Fellowships Program, Legislative Program, and Standards in Higher Education. A study action program is conducted by locals in all fifty states on topics of current interest to women. In 1958 the AAUW established the Educational Foundation. Each year fifty fellowships are bestowed upon women entering graduate school, and fifty women from foreign countries are brought to the United States to receive a college education. The Adult Counselor Program was initiated to develop techniques for counseling women who are seeking employment. The AAUW provides financial grants for public service projects and in 1969 established the Coretta Scott King Award for distinguished public service by a woman.

At present the AAUW has a nationwide membership of over 190,000. Its national headquarters is located at Washington, D.C. Currently Dr. Marjorie Bell Chambers is president, with Alice L. Beeman serving as general director. The organization's official journal is *AAUW Journal*.

**AMERICAN ASSOCIATION ON INDIAN AFFAIRS.** See Association on American Indian Affairs.

**AMERICAN AUTOMOBILE ASSOCIATION (AAA).** Founded in 1902 at New York City by the representatives of several eastern-seaboard motor clubs for the purpose of promoting better roads and safer driving. At the time of AAA's formation there were only 20,000 automobiles in use in the United States and less than 150,000 miles of highway in existence. Throughout its history the AAA has agitated and lobbied for the construction of more and better roads.

This organization was instrumental in securing enactment of the Federal Highway Act of 1916, which initiated the construction of the first national network of arterial highways. It also played a key role in obtaining passage of the Interstate Highway System Act of 1956. The AAA monitors government legislation and represents the interests of motorists before federal agencies. To implement auto safety, the AAA promoted the use by states of uniform traffic signs; sponsored the School Safety Patrol by distributing thirty million pieces of equipment; and supports the school driver training program by cooperating with six thousand auto dealers in providing free cars for participating secondary schools. The AAA makes its judgment known relative to the effectiveness of safety equipment on automobiles; alerts its members in regard to rulings by government agencies; issues information concerning the price and availability of gasoline; and by lobbying, seeks to restrict the use of gasoline tax and other taxes levied on motorists for funding highway construction or maintenance and not for other purposes (such as mass transit). Recently it has opposed permitting larger trucks on the highways since they constitute a danger to motorists driving passenger cars. It also initiated the DWI (Drive While Intoxicated) COUNTERATTACK program to promote the establishment of rehabilitation centers for those arrested while driving under the influence of alcohol.

The AAA provides a variety of services to its seventeen million dues-paying members: travel information, maps, tourist guides, hotel and motel reservations, emergency road service, bail bond, and both auto and travel insurance. Permanent committees exist relative to Emergency Road Service, Highway Traffic and Safety, National Touring Board, and World Wide Travel. Current national headquarters is located at Falls Church, Virginia, and there are over nine hundred regional and local offices throughout the country. The present chief administrator is J. B. Creal. AAA publications include *Sportsmanlike Driving*, which is used as a manual in many driver-training programs, maps, tour books, and local newsletters.

**AMERICAN BAR ASSOCIATION (ABA).** Founded in 1878 at Saratoga Springs, New York, by a group of two hundred lawyers for the purpose of upgrading the legal profession. Headquarters was eventually moved to Chicago, where it remains. According to its constitution, the purposes of the ABA are to see that the U.S. Constitution is upheld; advance the science of jurisprudence; further the administration of justice; seek uniformity in statutory law; ensure that legal knowledge is applied for the benefit of the general public; protect the honor of the profession; create goodwill between lawyers and lay citizens; and promote the interests of the bar.

The ABA is governed by the House of Delegates (established in 1934), which is elected by the Assembly (an annual meeting of the general membership and affiliated organizations). The U.S. attorney general and solicitor general of the United States are automatically members of the House. In turn, the 340-member House, the legislative and policy-making body of the ABA, elects the president, selects the twenty-two-member board of governors, and meets twice yearly to review or confirm decisions regarding the bar on pertinent issues. Specific studies on legal specialties are conducted by a number of standing or special committees. The ABA established the American Bar Foundation in 1952 to fund legal research and publish its findings for the benefit of its membership.

Through its governance machinery, the ABA has taken public stands on many controversial issues. It has affirmed strong support for the United Nations; endorsed the equal rights amendment to the U.S. Constitution; suggested labor legislation to implement post-impasse procedures so as to prevent strikes harmful to the public interest; proposed laws to grant compensation for victims of crimes; opposed no-fault insurance; recommended that possession of marijuana not be considered a criminal offense; approved passage of the Earned Amnesty Act of 1974 as it pertained to Vietnam war resisters; and supported amendments to the Consumer Protection Act of 1971 to ensure proper judicial review upon implementation. The ABA also recommended uniform laws in the fifty states relative to abortion, divorce, jury selection, probate codes, and voting requirements. It took no official position on the issue of capital punishment.

The ABA has sought to improve both the quantity and quality of legal services available to the public. Efforts have been made to raise the competency of lawyers through the Center for Professional Discipline. Commissions have made recommendations regarding prison reform, aid to the mentally retarded, review of criminal justice standards, and the inclusion of law-related subjects in the curriculum of elementary and secondary schools.

Because some 175,000 lawyers, representing 45 percent of those in the legal profession, belong to the ABA, its official position on vital issues is significant. Moreover since a large number of state legislators, members of Congress, and judges are lawyers, they are no doubt influenced by ABA's stands. Opinion is thus influenced or even molded at the professional level where its impact on society is subtle but important. Also its approval or disapproval of potential nominees for the U.S. Supreme Court affects the decision of the president in terms of his ultimate appointee to fill any vacancy on the nation's highest tribunal.

The ABA has its national headquarters at Chicago with an office in Washington, D.C. Current executive secretary is Bert H. Early, with John B. Tracey serving as a lobbyist in the nation's capital. ABA publications include *American Bar Journal*, *American Bar News*, *American Criminal Law Review*, *Business Lawyer*, and *International Lawyer*.

**AMERICAN BEAT CONSENSUS (ABC).** Founded in 1959 at Chicago by William Lloyd Smith, owner of a small bookstore, to promote the nonconformist philosophy and lifestyle of the beatniks. Designating himself a presidential candidate in 1960, Smith ran on a platform calling for an economic system that would upgrade the working class and permit everyone to pursue their own lifestyle. It also proposed a $10 billion federal subsidy for artists. In a jocose manner, the platform recommended, "Forget the budget, just balance the debt. Make peace with everybody, because all beatniks are cowards. Legalize nepotism, favoritism, excess profits, and mink coats."

Although this ostensible one-man political party was not officially listed on any state ballot (thus receiving no recorded vote), it was significant in that it represented the avant-garde, the forthcoming hippie, or subculture, of the New Left movement, which altered the lifestyle of many young people and spawned political parties that did have a considerable impact on the national scene.

**AMERICAN BIMETALLIC LEAGUE (ABL).** Founded in 1889 at St. Louis, Missouri, by Congressman Richard "Silver Dick" Bland (D-Mo.) and other silverites for the purpose of promoting the free and unlimited coinage of silver. Adoniram J. Warner of Ohio served as president. Although never exceeding one thousand members, the ABL was extemely well financed by contributions from western silver mine owners, and it quickly became an effective lobby and pressure group for bimetallism.

Its first political triumph came when the ABL was instrumental in securing enactment of the Sherman Silver Purchase Act of 1890, which authorized the Treasury Department to acquire 4.5 million ounces of silver per month. When the measure was later repealed during the panic of 1893, the ABL initiated an intense publicity campaign for the remonetization of silver. Of immense help in this effort was the widely circulated pamphlet financed by ABL and written by one of its publicists, William H. Harvey, *Coin's Financial School* (1893).

As a last resort, in case it failed to win over a major party to its cause, the ABL founded the American Bimetallic Party in 1896. With the aid of Senator Henry Moore Teller (R-Colo.) and other western silverites in the GOP,* this became the nucleus of the Silver Republican Party.* The success of ABL pressure, propaganda, and money was evident, however, when the Democratic Party* adopted a free-silver platform at its Chicago convention in 1896 and nominated William Jennings Bryan of Nebraska for president. Additional dividends came when both the Populist Party* and Silver Republicans followed suit in the nomination of Bryan. Silver mine owners in the ABL were major contributors to the Great Commoner's campaign but could not gain the victory for the Democratic-Populist-Silver Republican fusionist candidate. Soon after the election of 1896, the ABL disbanded; as a narrow interest-group lobby, it was no longer interested in populism or other issues of the day.

For further information, see Lawrence J. Scheidler, "Silver and Politics, 1893–1896" (Ph.D. dissertation, Indiana University, 1936); Fred Wellborn, "Silver Republican Senators, 1889–1891," *Mississippi Valley Historical Review* 14 (1928): 462; Jeannette P. Nichols, "Bryan's Benefactor: Coin Harvey," *Ohio History Quarterly* 67 (1958): 299; and Stanley L. Jones, *The Presidential Election of 1896* (1964).

**AMERICAN CIVIL LIBERTIES UNION (ACLU).** Founded in 1920 at New York City by a group of civil libertarians, including: Roger Baldwin, Clarence Darrow, John Dewey, Felix Frankfurter, Jane Addams, Jeannette

Rankin, Robert Morss Lovett, Arthur Garfield Hays, Reverend John Haynes Holmes, Reverend Henry F. Ward, Rabbi Judah Magnus, Monsignor John Ryan, James Weldon Johnson, Helen Keller, Alexander Meiklejohn, Norman Thomas, and Oswald Garrison Villard. Growing out of the American Civil Liberties Bureau, started by Norman Thomas and Roger Baldwin in 1917 to defend conscientious objectors of World War I, the ACLU was formed to counter the activities of Attorney General A. Mitchell Palmer and other government agencies during the hysteria of the red scare.

Often associated specifically with liberal or left-wing causes, the ACLU nevertheless has defended the right of free speech for all manner of groups. It has argued more cases before the U.S. Supreme Court than any other entity except the federal government itself. Famous cases in which it has been involved include the defense of Sacco and Vanzetti (1920); the Scopes trial (1925); the Scottsboro boys (1931); and the Bonus Army* (1932). It also succeeded in getting a decision in 1933 that James Joyce's novel, *Ulysses*, was not obscene literature, and it defended religious freedom in *Virginia State Board of Education* v. *Barnette* (1943), where the latter, a Jehovah's Witness, won the right not to participate in the pledge of allegiance to the flag.

Since the ACLU views political protest as an extension of free speech, it supports the unrestricted right of individuals or groups to express their opinions or to participate in demonstrations. It has thus defended members of the Communist Party of the United States of America,* German-American Bund,* right-wing Nazi groups, controversial political figures such as Alabama's Governor George C. Wallace, prize fighter Muhammad Ali, and radical dissenters of every era. The ACLU has repeatedly defended the civil rights of minorities and anti-Vietnam War protesters while opposing all government steps such as surveillance, electronic eavesdropping, and "no knock" searches, to maintain national security or to interfere with the exercise of constitutional rights (personal liberty, assembly, free speech, and right of petition) to maintain law and order. It won many cases during the 1960s by appealing to the Warren Court.

Using litigation and through initiating test cases, the ACLU seeks to reform society in accord with its own libertarian outlook. In seeking its goal, the ACLU has greatly expanded the concept of individual rights under the First Amendment as against those of society, while simultaneously limiting the power of government to implement laws intended to ensure domestic tranquility. It has done much to ensure and expand the legal rights of the poor, criminals, prisoners, and racial minorities. It has consistently opposed capital punishment, regarding it as a form of cruel and unusual punishment, and has worked to decriminalize such offenses as the personal use of marijuana.

In 1975 the ACLU filed a $500 million class-action damage suit against the Central Intelligence Agency (CIA) and National Security Agency, charging that these federal agencies illegally opened the mail and intercepted overseas telephone calls and cables of so-called dissidents. In 1976 it initiated a campaign to prevent passage of congressional legislation that would stiffen penalties for revealing the contents of secret documents, such as the Pentagon Papers, and conducted a campaign to secure laws to terminate or rigidly control covert operations of both the CIA and Federal Bureau of Investigation (FBI).

The work of the ACLU is financed in part by the dues of some two hundred thousand members located in all parts of the United States. It employs a professional staff at its New York City headquarters and maintains lobbyists in Washington, D.C. The ACLU also has available the services of some five thousand cooperating attorneys who represent the organization in thousands of cases annually. ACLU policies are determined by an eighty-member board of directors, of which Edward J. Ennis is chairperson; a National Advisory Council, chaired by former U.S. Attorney General Ramsey Clark; and an executive department headed by Aryeh Neier, executive director.

In 1966 ACLU founded the American Civil Liberties Union Foundation (ACLUF) as a nonprofit affiliate for obtaining tax-deductible contributions to fund its widespread activities. Currently the ACLUF is financing court action in some six thousand cases involving such issues as protecting individual privacy (credit, tax, and medical records); exposing wiretapping by the FBI, CIA, and Internal Revenue Service; fighting censorship by federal and state agencies (including school boards); preventing police brutality; and defending the civil rights of homosexuals, ex-convicts, prisoners, migrant farm workers, and mental patients.

The ACLU, the most renowned organization advocating unlimited political freedom under the Bill of Rights, publishes policy statements, pamphlets, and the magazine *Civil Liberties*.

For more information, see Morris L. Ernst, *The First Freedom* (1946); Lucille Milner, *Education of an American Liberal* (1954); Charles L. Markmann, *The Noblest Cry* (1965); and William H. McIlhany, *The ACLU on Trial* (1976).

**AMERICAN COALITION OF PATRIOTIC SOCIETIES (ACPS).** Founded in 1929 at New York City by John B. Trevor, its first president, for the purpose of promoting restrictions upon immigration into the United States. Trevor had previously formed the Citizen's Committee on Immigration Legislation, which lobbied for passage of the National Origins Act of 1924. This measure established immigration quotas relative to the number of hyphenate Americans residing in the United States as of the 1890 census. The quota system favored those wishing to emigrate from northern and western Europe while discriminating against those from eastern and southern Europe. In 1929 the ACPS supported federal legislation that limited annual immigration into the United States to a total of 150,000.

In the era of xenophobia and racism that followed World War I, the ACPS had thousands of members who feared that the United States would be inundated by peoples who were considered either inferior or non-assimilable. The red scare of the 1920s tended to reinforce this feeling among masses of native Americans. The Immigration Act of 1965 abolished the national-origins quota system and raised the overall total to 170,000 (and an additional 120,000 from the Western Hemisphere). Since the termination of the Vietnam war, Congress has also permitted large numbers of Vietnamese refugees to settle permanently in the U.S.

The influence of ACPS, which has a relatively small membership, has diminished considerably. Although it still vows to "keep America American," ACPS's impact on Congress is negligible. Its general political orientation is that of right-wing conservatism. Among its present objectives are deportation of undesirable aliens, no issuance of Social Security cards to aliens who have gained illegal entry into the United States, and nullification of the Panama Canal Treaty of 1978. It also advocates a strong Federal Bureau of Investigation, revitalization of the Central Intelligence Agency, and restoration of the Internal Security Committee of the House of Representatives as a permanent committee. Domestically it favors measures that expose or combat socialism and communism. In terms of the international stance of the United States, ACPS favors military preparedness as a means of preserving America's strength abroad.

Present national headquarters is located in New York City. Current president is Asa E. Phillips, Jr., with John B. Trevor, Jr., serving as acting secretary.

**AMERICAN COLONIZATION SOCIETY (ACS).** Founded in 1816 at Washington, D.C., by Robert Finley, a Presbyterian clergyman, for the purpose of returning freed slaves to Africa. Although never large in membership, the organization attracted the support of such prominent individuals as Henry Clay, James Monroe, Thomas Jefferson, and John Randolph. Financial support to carry out this endeavor came primarily from slave owners in Kentucky, Maryland, and Virginia, who did not desire to see emancipated slaves settle in the United States. Others who supported the efforts of the ACS opposed slavery as an institution but thought it desirable to return former slaves to Africa.

In 1821 the ACS acquired by purchase Cape Mesurado, a strip of land on the west coast of Africa, an area subsequently named Monrovia. In 1827 the ACS failed in its efforts to get Congress to help fund the mass colonization of blacks to Africa. Colonization was linked to a proposed plan of compensated emancipation, which Henry Clay sought unsuccessfully to get enacted in Kentucky. By 1831 the ACS had transported only 1,420 blacks to Monrovia, a number constituting less than one-third of the slaves born in the United States each year.

In 1847 the blacks who had been resettled from the United States declared their independence and established the Republic of Liberia. The colonization program of the ACS ceased after the conclusion of the Civil War, but aid to Liberia continued until 1912. At that time the ACS dissolved.

For further information, see P. J. Saundenraus, *The African Colonization Movement, 1816-1865* (1961).


**AMERICAN COMMONWEALTH POLITICAL FEDERATION (ACPF).** Founded in 1935 at Chicago by a coalition of liberal, left-wing organizations for the purpose of forming a new political party. Groups instrumental in organizing the ACPF included the League for Independent Political Action,* Farmer-Labor Political Federation,* Wisconsin Progressive Party,* and Minnesota's Farmer-Labor Party.* Others included farm leaders, union leaders, socialists, and intellectuals. Seventy-five delegates, representing eleven states, assembled to bring about the creation of a major third party for the 1936 presidential election. Officers selected at this convention were Thomas Amlie, chairperson; John H. Bosch, vice-chairperson; Paul H. Douglas, treasurer; Howard Y. Williams, national organizer; and Alfred Bingham, executive secretary.

The party platform adopted contained planks calling for public ownership of major industries; an increase in federally financed public works; unemployment insurance and old-age pensions; legislation to outlaw the yellow-dog contract; guaranteed cost of production to farmers; a mortgage moratorium and government refinancing of loans at low interest; a cash bonus for veterans; higher taxes on wealth; nationalization of banks; federal aid to education; equal protection of civil rights for minorities; a constitutional amendment specifically authorizing Congress to provide for the general welfare; and the establishment of an international agency to foster peace.

A national convention was convened in 1936 at Chicago, but plans for creating a third party never materialized. The relatively small membership of the ACPF divided their allegiance between the National Union Party* and the Socialist Party of America.* Some, such as Dr. Paul H. Douglas, a professor of economics at the University of Chicago, gave their support to the New Deal policies of Franklin D. Roosevelt. The leftward direction of the Roosevelt administration did much to dissipate the ranks of the ACPF. F.D.R.'s overwhelming reelection in 1936 aborted any attempt to form a new party and caused the final demise of the ACPF in 1937.

For further information, see Donald R. McCoy, *Angry Voices: Left-of-Center Politics in the New Deal* (1958).

**AMERICAN CONSERVATIVE UNION (ACU).** Founded in 1964 at Washington, D.C., by a group of one hundred right-wing, anti-Communist conservatives for the purpose of promoting their brand of conservatism as a political philosophy best suited for the United States. In a statement of principles the ACU declared its uncompromising support for "capitalism . . . [as] the only economic system of our time that is compatible with political liberty." It also affirmed the conviction that "our national security is threatened by the international Communist movement."

Specifically the ACU advocated the reduction of taxes, curtailment of federal spending, revenue sharing, continuation of the war in Vietnam, U.S. retention of the Panama Canal, nonrecognition of the People's Republic of China, military preparedness, and cessation of efforts to achieve a détente with the Soviet Union.

In 1964 the ACU worked for the nomination of Senator Barry M. Goldwater (R-Ariz.) as the Republican presidential candidate. In 1968 the ACU supported the presidential candidacy of Richard M. Nixon. After helping to elect Nixon as president, the ACU became disenchanted with him because of his domestic and foreign policies. It strongly disapproved of Nixon's proposed visit to the People's Republic of China and criticized the Nixon administration for its huge budget deficits, wage and price controls, welfare spending, and failure to reduce the size of the government bureaucracy. As a result of its disillusionment with Nixon, the ACU endorsed the presidential candidacy of Congressman John Ashbrook (R-Ohio) in 1972. ACU power within the Republican Party* was not strong enough to prevent Richard Nixon from being renominated as the GOP's presidential nominee.

In 1975 the ACU, along with the Young Americans for Freedom,* sponsored the Conservative Political Action Conference in Washington, D.C. Among the five hundred delegates present were such prominent conservatives as Senator Goldwater, Congressman Ashbrook, Senator Carl Curtis (R-Nebr.), Senator James Buckley (Conservative-N.Y.), anti-equal-rights-amendment activist Phyllis Schlafly, political scientist and columnist Kevin Phillips, senior editor F. Stanton Evans of the *Indianapolis News*, and Ronald Reagan, a former governor of the state of California. Although those assembled voiced dissatisfaction over the domestic and foreign policies of the Ford administration, they took no steps to form a third party. Instead the thirteen-member Committee on Conservative Alternatives was established with authority to "call another meeting if necessary to chart more explicitly the future course of conservatism."

When Ronald Reagan entered the presidential primaries in an effort to win the 1976 Republican presidential nomination, the ACU supported him over President Ford. In an attempt to thwart this challenge, President Ford dropped Vice-President Nelson Rockefeller (whom the ACU disliked intensely) from the ticket and replaced him with Senator Robert Dole (Kans.). Although this move pleased the ACU, it weakened the ticket nationally.

When Ford was ultimately renominated, many ACU Reagan supporters refused to campaign energetically for the incumbent president. This lack of support contributed to Ford's defeat by Jimmy Carter, the presidential nominee of the Democratic Party.*

With permanent headquarters in Washington, D.C., the ACU has affiliated chapters in twenty-three states representing some seventy thousand members. It supports the Conservative Victory Fund to nominate and elect candidates in agreement with its political philosophy. Many ACU members are involved in other groups such as the Conservative Caucus,* National Conservative Political Action Committee, and the Committee for the survival of a Free Congress. When Congressman Philip Crane (R-Ill.), an ultra-conservative, announced his intention of seeking the Republican presidential nomination in 1980, many ACU members indicated their support for him. After Ronald Reagan received the Republican presidential nomination, most in the ACU gave their support to the former governor of California. Currently M. Stanton Evans presides as chairman of the board of directors, with James C. Roberts serving as executive director. The ACU publishes a monthly magazine, *Battle Line*.

For more information, see Alan Crawford, *Thunder on the Right* (1980); George Nash, *The Conservative Intellectual Movement in America since 1945* (1976).

**AMERICAN COUNCIL OF CHRISTIAN CHURCHES (ACCC).** Founded in 1941 at Valley Forge, Pennsylvania by the Reverend Carl McIntire to promote strict fundamentalism and to oppose both modernism and communism. McIntire, who was defrocked by the United Presbyterian church in 1936, was the prime mover behind the ACCC until 1969. At that time, his right-wing leadership so alienated many within the ACC that the organization severed its ties with him.

To further his own religious and political beliefs, Reverend McIntire started the weekly *Christian Beacon* in 1936; organized his own Bible Presbyterian church in 1937; founded Faith Theological Seminary (which moved to Elkins Park, Pennsylvania, in 1952); and initiated the "Twentieth Century Reformation Hour" radio program in 1955. He wrote *Author of Liberty* (1946), which claimed that the United States was God's chosen vehicle to save the world. McIntire blamed Communist infiltration for most of the nation's woes. His views became increasingly anti-liberal, anti-ecumenical, anti-United Nations, and anti-Communist. He championed states' rights, use of nuclear weapons, and total victory in Vietnam. In 1960 he conducted a vitriolic campaign against Senator John F. Kennedy (D-Mass.), the presidential nominee of the Democratic Party,* because of Kennedy's Roman Catholicism.

The appeal of ACCC, at the time when McIntire determined its policies, was based upon the fears generated by the cold war. Fundamentalist Christians often were persuaded that liberalism was tantamount to communism and therefore should be hated. Public opinion among the less educated no doubt was influenced to the extent that popular support for the Korean and Vietnam wars did exist. In the same vein, the grass-roots member of an ACCC affiliate opposed diplomatic recognition of the People's Republic of China or détente with the Soviet Union. The ACCC still resists modernism, socialism, and communism but has softened its message considerably.

With current national headquarters in Valley Forge, the ACCC conducts radio and television missions and promotes lay activity on behalf of some fifty affiliates (representing a million and a half members). Currently Donald L. Gorham serves as general secretary. The ACCC publishes the following monthly magazines: *ACCCent, California ACCCent, Southern ACCCent*, and *Crusader*.

For further information, see Brooks R. Walker, *The Christian Fright Peddlers* (1964).

## AMERICAN COUNCIL OF YOUNG POLITICAL LEADERS (ACYPL).
Founded in 1966 at Washington, D.C., by the Young Republican National Federation* and the Young Democrats of America* for the purpose of promoting international understanding of the American political system. On a bipartisan basis, the ACYPL sponsors an exchange program, seminars, and overseas tours so that young (under forty years of age) American politicians might meet with their counterparts in foreign countries. The aim is to foster a better understanding of U.S. politics and to acquaint future American leaders with foreign political systems. Special conferences are arranged so that Americans might meet foreign officials and thus acquaint themselves with the internal problems of host countries.

The present national headquarters of ACYPL is located at Washington, D.C. Current executive director is R. Spencer Oliver.

## AMERICAN COUNCIL ON ALCOHOL PROBLEMS. See Anti-Saloon League of America.

## AMERICAN COUNTRY LIFE ASSOCIATION (ACLA). Founded in
1919 at Baltimore, Maryland, by a provisional committee headed by Kenyon L. Butterfield, president of Massachusetts Agricultural College, for the purpose of promoting improvements in the quality of rural life. The formation of the ACLA came as an outgrowth of the Country Life Commission (CLC) appointed by President Theodore Roosevelt in 1908. The chairman of the CLC was Liberty Hyde Bailey, dean of the College of Agriculture at Cornell University. Other prominent members included Kenyon Butterfield, Walter Hines Page, editor of the *World's Work*; Gifford Pinchot, chief of the U.S. Bureau of Forestry; Charles S. Barrett, president of the National Farmers

Union;* William A. Beard of California; and Henry Wallace, owner and editor of the *Wallaces Farmer*.

After conducting hearings and investigating conditions in rural America, the CLC submitted its report to President William Howard Taft in 1909. The report concluded that farmers needed better farm-to-market roads, easy access to credit, protection from trusts, more knowledge about markets, and relief from discriminatory taxation. It also recommended the formation of voluntary associations to increase the economic power of the rural sector. Furthermore it called upon the federal government to regulate corporations; initiate parcel post and postal savings programs; fund research and distribute information on all aspects of agriculture so that farmers might be more fully informed; coordinate extension work; expand rural health centers; construct more highways; reduce railroad fares; and prevent the interstate transportation of liquor into states where its sale was prohibited. Its general political orientation was that of the progressive movement prominent at the beginning of the twentieth century.

Some of these recommendations were enacted into legislation during the administrations of Taft and Woodrow Wilson. The ACLA found a receptive ear in 1921 to its suggestion that more federal assistance be given to farmers. At that time Henry C. Wallace, the son of the original member of the CLC, was secretary of agriculture in the administration of Warren G. Harding. Legislation was passed to help farmers ride out the economic slump that hurt the rural sector after the conclusion of World War I.

The influence of the ACLA waned when Calvin Coolidge became president. Coolidge resisted all pleas for federal intervention to better the lives of farmers. Herbert Hoover was receptive only to the point of promoting his Federal Farm Board project. During the administration of Franklin D. Roosevelt, rural America benefited from a host of federal legislation. At this time Henry A. Wallace, Henry C.'s son, was secretary of agriculture.

Since World War II, the ACLA has had only a limited membership. Currently it numbers about 175. Members come from the ranks of agriculturists, educators, individuals interested in preserving rural life, and the clergy. At its national conference in 1963, ACLA devoted its attention to rural poverty. By arousing public awareness of this problem, the ACLA helped stimulate congressional response to President Lyndon Johnson's request for federal assistance to the poverty stricken in rural areas. The ACLA also cooperated with President Johnson's specially appointed Commission on Rural Poverty which was formed in 1966.

In recent years the political impact of the ACLA has waned. Its annual meetings have been turned into forums but attract little national attention. Present national headquarters is located is Sioux Falls, South Dakota. Current president is Gene Wunderlich.

For further information, see William L. Bowers, *The Country Life Movement in America, 1900–1920* (1975).

**AMERICAN EQUAL RIGHTS ASSOCIATION (AERA).** Founded in 1866 at New York City by a group of suffragists and delegates of the National Equal Rights League* (NERL) for the purpose of promoting Negro and woman suffrage. The merger movement took place at the Eleventh National Woman's Rights Convention. Leaders of the women's suffrage movement were Elizabeth Cady Stanton, Susan B. Anthony, and Lucretia Mott. Mott served as president, and Frederick Douglass, head of the NERL, was chosen vice-president.

The object of the AERA was to gain the vote for both blacks and women. It coordinated campaigns in Kansas and New York and coalesced the efforts of former abolitionists and others seeking legal equality for ex-slaves. Some dissension existed within the AERA, since many white women within the organization were interested in black suffrage only as a means to get the vote for women. Blacks within AERA also wanted the organization to fight for full civil rights for blacks, as well as gaining the right to vote.

After Congress passed the Fifteenth Amendment to the U.S. Constitution, which did not include women, the suffragists withdrew from the AERA, causing the organization to die. The NERL continued to fight for ratification of the Fifteenth Amendment. The suffragists withdrawing from the defunct AERA tended to join either the National Woman Suffrage Association* or the American Woman Suffrage Association.* Both organizations were dedicated solely to woman suffrage, although they differed in strategy.

For further information, see Ellen C. DuBois, "A New Life: The Development of an American Woman Suffrage Movement, 1860–1869" (Ph.D. dissertation, Northwestern University, 1975); and Elizabeth Cady Stanton, Susan B. Anthony, and Matilda Joslyn Gage, eds., *History of Women Suffrage* (1882 [1969]), vol. 2.

**AMERICAN FARM BUREAU FEDERATION (AFBF).** Founded in 1920 at Washington, D.C., by the heads of state farm bureaus and a group of agricultural leaders for the purpose of promoting the economic welfare of commercial farmers. A prime mover was Henry C. Wallace, editor of *Wallaces Farmer* and secretary of agriculture in the Harding-Coolidge administrations from 1921 to 1923 (the time of his death). James R. Howard, president of the Iowa Farm Bureau, became the first national president.

The first state farm bureau began in Broome County, New York, in 1911. Following passage of the Smith-Lever Act of 1914, which established federal support for state extension services, county agents led the movement to organize countywide farm bureaus. As local units grew, they federated into state groups, and in 1920 they affiliated to form the AFBF. The heads of state bureaus made up the AFBF's board of directors.

Membership in the AFBF is by families. The number of members grew from 325,000 in 1921 to the present total of 1.8 million. Traditionally

representing the family farm, the AFBF does recognize the need for supporting the economic interests of large-scale operators and agribusiness. The
AFBF provides services for its members, including insurance, machinery,
fuel, seeds, and chemical fertilizers at discount prices.

During the 1920s the AFBF championed federal intervention on behalf of
the farmer. It endorsed the McNary-Haugen bill, which was twice vetoed by
President Calvin Coolidge. To help bolster its political power, the AFBF
was instrumental in forming the bipartisan farm bloc in Congress. Under
the leadership of Edward A. O'Neal of Alabama, the AFBF wielded great
political influence in the administration of Franklin D. Roosevelt. For example, it helped formulate the Argicultural Adjustment Act of 1933, one of
the most significant New Deal farm measures, and it was instrumental in
gaining passage of the Soil Conservation and Domestic Allotment Act of
1936 and the Agricultural Adjustment Act of 1938.

When O'Neal resigned as president in 1947, after serving for fifteen
years, Allan B. Kline became his successor. At this time, the pro-New Deal
farm policy position of the AFBF changed to one of opposing high, rigid
price supports in favor of flexibility and less government control over commodity production. During the administration of Harry S. Truman, the
AFBF vigorously opposed the Brannan plan and contributed much toward
its legislative defeat. During the administration of Dwight D. Eisenhower,
when Ezra Taft Benson served as agriculture secretary, the AFBF (then
headed by Charles B. Shuman) championed agriculture based upon a free
market rather than continued federal subsidies tied to production controls.
The AFBF opposed the farm programs of John F. Kennedy and Lyndon B.
Johnson, which reversed the trend toward lower price supports and fewer
controls. When Richard M. Nixon and Gerald R. Ford, during their respective
terms in office, returned to a greater free market policy in agriculture, the
AFBF applauded these efforts. The AFBF in recent years has not endorsed
or supported the protests of the American Agriculture Movement,* which
seeks to restore high federal subsidies and strict production controls.

The AFBF lauded the farm export policies of Ezra Taft Benson and Earl
Butz (the latter served as secretary of agriculture in the Nixon and Ford administrations). It has been critical of the Carter administration for not expanding agricultural exports. Because the farm population is currently less
than 4 percent of the nation's total population, AFBF's political influence
has waned accordingly. Its counsel in the halls of Congress receives less and
less attention as the urban population continues to grow.

Present national headquarters of the AFBF is located at Park Ridge, Illinois. Allan Grant, owner of a 640-acre farm and former head of the
California Farm Bureau, serves as the current president. The AFBF
publishes the weekly *Farm Bureau News* and a monthly, *American Farmer*.

For further information, see Samuel R. Berger, *Dollar Harvest: The
Story of the Farm Bureau* (1971).

**AMERICAN FEDERATION OF LABOR COMMITTEE ON POLITICAL EDUCATION.** See Committee on Political Education.

**AMERICAN FEDERATION OF LABOR-CONGRESS OF IN-DUSTRIAL ORGANIZATION POLITICAL ACTION COMMITTEE.** See Political Action Committee.

**AMERICAN FIRST PARTY.** See Christian Nationalist Party.

**AMERICAN INDEPENDENT PARTY (AIP).** Founded in 1968 at Montgomery, Alabama, by Governor George C. Wallace as his personal vehicle for seeking the presidency by the independent party route. First elected governor of Alabama as a Democrat in 1962, Wallace achieved national notoriety in 1963 as a foe of racial integration. On the campus of the University of Alabama, he uttered the defiant words, "Segregation now! segregation tomorrow! segregation forever!" Capitalizing on an incipient white backlash related to civil rights demonstrations, Wallace entered three Democratic Party* primaries in 1964. He surprised opponents by polling 30 percent of the vote in Indiana, 45 percent in Maryland, and 35 percent in Wisconsin.

In 1968 Wallace formed the AIP with headquarters in the state capital of Alabama. Without benefit of a nominating convention, Wallace declared himself the party's presidential nominee, personally chose General Curtis E. LeMay as his vice-presidential running mate, and dictated the contents of the AIP platform, which condemned campus disorder, crime in the streets, urban riots, wasteful welfare expenditures, the Civil Rights Act of 1964, big government, federal bureaucracy, the Supreme Court, and those military planners who "have fostered the 'no-win' policy" in Vietnam.

Specific planks pledged restoration of power to local and state governments, a retreat from socialism, support for law-enforcement agencies, suppression of the drug traffic, reduction of taxes for the middle class, tax incentives for industry, a federal program for job training and retraining, productive public works, guarantee of a sound financial basis, improvement of Medicare, more assistance to the elderly, abrogation of the nontax status for "giant foundations," farm price supports at 90 percent of parity, limitations on the importation of foreign agricultural commodities, creation of a national feed grain authority, an "equitable" minimum wage, insistence on local control of schools, development of low-cost mass transportation, promotion of effective programs to abate air and water pollution, assurance of a "balance of force" in the Middle East, continued support for the North Atlantic Treaty Organization, building of a strong national defense, and the negotiation on an "honorable conclusion of hostilities in Vietnam."

The AIP platform remonstrated against domestic gun control, protested federal intrusion into the internal affairs of labor unions (to enforce affirmative-action programs), and disapproved of foreign aid to nations that opposed the United States "militarily in Vietnam and elsewhere." Relative to Cuba, which he labeled a "red satellite," the platform promised to "frustrate Castro's attempt to export subversion." It called for an amendment to the U.S. Constitution requiring federal judges to "face the electorate" on their records "at periodic intervals," and it proposed that members of the Supreme Court and courts of appeals also be reconfirmed at "reasonable intervals."

Assuming the posture of an angry, old-time populist, George Wallace conducted a whirlwind campaign in which he lashed out repeatedly against the self-styled elitists who were usurping power from the American people. These political villains at times he dubbed "theoreticians," "pseudo-intellectuals," and "liberals and left-wingers." He severely castigaged them for their alleged arrogance, permissiveness, unconstitutional views, treasonous behavior, and general lack of common sense. Appealing to the prejudices, patriotism, and economic self-interest of such groups as blue-collar workers, small-town residents, senior citizens, white southerners, pro-Vietnam supporters, and those throughout the country not reconciled to integration, the Alabamian articulated their grievances by serving as their spokesman. Loyal followers admired his pugnacious quality and willingness to "stand up for America." They cheered his attacks on anarchists, arsonists, anti-war activists, looters, and military revolutionaries. Wallace incurred the wrath of young protesters seeking to disrupt his political rallies by deliberately taunting them. The vocal politician seemed to enjoy confrontations and exploited them to prove he was a courageous champion of all so-called decent Americans. He seethed with indignation when censuring "sick politicians" for prohibiting prayer in public schools while allowing pornography to be sent through the mails. Pro-Wallace zealots hailed him as a hero, while outraged critics portrayed him as a bigoted racist, an inflammatory ignoramus, and a dangerous proto-fascist in the mold of Huey Long.

The Wallace-LeMay ticket was on the ballot in all fifty states in 1968 and drew a popular vote of 9,901,151, 13.54 percent of the total vote cast. In winning the states of Alabama, Arkansas, Georgia, Louisiana, and Mississippi, Wallace netted forty-six electoral votes. By depriving the nominee of the Democratic Party, Hubert H. Humphrey, these crucial votes in the electoral college, Wallace contributed to Republican Richard Nixon's narrow victory in the presidential contest.

Early in 1969 two factions began to develop in the AIP. One group, drawing its members from an organization called the Association of Wallace Voters, met in Dallas, Texas, to establish a permanent AIP. It chose avowed segregationist T. Coleman Andrews of Virginia as its national chairman. Another faction met later that same year at Louisville, Kentucky. It called itself "the National Committee of Autonomous State Parties, known as the American Independent Party, American Party, Independent Party, Conservative Party, and Constitutional Party." Although its members had backed Wallace, they desired a permanent party not in the control of one man. This wing of the AIP selected William L. Shearer, editor of the *California Statesman*, as its national chairman.

In 1972 Governor Wallace began running in the presidential primaries of the Democratic Party. Using the slogan, "Send them a message," his campaign began to gain momentum when suddenly it was brought to a halt. Assassin Arthur H. Bremer felled the Alabama governor with gunshot wounds on a parking lot in Maryland. Although surviving, Wallace left the campaign trail to recover from his crippling injuries, forever to be a paraplegic.

Temporarily united, all factions of the AIP met at Louisville in 1972 to hold their national convention. The assembled delegates wanted to nominate Wallace, but in an address by telephone from his hospital bed, he declined the offer. The presidential nomination was then bestowed upon former California Congressman John G. Schmitz, who was a member of the John Birch Society,* with second place on the ticket going to farm magazine publisher Thomas Jefferson Anderson of Pigeon Forge, Tennessee.

The 1972 platform reiterated its stance on such issues as prayer in the schools, local government, anti-gun legislation, the federal judiciary, welfare chiselers, and socialism. It sharply attacked the women's movement, draft dodgers and deserters, drug users, and advocates of sex education. Various planks opposed legalization of marijuana, liberalized abortion laws, pornography, deficit spending, compulsory arbitration, and U.S. participation in international organizations and agencies (such as the United Nations, the International Monetary Fund, and the World Bank). Promises were made to preserve the neighborhood school (by terminating school busing to achieve racial balance), reform Social Security, reduce unemployment, stop imports from "slave" nations, expand private health-care programs, protect consumers, improve the environment, end secrecy in government, collect all foreign debts (including those from previous wars), bolster national defense, lower taxes, plug tax loopholes for the rich, permit individual ownership of gold, curtail foreign aid, sever diplomatic contacts with the People's Republic of China, support South Africa and Rhodesia, implement a policy of neutrality in the Middle East, revitalize the Monroe Doctrine with regard to Latin America, and limit interventions abroad to prevent the sacrifice of American freedoms on the "altar of international involvement." Presidential aspirant John Schmitz summarized his position succinctly when he asserted, "Never go to war unless you plan to win . . . those who go to work ought to live better than those who don't . . . treat our friends better than our enemies."

On the ballot in thirty-three states, the AIP-AP ticket polled a popular vote of 1,090,673, representing 1.40 percent of the total vote cast. The Schmitz-Anderson ticket drew most of its support from the Far West and Deep South. It attracted from 3 to 6 percent of the overall vote in the states located in those regions.

After the 1972 election, factionalism again split the AIP. William K. Shearer, who was party chairman in California, maintained control of the AIP, while Thomas J. Anderson gained the leadership of a rump group calling itself the AP. In 1976 the AP held its national convention in Salt Lake City, Utah, and named Anderson its presidential nominee and Rufus Shakleford of Florida for vice-president. The AP's platform stated its opposition to abortion, gun control, federal welfare programs, foreign aid, the equal rights amendment (ERA), government spending, and the expansion of federal power. While campaigning, Anderson called for U.S. withdrawal from the United Nations and cessation of both trade and diplomatic recognition relative to all Communist countries.

The AIP convention met at Chicago later in 1976 to nominate Lester Maddox, former governor of Georgia, as its presidential standard-bearer. Chosen for the vice-presidency was William Dyke of Wisconsin, a former mayor of Madison. The AIP's platform took positions against abortion, the ERA, legalizing the use of any drugs, gun control legislation, foreign aid, government bureaucracy, lenient courts, laxness in law enforcement, American contacts with Communist nations, and U.S. participation in the United Nations. Lester Maddox, a bitter foe of integration and a political enemy of Jimmy Carter, told the assembled delegates, "Politically, morally, and spiritually, America is on the rocks." He then pledged, "I'll make sure that America is not second to Russia, not second to China, and not second to Castro, but first."

The AIP ticket of Maddox and Dyke polled a total of 170,531 popular votes, 0.2 percent of the national vote. Its largest vote was in California, with 51,098. Rival AP candidates Anderson and Shakleford drew only 160,773 popular votes (0.2 percent). Their best showing was in Utah, where they received 2.5 percent of that state's popular vote. Neither the AIP nor the AP won any electoral votes, and so they had no impact on the national election. (See table 1.)

Without the dynamic personality and strong leadership of George Wallace, or someone like him, the AIP degenerated into a bifurcated party

**TABLE 1 American Independent Party Presidential Candidates and Votes, 1968-1976**

| YEAR | CANDIDATE | TOTAL POPULAR VOTE |
|------|-----------|--------------------|
| 1968 | George Wallace | 9,901,151 |
| 1972 | John G. Schmitz | 1,901,673 |
| 1976 | Lester Maddox | 170,531 |

with right-wing ideologues in control of both factions. Negative in outlook, its adherents currently possess conspiratorial and ultraconservative views that cannot attract large numbers of voters.

For further information, see Marshall Frady, *Wallace: Across a Darkling Plain* (1968), and Theodore White, *The Making of a President, 1968* (1968).

**AMERICAN INDIAN DEFENSE ASSOCIATION.** See Association on American Indian Affairs.

**AMERICAN INDIAN MOVEMENT (AIM).** Founded in 1968 at the Pine Ridge Indian Reservation in South Dakota by Russell Means, a twenty-nine-year-old Oglala Sioux, and Dennis Banks, a thirty-six-year-old Chippewa, for the purpose of initiating a movement to liberate American Indians. According to the revolutionary rhetoric of its leaders, the intent of AIM was, first, to regain land from the United States that had been wrongfully acquired from Indians and, second, to reestablish an Indian nation.

In 1972 AIM sponsored a sit-in at the U.S. Bureau of Indian Affairs (BIA) in Washington, D.C., to protest the way the federal government treated Indians. Those participating in the demonstration protested specifically against the existence of tribal councils on the grounds that they led to paternalistic control over Indians by the BIA. The policy of permitting tribal councils was authorized by federal legislation in 1934 as a means of implementing democratic government among the various Indian tribes still in existence. The sit-in terminated when federal officials promised to investigate the Indians' complaints relative to BIA's alleged maladministration. Upon withdrawing from the BIA building, the small band of protesters removed the contents of certain files, taking these materials with them, and generally left the offices in a shambles.

From February 27 to May 8, 1973, some 250 members of AIM forcefully seized the hamlet of Wounded Knee, located on the Pine Ridge Reservation. This was the site where, in 1890, the U.S. Seventh Cavalry plundered an Indian village in revenge for the destruction of General George Custer and his force at the battle of Little Big Horn (1876). Leaders of this occupation included Means, Banks, Leonard Dog Crow, Carter Camp, and Stanley Holder. They demanded removal of the elected president of the Oglala Tribe Council, Richard Wilson; called for an investigation of the BIA by Senator Edward Kennedy (D-Mass.); and directed Senator William Fulbright (D-Ark.), chairman of the Senate Foreign Relations Committee, to conduct hearings so as to determine the legality of some 371 treaties between the U.S. government and various Indian nations. The tribal council resented the charge that they were BIA puppets and, in turn, claimed that AIM represented only a radical minority faction bent on gaining control over the tribe by illegal use of force.

Despite mediation attempts by Senator George S. McGovern (D-S.D.), violence broke out between AIM occupiers and federal law-enforcement officers. Eventually agents from the Federal Bureau of Investigation and a group of U.S. marshals combined their attacks to break the siege by armed force. Some 120 AIM militants were compelled to surrender. Means and Banks subsequently were indicted by a grand jury for their roles in this incident, but when the case went to trial in St. Paul, Minnesota, a federal judge dismissed all charges on the basis that the government mishandled the case. Banks was later tried and convicted on riot and assault charges stemming from another incident in Custer, South Dakota. He jumped bail and became a fugitive until recaptured in 1976.

Because of their involvement at Pine Ridge, Carter Camp, Leonard Dog Crow, and Stanley Holder were placed under arrest and tried in a federal court in Cedar Rapids, Iowa. They were convicted of interfering with and robbing a U.S. postal inspector. Each was given an eighteen-month prison sentence. AIM has conducted a campaign to raise funds in order to appeal the convictions in higher courts.

Some 240 deaths have occurred at Pine Ridge over the past several years. Opponents of AIM claim that the group is responsible for these murders, but AIM maintains that its members are the ones who are being killed deliberately by tribal or outside police. In 1976 the AIM-backed Al Trimbale was elected tribal chief. Lawlessness, however, continued on the reservation. When outside law officials were sent in to restore order, they were frequently attacked by unknown assailants. Because of its militancy and the radical nature of its ideology, AIM has remained relatively small in numbers. Non-Indian left-wing groups have supported the Indian movement, but most Indians have utilized other, more legitimate means to regain lands, secure enforcement of their treaties, or improve their economic conditions.

For further information, See Carol Quigley, *The Tragedy in Hope* (1975).

**AMERICAN INDO-CHINA VETERANS LEGION (AIVL).** Founded in 1971 at West Hartford, Connecticut, by a group of Vietnam war veterans for the purpose of promoting more benefits for former members of the U.S. armed forces. One of the prime movers of AIVL was Harvey A. Dennenberg, currently serving as its national commander.

The AIVL lobbies to secure greater benefits for Vietnam veterans on both the federal and state levels. It was successful in Connecticut in gaining 100 percent tuition waivers for Vietnam-era servicemen and women who chose to pursue vocational training or embark on higher-education programs. It was also a contributing factor in securing the establishment of the Office for Veterans Affairs for Education under the authority of the commissioner of higher education.

AILV seeks to enlarge its membership beyond Connecticut so as to broaden its influence and become a powerful spokesperson for Vietnam veterans. Present national headquarters is located at West Hartford, Connecticut.

**AMERICAN INSTITUTE OF INTERNATIONAL AFFAIRS.** See Council on Foreign Relations.

**AMERICAN LABOR PARTY (ALP).** Founded in 1936 at New York City by a group of socialist-oriented labor leaders to divert votes from Norman Thomas to Franklin D. Roosevelt in that year's presidential election. It also endorsed Herbert Lehman, the gubernatorial candidate of the Democratic Party.* Prime movers in the initial organization of the ALP were David Dubinsky of the International Ladies' Garment Workers' Union, who became state chairperson, and Emil Rieve of the American Federation of Hosiery Workers.

The ALP existed as a state party in New York, with most of its membership in New York City, but its political stand and number of votes cast had national significance in key elections. It contributed to the mayoral victories of Fiorello H. La Guardia in 1937 and 1941 and in 1938 elected Vito Marcantonio to Congress. In a special election on February 18, 1948, to fill a vacancy in the Twenty-fourth Congressional District in the Bronx, ALP candidate Leo Isacson won by leading the field against candidates representing the Democratic, Republican,* and Liberal parties.* This victory seemed to indicate a considerable increase in the power and influence of Henry A. Wallace, whom the ALP had endorsed for the presidency.

In 1944 Sidney Hillman, head of the Political Action Committee,* ousted Dubinsky as state chairperson in a bitter intraparty struggle. Dubinsky claimed that Communists had gained control of the party, and as a result of this ideological split he, along with such notables as brain-truster Adolf Berle and renowned educator George S. Counts, left the ALP and joined with other non-Communist liberals to form the Liberal Party. Under Hillman's control, union leaders who now gained ascendancy within the ALP included Michael Quill, president of the Transport Workers Union of America, and Joseph Curran, president of the National Maritime Union of America. Curran quit the ALP in 1946 and Quill in 1948, both claiming that the Communists wielded undue power in the party.

In the mid-term elections of 1946 the ALP sponsored rallies at which Secretary of Commerce (and ex-Vice-President) Henry A. Wallace frequently spoke. When President Harry S. Truman suddenly fired his commerce secretary for taking a pro-Soviet stand on foreign policy issues, the ALP was one of the leading groups to urge Wallace to form a third party in opposition to the Truman Doctrine. In 1948 the ALP backed Wallace, who was also the presidential nominee of the Progressive Party,* and championed abolition of the House Committee on Un-American Activities, opposed the

Marshall Plan, condemned the peacetime draft, demanded cessation of stockpiling of atomic bombs, and called for peaceful relations with the Soviet Union. In a losing cause Henry Wallace drew 509,559 votes in New York (half his total). The ALP's endorsement of Wallace may in actuality have hurt him as much as it helped.

In 1949 Marcantonio, who had become state chairperson in 1948, lost the race for mayor in New York City, and in 1950 he also lost his seat in Congress. The ALP once again supported the Progressive Party presidential nominee in 1952, Vincent W. Hallinan of California, but he drew a national vote of only 140,023. Failing to draw at least 50,000 votes in 1954, the ALP lost its place on the New York ballot. By 1956 it had ceased to exist.

For further information, see Matthew Josephson, *Sidney Hillman: Statesman of American Labor* (1952); Max D. Danish, *The World of David Dubinsky* (1957); and Alan Shaffer, *Vito Marcantonio, Radical in Congress* (1966).


**AMERICAN LEAGUE AGAINST WAR AND FASCISM (ALAWF).** Founded in 1933 at New York City by the delegates of the First United States Congress against War (FUSCAW) for the purpose of uniting liberals and left-wing adherents into a common front against fascism. The antecedents of ALAWF stemmed from the 1932 Amsterdam World Congress against War. This conclave gave birth to the World Committee against War, which in turn spawned the American Committee for the Struggle against War. This latter organization convened the FUSCAW, parent of the ALAWF.

Prominent Communists were much in the forefront within the ALAWF. Its first chairman was Dr. J. B. Mathews, who later renounced his communism and became director of research for the House Un-American Activities Committee (HUAC). Other Communists on the executive committee included Clarence Hathaway, editor of the *Daily Worker*, Israel Amter, Max Bedacht, Ella Reeve Bloor, and Langston Hughes. Until 1937 when the ALAWF changed its name to the American League for Peace and Democracy (ALPD), the Communist Party of the United States of America* (CPUSA) was an official affiliate. Even after 1937 the CPUSA, with Earl Browder at its head, dominated ALPD's policies and funded many of its activities.

In 1939 the ALPD came under investigation of HUAC, then chaired by Congressman Martin Dies (D-Tex.). Dr. Harry Freeman, chairman of ALPD at the time, appeared before HUAC to deny that his organization was a Communist front or that it took its orders from the Comintern. Subsequent actions by the ALPD were to cast doubt on the accuracy of these assertions.

During the Spanish Civil War, the ALPD had agitated for U.S. assistance to the Spanish Republic. Many of its members either joined or helped recruit soldiers for the Abraham Lincoln Brigade to fight against General Franco's fascist troops. The ALPD called upon Congress to repeal the Neutrality Act so that the Spanish Republic might receive arms and munitions. But in 1939, after Hitler and Stalin announced the Nazi-Soviet Pact, the ALPD suddenly reversed its position. It now demanded strict adherence to the Neutrality Act, denounced rearmament as militarism, and joined the chorus of isolationists insisting that the United States not get involved in Europe's affairs. The ALPD was further embarrassed when it had to justify Soviet action in the Russo-Finnish War. It was apparent that Finland was the victim of Soviet aggression, yet ALPD spokespeople defended Russia's annexation of Finn territory.

The demise of the ALPD came in 1941. When the Germans invaded the Soviet Union in that year, the ALPD again reversed its isolationist position and demanded repeal of the Neutrality Act so that military supplies might be sent immediately to Russia. Furthermore the ALPD insisted that the United States increase its military strength and intervene in the war on the side of the Soviet Union. This about-face scuttled the ALPD, since its slavish adherence to a party line dictated by Moscow ruined its credibility among the non-Communist Left.

The period of the ALPD's greatest influence was from 1935 until 1939. It provided a vehicle for Communists to secure liberal and left-wing support for opposition to the growing menace posed by such fascist leaders as Hitler, Mussolini, and Franco. ALPD membership in 1939 numbered about twenty thousand representing some three hundred local chapters or affiliates. Although never large in size, it was able to utilize liberal spokespeople to get its message across to the American people. ALPD's refusal to condemn the Soviet invasion of Finland or to censure Russian seizure of Estonia, Latvia, and Lithuania prompted many individuals of the non-Communist Left to disassociate themselves from an organization too prone to defend Soviet actions, regardless of its consequences.

For more information, see Earl Latham, *The Communist Controversy: From the New Deal to McCarthy* (1966).

**AMERICAN LEAGUE FOR PEACE AND DEMOCRACY.** See American League against War and Fascism.

**AMERICAN LEAGUE TO ABOLISH CAPITAL PUNISHMENT (ALACP).** Founded in 1927 at Boston, Massachusetts, by a group of lawyers and intellectual leaders for the purpose of promoting the abolition of capital punishment in the United States. Prime movers in the formation of ALACP included Herbert Ehrmann, a defense attorney in the celebrated Sacco-Vanzetti case; Sarah Ehrmann, who served as executive director from

1949 to 1967; Clarence Darrow, the famed criminal lawyer and the organization's first president; and Lewis E. Lawes, warden of New York's Sing Sing prison and the second president of ALACP.

By 1972 the ALACP had thirty-seven state chapters with over eight thousand members. Membership was constituted primarily of those in the legal profession, the clergy, criminologists, penologists, legislators, and those involved in social welfare work. Several permanent committees were established: Publications, Research and Statistics, State Liaison, and International Organization Liaison. Members served as expert witnesses before state legislative committees and those of the U.S. Congress dealing with penal codes. The ALACP has been influential because of its lobbying and through studies that made an impact on the American judiciary. It worked constantly to abrogate the death penalty in the several states and to have it abolished from the Federal Penal Code. Its greatest success came in 1972 when the U.S. Supreme Court outlawed many areas where capital punishment could be used as punishment for a crime.

The greatest impact of the ALACP has been on lawmakers and the legal profession. By convincing lawyers and judges of the necessity to abolish capital punishment, it has influenced the thinking of many who were in a position to take action. The general public knows little of ALACP nor does it accept its argument that capital punishment should be totally abrogated. Because of public pressure and the growing incidence of murder, some state legislatures have reintroduced the death penalty.

Present national headquarters is located in Boston. The current president is Dr. Hugo Bedau, a philosophy professor at Tufts University. Publications include special reports and the *ALACP News-Notes*.

For further information, see Herbert Ehrmann, *The Case That Will Not Die* (1969).


**AMERICAN LEGION (AL).** Founded in 1919 at Paris, France, by an assembled group of American veterans summoned to a caucus by Lieutenant Colonel Theodore Roosevelt, Jr., for the purpose of promoting the interests of former members of the U.S. armed forces. As the Father of the American Legion, Roosevelt presided over the Legion's first convention that same year at St. Louis, Missouri. At this meeting a constitution was adopted, which stated the objectives of the Legion:

To uphold and defend the Constitution of the United States of America; to maintain law and order; to foster and perpetuate a one hundred percent Americanism; to preserve the memories and incidents of our associations in the great wars; to inculcate a sense of individual obligation to the community, state, and nation; to combat the autocracy of both the classes and masses; to make right the matter of might; to promote peace and good will on earth; to safeguard and transmit to posterity the principles of justice, freedom, and democracy; to consecrate and sanctify our comradeship by our devotion to mutual helpfulness.

Chartered by Congress the same year it was formed, the Legion subsequently became the largest and most powerful of all the veterans' organizations. With a current membership of nearly three million, the Legion represents men and women who served in World War I, World War II, Korea, and Vietnam. The AL carries on a vast program both to influence public opinion and to gain government benefits for veterans and their dependents. The AL seeks to implement specific goals through a number of committees (called commissions): Americanism; Children and Youth; Economic; Finance; Foreign Relations; Internal Affairs; Legislative; National Security; Public Relations; and Veterans Affairs and Rehabilitation. The last was established in 1970 to handle problems dealing with disability compensation, hospitalization, and vocational training.

The AL has always been politically active in seeking federal legislation to further its aims and objectives. It constitutes a powerful lobby on issues relating to veterans' affairs, national defense, and certain aspects of foreign policy. Overall its political stance has been conservative on domestic affairs and hawkish relative to foreign relations. The AL was instrumental in gaining passage of the National Defense Act of 1920, Soldiers' Bonus Act of 1924, G.I. Bill of Rights (1944), and the Veteran's Preference Act of 1944. It was persuasive in getting a presidential proclamation in 1921 declaring November 11 as Armistice Day (now Veterans Day). Recently the AL, with other groups, succeeded in acquiring greater benefits for Vietnam veterans.

The AL has always advocated a strong national defense for the United States. In the 1930s when the isolationists and pacifists were strong, the AL consistently supported President Franklin D. Roosevelt in his attempts to keep the nation militarily prepared. Following World War II the AL counseled military strength as a means of keeping the Soviet Union in check during the cold war era. During the Truman-MacArthur controversy at the time of the Korean War, many Legionnaires supported the idea of using atomic weaponry to win the war. The concept of *détente* with the Soviet Union and diplomatic recognition of the People's Republic of China were long viewed by the AL with suspicion. The AL supported Presidents Lyndon Johnson and Richard Nixon in their prosecution of the Vietnam war. It was critical of anti-war protesters, civil rights demonstrations, lawlessness in the cities, and those who advocated withdrawal from Vietnam. When President Jimmy Carter proposed amnesty for draft dodgers and deserters, the AL opposed it.

The AL has always sought to promote patriotism and love of country. Its National Commission on Americanism conducts the High School Oratorical Contest, operates both Boys State and Boys Nation, and bestows school medal awards to students on the elementary, junior high, and senior high levels. Since 1926 the Legion has supported baseball for boys (currently involving some seventy thousand), sponsors four thousand scouting groups (Cub Packs, Scout Troups, and Explorer Units); and, in cooperation with the National Education Association* and the National Congress of Parents and Teachers* sponsors American Education Week. The AL played a leading role in formulating the present flag code used in the United States. It also joined with the Freedoms Foundation at Valley Forge* to create the John Morton Cold War Briefing Room to educate the public relative to the implications of the threat from Communist nations. A monthly newsletter, *Firing Line*, was published to warn the general public about subversive activities within the United States.

The Legion conducts a huge social welfare program for children. Its National Commission on Children and Youth finances Legion-operated institutions for the care of children of disabled veterans when the latter are unable to do so. The AL is also a large contributor to the American Heart Association and the National Association for Mental Health. In 1954 the AL established the American Legion Child Welfare Foundation for broadening the scope of its work. Since 1921 the Legion has sold red poppies to help finance these endeavors.

The AL has an auxiliary for women (primarily wives and mothers of members); the Press Association; Forty-and-Eight (a fraternal group); Post-Mortem Club (for former national and state officers); Society of American Legion Founders; and the Sons of the American Legion. Although the AL has sixteen thousand posts throughout the country, its membership has declined since the post-World War II era. Once extremely powerful in terms of lobbying and political ability, its influence has waned somewhat in recent years. Present national headquarters is located at Indianapolis, Indiana. Robert E. L. Eaton of Maryland is currently serving as national commander. Its official publication is a monthly, *American Legion Magazine*.

For more information, see Richard S. Jones, *A History of the American Legion* (1947), and Roscoe Baker, *The American Legion and American Foreign Policy* (1954).


**AMERICAN LEGISLATORS ASSOCIATION.** See Council of State Governments.


**AMERICAN LIBERTY LEAGUE (ALL).** Founded in 1934 at Washington, D.C., by a group of businessmen for the purpose of promoting opposition to the New Deal. Prime movers in its formation were John Jacob Rascob, former head of General Motors and an ex-national chairman of the Democratic Party,* and R. R. M. Carpenter, a retired du Pont vice-president. Jouett Rouse, who was president of the Association against the

Prohibition Amendment* (AAPA), assumed the presidency of the ALL. William H. Stayton, who had founded the AAPA, became ALL's executive secretary.

In the summer of 1936, the high tide of its activity, membership in ALL totaled almost 125,000. Most members were college educated and were either self-employed professionals or business executives. The Lawyer's Division was created in 1936 to do research on the constitutionality of New Deal legislation. Some 345 campus chapters were formed by 1936 with over 10,000 members. The Farmer's Independent Council was also established as a subsidiary organization, but it enrolled relatively few farmers. Prominent political figures associated with the ALL included, Alfred E. Smith, a former governor of New York and the Democratic nominee for president in 1928; John W. Davis, a corporation lawyer and the Democratic nominee for president in 1924; and Congressman James W. Wadsworth, Jr. (R-N.Y.). Leading business persons who joined included J. Howard Pew of the Sun Oil Company; Ernest Woodword of the Jello Company; Edward Hutton of General Foods; and Irénée du Pont of the E. I. du Pont de Nemours and Company.

The political philosophies guiding the policies of the ALL were those of laissez-faire economics, rugged individualism, and social Darwinism. Because its members were wealthy, the ALL made use of a large public relations staff to bombard the media with anti-New Deal materials. Advertisements were published in newspapers, time was purchased on the radio, and tons of pamphlets were distributed to the general public in an attempt to undermine the New Deal policies being implemented by President Franklin D. Roosevelt. The ALL was critical of deficit spending, public works, high taxes, and the growing government bureaucracy.

In 1936 the ALL made a special effort to prevent the reelection of President Roosevelt. It spent much money in distributing anti-Roosevelt campaign literature and in assisting anti-New Deal candidates. These efforts were a failure. Democrats, in fact, made a point of identifying the ALL with the Republican Party* so as to pin the rich-man label on the GOP. Governor Alfred M. Landon of Kansas, the Republican nominee for the presidency, regarded ALL's endorsement as a virtual "kiss of death." Following Roosevelt's landslide victory over Landon in 1936, the ALL began to lose its membership. By 1940 it was moribund and that year it finally disbanded.

For more information, see Frederick Rudolf, "The American Liberty League, 1934–1940," *American Historical Review* 56 (October 1950): 19–33, and George Wolfskill, *The Revolt of the Conservatives: A History of the American Liberty League, 1934-1940* (1962).

**AMERICAN LIBRARY ASSOCIATION (ALA).** Founded in 1876 at Philadelphia by Melvin Dewey, the originator of the Dewey Decimal System of classification, and a group of librarians for the purpose of promoting free libraries and to upgrade the professional status of librarians. The problems it sought to remedy included lack of libraries in many communities, inadequate facilities in those that did exist, poor financing, and untrained personnel.

To ensure that libraries could serve their respective communities well, the ALA initiated the first training programs for librarians, implemented uniform systems of book classification, and pressed for the establishment of libraries in elementary and secondary schools. To deal with all aspects of operating a library, as well as related problems, various committees were established, including: Accreditation, Audio-Visual, Awards, Chapter Relations, Editorial, Instruction in the Use of Libraries, Intellectual Freedom, International Relations, Legislation, Organization, Reference and Subscription Books, Planning, and Standards. The ALA was instrumental in promulgating National Library Week to publicize the usefulness of public libraries.

The ALA monitors federal legislation, deals with federal agencies, maintains professional lobbyists in Washington, D.C., and provides a myriad of services to libraries throughout the nation. It utilizes its influence to secure greater federal funding for libraries and supplies information to its members relating to state and local financing. One of the areas where it often clashes with public opinion in small towns relates to the issue of intellectual or academic freedom. The ALA has fought to prevent local pressure groups from banning certain books, magazines, and films. Whenever possible these disputes are settled locally, but the ALA has initiated court cases to test the validity of locally imposed censorship.

The ALA has joint committees with other organizations such as the Association of American Publishers, Canadian Library Association, Catholic Library Association, Children's Book Council, and National Education Association.* Within the ALA there are divisions based upon special types of libraries and the various types of administrative duties connected with the operation of a library. It is also affiliated with other groups, such as the American Association of Law Libraries, American Theological Library Association, Music Library Association, and the Theatre Library Association.

Current national headquarters is located in Chicago, with Robert Wedgeworth serving as executive director. Present membership exceeds forty thousand; almost all professional librarians are members. The ALA conducts meetings and seminars and holds semiannual conferences. Its publications include a semimonthly, *Booklist and Subscription Books Bulletin*, monthly *American Libraries*, and a periodical review of current books, *Choice*.

**AMERICAN MEDICAL POLITICAL ACTION COMMITTEE (AMPAC).** Founded in 1961 at Chicago by the American Medical Association

(AMA) for the purpose of promoting greater involvement or participation by physicians in the political process. Supported by its parent, the AMA, the AMPAC has established various state political action committees to work for the election of local, state, and national candidates who espouse programs beneficial to the medical profession. Members of the AMA are encouraged to take part in political campaigns, contribute funds, canvass, sponsor rallies, and vote for candidates pledged to support the AMA position on certain issues.

AMPAC's motto is, "Politics is not something to avoid or abolish or destroy. . . . We must master its ways or we shall be mastered by those who do." Disapproving of national health insurance because it would be similar to a nationalized medical service, the AMPAC backs candidates who promote alternative systems. The AMPAC seeks the election of public officials who would preserve the individual freedom of doctors and limit the amount of federal control involved in the practice of their profession. In this area it runs counter to the views of many liberals and those in the lower economic groups who desire more extensive and less expensive medical services for the poor. The AMPAC resists programs designed to set fees or to impose rigid government controls of the activities of the medical profession.

To educate AMA members relative to the manner in which to participate more effectively in politics, the AMPAC distributes these booklets: *A Guide to Congressional Campaigns: A Winning Perspective, Helping Your Candidate Win*, and a *Handbook for Candidate Support Committees*. It has also produced films, including *Your Place in Political Action, Managing the Campaign for the House of Representatives*, and *How the Opinion Maker Makes Opinion*.

Present AMPAC headquarters is located at Chicago, with lobbyists stationed in Washington, D.C. The AMPAC, in carrying out the policies of the AMA, endorses political candidates, aids in their campaigns, and raises funds. Current AMPAC chairman is Dr. James C. MacLagan, with William L. Watson serving as executive director and treasurer. AMPAC publications include a newsletter, *Political Stethoscope*, and a leadership bulletin, *Across the Boards*.

**AMERICAN MUNICIPAL ASSOCIATION.** See National League of Cities.

**AMERICAN NATIONAL PARTY (ANP).** Founded in 1876 at Syracuse, New York, by the National Christian Association* for the purpose of promoting a Christian political philosophy. Its nominees for the national election of 1876 were James B. Walker for president and Donald Kirkpatrick for vice-president. The ANP platform supported prohibition; called for abolition of all secret societies; demanded legislation to curb monopolies; advocated a sound money system; proposed elimination of the electoral college, with direct election of the president and vice-president; insisted that American Indians be treated justly and fairly; and contended that the Bible ought to be read and studied in all public schools. Running on this platform, the ANP presidential ticket drew only 2,636 popular votes.

The ANP nominees in 1880 were John W. Phelps of Vermont for president and Samuel C. Pomeroy of Kansas for vice-president. Reiterating much of its previous platform, one plank specifically asserted, "Expose, withstand, and remove secret societies, Freemasonry in particular, and other anti-Christian movements, in order to save the churches of Christ from being depraved." The presidential ticket in this national election received 700 votes.

In 1884 the ANP nominated only a presidential candidate, Peter D. Wigginton, who garnered fewer than 100 votes. Following this debacle, the party disintegrated. The ANP represented the attitude of certain Christians who believed they could impose their morality upon the nation through politics. Its anti-Mason position was a throwback to earlier days when Christians considered the Masons, and others who held secret rituals, as a threat to the Christian church in America. The party's base of popular support was too narrow and thus lacked wide appeal.

**AMERICAN NAZI PARTY.** See National Socialist White People's Party.

**AMERICAN NEGRO LABOR CONGRESS.** See National Negro Congress.

**AMERICAN PAROLE ASSOCIATION.** See National Council on Crime and Delinquency.

**AMERICAN PARTY (1856).** See Know-Nothing Party.

**AMERICAN PARTY (1968).** See American Independent Party.

**AMERICAN PEACE SOCIETY (APS).** Founded in 1828 at Boston by pacifist William Ladd, who headed the organization until his death in 1841, for the purpose of promoting world peace. The APS, whose membership was never large, nevertheless utilized the right of petition and lobbying techniques in an attempt to secure implementation of its peace policy.

Ladd wrote two books from which the APS derived its objectives: *A Brief Illustration of the Principles of War and Peace, by Philanthropos* (1831) and *Essay on a Congress of Nations* (1840). Three proposals emerged from these books, which the APS sought to have implemented. It advocated the abolition of war as a means of solving international disputes, formation of a congress of nations, and the establishment of an international court to adjudicate differences between nations.

The last two proposals, made by Ladd and championed by the APS, were significant in that they suggested the creation of international institutions to resolve disputes. The congress of nations concept came to fruition in the League of Nations and the contemporary United Nations. The International Court at the Hague was established at the turn of the century, but the United States never accepted its jurisdiction. The U.S. Congress did, however, endorse the United Nations' International Court of Justice.

Divisions within the ranks of the APS occured when the United States was involved in a war. Such disruptions took place during the Civil War, World War I, and World War II. Members who were not pacifists tended to regard these actions as defensible and thus supported the war effort. Following World War I, the APS ardently supported U.S. membership in the League of Nations and participation in the International Court at the Hague, but public opinion ran counter to the APS's position, and neither took place. During the period of isolationism in the 1920s and 1930s, the APS found a fertile field for advocating disarmament. Following World War II, the general acceptance of the United Nations by the public at large was more responsible for U.S. membership than were the efforts of the APS. Since the establishment of the United Nations, the activities of the APS have diminished considerably.

Present national headquarters is located in Washington, D.C. Membership totals about a hundred. Evron K. Kirkpatrick currently is serving as president. The APS publishes a quarterly journal, *World Affairs*.

For further information, see Elton Atwater, *Organized Efforts in the United States toward World Peace* (1936).

**AMERICAN PROTECTIVE ASSOCIATION (APA).** Founded in 1887 at Clinton, Iowa, by Henry F. Bowers as a secret society to neutralize the growing political activity of Roman Catholics. It opposed Catholic parochial schools; hiring of Catholic teachers in the public schools; Catholics' holding political office; tax exemptions for church property; unrestricted immigration; enlistment of aliens in the armed forces; and liberalized naturalization procedures. In addition, it demanded competency tests in the English language and extended residency requirements for obtaining citizenship or qualifying for the franchise.

Its name has become synonymous with the nativist movement of the 1890s, but the actual influence of the APA on the political and legislative process was overrated by contemporaries. Although it claimed credit for Republican* gains in the mid-term elections of 1894, Democratic Party* losses more accurately may be attributed to the economic hardships following the panic of 1893. Even the congressional decision to terminate federal support for Indian schools operated by Catholics was in the making before APA began its intense lobbying.

The notoriety achieved by APA sprang largely from press reports that

frequently attributed to it the work of other nativist groups, including the
Loyal Orange Lodges and similar anti-Catholic, anti-immigration organizations. At its peak in late 1894 and early 1895, the APA probably enrolled no
more than a hundred thousand members, mostly from the Midwest, yet it
claimed a membership of two and one-half million. When it became clear
that the APA could neither influence legislation nor deliver votes for its
favorite candidates, the organization went into decline. Most white, Anglo-
Saxon, Protestant voters had nothing to do with APA because of its in-
tolerant hate mongering. Internecine squabbling in 1896 over endorsement
of the Republican presidential candidate, William McKinley, rather than
that of William Jennings Bryan, hastened the death of the APA. By the turn
of the century, it was a moribund remnant of its former self, and it soon
faded out of existence.

For further information, see John Higham, *Strangers in the Land:
American Nativism, 1860-1925* (1955), and Donald L. Kinzer, *An Episode
in Anti-Catholicism: The American Protective Association* (1964).

**AMERICAN PROTECTIVE TARIFF LEAGUE.** See Trade Relations
Council of the United States.

**AMERICAN REPUBLICAN PARTY.** See American Independent Party.

**AMERICAN SECURITY COUNCIL (ASC).** Founded in 1955 at
Washington, D.C., by a group of retired officers of the U.S. armed forces
for the purposes of promoting national security. The membership rolls of
the ASC listed such prominent officers of the military establishment as
General Lewis W. Walt of the U.S. Marine Corps, Admiral John J. Bergen,
Admiral Robert L. Dennison, and Rear Admiral Chester C. Ward. Included
also were four former chairmen of the Joint Chiefs of Staff: General
Lyman L. Lemnitzer, General Nathan Twining, General Earle G. Wheeler,
and General Maxwell D. Taylor.

Civilian members of the ASC included such notable individuals as Lloyd
Wright, a former president of the American Bar Association*; James D.
Atkinson, professor of government at Georgetown University; G. Duncan
Bauman, publisher of the *St. Louis Globe-Democrat;* Clare Booth Luce,
former congresswoman and U.S. ambassador to Italy; Dr. Eugene P.
Wigner, physicist from Princeton University; Dr. Edward Teller, a nuclear
scientist and the "father" of the hydrogen bomb; and Dr. Stefan T.
Possony, director of International Studies at the Hoover Institution on
War, Revolution, and Peace.

Financed by grants and contributions from corporations, universities,
and other institutions involved in national defense research, the ASC maintains a library, disseminates information, sponsors radio and television
broadcasts, and provides newspapers with news relating to the internal

security of the United States. It also issues reports, provides expert witnesses to testify before congressional committees, and seeks to enlighten public opinion on the need to keep the nation's military strength at a level to ensure world power status for the United States. Because of the technical nature of military weaponry, the ASC exerts more influence on Pentagon officials, the White House, and Congress than it does on the general public.

The ASC supports Radio Free Europe and a series of broadcasts within the continental United States. In 1976 it initiated Bicentennial Operation Alert, a project designed to alert the American public to the dangers it saw in détente with the Soviet Union and to the risk involved in permitting the strength of the U.S. armed forces to deteriorate relative to the growing military prowess of potential adversaries. It has proclaimed reservations on the Strategic Arms Limitation Treaty of 1979, maintaining that the United States yielded more concessions than it received. This attitude is consistent with its suspicions that the Soviets may secretly violate the agreement because the United States is unable to monitor and detect such violations.

Present national headquarters of the ASC is located at Washington, D.C., with John M. Fisher as president. Current membership is thirty-five hundred. The ASC issues research reports at regular intervals and publishes the *Washington Report*, a weekly.

**AMERICAN SOCIETY FOR PUBLIC ADMINISTRATION (ASPA).** Founded in 1939 at Washington, D.C., by a group of public administrators for the purpose of promoting professionalism in public service. The ASPA attraced public officials and administrators from local, state, and federal government. Educators and others involved in public management also found it important in terms of setting standards, facilitating the effective training of officials in public service jobs, and upgrading the working conditions of those in administrative positions.

The ASPA has permanent committees: Comparative Administration; Continuing Education and Training; International; and Public Issues. It operates a placement bureau, conducts research, issues special reports, disseminates information to the public, monitors legislation, and keeps members informed on issues relating to public management. Regional and national conferences are held to keep members informed and to influence public opinion favorably toward public officials who are often regarded as faceless bureaucrats.

Present national headquarters of the ASPA is in Washington, D.C. Membership, which is nationwide, exceeds ten thousand. The current president is Nesta M. Gallas, with Seymour Berlin serving as executive director. ASPA is affiliated with the National Association of Schools of Public Affairs and Administration and the Conference of Minority Public Administrators. The ASPA issues a monthly, *Public Administration News*, and a bimonthly *Public Administration Review*.

**AMERICAN SOCIETY FOR THE PREVENTION OF CRUELTY TO ANIMALS (ASPCA).** Founded in 1866 at New York City by Henry Bergh, who served as its president until 1888, for the purpose of promoting humane treatment of animals. Under Bergh's leadership, the ASPCA lobbied successfully in New York to get the state legislature to enact the first stringent anti-cruelty law. Passed in 1866, it forbade inhumane or cruel treatment to animals. The law did much to protect horses, which were often beaten and forced to haul loads beyond their pulling capacity.

Because the ASPCA was given the legal authority to enforce New York's anti-cruelty law, it immediately set about to end the practice of whipping horses; stopped dogfights and all other types of animal fights staged for amusement; required sportsmen to substitute clay pigeons for real ones; and campaigned against the use of bird feathers as adornments on hats. Following the New York example, ASPCA chapters were formed in other states to achieve similar goals.

As membership grew, the ASPCA broadened its work to include the establishment and operation of animal hospitals (1912); providing school children with free educational materials relating to the humane treatment of pets (1916); inaugurated dog obedience classes (1944); opened an animal port at Kennedy International Airport (1958); started a special adoption service for dogs and cats (1962); acquired patents for equipment for the humane slaughter of food animals and made them available royalty free to meat packers (1964); began the use of closed-circuit television in animal shelters (1971); and recently embarked on a national program for controlling animal overpopulation by encouraging the neutering of pets, now mandatory for all pets secured from ASPCA shelters.

The ASPCA gives free care to more than a quarter of a million animals yearly. Its Henry Bergh Memorial Hospital in Manhattan is the most advanced veterinary center in the world. ASPCA members lobby on the local, state, and federal level to gain protective legislation for animals. Some eight thousand members support the work of the organization through contributions. Present national headquarters is located in New York City. Currently Alistair B. Martin is president, with Encile E. Rains serving as both executive vice-president and general director. George W. Foy is employed as a lobbyist in Washington, D.C. Departments within the ASPCA include Humane Education, Humane Work, Hospital and Clinic, License, Public Relations, and Special Activities. The ASPCA holds an annual convention and publishes *Animal Protection*.

**AMERICAN SOCIETY OF SANITARY ENGINEERNG (ASSE).** Founded in 1906 at Washington, D.C., by a group of twenty-two plumbing inspectors and sanitary engineers for the purpose of promoting professionalism in the field of sanitary engineering. Goals included improvement in the science of sanitary engineering, protection of the public, upgrading the profession, and increasing the job benefits of those working in the field of plumbing or sanitation.

With a slogan of "Prevention Rather Than Cure," ASSE initiated a successful national program for securing standardized laws and municipal codes regulating water and sewage installations. It sponsored research related to water pollution; causes of epidemics (such as hepatitis and polio), garbage disposal, irrigation, and disposition of nuclear wastes. ASSE has a number of permanent committees: Adequate Plumbing Requirements; Air-Conditioning, Water Supply, and Waste; Apprentice Education; Atomic Energy; Buildings; Cross-Connections; Detergents; Drainage; Explosions; Garbage Disposal; Health Protection and Disease Prevention; Hot Water Damage; Irrigation and Lawn Sprinklers; Mobile Homes and Parks; National Defense and Safety; Plumbing and Disease Organisms; Pressure and Temperature Control Valves; Radioactive Waste Disposal; Rainwater Disposal; Refrigeration; Sewage Disposal; Solar Water Heating; Sterilization of Food and Drink; Swimming Pools; and Water Conservation.

ASSE's refresher course, initiated in 1946 and held prior to each annual convention, reviews basic principles and introduces new techniques to its members. Membership, nearly three thousand in thirty local chapters, is drawn from the ranks of architects, building designers, building inspectors, engineers, health inspectors, plumbers, plumbing contractors, and sanitary engineers. At its national convention papers are delivered and discussions are held with representatives of other organizations, such as the National Bureau of Standards, the International Association of Plumbing and Mechanical Officials, the National Sanitation Foundation, Building Officials Conference of America, the American Society of Plumbing Engineers, and the American Supply Association.

The ASSE continually tests plumbing equipment and certifies that it meets established standards by awarding it a seal of approval. The Seal Control Board, set up to implement this program, assists manufacturers in complying with its requirements. Revocation of the seal of approval is widely publicized and therefore acts as a deterrent to use of ineffective or unsafe equipment by builders. Representatives of ASSE also testify at local, state, and federal hearings held by government officials and thus are influential in establishing codes for the prevention of water pollution.

Present national headquarters is located in Cleveland, Ohio. Current president is Wylie M. Mitchell, with Sanford Schwartz serving as executive secretary. In addition to special reports, ASSE publishes a monthly, *News Letter*, and an annual, *Year Book*.

**AMERICAN UNION AGAINST MILITARISM (AUAM).** Founded in 1914 at New York City by a group of pacifists and antiwar advocates for the purpose of preventing U.S. involvement in World War I. Prime movers in the formation of the AUAM were Lillian D. Wald, its president, Crystal Eastman, a member of its executive committee, and Florence Kelley, a pacifist and renowned social reformer. Other important members of the AUAM included Jane Addams, Roger Baldwin, Scott Nearing, and Norman Thomas. Its basic political orientation was pacifist and leftwing.

The initial goal of the AUAM was to persuade President Wilson to mediate an end to World War I. When the Wilson administration moved toward preparedness, the AUAM opposed all efforts toward preparing the nation militarily. It lobbied unsuccessfully against passage of the National Defense Act of 1916, which increased the size of the U.S. armed forces. Once the United States was involved in the war, the AUAM also opposed passage of the Selective Service Act of 1917. This opposition, at a time when wartime patriotism was high, made the AUAM and its activities unpopular with the mass population.

Because of its opposition to war and—as the AUAM viewed it—imperialistic ventures, public opinion generally regarded this organization as radical and un-American. Since anti-war statements were not popular, AUAM members were harassed and intimidated by public officials. As a result, the AUAM turned its attention to the preservation of civil liberties and the right of free speech. The AUAM was instrumental in forming the American Bureau for Conscientious Objectors and the Civil Liberties Bureau. From the latter organization emerged the American Civil Liberties Union.*

The AUAM was not large in terms of numbers—membership was never more than a few hundred—but those belonging were articulate people of prominence. They had access to the press and literary journals of the time. A few were pacifists, some were socialists, most were liberals, and a small minority were left-wing radicals opposed to capitalistic imperialism. The views expressed by the AUAM did not represent those of the masses but rather those of a few intellectuals and social reformers. The AUAM was in disarray during World War I, and by the end of the conflict it was moribund.

For more information, see R. L. Duffus, *Lillian Wald, Neighbor and Crusader* (1938); Horace C. Paterson, *Opponents of War, 1917–1918* (1957); and Max Eastman, *Love and Revolution* (1964).

**AMERICAN VEGETARIAN PARTY (AVP).** Founded in 1948 at Chicago by Dr. John Maxwell, owner of a vegetarian restaurant, and Symon Gould, editor of the *American Vegetarian*, for the purpose of promoting vegetarianism in the United States.

In 1948, Maxwell ran as the AVP's presidential candidate with Gould as his vice-presidential running mate. The AVP platform called for prohibitions on the eating of meat, advocated federal ownership of all natural resources, and demanded government pensions of one hundred dollars per month for each individual over sixty-five years of age. The AVP presidential ticket polled four votes.

AVP candidates repeatedly entered the presidential elections until 1960. Their popular vote was always miniscule in number. The party ceased to exist in 1960 when Gould died. The AVP had no connection with the American Vegetarian Union. It represented a one-issue party that failed to attract a national membership.

**AMERICAN VETERANS COMMITTEE (AVC).** Founded in 1943 at Washington, D.C., by a group of World War II veterans for the purpose of promoting a better America for war veterans. Its stated objective was "To achieve a more democratic and prosperous America and a more stable world. Citizens first, veterans second." One of the prime movers in the formation of the AVC was Charles G. Bolte, who represented the organization's liberal orientation.

Since the AVC regarded the American Legion* and Veterans of Foreign Wars of the United States* as too conservative on domestic and international issues, the founders of AVC desired a new organization to represent the views of more liberally oriented individuals. It lobbied not only for increased benefits to veterans but also championed civil rights, support for the United Nations, reapportionment, and revision of outdated state constitutions. In an era of Jim Crowism it refused to charter segregated local units. Because some of its members were affiliated with the American Civil Liberties Union,* it also vigorously opposed all forms of censorship. In general, the AVC has taken the position that veterans fare best not by special legislation but when social reforms are achieved on a national level.

Total membership in AVC today is about twenty-five thousand. Members represent veterans from World War II, Korea, and Vietnam. The AVC is less influential than larger veterans' organizations. Its liberal, left-wing orientation restricts its membership base and diffuses its activities. Present national headquarters is located in Washington, D.C. Current executive director is June A. Willenz. The AVC helped found and is affiliated with the World Veterans Federation.

For further information, see Charles G. Bolte, *The New Veteran* (1945).

**AMERICAN VETERANS OF FOREIGN SERVICE.** See Veterans of Foreign Wars of the United States.

**AMERICAN VETERANS OF WORLD WAR II-KOREA-VIETNAM.** See AMVETS.

**AMERICAN WOMAN SUFFRAGE ASSOCIATION (AWSA).** Founded in 1869 at Cleveland, Ohio, by Lucy Stone, Julia Ward Howe, Henry

Blackwell (Stone's husband), the Reverend Thomas J. Higginson, the Reverend Henry Ward Beecher, and other supporters of civil rights for the purpose of advocating ratification of the Fifteenth Amendment and agitating for woman suffrage. The formation of the AWSA the same year as the founding of the National Woman Suffrage Association* (NWSA) signaled a breach in the woman suffrage movement. The AWSA supported ratification of the Fifteenth Amendment to the U.S. Constitution, which gave black freedmen the right to vote, even though women were not included. The NWSA, having failed to secure inclusion of the franchise for women, fought to defeat the amendment. Another difference centered around the AWSA's conservative approach to such reforms as the labor union movement, the greenback issue, and liberalization of divorce laws. AWSA leaders opposed endorsement of such issues and instead focused only on the subject of woman suffrage.

Lucy Stone had long been involved in the fight for equal rights for women. In 1850 she called the first national woman's rights convention and in 1868 was instrumental in forming the American Equal Rights Association,* which sought the vote for both black males and women. While serving as president of the New Jersey Woman Suffrage Association in 1868, Stone helped found the New England Woman Suffrage Association. In 1870 she started a weekly newspaper, the *Woman's Journal*, which for the next forty-seven years she edited and financed, along with her husband and her daughter, Alice Stone Blackwell. It was called by its followers the "voice of the woman's movement."

Finding it difficult, if not impossible, to secure congressional enactment of a woman suffrage amendment to the U.S. Constitution, the AWSA worked hard to gain the vote by passage of state laws. In 1890 it won a significant victory when Wyoming granted the franchise to women. That same year the AWSA and the NWSA merged in order to unite the woman suffrage movement. In the new organization, named the National Woman Suffrage Association, Stone became chairperson of the executive committee. Although her personal relations with the leaders of the former NWSA were not cordial, the woman suffrage movement benefited by the new-found unity.

For more information, see Elinor Rice Hays, *Morning Star: A Biography of Lucy Stone* (1961).

**AMERICAN WORKERS PARTY.** See Conference for Progressive Labor Action.

**AMERICANS FOR CONSTITUTIONAL ACTION (ACA).** Founded in 1958 at Washington, D.C., by Senator Karl Mundt (R-S.D.) and retired Admiral Ben Moreell, who at the time was chairman of the board of directors of Jones and Laughlin Steel Corporation, for the purpose of promoting the election of true conservatives to public office. The ACA was patterned after its liberal counterpart, the Americans for Democratic Action.* ACA supports candidates who, in its judgment, display "allegiance to the original spirit and principles of the Constitution." Among the original trustees of the ACA were two generals associated with Douglas MacArthur during World War II, Thomas A. Lane and Bonner Fellers, and two well-known actors, John Wayne and Walter Brennan.

Membership in ACA is relatively small because it stands for ultra-right-wing conservatism. Its members represent the Ronald Reagan faction within the Republican Party* and consider the welfare state as being only one step removed from socialism. They believe government is too big, that federal bureaucracy regiments the lives of individuals, and that taxes should be drastically cut. Relative to foreign policy the ACA is hawkish regarding the Soviet Union and the People's Republic of China. It supports treaty commitments to Taiwan, desires the United States to keep total control over the Panama Canal, and views disarmament or détente with dismay.

The ACA issues the *ACA-Index*, which rates the voting records of members of Congress according to its own criteria. Two senators, John Tower (R-Tex.) and Barry Goldwater (R-Ariz.), once received scores of 100 percent and 98 percent, respectively. Five Democratic* senators have received the lowest rating: Daniel K. Inouye (Ha.), Edward Kennedy (Mass.), Russel B. Long (La.), Gaylord Nelson (Wis.) and Abraham Ribicoff (Conn.).

To promote the election or reelection of conservative candidates to Congress, the ACA also bestows endorsements, provides campaign services, and grants financial assistance. In addition it presents biennial distinguished service awards to selected members of Congress deemed worthy of such recognition. Whereas the ACA has been successful in specific congressional campaigns, its political base is too narrow in ideological terms to win mass support. Its pride in purity of principles over pragmatic politics renders the ACA less effective in elections. It also serves to split the Republican Party by separating the right wing from the moderates and more liberal members of the GOP.

Present national headquarters of ACA is located in Washington, D.C. Current president is Charles A. McManus, Jr. To keep its members abreast of current legislation, the ACA issues *ACA Congressional Record Digest and Talley*.

**AMERICANS FOR DEMOCRATIC ACTION (ADA).** Founded in 1947 at Washington, D.C., by representatives from the Union for Democratic Action (UDA) for the purpose of promoting both New Deal liberalism and a type of internationalism that had been advocated by President Franklin D. Roosevelt. The UDA, an organization of pro-New Deal liberals formed during World War II, invited 150 supporters of FDR to a conference. At this meeting, a committee of twenty-five was selected to set up the new national organization to be known as the ADA. Wilson Wyatt, who would become ADA's first national director, and economist Leon Henderson were co-chairmen of this committee. Other members included Mayor Hubert H. Humphrey of Minneapolis; radio commentator Elmer Davis; Reinhold Niebuhr, noted theologian; Franklin D. Roosevelt, Jr.; Walter White, president of the National Association for the Advancement of Colored People*; David Dubinsky, president of the AFL's International Ladies' Garment Workers' Union; Walter P. Reuther, president of the CIO's United Automobile Workers of America; and James Loeb, Jr., secretary of the parent UDA. Charter members of the ADA included such prominent people as Eleanor Roosevelt, Stewart Alsop, Chester Bowles, Joseph P. Lash, Sidney Hook, Gardner Jackson, Arthur M. Schlesinger, Jr., Jerry Voorhis, Chet Holifield, Bishop G. Bromley Oxnam, and Emil Rive, president of the CIO's Textile Workers of America.

A six-point statement of principles adopted by the ADA called for expansion of New Deal programs, protection of civil liberties, support for the United Nations, and U.S. aid to "freedom-loving peoples the world over." The statement also asserted, "We reject any associaton with Communists or sympathizers with Communism in the United States as completely as we reject any association with Fascists or their sympathizers." This caveat to Communists alienated some pro-Russian left wingers and fellow travelers, but it prevented the ADA from becoming either a Communist front or an organization dominated by those whose real loyalty lay with the Communist Party of the United States of America.*

In 1948 the ADA supported the reelection of President Harry S. Truman. In so doing, it did much to convince liberals not to vote for Henry A. Wallace, the presidential candidate of the Progressive Party of 1948.* By influencing many liberals to remain loyal to the Democratic Party,* the ADA contributed substantially to Truman's so-called miracle victory over Governor Thomas E. Dewey of New York, the presidential nominee of the Republican Party.* In 1952 and 1956, ADA endorsed Adlai E. Stevenson for president; in 1960, John F. Kennedy; in 1964, Lyndon B. Johnson; in 1968, Hubert H. Humphrey; and in 1972, George McGovern (with some reservations). In 1976 Jimmy Carter was not the ADA favorite among the Democratic presidential contenders, and it was critical of Carter's commitment to reduce government spending, which would curtail many social welfare programs. The ADA supported Senator Edward Kennedy (D-Mass.) in his effort to win the 1980 Democratic presidential nomination. After Jimmy Carter won renomination, it again endorsed him but without enthusiasm. Some members, such as historian Arthur M. Schlesinger, Jr., endorsed independent candidate John Anderson.

The ADA has long championed social welfare measures and federal legislation to reduce unemployment. It supports anti-poverty programs, increased Social Security benefits, a higher minimum wage, national health insurance, low-cost housing, consumer protection, environmental control, and affirmative rights for minorities. ADA members have often been in the vanguard of those making proposals that have found their way into the Fair Deal of Harry Truman, the New Frontier of John F. Kennedy, and the Great Society of Lyndon B. Johnson.

During the 1960s, leadership of the ADA gravitated toward the Left. Key spokespeople were economist John Kenneth Galbraith; Michael J. Harrington, a Socialist turned Democrat; Congresswoman Bella S. Abzug (D-N.Y.), an activist in the women's movement; and Allard K. Lowenstein, an organizer of both the Anti-war Vietnam Summer and the "dump Johnson" movement in 1968. In 1972 following President Richard M. Nixon's reelection, the ADA was among the first groups to call for his impeachment.

In 1975 the ADA created the Democratic Conference as a coalition of liberal Democrats and trade union leaders. Its purpose was to find common ground so as to avoid a split at the Democratic National Convention. To influence the primary elections in 1976, the ADA issued the following campaign pamphlets: *Presidential Candidates' Voting Record*; *Senator Henry M. Jackson: Liberal?*; *Transcript of George Wallace Interview with Foreign Journalists, Montgomery, Alabama, March 3, 1975*; and *Wallace: Worse Than You Think*.

Membership in ADA, which today totals nearly sixty-five thousand, is composed mostly of professionals, educators, intellectuals, trade union leaders, and liberal Democrats. Its greatest influence is in its ability to formulate liberal domestic and international policies, which, in turn, are adopted as part of the Democratic Party's political platform. Its members, highly articulate, publicize their position with a great deal of skill and effectiveness. Thus public opinion, particularly that of the left wing, is mobilized for congressional and national elections.

Present national headquarters is located in Washington, D.C. The current national chairman is Congressman Donald M. Fraser (Democratic Farm Labor [DFL]-Minn.). Publications include a monthly, *ADA World*; a semimonthly, *Legislative Newsletter* (which ranks members of Congress according to ADA's liberal criteria); and an annual, *Program for Americans*.

For further information, see Clifton Brock, *Americans for Democratic Action* (1963), and Jack T. Ericson, ed., *The Americans for Democratic Action Papers, 1941–1965: A Guide to the Microfilm Edition of the Original Records in the State Historical Society of Wisconsin* (1978).

**AMERICANS FOR ENERGY INDEPENDENCE (AFEI).** Founded in 1975 at Washington, D.C., by Admiral Elmo R. Zumwalt, former chief of U.S. naval operations, for the purpose of promoting a national policy of oil independence for the United States. Admiral Zumwalt served as AFEI's first president. The primary motivation for the formation of AFEL was the Arab (OPEC) oil cartel embargo of 1975, which caused a shortage of gasoline throughout the nation.

Membership in AFEI is relatively small, numbering no more than one hundred, but members represent important segments of business, the petroleum industry, and government. Former President Gerald R. Ford is a member. The AFEI lobbies for federal legislation that would foster research for alternative sources of energy. The AFEI also seeks to focus public attention on the need for an overall energy program so that the United States does not remain dependent upon oil imported from other countries.

Present national headquarters is located in Washington, D.C. Current president is Endicott Peabody, a former governor of Massachusetts.

**AMERICANS FOR INDIAN OPPORTUNITY (AIO).** Founded in 1970 at Washington, D.C., by a group of American Indians for the purpose of promoting social and economic benefits for Americans of Indian ancestry. The AIO is governed by a thirty-three-member board of governors, which includes such nationally known individuals as I. W. Abel, president of the United Steelworkers of America; Maria Tallchief Paschen, former prima ballerina of the New York City Ballet Company; and the Reverend Theodore M. Hesburgh, president of Notre Dame University.

The AIO operates on many levels to advance the cause of American Indians. It provides technical assistance to local tribes; initiates educational projects; supports job-training programs; seeks government funding to develop economic opportunities for Indians; lobbies for federal legislation; monitors government agencies; provides information to non-Indians on Indian problems; fosters preservation of Indian culture; serves as a catalyst for Indian action; and helps to coordinate the activities of Indians, Eskimos, and Aleuts. The AIO established the Native American Legal Defense and Education Fund and in 1973 inaugurated experimental programs to develop models for metropolitan relocation. It is also trying to find solutions for other reservation problems.

The AIO desires to see American Indians cease being wards of the government but realizes that many Indians are not prepared to earn a living in a non-Indian society. It fosters self-help whenever possible and promotes local programs that prepare Indians for independent living outside of the tribe. The AIO is seeking to promote social integration while at the same time preserving Indian culture and self-pride. AIO-sponsored programs have rendered assistance to over three hundred Indian tribes throughout the United States. National conferences are held periodically to inform the public about the needs of American Indians.

Present national headquarters is located in Washington, D.C. Currently La Donna Harris, a Comanche and the wife of Fred R. Harris, former senator from Oklahoma, is president of AIO, with James MacDonald serving as executive director.

**AMNESTY INTERNATIONAL (AI).** Founded in 1961 at London, England, by Peter Beneson, a British lawyer, for the purpose of facilitating the release of political prisoners all over the world. The U.S. affiliate was formed in 1966 at New York City. AI's primary objective is to seek the release of "prisoners of conscience" who are imprisoned for expressing political or religious views that do not advocate violence. By disseminating information and publicizing such cases, the AI tries to focus world opinion on the countries involved so as to attain freedom for prisoners so held.

To obtain information about individuals held captive solely for political or religious reasons, AI monitors trials, gives legal assistance to victims of persecution, and observes the treatment that prisoners are given in prison. AI espouses no particular ideology. Through its efforts some ten thousand political prisoners have been freed. It uses its influence with the United Nations, Council of Europe, UNESCO, Inter-American Commission on Human Rights, and the Organization of African Unity. For those political prisoners for whom freedom cannot be gained, AI keeps in contact with them through letters and visitations so that they will not feel abandoned. Currently it is focusing its attention on the Soviet Union, where political dissidents and those of the Jewish faith have been imprisoned for expressing their beliefs. In 1977 AI was the recipient of the Nobel Peace Prize in recognition for its humanitarian work.

Some 170,000 volunteers carry out the activities of AI. Honorary chairmen of AI include Roger Baldwin, Sean McBride, Victor Reuther, and Michael Straight. Chairman of the board of directors is A. Whitney Ellsworth. Members of the National Advisory Council include such well-known persons as Joan Baez, Daniel Bell, Zbigniew Brzezinski, William F. Buckley, Jr., Jules Feiffer, Lillian Helman, Arthur Miller, Frank Mankiewicz, and former Senator Jacob Javits (R-N.Y.). Current secretary-general of AI is Martin Ennals, with Dr. Amelia Augustus serving as executive director of the U.S. affiliate in New York City.

The AI supports the human-rights policy of President Jimmy Carter, which seeks to protect the civil liberties of political dissenters, and seeks its implementation wherever possible. It desires to see the Helsinki Agreement, of which the Soviet Union was a signatory with the United States, enforced relative to human rights in Eastern Europe and publicizes violations to arouse world public opinion. Periodically it appeals to members of the United Nations to comply with the U.N.'s Universal Declaration of Human Rights. Investigators are constantly seeking cases where human rights are violated for political or religious reasons. In the United States the AI publishes a bimonthly, *Amnesty Action*, and a quarterly, *Chronicle of Current Events*.

**AMVETS.** Founded in 1944 at Kansas City, Missouri, by leaders of eighteen smaller veterans' organizations for the purpose of promoting greater benefits for men who served in the U.S. armed forces during World War II. The organization was originally named the American Veterans of World War II but altered its name to AMVETS after it was so dubbed by a newsman. AMVETS was chartered by Congress in 1946. Its charter was amended in 1950 to make Korean War veterans eligible for membership and again in 1966 to include Vietnam war veterans. In 1946 AMVETS AUXILIARY was formed for female veterans and relatives of males belonging to the parent organization.

With a motto of "We Fought Together—Now Let's Build Together," AMVETS maintains a staff to assist its 250,000 members in all matters relating to veterans' affairs. It lobbies in Congress for increased government benefits to veterans and monitors federal programs geared to aid veterans. It was instrumental in securing enactment by Congress of the Korean G.I. Bill of Rights and the Cold War Bill of Rights so that veterans of Korea and Vietnam might enjoy similar benefits as those who served in World War II. AMVETS seeks to improve job training, maintain veteran preference in civil service positions, and improve medical facilities at hospitals operated by the Veterans Administration. AMVETS was opposed to giving amnesty to draft dodgers or deserters. It supports a strong national defense program so that the United States will never have its security threatened.

AMVETS maintains these permanent committees: Americanism; Armed Forces; Brotherhood; Civil Defense; Civil Service and Employment; Domestic Affairs, Employment of the Handicapped; Hospital and Service; International Affairs; Legislative; Traffic Safety; and Veterans Rehabilitation. To publicize the last one, AMVETS cooperates annually with the President's Committee on Employment of the Handicapped to sponsor a nationwide poster contest to inform the public about this program.

AMVET's volunteers, called Green Hats, render assistance to hospitalized veterans, retarded children, and orphans. They also sponsor a Blood for Veterans Week. Starting in 1952 AMVETS funded a $250,000 scholarship program. It also administers the Youth Program, as well as one called Positive Americanism. Programs are sponsored in conjunction with the United Nations and the Freedoms Foundation at Valley Forge.* In addition to fellowship and seeking federal benefits, AMVETS provides such services for its members as life insurance, hospital coverage, discounts on medical prescriptions, and travel tours.

AMVETS AUXILIARY sponsors programs to assist hospitalized

veterans, child welfare centers, and projects to promote patriotism. Junior AMVETS was organized for children and the Sad Sacks for fun activities.

In 1954 AMVETS began bestowing the Silver Helmet Award. This replica of a World War II soldier's helmet is given to Americans who make outstanding contributions to public service. The first recipient was General George C. Marshall. The Silver Helmet was also awarded to the following presidents: Herbert C. Hoover, Harry S. Truman, Dwight D. Eisenhower, John F. Kennedy, Lyndon B. Johnson, and Richard M. Nixon. Other recipients included such prominent individuals as Dr. Ralph Bunche, Eleanor Roosevelt, J. Edgar Hoover, Senator Henry M. Jackson (D-Wash.), Joe DiMaggio, Bob Hope, Martha Raye, Red Skelton, and Danny Thomas.

National headquarters of AMVETS is located in Washington, D.C. Current national director is R. B. Gomulinski. National headquarters of AMVETS AUXILIARY is located in Old Orchard Beach, Maine. Current executive secretary is Rita J. Potvin. AMVETS is affiliated with the AMVETS National Service Foundation and the World Veterans Federation in Paris. Publications by AMVETS include *Newsletter* and a bimonthly magazine, *National AMVETS.*

**ANARCHIST FEDERATION (AF).** Founded in 1960 at New York City by a group of anarchists, syndicalists, and former members of the Industrial Workers of the World (IWW) for the purpose of promoting anarchism in the United States. Prime movers in this fusion movement included Murray Brookchin, a former organizer for the IWW and the Congress of Industrial Organizations; Walter Coughey, an advocate of linking anarchism to ecology (liberation from pollution); Paul Spencer, editor of an anarchistic journal, *Good Soup*; Charles T. Smith, a Harvard University graduate and former Episcopalian turned Eastern Orthodox; and Mike Itkin, a Jew who became a priest in a sect called the Old Roman Catholic church.

With a relatively small membership, never exceeding one thousand during its high tide during the 1960s, the AF represents a wide variety of viewpoints. Most members believe in the overthrow of capitalism and the abolition of government, but there is no ideological agreement as to the means to achieve these goals. Some members are pacifists and preach gradual change. Others are more militant and believe in direct action, including individual acts of terror. Many are anti-political, some are romantic utopians, and a few are nihilists. Those formerly associated with the IWW still believe in syndicalism and desire to make the trade union movement the vanguard of the revolution. The hero of this group is William "Big Bill" Haywood, a leader of the Western Federation of Miners and a founder of the IWW.

One faction within the AF was led by Sam Weiner. Championing extreme individualism, he formed a short-lived organization, the Libertarian League. An affiliate of AF for teenagers was established in 1964. Calling itself the Resurgence Youth Movement, its mimeographed magazine,

*Resurgence*, was filled with calls for violence. Anti-establishment and prone to civil disorder, this group did widespread property damage during the anti-Vietnam war protests until police subdued its activities.

Because of the nature of its beliefs, the AF has no national headquarters nor does it have an organizational structure. During the 1960s and 1970s, when the anti-Vietnam war protests were going on, some radicals and followers of the New Left joined the anarchist movement. But once the war in Vietnam terminated, most students left the AF, and it has subsequently become moribund. Anarchism has never had many adherents in the United States because anarchists cannot work within the democratic system. Their demands for free speech and the right to demonstrate their opposition to government become a problem when their very activities are aimed at abolition of the democratic system. For this reason anarchists generally have been regarded as radical eccentrics who must be tolerated when they are peaceful and suppressed when they become violent. Those anarchists who practice terrorism tend to make the entire movement suspect to the general public. Anarchist influence in America has been insignificant and over the years has won few converts among the masses.

For more information, see James Joll, *The Anarchists* (1964).

**ANTI-DEFAMATION LEAGUE OF THE B'NAI B'RITH (ADL).** Founded in 1913 at Chicago by Sigmund Livingston, an attorney from Bloomington, Illinois, who served as its director until 1946, for the purpose of preventing derogatory stereotyping of Jews in the press, vaudeville, and movies. ADL operates in conjunction with its parent organization, the B'nai B'rith. The objectives of ADL were "to stop, by appeals to reason and conscience, and if necessary, by appeal to law, the defamation of the Jewish people" and "to secure justice and fair treatment to all citizens alike and to put an end forever to unjust and unfair discrimination against, and ridicule of, any sect or body of citizens."

In 1914 the ADL aroused considerable controversy by seeking to persuade educators not to use William Shakespeare's *Merchant of Venice* (either read in class or performed on stage) on the grounds that it demeaned Jews through the character of Shylock. During the 1920s ADL publicly accused the Ku Klux Klan* of anti-Semitism and was instrumental in securing enactment of anti-hood laws in some states of the South. ADL sought to refute the so-called Protocols of the Elders of Zion (a spurious document concocted by the Tsarist police in 1905 purporting to outline a Jewish conspiracy to enslave the world) when they were published in Henry Ford's weekly journal, the *Dearborn Independent*. When Adolf Hitler came to power in 1933, the ADL worked incessantly to counter Nazi racist propaganda and strove to expose the anti-Semitism of the German-American Bund.

After World War II, the ADL was instrumental in securing abolition of the enrollment quota system whereby Jews were discriminated against when seeking to enter institutions of higher learning. The ADL has been vigorous in opposing current activities of Klan groups and neo-Nazi organizations such as the National Socialist White People's Party.* It has also taken steps to counter negative Arab opinion relative to the existence of Israel as a nation-state in the Middle East. ADL seeks to prevent "anti-Zionism" from becoming a subterfuge for a new type of anti-Semitism. It denies "dual loyalty" on the part of American Jews' supporting Israel and strives to refute charges that American Jewry constitutes a "Zionist pressure bloc." The ADL believes that information should continually be disseminated relative to the Holocaust so that the younger generation of Americans will realize what once took place because of bigotry and anti-Semitism.

Commencing in 1948, the ADL began bestowing an annual America's Democratic Legacy Award. The first medallion was awarded to President Harry S. Truman. Interestingly, the award also went to Henry Ford II in 1951 and to the Ford Foundation in 1954. In 1946 the national headquarters of ADL was moved to New York City, and in 1965 it absorbed the Institute for Democratic Education.

The ADL maintains a staff of some 250, lobbies, and operates twenty-eight regional offices throughout the country. Its present membership totals nearly 170,000. Permanent committees exist to deal with Civil Rights; Community Service; Planning and Development; Program; and Public Relations. The ADL publishes *Facts*, which contains reports on activities of anti-Semitic organizations; *Rights*, which presents information on specific cases of discrimination against Jews; *Law*, which monitors civil rights legislation and court decisions; and its official monthly, *ADL Bulletin*.

**ANTI-ENLISTMENT LEAGUE.** See War Resisters League.

**ANTI-FEDERALIST PARTY (AFP).** Formed in 1787 after the writing of the U.S. Constitution at the Philadelphia convention for the purpose of preventing its ratification by the states. Its antecedents stem from the colonial and confederation periods, when farmer-small property holder factions fought against political domination by the merchant-planter class. The farmer-small property holder groups within the various states favored retention of the Articles of Confederation.

The Anti-Federalists represented small farmers or small property holders. They were generally less educated than those in the Federalist Party* and tended to be in the debtor class. They also believed in direct democracy, states' rights, a monetary policy favorable to debtors, low taxes, and cheap land. The Anti-Federalists coalesced into a party when the Constitution was presented to the states for ratification. Primary opposition to the document stemmed from the fear that the new federal government was too centralized and too powerful. It was also believed that the Constitution would favor unduly the economic interests of merchants, lawyers, and planters over that of small farmers and property owners. Prominent spokesmen for the Anti-Federalists included Richard Henry Lee, George Mason, and Patrick Henry of Virginia; Elbridge Gerry of Massachusetts; and George Clinton of New York.

Adherents to the Anti-Federalist Party were defeated in their attempt to prevent the states from ratifying the new Constitution. Many of their arguments were refuted by Alexander Hamilton, James Madison, and John Jay in *The Federalist Papers* (1787). The opposition of the Anti-Federalists did serve to force the Federalists to support ten amendments that subsequently became the Bill of Rights. Their fight against ratification also helped forge a two-party system and established the concept of a loyal opposition. Upon losing to the Federalists, the Anti-Federalist Party disbanded. Its members generally entered the Democratic-Republican Party,* which was formed by Thomas Jefferson during the Federalist administration of George Washington.

For further information, see Jackson Turner Main, *The Antifederalists: Critics of the Constitution, 1781-1788* (1961); Cecelia M. Kenyon, *The Anti-Federalists* (1966); and Robert Allen Rutland, *The Ordeal of the Constitution: The Anti-Federalists and the Ratification Struggle of 1787-1788* (1966).

**ANTI-IMPERIALIST LEAGUE (AIL).** Founded in 1898 at Washington, D.C., by a group of anti-war partisans for the purpose of opposing the Spanish-American War and the acquisition of foreign territory as a result of military conquest. Prime movers in the formation of the AIL were Carl Schurz, an editorial writer for *Harper's Weekly*, and Moorfield Storey, a lawyer, reformer, and author of *Our New Departure* (1901). Although relatively small in number, the AIL attracted the support of such individuals as industrialist Andrew Carnegie, writer Samuel Clemens (Mark Twain), and Samuel Gompers, president of the American Federation of Labor.

The AIL lobbied and sought to rally public opinion against ratification of the Treaty of Paris in 1898, by which Spain ceded to the United States Guam, Puerto Rico, and the Philippine Islands in return for a cease-fire and $20 million. AIL opposed such a settlement, arguing that imperialism would make the United States prone to military ventures; that colonialism would be undemocratic because it meant ruling other peoples; and that alien populations could not be incorporated into the American system. The AIL supported Filipino aspirations for total independence as articulated by rebel leader Emilio Aguinaldo.

Many members of the AIL supported William Jennings Bryan, the presidential nominee of the Democratic Party,* in the national election of 1900. Bryan campaigned on an anti-imperialist platform that contained the caveat, "We assert that no nation can long endure half republic and half empire, and we warn the American people that imperialism abroad will lead quickly and inevitably to despotism at home." When President McKinley won reelection, the AIL accepted the results as a national referendum. Defeated despite a vain attempt to influence public opinion to the contrary, the AIL disbanded.

For more information, see Robert L. Beisner, *Twelve Against Empire: Anti-Imperialists, 1898-1900* (1968).

**ANTI-MASONIC PARTY (AMP).** Founded in 1826 in western New York by opponents of Freemasonry for the purpose of ending the political control of those who belonged to secret societies. Impetus for the formation of the AMP arose when a former Mason, William Morgan, met a strange death after writing a book revealing the secret oaths and rituals of the Masonic Order to which he had once belonged. By 1828 the AMP had won four senate and seventeen assembly seats in the New York state legislature. Thereafter it became part of an anti-Jackson coalition in the Empire State after Andrew Jackson defeated John Quincy Adams for the presidency.

From New York the AMP spread to other states and was soon a national party. By claiming that Masons and other secret societies were undemocratic and aristocratic, it attracted many poor farmers, laborers, and those to whom egalitarianism had wide appeal. Many evangelical Christians also joined the AMP, since they believed that Masonry was anti-Christian and an evil that needed to be eliminated. The AMP stressed that Masons in politics tended to corrupt the American system by secretly favoring one another and enacting legislation for the benefit of a privileged elite. The grass-roots appeal of the AMP tended to be based on class lines in an era when the franchise was being broadened.

At its first national nominating convention (the first ever held by a political party), Thurlow Weed and William H. Seward tried to promote a presidential candidate whom the National Republican Party* could also select for the presidential election of 1832. A fusion candidate, it was hoped, could prevent the reelection of Andrew Jackson. When Henry Clay, who would be the National Republican candidate, refused to repudiate Masonry, the AMP chose William Wirt of Maryland to head its ticket. Amos Ellmaker of Pennsylvania was chosen as his vice-presidential running mate. In a three-way presidential race that saw Andrew Jackson reelected, Wirt polled only 33,189 popular votes and 7 electoral votes (carrying only Vermont).

By 1835 the AMP had disappeared in some states, having assimilated or fused with the new Whig Party.* In that same year the AMP nominating convention, meeting at Harrisburg, Pennsylvania, nominated William Henry Harrison (who was also a Whig nominee) as their presidential candidate. Selected as his vice-presidential running mate was Francis Granger of New York. In a presidential contest won by Martin Van Buren, Harrison drew 549,508 popular and 73 electoral votes.

Following the 1836 presidential election the AMP disintegrated, with most of its adherents joining the Whig Party or subsequently becoming affiliated with the Know-Nothing Party.* During its relatively short life, the AMP reflected the strength of the egalitarian movement. Its initiation of a nominating convention and appeal to participation in politics by the masses contributed to the democratization of the political process.

For more information, see Lorman Ratner, *Anti-Masonry: The Crusade and the Party* (1969).

**ANTI-MONOPOLY PARTY (AMP).** Founded in 1884 at Chicago by an assembled group calling themselves the Anti-Monopoly Organization of the United States for the purpose of nominating a presidential candidate. The AMP was the outgrowth of a series of state parties formed after the panic of 1873. A moving force behind the formation of these parties was the Grange* movement and the belief of the farmers and debtor class that railroads, banks, and big business dominated the nation's economy to the detriment of rural and working people.

At its 1884 nominating convention, the delegates of the AMP nominated Benjamin F. Butler of Massachusetts as its presidential candidate. Absolom Madden West of Mississippi was chosen as the vice-presidential nominee. The AMP's platform included demands for the federal regulation of monopolies in interstate commerce; graduated income tax; an eight-hour workday; a low tariff; direct election of U.S. senators; a ban on the importation of foreign contract labor; government aid to farmers; establishment of a department of labor; and payment of the national debt.

In the national election of 1884, in which Grover Cleveland won the presidency, Benjamin Butler polled only 175,066 (1.8 percent) of the popular votes. He no doubt would have won even fewer had he not also been the presidential nominee of the Greenback Party.* Although many of the planks advocated by the AMP eventually were enacted into law, the poor showing at the polls caused the AMP to die shortly after the election. Many of its adherents eventually gravitated into the Populist Party.*

For more information, see Hans L. Trefousse, *Ben Butler* (1957).

**ANTI-SALOON LEAGUE OF AMERICA (ASLA).** Founded in 1895 at Washington, D.C., by the Reverend Howard Hyde Russell of Ohio, the Reverend A. J. Kynett of Pennsylvania, Methodist Bishop Luther B. Wilson of Washington, D.C., Roman Catholic Archbishop John Ireland of

Minnesota, and other prohibitionists. ASLA's purpose was to serve as a nonpartisan, single-issue alternative to the Prohibition Party,* whose growing involvement with other issues alienated those who saw the liquor problem as the main threat to the welfare and morality of most Americans. The founding meeting had been preceded by the formation of local anti-saloon leagues in Ohio and Washington, D.C., two years before.

Under the leadership of Russell, who became the first national superintendent, the ASLA created or absorbed affiliates in nearly every state by 1903. Under the Reverend Purley A. Baker, who succeeded Russell in that year, the ASLA established a position of power by defeating an uncooperative Republican* governor in the Ohio state election of 1905. Baker remained at the head of the organization until his death in 1924; the Reverend F. Scott McBride succeeded him and held the position until 1933. Other prominent leaders included the Reverend Edwin C. Dinwiddie, the first legislative superintendent; Dr. Ernest H. Cherrington, editor-in-chief of ASLA's paper, the *American Issue*; Southern Methodist Bishop James Cannon, Jr., chairman of the legislative committee; and Wayne B. Wheeler, general counsel and legislative superintendent during the 1920s.

The ASLA was one of the most effective temperance organizations and successful pressure groups in American history. Following a threefold program —"Agitation, Legislation, and Law Enforcement"—it attacked the liquor industry on every front. Its printing press at Westerville, Ohio, churned out millions of pages of propaganda. Using classic balance-of-power techniques, the league swung its minority bloc of votes so as to obtain maximum influence upon candidates and legislators. Those running for offices at all levels were supported or opposed solely according to their stance on the prohibition issue. With political adroitness and perfect opportunism, ASLA demanded local option laws in wet states while working for statewide prohibition in local-option states.

A centralized structure, with a salaried superintendent in each state appointed by the national superintendent, kept state leagues responsible to the directives of the national leadership. The indispensable foundation of ASLA's vast political power was the large number of evangelical Protestant churches that contributed money and influenced votes. With this backing, ASLA's pressure politics contributed much toward getting prohibition adopted in nineteen states by 1917. The league was also largely responsible for federal enactment of the following major pieces of legislation: the Webb-Kenyon Interstate Liquor Act of 1913, which prohibited shipment of liquor into dry states; passage by Congress of the Eighteenth (prohibition) amendment in 1917; ratification by the states of the Eighteenth Amendment by 1920; the National Prohibition Enforcement Act of 1919 (Volstead Act); and the Jones Act of 1929, which increased penalties for bootlegging and illegal sales of alcoholic beverages.

In 1919 the ASLA joined with temperance groups in other countries to form the World League against Alcohol. At home, the league endorsed the election of Herbert C. Hoover to the presidency in 1928 because he, unlike Governor Alfred E. Smith of New York (the Democratic Party* nominee for president), supported the "great experiment." At this point the ASLA reached the peak of its power and prestige. Thereafter under the adverse economic conditions of the Great Depression and shock of scandal attaching itself to Bishop Cannon, the financial coffers and political power of ASLA decreased rapidly.

After failing to stop either the election of Franklin D. Roosevelt, who favored repeal (and approved legislation legalizing the manufacture and sale of beer) and subsequent ratification of the Twenty-first (repeal) Amendment in December 1933 the ASLA split into two branches. One, the Temperance Education Foundation, served as custodian of most ASLA records until they were turned over to the Ohio State Historical Society in 1974. The other, after being known for a time as the National Temperance League, is now the American Council on Alcohol Problems (ACAP), whose national headquarters is located in Washington, D.C., with George W. Lewis, Jr., serving as executive director. As an interchurch federation of some eighty denominational and state councils as affiliates, the ACAP sponsors programs in "alcohol education and citizenship action without regard to conflicting views on any other social questions." It utilizes television and radio, operates a speakers' bureau, provides counseling services, funds research, publishes educational materials, and issues a bimonthly magazine, *American Issue.*

For further information, see Peter Odegard, *Pressure Politics: The Story of the Anti-Saloon League* (1928); Virginius Dabney, *Dry Messiah: The Life of Bishop Cannon* (1949); James H. Timberlake, *Prohibition and the Progressive Movement, 1900-1920* (1963); and Norman H. Clark, *Deliver Us from Evil: An Interpretation of American Prohibition* (1976).

**ARMED FORCES OF PUERTO RICAN NATIONAL LIBERATION.** See Fuerzas Armádas de Liberacíon Nacional Puertorriqueña.

**ARMY OF THE PHILIPPINES, CUBA, AND PUERTO RICO.** See Veterans of Foreign Wars of the United States.

**ASSOCIATION AGAINST THE PROHIBITION AMENDMENT (AAPA).** Founded informally at Washington, D.C., during the ratification of the Eighteenth (prohibition) Amendment in 1918, the AAPA was formally incorporated in 1920. The founder and first president was Captain William H. Stayton, a former naval officer of elitist and conservative views. The purpose of the organization was to oppose the centralizing effect of national prohibition, which its right-wing members saw as undermining the principle of local (state) self-government. This constitutional argument remained the basic position of AAPA throughout its history, although some members were equally opposed to the very idea of prohibition.

As a nonpartisan, nonsectarian, and nonprofit corporation, membership in the AAPA was open to all except those who made their living from the liquor industry. It nevertheless remained recognizably upperclass, with many members being drawn from the top echelon of such corporations as du Pont and General Motors. By 1926 the AAPA claimed a membership of 726,000 in twenty-five states, with the largest numbers being in New York, Ohio, Illinois, and California.

Originally envisioning itself as a voting bloc, over a period of time the AAPA came to focus more on publicity and lobbying than specific political activity. After it failed to prevent ratification of the Eighteenth Amendment, the AAPA worked for modification of the Volstead Act to permit manufacture and sale of beer with a low alcoholic content. This effort also proved to be unsuccessful.

In 1928 the AAPA underwent reorganization when overall direction was taken from Captain Stayton and given to Henry H. Curran, a New York lawyer, and to an executive committee headed by Pierre S. du Pont. Other steps toward revitalization included enlarging the board of directors, soliciting contributions from wealthy supporters, and establishing departments within the AAPA on research, information, politics, finance, and accounting. With renewed effort, a massive publicity campaign was launched to advertise the failure of prohibition. From 1928 to 1930 the AAPA distributed nearly four and one-half million pieces of anti-prohibition literature.

Two prominent members of AAPA were identified closely with the hierarchy of the Democratic Party*: John J. Rascob, chairman of the Democratic National Committee,* and Jouett Shouse, head of the National Committee's executive council. Shouse replaced Curran at the helm of AAPA in 1932 and immediately focused all of AAPA's energies on raising money (some $300,000) and campaigning for Democrats pledged to repeal. Thus the AAPA not only helped make prohibition an important issue in the 1932 national election but also aided in sending Franklin D. Roosevelt to the White House.

Interpreting the Democratic victory as a mandate for repeal, the AAPA pressured Congress for quick passage of the Twenty-first (repeal) Amendment and immediate enactment of legislation legalizing sale of beers and wines at 3.2 percent or less in alcoholic content. AAPA's proposed version of the Twenty-first Amendment was the one accepted. Its recommended procedure for ratification called for state conventions. The AAPA then circulated model statutes for the creation of these conventions, specifying at-large election of delegates pledged for or against repeal, a method that was adopted by twenty-five states. Various AAPA chapters helped draw up pro-repeal slates in several states, and the organization spent some $250,000 to get them elected. Many AAPA leaders were in fact elected delegates to the various state ratification conventions of 1933.

On December 6, 1933, the day after the Twenty-first Amendment was ratified, officially repealing prohibition, the AAPA directors met to dissolve their organization. Although they had been successful in their primary objective, AAPA leaders soon perceived that the trend toward governmental centralization, which they had fought to reverse, was continuing under the aegis of the New Deal. Consequently many former members of AAPA helped form a new organization, the American Liberty League.*

For further information, see Dayton E. Heckman, "Prohibition Passes: The Story of the Association Against the Prohibition Amendment" (Ph.D. dissertation, Ohio State University, 1939); David E. Kyvig, "In Revolt against Prohibition: The Association against the Prohibition Amendment and the Movement for Repeal, 1919-1933" (Ph.D. dissertation, North-western University, 1971); and Fletcher Dobyus, *The Amazing Story of Repeal* (1940).

**ASSOCIATION FOR HUMANE ABORTION.** See Association for the Study of Abortion.

**ASSOCIATION FOR THE STUDY OF ABORTION (ASA).** Founded in 1965 at New York City by Dr. Alan F. Guttmacher, M.D., a pioneer in family planning, for the purpose of promoting legalized abortion. Formed originally as the Association for Human Abortion, the name was changed to ASA within the first year of its existence. The ASA seeks to influence public opinion, members of Congress, and federal judges so as to gain universal acceptance of legalized abortion. It tries to refute the moral arguments against abortion as articulated by the National Right to Life Committee* and the Respect Life Committee of the National Conference of Catholic Bishops.

The ASA membership, which totals nearly twenty-two thousand, is drawn primarily from the ranks of professionals. The largest groups represented are the clergy, physicians, lawyers, and social workers. The ASA submitted legal briefs and thus helped to formulate judicial opinions in the cases of *Doe* v. *Bolton* (1973) and *Roe* v. *Wade* (1973). Both decisions by the Supreme Court gave legal approval for abortion on grounds other than the standard justification of preserving the mother's health or saving her life. The ASA lobbies for liberalized abortion laws in the states and on the national level. It has endorsed the Revised Uniform Abortion Act as proposed by the American Bar Association.* ASA members mounted a campaign to prevent enactment of a constitutional amendment forbiding abortion and seeks reversal of congressional legislation which prevents federal funds to be used for financing abortions.

Two permanent committees exist in ASA: Clergymen's Advisory and Research. ASA has been most successful in influencing medical and judicial opinion. It has been less successful in influencing mass public opinion. The ASA works with other organizations with similar goals and has been assisted by the National Organization for Women* on numerous occasions.

Present national headquarters of ASA is located in New York City. Current president is Dr. Robert E. Hall, M.D., with Jimmye Kimmey serving as executive director. ASA publications inlcude two quarterlies, *ASA Bibliography* and *ASA Newsletter*.

**ASSOCIATION ON AMERICAN INDIAN AFFAIRS (AAIA).** Founded in 1936 at New York City as a result of a merger of the National Association on Indian Affairs and the American Indian Defense Association to form the American Association on Indian Affairs for the purpose of promoting the economic, social, and legal welfare of American Indians. In 1946 the name was changed to the AAIA. Permanent committees are: Public Education; Welfare; Indian Community Development; Tribal and Government Relations; and Legal Defense.

The AAIA disseminates information in an attempt to influence public opinion relative to problems confronting American Indians. It also attempts to secure favorable legislation from Congress so that Indians might make improvements in their job opportunities, health standards, and educational levels. The AAIA is concerned with the preservation of Indian culture while at the same time seeking to improve the living standards of those residing in a tribal setting. It also provides legal counsel in order to ensure that both the rights of tribes and individual Indians are not violated by non-Indians.

Under AAIA auspices, programs are conducted in community planning, improvement of health facilities, betterment of education, legal defense, and securement of government assistance when needed. In 1963 the AAIA started the American Indian Arts Center in New York City to promote public interest in Indian arts and crafts. It was hoped that Indians might profit more by selling their own art than through trading centers operated by non-Indians.

Present national headquarters is located in New York City. Current president is Dr. Alfonso Ortiz, a Tewa Indian and a professor of anthropology at the University of New Mexico, with William Byler serving as executive director. Membership in AAIA totals over sixty thousand. It publishes a monthly newsletter, *Indian Affairs*, and a quarterly journal, *Indian Family Defense*.

## _B

**BIPARTISAN CONGRESSIONAL CLEARINGHOUSE (BCC).** Founded in 1970 at Washington, D.C., by Mark Talisman, an aide to Congressman Charles A. Vanik (D-Ohio), for the purpose of electing anti-Vietnam War candidates in the mid-term elections of 1970. The BCC sought to coordinate the efforts of anti-war student groups so as to promote the election of candidates pledged to end the war in Vietnam. At one point, some two hundred college affiliates were in existence.

Students were encouraged to gather signatures on anti-war petitions, campaign for candidates supported by the BCC, and participate in fund-raising activities. Some $70,000 was raised in this fashion to support the political campaigns of BCC-endorsed candidates. Although it is difficult to ascertain just how many candidates the BCC was responsible for electing, it no doubt contributed to the election of some candidates committed to terminate the war as quickly as possible. When the United States withdrew from the Vietnam war during the administration of Gerald R. Ford, the BCC disbanded.

**BIRCH SOCIETY, JOHN.** See John Birch Society.

**BLACK CONGRESSIONAL CAUCUS (BCC).** Founded in 1971 at Washington, D.C., by Senator Edward Brooke (R-Mass.) and Walter Fauntroy (D-D.C.), along with twelve black members of the House of Representatives, for the purpose of forming a black voting bloc in Congress. BCC members in the House included Shirley Chisholm (D-N.Y.), William Clay (D-Mo.), Cardiss Collins (D-Ill.), John Conyers, Jr. (D-Mich.), Ronald Dellums (D-Calif.), Charles Diggs, Jr. (D-Mich.), Augustus Hawkins (D-Calif.), Ralph Metcalfe (D-Ill.), Ferren Mitchell (D-Md.), Robert N. C. Nix (D-Pa.), Charles Rangel (D-N.Y.), and Louis Stokes (D-Ohio).

The primary purpose of the BCC was to increase the power of black members of Congress by voting as a bipartisan bloc. In this manner, votes on pending legislation of benefit to blacks would not become partisan, and vote trading could be done to win additional votes for measures of value to blacks. Unity among black members of Congress would also make it possible for them to approach the president with more authority. All blacks subsequently elected to Congress are invited to membership. White members of Congress who represent districts with large black constituencies have not been accepted as members.

The BCC has had considerable success in gaining support from liberal Democrats. Senator Edward M. Kennedy (D-Mass.) has championed most of the demands it has made. The BCC was instrumental in securing passage of the Humphrey-Hawkins Act in 1978, which committed the federal government to a policy of guaranteeing full employment, albeit in an amended version. It has advocated the appointment of more blacks to governmental posts and desires a U.S. foreign policy that would isolate Rhodesia and South Africa. It also has called for a pro-African policy aimed at furthering self-determination for Africa. The BCC supports affirmative-action programs and government projects aimed at reducing unemployment among blacks.

BCC representatives have sought and received meetings with Presidents Richard M. Nixon, Gerald R. Ford, and Jimmy Carter. BCC spokespersons have been critical of all three presidents: Nixon for cutting welfare programs, Ford for not restoring them, and Carter for giving a higher priority to his anti-inflation program than one geared to reducing unemployment among blacks. Because most members of the BCC are Democrats, it has more influence within the Democratic Party* than it does the Republican Party.* In 1972 the BCC was a moving force in promoting the first National Black Political Assembly.* The present chairman of the BCC is Congressman Cardiss Collins (D-Ill.)

**BLACK PANTHER PARTY (BPP).** Founded in 1966 at Oakland, California, by Bobby Seale and Huey P. Newton for the purpose of liberating blacks from what they considered to be an inferior, colonial status. This militant black nationalist party adopted a paramilitary stance (with guns and uniforms) and espoused a revolutionary philosophy justifying the use of violence. Born in a ghetto and with a membership of young people, it adopted a platform reflecting the revolutionary theories of Karl Marx, Vladimir Lenin, Mao Tse-tung, and Frantz Fanon. Specific planks contained the following demands:

We want power to determine the destiny of our Black Community; . . . We want full employment for our people; We want an end to the robbery by the CAPITALIST of our Black Community [later the word *capitalist* was changed to *white man*]; We want decent housing . . . ; We want education for our people that exposes the true nature of the decadent American society . . . ; We want all black men to be exempt from military service; We want an immediate end to POLICE BRUTALITY and MURDER of black people; We want freedom for all black men held in federal, state, county, and city prisons and jails; We want all black people when brought to be trial to be tried in a court by a jury of their peer group . . . ; We want land, bread, housing, education, clothing, justice, and peace. And as our major political objective, a United Nations-supervised plebiscite to be held throughout the black colony in which only the black colonial subjects will be allowed to participate, for the purpose of determining the will of the black people as to their national destiny.

The BPP had members in a few of the major cities of the United States but represented only a tiny fraction of the black community. Its revolutionary stance was criticized by some civil rights leaders as counterproductive, if not futile. Armed confrontations between Black Panthers and police took place in Oakland, Chicago, Los Angeles, and New York City. In Chicago, BPP leaders Fred Hampton and Mark Clark were killed in a police raid on their headquarters. After shootouts in Oakland, Huey Newton and Eldridge Cleaver, BPP's minister of information, were indicted for allegedly shooting several policemen. In this incident, the BPP treasurer, Bobby Hutton, was killed. Seale was exonerated, but Newton served twenty-two months in prison until the conviction was reversed on appeal in 1970. Two subsequent trials ended in a hung jury, and all charges were then dropped. Newton later was charged with shooting a seventeen-year-old girl. In 1975 he fled to Cuba as an exile. In 1978 Newton returned to the United States to stand trial. At this time he took over the BPP leadership from Elaine Brown.

In 1968 Eldridge Cleaver ran for the presidency as the nominee of the Peace and Freedom Party.* In 1971 he was expelled from the BPP following an internal struggle for power. Cleaver fled to Algeria in 1973 to avoid imprisonment for violating his parole. He returned voluntarily in 1975 to face the pending charges against him. Feeling confident of a fair trial, Cleaver asserted, "With all its faults the American system is the freest . . . in the world."

In 1972 four members of the BPP hijacked a Delta Airlines plane and forced it to fly to Algeria; there they demanded $1 million in ransom. George Wright is still a fugitive, but Melvin and Jean Carol, George Brown, and Joyce Tillerson were apprehended. After being tried and convicted, all were given prison sentences.

Protesting against surveillance by the Federal Bureau of Investigation and harassment by other law-enforcement agencies, the BPP remained highly controversial until it renounced the use of violence. In 1973 Bobby

Seale ran unsuccessfully for Oakland's office of mayor. Discarding guns, black berets, and battle fatigues, the BPP switched from bullets to ballots in an attempt to gain legitimate acceptance from the electorate. It initiated public service programs such as free breakfasts and health clinics. Members thereafter had to accept twenty-six rules of discipline. One of these stated that "no party member can have narcotics or weed in his possession while doing party work." Also promulgated were eight "points of attention," which instructed members of the BPP to "Speak politely; Pay fairly for what you buy; Return everything you borrow; Pay for anything you damage; Do not hit or swear at people; Do not damage property or crops of the poor, oppressed masses; Do not take liberties with women; and If we ever have to take captives, do not ill-treat them."

The BPP has all but disappeared except in Oakland, where it remains small and ineffective at the polls. Its formation represented part of the radical and militant activities of the civil rights and anti-Vietnam movements when left-wing groups sought to incite a Marxian type of socialist revolution. Although few were attracted to the BPP, those who were tended to be a mixture of idealists, idealogues, youths wanting action, adventure seekers, and some seeking retribution. The BPP should not be confused with the Lowndes County Freedom Organization,* which also became known as the Black Panther Party because of its use of the black panther as its party symbol.

For more information, see Eldridge Cleaver, *Soul on Ice* (1968); Gene Marine, *The Black Panthers* (1969); and Huey P. Newton, *To Die for the People: The Writings of Huey P. Newton* (1971).

**BLACK PANTHERS.** See Black Panther Party.

**BLACK POLITICAL CONVENTION.** See National Black Political Assembly.

**BLIND FEDERATION.** See National Federation of the Blind.

**BONUS ARMY (BA).** Founded in 1932 at Washington, D.C., by Walter E. Waters and other veterans of World War I for the purpose of promoting passage by Congress of the Patman bill, which would have made it possible for ex-servicemen to receive cash for the certificates they received pursuant to enactment of the Adjusted Compensation Act (Soldiers' Bonus Act) of 1924. Because of the economic hardships of the Great Depression, some fifteen thousand veterans descended upon Washington, D.C. in 1932 to lobby and demonstrate for passage by Congress of the measure sponsored by Congressman Wright Patman (D-Tex.), whereby the federal government would redeem immediately bonus certificates worth $2 million.

The Patman bill was approved by the House of Representatives but was rejected by the Senate. President Herbert C. Hoover had voiced his disapproval of the measure, thus helping to defeat it in the upper chamber. After the Senate action, some two thousand veterans remained in Washington, D.C., to protest. The District of Columbia police asked for federal troops to ensure that no civil disorder would take place. Up to this time bonus marchers had carried flags while conducting peaceful demonstrations. President Hoover ordered army troops to the scene, but with orders not to use force or precipitate violence. In carrying out this assignment General Douglas MacArthur, chief of staff of the U.S. Army, disregarded the president's order. Believing that the bonus march constituted an attempt by Communists to overthrow the government, MacArthur routed the remnants of the BA. He ordered their hastily constructed shacks on the Anacosta Flats burned and all demonstrators driven from the District of Columbia.

During the course of the army's action, several people were inadvertently killed. This excess show of force created much adverse publicity for the Hoover administration. It established an image in the public's eye of a hardhearted president who ordered troops to drive destitute veterans from the capital and thus prevent them from petitioning the government. This incident no doubt contributed to Herbert Hoover's defeat in 1932. Congress eventually redeemed the bonus certificates in 1936 when it overrode a veto by President Franklin D. Roosevelt.

For more information, see Roger Daniels, *The Bonus March* (1971); W. C. White, *B.E.F.: The Whole Story of the Bonus Army* (1933).

**BONUS EXPEDITIONARY FORCE.** See Bonus Army.

**BONUS MARCHERS.** See Bonus Army.

**BRECKINRIDGE DEMOCRATS.** See National Democratic Party.

**BROOKINGS INSTITUTION (BI).** Founded in 1916 at Washington, D.C., by Frederick A. Cleveland, then chairman of President William Howard Taft's Commission on Economy and Efficiency, and Charles D. Norton, vice-president of the National Bank of New York City, for the purpose of promoting research relative to American education, domestic problems, and international relations. The first chairman was Frank J. Goodnow, who at the time was president of Johns Hopkins University.

Formed originally as the Institute for Government Research, the BI was renamed when it merged with both the Institute of Economics and the Robert Brookings Graduate School of Economics and Government. It was named Brookings after a St. Louis businessman who had served on the War Industries Board during World War I and who gave generous financial support to the BI.

The BI is a nonpartisan, nonprofit institution with no membership. It initiates studies in all areas of economics, government, and foreign affairs. Divisions exist dealing with Economic Studies, Governmental Studies, Foreign Policy Studies, and Advanced Study. It also maintains a library and operates the Social Science Computation Center. BI's first published study, *Problems of a National Budget* (1920), was so influential that it was instrumental in inducing Congress to enact the Budget and Accounting Act of 1921. In the 1930s BI sponsored research that contributed to the enactment by Congress of the Reciprocal Trade Agreements Act of 1934. Its *Three Years of the Agricultural Adjustment Administration* (1937) was an objective evaluation of New Deal farm policy, which broadened public support when the AAA was found to be an effective economic mechanism.

When the Full Employment Act of 1946 established the Council of Economic Advisers, Edwin G. Nourse, then vice-president of BI and one of its original staff members, became its first chairman. Because of a request from Senator Arthur Vandenberg (R-Mich.) in 1947, the BI worked out an administrative program for implementing the Marshall Plan. Its recommendations for labor reform were incorporated into the Taft-Hartley Act of 1948. The BI study, *Presidential Transitions* (1959), was utilized by President-elect John F. Kennedy as a guide for assuming the responsibilities of his office. And the BI's *Proposed Studies on the Implications of Peaceful Space Activities for Human Affairs* (1958) suggested a research agenda for the National Aeronautics and Space Administration that was eventually carried out. Special studies on contemporary problems by the BI contribute to public opinion and greatly influence lawmakers and occupants of the White House.

The BI supports advanced study by scholars and provides expert training for officials in government, business, and labor. In 1964 the BI was the recipient of an Award for Merit bestowed by the Public Personnel Association. Headquarters is in Washington, D.C., and current president of BI is Kermit Gordon, with Walter G. Held serving as director of administration. Prominent members of the board of directors include Douglas Dillon, chairman; Robert S. McNamara, former secretary of defense in the administrations of Presidents Kennedy and Johnson and past president of the International Bank for Reconstruction and Development; John Fischer, associate editor of *Harper's Magazine*; and George M. Elsey, president of the American National Red Cross.

In addition to periodic studies, the BI publishes "Brookings Papers on Economic Activity," its *Annual Report*, and the quarterly *Brookings Bulletin*.

For further information, see Charles B. Saunders, Jr., *The Brookings Institution, A Fifty-Year History* (1966).

**BULL MOOSE PARTY.** See Progressive Party (1912).

**BULL MOOSERS.** See Progressive Party (1912).

**BUSINESS AND PROFESSIONAL WOMEN'S CLUBS, INC., THE FEDERATION OF.** See National Federation of Business and Professional Women's Clubs.

**BUSINESS-INDUSTRY POLITICAL ACTION COMMITTEE (BIPAC).** Founded in 1963 at New York City as an outgrowth of the Political Action Division of the National Association of Manufacturers* for the purpose of promoting the free enterprise system and fiscal responsibility in government. With Robert L. Humphrey as its prime mover and first president, the BIPAC was organized to counter the political influence of the AFL-CIO Committee on Political Education.* The original board of directors included such businessmen as Clifford Backstrand of Armstrong Cork, Lancaster, Pennsylvania; J. R. Fluor of Fluor Corporation, Los Angeles, California; J. B. Lanterman of Amsted Industries, Chicago, Illinois; H. C. Lumb of Republic Steel, Cleveland, Ohio; and R. D. Poindexter of Superior Iron Works and Supply, Shreveport, Louisiana. In 1966 the board was enlarged to include at least one representative from each state.

The BIPAC seeks to represent the viewpoint of business and to foster free enterprise in the United States. Thus it promotes a political program whose tenants include removal or reduction of government controls over business, reduction in federal spending, an anti-inflation fiscal policy, and curtailment of the power of federal bureaucracies. Through its Congressional Candidate Review Committee (consisting of three Democrats* and three Republicans*), BIPAC endorses designated members of Congress for reelection and also may provide financial assistance for political campaigns. From 1963 to 1975 the BIPAC has contributed over $2 million to the campaigns of some seven hundred congressional candidates in all fifty states. Of these, over two-thirds have been successfully elected or reelected. BIPAC does not endorse or contribute to presidential candidates.

BIPAC is supported financially by contributions from individual members who subscribe to its conservative political principles. Although the membership is relatively small, its involvement in political campaigns has been significant in terms of results. In 1970 BIPAC's national headquarters was moved to Washington, D.C. Current executive chairman is Harold S. Mohler. BIPAC publications include a *Newsletter* and the bimonthly *Politics.*

**BYRD MACHINE (BM).** Founded in 1926 at Richmond, Virginia, by Governor Harry F. Byrd, Sr., for the purpose of gaining personal control of the state's Democratic Party.* Byrd served as governor from 1926 to 1930, was a Democratic National Committeeman from 1928 to 1940, and was elected to the U.S. Senate in 1933, where he served until his retirement in 1965.

As boss of his machine, Byrd kept a low profile so that the voting public was seldom aware of his enormous power. Under his domination the BM advocated states' rights, racial segregation, and conservative fiscal policies. As chairman of the Senate Finance Committee and because of seniority, Byrd was a powerful critic of big government and deficit spending. Considered a reactionary rightwinger by his political opponents, Byrd was known for his opposition to the New Deal, Fair Deal, and New Frontier programs. Since he was constantly reelected, his activities in the Senate went beyond Virginia state politics. After the 1954 *Brown* v. *Topeka Board of Education* decision by the U.S. Supreme Court outlawing segregation in the public schools, Byrd led southerners in a fight to prevent the integration of educational facilities.

When Byrd retired from the U.S. Senate in 1965, he chose his son, Harry, Jr., as his successor. The younger Byrd never wielded the power held by his father. When Harry, Sr., died ten months after retirement, the political machine he had formed disintegrated.

For more information, see James W. Ely, Jr., *The Crisis of Conservative Virginia: The Byrd Organization and the Politics of Massive Resistance* (1976).

# C

**CARNEGIE ENDOWMENT FOR INTERNATIONAL PEACE (CEIP).**
Founded in 1910 at New York City by steel magnate Andrew Carnegie for
the purpose of promoting world peace. Prime movers in its formation were
Elihu Root, CEIP's first president; Nicholas Murray Butler, president of
Columbia University; and Professor James T. Shotwell, also of Columbia
University and founder of the outlawry-of-war movement. From Carnegie's
original endowment the CEIP now has assets totaling $35 million.

The CEIP has initiated and funded studies relating to international arbitration, organization, and law. It has never adopted a dogmatic pacifist
position but seeks to promote international arbitration or peaceful
mechanisms for maintaining amity between nations. The CEIP supported
the outlawry-of-war movement and was influential in securing U.S. ratification of the Kellogg-Briand Peace Pact of 1928, a treaty in which signatory
nations renounced war as a means of settling international disputes. Butler,
CEIP president from 1925 to 1945, was awarded the Nobel Peace Prize in
1931, along with Jane Addams, for his work in promoting the world peace.

The CEIP supported U.S. membership in the League of Nations and the
International Court during the 1920s and 1930s but was never able to sway
public opinion sufficiently to achieve these goals. Also in the 1930s CEIP
backed the Neutrality Acts but at the same time advocated preparations for
national defense. It supported U.S. membership in the United Nations and
helped prepare the public for this action in 1945. It also supported the Marshall Plan and the formation of the North Atlantic Treaty Organization in
1948.

In contemporary times the CEIP funds programs aimed at strengthening
the United Nations. It also finances research related to arms control,
developing models for postindustrial societies, finding solutions to the problems facing underdeveloped nations, and codification of international law.
Many of its studies provide information upon which the State Department
and congressional committees can make foreign policy decisions.

The CEIP helps train diplomats for countries just achieving national independence. It assists in carrying out the German Marshall Fund of the United States; sponsors the Face to Face program where citizens talk directly to government officials; conducts forums where diplomats of various nations can meet to exchange views; has initiated the Rhodesia Project to study international sanctions; and operates the James Thompson Shotwell Library. CEIP funds help support the activities of the Arms Control Association and the Student Committee on International Affairs.

Present national headquarters is located in New York City with branch offices in Washington, D.C., and Geneva, Switzerland. Current president is Thomas Lowe Hughs. The CEIP publishes a journal, *Foreign Policy*.

For more information, see Nicholas Murray Butler, *Across the Busy Years*, 2 vols. (1939-1940).

**CATHOLIC WAR VETERANS OF THE UNITED STATES OF AMERICA (CWV-USA).** Founded in 1935 at Washington, D.C. by the Right Reverend E. J. Higgins, a former U.S. Army chaplain, for the purpose of promoting the welfare of war veterans belonging to the Roman Catholic church. With the motto, "For God, Country, and Home," the CWV-USA dedicated itself to promoting Catholicism and Americanism while opposing "atheistic Communism" and "paganism" in American society.

The CWV-USA has worked with other veteran organizations to secure greater benefits for those who have served in the armed forces of the United States. It supports a strong national defense posture and has regarded Communist nations as being potential threats to U.S. security. It supports welfare and rehabilitation programs for its members and their families; cares for orphans and widows; and funds scholarships for high school seniors. In 1949 the Ladies Auxiliary was formed for mothers, widows, sisters, and close relatives of the CWV-USA; its national headquarters are located in Washington, D.C., and it has some ten thousand members. Special committees are: Americanism: Catholic Action; Civics; Education; Legislation; Welfare; and Youth Activities. Its current national secretary is Lorraine Satterfield.

The CWV-USA also has its national headquarters in the nation's capital. Present membership totals over one hundred thousand. Current national commander is Neil G. Knowles. The CWV-USA issues a bimonthly publication, *Catholic War Veteran.*

**CATHOLIC WORKERS MOVEMENT (CWM).** Founded in 1933 in New York City by Dorothy Day and Peter Maurin for the purpose of promoting radical social reform in the United States. Maurin, a French-born Catholic, proposed that the poor could be helped by a system of communal farms and urban houses of hospitality, similar to the storefront churches or missions of the Salvation Army. Day, who joined the Roman Catholic church in 1927, had formerly been a nurse, journalist, and member of the Socialist Party of America.* She had written for such socialist and radical journals as the *Call* and the *Masses*.

The same year the CWM was founded, Day and Maurin started their own journal, *Catholic Worker*, whose editorial stance was radical and anti-capitalist. It advocated pacifism, disarmament, destruction of all weapons, and refusal to register for military conscription, and it opposed U.S. involvement in any war. CWM members refused to pay taxes that would go toward preparing for war, practiced civil disobedience, and refused to serve in the armed forces when drafted.

Other notable CWM leaders have been David Miller, who, influenced by the teachings of Father Daniel Berrigen, publicly protested the war in Vietnam by burning his draft card; Ammon Hennacy, a Christian anarchist who carried on what he called a "One Man Revolution"; and Roger LaPorte, a Hunter College student whose self-immolation by fire in front of the United Nations building was carried out as a personal protest against the Vietnam war. During the Vietnam conflict the CWM headquarters on Manhattan's Lower East Side became a haven for draft dodgers, conscientious objectors, and militant protesters.

The circulation of the *Catholic Worker* at one time was over one hundred thousand. This figure, however, did not represent CWM membership. Considering the number of Roman Catholics in the United States, its membership represented only a tiny fraction of the Catholic population. Its radical and anarchistic orientation attracted only a few ideologues, and once the civil rights and anti-Vietnam War activism declined, membership fell even more.

Founders Day and Maurin made their greatest impact on Catholic opinion through their humanitarian work. They both voluntarily lived in poverty while trying to help the poor and needy. The CWM operated the St. Joseph's House of Hospitality, a model that was imitated by others in different cities, and a communal farm in Staten Island. CWM's agitation that the Roman Catholic church take a greater interest in social reform had some effect upon both the hierarchy and laity of that church body. Because of its radical socialist and pacifist orientation, the CWM has little impact on public opinion in general or in terms of political influence.

A handful of people still continue to operate out of their New York City headquarters. The *Catholic Worker* continues to be published but with a relatively small circulation.

For more information, see Dorothy Day, *The Long Loneliness* (1952); Robert Coles and John Erickson, *A Spectacle Unto the World: The Catholic Worker Movement* (1974); and Neil Betten, *Catholic Activism and the Industrial Worker* (1976).

**CENTER FOR COMMUNITY CHANGE (CCC).** Founded in 1968 at Washington, D.C., by Jack T. Conway, Leonard Lesser, Richard W. Boone, and Benjamin Goldstein for the purpose of helping the poor and disadvantaged. Its stated objectives were "to provide technical assistance to community organizations of the poor seeking to improve their communities, to act as their advocates, and to analyze national issues affecting the poor and disadvantaged."

The impetus for CCC's formation was the plethora of welfare programs spawned by President Lyndon B. Johnson's Great Society (anti-poverty) program. Financial resources were available, but many local community organizations did not know how to apply for federal assistance. The CCC, which has no membership as such, was established to monitor federal legislation and then give technical assistance to groups needing help. In 1977 the CCC, along with the League of Women Voters* and the National Urban Coalition, set up the National Clearinghouse on Revenue Sharing to monitor the distribution of some $30.2 billions in federal funds. In this venture, CCC hopes to ensure that the poor receive some benefit from federal funding acquired by local communities. It also seeks to involve citizens in the decision-making process as to how revenue-sharing funds are spent in the local community.

Present national headquarters of CCC is located in Washington, D.C. The current president is Jack T. Conway, with Leonard Lesser serving as secretary and general counsel. Soon after its founding the CCC absorbed the Citizen's Crusade against Poverty. Publications issued by the CCC include its *Annual Report* and the bimonthly *Monitor*.

**CENTER FOR THE STUDY OF RESPONSIVE LAW.** See Public Interest Research Group.

**CERMAK MACHINE.** See Democratic Central Committee of Cook County.

**CHAMBER OF COMMERCE OF THE UNITED STATES (CCUS).** Founded in 1912 at Washington, D.C., by Charles Nagel, secretary of commerce and labor in the administration of William Howard Taft, and representatives of business organizations and trade associations, for the purpose of forming a federation that would serve as the "Voice of Business." One of the prime movers in the formation of CCUS was President Taft, who believed that there should be a single voice to promote the interests of the business community. The CCUS's first president was Harry A. Wheeler, who at the time also served as president of the Chicago Association of Commerce and was vice-president of the Union Trust Company.

The CCUS sought to promote the free enterprise system by informing the government of its views and disseminating information to the general public. It has become the most influential and widely known advocate for business in the country. Prior to World War I, the CCUS called for the establishment of an international council of reconciliation to prevent wars. But once the United States intervened in the European conflict in 1917, the CCUS organized the War Service Committee to assist the Council of National Defense. It also approved the levying of an excess-profits tax by the federal government. In the immediate postwar period and during the 1920s, the CCUS urged legislation prohibiting strikes against public utilities, but it opposed compulsory arbitration. It also fought against government ownership of the railroads (Plumb plan) and was instrumental in securing congressional passage of the Transportation Act of 1920, which returned the railroads to private control.

During the administrations of Warren G. Harding and Calvin Coolidge, the CCUS endorsed proposals to aid agriculture; favored high protective tariffs; encouraged development of the airline industry; worked against regulatory legislation; and sought to prevent unionization of major industries by championing the "American [open shop] System." Immediately after the stock market crash of 1929, the CCUS cooperated closely with President Herbert C. Hoover to minimize the negative effects of the Great Depression. The CCUS supported enactment of the National Industrial Recovery Act of 1933, but after it was declared unconstitutional in 1935 the chamber became increasingly anti-New Deal. It decried the "drift toward socialism," criticized the growing national debt caused by deficit spending, and disliked the antitrust investigations of the Temporary National Economic Committee headed by Senator Joseph O'Mahoney (D-Wyo.).

During World War II the CCUS recruited businessmen to serve in government as "dollar-a-year-men." It also assisted industries in retooling for war, cooperated in salvaging industrial scrap, and promoted the sale of war bonds. In the post-World War II era, the CCUS has supported national defense expenditures; encouraged international trade and monetary stabilization; opposed President Harry S. Truman's seizure of the steel industry; endorsed the Taft-Hartley Act of 1948; and promoted state right-to-work laws to curtail the power of labor unions. The CCUS favored the efforts by President Richard M. Nixon to strengthen local government by revenue sharing but opposed his policy of wage and price controls. It approved of President Gerald R. Ford's attempt to lower federal expenditures and the anti-inflation campaign initiated by President Jimmy Carter. Recently the CCUS has agitated for greater tax incentives for investors but has opposed common-site picketing and the strengthening of the Consumer Protection Agency.

The CCUS has about thirty permanent committees; among them are Anti-trust and Government Regulations; Consumer Affairs and Environmental Control; Human and Natural Resources; International Relations;

and Trade with Foreign Countries. Recommendations made by committees are considered periodically by a sixty-five-member board of directors responsible for deciding CCUS policy on all issues.

In 1973 the CCUS selected ten issues on which crucial votes were taken to rate members of Congress. Among the issues selected were the overriding of President Nixon's veto of the increase in the minimum wage (opposed by the CCUS), delay in building the Alaskan oil pipeline (opposed), and enactment of budget reform and trade legislation (supported). The CCUS does not endorse congressional candidates or contribute to presidential campaigns. It does lobby, offers expert testimony before congressional committees, provides news media with information, and supplies schools and other organizations with films and factual data. It also conducts research and publishes special reports, monitors federal legislation and the operations of government agencies, and reports on this to its affiliates.

Currently the CCUS has a membership of more than seventy thousand business firms and individuals. It has over twenty-five hundred local, state, and regional chambers of commerce, as well as some one thousand trade and professional affiliates. The CCUS's annual budget is about $16 million, which comes from dues based on the size and amount of capital investment of a given business. Its Legislative Action Department employs paid lobbyists, and the American Chamber of Commerce Researchers Association, founded in 1962 at Nashville, Tennessee, supplies technical information and statistical data to member organizations. Programs are also carried out to train business executives and to alert them to the need for participation in the political process.

The present national headquarters of the CCUS is located in Washington, D.C., with regional offices in six other cities. Current president is Richard Lesher, with Arch N. Booth serving as executive vice-president. Organizations with which the CCUS cooperates include the American Chamber of Commerce Executives, Association of American Chambers of Commerce in Latin America, Junior Chamber International, and the United States Council of the International Chamber of Commerce. CCUS publications include the weekly *Congressional Action,* monthly *Nation's Business*, and bimonthly *Washington Report.*

**CHICAGO BOSS SYSTEM.** See Democratic Central Committee of Cook County.

**CHRISTIAN AMERICAN PATRIOTS.** See Christian Party.

**CHRISTIAN ANTI-COMMUNISM CRUSADE (CACC).** Founded in 1953 at Waterloo, Iowa, by Dr. Fred C. Schwartz and the Reverend Dr.

William E. Pietsch as a tax-free, nonprofit organization to alert Americans to the menace of communism. In 1958 CACC moved its permanent headquarters to Long Beach, California, where Dr. Schwartz, a medical doctor (also a practicing psychiatrist) as well as a Baptist lay preacher, became president of the organization. He rose to national prominence after testifying in 1957 as an expert on communism before the House Committee on Un-American Activities and because of his widely read 1960 publication, *You Can Trust the Communists (To Be Communists).*

The CACC sought to alert Americans to the dangers of communism and thus prevent the spread of its ideology at home and ensure its containment abroad. In 1961 the CACC sponsored a massive, outdoor rally at the Hollywood Bowl featuring movie stars and prominent political personalities. "Schools of Anti-Communism" were conducted by CACC all over the country during the 1950s and 1960s. Such "schools" were held under the auspices of local churches (usually fundamentalist in character), civic organizations, and right-wing groups (such as the John Birch Society*). They were one-week symposiums consisting of lectures, films, and dissemination of anti-Communist literature. Participating faculty frequently included Juanita Castro, sister of Cuba's Communist premier; James D. Atkinson, professor of government at Georgetown University; Herbert Philbrick, a former counterspy for the Federal Bureau of Investigation; Walter H. Judd, ex-congressman from Minnesota and a leading spokesperson for the "China lobby"; Dr. Joseph Dunner of Yeshiva University; Dr. J. C. Bales of Harding College; and Eugene Lyons, a senior editor of *Reader's Digest.*

At the high tide of its activities in 1961, the CACC received nearly $800,000 in contributions. Some came from the general public but most was donated by such major contributors as the Allen-Bradley Company, Deering-Miliken Foundation, Lilly Endowment, and the Charles Stewart Mott Foundation. With these funds the CACC financed anti-Communist activities in Brazil, Mexico, India, Japan, and some seventeen other foreign nations. Due to the lessening of international tensions and the public's decreasing interest in anti-Communist crusades, the work of the CACC declined drastically in the 1970s. Although it is still in existence, the CACC is dormant at this time. Its impact on mass public opinion during the height of the cold war was considerable. Its influence contributed to a prolonged support of the Vietnam war and in maintaining a hard-line approach toward both the Soviet Union and the People's Republic of China, manifest in the policy of nonrecognition.

The CACC supports a newspaper in India, publishes occasional pamphlets, and issues a semimonthly, *News Letter.*

For further information, see Brooks R. Walker, *The Christian Fright*

*Peddlers* (1964); Robert Schoenberger, ed., *The American Right Wing: Readings in Political Behavior* (1969); and Gary K. Claybough, *Thunder on the Right: The Protestant Fundamentalists* (1974).

**CHRISTIAN CRUSADE (CC).** Founded in 1950 at Tulsa, Oklahoma, by the Reverend Billy James Hargis for the purpose of stopping the spread of communism everywhere in the world. Hargis, who became a minister in the Church of Christ at eighteen years of age, served several pastorates until he launched his crusade against communism. Originally called the Christian Echoes National Ministry, Inc., the CC's first overseas venture was a "Bible Balloon Project" carried out in 1953. Over a million quotations from Holy Scripture, translated into seven languages, were distributed in so-called Iron Curtain countries by balloons.

The CC utilized all forms of media to get its message across to as many Americans as it could reach. Making use of radio, television, right-wing forums, and CC-sponsored evangelistic meetings, Hargis berated all those he believed in some way contributed to the spread of communism in the United States. Over the years his verbal assaults have been leveled at communists, socialists, left-wingers, liberals, civil rights militants, anti-Vietnam War protesters, the Warren Court, "doves," supporters of disarmament, advocates of federal welfare programs, clergy espousing the social gospel, the United Nations, and the National Council of Churches of Christ in the U.S.A. As spokesman for CC, the Reverend Hargis has linked Christian fundamentalism with laissez-faire capitalism and jingoistic nationalism. As a bulwark against communism, the United States, according to Hargis, should suppress this ideology at home and prevent its expansion abroad.

To get his message across to the general public, the Reverend Hargis authored such widely sold books as *The Facts about Communism and Our Churches* (1962), *The Total Lie* (1962), and *The Real Extremists—The Far Left* (1964). To enlighten Christians he initiated a so-called Christian Anti-Communist Youth University and a series of Anti-Communist Leadership Schools for clergy and lay people. The former consisted of a two-week seminar and the latter an intensive one-week course on the evils of communism. In order to reach a greater audience the CC owns an FM radio station, purchases broadcast time on hundreds of AM stations (including several in Mexico), and produces programs for television.

Other activities of CC include operation of the American Christian College and construction of the Cathedral of the Christian Crusade (with an accompanying Christian Crusade Museum). CC also owns the Summit Hotel in Manitou Springs, Colorado, and supports the David Livingston Missionary Foundation. In addition it produces films and recordings, maintains a library, publishes countless pamphlets and brochures, and issues the *Christian*

*Crusade Weekly*. Financial support for these endeavors comes primarily from public donations and monetary gifts from individual donors.

The origin and high point in activity of the CC paralleled the most crucial years of the cold war. Reflecting the concern of Christians related to the spread of communism, the CC no doubt contributed to the general support of the Korean War and diplomatic nonrecognition of the People's Republic of China. Critics charged the CC with oversimplification (it claimed, for example, that monolithic communism constituted an international conspiracy), exploitation of anti-Communist fears (for monetary gain), and needlessly fostering an extremist mania that threatened to touch off an atomic crusade against the Soviet Union and Red China.

For more information, see John H. Redekop, *The American Far Right: Billy James Hargis and the Christian Crusade* (1968).

**CHRISTIAN FREEDOM FOUNDATION (CFF).** Founded in 1950 in Buena Park, California, by H. Edward Rowe for the purpose of promoting Christian principles in politics. Originally more of an educational than political organization, the CFF disseminated information on how to apply Christian precepts to government and economics. In 1974, the CFF was reoriented more toward politics by Congressman John Conlon (R-Ariz.).

In 1977 the CFF's headquarters was moved to Washington, D.C. Under the leadership of Conlon, Bill Bright, head of the Campus Crusade for Christ, and Russ Walton, editor-in-chief of Third Century Publishers, a mansion was purchased in the nation's capital and named the Christian Embassy. Billy Graham and Norman Vincent Peale were named honorary members of the advisory council. The CFF seeks to elect "godly" leaders to political office. It has issued a pamphlet, *Your Five Duties as a Christian Citizen*, and its *Christian Index*, which lists how members of Congress voted relative to the preservation of "individual freedom, free competitive enterprise, and constitutional government." The criteria utilized by the CFF are based on fundamentalist religious precepts and conservative economic principles.

Some clergymen oppose this attempt to organize Christians into a voting bloc, particularly when the economics are rightwing and the theology fundamentalist in nature. Opponents to CFF contend that religion and politics should not be mixed, but that Christian citizens should apply individual moral judgment when casting votes.

**CHRISTIAN FRONT (CF).** Founded in 1939 at Royal Oak, Michigan, by the Reverend Charles E. Coughlin, a Roman Catholic priest serving a parish at the Shrine of the Little Flower, for the purpose of preventing U.S. intervention into the war in Europe. Father Coughlin was also the founder of the

National Union for Social Justice* and one of the prime movers in the formation of the Union Party.* CF affiliates grew throughout the United States but, because membership rolls were kept relatively secret, no accurate totals are known. Since the famed "Radio Priest" had a vast audience, it can be assumed that he had a significant following.

The local CF chapters varied in outlook and activity. Most attracted members motivated by a fear of communism. Some drew adherents because of their isolationist and anti-interventionist stance. Others appealed outright to ethnic hyphenates who were pro-German and pro-Italian in sympathies or were motivated by a strong anti-English bias. A few local groups were militant and prone to violence. At Brooklyn, New York, where members of the German-American Bund* may also have been involved, seventeen CF members were arrested for possession of guns and bombs.

Father Coughlin tended to espouse extreme views, which gradually eroded much of his mass support. His rhetoric became increasingly more pro-fascist and anti-Semitic in tone. It was one thing to attack bankers, munitions makers, and Communists, or even to criticize President Franklin D. Roosevelt's foreign policy, but Americans by and large did not accept his sympathetic views with regard to Hitler and Mussolini. His shrill rantings frightened many Americans who regarded Hitler's nazism as a peril to the United States and Europe.

The activities of the CF were kept under surveillance by the Federal Bureau of Investigation. In 1941, prior to the attack on Pearl Harbor, Father Coughlin's magazine, *Social Justice*, was banned from the U.S. mails as constituting seditious literature. This action, coupled with orders from the hierarchy of the Roman Catholic church that the priest no longer speak or publish on political subjects, brought an end to Father Coughlin's crusade. The impact of the CP and its influence on public opinion is difficult to assess. It no doubt contributed to isolationist, anti-interventionist sentiment, which in turn made it difficult for President Roosevelt to render aid to Great Britain or mobilize the nation for war. After December 11, 1941, when Germany and Italy declared war on the United States, the CF immediately collapsed.

For further information, see Charles J. Tull, *Father Coughlin and the New Deal* (1965), and Sheldon Marcus, *Father Coughlin: The Tumultuous Life of the Priest of the Little Flower* (1973).

**CHRISTIAN NATIONALIST CRUSADE.** See Christian Nationalist Party.

**CHRISTIAN NATIONALIST PARTY (CNP).** Founded in 1947 at Eureka Springs, Arkansas, by the Reverend Gerald Lyman Kenneth Smith to oppose communism, desegregation, and American Jewry. The CNP was formed as an outgrowth of the Christian Nationalist Crusade, which had been created in 1946 by a merger of organizations headed by Gerald L. K. Smith; Kenneth Goff, Christian Youth for America; Frederick Kister, Christian Veterans of America; Larry Asman, Christian Veterans Intelligence Service; Jeremiah Stokes, Salt Lake City Pro-American Vigilantes; and the Reverend Arthur W. Terminiello, known as the "Father Coughlin of the South."

Gerald L. K. Smith had been a member of Dudley Pelley's Christian Party,* an associate of Huey Long in the Share Our Wealth Movement,* and a participant in Father Charles E. Coughlin's National Union for Social Justice.* In 1948 Smith ran as the presidential candidate of the CNP, with Henry A. Romer as his vice-presidential running mate, and drew only forty-two votes. The CNP platform called for "deportation of all supporters of the political Zionist movement"; pledged itself to "unending warfare against every phase of and facet of atheistic Communism" (then claimed "that behind Communism stands the organized Jew"); supported a constitutional amendment legalizing segregation of blacks; backed a program of financing migration of blacks back to Africa; demanded U.S. withdrawal from the United Nations; denounced the harsh treatment of defeated Germany; urged pensions for the aged and infirm; favored guaranteed cost of production for farmers; and called for greater benefits to veterans.

In 1952 the CNP nominated General Douglas MacArthur as its presidential candidate, with Jack B. Tenney of California as his running mate. The ticket, without the support of General MacArthur, who displayed no sympathy for their cause, attracted 13,883 popular votes. The Reverend Smith ran for the presidency again in 1956, this time paired with Charles F. Robertson of California, and pulled eight votes. Although the CNP became defunct after such a poor showing, the anti-Semitic crusade of Gerald L. K. Smith continued unabated. He continued to publish the *Cross and the Flag*, with thirty thousand subscribers, which contained virulent attacks upon Jews, blacks, and the leading liberal political figures of the day.

Under Smith's direction a sixty-seven-foot-high statue of Christ was constructed atop Magnetic Mountain near Eureka Springs, Arkansas.

For further information, see Ralph Lord Roy, *Apostles of Discord* (1953), and Roland L. DeLorme and Raymond G. McInnis, eds., *Anti-Democratic Trends in Twentieth-Century America* (1969).

**CHRISTIAN PARTY (CP).** Founded in 1936 at Asheville, North Carolina, by William Dudley Pelley for the ostensible purpose of leading the nation out of the Great Depression. Dubbed the "Chief," Pelley patterned the CP after the Christian American Patriots, also known as the Silver Shirts, which he had started in 1933. The latter group, whose goal was to transform America into a fascist-type nation, claiming 2 million members, wore silver shirts, blue corduroy knickers, and gold-colored stockings.

Ultra-right-wing and quasi-fascist in orientation, the CP was avowedly racist and claimed that the nation needed a strong man to lead it back to prosperity. Presumably, Pelley was to be the president-dictator who would take from the rich and give to the poor.

In 1936 Pelley ran as the CP nominee for president with Willard W. Kemp as his vice-presidential running mate; he drew 1,598 popular votes. With the slogan "For Christ and the Constitution," the CP platform called for mass redistribution of the nation's wealth, racial segregation, disfranchisement of Jews, and laws forbidding Jews to hold property in the United States.

Pelley's admiration for Hitler prompted him to take a pro-Nazi stance in 1939 relative to the war in Europe. He opposed aid to Great Britain or the Soviet Union and fought against U.S. intervention in World War II. After Germany declared war on the United States on December 11, 1941, the CP fell into disfavor with the public and soon ceased to exist. Pelley was indicted for sedition in 1942 but was never convicted. His demagogic appeal had been to exploit the fears of the poor and uneducated in the South during the hard times of the 1930s. After the United States became a participant in World War II, Pelley's views seemed unpatriotic and thus doomed the CP to extinction.

For further information, see George Thayer, *The Farther Shores of Politics* (1968).

**CHURCH OF GOD PARTY.** See Theocratic Party.

**CHURCH PEACE UNION.** See Council on Religion and International Affairs.

**CIO-POLITICAL ACTION COMMITTEE.** See Political Action Committee.

**CITIZENS COMMITTEE FOR THE RIGHT TO KEEP AND BEAR ARMS (CC).** Founded in 1971 by Alan M. Gottlieb at Seattle, Washington, for the purpose of defending the right of Americans to purchase and possess firearms. Gottlieb has served as executive secretary since its inception. In 1974 the national headquarters was moved to Bellevue, Washington. Current membership totals some thirteen thousand, with chapters in forty-one states.

The CC believes that the Bill of Rights guarantees absolutely the right of American citizens to keep and bear arms, citing the Second Amendment to the Constitution: "A well regulated militia, being necessary to the security of a free State, the right to the people to keep and bear arms, shall not be infringed." With strong ideological fervor, the CC contends that federal and state governments have no constitutional right to impose any legislative or statutory restrictions on the right of individual citizens to own guns. It maintains this position despite the fact that federal laws exist relative to the manufacture, sale, transport, and possession of firearms, and most states impose regulations or require gun registration. In addition, the absolute character of the Second Amendment has been modified by the U.S. Supreme Court due to the obsolescence of the militia provision, the absence of frontier conditions, and the markedly increased use of guns to commit felonious crimes. Congress enacted the Omnibus Crime Control and Safe Streets Act in 1968 in an attempt to decrease violence where firearms come into use. The CC, however, has opposed all such actions. It constantly seeks to repeal anti-gun provisions of current laws while working to prevent new gun-control legislation at both the federal and state levels.

In its efforts to preserve absolute prohibitions on gun control, the CC established the Legal Action Fund to challenge the legality of any such regulatory laws. Senator Barry Goldwater (R-Ariz.), a member of its Congressional Advisory Committee, works actively to repeal existing federal legislation and to prevent passage of even more stringent laws. The CC created the Political Victory Fund in 1974 to defeat the so-called Terrible Thirty, a designation for those members of Congress wishing to outlaw "Saturday night special" hand guns (cheaply made pistols often sold through the mails) and impose strict controls over the sale of all firearms. Among them were Birch Bayh (D-Ind.), Edward Brooke (R-Mass.), Shirley Chisholm (D-N.Y.), Michael Harrington (D-Mass.), Edward Kennedy (D-Mass.), George McGovern (D-S.D.), Bertram Podell (D-N.Y.), Ogden Reid (D-N.Y.), Peter Rodino (D-N.J.), and Adlai E. Stevenson III (D-Ill.).

The CC is most powerful politically in rural areas where hunting is still considered a safe and honorable pastime. It is weakest in heavily populated urban communities where the crime rate is high. The CC has been able to mobilize right-wing groups in support of its objectives and has lobbied effectively against all-inclusive registration or the banning of hand guns. Through its monthly magazine, *Point Blank*, the CC keeps its members informed about pending gun-conrol legislation, provides hunting news, and lists the locations and dates of competitive shooting meets throughout the country.

For further information, see Robert J. Kukla, *Gun Control* (1974).

**CITIZENS CONFERENCE ON STATE LEGISLATURES (CCSL).** Founded in 1965 at Kansas City, Missouri, by twenty-five public-spirited citizens representing all sectors of the general population for the purpose of upgrading and increasing the quality of state legislatures throughout the nation. Prime movers in the formation of CCSL were John W. Gallivan, publisher of the *Salt Lake Tribune*, who became chairman of the twenty-three-person board of trustees, and John A. Anderson, Jr., the former governor of Kansas, who was chosen president of the CCSL. Other prominent individuals serving as trustees include Brady Black, editor of the *Cincinnati Inquirer*; Dr. Howard R. Bower, chairman of the Department of Economics at Claremont College; Mrs. Robert J. Phillips, former president of the League of Women Voters of the United States*; Terry Sanford, president of Duke University and former governor of North Carolina; Charles B. Shuman, former president of the American Farm Bureau Federation*; and Jesse Unruh, former Speaker of the California Assembly.

The primary objective of the CCSL is to influence public opinion so that there will be widespread support for the reform of state legislatures. It is financed by grants from foundations and contributions from organizations interested in increasing the effectiveness of state government. In 1969, the CCSL received a $150,000 grant from the Ford Foundation to conduct its Legislative Evaluation Study, the first comprehensive analysis and comparison of all fifty state legislatures. It resulted in a published report, *State Legislatures: An Evaluation of Their Effectiveness* (1971), and was then republished in a paperback edition as *The Sometime Governments* (1971) for general distribution to the public.

Under the leadership of Horace E. Sheldon, director of governmental affairs for the Ford Motor Company and chairman of CCSL's Program Development Committee, studies also have been made in order to initiate reforms relative to adequate compensation for legislators; the holding of annual sessions; staffing; proper facilities; standardized rules of procedure; open committees; and manageable membership size. Additional studies of state constitutions have led to further recommendations for revisions permitting needed changes in the legislative process.

CCSL-sponsored task forces have been formed to investigate various areas: Statehouse Reporting, Legislative Libraries, and Public Education. Under the auspices of CCSL, public opinion has been sampled, a News Media Conference was held to increase understanding and cooperation between news people and state legislators. Recent projects are aimed at securing fundamental reforms in all fifty state legislatures. To achieve this goal, CCLS conducts meetings, produces films, provides informational material to educators, disseminates data to the public, conducts research, has developed a bibliography on pertinent subjects, and issues special reports for the enlightenment of state legislators.

Present national headquarters of the CCSL is located in Kansas City. A professional staff carries on the work of the CCSL under the guidance of executive director Larry Margolis.

**CITIZENS' COUNCILS OF AMERICA (CCA).** Founded in 1954 at Indianola, Mississippi, by Robert B. Patterson and thirteen other supporters of racial segregation for the purpose of opposing implementation of the

U.S. Supreme Court decision in *Brown* v. *Board of Education of Topeka* (1954). This group of arch-segregationists met in 1956 at New Orleans with sympathetic representatives of the other southern states to form a regional CCA. Patterson was chosen to serve as executive director. Integrationists and black leaders of the civil rights movement dubbed this organization the "White Citizens' Councils."

The CCA championed states' rights and the preservation of "racial integrity" through the continuance of legal segregation. It labeled "race-mixing" a Communist plot and utilized legal roadblocks, economic boycotts, protest marches, and political action to hamstring efforts toward desegregation. When restaurants, for instance, would integrate, the CCA immediately organized boycotts to discourage white patrons from entering the establishments. The CCA helped establish private schools when public schools became integrated. In 1956 it pressured nineteen southern U.S. senators and eighty-one southern members of the House of Representatives to sign a "Southern Manifesto" approving the "motives of those states which have declared their intention to resist forced integration by any lawful means." Some of the more progressive southern members of Congress, speaking out for compliance relative to desegregation, were defeated at the polls through campaigns led by the CCA.

When the CCA was controlled by a middle-class professional type of membership, its actions, though vigorous, were generally nonviolent in nature. During the 1960s, an influx of uneducated blue-collar workers and "redneck" small farmers led to the illegal use of force, even though not sanctioned officially by the CCA. Despite frantic efforts by the CCA to influence Congress, it could neither prevent passage of the Civil Rights Acts of 1957, 1960, and 1964 nor stop their implementation in the South.

CCA members tended to throw political support to pro-segregationists such as Governor Orval Faubus of Arkansas, Governor George C. Wallace of Alabama, and Governor Lester Maddox of Georgia. Many who were stalwarts in the CCA were also prominent backers of the American Independent Party* (AIP). In contributing to the vote amassed by Governor Wallace as the presidential candidate of the AIP in 1968, the CCA influenced the outcome of the national election, which saw Republican* Richard M. Nixon narrowly win over Democrat* Hubert H. Humphrey. Although the CCA continues to exert political pressure on candidates, its influence currently is limited primarily to local elections. CCA members opposed the anti-integrationist stand of Governor Jimmy Carter of Georgia but could not mount sufficient southern opposition to prevent his nomination for the presidency by the Democratic Party* in 1976 or his election as president.

Currently the CCA consists of some several hundred small groups located in sixteen states, mostly in the South. Organized as a federation, its national headquarters is located in Jackson, Mississippi, with L. W. Hollis serving as executive director. It supports a small, permanent staff, supervises a system of private schools, maintains a library, supplies speakers, publishes a newspaper, and issues a monthly magazine, *Citizen*.

For more information, see Hodding Carter, *The South Strikes Back* (1959), and Neil R. McMiller, *The Citizens' Council: Organized Resistance to the Second Reconstruction* (1971).

**CITIZEN'S PARTY (CP).** Founded in 1980 at Washington, D.C., by Barry Commoner, a leading environmentalist, and a group of populist-oriented citizens for the purpose of building a new grass-roots party as an alternative to the major political parties. Commoner, who operates his Center for the Biology of Natural Systems in St. Louis, became the CP's first presidential nominee. His vice-presidential running mate was LaDonna Harris, the wife of former Oklahoma Senator Fred Harris. The CP's liberal, left-wing stance earned it less than 1 percent ratings in the polls, but in spite of this lack of popularity its presidential ticket appeared on the ballot in thirty-one states. The only major union leader to endorse the CP was William Winpisinger, president of the International Association of Machinists.

The CP platform advocates the attainment of "economic democracy" by nationalizing the railroads; transforming privately owned oil companies into public utilities; placing a freeze on oil prices; bringing workers into the management of automobile companies; ratification of ERA; federal guarantees of full employment; reductions of from 30 to 50 percent in defense spending; comprehensive national health insurance; and government support for finding energy alternatives to nuclear power.

Few voters had heard of the CP until it aired a radio ad on some 600 stations across the country that aroused both interest and indignation. This controversial advertisement contained a barnyard term which shocked many listeners. A cartoon drawn by Don Wright appearing in the *Miami News* pictured a bull with a caption (words supposedly coming from the animal's mouth) saying "Commoner Dung." When some stations sought to delete the offensive word, the Federal Communications Commission refused to allow them to do so. Written for its shock value, the radio ad got the attention desired, but did little to win many votes for the CP. The final tally gave the CP presidential ticket 221,083 popular votes (less than 1 percent) and no electoral votes.

For more information, see Nicholas von Hoffman, "The Third Man Theme," *The New York Times Magazine* (September 28, 1980), 96-1-1; and "The Third Party Challengers," *Newsweek*, vol. 96 (October 20, 1980), 31–32.

**CITY MANAGERS' ASSOCIATION.** See International City Management Association.

**COALITION FOR A DEMOCRATIC MAJORITY (CDM).** Founded in 1973 at Washington, D.C., by Ben J. Wattenberg for the purpose of reorienting the Democratic Party* away from the New Politics of Senator George H. McGovern. Formation of the CDM was prompted by the overwhelming defeat of McGovern in the presidential election of 1972. Democrats adhering to the CDM desired to move away from the New Left, the McGovern reforms, and the radical social philosophy of the McGovern supporters so that the Democratic Party might continue to hold the loyalty of the average American voter.

The first chairman of the CDM was Ben Wattenberg, a former aide to Senator Henry M. Jackson (D-Wash.). The first executive director was Congressman Thomas S. Foley (D-Wash.). Other members included Congressmen Richard W. Bolling (D-Mo.), James G. O'Hara (D-Mich.), Jim Wright (D-Tex.); John P. Roche, former special assistant to President Lyndon B. Johnson; Charles S. Murphy, former speech writer for President Harry S. Truman; Eugene V. Rostow, former under secretary of state in the Johnson administration; Albert Shanker, president of the New York City chapter of the American Federation of Teachers; Bayard Bustin, director of the A. Philip Randolph Institute; Midge Decter, literary editor of *World Magazine*; Richard Schifter, vice-president of the Maryland state board of education; Max M. Kampelman, former legislative counsel to Senator Hubert H. Humphrey (D-Minn.); Robert Keefe, former administrative assistant to Senator Birch Bayh (D-Ind.); Leon Keyserling, economist; Jeane Kirkpatrick, professor at Georgetown University; Penn Kemble, former chairman of Frontlash; and Seymour Lipset, noted political scientist.

Following the defeat of George McGovern as the presidential candidate of the Democratic Party, the CDM sought to change the rules under which delegates were selected to the Democratic National Convention. They were instrumental in organizing sentiment to change the McGovern reforms, both to eliminate restrictions on the way delegations were selected and remove the quotas relative to representation of women, youth, and minority groups. CDM seeks to move away from the so-called New Politics and to return to a moderate position attractive to the majority of voters. It defends compromise, law and order, a strong national defense, consideration for the social and moral values of ordinary people, and a departure from the counterculture advocates associated with the New Left politics. Members of the CDM oppose extremism, desire welfare reform, support free enterprise, and caution against permitting the Soviet Union from attaining military supremacy over the United States. It supports the criticisms of the Strategic Arms Limitation Treaty agreement as negotiated by President Jimmy Carter and as made by Senator Sam Nunn (D-Ga.), Admiral Elmo Zumwalt, former chief of naval operations, and Paul Nitze, former deputy defense secretary. The CDM represents Democrats who eschew radicalism and idealistic disarmament.

Present national headquarters is located in Washington, D.C. Current chairman is Ben Wattenberg, with Senator Henry Jackson (D-Wash.) serving as honorary chairman. Membership totals about two thousand, representing Democrats from all parts of the country. The CDM has been instrumental in moving the Democratic Party away from the left-wing stance of 1972 toward a more moderate centrist position.

**COALITION FOR HUMAN NEEDS AND BUDGET PRIORITIES (CHNBP).** Founded in 1973 at Washington, D.C., by representatives of twelve organizations for the purpose of getting Congress to alter the budget priorities as submitted by President Richard M. Nixon. Within a very short while, some one hundred additional organizations were affiliated with the CHNBP. These affiliates represented church, citizens, community, consumer, environment, housing, labor, medical, minorities, public affairs, social welfare, women, and youth organizations.

Prime movers in the formation of CHNBP were Mayor Henry M. **Maier** of Milwaukee, who became its national chairman, and Barbara **Williams**, administrative assistant to Congressman Ronald V. Dellum (D-Calif.). The basic objective of this massive coalition was to prevent President Nixon from cutting the national budget so as to pare down or exclude appropriations desired by CHNBP. It lobbied for continuation and even expansion of federally funded programs dealing with unemployment; manpower training; housing and rent subsidies; model cities; urban renewal; health; the Office of Economic Opportunity; and education.

Some of the more well-known organizations that make up CHNBP are the American Baptist Convention, the Jewish Committee, the Catholic Committee on Urban Ministry, the National Council of Senior Citizens,* the Consumer Federation of America,* the National Farmers Union,* the United Mine Workers of America, the National Urban League, National Welfare Rights Association, the National Women's Political Caucus,* and the National Student Lobby.* Policies for CHNBP are decided by a forty-member board of directors, who also do the lobbying. Lobbyists of the member organizations are called upon to exert influence on members of Congress or the White House.

The CHNBP headquarters is located in Washington, D.C., and it operates on a $10,000 per month budget financed by voluntary contributions from member organizations. The CHNBP informs coalition members of the status of important legislation by its *National Priorities Newsletter*.

**COMMISSION ON INTERRACIAL COOPERATION.** See Southern Regional Council.

**COMMITTEE FOR A FREE CHINA.** See Committee of One Million.

**COMMITTEE FOR ECONOMIC DEVELOPMENT (CED).** Founded in 1942 at Washington, D.C., by Jesse Jones, secretary of commerce, and a group of businessmen for the purpose of preparing plans for postwar reconversion following the termination of World War II. Members of the business community involved in the formation of CED included Paul G. Hoffman, president of Studebaker Corporation; William G. Benton, co-founder of Benton and Bowles; Marion Folsom, treasurer of Eastman Kodak, member of the Business Advisory Council and later secretary of health, education and welfare in the Eisenhower cabinet; and Ralph Flanders, president of Jones and Lamson Machine Company and later a U.S. senator from Vermont.

Initially CED set up over two thousand regional committees to carry out postwar planning. In 1945 it reorganized as a permanent, independent organization with a board of trustees composed of two hundred people drawn from the ranks of chairmen of boards of directors, heads of major corporations, leaders in finance, and university presidents. On a rotation basis, twenty new members are brought in each year to represent all sectors of the business community. Its permanent committees are: Decision Making for National Security; Economic and Social Impact of the New Broadcast Media; Financing the Nation's Housing Needs; Improving Productivity in Government; Improving the Quality of the Environment; Management and Financing of Colleges; Organization and Financing of a National Health Care System; and United States and Japan in a New World Economy.

CED does not speak as the voice of business but rather endeavors to foster research and planning on a nonpartisan basis for the solution of domestic and international problems. As a business-academic cooperative venture, top scholars are utilized for research projects. The fifty-member Research and Policy Committee has issued over one hundred "Statements on National Policy." One of these statements, issued in 1945, led to the Bretton Woods Agreement and the establishment of the World Bank and International Monetary Fund. Recommendations from a 1946 statement were incorporated into the Employment Act of 1946, which created the President's Council of Economic Advisers and the Joint Economic Committee of Congress.

The trustees of CED were influential in seeking both public and congressional support for the Marshall Plan. CED's Paul Hoffman was selected to implement the European Recovery Plan as enacted by Congress in 1947. The CED was also instrumental in securing widespread support for the General Agreement on Tariffs and Trade (1947). In 1971 President Richard M. Nixon applied a wage-price freeze as a result of CED's statement, "Further Weapons against Inflation: Measures to Supplement General Fiscal and Monetary Policies." Other CED studies have related to improving the public welfare system, new directions for the American institutions of higher learning, and means of increasing East-West trade. Historically, CED research studies served to focus public attention on specific problems and their proposed solutions. Its reports, read by policy makers, are very influential in determining national policies as they relate to the broad spectrum of economic stability and international trade.

Present CED headquarters is located in New York City. The current chairman of the board of trustees is Emilio G. Collado, with Alfred C. Neal serving as president. In addition to its statements, special studies, and reports, CED publishes a *Newsletter*.

For further information, see Frank V. Fowlkes, "Washington Pressure: CED's Impact on Federal Policies Enhanced by Close Ties to the Executive Branch," *National Journal*, June 17, 1972, 1015–1024, and Karl Schriftgiesser, *Business and Public Policy* (1967).

**COMMITTEE FOR FAIR DIVORCE AND ALIMONY LAWS (CFDAL).** Founded in 1965 at New York City by a group of divorced men for the purpose of promoting reform relative to laws pertaining to divorce, child custody, and alimony. Originally called Alimony Unlimited, it was renamed the CFDAL shortly after its formation.

CFDAL lobbies, provides expert testimony before congressional and legislative committees, and applies political pressure to gain its objectives. These goals include abolition of "Alimony Prison" (in those states where, by law, men failing to pay legally stipulated alimony to their ex-wives are given jail sentences); adoption of no-fault divorce; limitation of alimony to one year; equal child custody rights for men; uniform divorce laws in all states; and equal visitation rights. The CFDAL was instrumental in securing enactment of New York's Divorce Reform Act of 1966. It is now seeking enactment by Congress of its national uniform divorce, alimony, and child custody bill.

In 1972 the CFDAL established the Institute for the Study of Matrimonial Laws (ISML). CFDAL conducts research studies, initiates educational programs, sponsors seminars, and provides counseling service. The CFDAL also cooperates with other organizations, such as Fathers United for Equal Rights and the National Second Wives Committee. Some of the activities of CFDAL have been attacked by women's groups as being unfair to divorcées.

Present national headquarters of CFDAL is still located in New York City. Membership totals over five thousand, mostly men. Current president is Walter R. Lubkemeier, with Sylvia Allen serving as executive secretary. The CFDAL publishes the *CFDAL Newsletter* each month.

**COMMITTEE FOR NONVIOLENT ACTION (CFNA).** Founded in 1957 at Alamogordo, New Mexico, by Quaker activist Lawrence Scott and ten fellow pacifists for the purpose of demonstrating against the continued testing of atomic weapons. The CFNA was originally an ad hoc committee, Nonviolent Action against Nuclear Weapons. A year after their civil disobedience protest at the Alamogordo testing grounds, it was determined to make the CFNA permanent.

Membership in the CFNA has always been very small. Although members have been militant, they also practice nonviolence. They utilize civil disobedience techniques such as refusing to pay taxes as long as nuclear weapons are being made. Some members once attempted to stop an atomic missile test in the Pacific Ocean by sailing small vessels into the landing area. Other members have picketed Cape Kennedy, tried to prevent construction of an underground missile silo, protested against germ warfare research at Fort Detrick in Maryland, implemented a "Polaris Action" plan consisting of demonstrations at the New London, Connecticut, submarine base, and carried out a "San Francisco to Moscow Peace Walk."

For many years the national chairman of CFNA was Abraham J. Muste, a militant pacifist. The impact on public opinion of CFNA's activities is hard to assess. Most Americans reject the pacifists' desire for total disarmament and do not approve of civil disobedience. In 1967 the CFNA disappeared as an independent organization when it was absorbed by the War Resisters League.*

**COMMITTEE FOR THE NATION TO REBUILD PRICES AND PURCHASING POWER (CFTN).** Founded in 1933 at Chicago by General Robert E. Wood, president of Sears, Roebuck and Company, and a group of other leading businessmen for the purpose of promoting economic recovery during the Great Depression. Other prominent individuals involved in its formation were Frank E. Gannett, owner of a newspaper chain, James Henry Rand, Jr., president of Remington Rand, and Lessing Rosenwald, chairman of the board of directors at Sears.

The CFTN sought to convince the business community that the return of prosperity depended upon the progressive concept of positive government as a means of stimulating the economy. Serving as its spokesman, General Wood publicly praised many aspects of the New Deal in an era when many businessmen still believed in negative government and were skeptical or even hostile to the Keynesian fiscal policy intiated by President Franklin D. Roosevelt. Within the CFTN, there was never unanimity of opinion, but general support was given to the National Industrial Recovery Act of 1933, devaluation of the dollar, Agricultural Adjustment Act of 1933, Banking Act of 1933 (which created the Federal Bank Deposit Insurance Corporation), Civilian Conservation Corps, Reciprocal Trade Agreements Act of 1934, and the Securities Exchange Act of 1934. The CFTN was critical of section 7A of the National Industrial Recovery Act, which permitted collective bargaining through the formation of industry-wide unions, and opposed passage of the Revenue Act of 1935 because it imposed a graduated tax on corporate income.

Although the CFTN represented only a very small part of the business-industrial community, its activities did much to blunt the sharp criticism of the American Liberty League* and the National Association of Manufacturers.* The demise of the CFTN came about when Franklin D. Roosevelt initiated the so-called Second New Deal. This shift toward a welfare state caused consternation among businessmen who feared that the power of the federal government was expanding too rapidly. When President Roosevelt attacked businessmen as "economic royalists" during the presidential election of 1936, only a few within CFTN (such as General Wood) could support his reelection. Even this support was finally dissipated when in 1937 the Roosevelt administration claimed that businessmen were deliberately engaging in a "strike of capital" to sabotage the New Deal. This allegation alienated the last few members of the CFTN, who believed the president was unfairly blaming them for the recession of 1937.

For further information, see H. M. Bratter, "The Committee for the Nation," *Journal of Political Economy* 49 (1941): 531–553.

**COMMITTEE FOR THE NEW MAJORITY (CFNM).** Founded in 1975 at Washington, D.C., by William A. Rusher, publisher of the *National Review*, and other conservatives for the purpose of keeping an option open for the formation of a new third party. Leaders in the CFNM included Eli Howell, former aide to Senator James B. Allen (D-Ala.) and consultant to Governor George C. Wallace of Alabama; Howard Phillips, a former member of the Nixon administration and a supporter of California's former governor, Ronald Reagan, for the GOP's* presidential nomination; and Senator Jesse Helms (R-N.C.), chairman of the Conservation Political Action Conference, which authorized exploration of the possibility of forming a third party.

The CFNM, although relatively small in numbers, sought to prepare the way for fusion of the followers of Ronald Reagan and George Wallace if neither succeeded in gaining the nomination in his respective party. Reagan failed to gain the nomination from incumbent President Gerald R. Ford, and Wallace withdrew from the Democratic* primaries after losing out to Jimmy Carter in the first encounter with the Georgia governor.

Attempts to coalesce the Reagan and Wallace followers failed, and as a result the CFNM dissolved. The effort to unite conservatives of both major parties into a new third party continues but under different auspices and dissimilar circumstances.

**COMMITTEE OF AMERICANS FOR THE CANAL TREATIES (CACT).** Founded in 1978 at Washington, D.C., by a group of leading U.S.

citizens for the purpose of promoting ratification of the Panama Canal treaties between the United States and the Republic of Panama. Co-chairpersons of CACT were Jerry Apodaca, Margaret Truman Daniel, Averell Harriman, Andrew Heiskell, Henry Cabot Lodge, Hugh Scott, Stuart Symington, and Maxwell Taylor.

The CACT lobbied in the Senate and sought to influence public opinion to secure ratification of the treaties that would transfer the canal and canal zone to the Panamanians. Members of CACT included Elie Abel, Reuben Askew, George Ball, Shirley Temple Black, Tom Bradley, J. Lawton Collins, John Sherman Cooper, Gardner Cowles, C. Douglas Dillon, Thomas K. Finletter, Gerald R. Ford, Orville Freeman, Theodore Hesburgh, Philip Jessup, John McCloy, George Meany, Lauris Norstad, Stanley Rabinowitz, Ogden Reid, Matthew Ridgway, Nelson A. Rockefeller, Franklin D. Roosevelt, Jr., Walt Rostow, Dore Schary, Arthur M. Schlesinger, Jr., Theodore Sorensen, Jack Valenti, and Elmo Zumwalt.

The CACT received support for its position from the National Council of the Churches of Christ in the U.S.A. and the National Women's Political Caucus.* Endorsements were also received from Secretary of State Cyrus Vance, former Secretary of State Henry Kissinger, General George S. Brown, chairman of the Joint Chiefs of Staff, and actor John Wayne.

Although not totally responsible for the ratification of the Panama Canal treaties, the CACT did much to mobilize public opinion in favor of this action. CACT members were articulate and able to utilize all forms of the media to get their message across to the American people. The basic argument put forth for permitting Panama to have sovereignty over the canal and canal zone was that without such attention the goodwill of the Panamanians would be lost. That might produce a situation where the canal would be sabotaged. The United States could not protect it from guerrilla-type warfare and thus would be better to conclude an honorable transfer of the canal to Panama. The United States in turn received safeguards in terms of using the canal during future wars and was given the right to protect it in times of emergency. Since the treaties won ratification in the U.S. Senate in 1978 by a one-vote margin, the CACT played a key role in achieving this success.

During its brief life, John O. March, Jr., served as CACT's national director. Once the treaties were ratified, the CACT dissolved.

**COMMITTEE OF ONE MILLION (COM).** Founded in 1953 at Washington, D.C., by Congressman Walter Judd (R-Minn.) to oppose the seating of the People's Republic of China in the United Nations (U.N.). In addition to Judd, members of the original steering committee included Senator John Sparkman (D-Ala.), later chairman of the Senate Foreign Relations Committee; Congressman John W. McCormack (R-Mass.), later Speaker of the House; and Senator H. Alexander Smith (R-N.J.), chairman of the Senate's Far East subcommittee. Others who belonged to COM included Senator

Paul H. Douglas (D-Ill.), Senator Abraham A. Ribicoff (D-Conn.), Senator Jacob K. Javits (R-N.Y.), Congressman Thomas E. Morgan (D-Pa.), and Congressman Clement J. Zablocki (D-Wis.). New York public relations consultant Marvin Liebman served as executive secretary from its founding until 1969.

Impetus for the formation of COM, which was originally called the Committee of One Million against Admission of Communist China to the U.N. (stemming from a petition with one million signatures), came from what was formerly termed the China lobby and the occasion of the Korean armistice in 1953. Bipartisan in nature, COM sought to promote U.S. support for Chiang Kai-shek's Nationalist China (Taiwan) rather than bestow diplomatic recognition on the People's Republic of China. COM's primary aim was to prevent the People's Republic from occupying the China seat on the Security Council or in the General Assembly of the U.N. Although probably never achieving a membership of one million, COM did attract hundreds of thousands of supporters at the height of its popularity. It succeeded in influencing the foreign policy of three presidents: Dwight D. Eisenhower, John F. Kennedy, and Lyndon B. Johnson. During this time the United States gave military aid to Taiwan, refused to grant diplomatic recognition to the People's Republic, and succeeded in preventing representatives of the People's Republic from being seated in the U.N.

Two events in 1971 sounded the death knell for the COM. The first took place on July 15, when President Richard M. Nixon announced his intention to visit the People's Republic. The second occurred on October 25, when the U.N. General Assembly expelled Nationalist China from that body in order to seat the delegates from the People's Republic. On the eve of President Nixon's visit to the People's Republic in 1972, Walter Judd, along with Senator Barry Goldwater (R-Ariz.) and Senator Strom Thurmond (R-S.C.), formed the Committee for a Free China (CFFC). Other significant members of Congress who joined the CFFC included Senator James Buckley (R-N.Y.), Senator Carl Curtis (R-Neb.), and Senator Jesse Helms (R-N.C.). The CFFS fought to forestall U.S. diplomatic recognition of the People's Republic and to prevent President Gerald R. Ford from canceling the 1954 Mutual Defense Treaty with Taiwan. In 1978 when President Jimmy Carter announced that diplomatic recognition was being granted to the People's Republic, the CFFC initiated legal action to prevent nullification of the U.S.-Taiwan treaty. This was done on the basis of the International Security Assistance Act of 1978, which stipulated that "there should be prior consultation between Congress and the executive branch" before such a treaty could be altered or abrogated. The Supreme Court, however, in 1979 did not sustain this view when it ruled in favor of the Carter administration.

The power and influence of the COM was at its zenith during the McCarthy and post-Korean War eras. Its ability to arouse mass support did much to deter presidents from seeking to establish diplomatic relations with the People's Republic. It not only affected Sino-U.S. relationships but helped to prevent détente between the United States and the Soviet Union. COM constantly publicized the fact that the Soviet Union had enslaved millions behind the Iron Curtain by making Communist satellites out of previously free nations. COM's ability to influence public opinion against having closer ties with either the People's Republic or the Soviet Union began to erode seriously during the Vietnam war. When President Nixon initiated contacts with the People's Republic and sought to end the cold war by easing tensions with the Soviet Union, COM/CFFC was unable to alter these policies either by congressional action or by the impact of grass-roots opposition. As the high tide of anti-communism subsided in the 1970s, so did the political influence of the COM/CFFC. Present national headquarters of the CFFC is located in Washington, D.C. Current executive secretary is Lee Edwards.

For further information, see Ross Koen, *The China Lobby in American Politics* (1975), and Stanley D. Bachrack, *The Committee of One Million: "China Lobby" Politics, 1953-1971* (1976).

**COMMITTEE ON CONSERVATIVE ALTERNATIVES.** See American Conservative Union.

**COMMITTEE ON MILITARISM IN EDUCATION (CME).** Founded in 1925 at New York City by pacifists, isolationists, and anti-interventionists for the purpose of opposing any type of military conscription or training. Its prime movers were Roswell Barnes, John N. Sayre, Tucker P. Smith, Oswald Garrison Villard, and E. Raymond Wilson.

CME's principal objective in the 1920s was to eliminate Reserve Officer Corps Training (ROTC) in both private and land-grant educational institutions. Its success was limited to certain high schools and colleges, but overall its opposition to ROTC did not gain the support of the general public. It supported general disarmament, outlawry of war, and the Kellogg-Briand Pact of 1928. During the 1930s, CME supported the Neutrality Acts but opposed the Burke-Wadsworth Act for military conscription in 1940. It also opposed, but failed again, when the draft act was renewed in 1941. Never a large organization, it died after the Pearl Harbor attack.

**COMMITTEE ON POLITICAL EDUCATION (COPE).** Founded in 1955 at Washington, D.C., by the American Federation of Labor-Congress of Industrial Organizations (AFL-CIO) for the purpose of electing political candidates favorable to organized labor. COPE was an outgrowth of the AFL's Labor's League for Political Education* (LLPE) and the CIO's Political Action Committee* (PAC). When the LLPE and PAC were merged in 1955 as part of the overall merger of the AFL and CIO, Jack Kroll and

James McDevitt were named co-directors. Kroll had headed the PAC, and McDevitt had been the previous director of the LLPE.

Although claiming to be nonpartisan, COPE in fact predominantly supports Democrats.* For instance, in the 1972 national election, COPE endorsed 408 candidates for the U.S. Senate, House of Representatives, and state gubernatorial offices (60 percent of them winning), of whom only twenty-five were Republicans. Among presidential candidates it has supported Adlai E. Stevenson (1956), John F. Kennedy (1960), Lyndon B. Johnson (1964), Hubert H. Humphrey (1968), and Jimmy Carter (1976 and 1980). In the 1972 presidential election between GOP* incumbent Richard M. Nixon and the Democratic nominee, Senator George McGovern of South Dakota, COPE remained neutral. The thirty-five-member AFL-CIO Executive Council decides on presidential endorsements, and COPE implements the policy. Support for other candidates is made at the state or local level.

COPE provides financial support, loaning of COPE staff members, free campaign literature, television time purchased by labor unions, publicity in labor publications, and campaign workers recruited from the ranks of the AFL-CIO. COPE is the political voice for the sixteen million members of 177 AFL-CIO affiliates, which represent 76 percent of organized labor. COPE supports political candidates who favor such legislation as the strengthening of collective bargaining, the raising of minimum wages, increases in Social Security payments, federal funding for vocational education, Medicare, better unemployment benefits, new codes for industrial safety, and programs geared to promote full employment.

In order to strengthen its relationship with the Democratic Party, COPE director Alexander E. Barkin established the Coalition for a Democratic Majority* in 1972. COPE was opposed to the New Politics and the McGovern reforms instituted at the 1972 Democratic National Convention (especially the quota system for delegates). It hopes to regain for organized labor its traditionally powerful place within the inner ranks of the Democratic Party. In 1973 the AFL-CIO renamed its Department of Organization the Department of Organization and Field Services. It was fashioned to work with COPE to maximize organized labor's political power. To coordinate its political activity further, a seven-member Legislative Department, headed by Andrew J. Biemiller (who formerly served in the House of Representatives as a Democrat from Wisconsin), implements legislative policy as determined by the AFL-CIO's Executive Council and president Lane Kirkland. The AFL-CIO has five registered lobbyists operating in the nation's capital, and so do some forty affiliates.

In 1975 COPE demonstrated its effectiveness when it helped to elect Democrat John Durkin to the U.S. Senate in a special election held in New Hampshire. This election was significant because in the original Senate election of 1974 Durkin had been declared the loser by two votes. Durkin's opponent was supported by William Loeb's *Manchester Union Leader* which leaders of organized labor regarded as an enemy. In 1976 COPE spent millions of dollars to elect Jimmy Carter and a Democratic Congress so that it might obtain passage of a common-site picketing bill. This measure had been enacted by Congress by 1976 but was vetoed by President Gerald R. Ford. To the surprise of George Meany and COPE officials, the common-site bill failed to pass Congress in 1977.

Since its existence, COPE has succeeded in helping to elect many presidents and members of Congress favorable to its cause. But this has not meant that the AFL-CIO has gained everything it wants. It has always been successful in getting the minimum wage raised, but it failed to stop passage of the Landrum-Griffin Act of 1959, and it could not get section 14-b of the Taft-Hartley Act repealed (which would have nullified right-to-work laws sanctioning a nonunion shop).

Many AFL-CIO officials voiced considerable criticism of President Carter over high unemployment, inflation, and the administration's refusal to provide tariff protection for U.S. steel and automobile companies. Most labor leaders backed Senator Edward Kennedy (D-Mass.) in 1980 when the latter attempted to win the Democratic presidential nomination from Jimmy Carter. Once Carter was renominated, AFL-CIO officially endorsed the incumbent, although the International Brotherhood of Teamsters broke ranks to support the presidential nominee of the Republican Party.*

For further information, see Terry Catchpole, *How to Cope with COPE: The Political Operation of Organized Labor* (1968), and Douglas Caddy, *The Hundred Million Dollar Payoff* (1974).

**COMMITTEE TO DEFEND AMERICA BY AIDING THE ALLIES (CDAAA).** Founded in 1940 at Emporia, Kansas, by William Allen White, the noted editor of the *Emporia Daily Gazette*, for the purpose of promoting public support for the foreign policy of President Franklin D. Roosevelt. White acted as national chairman, and Clark Eichelberger served as executive director.

The impetus for the formation of CDAAA, often called the William Allen White Committee, stemmed from an appeal by President Roosevelt for an organization to counter the isolationist appeal of the America First Committee.* The CDAAA served as a nonadministration voice to defend the president's interventionist policies. Its membership was relatively small, but its spokespeople were articulate and able to utilize the media of the times to great effect. Important members included Walter Lippmann, noted columnist for the *New York Herald Tribune*; Dr. Paul H. Douglas, a professor of economics at the University of Chicago; and General John J. Pershing, the commander of the American Expeditionary Force in World War I.

Although loosely organized, the CDAAA was very successful in countering the isolationist sentiment of the era. It sent speakers throughout the country, utilized the radio, and got newspapers to run articles written to generate public support for giving military aid to Great Britain. CDAAA spokespeople emphasized the fact that only Great Britain stood between Hitler's Germany and the rest of the world. CDAAA's efforts were successful in gaining public acceptance for revision of the Neutrality Acts, the "destroyer deal," Lend-Lease, and the Burke-Wadsworth (conscription) Act. Much credit is due the CDAAA for alerting the public to the need for war mobilization and preventing Great Britain from going down to defeat at the hands of Nazi Germany.

For more information, see William Allen White, *Autobiography* (1946), and Walter Johnson, *William Allen White's America* (1947).

**COMMITTEE TO SUPPORT MODERATE REPUBLICANS.** See Republicans for Progress.

**COMMITTEES OF CORRESPONDENCE (CC).** Founded in 1772 at Boston by the Boston town meeting for the purpose of promoting unity and exchanging views among the colonies. The prime mover was Samuel Adams upon whose motion the town meeting acted. Within a very short time other committees were formed in the colonies of Connecticut, New Hampshire, Rhode Island, South Carolina, and Virginia. Prime movers in Virginia included Patrick Henry, Richard Henry Lee, and Thomas Jefferson.

The CC fostered unity and served to encourage colonial opposition to British policies in America. The colonists were instrumental in sustaining a fairly wide boycott of British goods and in organizing demonstrations against the British troops. Some members of the Boston CC took part in the Boston Tea Party and followed Samuel Adams in his agitation for a revolution. After 1775 many of the CC transformed themselves into Committees of Safety for the purpose of harassing the British. These so-called Minutemen took part in the Battle of Lexington and Concord in Massachusetts. They were disbanded in favor of a Continental Army after 1776. During its brief existence, the CC did much to arouse colonial sentiment in favor of independence and thus make the American Revolution possible.

For more information, see John C. Miller, *Sam Adams: Pioneer in Proppaganda* (1936), and Pauline Maier, *From Resistance to Revolution, 1765-1776* (1972).

**COMMITTEES OF SAFETY.** See Committees of Correspondence.

**COMMON CAUSE (CC).** Founded in 1970 at Washington, D.C., by John W. Gardner for the purpose of promoting reform in government and inducing Congress to be more responsive to the needs of the nation. Dr. Gardner, who served as chairman of CC's board of directors until 1978, had been president of the Carnegie Corporation (1955-1965); served as secretary of health, education and welfare in the cabinet of President Lyndon B. Johnson (1965-1969); and was chairman of the Urban Coalition Action Council of New York (1969-1970), from which the concept of CC stemmed.

CC determines policy by periodic referendums of its members (polling by mail) and then lobbies for desired reforms or legislation. Membership dues support an annual average budget of $5 million, and volunteer workers supplement lobbying carried out by paid members of the permanent staff. Chief lobbyist is Mike Cole, one of the most successful in the nation's capital. CC is in effect a citizen's lobby and as such has been highly successful.

CC has played a significant role in securing the vote for eighteen year olds; gaining congressional approval of the equal rights amendment to the U.S. Constitution; easing residential requirements for voters; forcing candidates for federal office to disclose sources of major campaign contributions; getting Congress to legalize one dollar checkoffs for presidential campaigns on Internal Revenue forms 1040 and 1040A; forcing congressional committee hearings to be opened to the public unless the committee specifically votes to go into executive session; and obtaining termination of the oil depletion allowance as part of a tax reform law.

CC has fought against the seniority system, wants chairpersons of congressional committees selected each session, and has proposed a series of reforms for state legislatures. It has succeeded in securing federal financing (supplementary in nature) for presidential campaigns; curbing excessive military spending; strengthening environmental laws; ensuring congressional monitoring of the Central Intelligence Agency and the Federal Bureau of Investigation; reducing the powers of the executive office; and ensuring federal support of welfare programs. It also seeks the enactment of an energy program, passage of a national health insurance program, and legislation protecting the confidentiality of news sources. It has agitated for many years for reform of lobbying disclosure laws.

Although nonpartisan, CC is oriented toward political liberalism. It secures considerable cooperation from key leaders within the Democratic Party.* CC membership fluctuates between 200,000 and 320,000. It reached its highest figure when it was agitating for the impeachment of President Richard M. Nixon. Present national headquarters is located in Washington, D.C. Current national chairman is David Cohen, with Fred Wertheimer serving as vice-president. CC publications include *In Common: Report from Washington* and *Frontline*.

For further information, see Norman J. Ornstein and Shirley Elder, *Interest Groups and Policymaking* (1978).

**COMMONGOOD PARTY.** See People's Party (1971).

**COMMONWEAL OF CHRIST.** See Coxey's Army.

**COMMUNIST LABOR PARTY.** See Communist Party of the United States of America.

**COMMUNIST PARTY OF AMERICA.** See Communist Party of the United States of America.

**COMMUNIST PARTY OF THE UNITED STATES (MARXIST-LENINIST).** See Communist Party of the United States of America.

**COMMUNIST PARTY OF THE UNITED STATES OF AMERICA (CPUSA).** Founded in 1919 at Chicago by John Reed, Benjamin Gitlow, and some eighty left-wing radicals for the purpose of forming a Marxist organization based on the Soviet model. Calling themselves the Communist Labor Party (CLP), this group selected Alfred Wagenhaupt as executive secretary and designated Cleveland, Ohio, as their national headquarters. Meeting simultaneously in Chicago, a rival faction assembled under the auspices of the Russian Federation formed the Communist Party of America (CPA) and chose Chicago for their permanent headquarters. Louis C. Fraina was named national secretary of CPA and editor of its publication, *The Communist.*

Both parties accepted the teachings of Karl Marx and Friedrich Engels, and each embraced the ideology of the Bolshevik Revolution as delineated by Vladimir Ilyich Lenin and Leon Trotsky. Both parties joined the Third Communist International (Comintern), and each sought the special approval of the Kremlin. The CLP favored collaboration with Socialists and trade unions, such as the Industrial Workers of the World* (IWW), while the CPA opposed it.

Implementing a directive by Lenin to cooperate with trade unions and parliamentary groups of the Left, some sixty Communists held a secret meeting at Woodstock, New York, in 1921, to reorganize the CPA. Representing about twenty thousand members, all of whom operated in secret cells, the CPA declared that it would "systematically and persistently propagate the idea of the inevitability of and necessity for violent revolution" while seeking to "prepare the workers for armed insurrection as the only means of overthrowing the capitalist state." William A. Weinstone was chosen national secretary, but was soon replaced by Jay Lovestone (who was expelled from the party in 1929 for deviationism).

Prodded by officials of the Communist Party of the Union of Soviet Socialist Republics (CPUSSR) to end their factionalism, both parties held a covert unity conference at Bridgman, Michigan, in 1922. Harassed by the

Federal Bureau of Investigation, then headed by William J. Burns, members of the newly formed United Communist Party (UCP) emulated the Russian example of czarist days and went underground. Nevertheless some Communists were jailed or deported. Alfred Wagenhaupt, the executive secretary, was imprisoned, and Charles E. Rutherberg and John Reed, author of *Ten Days That Shook the World* (1919), fled ultimately to the Soviet Union. Both lived in Russia as exiles, and Reed was honored at his death in 1920 by being entombed within the Kremlin Wall.

To establish itself as a legal political party, the UCP formed the Workers Party of America (WPA). In 1924 the WPA, also known as the Workers (Communist) Party of America,* nominated William Z. Foster for president and Benjamin Gitlow as his vice-presidential running mate. Seeking the coalescence of all radical and revolutionary groups under one banner, the WPA platform called for emulation of the Soviet Union so that a "Communist social system" could be erected in America to guarantee for "workers and farmers the fruits of their toil." It also demanded nationalization of all major industries, government support for the unemployed, cessation of all federal strike-breaking activities, release of all political prisoners, an end to U.S. imperialism, self-determination for America's overseas possessions, and immediate diplomatic recognition of the Soviet Union. In the national election of 1924 the WPA ticket drew 36,386 popular and no electoral votes.

In 1928 the same team of Foster and Gitlow was named by the WPA as its presidential and vice-presidential slate. This time the pair drew only 21,181 votes.

For the national election of 1932, at the depth of the Great Depression, the Communist Party, U.S.A. (CPUSA)—it had again changed its name in 1925—once more slated William Z. Foster as its presidential nominee. This time, James W. Ford was selected to run with him. Seeking to appeal to the millions of unemployed workers and dispossessed farmers, the CPUSA platform militantly declared, "Only a revolutionary workers' and farmers' government can break through this paralysis of the capitalist crisis and start economic activity going full speed for the benefit of the masses of workers and farmers." Pointing to Communist Russia as a model, it claimed that "the Soviet Union stands out as proof that the workers can rule, not only in their interests, but in the interests of all those who are oppressed by capitalism." At a time when discontent and disillusionment were at their zenith, Foster and Ward attracted only 102,785 out of some 40 million votes cast in the election that saw Franklin D. Roosevelt overwhelmingly defeat Herbert C. Hoover.

Most of the CPUSA popular vote came from New York City where the International Workers Order (IWO) had an active membership of over twenty-five thousand. The IWO, a Communist front organization, was formed in 1930 and attracted members because it provided life insurance at low rates. It disbanded in 1950 when the state of New York revoked its insurance license.

Earl Browder paired with James W. Ford in 1936 to constitute the CPUSA presidential ticket for that year. Disdainful of the New Deal, the party's platform called for a guaranteed annual minimum wage, a thirty-hour work week; paid vacations; maternity and health insurance; massive public works; low-cost public housing; a moratorium on farmers' mortgages with government refinancing at low interest; a graduated land tax with total exemption from taxes for small farmers and rural cooperatives; federal regulation of farm prices; heavy taxation of the rich; civil rights for minorities; abolition of military training in the Civilian Conservation Corps; independence for Puerto Rico; a policy of nonrecognition relative to Japanese territorial acquisitions; an end to U.S. intervention in Latin American affairs; support for a collective stand of the United States and the League of Nations against the imperialism of Germany, Italy, and Japan; and an appeal to workers to assist in establishing the type of socialism practiced by the Soviet Union as a means of solving America's economic problems. Running on the slogan "Communism is twentieth-century Americanism," Browder and Ford had little appeal in the year that witnessed a Roosevelt landslide over Republican* Alfred M. Landon. Their vote totaled only 80,159.

The robot-like parroting by the CPUSA of the official party line set by Moscow was most evident in 1939, when Joseph Stalin and Adolph Hitler agreed to the Soviet-Nazi Nonaggression Pact. Prior to this alliance, the CPUSA, with its Popular Front against fascism, had championed U.S. opposition to Hitler. But in view of the U.S.S.R.-German agreement, American Communists suddenly reversed their interventionist position. The CPUSA failed to condemn the German invasion of Poland because the Red Army also occupied part of that same country, and it remained silent when the Soviet Union absorbed Estonia, Latvia, Lithuania, and a portion of Finland (the last as a result of military conquest in 1940). When the Third Reich defeated France and sought to conquer Great Britain through intensive bombing, the CPUSA joined with American isolationists to oppose vigorously all aid to Britain, military conscription, and any form of industrial mobilization.

In the national election of 1940 Earl Browder was once again the CPUSA's presidential nominee. With his usual running mate, James Ford, his campaign focused on the theme "Keep America out of the imperialist war." The platform demanded a halt to anti-Soviet policies; cessation of mobilization; opposition to the draft; immediate suspension of all shipments of munitions and armaments to "imperialist belligerents"; and a condemnation of the scheme by capitalists "to drag the American people into the European war on the side of Great Britain." Despite the duo's insistence that a "vote for the Communist Party is a vote against imperialist war," Browder and Ford garnered only 46,251 votes. In his memoirs, *I Confess*

(1940), Benjamin Gitlow renounced the CPUSA with the admission, "We all accepted, without reservation, the right of the Russian Bolshevik leaders to boss our party."

When Hitler's mighty Wehrmacht launched a full-scale invasion into the Soviet Union on June 22, 1941, the CPUSA made a hasty about-face. Its leaders now frantically implored the U.S. government to render immediately all-out aid to the hard-pressed Soviets. They called for quick mobilization and assistance to Britain, which was now the Soviet Union's ally.

To further the war effort, Stalin ostensibly dissolved the Comintern in 1943, even though the CPUSA had apparently withdrawn already in 1940 (due to the Smith Act). Now American Communists could claim that no international revolutionary organization existed. To transform itself further into a loyal American organization and thus promote Soviet-American friendship, the CPUSA tactfully adopted the name Communist Political Association (CPA). During the course of the war, the party line emphasized cooperation with liberals and left-wing groups of all kinds in order to further the war effort and thereby ensure the survival of the Soviet Union.

Soon after the termination of World War II, "Browderism" was denounced by the Kremlin. No longer useful, at least in Moscow's eyes, Earl Browder was deposed as party leader and ultimately expelled. The new head of the CPUSA was William Z. Foster, chairperson, and Eugene Dennis was national secretary. The Communist International (now dubbed the Cominform) was officially reestablished in 1947, and the CPUSA rigidly adhered to its ideological dictums.

As the cold war intensified in the postwar era, members of the CPUSA vociferously attacked the Truman Doctrine, aid to Greece and Turkey, the U.S. loan to Great Britain, the Marshall Plan, and the North Atlantic Treaty Organization. All U.S. efforts to prevent Soviet domination of Europe were thus condemned, but no criticism was made of the Soviet Union when it rang down an Iron Curtain in Eastern Europe and created a permanent system of puppet regimes as Soviet satellites.

The CPUSA decided not to enter a presidential slate in the 1948 election. Instead it endorsed Henry A. Wallace, the presidential nominee of the Progressive Party.* The CPUSA platform urged the termination of the cold war by abandoning the Marshall Plan; stopping military aid to Nationalist China, South Korea, and Western Europe; ending U.S. militarism; restoring a policy of international cooperation with the Soviet Union; and recognizing that American Communists were not foreign agents. The support of the CPUSA did not help Henry Wallace, but it did publicly pin a red label on him that he was never able to remove, particularly since he did not repudiate their endorsement. After he had suffered defeat at the polls, Wallace denounced the CPUSA for meddling in his campaign.

In 1949 eleven top CPUSA officials were convicted under the Smith Act for conspiring to overthrow the U.S. government by force. Seven were eventually imprisoned, but four, including Gus Hall, fled the country. Discovered in Mexico, he was captured in 1951 and sent to prison. Other anti-Communist measures enacted during that era included the McCarran Internal Security Act of 1950 and the Communist Control Act of 1954. The Korean War, evidence of wartime espionage in the United States and Canada, loyalty programs, loyalty oaths, purges of Communists by labor unions, congressional investigations, and infiltration by the FBI tended to decimate the ranks of the CPUSA. Further defections occurred in 1956 when Soviet leader Nikita Khruschev denounced Stalinism at the Twentieth Congress of the CPUSSR. Chairman Khruschev's announcement of a policy of coexistence with capitalistic countries caused further consternation among the party faithful in America. The exodus from the CPUSA increased even more in 1956 when the Hungarian Revolution was crushed by Red Army tanks and other repressive measures taken by the Soviets to maintain their control over the satellite nations of Eastern Europe. The nadir of the CPUSA was reached in 1958 when the *Daily Worker*, issued on a regular basis since 1924, stopped publication.

The rise of the New Left as a political movement—linked with civil rights, free speech, and the anti-Vietnam war protest during the 1960s and 1970s—created an atmosphere of radicalism in which the CPUSA revived. Gus Hall, after his release from prison (now regarded by radicals as a kind of martyr), again took charge of the party. In 1968 he, with Charlene Mitchell as his running mate, ran for the presidency. The CPUSA ticket polled 1,075 votes. Hall, paired with Jarvis Tyner, carried the CPUSA standard in 1972 and again in 1976. In 1972 they pulled 25,229 popular votes, and in 1976, a total of 58,992. Membership in CPUSA still remained very small due to many factors: negative image as a mouthpiece for Moscow; its anti-Israeli policy (and anti-Semitism in the Soviet Union); its doctrinaire stance; and intraparty dissension stemming from Maoism and the Sino-Soviet rift over geographical boundaries. Also younger radicals regarded it as too conservative.

In 1965 a rival organization was founded, the Communist Party of the United States (Marxist-Leninist) [CPUSA-ML], whose national headquarters was located in Los Angeles. A. M. Hoffman served as chairperson of the central committee. It published a biweekly, *People's Voice*, and a bimonthly, *Red Flag*. The CPUSA-ML reflected the Maoist stance of the Communist Party of the People's Republic of China and denounced the so-called revisionism of both CPUSA and the CPUSSR. With but a miniscule membership, the CPUSA-ML advocated overthrow of the American capitalistic system in favor of a socialist system patterned after the Red Chinese model; self-determination for American blacks; an end to U.S. imperialism; and U.S. support for the Third World.

American Communists, of whatever faction, have always been confronted with a basic dilemma. On the one hand, they have espoused a revolutionary ideology, but they have had to give lip-service to the democratic system of elections and rule by the majority. They have also been plagued by continual switches in party line caused by changes of policy in Moscow or Peking. This has resulted in embarrassments, purges, and having to defend positions not necessarily in the best interests of the United States. Communist parties in America, therefore, have had great difficulty operating as legitimate political parties. They cannot win the support of the electorate in the same manner as those committed to the principles of the U.S. Constitution. For this reason, the CPUSA never acquired a large constituency.

In 1980 Gus Hall once again ran as the presidential nominee of the CPUSA with black activist Angela Davis as his vice-presidential running mate. Hall's views were made known through a book titled, *Basics for Peace, Democracy and Social Progress* (1980). It repeats the Communist Party line that capitalism is oppressive and that the U.S. is an imperialist nation. No criticism of the Soviet Union's invasion of Afghanistan is made.

Angela Davis, a lecturer on feminism and black studies at San Francisco State University and co-chairperson of the National Alliance Against Racism and Political Repression, did little stumping outside of issuing weekly press releases. She was especially critical of President Carter both for initiating draft registration and ordering a U.S. boycott of the 1980 Olympics held in Moscow. The latter was done to protest the invasion of Afghanistan by the Soviet Union. When asked by reporters if she had given up her revolutionary views, Angela Davis replied, "We cannot avoid being inside the system. It's important that we protect all the democratic channels that remain open."

When the 1980 vote tally was complete, it revealed the Hall-Davis ticket drew only a smattering of votes (See table 2.)

**TABLE 2 Communist Party of the United States (CPUSA) Presidential Candidates and Votes, 1924-1980**

| YEAR | CANDIDATE | TOTAL POPULAR VOTE |
|------|-----------|--------------------|
| 1924 | William Z. Foster | 36,386 |
| 1928 | William Z. Foster | 21,181 |
| 1932 | William Z. Foster | 102,785 |
| 1936 | Earl Browder | 80,159 |
| 1940 | Earl Browder | 46,251 |
| 1968 | Gus Hall | 1,075 |
| 1972 | Gus Hall | 25,229 |
| 1976 | Gus Hall | 58,992 |
| 1980 | Gus Hall | 43,871 |

For more information, see Earl R. Browder, *What Is Communism* (1936); Irving Howe and Louis Coser, *The American Communist Party: A*

*Critical History* (1957); Theodore Draper, *American Communism and Soviet Russia* (1960); Joseph Starobin, *American Communism in Crisis, 1943-1957* (1972); and Philip J. Jaffe, *The Rise and Fall of American Communism* (1975).

**COMMUNIST PARTY, U.S.A.** See Communist Party of the United States of America.

**COMMUNIST POLITICAL ASSOCIATION.** See Communist Party of the United States of America.

**CONFERENCE FOR PROGRESSIVE POLITICAL ACTION (CPPA).** Founded in 1922 at Minneapolis by representatives of the Farmer-Labor Party,* railroad brotherhoods, socialists, and other trade union groups for the purpose of furthering the election of pro-labor candidates to political office. The CPPA was modeled after the Nonpartisan League* but was designed to be national in scope and socialist in orientation to act as a political umbrella and enroll the support of the entire labor and liberal-left movement. In many ways, it was an attempt to instill some vigor into the seemingly dormant progressive movement.

The platform of the CPPA called for direct election of the president; repeal of the Transportation Act of 1920 (members favored the Plumb plan, designed to nationalize the railroads); higher income tax rates in the upper brackets; increased inheritance taxes; abolition of child labor; legislation outlawing the use of court injunctions to break up strikes; amnesty for opponents of World War I who were imprisoned; unilateral disarmament on the part of the United States; and protection of the civil rights of dissenters (a protest against the techniques employed during the Palmer raids).

The CPPA served as the nucleus for the 1924 Progressive Party,* which nominated Senator Robert M. La Follette (R-Wis.) for the presidency and Senator Burton K. Wheeler (D-Mont.) as his vice-presidential running mate. This ticket received the endorsement of the Farmer-Labor Party, Nonpartisan League, Socialist Party of America,* and American Federation of Labor. Nevertheless, the La Follette-Wheeler team ran third behind the victorious Republicans* (Coolidge-Dawes) and Democrats* (Davis-Bryan). Although La Follette drew 4,832,532 popular votes, he received only thirteen electoral votes. This blow, coupled with the death of La Follette in the summer of 1925 (and that of Eugene Debs in 1926), caused the CPPA to disband. With a stance considered too radical by the general voters of that era and a political base too narrow for survival, the attempt by the CPPA to give birth to a permanent third party failed dismally.

For further information, see Richard T. Ruetten, "Senator Burton K. Wheeler and Insurgency in the 1920s," in Gene M. Gressley, ed., *The*

*American West: A Reorientation* (1966), and James Weinstein, *The Decline of Socialism in America, 1912-1925* (1967).

**CONGRESS OF INDUSTRIAL ORGANIZATION-POLITICAL ACTION COMMITTEE.** See Political Action Committee.

**CONGRESS OF RACIAL EQUALITY (CORE).** Founded in 1942 at Chicago by James L. Farmer under the auspices of the Fellowship of Reconciliation* for the purpose of promoting civil rights in the United States. Formed originally as the Chicago Committee of Racial Equality and under Farmer's leadership, CORE utilized moral suasion and Gandhian tactics of passive resistance to break down segregation in American society. In 1960 it initiated the sit-in technique at Greensboro, North Carolina, designed to compel desegregation in restaurants. To further the integration of public transportation, CORE members participated in freedom rides, whereby buses were boarded and segregation in seating ignored. CORE also sponsored many other types of peaceful demonstrations, such as sing-ins, boycotts, and quiet protest marches. Its membership at this time rose to 180,000 (both black and white). Its tactics brought some arrests and police harassment in the South, but it did contribute much to the public pressure for enactment of the Civil Rights Act of 1964.

In 1965 under the leadership of Floyd McKissick, it increased its agitation for an end to racism, discrimination in jobs, and police brutality. It became increasingly concerned with the promotion of black nationalism. Initiating a more militant policy of black power, McKissick expelled whites from CORE and began to champion a more radical program. Coinciding with the rising anti-Vietnam war movement, CORE's protest marches became violent, and often property was damaged. Some older civil rights leaders believed that CORE's activity was alienating public opinion and thus becoming counterproductive.

Under its current national director, Roy Innis, who took office in 1968, CORE advocates a policy of dual citizenship for blacks who live in America but want to preserve their cultural heritage. Dual citizenship serves to promote pan-Africanism and preserves the right to return to Africa. Innis himself holds citizenship in Uganda as well as the United States and has become involved in the cause of African nationalism and the advancement of the Third World.

CORE's present national headquarters is located in New York City. Current membership is relatively small, and its activity is now centered on voter registration, improvement of slums, job opportunities, and electing blacks to political office. Published bimonthly is the magazine *CORE-lator*.

For more information, see August Meier and Elliot Rudwick, *CORE: A Study in the Civil Rights Movement, 1942-1968* (1973).

**CONGRESS ON POPULATION AND ENVIRONMENT.** See Council on Population and Environment.

**CONSERVATIVE CAUCUS, THE (TCC).** Founded in 1974 at Washington, D.C., by a group of concerned conservatives for the purpose of promoting conservatism as an action-oriented political philosophy. Prime movers in the formation of TCC were Governor Meldrim Thomson, Jr. (R-N.H.), its first national chairman; Howard Phillips, who served in the Nixon administration and was its first national director; Senator Jesse Helms (R-N.C.); and William Rusher, publisher of the *National Review*. Regarding itself as a nonpartisan, grass-roots lobby, TCC seeks to implement conservative principles by supporting or opposing measures in line with its political philosophy and to further the election of those who support its views.

TCC has favored tax reduction; elimination of government regulations; abolition of the federal bureaucracy; extension of proposition 13 (as passed in California) to other states; the impeachment of former U.N. Ambassador Andrew Young; and continued U.S. support for Rhodesia, South Africa, South Korea, and Taiwan. It has opposed ratification of the Panama Canal treaty; national health insurance; gun-control legislation; common-situs picketing; the equal rights amendment and the extension of time for its ratification; election day registration; subsidization of United Nations activities; enactment of the Public Disclosure Lobbying Act; creation of a consumer protection agency; a constitutional amendment giving the District of Columbia two senators; a requirement by the Federal Communications Commission that television and radio broadcasters be required to consult with homosexual groups over programming; and any attempt by the Internal Revenue Service to withdraw the tax-exempt status of private schools formed deliberately to elude desegregation laws.

In 1977 TCC created the Citizens Cabinet to monitor the activities of President Jimmy Carter's cabinet. This monitoring was done by keeping track of the policies and programs developed by Carter's cabinet and how they were implemented. This "shadow cabinet" consisted of William Rusher, attorney general; Governor Meldrim Thomson, secretary of state; Professor Hans Sennholz of Grove City (Pa.) College, secretary of the treasury; Congressman Larry McDonald (D-Ga.), secretary of defense; former Lieutenant Governor John Harmer of California, secretary of commerce; former Congressman Ron Paul (R-Tex.), secretary of labor; Congressman Steve Symms (R-Idaho), secretary of agriculture; former U.S. Welfare Commissioner Robert Carleson of California, secretary of health, education and welfare; John McClaughry of Vermont, secretary of housing and urban development; Sam Husbands, Jr., of California, secretary of transportation; and Henry Hazlitt, chairman of the Council of Economic Advisers.

To expand and seek replacements for the Citizens Cabinet in 1978, a Citizens Cabinet Organizing Committee (CCOC) was formed to make the selections. The membership of the CCOC included Edwin Feulner, president of the Heritage Foundation; Frances Watson, president of the Conservative Democrats of America; Joseph Coors of the Adolph Coors Company; Richard Dingman, director of the House Republican Study Committee; Morton Blackwell, editor of the *New Right Report*; Louis Jenkins of Louisiana, president of the American Legislative Exchange Council; Congressman Robert Stump (D-Ariz.); Paul Weyeich, director of the Committee for Survival of a Free Congress; and Dr. John McCarty, director of the Association of Private Colleges.

The 1978 Citizens Cabinet not only monitored the Carter cabinet but developed conservative proposals for governing the nation. In this cabinet, Senator Carl Curtis (R-Nebr.) succeeded Dr. Sennholz as secretary of the treasury. Dr. Sennholz, in turn, replaced Henry Hazlitt as chairman of the Council of Economic Advisers. State congressman Clay Smothers of Texas succeeded Ron Paul as secretary of labor, with Paul becoming energy secretary. Barbara Keating, the 1974 nominee of the Conservative Party* for the U.S. Senate, replaced John McClaughry as secretary of housing and urban development. Dr. Howard Hurwitz of New York replaced Robert Carleson as secretary of health, education and welfare. Richard Viguerie, publisher of *Conservative Digest*, succeeded John Harmer as commerce secretary. General Daniel O. Graham, former chief of the U.S. Defense Intelligence Agency, was appointed director of the Central Intelligence Agency. Congressman Robert K. Dornan (R-Calif.) became the U.N. ambassador in the new Citizens Cabinet. All other positions remained the same as the 1977 appointments.

In 1978 TCC held a national convention at Atlanta, Georgia, where a series of workshops was held on such topics as opposing Cuban imperialism, defeating communism in Chile, aiding anti-Marxist forces in Nicaragua, Chinese communism, strengthening the U.S. position in Korea, rebuilding U.S. alliances in Asia, Marxist terrorism in Rhodesia, countering Soviet strategy for Africa, anti-communist prospects in West Germany, the Soviet military threat and future of NATO, the future of Iran, stopping U.S. subsidy of U.N. activities, and free-market approaches to oceanic and space resources. Plaques were given to honor Congressman Arlan Strangeland (R-Minn.) for his opposition to election-day voter registration and to Congressman Larry McDonald (D-Ga.) and Senator Orin Hatch (R-Utah) for their role in fighting against ratification of the Panama Canal treaty.

TCC represents the right wing of the political spectrum and has members (currently over three hundred thousand) belonging to both the Democratic* and Republican* parties. In general it opposes the welfare state and champions a free market economy with a minimum of government interference.

More recently it has opposed easy abortion and supports restrictions on the activities of homosexuals. It is strongly anti-Communist in orientation and opposes détente with the Soviet Union or diplomatic relations with the People's Republic of China.

Present national headquarters of TCC is located at Falls Church, Virginia, with a Project Office in Boston. It is governed by a six-member board of directors with the assistance of a national advisory board made up of twenty-one members of Congress. Meldrim Thomson currently is national chairman, with Howard Phillips serving both as national director and chairman of the board of directors. Senator Gordon Humphrey (R-N.H.) is chairman of the Congressional Policy Council. TCC publications include *Leadership Manual, Senate Report,* and a quarterly, *Member's Report.*

**CONSERVATIVE PARTY (CP).** Founded in 1962 at New York City by a group of concerned conservatives for the purpose of maximizing the right-of-center vote in the state of New York. Its objectives were to offer alternative candidates to those nominated by both the Liberal Party* and the Democratic Party,* and to counter the influence of liberals within the Republican Party.* The latter were identified as Governor Nelson Rockefeller, Senator Jacob Javits, and Mayor John Lindsay, who later turned Democrat. Original organizers of the CP included Kieran O'Doherty, a GOP committeeman from Queens who served as CP's first state chairman and its 1962 candidate for the U.S. Senate; J. Daniel Mahoney, a New York City attorney and its current state chairman; David H. Jaquith, president of the Syracuse board of education and CP's gubernatorial candidate in 1962; Suzanne La Follette, journalist and niece of Wisconsin's famous Senator Robert M. La Follette; William F. Rickenbacker, business analyst and son of the World War I aviator hero Captain Eddie Rickenbacker; Frank S. Meyer, writer for the *National Review*; and Professor Henry Paolucci of Iona College of New Rochelle, who unsuccessfully challenged Robert F. Kennedy in the 1964 election for the U.S. Senate.

The CP drew its voter strength primarily from the middle class (usually home owners and veterans) who tended to be either urban-oriented Roman Catholics or upstate Protestants. Opposed to both right-wing radicalism and left-wing extremism, the CP's platforms stressed such issues as tax reduction; balanced budgets; reform of social welfare programs; tougher anti-crime laws; enactment of right-to-work legislation; abolition of featherbedding; preservation of neighborhood schools; elimination of import restrictional reduction of tariffs; curtailment of foreign aid; non-recognition of Communist regimes; maintenance of a strong national defense posture with an up-to-date nuclear arsenal; and continuation of military assistance to nations resisting a Communist takeover.

The CP first gained national attention in 1965 when its New York City mayoralty candidate, William F. Buckley, Jr., the noted lecturer, publisher, writer, and television personality, drew 341,226 votes in losing to John Lindsay. This constituted some 15 percent of the votes cast in all five boroughs despite a CP registration of only a little over 31,000. In 1966 CP gubernatorial candidate Dr. Paul L. Adams outpolled his Liberal Party counterpart, Franklin D. Roosevelt, Jr., by 2,789 votes. This achievement gained third place on the New York State ballot for the CP right beneath the Republican and Democratic parties. The CP attained its greatest victory in 1970 when James Buckley, a forty-seven-year-old business executive and younger brother of William, triumphed over GOP incumbent Charles Goodell for a seat in the U.S. Senate. Once elected, Buckley announced his intention to vote with the Republican Party to organize the Senate. While serving in the upper chamber, he subsequently accepted Republican committee assignments and held the post of vice-chairman of the GOP Senate Reelection Committee in 1974. This precedent seemed to indicate that CP candidates intended to work within the Republican Party and not act as unaligned independents. Further evidence of the alliance between the CP and GOP was the fact that in 1980 James Buckley won the Republican nomination for the U.S. Senate from Connecticut. Elsewhere former CP candidates also were running as Republicans.

Present CP headquarters is located in New York City. Current executive director is Serphin R. Maltese. Party strength in terms of confirmed adherents stands currently at about 130,000. The future impact of the CP on Republican policies and its influence on national politics will depend upon its continued ability to attract voters in the Empire State.

For more information, see J. Daniel Mahoney, *Action Speaks Louder—The Story of the New York Conservative Party* (1967).

**CONSERVATIVE PARTY OF NEW YORK.** See Conservative Party.

**CONSERVATIVE UNION.** See American Conservative Union.

**CONSTITUTION PARTIES OF THE UNITED STATES.** See Constitution Party.

**CONSTITUTION PARTY (CP).** Founded in 1952 at Los Angeles, California, by representatives of various right-wing groups for the purpose of promoting states' rights and the decentralization of the federal government. Its platforms opposed the exercise of federal power relative to civil rights, welfare programs, and regulation of private enterprise. Federal intervention into these areas was viewed as a dangerous drifting toward socialism. Subsequently members supported such measures as reduction of federal expenditures, balanced budgets, tax cuts, restrictions on immigration, and the right of (Christian) prayer in the public schools. In the realm of foreign policy, demands were made for withdrawal of diplomatic recognition from Communist countries, nonparticipation in the United Nations, curtailment of foreign aid, and abrogation of U.S. commitments related to international agreements on trade and tariff. The CP also has consistently advocated that the United States maintain a strong military establishment and, if it went to war, the goal should be total victory.

The CP presidential nominee in 1952 was General Douglas MacArthur, who ignored the designation. In some states Vivien Kellems ran as the vice-presidential nominee, in others it was Jack Tenny, and in still others it was Harry F. Byrd. The CP ticket was on the ballot in Arkansas, California, Colorado, Missouri, New Mexico, North Dakota, Tennessee, Texas, and Washington. It polled 17,220 popular votes (0.03 percent). Its greatest number of votes, 3,504, came from California. In a few states the CP ticket was listed on the ballot as the America First Party.

In 1956 only the CP of Texas ran its own slate of candidates in the presidential election. William E. Jenner, former Republican senator from Indiana, headed the ticket, and Mayor J. Bracken Lee of Salt Lake City was designated the vice-presidential nominee. In a state noted for its right-wing conservatism, the Jenner-Lee ticket polled 30,999 votes. It had no influence on the national election but did reflect a conservative trend in Texas. Other CP state affiliates in 1956 tended to endorse the nominees of the States' Rights Party.* This team of T. Coleman Andrews and Thomas H. Werdel drew a popular vote of 111,178 (primarily in five southern states). (See table 3.)

By 1960 the CP was really no longer a national party, if in fact it ever had been. The CP of Texas nominated Charles L. Sullivan of Mississippi as its presidential candidate and Merritt B. Curtis of the District of Columbia as his vice-presidential running mate. The CP of Washington placed Curtis at the head of its presidential ticket and paired him with B. N. Miller. The Sullivan-Curtis ticket drew 18,169, and the Curtis-Miller duo attracted only 1,240 popular votes.

**TABLE 3 Constitution Party Presidential Candidates and Votes, 1952-1964**

| YEAR | CANDIDATE | TOTAL POPULAR VOTE |
| --- | --- | --- |
| 1952 | Douglas MacArthur | 17,220 |
| 1956 | William E. Jenner | 30,999 |
| 1960 | Charles L. Sullivan | 18,169 |
| 1964 | Joseph B. Lightburn | 5,090 |

In 1964 the CP presidential ticket was headed by Joseph B. Lightburn of West Virginia, with Theodore C. Billings of Colorado serving as his vice-presidential running mate. This ticket drew only 5,090 popular votes. The demise of the CP came in 1968 when its nominees were Richard K. Troxell of Texas for president and Merle Thayer of Iowa for vice-president. This duo, which was only on the ballot in North Dakota, attracted a mere thirty-four popular votes. Following this debacle, the CP became moribund. It thus exemplified the fate of a party too far to the right on the political spectrum to attract a national following.

**CONSTITUTIONAL UNION PARTY (CUP).** Founded in 1860 at Baltimore, Maryland, by a group of delegates representing factions of the Whig* and Know-Nothing* parties from the border states for the purpose of forming a new political party dedicated to the preservation of the Union. Fearing that a North versus South sectionalism over the slavery issue would cause civil war and that they would be caught in the middle, the CUP platform declared:

*Whereas*, Experience has demonstrated that Platforms adopted by the partisan Conventions of this country have had the effect to mislead and deceive people, and at the same time to widen the political divisions of the country, by the creation and encouragement of geographical and sectional parties, therefore *Resolved*, that it is both the part of patriotism and of duty to recognize no political principle other than The Constitution of the Country, The Union of the Country, and The Enforcement of the Laws.''

The two main contenders for the CUP presidential nomination were former Senator John Bell of Tennessee and Governor Sam Houston of Texas. Bell, a former Whig and a southern moderate, was nominated on the second ballot. He opposed both abolitionism and the extension of slavery. As his vice-presidential running mate, the convention selected former Senator Edward Everett of Massachusetts.

In a four-way presidential contest where Abraham Lincoln represented the Republican Party,* Stephen A. Douglas the Democratic Party,* and John C. Breckinridge the National Democratic Party,* Bell polled 592,906 popular votes. This constituted the smallest total of all the candidates (12.6 percent) and yielded only thirty-nine electoral votes (Virginia, Kentucky, and Tennessee). With the advent of the Civil War the CUP died. It was a quickly organized party that sought to preserve the Union by avoiding the issue of slavery and maintaining the status quo. This strategy would not work in an era when the free soil versus slavery question was uppermost in the minds of the voters.

For further information, see John B. Stabler, *A History of the Constitutional Union Party: A Tragic Failure* (1954).

**CONSUMER FEDERATION OF AMERICA (CFA).** Founded in 1967 at New York City by representatives of fifty-six consumer groups for the purpose of promoting the interests of consumers. Organized on the basis of a confederation, it currently has some 200 member organizations. These include about 150 local organizations and fifty national. Permanent committees exist relative to: Communications; Credit; Education; Environment; Energy and Natural Resources; Federal and State Legislation; Food and Marketing; Health Drugs; Housing; Low Income Consumers; Medical; Practices and Policies; and Transportation.

The CFA lobbies in Congress for legislation relating to consumer protection. It seeks more stringent laws in the areas of food and drugs, credit, insurance, guarantees and warranties, safety, labeling and pricing, service, environment, home improvements, and transportation. It not only works for the enactment of regulatory legislation but monitors the federal agencies whose responsibility it is to enforce them. The FCA initiates research studies, disseminates information to influence public opinion, and coordinates lobbying activities of member organizations. It concerns itself with all measures affecting food prices and for a long time has urged the creation of a federal consumer protection agency. To induce public officials to serve the needs of the buying public better, it bestows annually both a Distinguished Public Service Award and a Distinguished Public Service Award for Leadership in Consumer Affairs.

Present national headquarters is located in Washington, D.C. Current national director is Kathleen O'Reilly. The former national director, Carol Tucker, once served as assistant secretary of agriculture in charge of Food and Consumer Service (1977-1981). CFA publications include a monthly, *CFA News and Comment*; a semiannual, *Directory of State and Local Government and Non-Government Consumer Organizations*; and its *Annual Voting Record of the U.S. Congress*.

For more information, see Judith Smith, ed., *Political Brokers: People, Organizations, Money and Power* (1972).

**CONTINENTAL ASSOCIATION (CA).** Founded in 1774 at Philadelphia by the First Continental Congress for the purpose of initiating a boycott on British goods as a means of forcing Parliament to repeal the Coercive Acts (Intolerable Acts). As part of the Declaration and Resolves adopted by the Continental Congress in 1774 was the injunction for all the American colonies to "enter into a nonimportation, nonconsumption, and nonexportation agreement or association." The CA was an outgrowth of an idea promulgated by the Suffolk Resolves (adopted by Suffolk County, Massachusetts) calling for civil disobedience and economic pressure to force the British Parliament to respect the principle of self-rule.

By 1775 the CA had been established in all of the thirteen colonies. The

Committees of Correspondence* helped disseminate information, and groups such as the Sons of Liberty* helped enforce a boycott of British goods. Although the CA failed in its prime objective, it did help to unite the colonies by fostering a nascent nationalism and set the stage for the Second Continental Congress. The latter issued the Declaration of Independence in 1776 and governed the nation during the American Revolution.

For more information, see Pauline Maier, *From Resistance to Revolution* (1972).

**COOK COUNTY MACHINE.** See Democratic Central Committee of Cook County.

**CORE.** See Congress of Racial Equality.

**COUNCIL OF ENERGY RESOURCES TRIBES (CERT).** Founded in 1978 at Washington, D.C., by Peter MacDonald, a Navaho Indian, for the purpose of promoting the economic benefit of Indian tribes holding energy-rich lands. Immediately after being formed, CERT sought foreign financial assistance from the Organization of Petroleum Exporting Countries (OPEC). To counter such outside influence, a federal grant of $200,000 was given to CERT for organizing tribes owning lands that contained oil, coal, uranium, natural gas, or other valuable minerals.

CERT represents tribes that own 25 to 40 percent of all U.S. uranium, 33 percent of all the nation's coal, and 5 percent of the oil and gas reserves. CERT seeks to protect the legal rights of these tribes and make sure that they benefit economically from these needed natural resources. Heretofore many Indian tribes were leasing their valuable lands for very small sums. CERT also has asked the federal government for funds to have Indians trained as engineers and technical experts. It has agitated for other fundamental legislation to protect Indian rights in general and to remedy the wrongs of the past.

Present national headquarters is located in Washington, D.C. Current president is Peter MacDonald. The CERT represents twenty-five tribes in ten states, the largest of which is the Navaho tribe (with 125,000 members). With future energy shortages, CERT will be even more instrumental in securing for American Indians greater economic benefits from the natural resources contained within their tribal lands.

**COUNCIL OF STATE GOVERNMENTS (CSG).** Founded in 1925 in Denver, Colorado, by Henry W. Toll, a Colorado state senator and first executive director (currently honorary chairman), for the purpose of promoting better state government. Formed originally as the American Legislators Association, it was renamed the CSG in 1933, and its national headquarters was moved first to Chicago and then in 1969 to Lexington, Kentucky. Regional offices are operated in New York City, Chicago, Atlanta, San Francisco, and Washington, D.C. In 1938 the National Governors' Conference* adopted the CSG as its secretariat. Other affiliated organizations served by CSG include the National Legislative Conference,* National Conference of Lieutenant Governors, National Association of State Budget Officers, National Association of State Purchasing Officials, National Conference of Court Administrative Officers, and the Council of State Planning Agencies.

Services performed for its member affiliates include conducting special research; issuing reports; monitoring congressional legislation and federal agencies; assisting state legislators; conducting training programs; sponsoring forums and workshops; and establishing commissions to promote both interstate cooperation and that between the federal government and the states. Special project reports issued in 1974 included *State-Local Employee Labor Relations*; *The States and Criminal Justice*; *Consumer Protection in the States*; *State Control of Drug Abuses*; and *Environmental Quality and State Governments*.

Current officers of the CSG are Governor Calvin L. Rampton of Utah, president; state senator John J. Marchi of New York, chairman; and Brevard Crihfield, executive director. CSG publications include a monthly, *State Government News*, a quarterly, *State Government*, and a biennial, *The Book of the States*.

**COUNCIL ON FOREIGN RELATIONS (CFR).** Founded in 1921 at New York City by the merger of a pro-League of Nations discussion group with the American Institute of International Affairs (AIIA) for the purpose of enlightening the public, promoting research, and providing a forum where scholars and leaders of all segments of society could exchange ideas on foreign policy matters. The AIIA had been founded in 1919 to parallel the establishment of the Royal Institute of International Affairs in Great Britain. The AIIA, which supported U.S. entry into the League of Nations and World Court, was formed by the following people (who became prime movers in the CFR): General Tasker H. Bliss, a delegate to the Paris Peace Conference; Archibald Cary Coolidge, professor of history at Harvard University; James T. Shotwell, professor of history at Columbia University; George Louis Beer, professor of history at Columbia University; James Brown Scott, expert on international law; Stanley K. Hornbeck, State Department specialist on the Far East; and Thomas W. Lamont, adviser on financial affairs to President Woodrow Wilson. In 1922 the CFR started publishing a quarterly journal, *Foreign Affairs*, with Professor Coolidge as editor. Hamilton Fish Armstrong served as his assistant and later was its editor for fifty years. Current editor of this prestigious journal is William P. Bundy.

The CFR has 1,551 members who are elected by the board of directors. Choice for membership is based upon an assessment of the candidate's experience or expertise in the field of international relations. At present the largest number of members has been selected from business (39 percent), academia (24 percent), and government (13 percent). A majority of the membership is eastern; 43 percent are from New York City, 23 percent from Boston and Washington, D.C., and 43 percent from other parts of the nation.

The CFR sponsors conferences and forums, initiates research projects, issues special studies, and arranges for thirty-six committees, located throughout the country, to meet and hold discussions. It conducts the International Affairs Fellowship Program, awarding annual grants for research in international relations. The CFR has had a significant impact on U.S. foreign policy because of the prominent status of its members. Its publications are read by policy makers in government and throughout the academic world.

Current national headquarters is located in New York City. David Rockefeller is the present chairman of the board of directors, with Bayless Manning serving as president. In 1973 the CFR revived the AIIA as an auxiliary to foster cooperation with other such organizations in foreign countries. In addition to *Foreign Affairs*, the CFR publishes annually the *Political Handbook and Atlas of the World* and *Documents on American Foreign Relations*.

For further information, see Hamilton Fish Armstrong, *Peace and Counterpeace: From Wilson to Hitler* (1971).

**COUNCIL ON POPULATION AND ENVIRONMENT (COPE).** Founded in 1969 at Chicago by the first Congress on Optimum Population and Environment for the purpose of promoting environmental and population control. A prime mover in the formation of COPE was Dr. Paul Erlich, a noted ecologist. Its purpose was to coordinate the activities of the many groups working to achieve such goals as elimination of pollution, smog control, pure water, and zero-growth population. COPE is funded by grants from private foundations and corporations to serve its affiliates and to enlighten public opinion on the subjects of ecology and environmental control.

In 1972 COPE sponsored a series of monthly luncheon dialogues in various cities with community leaders to publicize its aims and objectives. In 1973 it produced a series of television programs that dealt with problems relating to regional transportation and smog control. The following year Project TRUST (To Reshape Urban Systems Together) was launched to educate the public on how urban communities could achieve environmental control. To influence public opinion, COPE sponsors forums and provides speakers to publicize the need for an ecologically safe environment and population control.

Present national headquarters is located in Chicago. Some twenty-five organizations are affiliated with COPE. Current president is James D. Hemphill, with James Malone serving as executive director. COPE issues a *Newsletter*, and under its auspices a book, *Population, Environment, and People*, was published (1971).

**COUNTRY LIFE ASSOCIATION.** See American Country Life Association.

**COUNTRY PEOPLE'S CAUCUS.** See People's Party (1971).

**COUNTRY PEOPLE'S PARTY.** See People's Party (1971).

**COX MACHINE (CM).** Founded in 1888 at Cincinnati by George Barnsdale Cox for the purpose of gaining political control over the city in which he lived. "Old Boy" Cox, a member of the Republican Party,* fashioned his political machine after Tammany Hall.* Cox, whose only elective office was that of city councilman, ran his machine with a tight hand until 1910. Control of Cincinnati gave him considerable political power in Ohio and within the high councils of the GOP. Since Ohio was a pivotal state and a "mother of Presidents," Cox's influence in national party affairs was considerable.

In 1911 Cox was indicted but never tried for perjury in connection with an investigation of corruption in Cincinnati. As is often the case with political bosses, their power and prestige is frequently used for personal aggrandizement. And domination of the city council in many cases leads to fraud and corruption. This seemed to be the case with the Cox machine, although no trial was ever held. When Cox left politics in 1911 to pursue his business interests, the machine he built collapsed shortly thereafter.

For more information, see Zane Miller, *Boss Cox's Cincinnati: Urban Politics in the Progressive Era* (1968).

**COXEY'S ARMY (CA).** Founded in 1894 at Massillon, Ohio by Jacob S. Coxey for the purpose of promoting federal aid to the unemployed. Coxey, a reformer and businessman, was concerned that he had to lay off some fifty workers at his sandstone quarry due to the adverse economic conditions caused by the panic of 1893. He decided to gather a group of unemployed workers and lead them in a protest march to the nation's capital. Marching from Massillon to Washington, D.C., his band of unemployed never totaled more than five hundred.

Coxey intended to petition Congress to enact two measures to combat unemployment: the good roads bill and a non-interest-bearing bond bill. The former would have authorized the Treasury Department to issue $500 million in fiat money to fund a massive program of improving country roads. Thus many jobless men would be put to work, and rural areas would benefit from improved roads. The second proposal would have permitted state and local governments to issue bonds, which in turn could be deposited with the federal government as security for loans of legal tender currency. Public works funded in this manner were to employ the jobless at a rate of not less than $1.50 for an eight-hour work day.

It was expected that Coxey's "army," dubbed the "Commonweal of Christ," would reach a hundred thousand before arriving at the nation's capital. Actually only a small group ever materialized. When Coxey and his tiny band arrived in Washington, D.C., they were not welcomed by either President Grover Cleveland or by members of Congress. As Coxey and his men marched before the White House, they were arrested ostensibly for "walking on the grass." After some marchers were arrested for trespassing, the rest of Coxey's Army disbanded immediately.

Despite the fact that his "petition in boots" had failed, Coxey continued his political activity. In 1894 he ran for Congress as a Populist Party* candidate but lost. In 1897 he ran as an independent in Ohio's gubernatorial election, and once more was defeated. In 1914 he organized another "army" for a march to Washington, D.C., and this time was permitted to present his petition to President Woodrow Wilson. Running as an independent candidate for the U.S. Senate in 1916, he again lost. Coxey visited President Warren G. Harding in 1922 to urge stricter regulation of banking procedures and the abolition of the Federal Reserve System. Coxey was defeated in 1924, 1926, and 1928—the first two times running for the House of Representatives and the third for the U.S. Senate. In 1932 Coxey was nominated for the presidency by the Farmer-Labor Party* with Julius J. Recter as his vice-presidential running mate. The Coxey-Recter ticket drew only 7,431 popular votes. Coxey was finally successful in winning elective office when he was elected mayor of Massillon in 1931; he served until 1933.

Coxey's Army had some impact on public opinion and prompted Congress to take steps toward monetary reform, improvement of roads, and reduction of interest rates. Coxey's public works proposals did not come to fruition until the New Deal. In 1944, on the fiftieth anniversary of his original protest march, Coxey was invited to Washington, D.C., by President Franklin D. Roosevelt. On the steps of the Capitol, Coxey delivered the speech that he had intended to make in 1894. Public works projects that seemed so radical fifty years before were now accepted as a normal part of the welfare state that came into being during the Roosevelt administration.

For more information, see Jacob S. Coxey, *Coxey's Own Story* (1914), and Donald L. McMurray, *Coxey's Army: A Study of the Industrial Army Movement of 1894* (1968).

**CRAZIES.** Founded in 1968 at Washington, D.C., by a small group of anti-Vietnam war protesters to utilize violence as a means of demonstrating their opposition to the war and toward American society in general. Whether spontaneous or premeditated, a tiny group of demonstrators left a protest march being carried out under the auspices of the Mobilization Committee to End the War in Vietnam* to conduct a violent rampage of their own. Their conduct was so irrational as to be dubbed "crazy" (hence the name attached to those who adhered to this militant group). Leaderless and without a national headquarters, several hundred radical extremists nevertheless identified with this organization.

Most of the actions by Crazies were anarchistic and nihilistic in orientation. They engaged in trashing (breaking windows); shouting down speakers at political rallies; disrupting college and high school classes; inciting violence and destroying property. Seemingly irrational, their commitment to a revolutionary type of violence seemed to be the primary objective of the Crazies. The most organized of their activities was the staging of a "counter-inaugural" at Washington, D.C., in 1969 during the presidential inauguration of Richard M. Nixon. Most Crazies had belonged to such groups as the Students for a Democratic Society,* Du Bois Clubs of America,* or the group known as the Weatherman.*

The political impact of the Crazies on public opinion was negative and counter-productive. They proved embarrassing to the anti-Vietnam War movement because they sought to turn peaceful protest marches into violent rampages. Once the United States terminated its involvement in the war, the Crazies disbanded. A few joined the guerrilla bands of the Weatherman and went underground. Their short-lived existence reflected the extremism of some young militants during an era when radicalism was rampant.

For further information, see William H. Orrick, Jr., *Shut It Down! A College in Crisis* (1969), and Sidney Hyman, *Youth in Politics, Expectations and Realities* (1972).

**CRUMP MACHINE (CM).** Founded in 1909 in Memphis, Tennessee, by Mayor Edward H. "Boss" Crump for the purpose of solidifying his political control of the city and surrounding Shelby County. His Democratic political machine controlled Memphis for the next fifty years and made him at one point the virtual political dictator of the state of Tennessee. Crump kept absolute personal control over his machine and politically punished those who thwarted his will or disobeyed his orders. His chief lieutenants were Frank Rice, who supervised each ward in Memphis, and Will Hale, who kept an eye on Shelby County. They made sure local officials fostered programs which benefitted the Crump machine and alloted any patronage to its members.

Crump served as mayor from 1909 to 1916, when he was ousted from office by petition for not enforcing the state's prohibition law. At this time, he was elected county trustee, a position that combined the jobs of tax collector and treasurer. Crump held that post for the next eight years, during which he also became a millionaire. He owned an insurance company, two large Mississippi cotton plantations, a Coca-Cola franchise, and sizable shares of stock of several banks.

In 1928 Crump's machine supported Governor Alfred E. Smith for the presidency. The Democratic Party's* presidential nominee won in Shelby County but lost the state's popular vote to Republican Herbert C. Hoover. In 1930 Crump was elected to the U.S. Congress from Tennessee's Tenth District (which was Shelby County). He held that seat until 1935. While in the House of Representatives, he gained control over the Tennessee congressional delegation and the state house. He formed an alliance with Senator Kenneth D. McKellar (D-Tenn.) and won the friendship of both Senator Cordell Hull (D-Tenn.) and Congressman Joe Burns (D-Tenn.), who was House majority leader.

By 1936 Crump had achieved almost total political control over his state even though he held no office. His sole political title was that of Tennessee's committeeman on the Democratic National Committee.* This power, with a few setbacks, lasted until 1948. He personally selected the politician who would be mayor of Memphis, controlled all Shelby County offices, and for all practical purposes dictated who would be governor. The source of his power was the ability to deliver votes, particularly in Shelby County. Because the state had a poll tax, the CM paid the tax for black voters and made sure they got to the polls to vote as directed. Ballot boxes were stuffed, repeater voters were used, and the patronage spoils system were all resorted to in winning local and state elections.

Crump personally was a showman. He often dressed in striped pants, plaid jacket, and two-toned shoes, and he always carried one of his forty-odd canes. His showmanship was also evidenced in the Memphis Cotton Carnival, which he started in 1932 (President Franklin D. Roosevelt visited in 1938), the Mid-South Fair, and the annual Crump Charity Game. Under Crump's control, the city of Memphis was wide open, corrupt, and segregated. Little dissent was tolerated, no labor union organizers were allowed, and all federal public works monies were channeled through Crump's machine.

In 1937, Crump's political power was curtailed to some degree when Tennessee adopted the county-unit system. This reduced Shelby County's voting power from 25 percent to 13 percent of the state's total vote. In 1945 Crump's political power was further weakened when returning black war veterans ceased being voting pawns in the hands of the CM. In 1946 the East Tennessee Republicans also stopped cooperating with Crump. The tide against Crump increased in 1948 when Harry Truman campaigned on a strong civil rights plank and Estes Kefauver won the U.S. Senate seat in Tennessee. Both drew black votes away from candidates run by the CM.

Further erosion of Crump's power took place in 1952 when Senator McKellar lost his bid for reelection and Dwight D. Eisenhower, the presidential nominee of the Republican Party,* won Tennessee's electoral votes.

By 1954, the year Boss Crump died, his machine no longer controlled the state, but it still ran Shelby County and the city of Memphis. The surviving remnants of the CM were destroyed politically in 1959 when all of its members lost their city and county offices.

At the zenith of his power, Crump was courted by presidents and political hopefuls. Marred by corruption and dominated by Crump's personal predilections, the machine ran roughshod over the people and made a mockery of the democratic process. Its demise resulted from a successful reform movement that ended the political careers of Crump's cronies, thereby destroying one of the most powerful and corrupt machines ever to exist in American politics.

For more information, see William D. Miller, *Mr. Crump of Memphis* (1964), and Fred Hutchins, *What Happened in Memphis* (1965).

# _D_

**DALEY MACHINE.** See Democratic Central Committee of Cook County.

**DEMOCRATIC ADVISORY COUNCIL (DAC).** Founded in 1957 at Washington, D.C., by Paul M. Butler, then chairman of the Democratic National Committee,* for the purpose of permitting prominent Democrats outside of Congress to contribute to the formulation of party policy. Committees within the DAC were established on foreign policy, headed by Dean Acheson; economic policy, headed by John Kenneth Galbraith; and labor policy, headed by George M. Harrison. Other members included Harry S. Truman, Adlai E. Stevenson II, Averell Harriman, David Lawrence, Herbert Lehman, G. Mennen Williams, Paul Ziffren, Benjamin Cohen, William Benton, Chester Bowles, James B. Carey, Philip Jessup, Hans J. Morgenthau, James G. Patton, John Snyder, Marriner S. Eccles, Leon H. Keyserling, Arthur M. Schlesinger, Jr., Robert C. Weaver, Wilson Wyatt, Sidney Hillman, Jack Kroll, Jacob Potofsky, Walter Reuther, Thomas Finletter, and Jacob Arvey.

Known originally as the Democratic Advisory Committee, the name was quickly changed to Democratic Advisory Council during the first year of its existence. It generally represented the moderate to liberal position within the Democratic Party.* Meeting every three months, it periodically issued policy statements on the issues of the day. In 1957 such statements were issued relative to the need for a cloture rule to end Senate filibusters, civil rights legislation, and statehood for Alaska and Hawaii. The council proposed a space program to rival that of the Soviet Union, criticized Arkansas officials for their handling of the Little Rock school integration, called for revision of the immigration law, proposed programs to stimulate economic growth, and chastised the Eisenhower administration for its foreign policy based on the concepts of liberation and massive retaliation.

In 1958 twelve position papers were issued; in 1959 twenty; and fifteen in 1960. Since the Democrats did not control the White House, these policy statements were not always implemented. Further obstacles existed to limit the influence of the DAC, since both Senate Majority Leader Lyndon B. Johnson (D-Tex.) and House Speaker Sam Rayburn boycotted DAC meetings. They did this because they resented the DAC's encroachment upon their leadership and thus simply ignored it. The only members of Congress who regularly attended its sessions were Senator Hubert H. Humphrey (D-Minn.) and Senator Estes Kefauver (D-Tenn.). Senator Johnson had presidential ambitions and believed the DAC was primarily a vehicle for promoting another presidential nomination for Adlai Stevenson. Stevenson did tend to dominate it, since he secured funding for its operation.

The life of the DAC was relatively short. When John F. Kennedy was elected president in 1960, it disbanded. It had been useful in building a case against the Republican Party* and in keeping the Democratic Party on a reasonably liberal course. Because it received considerable publicity from the *Washington Post* and *New York Times*, it no doubt influenced public opinion and thus helped Kennedy win the nomination and the presidency.

For more information, see John B. Martin, *Adlai Stevenson of Illinois* (1977).

**DEMOCRATIC (BRECKINRIDGE FACTION) PARTY.** See National Democratic Party.

**DEMOCRATIC CENTRAL COMMITTEE OF COOK COUNTY (DCC-CC).** Founded in 1930 at Chicago by Mayor Anton J. "Tony" Cermak for the purpose of controlling the Democratic Party* in Cook County. Cermak, a former coal miner who had come to America from Bohemia in 1889, built his political machine by organizing every ethnic and minority group in the Chicago area. Of the city's 3.3 million population at the time, over 1 million were foreign born, and 250,000 were black. Cermak also formed a saloon keeper's league to get the political support of the foes of prohibition. The power of Cermak's political machine was evident in 1931. Heading an ethnically balanced ticket, Cermak defeated Republican* William "Big Bill" Thompson in the mayoralty race. The Democrats have controlled city hall since that time due to the machine that Cermak built.

When Mayor Cermak was assassinated in 1933 while conferring with President Franklin D. Roosevelt at Miami, Florida, the Chicago political machine came under the control of two men. Edward J. Kelly, formerly a Cermak aide, became mayor (a post he held until 1947), and Patrick Nash assumed the position of DCC-CC chairman. The Kelly-Nash machine cultivated the loyalty of the ethnic population in every ward and precinct in Chicago. President Roosevelt assisted the Kelly-Nash machine by seeing that some 200,000 public-works jobs, under the auspices of the Works Progress Administration and the Public Works Administration, were available for the unemployed of Chicago. In return, the Kelly-Nash organization delivered Cook County's votes to FDR, which assured a Democrat victory in Illinois in 1936, 1940, and 1944. It was Mayor Kelly who organized the draft Roosevelt movement in 1940 when the Democratic National Convention was held in Chicago. As head of the Illinois delegation, Kelly assured Roosevelt of the nomination by getting the support of other city bosses to break the third-team barrier.

When Patrick Nash died in 1943, Mayor Kelly took over the chairmanship of the DCC-CC. The Kelly machine now slated candidates for alderman and county and state offices. Any Democrat hoping to win in a primary election invariably needed the endorsement of the DCC-CC. No Democrat could win in Illinois without large pluralities in Cook County to offset the downstate Republican vote.

In 1948 Mayor Kelly retired. The chairmanship of the DCC-CC went to Colonel Jacob Arvey, a lawyer, noted leader in the Jewish community, and World War II veteran. Under his leadership the DCC-CC slated the following candidates for the 1948 election (the year Harry S. Truman was running for reelection): businessman Martin J. Kennelly for mayor; Adlai E. Stevenson II, then a lawyer, for governor; and Dr. Paul A. Douglas of the University of Chicago for U.S. senator. All won due to heavy pluralities in Cook County.

The political fortunes of the DCC-CC declined in 1950. It had slated Daniel "Tubbo" Gilbert for the office of Cook County sheriff that year. Also running for reelection was Senator Scott W. Lucas (D) who was majority leader. When the news leaked out that Gilbert possessed financial wealth far beyond what his salary would enable him to garner, it caused the entire ticket to go down to defeat. The scandal helped Everett M. Dirksen to unseat Scott Lucas.

Because of this debacle, Jacob Arvey resigned in 1953, and his place as chairman of the DCC-CC went to Joe Gill. When Mayor Kennelly was induced not to run again in 1955, Richard M. Daley was slated. He had held local and state offices and possessed leadership qualities that made him the ideal successor as political boss. Daley, who served as mayor until his death in 1976, also assumed the chairmanship of the DCC-CC.

The makeup of the DCC-CC under Mayor Daley consisted of eighty persons. Fifty were committeepersons from Chicago wards and thirty were from the townships of suburban Cook County. All were elected to four-year terms by registered Democrats of Cook County (which comprises Chicago and its environs). Because Daley was both DCC-CC head and mayor, he personally could control patronage and slating, dictate policy, and run the city without major opposition from non-Democratic city council members. Boss Daley could help those to whom he was loyal and hurt those who offended him. Daley contributed much to John F. Kennedy's rise to power. He helped

Kennedy get the Democratic presidential nomination and then delivered Illinois in a close election. Republicans charged vote fraud in Cook County but were never able to get the electoral votes for Richard M. Nixon. In 1972 Daley handpicked the delegation to attend the Democratic National Convention at Chicago. Because of the reforms introduced by Senator George McGovern (D-S.D.), Daley's delegation was not seated. In 1972 when McGovern was the presidential nominee of the Democratic Party, Mayor Daley did not exert much supportive effort, and probably as a result Illinois went overwhelmingly for Richard M. Nixon.

Mayor Daley was considered a good administrator and personally honest. His machine, however, was involved in vote frauds and corruption. The DCC-CC suffered a setback in 1976 when it sought to unseat Daniel Walker, a Democratic governor who would not take orders from Daley. The result was the election of a Republican governor. When Daley died in 1976, control of the machine went to Michael A. Bilandic, as mayor, and George W. Dunne, president of the Cook County Board, who became chairman of the DCC-CC. In 1979 Jane Byrne defeated Mayor Bilandic in the Democratic primary and was subsequently elected mayor by an overwhelming majority. This was the first time a woman rose to such a powerful position within the Chicago Democratic machine. Mayor Byrne backed Senator Edward Kennedy (D-Mass.) for the Democratic presidential nomination in 1980. When President Jimmy Carter won renomination she endorsed him as did the DCC-CC.

For more information, see Mike Royko, *Boss Richard J. Daley of Chicago* (1971), and Len O'Connor, *Clout, Mayor Daley and His City* (1975).

**DEMOCRATIC NATIONAL COMMITTEE (DNC).** Founded in 1848 at Baltimore by the national convention of the Democratic Party* for the purpose of promoting the establishment of a nationwide party organization. The DNC was formed in response to a motion by J. D. Bright of Indiana. It was the outgrowth of action taken four years earlier when the Democratic National Convention established a temporary central committee to create unity among the various state parties. Original membership consisted of one representative (a man) from each state. Since 1920, a man and a woman from each state and territory are selected at the conclusion of a national convention to hold office until the next one convenes. Present membership totals 110. The first chairperson was Benjamin F. Hallett of Massachusetts, who served on a part-time basis. It was not until 1921 that a full-time national chairperson was selected—Cordell Hull of Tennessee (who would later serve as secretary of state in Franklin D. Roosevelt's cabinet). The current holder of that position is John White.

In 1932 the DNC formed the Young Democrats of America,* and in 1936 commenced publication of an official organ, *Democratic Digest*. It was not until 1951 that an executive committee was created, and at the same time permanent national headquarters was established in Washington, D.C., eliminating New York City as a dual site. Under the leadership of national chairman Paul Butler of Indiana, the Democratic Advisory Council* was set up in 1957. At the Democratic National Convention of 1972, held at Miami, Florida, the DNC implemented reforms authorized by the 1968 convention. A commission had been established to prepare new rules relative to the selection of delegates and the procedures governing the activities of the convention. The commission was originally headed by Senator George McGovern (D-S.D.), who was is turn succeeded by Congressman Donald M. Fraser (D-Minn.).

The rules changes adopted by the commission abolished the unit voting system, streamlined and shortened nominating procedures, and made the selection of delegates conform to specific quotas. The changes were designed to give more representation to women, young people, and blacks. In 1972 many state delegations arrived at the national convention without complying, thus creating controversy when the seating of certain delegates was challenged. Chicago's Mayor Richard J. Daley, who controlled the Democratic Central Committee of Cook County,* complained that the rules changes favored the nomination of George McGovern as the presidential nominee of the Democratic Party. The convention, he said, forced Illinois to seat a delegation not truly representative of his state's political strength. In 1976 many of the rules changes regarding the composition of delegations were repealed or substantially modified.

In addition to its preparations for national conventions every four years, the DNC plays a leading role in conducting the presidential campaign. It serves as a liaison between the national party and state groups; conducts party business between elections; coordinates congressional elections; disseminates information to the public; raises campaign funds; and provides materials to the various media. Intraparty struggles are sometimes evident in the composition of the DNC as factions attempt to gain control over the national organization. This internecine warfare was evident in 1980 when many members of the DNC preferred Senator Edward Kennedy (D-Mass.) as the party's presidential nominee over that of incumbent President Jimmy Carter. Current DNC chairperson is Charles T. Manatt, who worked hard to unify all elements of the Democratic Party behind Carter during the 1980 campaign. DNC's official publication is a biweekly, the *National Democrat.*

**DEMOCRATIC PARTY (DP).** Founded in 1832 at Baltimore, Maryland, by delegates from twenty-three states for the purpose of promoting the reelection of President Andrew Jackson. The formation of the DP was an outgrowth of the 1824 national election when Andrew Jackson challenged

John Quincy Adams, the presidential nominee of the Democratic-Republican Party.* In 1828 Jackson was victorious over the incumbent president, John Quincy Adams, and during his first term laid the foundations for the DP. The national nominating convention at Baltimore in 1832, the first ever held by the DP, in effect made official its existence as a nationwide political party.

The 1832 Baltimore convention did not actually nominate Andrew Jackson as its presidential candidate but rather concurred in the various nominations made by state legislatures. The delegates did vote to make Martin Van Buren of New York the official vice-presidential nominee. No platform was adopted; rather it was left to each state delegation to prepare a statement relative to the party's stand on the issues. The convention adopted two rules of lasting significance: presidential nominations hereafter were to be by a two-thirds vote of the delegates (altered in 1936), and state delegations were to be given the same number of votes as their electoral votes (changed in 1940).

In a three-cornered race in 1832, Andrew Jackson triumphed easily over Henry Clay, the presidential nominee of the National Republican Party,* and William Wirt, the candidate of the Anti-Masonic Party.* So dominant was Jackson's control over his party and Congress during the next four years that he virtually created an imperial presidency. He personally destroyed the Bank of the United States, an action that had economic repercussions, and as champion of the common people, waged rhetorical war on the "moneyed aristocrats." Jackson initiated mass participation in politics and influenced DP policy for the next several decades. He not only gave birth to the modern DP but left a legacy of Jacksonian Democracy that helped transform American society. He also continued the Jeffersonian tradition of agrarianism and states' rights as part of the DP political credo.

Vice-President Martin Van Buren was Jackson's personal choice to succeed him in the White House. The DP nominating convention convened in 1835 at Baltimore and unanimously chose Van Buren to head the presidential ticket. Richard M. Johnson of Kentucky was selected as the vice-presidential nominee. No platform was adopted by the convention, but it was understood that the campaign would revolve around the defense of Jackson's policies (with Van Buren safely cloaked in the Jacksonian mantle). Pitted against three candidates of the new Whig Party,* Van Buren was an easy victor in the presidential election of 1836.

Martin Van Buren was called "the Little Magician" because he was a master politician. He had been leader of the Albany Regency,* understood how to use the spoils system, and was a loyal Jacksonian. It was his misfortune that the panic of 1837 struck just as he assumed the presidency. When the Democrats met at Baltimore in 1840 to renominate Van Buren, they decided not to nominate a vice-presidential candidate. It was left to state leaders to decide on candidates attractive to their local areas. For the first time in history, a party platform was adopted. It was a short document that was negative and defensive in tone. The fundamental political philosophy being expressed was that of states' rights. It maintained that the Constitution did not confer upon the central government authority to carry out internal improvements, interfere with slavery, charter a national bank, or assume state debts. It defended the independent treasury and promised rigid economy in government. Pitted against Whig William Henry Harrison, with James G. Birney a minor candidate as the nominee of the Liberty Party,* Van Buren failed to be reelected by a slim margin.

When the Democrats met in their 1844 nominating convention at Baltimore, Van Buren was the leading contender, with Lewis Cass of Michigan close behind. For the first time in history, a dark-horse candidate, James K. Polk of Tennessee, was nominated for the presidency. As his vice-presidential running mate, the delegates chose Silas Wright of New York. When Wright refused to accept the nomination, it went to George M. Dallas of Pennsylvania. The platform appealed to the masses by declaring that the "American Democracy place their trust in the intelligence, the patriotism, and the discriminating justice of the American people." Various planks reiterated that the U.S. government was one of limited power without constitutional authority to carry on a general system of internal improvements, charter a national bank, interfere with or control slavery, or expend money except for the necessary expenses of the government. It opposed the policy of returning proceeds from the sale of public lands to the various states or tampering with the executive veto. Advocated were the reoccupation of the Oregon Territory and the reannexation of Texas. In a close presidential election, Polk won over the Whig, Henry Clay, and third-party candidate James G. Birney of the Liberty Party.

Meeting again at Baltimore in 1848, the Democrats chose Lewis Cass of Michigan, the advocate of squatter sovereignty, as their presidential nominee. For the vice-presidency the delegates named General William O. Butler of Kentucky. Of significance was the creation by the convention of the Democratic National Committee.* As before, the states' rights philosophy permeated the platform, which reemphasized the DP's opposition to a national bank, and distribution of public-land sales money to the states. Praise was bestowed upon President James K. Polk, who chose not to run for reelection, for his handling of the Mexican War and for getting the tariff lowered. Running against Zachary Taylor of the Whig Party and Martin Van Buren of the Free Soil Party,* Cass lost by just over 200,000 popular votes.

Assembling at their perennial convention site in Baltimore, the Democrats had many contenders for the 1852 presidential nomination. When a deadlock occurred among Lewis Cass, James Buchanan, William

L. Marcy, and Stephen A. Douglas, a dark horse, Franklin Pierce of New Hampshire, won the nomination. As his vice-presidential running mate, the delegates decided on William R. King of Alabama. The platform repeated once again the limited-government planks of previous documents and reaffirmed its opposition to internal improvements. It specifically stated that "Congress has no power under the Constitution to interfere with or control the domestic institutions [it was referring to slavery] of the several States." One plank applauded the Compromise of 1850 and another called for friendly relations with Mexico. Pitted against Whig Winfield Scott and Free Soiler John P. Hale, Franklin Pierce triumphed with a comfortable popular vote margin.

For the first time since its inception, in 1856 the DP held its national nominating convention in a city other than Baltimore, when the delegates assembled at Cincinnati, Ohio. President Pierce sought renomination but was challenged by James Buchanan of Pennsylvania and Stephen A. Douglas of Illinois. Buchanan emerged with the presidential nomination and was paired with John C. Breckinridge of Kentucky as his vice-presidential running mate. The platform repeated the limited-government arguments but underscored the stricture against federal interference with the institution of slavery. Secret societies were denounced (meaning the Know-Nothing Party*), as well as abolitionists. Endorsed were free trade; implementation of the Monroe Doctrine; construction of a road to the Pacific; U.S. expansion in the Gulf of Mexico region; and friendship with the peoples of Central America. In a three-way race with John C. Frémont, the nominee of the new Republican Party,* and former Whig Millard Fillmore, running as the candidate of the Know-Nothing Party, James Buchanan eked out a narrow win.

With the slavery issue supreme in the minds of southerners, the Democrats in 1860 gathered at Charleston, South Carolina. This was a disastrous national convention; a deadlock over the platform prompted a walkout of forty-five delegates from nine states. The southerners and pro-slavery advocates would not endorse the doctrine of popular sovereignty nor would they accept the slavery plank of previous platforms. Following the walkout, some ten days passed in an attempt to name a presidential nominee. Stephen A. Douglas could not attain the two-thirds needed for nomination. For the only time in history, a national nominating convention adjourned without having named a presidential candidate. A recess for six weeks was decided upon, after which the convention would reconvene in Baltimore.

After reassembling at Baltimore, even more dissension took place. Voting on the credentials of those who had bolted at Charleston produced a new walkout. These and previous dissenters would meet shortly thereafter to form the National Democratic Party* of 1860. The remnant of the DP convention nominated Stephen A. Douglas to head the presidential ticket, with Benjamin Fitzpatrick of Alabama as the vice-presidential nominee. When the latter declined to accept, the Democratic National Committee named Herschel V. Johnson in his stead. Following its usual reaffirmation of the principles of limited government, the platform of the decimated DP called for the construction of a transcontinental railroad, acquisition of Cuba, protection for all Americans who traveled abroad, and faithful execution of the Fugitive Slave Act. Popular sovereignty was endorsed as a way of handling the slavery issue in the territories, and a pledge was made that the DP "will abide by the decision of the Supreme Court of the United States upon those questions of Constitutional law." Stephen Douglas lost to fellow Illinoisan Abraham Lincoln, the Republican, in a four-cornered presidential race that included John C. Breckinridge, the National Democrat, and John Bell of the Constitutional Union Party.*

Factionalized and in disarray, the Democrats held their 1864 nominating convention in Chicago. Tainted by charges of treason and with Copperheads (Northern Democrats who supported the Southern cause and wanted to end the war) in their midst, the DP's only hope was that a war-weary nation would turn to them for peace. General George B. McClellan of New Jersey was easily nominated for the presidency on the first ballot. George H. Pendleton of Ohio was chosen as the vice-presidential nominee. The platform censured the Lincoln administration for "four years of failure to restore the Union by the experiment of war." Also criticized were "subversion of the civil by military law," "open and avowed disregard of states' rights," and disregard for prisoners of war. The demand was made "that immediate efforts be made for a cessation of hostilities." A concluding plank extended the sympathy of the DP to Union soldiers and sailors. McClellan was defeated by incumbent President Abraham Lincoln, who drew the votes of both Republicans and war Democrats by running as the nominee of the Union Party.*

The first post-Civil War convention of the DP was held in New York City at Tammany Hall.* Still tainted with the stigma of treason, the assembled delegates knew their chances for political victory were slim. When a boom for General Winfield Scott Hancock failed, the delegates turned to former Governor Horatio Seymour of New York as their presidential nominee. He was paired with General Francis P. Blair of Missouri, a former Republican. The platform sought to dismiss the issue of the Civil War by "recognizing the questions of slavery and secession as having been settled for all time to come by the war." Additional planks called for an end to Reconstruction and the restoration of the southern states to the Union; amnesty for political prisoners; payment of the national debt in greenbacks; reduction of the standing army and navy; economy in government; abolition of the Freedmen's Bureau; expulsion of corrupt men from office; a tariff for revenue; and the prohibition of the sale of public land to speculators. Praise was given to President Andrew Johnson for "resisting the aggressions of Congress" and to Chief Justice Samuel P. Chase for the "justice, dignity, and impartiality with which he presided over the court of impeachment." Although a vigorous war governor, Seymour lost the presidential election to Republican Ulysses S. Grant by a landslide vote.

The 1872 Democratic convention at Baltimore was one of the shortest on record. The delegates merely approved the presidential ticket previously selected by the Liberal Republican Party* (LRP), hoping that the split in the Republican Party might give the DP a chance for victory. Ratified for the presidential candidacy was Horace Greeley, editor of the *New York Tribune*, and for the vice-presidency, Governor B. Gratz Brown of Missouri. The LRP platform was adopted without debate. It demanded "equal and exact justice to all, of whatever nativity, race, color or persuasion, religion or politics"; universal amnesty; supremacy of civil authority over the military; civil service reform; limitation of one term for the presidency; a "speedy return to specie payment"; no more land grants to railroads; and payment of the public debt. Horace Greeley as the fusion DP-LRP candidate was overwhelmed at the polls by Republican President Grant.

When the Democratic delegates convened at St. Louis, Missouri, in 1876, it was the first time any national nominating convention had met west of the Mississippi River. The panic of 1873 and the Grant scandals gave the Democrats renewed hope for capturing the White House. Governor Samuel J. Tilden of New York was designated the presidential nominee, with Thomas A. Hendricks of Indiana picked as the vice-presidential candidate. Exploiting the corruption in the Grant administration, the platform repeatedly used the phrase "reform is necessary" when it enumerated such issues as carpetbag governments in the South (as part of Grant's Reconstruction program); failure to redeem greenbacks; waste of public lands through land grants to railroads; excessively high tariff; and civil service reform. The only positive plank endorsed benefits to veterans. In one of the most unusual presidential elections the nation ever witnessed, Tilden won the popular vote by over 250,000 more than Republican Rutherford B. Hayes and yet lost the presidency. In this famous disputed election, an electoral commission eventually awarded Hayes 185 electoral votes to Tilden's 184, thus depriving the Democrats of victory.

When the Democrats assembled at Cincinnati, Ohio, in 1880, most delegates assumed that Samuel J. Tilden would again be the presidential nominee. But Tilden withdrew his name for consideration, and the nomination went to General Winfield Scott Hancock of Pennsylvania. Second place on the ticket went to William H. English of Indiana. The platform bitterly described the previous presidential election as the "great fraud." Other planks called for hard money; tariff for revenue; civil service reform; exclusion of Chinese immigrants; public land for actual settlers; and decentralization of the government. In a three-man contest, Hancock faced Republican James A. Garfield and James B. Weaver of the Greenback Party.* Hancock lost by fewer than 2,000 votes to Garfield. It was another Democratic defeat, but the margin was so close as to indicate future victory four years hence.

Democrats were optimistic when they met at Chicago in 1884. Governor Grover Cleveland of New York was chosen the presidential nominee despite critical attacks by Tammany Hall delegates. Thomas A. Hendricks of Indiana got the nod for the vice-presidency. The platform had a states' rights orientation but softened its stand on the need to lower the tariff. Other planks demanded reduction in taxes; an end to corruption; "honest money"; the "diffusion of free education by common schools"; "repeal of all laws restricting the free action of labor"; public lands to be kept for homesteaders; exclusion of Chinese labor; improvements on the Mississippi River and other waterways; expansion of U.S. markets overseas; and more intimate commercial and political relations with Canada, Central America, and South America. There were three other presidential candidates in the field in 1884: Republican James G. Blaine, Greenbacker Benjamin F. Butler, and John P. St. John of the Prohibition Party.* Cleveland won by a narrow margin, the first Democrat elected president since before the Civil War.

It was a jubilant group of Democrats who assembled at St. Louis in 1888 to renominate President Grover Cleveland by acclaim. Because Vice-President Thomas Hendricks had died in office, he was replaced by Allen G. Thurman of Ohio. The platform lavished praise upon President Cleveland and gave support to his call for downward revision of the tariff. The Cleveland administration was further lauded for recovering 100 million acres of public lands for homesteaders; reconstruction of the U.S. Navy; "honest reform"; enactment of the Chinese Exclusion Act; and frugality in government. Additional planks endorsed home rule for Ireland and called for statehood for the territories of Dakota, Montana, New Mexico, and Washington. In facing Republican Benjamin Harrison, President Cleveland won the popular vote by a little over 90,000 but lost the election in the electoral college. Harrison's electoral vote was 233 to Cleveland's 168. The Democrats lost the election primarily on the tariff issue and were once again relegated to the role of loyal opposition.

At the 1892 Democratic convention held in Chicago, ex-President Grover Cleveland was nominated to head the ticket despite opposition from Tammany Hall. The choice of Adlai E. Stevenson of Illinois for the vice-presidency rounded out the ticket. The platform reflected the Jim Crow system that had developed in the South when it condemned any attempts to enact a force bill. It warned that "a horde of deputy marshalls at every polling place . . . would outrage the electoral rights of the people . . . [and lead to] the subjugation of the colored people to the party in power, and the reviving of race antagonisms." Condemned were the McKinley Tariff, the Sherman Silver Act, and any attempt to impose prohibition. Planks called for the use of both gold and silver as money and the construction of a canal through Nicaragua. In a rematch with Republican Benjamin Harrison, the incumbent president, Cleveland triumphed by a popular vote margin of over 350,000. Noteworthy was the fact the candidate of the Populist Party,* James B. Weaver, polled over 1 million popular votes.

Gathering once again at Chicago in 1896, the Democrats were split into silver (soft-money) and gold (hard-money) factions. The monetary issue had been aggravated by the panic of 1893, which plagued the Cleveland administration. The repeal of the Sherman Silver Act of 1890 in 1893 was dubbed the "crime of '93" by silverites. Despite President Cleveland's opposition to William Jennings Bryan of Nebraska, Bryan gained the support of many delegates with his electrifying Cross of Gold speech. At thirty-six years of age, the young Nebraskan was nominated for the presidency. His vice-presidential running mate was Arthur Sewall of Maine. The platform demanded "free and unlimited coinage of silver and gold at the present legal ratio of 16 to 1," enlargement of the regulatory powers of the Interstate Commerce Commission, and reduction of the tariff. Other planks opposed importation of foreign labor; favored admission of the territories of Arizona, New Mexico, and Oklahoma as states; condemned the trafficking by the government with banking syndicates; supported veterans' pensions; and upheld the Monroe Doctrine. Victory for Bryan seemed in the offing, since he was also the presidential nominee of the Populist Party. This advantage was partially offset when a group of gold Democrats and Clevelandites formed the National Democratic Party* of 1896 and ran John M. Palmer as their presidential candidate. Although Bryan headed a fusion ticket, he lost out to Republican William McKinley by a considerable popular vote margin.

With a determined show of harmony at Kansas City, Missouri, in 1900, the Democrats once more nominated William Jennings Bryan as their standard-bearer. Ex-Vice-President Adlai E. Stevenson was nominated to fill the second place on the ticket. Although a silver plank reiterated the DP's support for free and unlimited coinage of silver, the main thrust of the platform was aimed at condemning the territorial expansion of the United States following the Spanish-American War. An anti-imperialism plank asserted, "We are unalterably opposed to seizing or purchasing distant islands [the Philippines] to be governed outside the Constitution." Pledged were enactment of antitrust laws; creation of a Department of Labor as a cabinet position; direct election of U.S. senators; construction of a Nicaraguan canal; and reclamation for the arid lands of the West. Additional planks were critical of the Dingley Tariff, the Hay-Pauncefote Treaty, and the imposition of a government upon Puerto Rico. Challenging incumbent President William McKinley, the valiant Bryan again went down to defeat by a larger margin than four years previously.

When the Democrats met in St. Louis in 1904, they were confronted with a difficult task of nominating a presidential candidate who could dislodge the popular incumbent—Theodore Roosevelt. The lot fell to Alton B. Parker, the chief justice of the New York Court of Appeals. Paired with him was Henry G. Davis of Virginia. Although William Jennings Bryan was present at the convention, his influence was negligible. The platform, a lengthy document, described T.R.'s administration as being "spasmodic, erratic, sensational, spectacular, and arbitrary." It criticized American imperialism, the high tariff, government subsidies to private shippers, and the failure of the federal government to break up monopolies. Support was promised for reclamation; reciprocal trade with Canada; establishing an eight-hour workday for federal employees; constructing a Panama canal; improving waterways; election of U.S. senators by direct vote of the people; statehood for Arizona, New Mexico, and Oklahoma; "extermination of polygamy"; pensions for veterans; and reduction of the size of the U.S. Army. Relative to civil rights for Negroes in the South, one plank asserted, "To revive the dead and hateful race and sectional animosities in any part of our common country means confusion, distraction of business, and the reopening of wounds now happily healed." Alton Parker netted only 37.6 percent of the popular vote in a landslide loss to Roosevelt.

Bryanites regained control of the DP at its 1908 nominating convention at Denver, Colorado, the first national convention of a major party in a western state. William Jennings Bryan was given the presidential nomination on the first ballot. A two-time loser, he was paired with John W. Kern of Indiana, a man who had twice lost gubernatorial races in the Hoosier state. The platform claimed, " 'Shall the people rule?' is the overshadowing issue which manifests itself in all the questions now under discussion." Many commitments were made in subsequent planks, including: enactment of legislation prohibiting corporations from making unreasonable campaign contributions; immediate downward revision of the tariff; stricter regulation of railroads and telegraph; greater power to the Interstate Commerce Commission; stronger antimonopoly laws; an income tax; establishment of a postal savings bank; limitations on the use of labor injunctions; pensions for veterans; creation of a national bureau of public health; extension of agricultural, mechanical, and industrial education; direct election of U.S. senators; statehood for Arizona, New Mexico, and Oklahoma; setting of regulations for free grazing on public lands; improvement of internal waterways; federal aid to states for the construction of post roads; independence for the Philippines; prohibition of immigration from Asian countries; and the fostering of closer ties with Latin American nations. Criticism was leveled at the Roosevelt administration for the panic of 1907 and for incurring a fiscal deficit, and at the Speaker of the House of Representatives, Joseph G. Cannon, for being "more powerful than the entire body." Bryan lost to Republican William Howard Taft by a little over 269,000 popular votes in an election that saw Eugene V. Debs draw over 420,000 votes as the presidential nominee of the Socialist Party of America.*

It was a jubilant group of Democrats who assembled at Baltimore in 1912 for the national convention. A week before, the Republican Party had split when Theodore Roosevelt led a dissident group in a walkout to form the Progressive Party* of 1912. William Jennings Bryan was instrumental in getting the presidential nomination for Governor Woodrow Wilson of New Jersey, who won on the forty-fifth ballot. Governor Thomas R. Marshall of Indiana was named the vice-presidential nominee. The platform promised immediate downward revision of the tariff; "vigorous enforcement of the criminal and civil law against trusts and trust officials"; an amendment to the U.S. Constitution authorizing an income tax; enactment of a law prohibiting any corporation from contributing to political campaigns; inauguration of the presidential primary; adoption of a constitutional amendment limiting a president to one term; direct election of U.S. senators; legislation to prevent the abuse of the writ of injunction and establishment of the eight-hour workday for workers on all national public work; federal rate regulation of railroads, express companies, telegraph, and telephone companies; appropriations for vocational education; development of the nation's inland waterways; construction of post roads; conservation of natural resources; making speculation on commodity markets illegal; exemption from tolls of American ships engaged in coastal trade that pass through the Panama Canal; strengthening of government agencies supervising enforcement of the Pure Food and Drug Act; reform in the administration of civil and criminal law; independence for the Philippines; parcel post and extension of rural free delivery; and the "overthrow of Cannonism." Running as a progressive, Woodrow Wilson triumphed over a field of candidates in an exciting campaign that saw Theodore Roosevelt of the Progressive Party come in second; incumbent President William Howard Taft, the Republican, third; and Socialist Eugene V. Debs, fourth.

Europe was at war as the Democratic National Convention opened at St. Louis in 1916. President Woodrow Wilson was renominated 1,092 to 1, and Vice-President Thomas Marshall was so designated by acclamation. The platform lauded such achievements of the Wilson administration as the Federal Reserve System, Federal Trade Commission, Underwood Tariff, Seamen's Act, Rural Credits Act, and the Cotton Futures Act. It stressed patriotism and national unity with planks indicating support for woman suffrage; national preparedness; continued neutrality; development of a "stable, responsible government in Mexico"; promotion of a larger merchant marine; construction of more public highways; prison reform; alteration of the rules of the U.S. Senate to prevent filibusters; independence for the Philippines; flood-control projects in the lower Mississippi Valley; territorial status for Hawaii and Puerto Rico; and enactment of a federal child labor law. Conspicuously absent from the platform were planks dealing with a one-term limitation on the office of the presidency or a defense of states' rights. Wilsonian liberalism made the progressive concept of positive government a new tenet of the DP's political credo and indicated the abandonment of the Jefferson-Jackson commitment to states' rights and negative government. In what turned out to be an extraordinarily close election, President Wilson won by a popular vote of 580,000 over Republican challenger Charles Evans Hughes, but this translated into only a narrow twenty-three electoral-vote margin. Wilson won basically because of the slogan, "He kept us out of war."

Neither the nation nor the DP had a leader when Democrats met at San Francisco in 1920 to nominate a presidential candidate. Woodrow Wilson was an invalid in the White House, there was prolonged debate over the Treaty of Versailles, and reconversion following World War I was haphazard at best. Wilson wanted a third term, but the delegates bypassed him for Governor James M. Cox of Ohio. Second place on the ticket went to Franklin D. Roosevelt of New York, who had served as assistant secretary of the navy in the Wilson administration. The platform saluted President Wilson as a great war leader and placed the plank supporting U.S. entry into the League of Nations first. Other planks endorsed alteration of the rules in the U.S. Senate; revision of tax laws; creation of an effective budget system; retention by the government of the nitrogen plant at Muscle Shoals; quick ratification by the states of the Nineteenth (woman suffrage) amendment to the U.S. Constitution; elimination of sex discrimination relative to civil service jobs; federal assistance to disabled veterans; improvement of port facilities; self-determination for Armenia and Ireland; continuation of the policy of not permitting Asiatic immigrants to enter the United States; and independence for the Philippines. Because of disagreement, no plank on prohibition was included. In what amounted to a huge anti-Wilson protest vote, James M. Cox was resoundingly defeated by Republican Warren G. Harding.

Because of the Harding scandals, the Democrats meeting at New York City in 1924 had hopes for nominating a presidential winner. These hopes soon vanished as a deadlock ensued between Alfred E. Smith of New York and William Gibbs McAdoo of California. In a seventeen-day convention and after 103 ballots, the convention finally decided upon John W. Davis of West Virginia. The dubious honor of the vice-presidential nomination went to Governor Charles W. Bryan of Nebraska, the brother of William Jennings Bryan, who was making his last appearance at a Democratic convention (the Great Commoner died the next year). The platform claimed that "never before in our history has the government been so tainted by corruption." It sought to persuade voters that "a vote for [President Calvin] Coolidge is a vote for chaos." Various planks promised honest government: aid to farmers; adjustments in the tariff; lower rail and water rates; operation of the Muscle Shoals plants to maximum capacity; expansion of reclamation projects; recovery of the navy's oil reserves; conservation of wildlife; improved highways; adequate salaries for postal employees; limitations on campaign contributions; control of the narcotics problem; exclusion of Asiatics; independence for the Philippines; "humanizing the veterans' bureau"; "sweeping reductions of armaments by land and sea"; U.S. participation in the world court and League of Nations; vigorous enforcement of antitrust laws; flood control; fuller development of aviation; ratification of the child labor amendment; and friendly relations with Latin America. Planks criticized the Fordney-McCumber Tariff; Secretary of the Treasury Andrew Mellon's tax policies; the isolationist foreign policy of the Republican Party; subsidization of the merchant marine; the Lausanne Treaty; and abridgements on free speech. In an uninspiring campaign, John W. Davis lost in a landslide to incumbent President Calvin Coolidge, but he did succeed in gaining more popular votes than did Robert M. La Follette, the presidential nominee of the Progressive Party* of 1924.

The Democrats headed south for their national convention in 1928. At Houston, Texas, Governor Alfred E. Smith of New York emerged as the presidential nominee, with Senate minority leader Joseph T. Robinson of Arkansas as his vice-presidential running mate. The platform contained a states' rights plank, but the traditional low tariff stance was modified considerably. Other planks pledged reduction of internal taxes; enactment of the McNary-Haugen bill; improvement of deep waterways from the Great Lakes to the Gulf of Mexico and to the Atlantic Ocean; flood control; conservation of natural resources; improvement of highways; collective bargaining for labor unions; public works to reduce unemployment; compensation to federal employees for injury or disability; greater assistance to veterans; federal regulation of radio communications; abolition of the lame-duck session of Congress; public revelation of campaign contributions; enlargement of the Bureau of Public Health; independence for the Philippines; "honest enforcement" of prohibition; fulfillment of commitments to Armenia; and a foreign policy based upon the principles of "outlawry of war" and "freedom from entangling political alliances with foreign nations." No mention of the League of Nations was made, and the mild prohibition plank was nullified by Al Smith when he publicly declared himself a wet. Although Smith's Roman Catholicism became an issue, primarily in the South, his ties with Tammany Hall and his big-city profile hurt him even more at the polls. His loss to Republican Herbert C. Hoover in both the popular and electoral vote was overwhelming.

When the Democrats met at their national convention at Chicago in 1932, the nation was in the throes of the Great Depression. The presidential nomination went to Governor Franklin D. Roosevelt of New York. Selected for the vice-presidency was House Speaker John N. Garner of Texas. The platform blamed Hoover for the depression but gave little or no indication as to what a new Democratic administration would do. Various planks advocated "drastic reduction of governmental expenditures"; a federal budget "annually balanced"; sound currency; extension of federal credit to the states; reduction in the work week; unemployment and old-age insurance; rural credit and "effective control of crop surpluses"; an army and navy "adequate for national defense"; strengthened antitrust laws; "removal of government from all fields of private enterprise except where necessary to develop public works and natural resources in the common interest"; protection of the investing public; "full measure of justice and generosity for all war veterans"; a strengthened Corrupt Practices Act; repeal of the Eighteenth (prohibition) Amendment; modification of the Volstead Act; settlement of international disputes by arbitration; and collection of World War I debts from foreign nations. Governor Roosevelt broke tradition by coming to the convention in order to accept the presidential nomination personally. FDR went on to beat incumbent President Hoover by a whopping 57.42 percent of the popular vote.

Realizing that the New Deal was popular with the electorate, Democrats assembled at Philadelphia in 1936 to renominate President Roosevelt and Vice-President Garner by acclaim. They abolished the two-thirds rule and voted that all future nominations would be by simple majority. The platform pointed with pride to the many accomplishments of the Roosevelt administration, among them the Social Security Act, Wagner Act, Tennessee Valley Authority, Soil Conservation and Domestic Allotment Act, National Youth Administration, and the Works Progress Administration. The DP had now embraced an enlarged positive government as part of its political principles. Thus the Wilson-Roosevelt emphasis on big federal government eclipsed the Jefferson-Jackson belief in states' rights and local government. Various planks promised reduction of government expenditures; a balanced budget; a vigorous fight against crime; further flood control; a "clarifying amendment" to the U.S. Constitution relative to the relationship between the federal government and the states; expansion of the reciprocal trade agreements; opposition to the "despotism of Communism and the menace of concealed Fascism"; implementation of the Neutrality Act; and extension of the Good Neighbor policy. FDR polled 60.79 percent of the popular vote, overwhelming both the Republican challenger, Governor Alfred M.

Landon of Kansas, and William Lemke, the nominee of the Union Party.*

Prior to the time of the Democratic National Convention of 1940 at Philadelphia, World War II had broken out in Europe. Defying the no-third-term tradition, the delegates renominated President Roosevelt on the first roll call. Vice-President Garner was dropped in favor of Henry A. Wallace of Iowa as second man on the ticket. The first sentence of the platform's preamble set the tone of the entire document: "The world is undergoing violent change." Specific planks called for strengthening national defense; a pledge not to "participate in foreign wars"; enlarging the tenant-purchase program; refinancing existing farm debts; preserving and strenghtening the Ever-Normal Granary; expanding the food stamp and school lunch programs; enlarging rural electrification; encouraging the formation of cooperatives; including crops other than wheat in the crop insurance program; enforcing the Fair Labor Standards Act; attacking "unbridled concentration of economic power;" expanding tariff reciprocity; promoting public power; developing western resources; protecting the radio industry from censorship; continuing the fight against unemployment; expanding health facilities; increasing federal aid to education; accelerating slum clearance and the construction of low-rent housing; fair treatment of veterans; extending civil service to all positions in the executive branch of the government; self-government leading to statehood for Alaska, Hawaii, and Puerto Rico; creating an Indian claims commission; and ensuring "due process and the equal protection of the laws for every citizen, regardless of race, creed, or color." Although the Republican nominee, Wendell Wilkie, was a tough campaigner, FDR polled 54.70 percent of the popular vote.

The nation had been at war for four years when the Democrats convened their national convention at Chicago in 1944. President Roosevelt was renominated for a fourth term, but Vice-President Henry Wallace was dropped from the ticket and replaced by Senator Harry S. Truman of Missouri. The platform duly praised the accomplishments of the Roosevelt administration and then called for the United States to "join with the other United Nations in the establishment of an international organization"; continuation of the Good Neighbor policy; the "opening of Palestine to unrestricted Jewish immigration and colonization"; legislation assuring "equal pay for equal work, regardless of sex"; an equal rights amendment for women; continued federal aid to education; nondiscriminatory transportation charges; self-government for Puerto Rico and eventual statehood for Alaska and Hawaii; extension of the right of suffrage to the people of the District of Columbia; and postwar continuation of programs initiated under the New Deal. Endorsed also were the Four Freedoms and a statement on civil rights that declared, "We believe that racial and religious minorities have the right to live, develop, and vote equally with all citizens and share the rights that are guaranteed by our Constitution." Although ill and near death, FDR triumphed over his Republican adversary, Governor Thomas E. Dewey of New York, by winning 53.39 percent of the popular vote.

Gloom pervaded the convention hall at Philadelphia in 1948. President Harry S. Truman was nominated to head the ticket, although most delegates did not think he could win. Then a fight over the civil rights plank developed, and southerners bolted to form their own States' Rights Party* (Dixiecrats). After a rousing keynote speech, Senator Alben W. Barkley of Kentucky was selected for the vice-presidency by acclaim. The platform gave credit to the Truman administration for "resisting Communist aggression" by the Truman Doctrine, Marshall Plan, and aid to Greece and Turkey. It advocated international control of weapons; maintenance of armed forces "to assure our security against aggression"; immediate diplomatic recognition of Israel; reduction of the national debt; repeal of the Taft-Hartley Act; raising the minimum wage to 75 cents an hour; aid to war veterans; national health insurance; federal aid to education; extension of Social Security; flexible price supports for farmers; regional development of water, mineral, and other natural resources; acceleration of irrigation and reclamation projects; elimination of "unfair and illegal discrimination based on race, creed, or color"; admittance of 400,000 displaced persons to the United States; statehood for Alaska and Hawaii; equal rights for women; civilian administration of atomic energy; establishment of a national science foundation; and prosecution of those guilty of treasonable activities. The platform sought to blame the Republican-controlled Eightieth Congress for obstructing what later became the Fair Deal. In a four-cornered race in which Governor Thomas E. Dewey represented the Republican Party, Henry A. Wallace the Progressive Party* of 1948, and J. Strom Thurmond the States' Rights Party, President Truman astounded his opponents by winning a "miracle victory."

When the Democrats convened at Chicago in 1952, a presidential draft movement had gained such momentum that it resulted in the nomination of Governor Adlai E. Stevenson II of Illinois. Paired with him on the ticket was Senator John J. Sparkman of Alabama. To prevent future walkouts by dissidents, the delegates voted to bind all in attendance by a party loyalty pledge. Since the nation was involved in the Korean War, the platform pledged resistance to Communist aggression and "peace with honor." Promised also were assistance to Israel; encouragement to the nations of the North Atlantic Treaty Organization; a commitment not to abandon the peoples of Central and Eastern Europe; support for India and Pakistan; friendship with Japan and the German Federal Republic; military and economic assistance to Nationalist China; continuance of the Point IV program; trade expansion; aid to refugees from Communist countries; continued implementation of anti-inflation laws; elimination of tax loopholes;

price supports at 90 percent of parity for farmers; repeal of the Taft-Hartley Act; improvement of conditions for migratory workers; river basin development on a regional basis; extension of Social Security; unemployment insurance; federal aid for medical education and hospital construction; urban redevelopment of the school lunch program; establishment of day care centers; increased benefits for veterans; a new law relating to presidential succession; equal rights for women; civil rights for minorities; and statehood for Alaska and Hawaii. In one of the most high-level campaigns ever conducted, in the sense that neither candidate resorted to mud-slinging tactics, Adlai Stevenson lost to Dwight D. Eisenhower, the Republican presidential nominee, by over 6 million popular votes.

In 1956 at Chicago the Democrats once more chose Adlai E. Stevenson to be their standard-bearer. Instead of indicating his choice for a running mate, Stevenson permitted the delegates to select whomever they desired. The result was a close contest in which Senator Estes Kefauver (D-Tenn.) emerged the victor over Senator John F. Kennedy (D-Mass.). In a lengthy platform, the legislative record of the Democratic-controlled Congress was praised while the actions of the Eisenhower administration were condemned. Criticism was leveled at Secretary of State John Foster Dulles for his "brink of war" type of foreign policy, Secretary of Agriculture Ezra Taft Benson for initiating flexible price supports, and President Eisenhower for using force to implement integration in southern schools. Other planks indicated support for civil rights; repeal of the Taft-Hartley Act; a return to price supports at 90 percent of parity; tax relief for lower-income families; federal aid to education; elimination of discriminatory quotas in the immigration law; an equal rights amendment for women; statehood for Alaska and Hawaii; government assistance to Indian tribes; acceleration of the domestic civilian atomic power program; an end to government secrecy and harassment of federal employees by loyalty probes; assistance to Israel and Arab countries; revitalization of the North Atlantic Treaty Organization; and expansion of world trade. In a rematch between Stevenson and Eisenhower, the latter won again by an even greater margin than four years previously.

When the Democrats converged on Los Angeles in 1960, it was the first time that city had ever hosted a national convention of a major party. The front-runner, Senator John F. Kennedy of Massachusetts, was nominated for the presidency on the first ballot. For his vice-presidential running mate JFK chose Senator Lyndon B. Johnson of Texas, the Senate majority leader. In a twenty-thousand-word platform that was aimed at enunciating the challenges of the "New Frontier" and assailing the Republicans, the following planks charged the existence of a "missile gap"; an unbalanced military force; lack of an adequate civil defense; existence of anti-Americanism abroad; loss of foreign trade; the existence of a discriminating national-origins quota in the immigration law; insufficient assistance by the United States to underdeveloped countries; a lack of "food banks" throughout the world; deterioration of the Atlantic Community; domestic economic stagnation; inflation and unemployment; an anti-labor policy; inadequate assistance to farmers; lack of adequate medical care for older citizens; air and water pollution; failure to develop atomic energy; an unbalanced budget; and soaring crime rates. Calling itself the "party of hope" as distinguished from the GOP as the "party of memory," the platform included these pledges: to oppose Communist aggression; to create a "national peace agency"; increase the minimum wage to $1.25 per hour; enact equal rights legislation for women; modernize the armed forces; use civil injunction suits in federal court to implement civil rights; close tax loopholes; enact price supports for farmers at 90 percent of parity; provide federal assistance to state and local governments; promote economic growth; use public works to reduce unemployment; repeal "right-to-work" laws; use surplus food as "powerful instruments for peace and plenty"; provide medical care benefits as part of Social Security; expand highways and aid to railroads; protect consumers by the creation of a consumer counsel; establish a federal advisory agency to expand the cultural resources of the nation; and establish a fair employment practices commission. Utilizing television to great advantage and with the slogan, "Let's get the country moving again," JFK won an extremely close victory over the Republican nominee, Vice-President Richard M. Nixon.

Less than a year before the Democrats met at Atlantic City in 1964, Lyndon B. Johnson had become president after John F. Kennedy was assassinated. LBJ was renominated for a full term by acclamation. The choice for the vice-presidency went to Senator Hubert H. Humphrey of Minnesota. Labeling itself a "covenant of unity," the platform heaped praise on the accomplishments of both JFK's presidency and that of LBJ. Condemned were such extremists as the Communist Party of the United States of America,* the Ku Klux Klan,* and the John Birch Society.* Criticized also were the supposedly reckless statements made by Senator Barry Goldwater of Arizona, the presidential nominee of the Republican Party, about the use of nuclear weapons in the Vietnam War. Promises were made to assist local communities in finding new sources of tax revenue; "fair, effective enforcement" of the Civil Rights Act of 1964; maintenance of an "overwhelming supremacy" of nuclear weapons; strengthening the armed forces for "discouraging limited wars"; and jobs for "every man or woman who is willing and able to work." Johnson's victory over Goldwater was a tremendous landslide (61.05 percent of the popular vote).

The convention site at Chicago in 1968 resembled an embattled bastion. Police, soldiers, and National Guard troops fought with anti-Vietnam war protesters while doves battled hawks inside the convention hall. After many floor fights over credentials, rule changes, and a peace plank, Vice-President Hubert H. Humphrey was chosen as the DP's presidential nominee. Senator Edmund S. Muskie of Maine was named the vice-presidential candidate. Two basic issues were in the forefront of the platform: the war in Vietnam and crime in the streets. The Vietnam plank stated, "Stop all bombing of North Vietnam when this action would not endanger the lives of our troops in the field; this action should take into account the response from Hanoi." Pledges were made to equip and train the South Vietnamese so that they could defend themselves when U.S. troops were withdrawn; to "maintain a strong and balanced defense establishment adequate to the task of security and peace"; to coexist with the People's Republic of China; to aid Israel as long as it was "threatened by hostile and well-armed neighbors"; to suppress crime and violence in the streets without violating the right of free speech or due process; to enact tax reform for a "minimum income tax for persons of high income"; to reduce taxes for the poor; and to reform the electoral college. In a hotly contested election Hubert Humphrey lost to Republican Richard M. Nixon by a little over 500,000 popular votes.

At the 1972 national convention at Miami Beach, Florida, the credentials of 1,289 delegates (40 percent of the total) were challenged because the selection of the delegates was to have taken place under new rules authorized by the 1968 convention. Congressman James O'Hara chaired the Commission on Rules, and Senator George M. McGovern of South Dakota chaired the Commission on Party Structure and Delegate Selection. Among the eighteen guidelines for the selection of delegates was the stipulation that larger quotas of women, young people, and minorities than previously selected be represented in the various state delegations. Utilizing this rule change to his advantage, Senator McGovern won the presidential nomination on the first roll-call vote. He then selected Senator Thomas F. Eagleton of Missouri as his vice-presidential running mate. Less than a month after his nomination, Eagleton was induced to resign from the ticket when it became known that he had hospitalized himself for psychological reasons. In his place McGovern and the Democratic National Committee chose R. Sargent Shriver of Maryland, a former director of the Peace Corps in the Kennedy administration.

The New Left orientation of the 1972 platform was evident by its contents, despite the fact that the more radical proposals—a guaranteed annual income for a family of four of $6,500, an increase in the income tax in higher brackets, and a gay plank calling for the repeal of laws discriminating against lesbians and homosexuals—were defeated. Included in the platform were the redistribution of wealth through tax reform; guaranteed income; revenue sharing; reduction of military spending; the "immediate total withdrawal of Americans from Southeast Asia"; return to Congress of powers assumed by the chief executive; development of friendly relations with the nations of the Third World; amnesty for deserters and draft-dodgers; more local control over federal programs; expansion of public service employment; a ban on the sale of handguns; an end to wiretapping and electronic surveillance; ratification of the equal rights amendment; continuation of busing as a means of attaining desegregation of the schools; high price supports for small farm units; and abolition of the electoral college. In losing to incumbent President Richard M. Nixon by almost eighteen million popular votes, McGovern suffered a tremendous defeat.

Democrats were jubilant at their New York City convention in 1976. Both President Richard M. Nixon and Vice-President Spiro T. Agnew had been forced to resign from office. The incumbent, President Gerald R. Ford, had not been elected to office and would have difficulty overcoming the stigma of the Watergate scandals. After winning many primaries, Jimmy Carter, a former governor of Georgia, emerged as the front-runner. He won the presidential nomination on the first ballot. Selected as his vice-presidential running mate was Senator Walter F. Mondale of Minnesota.

The platform promised to "reduce adult unemployment to 3 percent within four years"; ensure price stability without mandatory controls; eliminate tax shelters; inaugurate zero-based budgeting; revise the Hatch Act;

The platform promised to "reduce adult unemployment to 3 percent within four years"; ensure price stability without mandatory controls; eliminate tax shelters; inaugurate zero-based budgeting; revise the Hatch Act; provide "partial public funding" for congressional elections; initiate a comprehensive national health insurance; substitute income maintenance for the present welfare system; support affirmative-action programs; ratify the equal rights amendment; protect citizens' privacy from governmental agencies; support busing as the last resort to achieve racial integration in the public schools; use federal subsidies to promote the construction of low-cost housing; develop a "national urban policy"; reform the criminal justice system; ban the manufacture and sale of handguns; provide a more flexible use of the Highway Trust Fund; lessen the reliance on nuclear energy; enforce antipollution laws strictly; initiate a program to store agricultural surpluses on the farm; end balance-of-power diplomacy; reform the international monetary system; insist on the "observance of human rights in countries which receive American aid"; reduce military spending; conclude the SALT agreement with the Soviet Union; achieve a just and lasting peace in the Middle East; reaffirm military support for the Republic of South Korea; negotiate a new Panama Canal treaty; establish normal diplomatic relations with Cuba; and involve black Americans in U.S. foreign policy decisions that affect Africa. Running on this platform, Jimmy Carter won a narrow victory over Gerald Ford in 1976 by pulling 50.1 percent of the popular vote.

From the time of Andrew Jackson to the presidency of Jimmy Carter, the DP has evolved into a different party. While continuing to champion egalitarianism, it has reversed its position on states' rights and limited government. It now stands for increasing the role of the federal government in a welfare state that concerns itself with the economic well-being of the masses. This stance has made it the predominant political party ever since the era of the New Deal.

In 1980 President Jimmy Carter won renomination only after beating down a serious challenge by Senator Edward Kennedy of Massachusetts. At the Democratic National Convention in New York City anti-Carter forces attempted to win approval of a rule that would release delegates from primary commitments and permit them to vote their consciences. When this failed, Jimmy Carter and Walter Mondale were once again named the party's presidential ticket. Senator Kennedy, while losing in his bid for the nomination, played an important role in formulating certain key planks in the final version of the platform.

Relative to the dire state of the domestic economy, the Kennedy forces secured a plank which rejected high interest rates and high unemployment as a means of fighting inflation. It also pledged an immediate twelve-billion-dollar anti-recession program to create at least 800,000 jobs. Other planks promised "targeted tax reductions" to stimulate production; continued promotion of racial integration but by using forced busing only as a judicial "tool of last resort"; faster progress towards eliminating substandard housing; federal support for mass transit systems; public works for urban areas with high unemployment; a five year extension of the revenue sharing program; establishment of an "income floor" for the poor; enactment of a comprehensive national health-insurance plan; ratification of the Equal Rights Amendment; withholding of party financial support for Democrats refusing to support ERA; continuation of affirmative action programs; rejection of a constitutional amendment banning federal funding for abortions; condemnation of the Ku Klux Klan* and American Nazi Party*; tax reform; gun-control legislation; development of renewable energy sources; orderly retirement of nuclear power plants; an increase in agricultural target prices to cover farmers' cost of production; raising the salaries of military personnel; upgrading the combat readiness of the armed forces; registration of nineteen-year-old men and women as a means to mobilize in an emergency; modernization of a strategic deterrent power through the MX, Trident, and cruise missile systems; maintenance of a strong North Atlantic Treaty Organization; ratification of the Strategic Arms Limitation Treaty II; taking care not to provide Israel's enemies with sophisticated offensive weapons; taking steps to create an independent Palestinian State; condemnation of Iran for seizing U.S. diplomatic personnel as hostages; developing closer ties with the People's Republic of China; vowing not to treat Africa as an appendage of great power competition; and promoting world concern for human rights as an enduring basis for a "world order."

In a campaign in which President Carter and Vice-President Mondale vigorously canvassed for votes, the results were catastrophic for the Democrats. The Democratic presidential ticket was overwhelmed at the polls by the Republican team of Reagan and Bush. In the popular vote the Carter-Mondale duo pulled 34,913,332 popular votes to that of 43,201,220

**TABLE 4 Democratic Party Presidential Candidates and Votes, 1828-1980**

| YEAR | CANDIDATE | TOTAL POPULAR VOTE |
|------|-----------|--------------------|
| 1828 | Andrew Jackson | 642,553 |
| 1832 | Andrew Jackson | 687,502 |
| 1836 | Martin Van Buren | 762,678 |
| 1840 | Martin Van Buren | 1,128,854 |
| 1844 | James K. Polk | 1,339,494 |
| 1848 | Lewis Cass | 1,220,544 |
| 1852 | Franklin Pierce | 1,601,474 |
| 1856 | James Buchanan | 1,836,072 |
| 1860 | Stephen A. Douglas | 1,375,157 |
| 1864 | George B. McClellan | 1,805,237 |
| 1868 | Horatio Seymour | 2,703,249 |
| 1872 | Horace Greeley | 2,834,125 |
| 1876 | Samuel J. Tilden | 4,288,546 |
| 1880 | Winfield S. Hancock | 4,444,260 |
| 1884 | Grover Cleveland | 4,874,621 |
| 1888 | Grover Cleveland | 5,534,488 |
| 1892 | Grover Cleveland | 5,551,883 |
| 1896 | William Jennings Bryan | 6,502,779 |
| 1900 | William Jennings Bryan | 6,358,133 |
| 1904 | Alton B. Parker | 5,077,911 |
| 1908 | William Jennings Bryan | 6,406,801 |
| 1912 | Woodrow Wilson | 6,293,152 |
| 1916 | Woodrow Wilson | 9,126,300 |
| 1920 | James M. Cox | 9,140,884 |
| 1924 | John W. Davis | 8,386,503 |
| 1928 | Alfred E. Smith | 15,000,185 |
| 1932 | Franklin D. Roosevelt | 22,825,016 |
| 1936 | Franklin D. Roosevelt | 27,751,597 |
| 1940 | Franklin D. Roosevelt | 27,244,160 |
| 1944 | Franklin D. Roosevelt | 25,602,504 |
| 1948 | Harry S. Truman | 24,105,587 |
| 1952 | Adlai E. Stevenson II | 27,314,649 |
| 1956 | Adlai E. Stevenson II | 26,028,887 |
| 1960 | John F. Kennedy | 34,221,344 |
| 1964 | Lyndon B. Johnson | 43,129,584 |
| 1968 | Hubert H. Humphrey | 31,271,839 |
| 1972 | George S. McGovern | 29,171,791 |
| 1976 | Jimmy Carter | 40,829,046 |
| 1980 | Jimmy Carter | 35,481,435 |

for the GOP victors, and in the electoral tally the Democrats won a mere 49 to 489 for the Republicans. In its exercise of sovereignty, the electorate had registered a massive protest and, in doing so, repudiated the stewardship of President Jimmy Carter. The latter won only six states and the District of Columbia, while netting only 41 percent of the popular vote. The Democrats lost control of the U.S. Senate, lost thirty-three seats in the House, and sustained significant losses in state elections. The election loss was one of the most severe setbacks for the Democratic Party in contemporary times. (See table 4.)

For more information, see Frank R. Kent, *The Democratic Party: A History* (1928); Edgar Eugene Robinson, *They Voted for Roosevelt* (1947); James C. N. Paul, *Rift in the Democracy* (1951); Horace S. Merrill, *Bourbon Leader: Grover Cleveland and the Democratic Party* (1957); Ralph M. Goldman, *The Democratic Party in American Politics* (1966); Richard P. McCormick, *The Second American Party System: Party Formation in the Jackson Era* (1966); Paolo E. Coletta, *William Jennings Bryan*, 2 vols., (1969); William Domhoff, *Fat Cats and Democrats: The Role of the Big Rich in the Party of the Common Man* (1972); and Robert A. Garson, *The Democratic Party and the Politics of Sectionalism, 1941-1948* (1977).

**DEMOCRATIC-REPUBLICAN PARTY (DRP).** Founded in 1792 at New York City by Thomas Jefferson and James Madison for the purpose of opposing the political program of Alexander Hamilton and the Federalist Party.* At first called Jeffersonian Republicans or just Republicans, the DRP evolved as an outgrowth of the Anti-Federalist Party* and a coalition of those seeking to prevent the implementation of Hamiltonian policies during the administration of George Washington. Although no specific date can be pinpointed for formation of the party, the congressional faction supporting the "republican interests" had evolved into a visible entity by 1792.

When Thomas Jefferson served as secretary of state in Washington's cabinet from 1790 to 1793, he exerted leadership over the DRP. After he retired to Monticello, apparently no longer interested in politics, James Madison assumed the leadership of the DRP. As a member of the House of Representatives, Madison led the loyal opposition against the Federalists. The adherents to the DRP were in fact sometimes referred to as "Madison's party."

The political program, or platform, of the DRP championed states' rights; opposition to a strong central government; narrow construction of the U.S. Constitution; frugality in government; low tariffs; elimination of a standing army and reduction of the navy; friendship with France; and support for economic programs favoring the rural-agrarian sector over that of the urban-industrial. Members of the DNP tended to vote as a bloc against such Hamiltonian-sponsored programs as internal improvements, funding the national debt, and establishing the Bank of the United States.

In 1796 the adherents to the DRP ran Thomas Jefferson against incumbent John Adams in the presidential election. Adams received seventy-one electoral votes to sixty-eight for Jefferson, so the latter beat out Federalist Thomas Pinckney for the vice-presidency. Upon assuming his office, Jefferson also resumed command over the DRP. Through the use of the congressional caucus and with the assistance of James Madison and James Monroe, party discipline was strengthened. A party newspaper, the *National Gazette*, edited by Philip Freneau, was used to attack President John Adams, Hamilton, and the Federalist Party. The Federalist Party was portrayed as an anti-Republican party consisting of Tories, cryptomonarchists, and aristocrats. The Federalist newspaper, the *Gazette of the United States*, edited by John Fenno, depicted the DRP as being made up of Anti-Federalists, Jacobins, and those who would cater to the mob.

By 1800 the DRP had developed into a party strong enough to win a presidential election. It was the first national election in which the contest was between two parties. Aside from its general position, the DRP based its campaign on the unpopularity of the Alien and Sedition Acts and the concessions made to Great Britain for agreeing to the Treaty of London (Jay's treaty). When the electoral college voted, it gave both Thomas Jefferson and Aaron Burr seventy-three votes to sixty-five for John Adams. Because of the party haggling, the election was settled after thirty-six ballots in the House of Representatives, when Alexander Hamilton convinced enough Federalists that Jefferson would make a better president than Burr.

The revolution of 1800 was really not a revolution at all but the first presidential election carried out under a two-party system. With Jefferson's triumph the DRP controlled both the executive branch and the Congress. With great skill, President Jefferson used the spoils system and patronage to develop a party that would stay in power until 1828. He won an easy reelection victory in 1804 over Charles C. Pinckney by an electoral vote of 161 to 14.

So strong was the DRP that its presidential nominee of 1808, James Madison, won handily over Charles C. Pinckney despite the unpopularity of the Embargo Act of 1807. The electoral vote was 122 for Madison to 47 for Pinckney (George Clinton received 6 and one elector did not cast a vote). Madison won reelection in 1812 by an overwhelming electoral count of 128 to 89 for DeWitt Clinton.

Claiming victory over Great Britain in the War of 1812, due to Andrew Jackson's brilliant triumph at New Orleans after the peace treaty had already been signed, the DRP presidential nominee, James Monroe, won over Federalist Rufus King by an electoral vote of 183 to 34 in 1816. In what was called the Era of Good Feeling, Monroe was reelected in 1820 by an astounding electoral vote of 231 to 1 (the one went to John Quincy Adams). This was the high tide of the DRP's power, but four years hence it would produce its last president. In 1824 the DRP split into factions. Andrew Jackson polled 153,544 popular and 99 electoral votes to lead the list of presidential aspirants. John Quincy Adams was second with 108,740 popular and 84 electoral votes. Because the election had to be settled in the House of Representatives, old-line members of the DRP, with Speaker Henry Clay's help, chose Adams.

By 1828 the DRP had died and there emerged the Democratic Party* of Andrew Jackson. During its existence the DRP produced the Virginia dynasty and established the fact that a two-party system could function under the Constitution. Under its guidance the nation prospered, expanded, and established its total independence from Britain.

For more information, see Joseph Charles, *The Origins of the American Party System* (1956); Noble E. Cunningham, Jr., *The Jeffersonian Republicans: The Formation of Party Organization, 1789-1801* (1957); William N. Chambers, *Political Parties in a New Nation: The American Experience* (1963); and Alfred Young, *The Democratic Republicans of New York, The Origins, 1763-1797* (1967).


**DEMOCRATIC STUDY GROUP (DSG).** Founded in 1975 at Washington, D.C., by a group of newly elected members of Congress for the purpose of influencing policy making within the Democratic Party.* Seventy-five freshmen were selected in the 1974 anti-Nixon landslide election. They were predominantly reform minded and desired to achieve the following goals: end the seniority system, initiate tax reform and revenue sharing, and enact a health insurance plan. The DSG held weekly meetings, with Congressman Jerome Ambro (D-N.Y.) serving as chairman and Congressman Martin Russo (D-Ill.) acting as secretary.

This group of first-termers did indeed have an effect on Congress. Three committee chairmen lost their positions due to the DSG's efforts. It was also instrumental in terminating the oil-depletion allowance; fixing energy-consumption standards for automobiles and appliances; blocking a salary increase for the director of the Office of Management and Budget; and preventing the new Library of Congress building from being taken for office use by members of Congress. The DSG also sought a larger role in the formulation of foreign policy, desired greater federal action to lower unemployment, supported welfare reform, and agitated for more governmental regulation of gas and oil. Members of the DSG wanted to utilize the Democratic caucus to increase party discipline in voting. While yielding to some of their demands, Speaker Carl Albert (D-Okla.) and other leaders of the House of Representatives did not yield entirely to the demands of the DSG.


**DEMOCRATS.** See Democratic Party.

**DEUTSCHAMERIKANISCHE VOLKSBUND.** See German-American Bund.

**DIRTY SHIRT PARTY.** See Workingmen's Party.

**DISABLED AMERICAN VETERANS (DAV).** Founded in 1921 at Cincinnati, Ohio, by Judge Robert S. Marx, himself a disabled veteran of World War I, for the purpose of promoting greater government benefits for former members of the U.S. armed forces who suffered from war-related disabilities. Originally called the Disabled Veterans of the World War, the organization's name was changed to DAV in 1942. At this time membership was opened to veterans of World War II and all future wars. From the initial membership of one hundred present at its formation, the DAV now has some four hundred thousand members.

In order to improve the lives of its members, the DAV has assiduously striven to secure from both government (federal, state, and local) and the private business sector such benefits as adequate medical care, rehabilitation, job training, and employment for disabled veterans. The DAV was instrumental in securing establishment of a federal Veteran's Bureau (now the Veterans Administration) after World War I and lobbied for enactment of the GI Bill of Rights for World War II veterans. It agitated for and helped secure these same benefits for veterans of the Korean and Vietnam wars. In 1932 Congress granted the DAV a federal charter, designating it the "official voice of the nation's wartime disabled."

The Disabled American Veterans Auxiliary (DAVA) was founded in 1922 for women veterans and the wives of men who were members of the DAV. Currently with forty thousand members, the DAVA works to implement the objectives of the parent organization as well as provide services for dependents, especially children. The DAV-DAVA sponsor a welfare program that was initially funded by sale of small, blue forget-me-not flowers, but since 1941 funding has been based upon donations for identotags, miniature license plates mailed to automobile owners to ensure return of lost keys. An annual scholarship is awarded to the outstanding disabled veteran of the year.

The DAV promotes Americanism and organizes volunteers to visit hospitals where veterans are treated. It monitors federal legislation and agencies dealing with disabled veterans. It seeks to influence Congress to increase benefits for disabled veterans and to maintain employment priority in the civil service. Much effort has been given to achieve reforms in the Veterans Administration and to secure better medical treatment for the permanently disabled.

Current national headquarters of both the DAV and DAVA are located at Cincinnati. Denver D. Adams serves as national adjutant of the former and L. Kit Seal of the latter. From 1922 to 1960 the DAV published a newspaper, *Disabled Veteran of the World War Weekly*. This has been replaced by a monthly, *Disabled American Veterans Magazine*.

**DISABLED VETERANS OF THE WORLD WAR.** See Disabled American Veterans.

**DIXIECRAT PARTY.** See States' Rights Party.

**DU BOIS CLUBS OF AMERICA.** See W. E. B. Du Bois Clubs of America.

# _E_

**EDUCATION FOR DEMOCRACY (EFD).** Founded in 1971 at Indianapolis, Indiana, by John A. Von Kannon, publisher of a magazine, the _Alternative_, for the purpose of promoting a right-wing and anti-Communist viewpoint. It attracted relatively few members and by 1975 had become dormant. At this time former Vice-President Spiro T. Agnew revived the EFD and moved its headquarters to Crofton, Maryland. Agnew had resigned his office after pleading _nolo contendere_ to charges of income tax evasion.

Under Agnew's leadership, the EFD was established into a nonprofit organization "to promote, encourage, and support the development of public understanding and appreciation of the advantages of a democratic society." Funding was secured by soliciting $1,000 contributions from wealthy donors who subscribed to the type of conservatism as espoused by Agnew. The EFD sponsors brainstorming sessions, engages in research, conducts conferences, and disseminates information to the public. Its impact on public opinion thus far has been limited to the right wing of the Republican Party* and those belonging to extremely conservative third parties.

**EMERGENCY PEACE CAMPAIGN (EPC).** Founded in 1935 at Buck Hills, Pennsylvania, by a small group of pacifists to promote unity among anti-war and peace groups. The nationally known clergyman, Reverend Harry Emerson Fosdick, served as chairperson, and Walter Van Kirk acted as executive director. Some of the more notable members included Devere Allen, Rufus Brown, Frederick J. Libby, Ray Newton, and former Congresswoman Jeannette Rankin (she was elected to Congress once more in 1941 and as a pacifist had the distinction of having voted against U.S. entry into both World War I and World War II).

The EPC agitated for passage of the Neutrality Act by conducting a "no foreign-war crusade" on radio. Although it contributed to the isolationist and anti-interventionist sentiment of the 1930s, it failed to unite the diverse anti-war elements into a single organization. By 1937 it became moribund.

**END POVERTY IN CALIFORNIA (EPIC).** Founded in 1933 at Los Angeles by Upton Sinclair to promote social and economic reform in California. In 1934 Sinclair, a socialist and renowned proletarian novelist, won the Democratic gubernatorial primary by beating George Creel (who had the support of James Farley, chairperson of the Democratic National Committee*). As the official Democratic Party* candidate for governor, Sinclair ran on a platform calling for the establishment of self-supporting agricultural colonies; state acquisition and operation of idle factories to provide jobs for the unemployed; old-age assistance; increased taxes on the wealthy; and the implementation of other welfare measures to alleviate the suffering caused by the Great Depression.

President Franklin D. Roosevelt disapproved of the socialist orientation of EPIC and consequently did not actively support Sinclair's campaign. In a hotly contested election, the Republican* incumbent, Governor Frank E. Merriam, won reelection by a plurality of some 200,000 votes over Sinclair. This belied the closeness of the contest, since Raymond Haight, the gubernatorial nominee of two other radical parties (the Commonwealth and Progressive), polled over 300,000 votes. Had the left-of-center votes of Sinclair and Haight been combined, the GOP candidate would have been defeated.

EPIC died when regular Democrats regained control over their party in 1936. Sinclair's movement typified the radicalism of this era in which state Democratic parties of the Far West were captured by socialist or quasi-socialist groups. These groups, like Sinclair's EPIC, seldom won at the polls, but their collective actions did contribute to the groundswell of pressure that forced President Roosevelt to initiate the so-called second New Deal (which included the Social Security Act, Revenue Act of 1935, Works Progress Administration, Banking Act of 1935, Rural Electrification Administration, Resettlement Administration, Public Utilities Act, Farm Mortgage Moratorium Act, Wagner Act, and Fair Labor Standards Act).

For further information, see Upton Sinclair, *The Autobiography of Upton Sinclair* (1968), and Floyd Dell, *Upton Sinclair: A Study in Social Protest* (1970).

**EQUAL RIGHTS DEMOCRATS.** See Equal Rights (Locofoco) Party.

**EQUAL RIGHTS (LOCOFOCO) PARTY (ERP).** Founded in 1836 at New York City by a group of dissidents within the Democratic Party* for the purpose of defeating Tammany Hall* candidates. The ERP was sometimes referred to as the Friends of Equal Rights or the Equal Rights Party. Opponents dubbed them locofocos, since this recently developed type of match was used for light when Tammany officials sought to terminate a meeting by turning off the gaslights.

The ERP's platform included demands for cessation of chartering state banks; a hard-money monetary policy; popular election of the president; free trade; limitations on federal power; destruction of monopolies; and protection for labor unions. One of the prime movers in forming the ERP was William Leggett, editor of the *New York Evening Post*. Some adherents had formerly been members of the Workingmen's Party.\* By nominating fusion candidates acceptable to the Whig Party,\* the ERP was able to defeat Tammany Democrats and thus gain political control of New York City.

The ERP endorsed Martin Van Buren and worked for his nomination and election as the presidential nominee of the Democratic Party. It also supported President Van Buren's independent treasury and his other policies. By 1848 the ERP dissolved, with most of its members remaining in the Democratic Party.

For more information, see Carl N. Degler, "Locofocos: Urban 'Agrarians'" *Journal of Economic History* 16 (1956): 322–343, and Fitzwillian Byrdsall, *The History of the Loco-Foco or Equal Rights Party* (1842).

**EQUAL RIGHTS PARTY (ERP) (1872).** Founded in 1872 at New York City by feminist Victoria Claflin Woodhull for the purpose of promoting woman suffrage. In 1870 Woodhull had announced her intention of running for president and two years later proclaimed the formation of ERP for the express purpose of nominating her as its presidential candidate. Frederick Douglass, the renowned black leader, was named her vice-presidential running mate but declined.

The party itself had no membership, no organization, and never held a formal convention. It was the personal vehicle of the outspoken Woodhull and consisted of her family, friends, and some suffragists from the ranks of the National Woman Suffrage Association.\* Woodhull, a one-woman leader in the fight for equal rights for women, served well as a publicity device to dramatize the exclusion of her sex from politics. At the time, she was disliked by many women because of her behavior and was not taken seriously by men because of her eccentricity. Woodhull's actions enhanced her notoriety more than it did women's rights, since the ERP was allowed to vanish even before the election of 1872 took place.

For further information, see Emanie Sachs, *"The Terrible Siren": Victoria Woodhull (1838-1927)* (1928); Johanna Johnston, *Mrs. Satan: The Incredible Saga of Victoria C. Woodhull* (1967); and M. M. Marberry, *Vicky: A Biography of Victoria C. Woodhull* (1967).

**EQUAL RIGHTS PARTY (ERP) (1884).** Founded in 1884 at San Francisco by feminist Belva A. Bennett Lockwood, a lawyer, to promote woman suffrage and civil rights. Bennett, who used her maiden name in politics, was named the party's presidential nominee with Marietta Lizzy Bell Stow as her vice-presidential running mate. The platform called for woman suffrage; equal rights for blacks, Indians, and immigrants; enactment of a federal temperance law; passage of uniform laws in all states relative to marriage and divorce; and a commitment on the part of the United States never to go to war. On the ballot in only a few states, the Bennett-Stow ticket drew a sparse 4,169 popular votes.

Meeting in Des Moines, Iowa, in 1888 Bennett was again nominated for the presidency, this time with Charles S. Wells as the party's vice-presidential nominee. The platform once more demanded woman suffrage, prohibition, and equal rights for all Americans, and it contained a peace plank and called for civil service reform. The Bennett-Wells ticket drew fewer than one hundred popular votes and thereafter the ERP collapsed.

For more information, see Madeleine Stern, *We the Women* (1963).

**ESSEX JUNTO (EJ).** Founded in 1778 at Essex County, Massachusetts, by a group of Tory clergymen, merchants, lawyers, and political leaders for the purpose of opposing the proposed revision of the state constitution. Extremely conservative and Tory in politics, with many opposing the American Revolution, the members of the EJ were so named by their political opponent, John Hancock. The EJ did not want their state constitution democratized since they feared that mass participation in elections would lead to mob rule.

At the time the federal government was formed under the U.S. Constitution, members of the EJ supported the conservative candidates of the Federalist Party.* They also supported the fiscal and monetary policies of Alexander Hamilton, who served as treasury secretary in the cabinet of President George Washington. When Thomas Jefferson became president in 1800 and the Congress came under control of the Democratic-Republican Party,* the members of the EJ planned to form a northern confederation; the states of New England were to secede and thus form the nucleus of a new nation. Timothy Pickering was a leader in this scheme, and he approached Aaron Burr about the possibility of having New York join this confederacy. Other leading members of the EJ were George Cabot, Harrison Gray Otis, and Theophilus Parson. When Alexander Hamilton was informed of the plot, he staunchly opposed it.

Because the War of 1812 had wrought extreme economic hardship on New England, members of the EJ again agitated for secession and for concluding a separate peace with Great Britain. State officials in Massachusetts called for a convention of New England states to meet at Hartford, Connecticut. Representatives from Massachusetts, Rhode Island, and Connecticut (unofficial observers from Vermont and New Hampshire were also present) assembled at the Hartford Convention in 1814. After airing their "public grievances and concerns," the Hartford Convention adopted a series of resolutions proposing to limit the president to one term; prohibit selection of a successive president from the same state; eliminate the three-fifths clause from the U.S. Constitution; and write a series of constitutional amendments to protect New England from the rising political power of the West.

Because the Hartford Resolutions were published after Andrew Jackson's brilliant victory over the British at New Orleans, the EJ was disgraced. Due to public disfavor and internal criticism from Federalists, the EJ disbanded soon thereafter. Its record of secret plotting to break up the United States helped bring the Federalist Party into disrepute. Ironically this northern agitation for nullification and secession was adopted by the South somewhat later. New England would then become the champion of national unity.

For more information, see Shaw Livermore, Jr., *The Twilight of Federalism: The Disintegration of the Federalist Party* (1962), and David H. Fischer, *The Revolution of American Conservatism* (1964).

# _F_

**FAIR CAMPAIGN PRACTICES COMMITTEE (FCPC).** Founded in 1954 at Washington, D.C., by representatives of the Democratic* and Republican* parties and a group of religious leaders for the purpose of promoting higher ethical standards in election campaigning. Membership is relatively small, but the committee's work is important and has contributed much to the elimination of unfair campaign techniques.

The FCPC accepts complaints and investigates them to determine whether they are true. It also monitors national elections and censures those making dishonest campaign charges or engaging in smear tactics. It seeks to educate voters by providing materials for schools, disseminating information on election laws, and sponsoring conferences of representatives of civic groups, churches, and educational organizations.

National headquarters of the FCPC is located in Washington, D.C. Current executive director is Samuel J. Archibald. The FCPC maintains a library and publishes a newsletter, _Fair Comment_, and an annual _Candidate's Manual_.

**FAIR PLAY FOR CUBA COMMITTEE (FPCC).** Founded in 1960 at New York City by C. Wright Mills, a sociologist and leader of the New Left movement, for the purpose of promoting better U.S. relations with Cuba. Membership was relatively small and came from the ranks of the radical left wing in terms of the political spectrum.

Mills, a Marxian and a professor of sociology at Columbia University, wrote _Listen Yankee: The Revolution in Cuba_ (1960). He and the FPCC felt that diplomatic recognition should be extended to Fidel Castro's Communist regime. The efforts of the FPCC had little effect on public opinion, which backed the nonrecognition policy of the U.S. government and the boycott of Cuba by the Organization of American States.

In 1962 Lee Harvey Oswald started a local chapter of the FPCC in New Orleans. Oswald later gained notoriety by assassinating President John F. Kennedy in Dallas in 1963. The FPCC became moribund shortly thereafter.

**FARM BUREAU.** See American Farm Bureau Federation.

**FARMER-LABOR PARTY (FLP).** Founded in 1919 at Chicago by John Fitzpatrick, president of the Chicago Federation of Labor; Edward N. Nockels, its first national chairperson; and other socialist-oriented labor leaders. Its goal was to unite the left-of-center labor movement into an effective third party.

Formed originally as the Labor Party, it was renamed the FLP in 1920. That same year a nominating convention was held in Chicago, at which time it nominated a presidential slate and wrote a platform. Supporters of Senator Robert M. La Follette (R-Wis.) sought to promote his candidacy, but delegates selected Parley P. Christensen of Utah as their presidential nominee. Chosen as his vice-presidential running mate was Max S. Hayes of Ohio.

The FLP platform called for free coinage of silver; unemployment insurance; federally financed public works; guaranteed cost of production for farmers; rural credit; old-age pensions; a five-year moratorium on mortgage foreclosures; an end to immigration; public ownership of railroads, telegraph and telephone, cable, and other utilities; a six-hour workday with minimum wages at $1.00 per hour; higher income tax rates on incomes over $10,000 per year; increased inheritance taxes; national implementation of the initiative, referendum, and recall; tariff reduction; equal rights for women; abolition of the Federal Reserve System; prohibition of convict labor; and government regulation of the stock market.

Other demands included outlawry of the yellow-dog contract and court injunctions against strikes; a constitutional amendment to eliminate the lame-duck session of Congress and abolish the electoral college; direct election of judges; general disarmament; independence for the Philippines; abolition of holding companies; abrogation of child labor; and the unqualified observance of the constitutional right of free speech by courts, police and government officials. The last demand was to protest the activities of Attorney General A. Mitchell Palmer and other law-enforcement officials during the height of the red hysteria.

The presidential ticket of the FLP was on the ballot in seventeen states. In South Dakota it ran a joint slate with the Nonpartisan League.* In the national election of 1920, which saw Warren G. Harding win by a massive landslide, Christensen and Hayes drew only 189,339 popular votes, 1 percent of the total vote cast. The FLP was further embarrassed because Eugene V. Debs, the presidential nominee of the Socialist Party of America,* polled over 900,000 votes even though he was in prison.

The demise of the FLP was hastened in 1921 when Communists gained control over the national organization, prompting many socialists, labor leaders, and left-of-center groups to withdraw. It subsequently caused the death of a party that championed radical reform at a time when the general public preferred a return to Harding's normalcy.

The Farmer-Labor Party of Minnesota, an independent entity, continued to exist. In 1922 its candidate for governor won, as did others running for local offices. During the 1930s it tended to support the New Deal. From 1948 to his death in 1978, it was a strong supporter of Hubert H. Humphrey. In recent years, it has become periodically an important ally of the Democratic Party.*

For further information, see Murray S. Stedman and Susan W. Stedman, *Discontent at the Polls: A Study of Farmers and Labor Parties, 1827-1948* (1967), and S. A. Rice, *Farmers and Workers in American Politics* (1969).

**FARMER'S EDUCATIONAL AND COOPERATIVE UNION OF AMERICA.** See National Farmers Union.

**FARMERS HOLIDAY ASSOCIATION (FHA).** Founded in 1932 at Des Moines, Iowa, by Milo Reno, president of the Iowa Farmers Union, for the purpose of promoting a general strike of farmers. The purpose of the strike (or holiday) was to get all farmers to withhold their agricultural commodities from market so as to drive up prices. It was hoped that, by not providing food to urban areas, farm income would rise.

This strike was never widespread, since most farmers rejected the idea. Some attempts were made to stop shipments of farm commodities in the Dakotas, Illinois, Iowa, Nebraska, and Wisconsin. FHA members also tried to enforce the strike by stopping trucks on the highway and forcibly dumping the food. In Iowa violence broke out when milk and butter were dumped. Sometimes FHA members with shotguns set up barricades, but these militant attempts invariably failed. The strike did serve to attract national attention to the economic plight of farmers, whose cost of production often exceeded the prices they received. Membership in the FHA dropped quickly after Congress enacted the Agricultural Adjustment Act of 1933. When farm income rose because of the New Deal farm programs, the FHA became defunct.

For more information, see John L. Shover, *Cornbelt Rebellion: The Farmers Holiday Association* (1965).

**FARMERS UNION.** See National Farmers Union.

**FEDERALIST PARTY (FP).** Founded in 1787 at Philadelphia for the purpose of securing ratification of the newly drawn Constitution of the United States. The formation of the party developed as an outgrowth of a nationalist faction within the Continental Congress that was discernible by 1781. To present reasons why the Constitution should be ratified by the states and to counter the arguments of the Anti-Federalist Party,* Alexander Hamilton, James Madison, and John Jay wrote *The Federalist Papers* (1787-1788).

With membership heaviest in New England and the Middle Atlantic states, the Federalists campaigned for the election of delegates to state conventions who favored ratification. They were successful in their first party venture. Once the Constitution was approved and the new government was established, the Federalists controlled the presidency and the Congress. President George Washington, himself a Federalist, also appointed members of the FP to fill judiciary posts. Alexander Hamilton, serving as secretary of the treasury, formulated a program that consisted of assuming state debts, funding the national debt, creating the Bank of the United States, promoting internal improvements, and enacting a tariff aimed at protecting American industry.

During George Washington's two terms as president, the Federalists established the government as a working entity. They favored a strong central government and thus emphasized federal supremacy over the states. The FP drew its adherents from the propertied, business, professional class that favored the republican form of government and limited franchise. Relative to foreign policy, the Federalists favored military preparedness and strong ties with Great Britain. Ratification of Jay's Treaty (1794) implemented this policy.

In the 1796 presidential election, Federalist John Adams was contested by Thomas Jefferson, the candidate of the Democratic-Republican Party.* Adams won by a narrow electoral victory of seventy-one to sixty-eight. His single term as president was filled with controversy because of disunity in the FP and strong opposition from the Democratic-Republicans. Adams refused to be drawn into a war with France and insisted on armed neutrality. Passage by Congress of the Alien and Sedition Acts (1798), due to its fear of the revolutionary ideology of the French Revolution, created an adverse public reaction. The FP had failed to enlarge its membership among the masses and thus set the stage for its defeat in 1800.

In the presidential election of 1800, Thomas Jefferson triumphed over John Adams after the House of Representatives chose him over Aaron Burr. In 1804 Jefferson easily attained reelection by winning over Federalist Charles C. Pinckney by an electoral count of 162 to 14. Despite the unpopularity of the Embargo Act of 1807, Federalist Charles C. Pinckney lost the presidential election of 1808 to James Madison by an electoral vote of 122 to 47.

Federalists in New England fiercely opposed the War of 1812. Reactionary Federalists such as the Essex Junto* conspired to bring about a secession of the New England states. The Federalist-inspired Hartford Convention of 1814 created a negative impact on public opinion. In the presidential election of 1812, President James Madison won reelection over fusion candidate DeWitt Clinton by an electoral count of 128 to 89. In 1816 the third of the Virginia dynasty, James Monroe, triumphed over the last Federalist presidential nominee, Rufus King, by an electoral vote of 183 to 34.

The FP had an admirable record during the first twelve years of the nation's history by forming a government under the U.S. Constitution, but its inability after 1800 to defeat any of the presidential nominees of the Democratic-Republican Party was catastrophic to its existence as a viable political alternative. Its faiure to attract voters representing a wider economic base, plus its ill-advised position at the Hartford Convention, hastened its demise. It ran state and local candidates in 1820, but by 1824 it was virtually moribund.

For more information, see Leonard D. White, *The Federalists* (1948); Stephen G. Kurtz, *The Presidency of John Adams: The Collapse of Federalism* (1957); John C. Miller, *The Federalist Era, 1789-1801* (1960); and Shaw Livermore, *The Twilight of Federalism* (1962).

**FEDERALISTS.** See Federalist Party.

**FEDERATION OF AMERICAN ZIONISTS.** See Zionist Organization of America.

**FELLOWSHIP OF RECONCILIATION (FOR).** Founded in 1914 at Cambridge, England, by a group of Quakers, Mennonites, and Christian pacifists from Britain and Germany. Its prime purpose was to promote the spread of pacifism as a way to prevent war. An American branch was organized in 1915 and within a year had a membership of about fifteen thousand, whose goal was to keep the United States out of World War I. Some of the leaders of the American FOR included such well-known personalities as Norman Thomas, Bayard Rustin, George Houser, and Abraham J. Muste. Muste converted from communism to pacifism and worked with the FOR for the next fifty-three years. By the time of his death in 1967 he had earned the appellation Mr. Pacifist.

Although relatively small, FOR has been a significant organization in terms of its positive action on behalf of Christian pacifism. It actively promotes pacifistic opposition to war and has been responsible for serving as the leavening agent for other organizations to agitate in a nonviolent way for both peace and the advancement of civil rights.

It was instrumental in organizing the American Civil Liberties Union,* the National Conference of Christians and Jews,* and the Congress on Racial Equality* (CORE). James Farmer, an active member of FOR, became the leader of CORE to promote racial integration by using Gandhian tactics of passive resistance.

FOR contributed to the isolationist, anti-interventionist sentiment of the 1930s and opposed U.S. involvement in the Korean war, and it was one of the first organizations to speak out against the war in Vietnam. FOR's Emergency Committee on Vietnam cosponsored demonstrations with the Vietnamese Buddhist pacifist movement and later joined with American anti-war protest groups. It initiated the Brothers Project to send medical aid to both North and South Vietnam. It also counseled and rendered assistance to draft dodgers and deserters, worked for the release of political prisoners in South Vietnam, and agitated for amnesty for all war resisters.

In an era when anti-Vietnam demonstrations sometimes turned into raging riots, the FOR consistently eschewed violence. It did condone civil disobedience and was instrumental in persuading some young men to refuse to enter the military service. Thus the FOR did contribute to the breakdown in the war effort and in so doing helped end U.S. involvement in the Vietnamese conflict.

Present headquarters of FOR is in Nyack, New York. Its current executive secretary is Alfred Hassler. FOR sustains its operations by soliciting contributions. It maintains a library and publishes a monthly magazine, *Fellowship.*

For further information, see Nat Hentoff, *Peace Agitator, The Story of A. J. Muste* (1963), and Charles Chatfield, *For Peace and Justice: Pacifism in America, 1914-1941* (1971).

**FIGHT FOR FREEDOM (FFF).** Founded in 1941 at New York City by the Reverend Henry W. Hobson and a group of interventionists to promote American military assistance to Great Britain. Formed in April and existing until the Pearl Harbor attack, the FFF was led by Hobson, an Episcopalian bishop. Most active on the eastern seaboard, the FFF sought to counter the influence of the America First Committee* (AFC) and other isolationists of the period. FFF membership was relatively small, but its attacks on the AFC were telling. It charged AFC spokesman Charles Lindbergh with being both anti-Semitic and pro-Nazi in his views. The FFF also sought to refute the anti-British assertions made by Senator Gerald P. Nye (R-N.D.). By working with such organizations as the Committee to Defend America by Aiding the Allies,* the FFF helped formulate public opinion in support of President Franklin D. Roosevelt's foreign policy. Without that support, Roosevelt would not have been able to prepare the United States for its participation in World War II.

**FILIPINO AMERICAN POLITICAL ASSOCIATION (FAPA).** Founded in 1965 at Los Angeles by a group of Americans of Filipino ancestry for the purpose of promoting better social and economic conditions for Filipino-Americans. With a membership of some three hundred, the FAPA lobbies for legislation, conducts voter-registration drives, and assists newly arrived immigrants. It seeks the full participation of Filipino-Americans in the mainstream of American life, enforcement of civil rights laws, and equal job opportunities. The FAPA sponsors leadership-training seminars and disseminates information to the general public relative to minority problems. It encourages its members to take part in community affairs and to participate peacefully in the democratic system. Present national headquarters is located in Los Angeles. Current president is T. A. Mendoza. The FAPA publishes a monthly, *Fil-Am Express.*

**FOREIGN POLICY ASSOCIATION (FPA).** Founded in 1918 at New York City by Paul U. Kellogg, the editor of *Survey,* and a group of internationalists for the purpose of promoting U.S. entry into the League of Nations. Originally called the League of Nations Association, this name was changed to FPA when the U.S. Senate failed to ratify the Treaty of Versailles (or approve entry into the league). Among its founders were such prominent personages as Norman Angell, Herbert Croly, Will Durant, and Alvin H. Johnson. Significant members included Charles and Mary Beard, John R. Commons, John Dewey, Felix Frankfurter, and Ida M. Tarbell. Under the leadership of Norman Hapgood, its first president, the FPA lobbied in Congress and disseminated information to the public in an attempt to secure U.S. entry into the League of Nations.

When all attempts to promote U.S. membership in the league failed, the FPA dedicated itself to enlightening the public on matters of foreign policy and international relations. Research was initiated, publications issued, the Editorial Information Service set up, and the Speakers Bureau established to provide experts for local organizations. Initial speakers included Professor Paul A. Douglas of the University of Chicago and Professor Philip C. Jessup of Columbia University. One of FPA's early speaker-discussion programs at the Astor Hotel was given a wide audience when NBC radio gave it national airing.

In 1956 the World Affairs Center was created to act as a clearinghouse for information on international affairs for organizations and groups involved in public education. The Great Decisions program in adult education was inaugurated in 1954. By 1975 over six hundred discussion groups, involving four hundred thousand people, were using materials furnished by FPA. This program was enlarged to include high schools and college students, as well as the facilities of National Public Radio. In 1974 the FPA sponsored the first National Conference on Great Decisions in United States Foreign Policy at Washington, D.C. It also created the Task Force on Innovation to devise new methods for keeping grass-roots America informed on vital issues relating to foreign policy.

Present national headquarters is located in New York City. Current president is historian Samuel P. Hayes. FPA publications include five issues per year of *Headline Series*, and an annual, *Great Decisions*.

**FRATERNAL ORDER OF POLICE (FOP).** Founded in 1915 at Pittsburgh, Pennsylvania, by Martin L. Toole and Delbert H. Nagle, plus twenty-one other policemen, for the purpose of promoting the betterment of conditions under which the police had to work. Formed originally as the United States Association of Police, it was renamed in the first year as the FOP. William H. Larkin was elected its first president, with Delbert Nagle chosen as vice-president. The constitution that was drawn up specifically claimed that the FOP was not a labor union, and it denounced the use of the strike weapon by police officers.

Within two years, the membership of the FOP numbered about eighteen hundred. When Delbert Nagle was elected president in 1916, he decided to expand the FOP into a national organization. The FOP held its first national convention at Pittsburgh in 1917. Delegates from four lodges were present when Nagle was elected president and a constitution was adopted. The constitution stated the objectives of the FOP to be for the "purpose of bettering existing conditions of policemen" and "for advancing social, benevolent, and educational understanding among policemen." Membership was open to all police officers regardless of race, creed, or color. The stipulation was made that any member who participated in a police strike would be expelled automatically. In 1918 the FOP began publishing *Journal*.

Since many cities had ordinances forbidding the formation of labor unions for police, the FOP grew dramatically all over the country. Local lodges were formed in most big cities to unite police in their agitation for higher pay and better working conditions. Attempts by the American Federation of Labor to incorporate the FOP were staunchly resisted. When the Boston police strike took place in 1919, the FOP supported the action of Governor Calvin Coolidge. This meant the FOP approved of Coolidge's use of the state militia to restore order and of the subsequent decision not to reinstate those policemen who went out on strike. This stand gained national publicity for the FOP since the general public tended to agree with Coolidge's pronouncement, "There is no right to strike against the public safety by anybody, anywhere, anytime."

During the so-called red scare of the 1920s, the FOP supported the endeavors of Attorney General A. Mitchell Palmer in arresting radical aliens for deportation. It was always a supporter of J. Edgar Hoover until his death in 1972. Between 1920 and 1923 the FOP agitated for a national law to ban the manufacture or sale of handguns. It has consistently been in the forefront of the fight for gun-control legislation. The first legislative victory of the FOP came in 1927 when its lobbying for an eight-hour workday measure was passed by the Pennsylvania state legislature.

At its 1931 annual convention, the FOP denounced *Lawlessness in Law Enforcement*, the report of the National Commission on Law Observance, headed by Attorney General George Wickersham. Resolutions passed by the delegates claimed that the Wickersham report contained charges that "are untrue in the face of the facts, altogether unwarranted, and a blunt libel against the many tens of thousands in police service."

As the Great Depression deepened, the FOP became more politically oriented. At its 1933 convention the main speaker was Father James R. Cox, who had been the 1932 presidential nominee of the Jobless Party.* He told the assembled delegates, "Municipal officials do not want you to have a strong organization, but you should not let police be the cat's paw in politics." At that same convention a resolution was passed condemning Herbert C. Hoover for having "demoralized social, economic, industrial, financial, and agricultural life." President Franklin D. Roosevelt, on the other hand, was praised for his "inspiring leadership and forceful policies in leading us out of chaos into normal national life."

During the 1930s the FOP tried desperately to prevent police salaries from being cut, but in most cases it lost. When the Revenue Act of 1936 was enacted by Congress, extending for the first time the income tax to public employees of states and municipalities, the FOP immediately called for its repeal. This too proved unsuccessful. But in 1947 it was successful in having the Social Security Act of 1935 amended to permit police to be excluded so as to protect pension systems already in existence. Immediately after the attack on Pearl Harbor, a resolution passed at the FOP's 1941 convention, unanimously pledging loyalty to President Roosevelt "without reservation, and with all of our moral, intellectual, physical, and financial resources." During the 1950s the FOP supported bipartisan anti-Communist programs but did not endorse the activities of Senator Joseph McCarthy (R-Wis.).

The FOP has always been concerned with the manner in which movies and television portray police. During the 1930s the FOP repeatedly protested that movies were depicting criminals as folk heroes while stereotyping police as both brutal and stupid. In 1956 the FOP was so incensed over a television play, "A Long Way Home," produced by Robert Montgomery, that it initiated an economic boycott of the sponsor. As a result, the Schick Razor Company withdrew its sponsorship of NBC's "Robert Montgomery Presents." In 1951 the FOP established the Public Relations Committee to promote a favorable image of the police and to monitor the media. Because of the honorable way police were depicted in "Dragnet," it awarded television producer Jack Webb a plaque for "presenting a true picture of police procedure in his television show."

During the civil rights demonstrations and anti-Vietnam war demonstrations of the 1960s, the FOP defended police officers against repeated charges of police brutality. It ran advertisements with a caption under the picture of a police officer reading, "Some call him pig! I call him officer and sir!" Enjoined both to keep crime down and enforce narcotics laws, the FOP was critical of the U.S. Supreme Court for its 1966 *Miranda* decision. The FOP claimed that the police were deprived of adequate means of catching and convicting criminals, with society the loser. As the number of police review boards over the nation increased, the FOP's Legal Defense Fund, established in 1943, came to the assistance of its members who were charged with police brutality. In 1962 when Attorney General Robert F. Kennedy asked for congressional legislation to make it easier to convict police accused of brutality, the FOP lobbied against such a law. Its Legislative Committee, formed in 1940, set about to propose legislation that would make it a crime to accuse falsely a police officer. FOP's Committee on Human Rights and Law Enforcement, set up in 1956, contended that police review boards often violated the civil rights of individual police officers. It prepared a pamphlet for dissemination to the public, *Police Review Boards: A Threat to Law Enforcement.*

In 1965 Senator John McClellan (D-Ark.) sponsored an FOP proposal that survivorship benefits of $25,000 be paid by the government if a police officer was killed enforcing a federal law. This measure was eventually altered so that the sum would be 75 percent of an officer's yearly pay and in that form was signed into law by President Lyndon B. Johnson. Continued lobbying by the FOP secured enactment in 1976 of the Public Safety Officers Benefit Act. It pays $50,000 to dependents of officers killed in the line of duty while enforcing any law. Following President Gerald R. Ford's approval of this legislation, Ford was endorsed for the presidency by Robert H. Stark, FOP's president. In recent years the FOP has worked to attain collective bargaining for police (it no longer enforces its no-strike clause), seeks to influence public opinion favorably for increases in wages, and has consistently opposed the hiring of homosexuals by police departments. The National Women's Auxiliary was established in 1941, and in 1955 a highway safety campaign was initiated.

National headquarters of the FOP are located in Tucson, Arizona. Membership totals over 128,000 in some eight hundred local lodges. Current president is Robert H. Stark. The FOP is affiliated with the National Conference of Public Employee Retirement System. It publishes a quarterly, *National FOP Journal*, and an annual, *Survey of Salaries and Working Conditions of Police in the U.S.*

For more information, see Justin E. Walsh, *The Fraternal Order of Police, 1915-1976* (1977).

**FREE DEMOCRACY OF THE UNITED STATES.** See Free Soil Party.

**FREE DEMOCRATIC PARTY.** See Free Soil Party.

**FREE LIBERTARIAN PARTY.** See Libertarian Party.

**FREE SOIL PARTY (FSP).** Founded in 1848 at Buffalo, New York, by an assemblage of delegates representing antislavery groups for the purpose of forming a political party dedicated to the principle of "Free Soil, Free Speech, Free Labor, and Free Men." The FSP represented a coalition of segments of the near-defunct Liberty Party* (1839), Conscience (anti-slavery) Whigs, and Barnburner faction of the Democratic Party.* The convention nominated ex-President Martin Van Buren for the presidency and Charles Francis Adams of Massachusetts as his vice-presidential running mate. The platform demanded "No more Slave States and no more Slave Territory," free homesteads for actual settlers, cheap postage, a revenue-producing tariff, and river and harbor improvements to promote commerce.

In a three-man presidential race with Zachary Taylor representing the Whig Party* and Lewis Cass the Democrats, Van Buren polled 291,263 popular and no electoral votes. This constituted the smallest total of the three, but this 10.14 percent of the popular vote did contribute to the defeat of the Democratic nominee. The Free-Soilers also elected Salmon P. Chase to the U.S. Senate and thirteen members to the House of Representatives.

In 1851 the nominating convention of the FSP met at Pittsburgh, Pennsylvania, to select John P. Hale of New Hampshire as the presidential candidate and George W. Julian as his vice-presidential running mate. Identifying themselves as the "Free Democracy of the United States" (or Free Democratic Party), the platform labeled slavery a "sin against God and a crime against man." Specific planks condemned the Fugitive Slave Act and the Compromise of 1850. It reiterated its demand for "no more Slave States, no more Slave Territory"; low postage rates; free homesteads; improvement of rivers and harbors; no abridgement of the rights of immigrants; no French intervention to be permitted in Mexico; recognition of Haiti's independence; and arbitration in the settlement of international disputes.

In the presidential election of 1852, Hale was pitted against Democrat Franklin Pierce and Whig Winfield Scott. The FSP candidate drew the smallest vote in losing to Pierce. Hale's total was 155,825 popular and no electoral votes, less than 5 percent of the total ballots cast. This poor showing doomed the FSP, which by 1854 was defunct. By 1856 most of its adherents found their way into the newly formed Republican Party.* Although short-lived, the FSP played a significant role in galvanizing anti-slavery sentiment so as to make it an important political issue. (See table 5.)

For more information, see Richard H. Sewall, *John P. Hale and the Politics of Abolition* (1965); Eric Foner, *Free Soil, Free Labor, Free Men: The Ideology of the Republican Party before the Civil War* (1970); and Frederick J. Blue, *The Free Soilers: Third Party Politics, 1848-1854* (1973).

**TABLE 5 Free Soil Party Presidential Candidates and Votes, 1848-1852**

| YEAR | CANDIDATE | TOTAL POPULAR VOTE |
|------|-----------|--------------------|
| 1848 | Martin Van Buren | 291,263 |
| 1852 | John P. Hale | 155,825 |

**FREE SPEECH LEAGUE (FSL).** Founded in 1902 at New York City by Theodore Schroeder and other civil libertarians for the purpose of defending the constitutional right of free speech. In a membership that never exceeded a few hundred, FSL's most notorious member was the anarchist Emma Goldman. Other noteworthy adherents were an array of liberals, including Leonard D. Abbott, Ernest Crosby, Bolton Hall, Charles Spahr, Benjamin Tucker, Brand Whitlock, and the famed muckraker Lincoln Steffens.

The FSL initially was formed in reaction to the public hysteria and governmental harassment of radical dissidents. It sought to ensure constitutional guarantees, especially of free speech, for those who advocated unpopular causes. This did not mean that the FSL endorsed such views, only the right to advocate them.

In 1911 the FSL officially incorporated as a legal entity, with Leonard Abbott serving as president. Its primary activity was to defend radicals and extremists when their unlimited right to speak was curtailed. It also fought to stop what it considered illegal deportations and strove to get sedition laws repealed as unconstitutional. FSL's spirited defense of opponents of World War I created an adverse public reaction. Critical sentiment ran so high in 1920 that the FSL became a casualty of the red hysteria. Most of its members gravitated into the similar but better organized American Civil Liberties Union.*

**FREEDOM AND PEACE PARTY (FPP).** Founded in 1968 at Chicago by Richard "Dick" Gregory, a former comedian and television star (and dissident member of the Peace and Freedom Party*), to focus public attention on civil rights and the need to end the war in Vietnam. Carrying the presidential banner of the FPP, Dick Gregory's campaign was more in the nature of a one-man speaking tour on college campuses. In countless such talks he denounced racism, U.S. imperialism, big business, and American materialism. He spoke with a mixture of seriousness, satire, and humor.

At the polls, Gregory drew 47,133 popular votes in the 1968 presidential election. Although his party ceased to exist, he continued speaking on college campuses, did some writing, and occasionally fasted to focus attention on causes that were of interest to him.

For more information, see Richard C. Gregory, *Dick Gregory's Political Primer* (1970), and Hanes Walton, Jr., *Black Politics* (1972).

**FREEDOM CENTER INTERNATIONAL (FCI).** Founded in 1958 at Salem, Oregon, by the Reverend Walter Huss (its first and current president) for the purpose of stopping the spread of atheistic communism. Formed originally as the Salem Anti-Communist Clinic, it soon was renamed the FCI. Its objective was to alert Christians and the general public to the dangers of communism. To achieve this, the FCI sponsored rallies and conferences and disseminated information on how to detect and combat Communists.

The Reverend Huss, formerly a clergyman associated with the International Church of the Foursquare Gospel (founded by Aimee Semple McPherson), modeled the FCI after Dr. Fred Schwartz's Christian Anti-Communism Crusade.* Membership in FCI is relatively small at present since the rampant anti-Communist hysteria of the cold war era no longer exists. FCI's appeal was mainly to those of a lower socioeconomic background and fundamentalist religious persuasion. It rallied public opinion for a time against recognition of the People's Republic of China, but that support has eroded. With national headquarters in Salem, the FCI publishes a newspaper, the *National Eagle*.

**FREEDOM DEMOCRATS.** See Mississippi Freedom Democratic Party.

**FREEDOM NOW PARTY (FNP).** Founded in 1963 at Washington, D.C., by Conrad L. Lynn, a New York lawyer and its national chairman, and other blacks, for the purpose of establishing an all-black political party. Its platform stressed civil rights and equal job opportunities. Candidates were selected to run in the 1963 off-year elections in the states of California, Connecticut, and New York. Neither black nor white voters gave it much support, and as a consequence all FNP candidates fared badly at the polls.

In 1964 it was decided to enter FNP candidates only in the state of Michigan. Since that state had a black population of over 750,000, it was hoped that the FNP would demonstrate to the Democrats* and Republicans* that black voters held the political balance of power. The state chairman of FNP, Albert Cleage, a Congregationalist minister, entered a slate of thirty-nine candidates for offices ranging from U.S. senator to county positions. Again the FNP candidates drew so few votes it doomed the existence of the party as a permanent entity. Its demise seemed to indicate that a political party appealing to just one race cannot succeed in a system where major parties solicit the votes of minorities.

For more information, see Hanes Walton, Jr., *Black Political Parties: An Historical and Political Analysis* (1972).

**FREEDOMS FOUNDATION AT VALLEY FORGE (FF-VF).** Founded in 1949 at Valley Forge, Pennsylvania, by E. F. Hutton of New York City,

Don Belding of Los Angeles, and Dr. Kenneth Wells (its first president) of Pennsylvania, for the purpose of promoting patriotism. Originally called Freedoms Foundation, its name was changed to FF-VF in 1953. The latter's key goal involves "promoting an understanding and appreciation of America's political, social, spiritual, and economic institutions, and encouraging Americans to become responsible citizens." The FF-VF carries out "national programs of information and education that preserve our heritage of free government and traditional American values." Its work is supported by dues-paying members and contributions from individuals, companies, organizations, and foundations.

With national headquarters near the site where George Washington established his winter quarters during the Revolutionary War, the FF-VF constructed an educational and research center covering 105 acres. The complex includes the Martha Washington Building, which serves as administrative headquarters; General Henry Knox Building, which honors recipients of the Congressional Medal of Honor; Alexander Hamilton Residence Building, where teacher and youth seminars are held; Visitor Center, dedicated by former President Gerald R. Ford (who is also Honorary Chairman); and the Douglas MacArthur Educational Building. The latter houses such special collections as the J. Edgar Hoover Research Library on communism; Albert W. Hawkes Library on the American Credo; Spirit of '76 Library; Norris D. Wright Collection on American History; Richard W. Sears Collection on Free Enterprise; George Washington Carver Collection on Negro Contributions to America's Heritage; and General MacArthur's Collection of U.S. Flags.

On Freedom Hill stands a monument called "The American Credo." Inscribed upon it is the following:

Political and economic rights which protect the dignity and freedom of the individual: Right to Worship God in One's Own Way; Right to Free Speech and Press; Right to Peaceably Assemble; Right to Petition for Redress of Grievances; Right to Privacy in Our Homes; Right of Habeas Corpus—No Excessive Bail; Right to Trial by Jury—Innocent Until Proven Guilty; Right to Move About Freely at Home and Abroad; Right to Own Private Property; Right to Free Elections and Personal Secret Ballot; Right to Work in Callings and Localities of Our Choice; Right to Bargain with Our Employers and Employees; Right to Go into Business, Compete, Make a Profit; Right to Bargain for Goods and Services in a Free Market; Right to Contract About Our Affairs; Right to the Service of Government as a Protector and Referee; and Right to Freedom from Arbitrary Government Regulation and Control.

Other facilities located at the FF-VF include The Faith of Our Fathers Chapel; Independence Garden; Ampitheatre of the Unknown Soldier; and Medal of Honor Grove. Exhibits on display include "Man's Search for Freedom," illustrating the twelve major documents playing a role in the development of the U.S. Constitution; "American Credo Display," dealing with the rights and responsibilities of American citizens; "A Nation to Be Proud of . . . ," highlighting lesser-known technological, agricultural, social, and artistic achievements; "Patriots Hall of Fame," honoring famous American men and women for their contributions to the development of the United States; and the "Famous Newspaper Carriers of America," depicting now-famous Americans who were once newsboys.

The FF-VF bestows awards to foster and promote the political, social, spiritual, and economic values it cherishes. Included among the current recipients are: Dr. Alton Ochsner, who received the George Washington Award (its highest) for "speaking clearly on vital issues of health and on the responsibilities of his [medical] profession"; Ambassador Shirley Temple Black, American Exemplar Medal for "combining her talent with dedication, hard work, and high personal standards to serve the public, her family, and her country"; Carl Karcher, Private Enterprise Exemplar Medal "for his spirited support of private enterprise and of our nation"; and Dr. Michael Marcase, the American Citizenship Medal "for bringing families into the search for solutions to educational problems."

In the field of journalism those honored included: Lee S. Anderson of the Chattanooga *News-Free Press*, the George Washington Honor Medal for an editorial titled, "How the System Works," which pointed out how "government interference in the free market results in reduced productivity and lower standard of living"; Millie Pogna in the Letters-to-the-Editors category, the George Washington Honor Medal for advocating that "school children should learn of the superiority of our free enterprise system and about their priceless American heritage"; Jeff MacNelly for a syndicated cartoon critical of excessive government regulations; and Jake Garn, the George Washington Honor Medal for a published article titled, "America's Stake in SALT II," which warned, "the Soviets have achieved strategic superiority by outspending us in the development of weapons systems."

In the category of Platform and Pulpit winners of George Washington Honor Medals included: Robert F. Kane for a critique labeled "The Escalating Arrogance of Judicial Power," which maintained, "our Constitution from time to time has been construed in ways differing from those intended by the Founding Fathers"; movie star James Stewart for asserting "we should think about the good things in our lives and remember that America is the best country anywhere, even with all of the problems"; and Gordon K. Van Vleck for a speech titled, "The Time to Resurrect Capitalism." Valley Forge Honor Certificate Awards were given to Nicholas P. Kriskes for his talk on "Myths of the British National Health Service" and Peter T. Flawn for "Democracy and Excellence in America."

Other categories where awards were given include Youth Public Addresses and Journalism, College Campus Programs, Advertising/Public Affairs, Corporate and Nonprofit Publications, and Electronic Communications/Film. In the later designation, one of the Motion Picture Principal Awards went to the National Film Board of Canada for its presentation, "The New Alchemist," and one of the Television Principal Awards went to ABC for its special, "John Denver's Rocky Mountain Reunion." Among Radio Programs, George Washington Honor Medal Awards went to KOIT-FM in San Francisco for the program, "Crime Versus Law and Order," and to WIND in Chicago for "Mid-America Views America: The State of the Union at Midyear."

Additional categories include Community and National Activities, Economic Education Programs, and Americana. Among the recipients of awards in the latter category were the Business Industry Political Action Committee* and the National Right to Work Legal Defense Foundation, Inc. Recognition is also given in the areas of government, patriots, education, and school programs. All awards are given on George Washington's birthday and are bestowed to "recognize accomplishments in terms of constructive words and deeds which support the United States social, political, and economic system; suggest solutions to basic problems; and contribute to responsible citizenship."

Academic programs sponsored by the FF-VF include graduate seminars, youth conferences, and American heritage workshops. The current president is Dr. Robert W. Miller. The FF-VF publishes its *Annual Nation Awards* yearly and a *Newsletter* on an irregular basis.

**FREE-STATE PARTY (FSP).** Founded in 1855 at Topeka by a group of anti-slavery settlers for the purpose of making Kansas a free state. Following enactment by Congress of the Kansas-Nebraska Act of 1854, both pro-slavery settlers from Missouri and anti-slavery groups from New England rushed into Kansas. The pro-slavery faction organized a state government at Lecompton and submitted its constitution to the U.S. Congress. The FST organized a rival government and wrote its own constitution, but it banned slavery in Kansas.

The result was constant warfare between the two groups until "bleeding Kansas" became a miniature civil war battleground. When the Lecompton constitution was submitted to Kansas voters in a referendum, the FSP was instrumental in persuading the settlers to reject it. The FSP ultimately triumphed in 1861 when Kansas joined the Union as a free state. Most adherents to the FSP later became affiliated with the Republican Party.*

For more information, see Alice Nichols, *Bleeding Kansas* (1954).

**FRIENDS OF THE EARTH.** See League of Conservation Voters.

**FRIENDS PEACE COMMITTEE (FPC).** Founded in 1892 at Philadelphia by the Society of Friends for the purpose of promoting peace. Pacifist John B. Garrett was the prime mover in its formation and served as its first president (until 1916). The organization was known as the Philadelphia Peace Association of Friends until 1916, when it was briefly renamed the Emergency Peace Committee. It was again renamed, this time the Committee on Peace and Emergency Service (1917-1929), and was once again altered to the Committee on Peace and Service (1920-1933). In 1933 it absorbed the Peace Committee of the Religious Society of Friends of Philadelphia and Vicinity to become the FPC.

The devout Quakers who make up FPC's membership are very small in number but exert considerable influence because of their willingness to suffer for their religious beliefs. Members of the FPC refuse to be drafted into the armed forces, protest the use of taxes for military purposes, practice civil disobedience, and utilize nonviolent demonstrations. They participate not only in anti-war protests but also those related to economic exploitation and racial discrimination.

The FPC uncompromisingly opposed U.S. participation in the Spanish-American War, World War I, World War II, Korean war, and Vietnam war. During Vietnam the FPC staged protest demonstrations, advised draftees not to serve in the armed forces, and joined with other anti-war groups to influence public opinion against continuing the Vietnam conflict. The FPC calls for total disarmament, an end to Reserve Officers Training Corps programs, and destruction of nuclear weapons, and it has initiated counter-recruitment programs to discourage enlistments in the voluntary armed services.

Members of the FPC testify and lobby against military appropriations; sponsor aid missions to war-torn countries; support voluntary family planning and population control; and have inaugurated the Proxy-Bank so that groups holding corporate stocks can vote their shares for peace-related proposals and against those related to war. In 1973 it began the Nonviolence and Children Program to educate children up to junior-high-school age on the moral reasons for renouncing war. The FPC maintains the Peace Information Center, conducts vigils, operates a speakers' bureau, and promotes programs for international peace.

The FPC is governed by a sixty-six-member board of trustees appointed by the Philadelphia Yearly Meeting of the Religious Society of Friends. George C. Hardin currently serves as executive secretary. FPC publications include special pamphlets and a monthly newsletter, *Peace*.

**FUERZAS ARMÁDAS DE LIBERACÍON NACIONAL PUERTORRI-QUEÑA (FALN).** Founded in 1950 at Jayuya, Puerto Rico, by Don Pedro Albizu Campos and other Puerto Rican revolutionaries for the purpose of winning independence through armed insurrection. Also referred to as the Armed Forces of Puerto Rican National Liberation, these militant nationalists staged a military revolt on October 30, 1950. Three days after it was suppressed by Puerto Rican police and National Guardsmen, two FALN commandos sought to assassinate President Harry S. Truman at the Blair House, where he was staying while the White House was undergoing repairs. The would-be assassins were Griselio Torresola (who was killed) and Oscar Collazo. Collazo was wounded during his capture, tried, and sentenced to death (later commuted to life imprisonment).

On March 1, 1954, another group of four FALN commandos engaged in violent activity within the United States. While seated in the spectators' gallery, they suddenly shouted, "Freedom for Puerto Rico." In an instant they began shooting at the 234 members of the House of Representatives who were present. Five Congressmen were wounded during this attack. Capitol police quickly captured the FALN revolutionaries: Lolita Lebrón, Rafael Miranda, Andrés Cordero, and Irving Flores. All were tried, convicted, and imprisoned for their armed assault on the members of Congress. By 1980 all had been released or pardoned.

Although illegal and operating underground, members of the FALN continued to plot for the day when Puerto Rico will become an independent nation. Their numbers are small, and their influence on the Puerto Rican population is not very strong. Most Puerto Ricans prefer commonwealth status, which confers U.S. citizenship and the right to live in the continental boundaries of the United States. If Puerto Rico became an independent nation, it would be subject to immigration quotas. Thus Puerto Ricans living in the United States would also have to decide whether to stay as U.S. citizens or return home as Puerto Rican citizens.

In 1975 the FALN renewed its activities, possibly in conjunction with the underground Weatherman,* with a series of bombings in Chicago, New York City, and Washington, D.C. To gain publicity, members claimed responsibility for these acts of terrorism. One of their acknowledged leaders, who was freed from jail through legal means, was Carlos Feliciano. Nothing is known of other members or their method of operation. Periodically they claim credit for bombings. The Committee for the Freedom of Puerto Rican Nationalist Prisoners was formed in 1976 in attempt to gain the release of those revolutionaries convicted for acts of terror.

Over the years a hundred or more bombings in such cities as New York, Chicago, San Francisco, and Washington, D.C., have been attributed to the FALN. In 1976 and 1978 police raids were made on explosives factories operated by the FALN. When the Federal Bureau of Investigation raided a suspected bomb factory in Jersey City, New Jersey, it discovered documents indicating the FALN was planning bombings at the 1980 nominating conventions of both the Democratic and Republican parties. Also in 1980 police in Chicago arrested eleven members of the FALN, including Carlos Alberto Torres, who was number one on the FBI's most wanted list, for possession of firearms (including sawed-off shotguns) and conspiracy to commit armed robbery. After conviction, eight members of the group, including Torres, received prison sentences of five years each. Luis Rosa and Alicia Rodriquez received thirty-year prison terms after being convicted of armed robbery and conspiracy. Marie Haydee Torres was extradited to New York where she was convicted of a bombing at the Mobil Oil Company building where one person was killed. She received a life sentence.

Members of the FALN, when brought to trial for theft, robbery, or terrorist activities, claim to be political prisoners not bound by American civil law. They do not participate in their trials and claim that convictions violate international law. This revolutionary stance contradicts legal procedure in the United States and runs counter to the democratic process. The cause of Puerto Rican independence has not been furthered by the violence perpetrated by the FALN. Its activities have resulted only in terror and tragedy.

# G

**GERMAN-AMERICAN BUND (GAB).** Founded in 1936 at Buffalo, New York, by Fritz Julius Kuhn for the purpose of promoting naziism among German-Americans living in the United States. The formation of *Deutschamerikanische Volksbund* (the bund's German name) stemmed from two other organizations, the Teutonic Society (1925) and the Friends of New Germany (1933). Kuhn, a member of both groups and leader of the second, also belonged to the German Nazi Party and envisioned himself a future American fuehrer.

While living in Germany, Kuhn had taken part in the famous beer hall putsch of 1923, the abortive attempt of Adolf Hitler to take over Bavaria. After emigrating to the United States in 1924, he became active in promoting German nationalism. Upon founding the GAB in 1936, Kuhn bestowed upon himself the title of *bundsfuehrer* and adopted the swastika as the bund's symbol. In a public statement he declared, "The German-American Bund is definitely a political organization. It is our purpose to fight for the honor of the new Germany and against the Jewish boycott. . . . Whatever we have accomplished until now is merely a preliminary to what we shall do in the future. . . . Our task is to create a united German front in America."

In the constitution of the GAB, members were admonished, "To be and remain worthy of our Germanic blood, our German motherland, and German brothers and sisters, and to cultivate our German language, customs, and ideals; and to be upstandingly proud of these principles." For organizational purposes the United States was divided into three *gaue* (districts): East, with headquarters in New York City, Midwest, with headquarters in Chicago, and West, with headquarters in Los Angeles. Local chapters were called *Ortsgruppen* (local groups) and were led by an *Ortsgruppenleiter* (local group leader). Seventy-eight local chapters were established, with a membership estimated at from six thousand to twenty thousand. The following auxiliary groups were also formed: *Jungendschaft* for boys,

*Frauenschaft* for girls, *Deutsche Verband* for businessmen, *Prospective Citizens League* for those desiring German citizenship, and a paramilitary unit (resembling the Brown Shirts of the German Nazis), the *Ordnungsdienst*. The GAB published a weekly magazine, *Deutsch Weckruf und Beobachter* ("German Awakener and Observer").

Membership in the GAB was never really large considering the millions of German-Americans living in the United States. Most Americans of German heritage were repulsed by naziism. In 1938 the GAB was investigated by both the House Committee on Un-American Activities and the New York State legislature. After Congress enacted the Alien Registration Act, the GAB was forced to register as an agent of a foreign government. Because of the anti-Semitism and pro-Nazi stance of the GAB, its rallies frequently erupted in violence when hecklers sought to disrupt meetings. Kuhn was regarded by many as a would-be Hitler and was therefore despised by onlookers.

In 1939 Fritz Kuhn was indicted and convicted of grand larceny for embezzling funds from the GAB. While in prison, he was also deprived of his U.S citizenship on the grounds that he was a subversive agent of a foreign country. Leadership of the GAB fell to Gerhard Wilhelm Kunze. When Germany declared war on the United States in 1941, Kunze fled to Mexico. Soon he was apprehended and returned to the United States. Subsequently Kunze was tried, convicted, and sent to prison for espionage. Many other GAB members were also arrested by the Federal Bureau of Investigation. Some were released but kept under surveillance, and a few were detained for the duration of World War II. By 1942 the GAB was totally defunct.

For more information, see Leland V. Bell, *In Hitler's Shadow: The Anatomy of American Naziism* (1973), and Sander A. Diamong, *The Nazi Movement in the United States, 1924-1941* (1975).

**GOLD BUGS.** See National Democratic Party.

**GOLD DEMOCRATS.** See National Democratic Party.

**GOP.** See Republican Party.

**GOVERNORS' CONFERENCE.** See National Governors' Conference.

**GRAND ARMY OF THE REPUBLIC (GAR).** Founded in 1865 at Springfield, Illinois, by Dr. B. F. Stephenson, a former surgeon of the Fourteenth Illinois Infantry, and a group of ex-Civil War soldiers for the purpose of promoting benefits for veterans. Others involved in the formation of the GAR were Congressman John A. Logan (R-Ill.), formerly a brevet general in the Union army during the Civil War, and Republican Governor

Richard J. Oglesby, also a former Union officer. These two politicians saw political advantage in organizing the veterans' vote for the Republican Party.*

The first GAR post was established at Decatur, Illinois, in 1866, and in a short time local posts sprang up all over the country. At its first national encampment in 1866 at Indianapolis, Indiana, General Stephen A. Hurlbut was elected commander in chief. Membership was opened to all men who had served in the U.S. Army, Navy, or Marines. In 1868 the GAR was instrumental in securing May 30 as Memorial Day in commemoration of those members of the Union armed forces who died during the Civil War.

Very shortly after its formation the Radical Republicans* (those favoring a harsh Reconstruction policy in the South) readily passed legislation providing pensions for Civil War veterans in return for GAR votes in electing Republicans to Congress. By "waving the bloody shirt" and advising veterans to "vote as you shot," the GAR was molded into a virtual political ally of the GOP. With the exception of Grover Cleveland's two terms as president, the GAR helped the Republicans control the White House from 1869 to 1912. President Cleveland incurred the wrath of the GAR by vetoing private pension bills, and this may have contributed to his defeat in the national election of 1888.

Membership in the GAR reached its height in 1890, when it totaled 408,489. In 1889 a southern organization was formed, calling itself the United Confederate Veterans, but none of its 50,000 members shared in any of the benefits gained by the GAR. The last national encampment of the GAR took place at Indianapolis, Indiana, in 1949. Six of the surviving sixteen Civil War veterans were able to attend. The last member of the GAR died in 1956.

For more information, see Mary R. Dearing, *Veterans in Politics: The Story of the G.A.R.* (1952).

**GRAND OLD PARTY.** See Republican Party.

**GRANGE.** See National Grange.

**GRAY PANTHERS (GP).** Founded in 1970 at Philadelphia by Maggie Kuhn and a group of senior citizens for the purpose of promoting a better way of life for older people. Maggie Kuhn, who was seventy years old at the time, was a former national official in the Young Women's Christian Asssociation of the United States of America. She was chosen president and still serves in that capacity.

The GP has a relatively small membership—its mailing list is around eight thousand—but it claims to speak for thirty-two million Americans over sixty years of age who represent about 15 percent of the total U.S. population. Operating from its headquarters in a church near the University of Pennsylvania, the GP seeks to influence public opinion so as to change the stereotype connected with aging. It has been critical of banks, nursing homes, mass-transit authorities, the American Medical Association, television, and Congress for discriminatory attitudes or inaction concerning the welfare of senior citizens. It lobbied successfully to get Congress to eliminate mandatory retirement at age sixty-five. It has also agitated for removal of restrictions on the amount of income an individual can receive without losing Social Security benefits. The GP lobbies for better Medicare benefits and federal housing for the aged.

One of the projects carried out by the GP was its media watch. Its members monitored television networks in order to see how older people were depicted. It claimed that television discriminated against old people; for example, contestants on giveaway programs were invariably young or middle-aged. It also criticized the portrayal of aged individuals as demeaning. Joining with Ralph Nader's Public Interest Research Group,* GP seeks to get additional television programming for senior citizens and more consideration by business and governmental agencies for the needs of those over age sixty.

Currently, the GP has local chapters in about twenty cities. Its prime objective is to change attitudes so that old age is viewed as a period in life when individuals should be respected for their longevity and sagacity.

For more information, see Henry J. Pratt, *The Gray Lobby* (1977).

**GREEN CROSS.** See National Safety Council.

**GREENBACK INDEPENDENT PARTY.** See Greenback Party.

**GREENBACK NATIONALIST PARTY.** See Greenback Party.

**GREENBACK PARTY (GP).** Founded in 1874 at Indianapolis, Indiana, by a group of delegates representing locals of the National Grange,* Knights of Labor, and various other rural or local labor organizations, for the purpose of promoting changes in monetary policy. The GP, known alternately as the Greenback-Labor Party (and listed on the ballot in some states as the Independent Party or the National Party), formed as a reaction to the panic of 1873. It also resisted actions by creditors to remove from circulation the nearly $400 million of paper money (greenbacks) issued by the U.S. government during the Civil War. Farmers and workers, representing the debtor class, desired to have greenbacks declared legal tender and remain permanently in circulation. The GP desired so-called cheap money (inflation) rather than dear money (deflation).

In 1876 the GP nominated an eighty-five-year-old philanthropist, Peter Cooper, as its presidential nominee. Samuel F. Cary of Ohio was chosen as his vice-presidential running mate. The platform demanded the issuance of U.S. notes (paper money) as legal tender, repeal of the Specie-Resumption Act of 1875, the cessation of the sale of gold bonds to foreign buyers, and the practice of issuing silver bonds. The ticket drew 81,737 popular votes. (See table 6.)

TABLE 6 Greenback Party Presidential Candidates and Votes, 1876-1888

| YEAR | CANDIDATE | TOTAL POPULAR VOTE |
|------|-----------|--------------------|
| 1876 | Peter Cooper | 81,737 |
| 1880 | James G. Weaver | 308,578 |
| 1884 | Benjamin Butler | 175,370 |
| 1888 | Anson J. Streeter | 146,935 |

The GP grew in strength, reflected by its gains in the mid-term election of 1878. It pulled over a million votes and elected fourteen of its candidates to Congress. With high expectations, in 1880 the GP nominated General James G. Weaver of Iowa as its presidential standard-bearer and Benjamin J. Chambers for the vice-presidency. In militant language the platform called for issuance of paper money for the "common good"; unlimited coinage of silver; an eight-hour workday; abolition of contract (prison) labor; abrogation of child (under fourteen) labor; Chinese exclusion; forfeiture of railroad land grants for nonfulfillment of contracts; breaking up monopolies; graduated income tax; reduction of military expenditures; and the enfranchisement of all citizens. The Greenbackers were disappointed when their ticket attracted only 308,578 votes.

Still militant in its representation of the lower class, the GP continued to attack both the Democratic* and Republican* parties in its 1884 platform. It nominated General Benjamin F. Butler, an erstwhile Radical Republican,* as its presidential candidate and chose Absolom M. West of Mississippi as his running mate. It defiantly charged that the "dominant parties are arrayed against the people, and are the abject tools of the corporate monopolies." A series of planks denounced trusts and demanded their dissolution and called for government regulation of interstate commerce; the establishment of a government postal telegraph system; a graduated income tax; cheap money; adequate pensions for disabled Civil War veterans; a revised tariff geared for raising revenue from the import of luxury items; woman suffrage; and a constitutional amendment reducing the terms of U.S. senators. The ticket pulled only 175,370 votes.

In 1888 the weakened GP fused with the Union Labor Party* to field a presidential ticket. It too fared rather badly at the polls, so in 1892 the remnants of the GP merged with the rising Populist Party.* The GP did not reemerge as a separate entity until 1918. At that time, it was brought back to life by Indiana reformer John Zahnd, who became the GP's perennial presidential candidate from 1924 until 1940 (paired with various vice-presidential nominees), but attracted so few votes as to be insignificant. No candidate was chosen for 1944.

The 1948 presidential ticket of John G. Scott of New York and Granville B. Leeke of Indiana drew a negligible vote. The last person to head the GP as a presidential nominee was Frederick C. Proehl of Washington. He was paired with J. Edward Bedell of Indiana in 1952 and with Edward K. Meador of Mississippi in 1956. In these elections, the GP platform attacked the Federal Reserve System as constituting "legalized robbery." Other planks were so extremist and right wing in outlook that they were ignored by the electorate. Proehl's total vote was so miniscule that the GP ceased to qualify on any single state ballot, and the GP disappeared from the American political scene.

During its zenith, the GP called attention to the need for currency reform, although its simplistic solutions were rejected by the mass of voters. The need for a flexible monetary system was correct, but inflation schemes based on issuing paper (fiat) money would have been disastrous. Nevertheless the GP's agitation did promote some remedial legislation to alleviate the plight of the debtor class. By the time the Populist Party was formed, the GP had lost the influence it once had wielded.

For further information, see Irwin Unger, *The Greenback Era* (1964) and Walter T. K. Nugent, *Money and American Society* (1968).

**GREENBACK-LABOR AND NATIONAL PARTY.** See Greenback Party.

**GREENBACK-LABOR PARTY.** See Greenback Party.

# H

**HARTFORD CONVENTION.** See Essex Junto.

**HOME PROHIBITION PARTY.** See Prohibition Party.

**HUMAN RIGHTS PARTY.** See People's Party (1971).

**IMMIGRATION RESTRICTION LEAGUE (IRL).** Founded in 1894 at Boston, Massachusetts, by a group of professional and upper-class nativists for the purpose of ending the U.S. policy of unrestricted immigration. Among its founders were John Fiske, noted historian and social philosopher (who served as honorary president); N. H. Shaler, a geologist; George F. Edmunds, a former U.S. senator from Vermont; Samuel R. Capen, a prominent Boston businessman; Robert T. Paine, a well-known philanthropist; Prescott Hall, a lawyer; and Robert DeCourcy Ward, a graduate student in science. Hall and Ward were Harvard men and descendants from old-line Yankee families. Hall was executive secretary, with Ward close at hand to supply information bolstering the position of the IRL.

This organization had 531 members in fourteen states by 1895. Although never large in terms of numbers, Hall and Ward's superb leadership made the IRL highly influential when it came to lobbying in Congress. The IRL's initial strategy was to seek enactment of literacy test legislation as an instrument to check the influx of undesirable immigrants. Those designated as racially inferior, hence not desirable, were the multitudes of people coming from Southern and Eastern Europe, among them Italians, Poles, Russian Jews, Greeks, Bulgarians, and other Slavic nationalities. IRL adherents believed that this alleged rabble possessed such degenerate characteristics as inferior intelligence, criminal behavior, clannishness, slovenly indolence, and proneness to disease. Presuming Nordics and Anglo-Saxons to be superior, members of the IRL decried intermarriage with allegedly racially inferior and culturally unassimilable Slavs.

In 1895 Senator Henry Cabot Lodge (R-Mass.) and Congressman Samuel McCall (R-Mass.) cosponsored the literacy test legislation proposed by the IRL. Immediate support came from the American Protective Association.* The measure passed in Congress but was vetoed by President Grover Cleveland.

The IRL nevertheless persisted in lobbying for other restrictions and was influential in securing enactment of the Immigration Act of 1903. Signed by President Theodore Roosevelt, it specifically excluded anarchists. Another bill signed into law in 1907 prohibited Japanese immigration from Hawaii. That same year, Congress provided for the establishment of a commission to investigate problems arising from unrestricted immigration. Headed by Senator William P. Dillingham (R-Vt.), this commission received much information from the IRL. This tactic proved of value when the Dillingham commission strongly recommended congressional approval of a literacy test. Congress did so in 1913, but it was vetoed by President William Howard Taft.

World War I spawned fear among native-born citizens that hyphenate Americans might not be loyal to the United States when their former homeland was a belligerent or an enemy in time of war. The IRL capitalized on the xenophobia to secure passage of yet another literacy test bill in 1915. It too was vetoed, this time by President Woodrow Wilson. Undaunted by failure, the IRL and other restrictionists achieved success in 1917 when Congress overrode President Wilson's veto of a literacy test act.

The IRL and other powerful anti-immigrant groups, including the Ku Klux Klan* and the American Federation of Labor, pressured Congress for additional limitations on immigration. The results were the enactment and implementation of the Immigration Acts of 1920 and 1921. The former permitted the deportation of radical aliens, and the latter imposed a quota system on all immigrants. Worked out by Senator Dillingham, the quota discriminated overtly against Southern and Eastern Europeans by basing entry percentages upon the 1890 census, which was a decade of high immigration from Northern and Western European nations. Extended in 1922, the so-called quota act was made permanent in 1924, when it was signed into law by President Calvin Coolidge.

Having attained its goal of restrictive legislation, the IRL disbanded in 1924. During the thirty years of its existence, the IRL played a significant role in securing legalization of restrictions based on ethnic and racial discrimination. Whether convinced by supposed scientific and sociological evidence (such as social Darwinism) or motivated by prejudice, the IRL did reflect the fears of an elite group against a lower class.

For further information, see Thomas J. Curran, *Xenophobia and Immigration, 1820-1930* (1975).

**INDEPENDENCE LEAGUE.** See Independence Party.

**INDEPENDENCE PARTY (IP).** Founded in 1908 at Chicago by publisher William Randolph Hearst for the purpose of promoting his candidacy for the presidency. The IP was an outgrowth of Heart's Independence League formed to aid his independent candidacy in the 1906 New York gubernatorial race. Hearst, who just barely lost the presidential nomination of the Democratic Party* in 1904, expected to head the IP ticket. Instead the delegates nominated Thomas Higsen of Massachusetts for the presidency and John Temple Graves of Georgia for the vice-presidency.

The platform contained planks championing the initiative, referendum, recall, and direct primaries; regulating the stock market; making blacklists and court injunctions against labor unions illegal; improving health and safety conditions in factories; initiating government ownership of public utilities; prohibiting child and convict labor; creating a department of labor; establishing a central governmental bank; reducing the tariff; creating an interstate commerce court; outlawing the rebate; breaking up monopolies; expanding parcel post service and establishing postal savings banks; developing a national system of good roads; creating a national department of public health; admitting Arizona and New Mexico to statehood; excluding Asiatics as immigrants; instituting popular election of U.S. senators and judges; enacting a graduated income tax; speedy building of a strong navy; and using arbitration for the settlement of international disputes.

In a presidential election in which Republican* William Howard Taft defeated Democrat William Jennings Bryan by over a million popular votes, the IP ticket of Higsen and Temple drew only 82,537 votes (0.55 percent), far fewer than polled by the candidates of either the Socialist Party of America* or the Prohibition Party.* The IP had no appreciable effect on the outcome of the 1908 presidential election. Because of its poor showing, the IP dissolved immediately.

For more information, see Kirk H. Porter and Donald B. Johnson, eds., *National Party Platforms, 1840-1960* (1961).

**INDEPENDENT CITIZENS COMMITTEE FOR THE ARTS, SCIENCES AND PROFESSIONS (ICC-ASP).** Founded in 1944 at New York City by Hannah Dorner, a public-relations counsel, for the purpose of promoting the reelection of President Franklin D. Roosevelt and the election of liberal and left-wing candidates to Congress. Dorner acted as its first executive director, and famed sculptor Jo Davidson served as chairman.

During its two-year existence, membership reached over ten thousand. Its members included James Cagney, Eddie Cantor, Aaron Copland, Bette Davis, Agnes DeMille, Albert Einstein, Edna Ferber, Oscar Hammerstein, Lillian Hellman, Langston Hughes, Max Lerner, Yehudi Menuhin, Paul Robeson, Edward G. Robinson, Carl Van Doren, and Orson Welles. The ICC-ASP sponsored personal appearances of movie stars and prestigious personages to raise campaign funds for candidates having received its endorsement.

The ICC-ASP tended to support liberal, pro-New Deal Democrats.* In

New York State it also supported candidates nominated by the Liberal Party*
and the American Labor Party.* It was at a political rally cosponsored by
the ICC-ASP in 1946 (for senatorial candidate James M. Mead and gubernatorial candidate Herbert H. Lehman) that Secretary of Commerce Henry
A. Wallace made his controversial Madison Square Garden speech on
foreign policy. Subsequently Wallace was dismissed from President
Truman's cabinet for his ostensibly soft attitude toward the Soviet Union.
This led to the formation by Wallace in 1948 of the Progressive Party.*

From its Washington, D.C., branch office, the ICC-ASP sought to influence national policy related to civil rights and peaceful uses of atomic
energy. Relative to foreign policy, it supported the United Nations and
friendship with the Soviet Union. In 1946 the ICC-ASP merged with the
National Citizens Political Action Committee* to form the Progressive
Citizens of America.*

For more information, see Curtis D. MacDougall, *Gideon's Army*, 3
vols. (1965).

**INDEPENDENT (GREENBACK) PARTY.** See Greenback Party.

**INDEPENDENT NATIONAL PARTY.** See Greenback Party.

**INDEPENDENT PARTY.** See Greenback Party.

**INDEPENDENT PROGRESSIVE PARTY (IPP).** Founded in 1947 at Los
Angeles by Elinor Kahn, its permanent chairperson, and a group of liberal
and left-wing political adherents for the purpose of promoting the presidential
candidacy of Henry A. Wallace. In 1948 it became the state auxiliary of the
Progressive Party.* The IPP worked to elect a state ticket and the presidential ticket of the Progressive Party, which consisted of Henry A. Wallace
running for president, with Senator Glen Taylor (D-Idaho) as his vice-
presidential running mate.

Members of the IPP found it difficult to win votes for the ticket because
of seemingly pro-Soviet views that Wallace and Taylor espoused. No IPP
candidates were elected to state office, and the Progressive Party presidential ticket polled only 190,381 votes in the state of California (its national
vote was 1,157,057). California was second to New York in terms of votes
won, but overall both states registered relatively small totals for Wallace
and Taylor.

In 1952 a small remnant of the IPP supported the last presidential ticket
of the Progressive Party. Vincent Hallinan, a lawyer famous for defending
radical causes, was the presidential nominee and Charlotte Bass, a black
civil rights activist, ran as the vice-presidential candidate. Their California
total was 24,692 (second to New York again) out of a national total of

140,023 popular votes. Following this poor showing at the polls, the IPP disbanded.

For more information, see Karl M. Schmidt, *Henry A. Wallace, Quixotic Crusader* (1960).

**INDEPENDENT REPUBLICAN PARTY (IRP).** Founded in 1864 at Cleveland, Ohio, by a small group of Radical Republicans for the purpose of preventing the reelection of Abraham Lincoln as president of the United States. Disappointed with the wartime leadership of Lincoln, this faction nominated John C. Frémont as its presidential nominee and chose General John Cochrane as his vice-presidential running mate. Frémont had been the presidential nominee of the Republican Party* in 1856. Prior to the election, friends of Frémont convinced him not to oppose Lincoln. Both candidates subsequently withdrew from the presidential race and supported the ticket of the National Union Party.*

For more information, see William F. Zornow, *Lincoln and His Party Divided* (1954).

**INDEPENDENT REPUBLICANS.** See Mugwumps.

**INDIAN RIGHTS ASSOCIATION (IRA).** Founded in 1882 at Boston by a group of humanitarians for the purpose of promoting civil rights for American Indians. Most notable among its founders was Helen Hunt Jackson. Her *Century of Dishonor* (1881), a critical assessment of U.S. Indian policy, first brought the plight of the Indians to the attention of the American public at large. After she was appointed to a special commission to investigate conditions among the Mission Indians of California, Jackson wrote a romantic novel, *Ramona* (1884), based upon her experiences. This work of fiction did elicit some sympathy for Indians from the reading public but not to the degree Jackson had desired.

Many Quakers were members of the IRA and their Mohawk Conference of the Friends of Indians (1886) did much to influence the attitude of Senator Henry Lauren Dawes (R-Mass.) and President Grover Cleveland. Dawes authored the Dawes Severalty Act of 1887, and Cleveland signed it into law. This measure sought to terminate the reservation system by authorizing the division of tribal lands into family farms of 160 acres. Citizenship was to accompany the gradual dissolution of reservations as Indians became independent yeoman farmers. Thus it was hoped that they would be integrated into the American society and become productive citizens instead of being wards of the federal government. The IRA promoted this program through its publication, *Council Fire*, and believed it would be to the Indians' best interest when implemented.

The expected benefits of the Dawes Act did not materialize. Instead when

Indian tribes were broken up, the base of their religion and culture was destroyed. When their lands were disbursed, they frequently lost ownership and became even more economically depressed than before. Assimilation did not take place; instead the plight of Indians worsened. The American public generally was not interested in the Indians so there was no pressure from public opinion to implement treaty rights or to provide federal assistance to tribes so that they might develop self-government.

In contemporary times, the IRA, whose membership is less than three thousand, has modified its stand. It now supports attempts by Indians to live in tribal communities or integrate into the mainstream of American society. It strives to inform Indians of their legal rights and to assist them in adjusting to new conditions. The IRA also informs non-Indians of problems confronting the native Americans. Present national headquarters is located in Philadelphia. Currently John Calwalder is president, and Theodore B. Hetzel serves as general secretary. The IRA publishes a monthly magazine, *Indian Truth.*

For more information, see Ruth Odell, *Helen Hunt Jackson* (1939), and Henry E. Fritz, *The Movement for Indian Assimilation, 1860-1890* (1963).

**INDUSTRIAL WORKERS OF THE WORLD.** See Anarchist Federation.

**INSTITUTE FOR DEMOCRATIC EDUCATION.** See Anti-Defamation League of the B'nai B'rith.

**INSTITUTE FOR GOVERNMENT RESEARCH.** See Brookings Institution.

**INSTITUTE FOR POLICY STUDIES.** See National Conference of Alternative State and Local Public Policies.

**INSTITUTE OF MEDICINE.** See National Academy of Sciences.

**INTERCOLLEGIATE SOCIALIST SOCIETY OF AMERICA.** See League for Industrial Democracy.

**INTERNATIONAL CITY MANAGEMENT ASSOCIATION (ICMA).** Founded in 1914 at Springfield, Ohio, by Charles E. Ashburner, its first president, and seven other city managers for the purpose of promoting the professional proficiency of municipal administrators and to raise the quality of local government. Originally called the City Managers' Association, its name was changed to International City Managers' Association in 1924, and to IMCA in 1969.

The IMCA sponsors training institutes, engages in research, and publishes special reports dealing with problems confronting local governmental units. Reports have dealt with a variety of topics: public relations; minorities; managerial techniques; personnel; administration; finance; local planning; fire and police protection; recreation and parks; and public works. The ICMA maintains administrative relationships with federal agencies, state municipal leagues, universities, and other public-interest groups. It provides the Management Information Service for some fifteen hundred cities that subscribe and operates the Minority Executive Placement Service to assist qualified members of minority groups to obtain managerial and administrative positions in local governments. The ICMA sponsors the publication of the Manager Profession Series of textbooks and operates the Academy for Professional Development for its members. Recently the ICMA has urged Congress to provide more federal assistance to cities so that they can cope better with such problems as unemployment, mass transportation, pollution, and housing.

The national headquarters of ICMA is located in Washington, D.C. Current membership totals nearly sixty-eight hundred and is drawn from the ranks of city managers, municipal executives, and county administrative officers. Richard H. Custer, the town manager of West Hartford, Connecticut, is serving as president, with Mark E. Keane as executive director. The ICMA publishes a monthly magazine, *Public Management*; a semimonthly, *ICMA Newsletter*; the annual *County Year Book*; and the annual *Municipal Year Book*.

For more information, see Clarence E. Ridley and Orin F. Nolting, *The City-Manager Profession* (1934), and Richard J. Stillman, *The Rise of the City Manager: A Public Professional in Local Government* (1974).

**INTERNATIONAL CITY MANAGERS' ASSOCIATION.** See International City Management Association.

**INTERNATIONAL CONGRESS OF WOMEN.** See Women's International League for Peace and Freedom.

**INTERNATIONAL DOWNTOWN EXECUTIVES ASSOCIATION (IDEA).** Founded in 1953 at Denver, Colorado, by businessman Philip Milstein, its first president, for the purpose of promoting the redevelopment of downtown Denver. Some one hundred other groups in cities throughout the United States, which organized for the identical purpose of promoting downtown redevelopment, have affiliated to make IDEA a national organization. One of the prime movers in this process was the Chicago Central Area Committee, which sought to do for Chicago what Milstein was doing for Denver.

IDEA seeks to stop the exodus from the central city by agitating for massive urban-renewal projects. It works to interest federal agencies or private investors in the construction of new buildings, promenade malls, parks, civic centers, recreational facilities, renovation of old buildings, and landscaping to beautify the inner core of cities. IDEA also promotes in-town residential neighborhoods, downtown housing for senior citizens, municipal parking facilities, and mass transit. Its members lobby with federal, state, and local governmental bodies for projects to prevent the deterioration of cities' inner core and for rebuilding rundown areas. It opposes redlining, a practice by banks in which they do not make loans to those buying property in certain generally run-down areas, which causes real estate values to decline and prompts both business and residents to relocate in the suburbs. The activities of IDEA have done much to make both the public and governmental bodies aware of what is needed to be done to prevent downtown areas from becoming economically depressed slums.

Present national headquarters of IDEA is located in Denver. Current president is Philip Milstein.

**INTERNATIONAL WORKING PEOPLE'S ASSOCIATION (IWPA).** Founded in 1883 at Pittsburgh, Pennsylvania, by Johann Most, a German anarchist and editor of *Freiheit*, for the purpose of promoting anarchism in the United States. The IWPA platform, written by Most, called for the "destruction of the existing class rule . . . by energetic, relentless, revolutionary, and international action." This manifesto furthermore proposed the "establishment of a free society based upon cooperative organization of production"; abolition of the profit system; education based on the equality of the sexes; equal rights without distinction of race or sex; and "regulation of all public affairs by free contracts between . . . autonomous (independent) communes and associations." The American Declaration of Independence was cited as justification for the use of armed violence to precipitate a revolution.

Membership in the IWPA seldom exceeded a few hundred, with its greatest strength in Chicago, New York City, Philadelphia, and St. Louis. Small bands of anarchists, sometimes meeting secretly, congregated among recent immigrants from Germany, Russia, and Eastern European countries. Prominent among its members were Emma Goldman, editor of *Mother Earth*; Alexander Berkman, who attempted to assassinate Henry Clay Frick in 1892; and Albert R. Parsons and August Spies, participants in the Haymarket Riot of 1886. Spies and Parsons were arrested, tried, and executed in 1887. Before his death, Parsons wrote *Anarchism, Its Philosophy and Scientific Basis* (1887).

The IWPA was never accepted as a legitimate American political party because of its commitment to violence. It was always in disrepute and its members subject to constant harassment or arrest. The sedition trials during

World War I destroyed what was left of the IWPA, and those isolated remnants that continued in existence until 1920 were decimated by the Palmer raids of that era. Before it became extinct, most of its small membership were either arrested or deported.

Because of its violent nature, anarchism did not lend itself to the American democratic system. The use of assassination as a political tool was not compatible with constitutional rights. Anarchists espoused the overthrow of government by force rather than change through democratic means, so they were never influential in American politics. They made themselves known, but their tactics were counterproductive and futile.

For further information, see Rudolph Rocker, *Johann Most* (1924); Emma Goldman, *Living My Life* (1931); Eunice M. Schuster, *Native American Anarchism* (1932); and Richard Drinnon, *Rebel in Paradise: A Biography of Emma Goldman* (1961).

**INVISIBLE EMPIRE OF THE KNIGHTS OF THE KU KLUX KLAN.**
See Ku Klux Klan.

**IWW.** See Anarchist Federation.

**JEFFERSONIAN DEMOCRATS.** See Democratic-Republican Party.

**JEFFERSONIAN REPUBLICANS.** See Democratic-Republican Party.

**JEWISH DEFENSE LEAGUE (JDL).** Founded in 1968 at New York City by Rabbi Meir Kahane for the purpose of fighting anti-Semitism and promoting "Jewish power." Originally named the Jewish Defense Corps, it was renamed JDL soon after its formation in Manhattan (its present headquarters is in Brooklyn). Kahane, an associate editor of the *Jewish Press*, was JDL's national leader until he emigrated to Israel in 1971, and even after his departure he remained influential in determining its course of action. Others who took part in the formation of the JDL were Bertram Zweibon, Irving Claderon, Murray Schneider, and Chaim Bieber.

With Rabbi Kahane in charge of JDL's activities, the group was militant and frequently resorted to violence to achieve its goals. Its original objectives were to oppose what it deemed anti-Semitism among blacks and radicals, protect synagogues from vandals, support Israel, and promote a return to the traditional Jewish way of life. With the slogan "Never Again" (referring to the Holocaust), it operated as a tightly knit, disciplined organization responding to Kahane's orders.

The JDL was controversial and was portrayed by some as a gang of self-styled vigilantes and Zionist terrorists. Kahane was jailed on several occasions for his acts, both in the United States and in Israel. In 1971 the JDL initiated a campaign it referred to as "Every Jew a .22," which called upon Jews in high-crime neighborhoods to arm themselves. Operation Haganah (Defense) was implemented whereby JDL members themselves policed Jewish areas in Brooklyn and the Bronx to stop muggings, rape, and robberies. A Chaya ("beasts") Squad was also formed to frighten anti-semites with physical force.

In 1969 the JDL opposed the reelection of New York City's mayor John

V. Lindsay becaused of his alleged softness on the law-and-order issue and ostensibly because he permitted anti-Semites to remain in his administration. It was critical of Governor Nelson A. Rockefeller (R-N.Y.) but was unsuccessful, as it was in the case of Lindsay, in organizing a Jewish bloc of voters to defeat either of them. The JDL advised Jews and what it labeled the "Orthodox Jewish establishment" (dubbed "Uncle Jakes" by Kahane) to cease choosing liberalism over Judaism when it came to politics. In 1972 the JDL supported Senator Henry Jackson (D-Wash.) in the Democratic presidential primary because of his pro-Israel and hawkish stand on the war in Vietnam. When Senator George McGovern (D-S.D.) won the presidential nomination of the Democratic Party,* it opposed him on the basis of his dovish stance, lukewarm position on aid to Israel, and advocacy of quotas and affirmative action (considered by the JDL to be reverse discrimination).

Much to the surprise of the Jewish community, the JDL backed President Richard M. Nixon's Vietnam policy, arguing that an American defeat there would jeopardize future U.S. military intervention to assist Israel. Also surprising, the JDL formed an alliance with the Italian-American Civil Rights League led by Joe Columbo, a reputed Mafia chieftain. Protests by the JDL included such actions as picketing, disrupting meetings, firebombings, attempted hijacking, harassment of Soviet officials, and confrontation with Nazi groups. Individual Jews criticized by the JDL included impresario Sol Hurok (for bringing Soviet artists to the United States) and Leonard Bernstein, conductor of the New York Philharmonic Orchestra, for his fund-raising activities on behalf of the Black Panthers.*

Under Kahane's leadership, the JDL advocated separateness for Jews (no marriages with gentiles); political action solely to promote Jewish interests; Jewish education (not sending children to the public schools); the establishment of Jewish identity centers; teaching the young to admire Jewish revolutionaries and heroes of the Palestine National Liberation Movement; and eventually for all Jews to emigrate to Israel. "Jewish Is Beautiful" rallies were held, young Jews were encouraged to undergo paramilitary training, and a program was initiated to liberate all Jews in the Soviet Union by opposing détente between the Soviet Union and the United States. The last policy prompted the JDL to oppose the foreign policy as formulated by Henry Kissinger and to denounce representatives of the Soviet Union whenever possible.

After Rabbi Kahane emigrated to Israel in 1971, he started a JDL chapter in his adopted homeland. His new slogan was "Not One Inch" relative to returning lands that Israel had acquired as a result of its wars with Arab nations. He supported Menachem Begin and his party and advocated violent counterattack relative to the terrorism of Yasir Arafat's Palestinian Organization. In the United States, the JDL formed the Committee against Israeli Retreat (CAIR) to mobilize American opinion in favor of Israel's stand. CAIR sought the resignation of Secretary of State Kissinger and opposed the reelection of President Gerald R. Ford in 1976. It also sought to organize a "Christian for Zion" movement among fundamentalist Protestants.

JDL membership was never very large. At one time, it claimed seven thousand members in seventeen U.S. cities. It was not recognized by the World Zionist Congress and was opposed in the main by the American Jewish Congress, B'nai B'rith* and its Anti-Defamation League,* Reform Conference of American Rabbis, Union of Hebrew Congregations, and the American Jewish Committees. Many American Jews opposed JDL's insistence upon cultural and racial apartness, its use of violence, its demand that Jewish political figures represent Jewish interests first and always, and its hard line relative to peace negotiations with Egypt and other Arab nations.

Current national director of the JDL is Bonnie Pechter, with Simon Greenstein serving as chief of security. Rabbi Kahane, whose ultramilitancy even alienated some within the JDL, formed a new group in 1978, the Conference of Jewish Activists, which has few members in chapters in New York City, Chicago, Milwaukee, Phoenix, and Tucson.

For more information, see Meir Kahane, *The Story of the Jewish Defense League* (1975).

**JEWISH SOCIALIST VERBAND OF AMERICA (JSVA).** Founded in 1921 at New York City by Abraham Cahan, editor of the *Jewish Daily Forward*, and a group of Jewish socialists for the purpose of promoting socialism among Yiddish-speaking Jews. Cahan and many JSVA members were also affiliated with the Social Democratic Federation.*

Relatively small in number, the JSVA aimed its appeal at Jews in the lower socioeconomic class. Its efforts to propagate socialism have met with little success. Most Jewish workers found trade unions of greater benefit than agitation for government ownership of industry. As a result, the JSVA appealed only to an extremely small portion of the Jewish community. Its left-wing stance prevented it from becoming politically influential among Jews, and its political rhetoric was influential only among those of a radical persuasion.

Present national headquarters is located in New York City. Current national chairman is Samuel Weiss. The JSVA publishes a monthly magazine, *Der Wecker*.

**JOBLESS PARTY (JP).** Founded in 1932 at St. Louis, Missouri, by Father James R. Cox of Pittsburgh for the purpose of initiating political action to alleviate the adverse economic conditions caused by the Great Depression. At its national convention held in St. Louis that same year, the delegates nominated Father Cox as their presidential nominee and chose V. C. Tisdal as his vice-presidential running mate.

The platform of the JB called for nationalization of all banks, confiscation of personal fortunes, government relief, and federally financed public works to provide jobs for unemployed workers. The radical nature of some of its planks prevented the JB from becoming a party with a large mass following. Those suffering from the depression were prone to vote for the presidential nominee of the Democratic Party,* Governor Franklin D. Roosevelt of New York, rather than to support an obscure third party.

Because of a lack of campaign funds, Father Cox had to suspend his canvass for votes even before election day. His popular vote total was 740. The JB dissolved after this debacle. Father Cox subsequently was appointed by President Roosevelt to serve on the Pennsylvania state board of the National Recovery Administration. The public works plank of the JB was implemented by Roosevelt through the many New Deal measures aimed at providing employment for the jobless.

**JOHN BIRCH SOCIETY (JBS).** Founded in 1959 at Indianapolis, Indiana, by Robert H. Welch, Jr., a retired candy manufacturer, for the purpose of stopping the spread of communism at home and abroad. The organization was named after Captain John Morrison Birch, a former Baptist missionary serving under General Claire Chenault in China, who was killed in 1945 by Communist guerrillas.

From the outset of its formation, the purpose of the JBS, as determined by its undisputed leader, Robert Welch, was to propagate an ultraconservative political philosophy and to fight communism with uncompromising tenacity. Among the campaigns the JBS promoted were opposition to Medicare; impeachment of Earl Warren (when he was chief justice of the Supreme Court); U.S. withdrawal from the United Nations; repeal of the income tax; termination of all foreign aid programs; end of U.S. participation in the North Atlantic Treaty Organization; abolition of cultural exchange programs with Communist nations; denial of diplomatic recognition for the People's Republic of China; elimination of welfare programs; and the reduction of taxes. The JBS also considered the black civil rights movement as being Communist inspired and stressed the need to return to law and order. Members of the JBS were instructed to infiltrate antagonistic liberal organizations, harass opposition speakers, utilize billboards, and make use of the "letter-writing weapon" in letters-to-the-editor columns.

Positioned on the Radical Right of the political spectrum, the JBS has been criticized by liberals and conservatives alike for its doctrinaire and extremist views. Robert Welch astounded many Americans by his allegation, published in a privately circulated document, *The Politician*, that President Dwight D. Eisenhower was a "dedicated conscientious agent of the Communist conspiracy." Other extremist views expounded by Welch were published in the *Blue Book*; *The American Story*; *The Truth about Vietnam*; *More Truth about Vietnam*; *To the Negroes of America*; *This Is It!*; *Two Revolutions at Once*; and in articles in its magazine, *American Opinion*. Generally Welch interprets history in conspiratorial terms, claiming that "insiders" are plotting to gain control over the world. According to Welch, the conspiracy started with the founding of the secret Order of Illuminatti, organized by Adam Weishaupt in Bavaria on May 1, 1776. From that time to the present, these insiders (presumably liberal intellectuals, socialists, syndicalists, communists, and other radical left-wing groups) have sought to achieve their aims by promoting the French Revolution, social reforms, free public education, the income tax, the Federal Reserve System, the New Deal, tax exemptions for so-called philanthropic and educational foundations, two world wars in the twentieth century, and the Vietnam conflict.

Within the United States, as Welch interprets history, the secret and sinister insiders have controlled the presidential nominations of both the Democratic* and Republican parties*; have subverted the U.S. Constitution; and have transformed the United States from a republic into a "mobocracy." In so doing they have ostensibly prepared the nation for a Communist takeover. Welch also coined the term *comsymp* for those who covertly sympathize with the Communists. By the phrase *principle of reversal*, he explains why some liberals denounce communism. It is, according to Welch, a tactic used by crypto-Communists to conceal their true allegiance to a foreign ideology. Welch strongly supported the anti-Communist crusade of Senator Joseph McCarthy (R-Wis.) and others who engaged in similar activities.

The JBS supported Senator Barry Goldwater (R-Ariz.) for the Republican presidential nomination in 1964. When Goldwater was selected as the GOP nominee, its members campaigned for him. After Goldwater's defeat, Senator John Tower (R-Tex.), a noted conservative, denounced the JBS for its interference. Conservative columnist William F. Buckley, Jr., also rejected the political philosophy of the JBS. The Goldwater campaign was the high tide of John Birchism. It had made a significant impact on the political scene, but its influence would wane continually after 1960.

Within the complex problems stemming from industrial-urban and complicated international issues, the JBS sought a return to a simpler and isolationist way of life. In seeking a revival of the "good old days," its members earnestly believe in the validity of self-reliance, moral virtues, individualism, and limited government. Its solution to conditions brought about by technology, political pluralism, and cultural diversity was to embrace an ideology of spiritual, constitutional, and political fundamentalism. The JBS defends patriotism, religion, and the family unit. In response to his critics, Robert Welch in 1972 asserted, "What we are talking about is the survival of the United States and its resistance to a takeover by a worldwide conspiracy.'' Welch's personal objective was to utilize the JBS to prevent that from happening.

After the Goldwater debacle in 1964, in which the GOP presidential candidate lost by landslide proportions, leaders within the Republican Party deliberately rid John Birchers out of their party. Consequently the JBS has little influence within the GOP, but it does support conservative Republicans as well as conservative Democrats. Membership dropped, which also limited its political effectiveness. Much of the power wielded by the JBS is today possessed by such groups as the Moral Majority.*

National headquarters of the JBS is located in Belmont, Massachusetts. Some eight hundred local chapters existed at one time in all fifty states. Membership at its height probably totaled more than one hundred thousand. It is much lower now, although no exact figures are known. At one time, regional offices were operating in San Marino, California; White Plains, New York; Dallas, Texas; and Washington, D.C. Many JBS chapters organized local Support Your Police Committees. The JBS operates the Western Springs Publishing Company and issues the following publications: the weekly *Review of the News*; the monthly *Bulletin*; and a monthly magazine, *American Opinion*.

For more information, see Harry Overstreet and Bonaro Overstreet, *Strange Tactics of Extremism* (1964); Benjamin R. Epstein and Arnold Forster, *Report on the John Birch Society* (1966); and Seymour M. Lipset and Earl Raab, *The Politics of Unreason: Right-Wing Extremism in America, 1790-1970* (1970).

**JOIN HANDS (JH).** Founded in 1968 at Los Angeles by Janice Bernstein, Ethel Haydon, and Nancy York for the purpose of promoting racial integration in the United States. Formed in the aftermath of the assassination of the Reverend Dr. Martin Luther King, Jr., JH sought to persuade individuals to take responsible action to eliminate discrimination against racial minorities. Starting out as a white organization, it soon became biracial and thus more effective in getting both individuals and business leaders involved in the civil rights movement.

Each member subscribes to a ten-point pledge to eliminate racial prejudice from his or her mind and to take personal action whenever possible to foster peaceful integration of the races. A business and industry pledge also commits business leaders personally to promote harmonious racial integration by ending job discrimination. JH seeks to gain members in many varied groups so as to implement its program in community service clubs, churches, fraternal organizations, and business associations. JH has had a positive influence on public opinion in securing fair employment for blacks, integrating schools, and ending job discrimination. In 1973 Mayor Tom

Bradley of Los Angeles (the city's first black mayor) appointed Janice Bernstein to Los Angeles's Human Relations Commission. While holding this position, she continues to serve as president of JH.

National headquarters is located in Los Angeles, California. JH publishes materials for affiliated organizations in twenty-five states. It promotes as widely as possible the use of its pledge. Financing of its activities comes from the sale of a bumper sticker with its three-hands symbol (white, brown, and black). The JH also maintains a bibliography on race relations and periodically disseminates information to the public by pamphlets.

# _K_

**KEEP AMERICA OUT OF WAR CONGRESS (KAOWC).** Founded in 1938 at New York City by Norman Thomas and a group of anti-interventionists to prevent repeal or modification of the Neutrality Act of 1935. Its director was John T. Flynn. Other notable members included Franz Boaz, Max Eastman, H. C. Englebrecht, Suzanna La Follette, and Oswald Garrison Villard.

The KAOWC attracted intellectuals, socialists, liberal isolationists, and pacifists who opposed U.S. involvement in any foreign war. Although relatively small in numbers, members nevertheless were influential in rallying public opinion against war mobilization and in preventing the U.S. government from assisting the victims of German and Italian aggression in the 1930s. They also opposed, but unsuccessfully, the Burke-Wadsworth Act (draft law), Destroyer Deal, Lend-Lease, and the undeclared-war phase of Franklin D. Roosevelt's foreign policy.

Following the attack on Pearl Harbor, the KAOWC disbanded and reformed after World War II as the Post-War World Congress (later changing its name to the Post-War World Council). It championed Soviet-American friendship and U.S. support for the United Nations. The cold war and disagreement over whether the United States was justified in entering the Korean war caused its ultimate demise.

For further information, see Michael Wreszin, _Oswald Garrison Villard: Pacifist at War_ (1965).

**KELLY-NASH MACHINE.** See Democratic Central Committee of Cook County.

**KNIGHTS OF COLUMBUS (K of C).** Founded in 1882 at New Haven, Connecticut, by Father Michael J. McGivney for the purpose of promoting fellowship among the laymen of the Roman Catholic church. Named after Christopher Columbus, the K of C seeks to foster knightly service to church, country, and others. It stresses charity, unity, fraternity, and patriotism. Besides engaging in many activities to propagate the faith, the K of C provides insurance protection for its members.

To counter anti-Catholic bigotry, the K of C initiated a campaign whereby advertisements refuting false allegations concerning Catholics are placed in prominent magazines. The K of C reflects official Catholic positions on contemporary issues. With the K of C New Jersey State Council employing a professional lobbyist, it advocates federal aid to parochial schools, legalizing bingo, maintenance of good relations between the Vatican and the U.S. government, and legislation making abortion illegal. During the presidential election of 1960, many K of C members were active in the campaign of Senator John F. Kennedy (D-Mass.) so that a Roman Catholic might be elected president. Their actions in getting out the Roman Catholic vote may have provided Kennedy with his narrow margin of victory.

In 1922 the K of C financed a legal fight that ultimately led to a U.S. Supreme Court decision declaring unconstitutional an Oregon law seeking to abolish parochial schools (*Pierce* v. *Society of Sisters*, 1922). It has funded similar legal endeavors in other states when attempts were made to outlaw parochial schools. The strong anti-Communist stance of Senator Joseph McCarthy (R-Wis.) prompted many K of C members to support his crusade. In 1952 the K of C was instrumental in securing inclusion of the words "under God" in the Pledge of Allegiance.

The Supreme Council Catholic Benevolent Legion merged with the K of C in 1968. Present national headquarters is located at New Haven, Connecticut. Currently John W. McDevitt serves as Supreme Knight. K of C publications include a weekly, *Knights of Columbus News*, and a monthly, *Columbia*.

For more information, see Donald F. Crosby, *God, Church and Flag* (1978).

**KNIGHTS OF THE GOLDEN CIRCLE (KGC).** Founded in 1854 at Cincinnati, Ohio, by George W. L. Bickley for the purpose of expanding slave territory. Bickley's motive is not known. When he was not promoting some scheme, he practiced medicine and law and taught school. The KGC was an outgrowth of the Continental Union, a secret organization formed previously by Bickley to be a successor to the Know-Nothing Party.* When this venture failed, Bickley transformed it into the KGC, revised the secret ritual, devised a "great seal," and named himself "general." His initial goal was to "colonize and finally annex northern Mexico to the domain of the United States."

Interest in the KGC came primarily from the South, although its membership was exceedingly small, where a few filibustering ventures (armed raids) were attempted. Southerners desired to acquire Cuba, northern Mexico, and portions of Central America in order to enlarge the areas where slavery could exist. This would permit more slave states and thus give the South political strength equal to that of the North. In 1860 members of the KGC were agitators for secession. When the Confederacy was formed, the KGC supported the southern war effort.

Fear of the KGC arose in the North and Midwest when rumors began to circulate in 1861 that secret cells were being formed to thwart the Union's war effort. Peace Democrats, or Copperheads, it was alleged, were joining the KGC to undermine efforts of the Lincoln administration to win the Civil War and reunite the nation. A fourteen-thousand-word report issued in 1864 by the judge advocate general, Joseph Holt, claimed that the KGC had evolved into the Order of American Knights (OAK), which in turn had transformed itself into the Sons of Liberty (SL). These three organizations, now one, were supposedly headed by Ohio Democrat Clement L. Vallandigham in the North and Midwest and by Confederate General Sterling Price in the trans-Mississippi sector. The Holt report estimated KGC-OAK-SL membership to be at least six hundred thousand. It charged this subversive organization with the following crimes: discouraging enlistments in the Union army; aiding soldiers to desert; protecting draft dodgers; circulating disloyal and treasonous literature; furnishing arms to rebels; cooperating with enemy raids; destroying government property; persecuting and even assassinating loyal Unionists; and seeking to establish a northwest confederacy.

The OAK had been founded in 1856 at New Orleans by Phineas C. Wright to promote states' rights and the American colonization of Central America. It went defunct and was revived by Wright in 1863 at St. Louis to oppose the "despotism" of the Lincoln administration. Wright named himself OAK's supreme commander and set about to counter the activities of the Union League.* With but a few local chapters of this secret society, its achievements were meager.

The SL was founded in 1863 by an Indiana politician, Harrison H. Dodd, at Indianapolis for the purpose of countering the Union League and to serve as a secret, protective society for harassed Democrats. Clement Vallandigham accepted the post as supreme commander. When arrested in 1864, he claimed the SL was not a subversive organization and that its membership was minimal.

It is now known that the KGC, OAK, and SL were never fused into a single organization. Historical evidence also indicates that the membership of all three was far less than that claimed by their opponents. No doubt some secret cells did exist and the members, as pro-Confederate sympathizers, tried to undermine the Union war effort. In any case, the military tribunal's action against Dodd, Vallandigham, and Wright in 1864, along with Lincoln's reelection and northern military victories, ended the life of all three organizations.

War hysteria in the North and Midwest was prompted by many factors. The many defeats suffered by the Army of the Potomac, the raids into Union states by General John H. Morgan, and the guerrilla warfare of William Clarke Quantrill and his Missouri bushwhackers caused alarm among the general populace. Amid this aura of fear, Republicans* and Union Leaguers attacked all Democrats* as Copperheads. It was a natural step to believe that Copperheadism would manifest itself in secret and subversive societies such as the KGC, OAK, and SL. The campaign tactic of "waving the bloody shirt" began in 1864 when Republicans claimed these traitorous groups were representative of the position of the Democratic Party.* This belied the fact that many War Democrats supported the Union and most Peace Democrats were not involved in treasonous activity. The statements and actions of a few pro-Confederate extremists made it possible for the Radical Republicans* to affix the treason label on the Democrats during the Civil War. For the next twenty years, the Grand Old Party* was able to exploit this political tactic.

For more information, see Ollinger Crenshaw, "The Knights of the Golden Circle: The Career of George Bickley," *American Historical Review* 47 (October 1941): 23–50; Bethina Meradith Smith, "Civil War Subversives," *Journal of the Illinois State Historical Society* 45 (Autumn 1952): 220–240; and Frank L. Klement, *The Copperheads in the Middle West* (1960).

**KNIGHTS OF THE WHITE CAMELIA (KWC).** Founded in 1867 at Franklin, Louisiana, by a group of white, racist southerners for the purpose of suppressing the civil rights of freedmen. The primary objectives of this secret society were to ensure segregation and to restore white supremacy in the post-Civil War South. During the post-Civil War Reconstruction period, blacks had been given the franchise, and many were elected to political office. The KWC sought to prevent blacks from exercising their right to vote by utilizing terror. Secretly and at night, the members of the KWC resorted to intimidating, flogging, and even lynching blacks.

The KWC's mode of operation was similar to that utilized by the Ku Klux Klan.* The KWC tended to be strongest in the lower South. Its national headquarters was located at New Orleans, but little was known about its leaders. No accurate figures exist on membership, since the KWC operated as a clandestine organization. When President Rutherford B. Hayes terminated military occupation of the South in 1877, the KWC disbanded. Many of its members, however, continued to enforce covertly the Jim Crow system of segregation until it became the norm.

**KNOW-NOTHING PARTY (KNP).** Founded in 1849 at New York City by Charles Allen as the secret Order of the Star Spangled Banner. As a fraternal organization, it restricted membership to native-born Protestants, developed lodge-like rituals, and conducted secret meetings. In response to queries about its activities, members were instructed to answer, "I know nothing." Hence the order came to be known popularly as the Know-Nothings.

Leadership of the Know-Nothings was taken over by New York businessman James W. Barker in 1852. He had previously formed a nativist organization called the Order of United Americans. Under Barker's direction, the Know-Nothings expanded all over the state of New York and subsequently became a national organization. In 1854 local and state councils formed a National Council (NC), which in turn promulgated a constitution to govern the order's affairs. Local recruitment was left to states, but the NC set requirements for the various degrees of membership.

Ostensibly a social and fraternal organization, the Know-Nothings soon were influential in determining the outcome of numerous local and state elections. Xenophobic in orientation, they were fiercely anti-immigrant, anti-Roman Catholic, and anti-Irish. Membership, which grew rapidly, was drawn from the both the North and the South. Attracted were rural Protestants, those fearing urban political machines that organized ethnic voting blocs, and workers who regarded aliens and immigrants as unfair competition in terms of jobs. It opposed both the Whig* and Democratic* parties, particularly the latter for its large Irish-Roman Catholic constituency. Some Know-Nothings resorted to intimidation and violence in an effort to prevent aliens or naturalized citizens from voting.

The secrecy and religious test for membership were antithetical to the democratic system. Intolerance toward Roman Catholics and a prejudice against immigrants (both aliens and naturalized) appealed to nativists and superpatriotic zealots. Abraham Lincoln observed, "Our progress in degeneracy appears to me pretty rapid, as a nation, we began by declaring that 'all men are created equal.' We now practically read it 'all men are created equal, except negroes.' When the Know-Nothings get control, it will read, ' all men are created equal, except negroes, and foreigners, and catholics.' "

By 1855 both the designations of Know-Nothing Party and American Party (AP) came into usage. At Philadelphia in 1855 the American National Council (ANC) met to write a party platform for the 1856 presidential election. As a national party, the ANC had difficulty resolving the differences between pro-slavery southerners and the anti-slavery northerners. The result was a plank stating that since it was "impossible to reconcile opinions," it was deemed best to "maintain the existing laws upon the subject of slavery."

Northern Know-Nothings found this slavery plank unacceptable and demanded another meeting of the ANC prior to the national convention and the nomination of a presidential ticket. Another such meeting did take place at Philadelphia, when the previous platform was replaced by a new one, which tried to skirt the slavery issue altogether. One plank asserted that states' rights should be preserved (thus protecting slavery) by "non-interference by Congress with questions appertaining solely to the individual States." Another blamed the Democrats for "reopening sectional agitation" by their "repeal of the Missouri Compromise" and "vacillating course on the Kansas and Nebraska question." Other planks declared that "native-born citizens should be selected for all state, federal, and municipal offices or employment"; no person should be elected if they "recognize any allegiance or obligation" to any "foreign prince, potentate or power" (implying the papacy); only citizens (not aliens) should have the right of suffrage in states and territories; naturalization laws should require twenty-one years of continual residence as a prerequisite for citizenship; and all laws should be enforced until repealed or declared unconstitutional by "competent judicial authority." The platform affirmed its belief in the need for separation of church and state; demanded investigations of political corruption; called for "strict economy" in government; and authorized state councils to alter membership requirements (eliminate oaths, degrees, and other obligations) and to encourage "a free and open discussion of all political principles embraced in our platform," an attempt to gain more of a following by eliminating secrecy.

Shortly after the new platform was approved in 1856, with an anti-slavery faction calling itself North Americans (NA) refusing to accept it, a nominating convention convened in Philadelphia. On the second ballot, former President Millard Fillmore was chosen standard-bearer of the Know-Nothing (American) Party. For his vice-presidential running mate the delegates selected Andrew Jackson Donelson of Tennessee. Since it was Fillmore who had signed the Fugitive Slave Act into law and because the platform was not sufficiently anti-slavery in tone, the NA faction (seventy-one in number) withdrew.

Holding their own nominating convention in New York City, the NAs hoped to influence the selection of the Republican Party's* presidential nominee by selecting a fusion candidate. The choice of the NA delegates was Nathaniel P. Banks of Massachusetts. He was an expedient choice, since he had been elected Speaker of the U.S. House of Representatives by a coalition of Know-Nothings and Republicans. Second place on the NA ticket was given to William F. Johnston of Pennsylvania. This coalition strategy did not work when later in 1856 the Republican Party nominated John C. Frémont for the presidency. Despite this setback, many NAs supported the Republican ticket in the general election.

When the final vote tally was counted in the 1856 presidential election, Millard Fillmore (the regular KNP-AP candidate) drew 873,053 popular votes, 21.53 percent of the total cast. Although a majority of the northern Know-Nothings supported Frémont, the Fillmore candidacy did draw away votes that normally might have gone to the Republicans. Thus the existence of the KNP-AP made it impossible for Frémont to defeat Democrat James Buchanan for the presidency at a time when sufficient anti-slavery sentiment existed to have done so.

Between 1856 and 1860, the KNP-AP disintegrated. Know-Nothingism as a national entity died with its one herculean campaign effort. The last meeting of the NC took place at Louisville, Kentucky, in 1857. State parties continued for a short time, but by 1860 most northern Know-Nothings had drifted into the Republican Party, and southern adherents tended to find their way into the Constitutional Union Party.*

For further information, see W. Darrell Overdike, *The Know-Nothing Party in the South* (1950); Ray A. Billington, *The Protestant Crusade, 1800-1860* (1964); and Jean H. Baker, *Ambivalent Americans: The Know-Nothing Party in Maryland* (1977).

**KU KLUX KLAN (KKK).** Founded in 1866 at Pulaski, Tennessee, by a group of ex-Confederate soldiers as a veterans' social club. In 1867 the KKK came under the leadership of a former southern general, Nathan Bedford Forrest. With its headquarters in Nashville, Tennessee, General Forrest served as the Klan's grand wizard until 1869. In that year, he ordered the Klan to disband because of the odious reputation it had acquired. The Klan, however, continued to exist as a clandestine organization until 1877. That year President Rutherford B. Hayes removed the last federal troops from the South, thus terminating Radical Reconstruction.

Almost from its inception in the post-Civil War era, the Klan resorted to violence in an effort to restore white supremacy and southern control over state governments. Garbed in white robes and hooded masks, Klansmen used torches, whips, ropes, and guns to terrorize or kill all who stood in opposition to them. Special objects of their wrath included newly enfranchised freedmen, carpetbaggers, scalawags, Freedmen Bureau officials, Republicans,* and members of the Union League.* Floggings, kidnappings, lynchings, and all manner of intimidation perpetrated by the KKK became so flagrant that the federal government sought to suppress the Klan and other similar groups, such as the Knights of the White Camelia.* Through enactment of the Force Act of 1870 and the Ku Klux Klan Act of 1871, Congress authorized President Ulysses S. Grant to impose martial law to curb the lawless acts of the Klan. These strict measures also imposed severe penalties for terrorism or other lawless activities associated with the

KKK. Even with such stringent legislation, it was difficult to apprehend members of the Klan because of their secrecy and the surreptitious manner in which they operated. Any members caught and brought to trial faced local juries who were loathe to convict Klansmen. Many people held a general sympathy for the KKK's cause; often secret Klansmen served as members of a jury, and Klansmen often coerced juries through threats of retaliation.

In 1915 interest spawned by D. W. Griffith's movie, *The Birth of a Nation*, based upon Thomas Dixon's novel *The Clansmen* (1905), prompted William Joseph Simmons to revive the Klan. This former Methodist clergyman launched the Invisible Empire of the Knights of the Ku Klux Klan in 1915 with a huge cross-burning ceremony atop Stone Mountain near Atlanta, Georgia. Whereas the first KKK prevailed only south of the Mason-Dixon line and never had more than five hundred thousand members, the second Klan existed in other parts of the country outside the South (especially in the Midwest) and reached a high tide of membership in 1925 with five million adherents. It has been estimated that at least 350 delegates at the 1924 Democratic National Convention were Klansmen and they, in part, were responsible for blocking the presidential nomination of New York's Governor Alfred E. Smith. The KKK also contributed to Al Smith's defeat in the national election of 1928, because the presidential nominee of the Democratic Party* was a Roman Catholic.

The second Klan, lasting from 1915 to 1944, was not only bigoted in its attitude toward Catholics and Jews, but like its predecessor, vented its hatred on blacks. The Klan defended the Jim Crow system of segregation and did everything it could to prevent blacks from voting. During the 1920s the Klan's racism manifested itself also with regard to immigrants. It opposed the influx of foreigners from Southern and Eastern Europe on the grounds that such alien peoples were innately inferior to the white, Anglo-Saxon, Protestant stock of Northern and Western Europe. Agitation by the KKK helped secure congressional passage of the Immigration Act of 1924, which established discriminatory quotas against Southern and Eastern Europeans and prohibited the immigration of all Japanese.

By its very nature, the leadership of the Klan was autocratic and prone to the use of illegal means to impose its will upon others. Simmons took the title of imperial wizard. State (Realm) leaders were called "grand dragons" and local (Klavern) heads were designated as "cyclops." Secret meetings usually took place at night, with cross burnings a regular ritual. When members paraded publicly, they sought anonymity by wearing white robes and hoods. Throughout the nation the KKK was accused of vigilante tactics, involvement in the lynchings of blacks, and intimidation of those refusing to accept its avowed moral standards. It sought to elect Klan members to local, state, and federal offices, while opposing those it deemed unfit on account of their race, religion, or liberal political philosophy. The Klan was very powerful in some states, once virtually controlling the state of Indiana.

The demise of the Klan commenced when states began to adopt laws to curb its illegal activities. Revelations of internal corruption and debauchery further propelled the Klan in its decline. Its final demise was caused by its pro-Nazi stance and informal alliance with the German-American Bund* in 1940. Ultimate dissolution came in 1944 when activities of the KKK were considered unpatriotic by the general public and subversive by the federal government.

Nevertheless, the Klan was revived for a third time in 1946 by Dr. Samuel Green, an Atlanta dentist. Membership remained very small until the 1954 desegregation decision by the U.S. Supreme Court in the case of *Brown* v. *Topeka Board of Education*. In conjunction with the Citizens' Councils of America* and other extremist groups, the KKK used violent means in trying to prevent racial integration in the public schools. Reorganized in 1961 by Robert M. Sheldon, who designated himself imperial wizard, the United Klans of America was formed. With headquarters in Tuscaloosa, Alabama it published a newspaper, the *Fiery Cross*, for some thirty-five thousand members in eighteen states. A rival Klan headed by James K. Venable of Tucker, Georgia, also came into existence. At one time it had nearly ten thousand members located in Alabama, Florida, Georgia, Louisiana, North Carolina, South Carolina, and Tennessee. Some scattered factions were formed by dissident members. These included such groups as Mississippi's White Knights of the KKK, Florida's Militant Knights of the KKK, and the Aryan Knights of the KKK in Texas.

A congressional investigation conducted by the House Committee on Un-American Activities in 1965 exposed to the public the violence and illegal means employed by Klan members to thwart implementation of the Civil Rights Act of 1964. They were charged with illegal possession of firearms, murdering civil rights demonstrators, arson, and bombing of black churches. Some members of the Klan who refused to testify or gave false testimony were cited for contempt of Congress (with accompanying jail sentences and fines). A few others were later indicted by grand juries and tried in federal courts.

Although subdued and extremely small in membership, some Klans continue to exist. Sheldon's United Klans of America still exists, as does a rival KKK headed by David Duke. Duke, in his twenties, is a graduate of Louisiana State University and lives in Baton Rouge. He seeks to give the Klan a professional image instead of the redneck portrait long identified with the KKK. As imperial wizard, Duke provides leadership for some eight thousand members of his group. Duke claims he does not hate blacks but merely wants to protect America's white heritage. He submitted a brief to the U.S.

Supreme Court in the case of the *Regents of the University of California* v. *Bakke* arguing that affirmative action is actually reverse discrimination. His Knights of the KKK, as it is called, conducts a "citizens' watch" along the U.S.-Mexican border in an attempt to prevent illegal aliens from entering the United States. Members oppose aid to Israel, denounce court-mandated busing as a means to achieve racial balance in the public schools, and call for U.S. withdrawal from the United Nations.

Compared to the KKK of the post-Civil War era and the 1920s, the contemporary Klans are relatively powerless; they are impotent politically and uninfluential nationally. The American Independent Party* attracted Klan support, but most other parties disdain their support. President Lyndon B. Johnson publicly denounced the KKK and indicated that the Democratic Party* had no room for them in its ranks. The KKK is repugnant to most Americans today because of its record of racism, bigotry, use of violence, and undemocratic mode of leadership. In addition, its secrecy and nightrider approach does not fit into the American political tradition of open debate, obedience to the law, and civil behavior.

For more information, see Arnold S. Rice, *The Ku Klux Klan in American Politics* (1962); David M. Chalmers, *Hooded Americanism: Ku Klux Klan, 1865-1965* (1965); William P. Randel, *The Ku Klux Klan, A Century of Infamy* (1965); Kenneth T. Jackson, *The Ku Klux Klan in the City* (1967); Eyre Damer, *When the Ku Klux Klan Rode* (1912 [1970]); and Marion Monteval [pseud.], *The Klan Inside Out* (1976).

# L

**LA RAZA UNIDA PARTY (RUP).** Founded in 1970 at Crystal City, Texas, by a group of Chicanos for the purpose of promoting the political interests of Mexican-Americans. The impetus for the formation of RUP stemmed from the Youth Liberation Conference held at Denver, Colorado, in 1969. Here one of its leaders, Rudolfo Gonzales, proposed using the term *la raza* ("the race") to further the concept of racial unity among Americans of Latin descent. The RUP was also, in part, an outgrowth of the Political Association of Spanish Speaking Organizations, which was successful in 1963 in electing a slate of city officials in Crystal City. The ticket was headed by Juan Cornego. One of the prime movers in the formation of RUP was Mario Compean, its current executive director, who viewed RUP as a means of electing more Chicanos to local and state offices while serving as a balance of power between Texas Democrats* and Republicans.*

In the local and state elections of 1972 and 1974, RUP candidates met with mixed results at the polls. RUP nominees won some county and city offices but did not win on the state level. RUP's gubernatorial nominee, Ramsey Muniz, drew 214,118 (6.3 percent) of the state's popular vote in 1972 and 93,292 (5.6 percent) in 1974. In both elections, the Democratic candidate won with a popular vote of over 1 million. Two Mexican-Americans, Eligo de la Garza and Henry B. Gonzales, were elected to the U.S. House of Representatives as nominees of the Democratic Party.* The RUP has been effective on the local level and, although it has not won state offices, its existence has forced the two major parties to nominate Mexican-Americans on their respective tickets in order to attract Latino votes. In this respect, the RUP has contributed toward increasing the political power of all Chicanos.

For more information, see John Staples Shockley, *Chicano Revolt in a Texas Town* (1973); Julian Samora, ed., *La Raza: Forgotten Americans* (1974); and F. Chris Garcia, ed., *La Causa Politica: A Reader* (1974).

**LABOR PARTY.** See Farmer-Labor Party.

**LABOR REFORM PARTY.** See National Labor Reform Party.

**LABOR'S LEAGUE FOR POLITICAL EDUCATION (LLPE).** Founded in 1947 at Washington, D.C., by William Green, president of the American Federation of Labor (AFL), and its executive board for the purpose of endorsing pro-labor candidates and thus aid their election. The LLPE evolved out of a periodically elected Nonpartisan Campaign Committee and was formally established at the AFL's sixty-sixth convention in 1948. LLPE's formation was prompted by enactment of the Taft-Hartley Act, which the AFL had strenuously opposed. The anti-union measure was passed over the veto of President Harry S. Truman. Provisions of the act included disclosure of union leaders' incomes, a cooling-off period to stop strikes, and prohibitions against unfair union practices. The task of the LLPE was to defeat members of Congress who had voted for it and elect candidates committed to its repeal. Joseph Keenan, secretary of the Chicago Federation of Labor, was appointed director of the LLPE.

In 1948 the LLPE did not endorse either President Truman or the Republican presidential nominee, Governor Thomas E. Dewey. Nevertheless George Harrison, chairperson of the AFL's Department of Political Direction, did work actively for the Democratic presidential ticket. The LLPE raised over $115,000, which was used for radio, television, and printed material, in support of an educational program aimed at electing pro-labor candidates to Congress. Despite this effort, the Taft-Hartley Act, dubbed the "slave labor act" by labor leaders, was not repealed when the new Congress convened in 1949.

The LLPE continued its program of seeking to influence public opinion against the Taft-Hartley Act and in favor of legislation advocated by the AFL. From 1950 to 1951 it raised just under $500,000 for this educational work. Funds were secured by contributions from local unions and individual union members.

In 1952, with James McDevitt serving as director, the LLPE raised another $249,257 to try to elect the presidential nominee of the Democratic Party.* In endorsing Governor Adlai E. Stevenson II, the AFL broke with its long-standing tradition of not allying with a particular political party. LLPE's efforts were of no avail since Dwight D. Eisenhower, the GOP* candidate, triumphed handily over his Democratic opponent. President Eisenhower appeased the AFL momentarily when he appointed Martin P. Durkin, president of the AFL's Plumbing and Pipefitting Union, as secretary of labor. Durkin resigned his post in October 1953 because the president would not support repeal of the Taft-Hartley Act. Eisenhower further alienated the AFL in 1959 when he signed the Landrum-Griffin

Labor Act, which imposed even greater restrictions on labor unions than had existed previously.

The separate existence of the LLPE came to an end in 1955 when it was merged with the Political Action Committee* of the Congress of Industrial Organization to form the Committee on Political Education.*

For further information, see Philip Taft, *Organized Labor in American History* (1964).

**LAND LABOR CLUBS.** See Single Tax Movement.

**LEAGUE FOR INDEPENDENT POLITICAL ACTION (LIPA).** Founded in 1929 at Chicago by a group of socialist-oriented liberals for the purpose of starting a new political party. Prime movers in its formation included the famous educator John Dewey, who was selected chairperson; James H. Maurer, president of the Pennsylvania Federation of Labor, vice-chairperson; Oswald Garrison Villard, editor of the *Nation*, treasurer; Howard Y. Williams, a Unitarian clergyman, executive secretary; and economist Paul H. Douglas of the University of Chicago, who frequently served as party spokesperson. Membership in the LIPA, drawn especially from the intellectual community, included Paul Blanchard, Paul Brissenden, Stuart Chase, W. E. B. Du Bois, Nathan Fine, Zona Gale, John Haynes Holmes, John Ise, Harry W. Laidler, Robert Morss Lovett, Alexander Meiklejohn, Reinhold Niebuhr, and B. C. Vladeck.

Disappointed over the alleged conservatism of both the Democratic* and Republican parties,* and the inability of the Socialist Party of America* to attract a national following, members hoped that the LIPA would serve as an instrument to coalesce the liberal Left into one unified third party. Biding its time, the LIPA endorsed various socialists running for Congress in 1930 while seeking to bring diverse elements of the non-Communist Left into some sort of union.

In 1932 the LIPA adopted a platform calling for massive social and economic intervention on the part of the federal government to end the Great Depression. Demanded were federally funded relief; public works to alleviate unemployment; public ownership of major industries; increased income taxes on large incomes; higher inheritance taxes; corporate taxation; a six-hour workday; easy rural credit; reduction in taxes on land; legalization of collective bargaining; an anti-lynch law; workers' insurance; old-age pensions; reduction of tariff rates; cancellation of war debts; prohibition of conscription; and universal disarmament. Since no viable national party could be formed, the LIPA endorsed Norman Thomas, the candidate of the Socialist Party of America, for its presidential nominee. Although Thomas drew poorly in an election that saw Franklin D. Roosevelt win the presidency, two LIPA members won elections: Elbert Thomas of Utah to the U.S.

Senate and Marion Zionchek of Washington to the House of Representatives.

During the early stages of the Roosevelt administration, the LIPA, whose membership was about two thousand, criticized the New Deal as ineffective. To bring about greater government action to aid the victims of the depression, the LIPA sought an alliance with other groups such as the Farmers Holiday Association,* the Nonpartisan League,* the Socialist Party of America, and the Conference for Progressive Labor Action.* In 1933 the LIPA formed the Farmer-Labor Political Federation* as an additional step toward starting a third party.

Preparing for the 1936 presidential election, the LIPA took part in organizing the American Commonwealth Political Federation,* which was to serve as a nucleus for a third party. No new third party ever materialized, partly because of the existence of the Union Party,* which had a greater following, and partly because President Roosevelt's so-called second New Deal had shifted dramatically to the Left. Many of the goals of the LIPA had in fact been achieved through the massive welfare and public-works programs of the New Deal. After President Roosevelt's landslide reelection in 1936, the LIPA dissolved. Many members became pro-New Dealers and joined the Democratic Party. One of them, Paul Douglas, was subsequently elected to the Chicago City Council and in 1948 to the U.S. Senate.

For further information, see Paul H. Douglas, *The Coming of a New Party* (1932), and Donald R. McCoy, *Angry Voices, Left-of-Center Politics in the New Deal Era* (1958).

**LEAGUE FOR INDUSTRIAL DEMOCRACY (LID).** Founded in 1905 as the Intercollegiate Socialist Society of America (ISSA) at New York City by Jack London, Upton Sinclair, Harry W. Laidler, and a small group of socialist intellectuals for the purpose of promoting socialism among college students. London, famous for his naturalistic novel, *The Call of the Wild* (1903), was ISSA's first president; Sinclair, whose muckraking novel, *The Jungle*, would appear in 1906, served as vice-president. Laidler, an undergraduate student at Wesleyan College in Connecticut, was a member of the executive board, which also included Clarence Darrow, known at that time for his defense of labor leaders; Thomas W. Higgenson, a former abolitionist; James Graham Phelps Stokes, a wealthy activist in the socialist cause; and William English Walling, a "millionaire socialist" and future author of *Socialism as It Is* (1912).

Patterning itself somewhat after the British Fabians, the ISSA established a series of study clubs on college campuses. Within a few years, some twelve to fifteen chapters existed, with a membership of less than one hundred. Although the ISSA was small in number, the names of those belonging to it composed a veritable who's who of the future left-of-center liberals in

America. They included Heywood Broun, Bruce Bliven, Paul H. Douglas, Morris Hillquit, Joyce Kilmer, Freda Kirchway, Walter Lippmann, Edna St. Vincent Millay, Harry A. Overstreet, John Reed, and Ordway Tead.

World War I and the red hysteria of the 1920s tended to bring socialism into disrepute. By 1921 the ISSA, which was moribund, was reorganized as the LID. With a less radical sounding name, the LID continued to use education as a means to promote socialism. Among LID's presidents were educator John Dewey; Robert Morss Lovett, professor of literature at the University of Chicago; and Florence Kelley, labor reformer and founder of local Consumers' Leagues. Norman Thomas, Socialist leader and later to be the perennial presidential candidate of the Socialist Party of America,* and Harry W. Laidler would serve as executive director (the latter until 1957). Those holding posts as treasurer in the early phase of LID's life were Stuart Chase (author and later a renowned economist) and Reinhold Niebuhr, pioneer of neoorthodoxy at the Union Theological Seminary in New York City. Although LID's membership roster was relatively small, it again reflected a high level of quality. Among its student members were Sidney Hook, Darlington Hoopes, Max Lerner, Talcott Parsons, Walter Reuther, William L. Shirer, and Irving Stone.

Although not winning mass converts to socialism, the LID conducted institutes, provided speakers, and disseminated information on college campuses. In 1927 it formed the Student Committee to Aid Sacco and Vanzetti, supported the anti-Reserve Officers Training Corps movement, and advocated unilateral disarmament on the part of the United States. In the 1930s LID contributed to the isolationist, anti-interventionist sentiment prevalent on college campuses.

Seeking a vehicle to attract young people to the cause of socialism, the LID in 1928 converted its ineffective Intercollegiate Student Council into a semi-autonomous organization, the Student League for Industrial Democracy (SLID). With Joseph P. Lash, later Eleanor Roosevelt's biographer, as one of its best leaders, SLID sought to radicalize students through a series of summer institutes. In its declaration of principles, SLID called for an "alliance between students and workers by the interchange of experience and knowledge." Its members, probably fewer than a thousand, sponsored Student Anti-War Week in 1935, supported strikes by unions, and published *Revolt* (a bulletin later renamed *Student Outlook*).

In 1935 SLID cut its ties with LID and merged with the American Student Union. The union fell prey to Communist control and in 1941 went defunct. The LID revived SLID in 1945 and hired Jesse Cavileer, a recent graduate of Syracuse University, to serve as national secretary. Under a succession of national secretaries, including James Farmer, later to head the Congress of Racial Equality,* and Gabriel Kolko, who would later become a radically oriented historian of the New Left school, SLID supported civil rights, conducted student conferences, and encouraged dialogue between students and labor leaders. Many SLID members were present in 1947 when the National Student Association* was founded. In 1960 SLID severed its relations with LID and transformed itself into the Students for a Democratic Society.*

The LID never condoned violence, always championed social democracy through participation in parliamentary procedure, and stressed the value of rational dialogue. Through its Student-Labor Institute, LID still encourages discussion between students and labor leaders. Currently Nathaniel M. Minkoss is president of LID, and Harry Gleischman serves as chairperson of the executive committee. The LID presents an award to individuals who have contributed in a constructive way to the labor movement. The last recipient so honored was Senator Henry M. Jackson (D-Wash). In addition to publishing educational materials, the LID also issues an *Annual Report* and a bimonthly *Bulletin*. Its headquarters is in New York City.

For further information, see the LID publication, *The League for Industrial Democracy: Forty Years of Education* (1945), and James Weinstein, *The Decline of Socialism* (1967).

**LEAGUE OF CONSERVATION VOTERS (LCV).** Founded in 1969 at Washington, D.C., by representatives of Friends of the Earth (FOE) for the purpose of promoting the nomination and election of political candidates who support environmental legislation. The FOE was formed earlier in 1969 at San Francisco by David Browder, a former director of the Sierra Club,* for the purpose of promoting the conservation of natural resources, ecology, and the preservation of wilderness areas. It has a membership of some twenty thousand. Browder, who is currently director of the FOE, and others of its leaders formed the LCV as a nonmember organization to serve as FOE's political arm.

Funds for the LCV activities come from the FOE, contributions from the public, and from a ten-dollar annual fee for receiving its environmental voting chart relative to members of Congress. The LCV not only keeps track of the voting records of members of Congress, pertaining to their votes on legislation affecting the environment, but it endorses candidates. When endorsements are made, based upon their pro-environment record, candidates receive campaign funds and free publicity. Candidates are selected on a nonpartisan basis; only their stand on environmental issues is taken into account. In this manner the LCV has been instrumental in helping to elect members of Congress who favor both protection and restoration of the environment.

National headquarters of the LCV is located in Washington, D.C. Current coordinator is Marion Edey. LCV publications include two biennials, *How Your Congressman Voted on Critical Environmental Issues* and *How Your Senator Voted on Critical Environmental Issues*.

**LEAGUE OF NATIONS ASSOCIATION.** See Foreign Policy Association.

**LEAGUE OF UNITED SOUTHERNERS (LUS).** Founded in 1858 at Montgomery, Alabama, by William Lowndes Yancy for the purpose of promoting states' rights and the protection of slavery. Membership in the LUS was relatively small, since it represented "Fire-eaters" who were already advocating secession from the Union unless the demands of slaveholders were met.

The LUS called for the repeal of all laws that restricted the slave trade, demanded protection for slavery in the territories, and wanted strict enforcement of the Fugitive Slave Act. The LUS served as a spokesman for the slaveholding planter class, and thus it was far more militant than the white non-slaveholding class.

Members of the LUS within the Democratic Party* were instrumental in splitting the party in 1860 rather than acquiesce to the nomination of Stephen A. Douglas for the presidency. Immediately after the national election of 1860, when Republican* Abraham Lincoln won the presidency, the LUS championed secession. William L. Yancey wrote the 1861 ordinance of secession that took Alabama out of the Union, and he served in the Confederate Senate until his death in 1863. Following the formation of the Confederate States of America, the LUS disbanded. Its influence among the leadership class of the South served to inflame passions. The LUS helped lead the southern states into the Civil War.

For more information, see C. P. Denman, *The Secession Movement in Alabama* (1933), and William Barney, *The Road to Secession: A New Perspective on the Old South* (1966).

**LEAGUE OF WOMEN VOTERS OF THE UNITED STATES (LWV-US).** Founded in 1920 at Chicago by the delegates of the last convention of the National American Woman Suffrage Association* (NAWSA) for the purpose of promoting participation in politics by American women. The NAWSA, having succeeded in securing passage and ratification of the Nineteenth (woman suffrage) amendment to the U.S. Constitution, gave birth to its successor, the League of Women Voters. Its name was changed to LWV-US in 1946, with its prime objective being to increase the "effectiveness of women's votes in furthering better government." The moving force in the formation of the LWV-US was Carrie Chapman Catt, who served as honorary national president from 1920 until her death in 1947. Its first president was Maud Wood Park.

The LWV-US is nonpartisan and does not endorse or oppose any parties or candidates. It has these permanent committees: Environment; Foreign Policy; Human Resources; Government; Congress; and Voters' Service. It champions specific legislation when its members arrive at a consensus, and through its League of Women Voters Education Fund it seeks to influence public opinion. It also lobbies in Congress for passage of laws it has endorsed. In so doing, it sometimes joins coalitions to ensure enactment of legislation it supports.

The LWV-US has supported and contributed to the enactment of the following legislation: Tennessee Valley Authority Act (1933); Social Security Act (1935); Pure Food, Drug, and Cosmetic Act (1938); ratification of the United Nations Charter (1945); General Agreement on Tariffs and Trade (1948); Economic Opportunity Act (1965); Water Resources Act (1965); Nuclear Nonproliferation Treaty (1969); and the District of Columbia Home Rule Act (1973). It contributed significantly to the passage by Congress of the equal rights amendment to the U.S. Constitution. Much effort has been made lobbying in the various states in order to get sufficient legislative approval to ratify it.

Much research on controversial issues is conducted by the LWV-US, and the results are disseminated to the voting public. It sponsored the television debate in 1976 between President Gerald R. Ford, the presidential nominee of the Republican Party,* and Jimmy Carter, the presidential candidate of the Democratic Party.* In 1980 the LWV-US again sponsored the presidential debates. The first pitted the GOP nominee, Ronald Reagan, against independent John Anderson. The second debate paired Reagan against President Jimmy Carter, the Democratic nominee. The LVW-US was criticized by some for not placing a vacant podium in the initial debate to indicate that President Carter had refused to debate if John Anderson was present. Likewise in the second event it met criticism from Anderson's followers for excluding their candidate from the encounter. To inform voters, the LWV-US issues such publications as the *National Voter, Facts and Issues*, and *Current Focus*.

Present national headquarters is located in Washington, D.C. Current president is Ruth C. Clausen. Membership totals about 140,000, with fifty state leagues and over 1,300 local chapters. Some 3,000 members are men. The LWV-US periodically issues studies and audiovisual aids.

For more information, see Mary Gray Peck, *Carrie Chapman Catt* (1944), and Norman J. Ornstein and Shirley Elder, *Interest Groups, Lobbying and Policymaking* (1978).

**LEAGUE TO ENFORCE PEACE (LEP).** Founded in 1915 at Philadelphia by a group of preparedness advocates for the purpose of promoting the need for the United States to bolster its national defense. Former President William Howard Taft was chosen president. Other prominent members were ex-President Theodore Roosevelt; Senator Henry Cabot Lodge (R-Mass.); Senator James W. Wadsworth (R-N.Y.); A. Lawrence Lowell, president of Harvard University; and Henry L. Stimson, who had served as secretary of war in Taft's cabinet.

LEP adherents sought to arouse public opinion so as to force President Woodrow Wilson to initiate steps to prepare the United States militarily. LEP spokesmen cited the fate of Belgium, then occupied by German troops, as an example of what could happen to an unprepared nation. Most members of the LEP were interventionists and believed that a German victory would be detrimental to the national self-interest of the United States. Members were so strong in their belief concerning mobilization that they initiated the Plattsburgh idea, the establishment of a military training camp for civilians at Plattsburgh, New York. Adherents to the LEP were often members or supporters of other such groups as the American Defense Society, American Rights Committee, and the National Security League.* The LEP did influence public opinion, but not sufficiently to force President Wilson to mobilize for war. After the United States became an active participant in World War I in 1917, the LEP disbanded.

For more information, see Ruhl J. Bartlett, *The League to Enforce Peace* (1944).

**LIBERAL PARTY (LP).** Founded in 1944 at New York City by a group of non-Communist liberals who withdrew from the American Labor Party* to form their own labor, left-of-center coalition in order to promote social reform and elect candidates to municipal, state, and federal offices. Prime movers in the formation of the LP were David Dubinsky, president of the International Ladies' Garment Workers' Union: Alex Rose of the United Hatters, Cap and Millinery Workers International Union; Adolph A. Berle, New Deal brain-truster; George S. Counts, former president of the American Federation of Teachers and professor of education at Columbia Teachers College; and Reinhold Niebuhr, professor of applied Christianity at the Union Theological Seminary. Dr. John L. Childs served as LP's first state chairperson, with Dean Alfange, who would be the party's 1946 candidate for the twenty-fourth district, acting as chief spokesperson in New York City.

Although a state party, the LP has played a key role in the outcome of several elections with national significance. In 1944, LP's endorsement of Franklin D. Roosevelt garnered the president over 320,000 votes and thus contributed to his successful bid for a fourth term. Although the LP did not help carry New York for Harry S. Truman (whom it endorsed) in 1948, its opposition to Henry A. Wallace's Progressive Party* persuaded many liberal Democrats* not to support it. Other key elections in which the LP played a decisive role included the 1949 defeat of the American Labor Party's congressional candidate, Vito Marcantonio; the 1951 election of Rudolph Halley as president of the New York City Council; the election of Herbert Lehman in 1950 to the U.S. Senate; the election of Averell Harriman in 1954 as governor; the presidential election of John F. Kennedy in 1960 (he carried New York); and the election of John Lindsay as mayor of New York

City in 1965 and 1969. Although it generally supports Democrats, the LP regularly endorsed Senator Jacob Javits (R-N.Y.). In 1980, after failing to gain renomination in the Republican primary, Javits became the LP candidate for the U.S. Senate. He pulled some 630,000 votes but came in third behind the Republican (who won) and the Democratic candidates.

In 1980 the LP also endorsed independent John Anderson as its presidential candidate. Anderson and former Governor Patrick J. Lucey of Wisconsin (his vice-presidential running mate) drew only 7 percent of the popular vote. This constituted 5,581,379 popular votes while winning no electoral votes.

Platforms of the LP consistently have supported the right of collective bargaining for labor unions, U.S. participation in the United Nations, civil rights, social welfare programs, and resistance to communism at home and abroad. The LP took no official stand on the Vietnam war so as to avoid intraparty dissension. The party is regarded by some as the political arm of the garment unions, but it has drawn considerable support from the intellectual community. State chairpersons of the LP have been John Childs, (1944-1947); Adolph Berle (1947-1955); George S. Counts (1955-1962); New York University psychology professor Timothy Costello (1962-1970); and currently the Reverend Donald Harrington.

For futher information, see Max D. Danish, *The World of David Dubinsky* (1957).

**LIBERAL REPUBLICAN PARTY (LRP).** Founded in 1872 by an insurgent group of reformers within the Republican Party* because of disenchantment with the administration of President Ulysses S. Grant. LRP leaders included editors Horace Greeley and Whitelaw Reid of the *New York Tribune*, Murat Halstead of the *Cincinnati Commercial*, Horace White of the *Chicago Tribune*, Henry Watterson of the *Louisville Courier-Journal*, and Samuel Bowles of the *Springfield* (Mass.) *Republican*. Among the political notables helping to form the LRP were Charles Francis Adams, B. Gratz Brown, Carl Schurz, Charles Sumner, Lyman Trumbull, and Supreme Court justices Salmon P. Chase and David Davis.

At its 1872 nominating convention at Cincinnati, the LRP selected Horace Greeley as its presidential nominee and B. Gratz Brown as his running mate. The party's platform upheld the Thirteenth, Fourteenth, and Fifteenth amendments but demanded amnesty for former Confederates and the end to Reconstruction. Additional planks called for civil service reform, resumption of specie payment, no further land grants to railroads, and no repudiation of the national debt.

The Democratic Party* also nominated the Greeley-Brown ticket and adopted the LRP platform almost completely. In the presidential race against Grant, who had been renominated by the regular GOP, this LRP-Democratic coalition lost by a margin of 763,664 popular votes (11.8 percent). It did win 66 electoral votes from six southern and border states. Following this defeat the LRP dissolved.

For further information, see Matthew T. Downey, "Horace Greeley and the Politicians: Liberal Republican Convention in 1872," *Journal of American History* 53 (1967):727; Glyndon G. Van Deusen, *Horace Greeley: Nineteenth Century Crusader* (1953); Martin Duberman, *Charles Francis Adams* (1961); and Earle D. Ross, *The Liberal Republican Movement* (1919 [1970]).

**LIBERAL UNION, THE.** See People's Party (1971).

**LIBERTARIAN LEAGUE.** See Anarchist Federation.

**LIBERTARIAN PARTY (LP).** Founded in 1971 at Westminster, Colorado, by David Nolan and Susan Nolan, and a small group of libertarians for the purpose of promoting libertarianism as a political philosophy. Prime movers in the formation of the LP included Dr. John Hospers, a professor of philosophy at the University of Southern California and author of *Libertarianism* (1971); Edward H. Crane III, a former supporter of Senator Barry Goldwater (R-Ariz.) and LP's first national chairman; Manuel Klausner, editor of *Reason*, a libertarian publication; R. A. Childs, Jr., a leading libertarian writer; Murray Rothbard, professor of economics at Brooklyn Polytechnic Institute; Theodore ("Tonie") Nathan, a businessman from Eugene, Oregon; and Jim Dean, executive editor of the *Santa Ana Register*.

The political philosophy advocated by the LP represents a synthesis of ideas stemming from Herbert Spencer's social Darwinism; Ayn Rand's objectivism; Thomas Jefferson's views on limited government; Herbert Hoover's rugged individualism; and the laissez-faire economics of Friedrich A. von Hayek. The LP's statement of principles asserts, "We, the members of the Libertarian Party, challenge the cult of the omnipotent state and defend the rights of the individual." Members of the LP oppose the welfare state and wish to see the size and influence of the government drastically reduced. They champion personal liberty and oppose any infringement on it for any purpose. Intellectually there is an essence of anarchism in the LP's political philosophy, but it does not advocate abolition of all government. They are a rather free-wheeling group, which is considered too eccentric by most middle-class Americans.

Within the first year of its formation, the LP had thirteen state affiliates. By 1976 its candidates were on the ballot in thirty-two states. In 1972 the LP held its first national nominating convention at Denver, Colorado. Assembled delegates selected John Hospers of California as its presidential nominee and Theodore Nathan of Oregon for the vice-presidency. The LP platform called for termination of the following: U.S. intervention in Vietnam; conscription; confiscatory taxes; compulsory education; the census; gun registration laws; federal censorship or surveillance; the tariff; wage and price controls; restrictions on the use of drugs; government regulatory agencies; the Federal Reserve System; foreign aid; and welfare programs. On the ballot in California, Colorado, and Massachusetts, the Hospers-Nathan ticket drew only 3,671 popular votes. They did receive one electoral vote, however, when a Republican* elector cast his vote for the LP candidates rather than for the Nixon-Agnew team.

Between 1972 and 1976 several LP candidates ran for state and local offices. One such unsuccessful attempt was made by Francine Youngstein, who sought the mayor's office in New York City. The LP's 1976 nominating convention was held in Washington, D.C., where Roger L. MacBride of Virginia was chosen as the presidential nominee and David P. Bergland of California was selected as his vice-presidential running mate. The platform called for termination of all welfare programs; nuclear disarmament; total amnesty for draft dodgers and deserters; cessation of antitrust suits; elimination of all government regulation; an end to busing to achieve racial balance in the public schools; no sale of arms to foreign nations; application of the homesteading concept relative to unclaimed property (such as planets of the solar system); international negotiations toward complete and general disarmament; abolition of the Bureau of Alcohol, Tobacco, and Firearms; opposition to government regulation and regimentation; an end to the doctrine of sovereign immunity whereby states may not be sued without their permission; no federal financing of abortions; opposition to restrictions placed on laetrile or artificial sweeteners; free trade; and termination of compulsory school attendance. The popular vote for this ticket totaled 183,187 (0.2 percent).

Heartened by the gains made between 1972 and 1976, the LP took steps to reach out to all sectors of the population. To reach college students it formed the Young Libertarian Alliance (YLA) in 1976, which by 1979 had chapters in 250 colleges and universities throughout the nation. The YLA publishes a newspaper for college students, *Outlook*, and periodically issues the *YLA Newsletter*. Also established in 1976 was the Center for Libertarian Studies (CLS). Located in New York City, its president is David H. Padden with J. Philip Sykes serving as executive director. Friedrich A. von Hayek, a Nobel Laureate economist at the University of Freiberg, is honorary chairman. The CLS publishes the *Journal of Libertarian Studies*, a quarterly; *Occasional Papers*, a periodic series of essays; a newsletter, *In Pursuit of Liberty*; the *Austrian Economic Newsletter*, featuring the Austrian school of free-market economics; and specially commissioned studies. The CLS also sponsors annual symposiums on crime and punishment; holds regional conferences; conducts seminars for lawyers and physicians; and operates a research fellows and summer fellows program. In 1977 the LP held a series of party meetings in various regions of the country. These included the New England, Rocky Mountain, and Southern conferences. Also formed in 1977 was the Libertarian Health Association, designed to recruit physicians and dentists.

In 1980 the LP selected Edward Clark, a lawyer for Atlantic Richfield Company, as its presidential nominee and David Koch, president of Koch Engineering Company, as its vice-presidential candidate. The party's platform contained planks calling for the following: a massive, permanent tax cut for all citizens; reduction of government spending; a phase out of Social Security; no registration and no draft; withdrawal of U.S. troops from all foreign bases; termination of all welfare programs; no government regulation of business; drastic curtailment of military spending; an immediate pay freeze for all government employees; ratification of the Equal Rights Amendment; legalize marijuana; repeal of anti-gay laws; end subsidies for nuclear power; no bailout of the Chrysler Corporation or other companies; disengagement from heavy defense commitments to Western Europe, Japan, and South Korea; dismantling of the Department of Education; eliminate all energy regulations; abolish the Federal Trade Commission, Securities Exchange Commission, Federal Communications Commission, and Interstate Commerce Commission; U.S. withdrawal from the North Atlantic Treaty Organization and the United Nations; and a freeze on the money supply and elimination of the Federal Reserve Board. The LP presidential ticket is on the ballot in all fifty states and because of its belief that the government should not fund political campaigns, it accepts no federal funds.

While on the ballot in all of the states, the LP presidential ticket drew only 881,612 popular votes (1 percent) and no electoral votes.

The current national headquarters of the LP is located in Washington, D.C. Present national chairman is David P. Bergland, with Mary Louise Hanson serving as national vice-chairperson. LP publications include *Freedom Today*, *Libertarian Review*, and *Laissez Faire Book Catalog and Reviews*.

For more information, see Robert L. MacBride, *A New Dawn for America* (1977), and Edward Clark, *A New Beginning* (1980).

**LIBERTY LEAGUE.** See American Liberty League.

**LIBERTY LOBBY (LL).** Founded in 1955 at Washington, D.C., by Curtis B. Dall for the purpose of promoting conservatism in politics. The LL takes a right-wing conservative position on domestic issues and a staunch anti-Communist stand relative to international affairs. The LL is opposed to high taxes; federal aid to education; civil rights legislation; national health insurance; federal farm subsidies; public power; public housing; participation in the United Nations; and importation of products produced by foreign "cheap labor." It also calls for repeal of the Sixteenth (income tax) Amendment to the U.S. Constitution; withdrawal of diplomatic recognition from the People's Republic of China; termination of the SALT agreement with the Soviet Union; termination of U.S. participation in the General Agreement on Tariffs and Trade; and an end to all foreign aid programs.

The national headquarters of the LL is located in Washington, D.C. Curtis B. Dall serves as chairman. Over two hundred thousand dues-paying members receive *Liberty Ledger*, a rating of voting records of members of Congress, and *Liberty Lowdown*, a confidential report on issues before Congress. The LL also publishes a monthly, *Liberty Letter*. The influence of LL tends to be greatest among right-wing conservatives. It has had a minimal impact on either Congress or the general public.

**LIBERTY PARTY (LP) (1839).** Founded in 1839 in Warsaw, New York, by a group of abolitionists to promote the end of slavery through political action. A prime mover in the formation of the LP was Myron Holley of New York. The delegates assembled at this convention nominated James G. Birney as their presidential nominee and Francis Julius LeMoyne as his vice-presidential running mate. When the two nominees declined to accept, the LP almost dissolved at its outset.

Joining with Myron Holley to call another nominating convention of the LP were Alvan Stewart and Henry B. Stanton. Meeting at Albany, New York, in 1840, the assembled delegates once more nominated James G. Birney as their presidential nominee, paired with Thomas Earle of Pennsylvania as his vice-presidential running mate. This time Birney, who had broken with William Lloyd Garrison and his faction of the American Anti-Slavery Society* (which did not believe in political action), accepted the LP nomination, as did Thomas Earle. The LP platform was basically a one-issue document, which called for the immediate abolition of the institution of slavery. Other issues were sidestepped with the statement, "We by no means lost sight of numerous other questions in which all are to be affected, directly or indirectly, by our Government." It was hoped that the LP would attract the anti-slavery votes of those who would not join an abolitionist organization. In a three-cornered presidential race in which William Henry Harrison represented the Whig Party* and Martin Van Buren the Democratic Party,* Birney polled a meager 7,069 popular votes.

Although the LP made a poor showing, it had begun to attract interest among political figures such as Gerrit Smith, Charles Torrey, and Salmon P. Chase. In order to have more time to persuade the electorate to support LP candidates, the decision was made in 1841 to run Birney again at the next presidential election. His nomination was made official at the LP's national convention held at Buffalo, New York, in 1843. At this time the delegates also named Thomas Morris of Ohio as the vice-presidential nominee. The platform claimed that "slavery is against natural rights" and that the U.S. government "has under the Constitution, no power to establish or continue slavery." Other planks supported general education; rigid public economy; freedom of speech, press, and right of petition; Irish independence; and an invitation to "colored fellow citizens to fraternity with us in the Liberty Party." The 1844 presidential race was another three-man contest in which James K. Polk stood as the Democratic Party* candidate and Henry Clay represented the Whigs.* Birney was once more last in the field with 62,300 popular and no electoral votes. But he was instrumental in causing Clay to lose New York, and hence Polk became the winner.

The LP met at a national convention in 1848 at Rochester, New York. Delegates nominated Gerrit Smith of New York for the presidency and Charles E. Foote of Michigan for the vice-presidency. Prior to the election, however, these candidates withdrew from the contest. The LP was short-lived not because slavery was an unimportant issue but because it ignored most other issues; thus its base was too narrow for broad popularity. The greatest contribution of the LP was to make the anti-slavery cause a political issue and thus set the stage for the electorate to voice their opinion by the ballot box. Most of the adherents of the LP gravitated into the Free Soil Party.*

For further information, see Ralph V. Harlow, *Gerrit Smith, Philanthropist and Reformer* (1939); Betty Fladeland, *James Gillespie Birney: Slaveholder to Abolitionist* (1955); and Dwight L. Dumond, ed., *Letters of James Gillespie Birney, 1831-1857*, 2 vols. (1966).

**LIBERTY PARTY (LP) (1932).** Founded in 1932 at St. Louis by Frank E. Webb, a socialist, for the purpose of promoting socialism as a remedy for the economic ills of the Great Depression. At its national convention in 1932 William H. Harvey of Arkansas, the famous Populist author of *Coin's Financial School* (1894), was selected as the presidential nominee, with Frank F. Hemenway of Washington as his vice-presidential running mate.

The platform proposed federal relief, public works, and the nationalization of all industry. There was an attempt by Harvey to merge the LP with the Jobless Party,* but a dispute over who would be the presidential nominee foiled this effort. Harvey tried to revive the old-time Populist fervor, but his ability to campaign was limited by his age; he was eighty-one years old. Also the LP had difficulty raising campaign funds since its members were often unemployed, and middle-or upper-class voters regarded the party as unduly radical.

The LP presidential ticket was on the ballot in Arkansas, California, Michigan, Montana, New Mexico, North Dakota, South Dakota, Texas, and Washington. The Harvey-Hemenway ticket drew a popular vote of 53,199 (0.13 percent) and no electoral votes. The LP ticket probably took votes that would have gone to Franklin D. Roosevelt, but Roosevelt's margin of victory over Herbert C. Hoover was so large that any such loss did not matter. Once the New Deal was inaugurated, the LP became defunct.

For more information, see Donald R. McCoy, *Angry Voices, Left-of-Center Politics in the New Deal Era* (1971).

**LIBERTY UNION.** See People's Party (1971).

**LOCOFOCO PARTY.** See Equal Rights (Locofoco) Party.

**LOWNDES COUNTY FREEDOM ORGANIZATION (LCFO).** Founded in 1966 at Haynesville, Alabama, by representatives of the Student Non-violent Coordinating Committee* (SNCC) for the purpose of involving southern blacks in politics. At a meeting called by Stokely Carmichael, senior field officer of SNCC, seven black candidates were nominated for county offices. The symbol on the ballot used by the LCFO was a black panther. The LCFO was not an affiliate of the official Black Panther Party,* but southern newspapers, which were hostile, linked the Lowndes County party to the Black Panthers.

Even though the population of Lowndes County, totaling 15,417, was 81 percent black, none of the LCFO's candidates was elected to office. This and other poor showings in local elections prompted the LCFO to seek a broader base. In 1969 it merged with the black-oriented National Democratic Party of Alabama.* This proved to be a highly effective move; thereafter black candidates were elected to state and congressional offices. The LCFO helped to initiate the movement for blacks to exert political pressure by separatist parties. In the black belts of the South, where blacks outnumber the white voters, it was important to get black candidates on the ballots. Since the regular Democratic Party,* which was then white-dominated, would not do so, this tactic of forming an independent party gave black candidates a chance of appearing on the ballot. When the Voting Rights Act of 1965 made it possible for blacks to vote, the LCFO helped initiate black participation in the democratic process.

For more information, see Hanes Walton, Jr., *Black Political Parties* (1972).

**LOYAL DEMOCRATS OF MISSISSIPPI (LDM).** Founded in 1968 at Jackson, Mississippi, by representatives of the National Association for the Advancement of Colored People* (NAACP) and the Mississippi Freedom Democratic Party* (MFDP) for the purpose of challenging the regular state

Democratic delegation at the national nominating convention of the Democratic Party.* Prime movers in the formation of the LDM were Charles Evers, then running for Congress, and Lawrence Guyot, chairman of the MFDP.

The basic objectives of the LDM were to force the regular state Democrats to open their party to blacks or face a challenge at the 1968 national convention. The LDM accepted liberal whites and thus was an integrated party. The regular Democrats constituted an all-white party and ignored black voters who were actually the majority in many black-belt counties in the delta. A secondary goal was to unite blacks and white liberals so that the LDM could win elections in areas where blacks outnumbered white Democrats.

The national convention's credentials committee did vote to seat the LDM delegation instead of the all-white delegation of the regular Democrats. This decision was endorsed by Vice-President Hubert H. Humphrey, the leading contender for the presidential nomination. The convention as a whole subsequently ratified this decision, and the LDM delegation was seated. This served notice on all southern delegations that any prohibitions on the full participation by blacks would not be tolerated by the Democratic Party, a victory of national significance.

The political fortunes of blacks rose when the LDM seven-candidate slate in Fayette, Mississippi, was elected to office in 1969. Of this group, Charles Evers was elected mayor by defeating a white Democrat who had held the office for eighteen years. As blacks began to register and run for offices, the regular Democrats realized that they had to hold the black vote or lose out to the emerging Republican Party.* Thus the LDM initiated a process in the South whereby blacks were brought into the major parties because the bloc voting of blacks forced the issue.

For more information, see Hanes Walton, Jr., *Black Political Parties* (1972).

**MARINE CORPS LEAGUE (MCL).** Founded in 1923 at New York City by Sidney W. Brewster and a group of former U.S. Marines meeting in a special caucus for the purpose of promoting fellowship and benefits for ex-Marines. Brewster, a retired Marine major, was commandant of the Marine Corps Veterans Association (MCVO), formed eight months earlier and now the nucleus of the newly organized MCL. The MCL was chartered by Congress in 1937. It looked upon itself as an alumni organization for all former Marines. Its mottos were, *Semper Fidelis* ("Always Faithful"), "Once a Marine—Always a Marine, and "All for One and One for All."

The MCL has consistently resisted efforts to abolish the marines or take away their distinct place as a special unit among the nation's armed forces. Through its influence on public opinion and the members of Congress, the MCL prevented both Presidents Franklin D. Roosevelt and Harry S. Truman from eliminating the Marine Corps as a separate branch of the armed forces. The MCL lobbies for legislation beneficial to its members. It has been instrumental, in conjunction with other veterans' organizations, in getting greater government benefits for ex-servicepeople. The MCL monitors federal agencies dealing with veterans and disseminates needed information to its members. It has always championed a strong national defense and supported U.S. entry into World War II, Korea, and Vietnam.

In 1954 the MCL dedicated the heroic-sized bronze statue at Washington, D.C., depicting the flag-raising at Iwo Jima (created by Felix DeWeldon). In 1964 the MCL started the Civic Action Fund for Vietnam to aid civilian victims of the war. The Young Marines and the Youth Physical Fitness program were initiated in 1965. The former organization, for boys from eight to seventeen years of age, stressed physical fitness and good citizenship. Its motto was "Our Youth Is the Future." The Youth Physical Fitness program operated in twenty states and involved over five million boys. A Youth Foundation was set up to fund sports activities as an important aspect of this project.

Special committees exist within the MCL relating to: Americanism; Service and Rehabilitation; Veterans Administration Volunteer Service; Young Marines; and Youth Physical Fitness. In the 1970s the MCL took an active interest in curbing drug abuse; sought an equitable system of amnesty for draft dodgers or deserters; opposed curtailment of services or reduction of facilities in hospitals operated by the Veterans Administration; and strove to secure the return from Vietnam of all American prisoners of war. In 1971 the MCL formed the United States Orienteering Federation to promote hiking, cross-country running, and military land navigation. The MCL has always fostered patriotism and brings to the attention of the general public the history of the U.S. Marines.

The national headquarters of the MCL is located in Arlington, Virginia. Membership (which includes both men and women) totals nearly twenty thousand in some 340 local detachments throughout the nation. The Marine Corps League Auxiliary was established for members' spouses. The Military Order of the Devil was established in 1939 as the honor society for MCL. Current national adjutant is Frank Starr. The MCL publishes a monthly, *Marines Magazine*.

**MAYORS CONFERENCE.** See United States Conference of Mayors.

**MEXICAN-AMERICAN POLITICAL ASSOCIATION (MAPA).** Founded in 1959 at Los Angeles by a group of Mexican-Americans for the purpose of promoting political activism among Chicanos. Its membership grew to nearly fifty thousand by 1960. The MAPA supported Viva Kennedy! Clubs, which were first organized by J. Carlos McCormick of the Alianza Hispano-Americano.* The political endorsement of John F. Kennedy by the MAPA was instrumental in getting a large share of the Latino vote for the presidential nominee of the Democratic Party.*

The political objectives of the MAPA were to get Mexican-Americans politically active, to get them to vote as a bloc, and to get Chicanos elected to local, state, and national offices. It wanted Americans of Mexican ancestry to become as active as blacks in order to make civil rights gains and win economic benefits for the Chicano community. In 1962 the MAPA was instrumental in securing the election of Edward Roybal, a Mexican-American, to the U.S. House of Representatives. In that same year it also helped to elect Philip Soto and John Mareno, both Chicanos, to the California state legislature at Sacramento. In 1968 it was instrumental in getting Alex Garcia elected to the state legislature. Once the Latin community displayed its political power, the Democrats and Republicans* began to nominate more Mexican-Americans, and thus the MAPA began to disintegrate as a political entity. It had succeeded in achieving its goals but in so doing eliminated a need for itself as a distinct Mexican-American organization. It was absorbed into the Political Association of Spanish Speaking Organizations, which eventually helped to promote the formation of the La Raza Unida Party* outside of California.

For more information, see Eugene P. Dvorin and Arthur J. Minsner, eds., *California Politcs and Parties* (1966).

**MIDWESTERN GOVERNORS CONFERENCE (MGC).** Founded in 1962 at Chicago by the governors of the midwestern states for the purpose of promoting interstate cooperation and regional benefits. The prime mover in the formation of the MGC was Governor William L. Guy (D-N.D.), who was elected its first chairman. At the initial conference, governors present represented the states of Illinois, Indiana, Iowa, Michigan, Minnesota, Missouri, Nebraska, South Dakota, and Wisconsin. Those states whose governors would join soon thereafter included Kansas, Kentucky, North Dakota, Ohio, Oklahoma, and West Virginia.

Annual conventions are held on a rotating basis, as is the chairmanship. The objectives of the MGC are not only to foster cooperation among the midwestern states but to help ensure that the Midwest as a region secures its share of benefits from the federal government. Midwestern governors sought to prevent the South and West from getting too many federal establishments, particularly relating to military bases, air force installations, and the space program. The MGC was concerned also with federal assistance relating to pollution, highways, and urban redevelopment. Since the Midwest is heavily agricultural, the MGC seeks higher federal price supports for farmers. Because the governors in MGC represent both the Democratic* and Republican* parties, it has been difficult for the conference to act in a bipartisan manner. Yet it has exerted some influence on the White House by encouraging its congressional delegations to ally when legislation affecting the Midwest is before the Congress. The national headquarters of the MCG is located in Chicago at the Midwestern office of the Council of State Governments.* Current chairman is Governor Richard F. Kneip (R-S.D.).

For more information, see John H. Fenton, *Midwest Politics* (1966).

**MINUTEMEN.** See Patriotic Party.

**MISSISSIPPI FREEDOM DEMOCRATIC PARTY (MFDP).** Founded in 1964 at Jackson, Mississippi, for the purpose of promoting political activism among blacks. Prime movers in the formation of MFDP were Robert P. Moses, Aaron Henry, Lawrence Guyot, and Fannie Lou Hamer. Blacks were not permitted to participate in the activities of the regular state organization of the Democratic Party,* so those in Mississippi were excluded from primaries and membership on the delegations attending the national nominating convention. But some Mississippi counties had more black voters than white, and thus because of the Voting Rights Act of 1965 (which authorized federal registrars), the MFDP challenged the propriety of an all-white delegation representing only a portion of Mississippi Democrats.

The MFDP sent a rival delegation to the 1964 Democratic National Convention at Atlantic City, New Jersey. It challenged the seats of the regular (all-white) Mississippi delegation. Seeking a compromise, President Lyndon B. Johnson, who wanted a second term, offered the MFDP two seats on the regular delegation as delegates at large. This offer was refused, so the MFDP had no representation at all. Yet its action served to draw national attention to the situation in Mississippi and set the stage for fuller participation by blacks four years hence.

In 1968 Charles Evers, Aaron Henry, and Hodding Carter promoted the formation of the Loyal Democrats of Mississippi* (LDM), which represented the MFDP, the National Association for the Advancement of Colored People,* and a group of white liberals who desired political integration. The LDM sent a rival delegation to the Democratic National Convention at Chicago in 1968. This time the delegation received the backing of Vice-President Hubert H. Humphrey, who was seeking the presidential nomination of the Democratic Party. The LDM delegation was also endorsed by Senator Eugene McCarthy (D-Minn.) and Senator George M. McGovern (D-S.D.), both of them also seeking the presidential nomination. The convention subsequently unseated the regular Mississippi delegation headed by Governor John Bell Williams for both failing to include blacks and refusing to sign a loyalty pledge. The LDM delegation was seated. Thus came to fruition the efforts of the MFDP, which now had become the official representative of its state.

By forcing regular Democrats to recognize the political power of blacks, the MFDP succeeded in getting full political participation for southern blacks. Its success, therefore, had national implications. It also, ironically, lost its reason for a separate existence.

For more information, see Leslie Burl McLemore, "The Freedom Democratic Party and the Changing Political Status of the Negro in Mississippi" (Master's thesis, Atlantic University, 1965), and Hanes Walton, Jr., *Black Political Parties: An Historical and Political Analysis* (1972).

**MISSISSIPPI VALLEY ASSOCIATION.** See Water Resources Congress.

**MOBILIZATION COMMITTEE TO END THE WAR IN VIETNAM (MOBE).** Founded in 1966 at New York City and San Francisco by anti-war activists to protest continuation of U.S. involvement in the Vietnamese conflict. Known alternately as the Spring Mobilization Committee and the National Mobilization Committee to End the War in Vietnam, MOBE evolved out of the milieu of the civil rights and free-speech movements. At the outset it was a nebulous coalition of protesters, with the Students for a Democratic Society* (SDS) playing a leading role in its formation. It staged huge anti-war marches in New York City and San Francisco in the spring of 1966. In 1967 MOBE organized a massive march on the Pentagon, which led to violence and mass arrests of some demonstrators.

By 1968 MOBE activities were coordinated by Rennard "Rennie" Davis, David Dellinger, and Tom Hayden (a former leader of the SDS). Plans were made to initiate a major protest against the war in Vietnam so as to coincide with the meeting at Chicago of the Democratic Party's* national convention. Demonstrations at Grant Park and the subsequent march were marked with violence and counterviolence on the part of the Chicago police. Davis, Dellinger, and Hayden were arrested and with five others (dubbed the "Chicago Eight") were tried for conspiracy to incite a riot. The additional five who were tried included Abbie Hoffman and Jerry Rubin, both leaders of YIPPIE; Bobby Seale of the Black Panthers*; John Froines, a professor of chemistry at the University of Oregon; and Lee Weiner, a graduate student in sociology at Northwestern University.

MOBE declined when Dellinger, Davis, and Hayden were convicted for conspiracy by a jury (later overturned on appeal). In 1969 a series of short-lived organizations, all ceasing to exist by 1970, came into existence out of the remnants of the original MOBE. These splinter groups were the New Mobilization Committee to End the War in Vietnam; the National Coalition against War, Racism, and Regression (later known as the People's Coalition for Peace and Justice); and the Vietnam Moratorium Committee, headed by Sam Brown, David Hawks, David Mixner, and Marge Sklencar, all former supporters in 1968 of the Eugene McCarthy for President movement.

MOBE's last project was a counterinaugural protest in Washington, D.C., timed to coincide with the presidential inauguration of Richard M. Nixon. Hundreds of thousands of marchers congregated in the nation's capital in January 1969 and, as before, certain agitators provoked violence. This was the last organized activity of MOBE before it went defunct. During its brief life it had contributed substantially to the anti-war sentiment that served to apply pressure on President Lyndon B. Johnson to withdraw from the presidential race and to initiate proposals at a Paris conference for U.S. withdrawal from Vietnam.

For further information, see Sidney Hyman, *Youth in Politics: Expectations and Realities* (1972); Daniel Walker, *Rights in Conflict* (1968); and Tom Hayden, *Rebellion and Repression* (1969).

**MORAL MAJORITY (MM).** Founded in 1979 at Lynchburg, Virginia, by a group of Christian clergymen and laymen for the purpose of promoting

morality and opposing "humanism, socialism, and moral permissiveness."
The prime mover in MM's formation was the Reverend Dr. Jerry Falwell,
pastor of Thomas Road Baptist Church in Lynchburg, preacher on the
"Old Time Gospel Hour" television program, and chancellor of Liberty
Baptist College. Others involved in MM's creation were Dr. Greg Dixon,
pastor of Indianapolis Baptist Temple; Dr. Tim LaHaye, founder of Christian
Heritage College at El Cajon, California; Alan Dye, tax attorney; Bob Billings,
past president of Hyles-Anderson College; Dr. Charles Stanley, pastor of
First Baptist Church of Atlanta, Georgia; and Dr. James Kennedy, pastor
of Coral Ridge Presbyterian Church at Fort Lauderdale, Florida.

The MM's motto is "Bringing Morality Back to America." Its objectives
are:

Mobilizing the grass roots of moral Americans into a clear, loud, and effective voice,
which will be heard in the halls of Congress, in the White House, and in state
legislatures across this land; informing the moral majority of Americans about what
is going on behind their backs in Washington; lobbying intensively in Congress to
defeat left wing, social welfare bills that would further erode our precious freedoms;
pushing for positive legislation which will insure a strong, enduring and free
America; and helping the moral majority of Americans in local communities fight
pornography, homosexuality, obscene school textbooks, and other burning issues
facing each and every one of us.

MM supports the Kemp-Roth Bill (for a 30 percent tax cut), prayer in the
public school, a balanced federal budget, elimination of federal interference
in the free enterprise system, an anti-abortion constitutional amendment,
and strengthening U.S. ties with both Israel and Taiwan. It opposes ratification of the Equal Rights Amendment, federal funding of abortions, losing
control of the Panama Canal, gay rights, sex education in the public
schools, forced busing to achieve racial balance, approval of the Strategic
Arms Limitation Treaty II, legalization of marijuana or prostitution, cutting defenses, continuation of the Department of Education, and undue
federal regulation of business.

MM has fifty state chapters and boasts a membership of over two
million, of which some 70,000 are members of the clergy. Membership is
drawn primarily from the ranks of evangelical or fundamentalist denominations and sects. Local chapters conduct registration drives, take part in
political campaigns, hold rallies, endorse candidates, and target for defeat
those whom it opposes. MM cooperates with other right-wing organizations, such as Christian Voice and Religious Roundtable, to raise campaign
funds and support the election of its endorsed candidates. In 1980 MM got
some four million people to register and influenced another ten million with
its political campaign. Of the forty candidates it endorsed, all won. Among

those targeted for defeat, and who did lose their seats in the U.S. Senate, were Frank Church of Idaho, George McGovern of South Dakota, John Durkin of New Hampshire, Birch Bayh of Indiana, John Culver of Iowa, and Gaylord Nelson of Wisconsin. The MM also claimed a major share of the credit for Ronald Reagan'a landslide victory over Jimmy Carter. Jerry Falwell traveled over 300,000 miles during the campaign to work for the election of Reagan and other conservatives endorsed by MM. The political success of MM was aptly demonstrated not only relative to the national election, but also on the state and local level where it was instrumental in electing pro-morality candidates.

National headquarters of MM is located in Washington, D.C., with an additional office in Lynchburg, Virginia. Dr. Ronald S. Godwin serves as vice-president and chief operations officer. MM publishes the bi-monthly newspaper *Moral Majority Report*.

For further information, see Lisa Myers, "The Power of the Christian Right," *Family Weekly* (October 26, 1980), 7–9 and "A Tide of Born-Again Politics," *Newsweek*, vol. 96 (September 15, 1980), 28–36.

**MORALITY IN MEDIA (MM).** Founded in 1962 at Yorkville, New York, by three clergymen as an interfaith, nonpartisan organization for the purpose of alerting parents to the presence of obscenity and pornography in television, movies, and magazines. Originally called Operation Yorkville, it was renamed MM in 1968 when its headquarters was moved to New York City. That same year the Reverend Morton A. Hill became MM's president.

In 1968 Father Hill was appointed by Lyndon B. Johnson to the Presidential Commission on Obscenity and Pornography. Father Hill and Dr. W. C. Link, now a member of MM's national planning board, coauthored the minority Hill-Link report, which dissented from the commission's general findings. The Hill-Link rejoinder claimed that smut, exploitation of sex, excess nudity, perversion, sadomasochism, violence, and general tastelessness in the media (movies in particular) had a corrupting influence on the manners and morals of young people.

Emphasizing the need for entertainment based on the principles of "love, truth, and taste," MM seeks to organize the protests of parents so as to raise the moral level of all media content aimed at children. To achieve its goals, MM has sponsored forums, promoted letter-writing campaigns, sent out petitions, and prepared news releases. Realizing that codes have deteriorated, that self-censorship or self-restraint on the part of the media is seldom practiced unless pressure is applied, MM hopes to arouse public opinion so as to induce compliance to rational regulations relative to media content. Aware that parents often do not know what their children view, MM endeavors to make parents cognizant of the negative influences to which their children are being constantly subjected.

In its *MM Newsletter* (issued eight times yearly) a "target of the month" is designated, the status of legislation is discussed, and excerpts from court decisions are printed. This magazine also honors an MM Man of the Month (one who has striven to implement the objectives of the organization) and a Prosecutor of the Month. MM serves as a center for disseminating information, keeps in contact with law-enforcement agencies, and operates a library and clearinghouse on the laws of obscenity. A membership of some forty-five thousand supports the work of MM with dues and contributions. Father Hill is currently president, with Rabbi Dr. Julius G. Neuman serving as chairperson.

MM has been successful in influencing public opinion and in securing some modification of television content. It helped bring about the family-hour in television, has prevented some movies that it considers objectionable from being shown on television (or at least run at an hour when children are in bed), and has contributed to local action in various states against pornographic magazines. MM believes that if concerned people make known their dislike of morally objectionable content, the media will be forced to react to society's wishes. As well as receiving opposition from large media interests, MM frequently is criticized by the liberal intellectual community for instigating censorship and thereby infringing on freedom of speech guaranteed by the First Amendment of the U.S. Constitution.

**MOVEMENT FOR A NEW CONGRESS (MFNC).** Founded in 1970 at Princeton, New Jersey (on the campus of Princeton University), by Dr. Henry Bienen, a Princeton professor, and William Murphy, a Princeton doctoral candidate, for the purpose of promoting the election of political candidates committed to ending the war in Vietnam. Some 350 local chapters were formed on college campuses all over the United States, representing thousands of students, to campaign in the mid-term election for congressional candidates opposed to the continuation of the Vietnam war.

Of the fourteen candidates for the U.S. Senate backed by MFNC, eight won and six lost. Of the fifty-four races for the House of Representatives in which a specific candidate was endorsed, twenty-four triumphed while thirty were defeated. The MFNC was instrumental in helping to reelect Senator Adlai Stevenson III (D-Ill.) and Senator Vance Hartke (D-Ind.) and in assisting John V. Tunney to defeat incumbent Senator George Murphy (R-Calif.). The record of the MFNC was mixed because its opposition in some instances actually helped a candidate. Much of the campaign oratory of President Richard M. Nixon and Vice-President Spiro Agnew was aimed at the disruption and campus violence carried on by student radicals. Thus the campaign was not entirely between hawks and doves but also between law-and-order advocates and those defending free speech even if it meant protest demonstrations.

The results of the 1970 elections indicated that the candidates of the Democratic Party* won 52 percent of the popular vote. In terms of actual seats gained, the Republicans* picked up two in the Senate and the Democrats gained nine in the House. Since the Democrats controlled both houses of Congress, the anti-war movement benefited to a small degree from the outcome of the off-year elections of 1970. Following the election, the MFNC disbanded.

**MUGWUMPS.** Founded in 1884 at New York City by dissidents within the Republican Party* for the purpose of opposing the election of James G. Blaine, the GOP nominee, to the presidency. Calling themselves Independent Republicans, they were dubbed mugwumps by Charles A. Dana of the *New York Sun*. Using the term derisively, Dana coined the label from the Algonquin Indian word *mugquomp*, meaning "big chief." The implication was that mugwumps had arrogated themselves to chiefs and would not maintain party loyalty unless their wishes were followed.

Leading mugwumps included Theodore Roosevelt, Carl Schurz, Charles W. Eliot, E. L. Godkin, George Curtis, Henry Ward Beecher, Andrew D. White, and Henry Cabot Lodge. Representing eastern, reform-minded Republicans, the mugwumps refused to campaign for Blaine because of his ostensible connection with corruption, big business, and the spoils system. Meeting at a convention in New York City, they branded Blaine a "representative of men, methods, and conduct which the public conscience condemns." In addition to the scandals associated with Blaine, they opposed his high tariff stand. The mugwumps called upon the Democratic Party* to nominate a presidential candidate whom they could support. When the Democrats nominated Governor Grover Cleveland of New York, the mugwumps endorsed him, saying that he was a symbol of "political courage and honesty and of administrative reform."

The mugwumps' support for Cleveland proved to be instrumental in the Democrats' victory over Blaine. The loss by Blaine of New York State, where the mugwumps were very strong, cost the GOP candidate the election and the presidency. Following the election of 1884, most mugwumps returned to the Republican Party. Their action anticipated the Progressive movement of the early twentieth century, in which Theodore Roosevelt was a primary leader.

For more information, see Lorin Peterson, *The Day of the Mugwump* (1961), and Gerald W. McFarland, *Mugwumps, Morals and Politics* (1975).

## N

**NADER'S RAIDERS.** See Public Interest Research Group.

**NATIONAL ACADEMY OF SCIENCES (NAS).** Founded in 1863 at Washington, D.C., by Alexander Dalls Bache, superintendent of the U.S. Coast Survey, and a group of scientists for the purpose of creating an "institution of scientists to guide public action in scientific matters." Of the original fifty members, most were formerly associated with an organization called *Lazzaroni* (an Italian word meaning "beggars"). Original members of the NAS included such prominent scientists as Bache, its first president; Joseph Dana, a physicist; James Dwight Dana, a geologist; Louis Agassiz, a naturalist; and Benjamin Peirce, a mathematician. According to its congressional charter, which it received soon after being organized, the NAS "shall, whenever called upon by any department of the Government, investigate, examine, experiment, and report upon any subject of science or art." Funds for such activity were to be provided by the federal government.

The NAS is a private organization that elects its members. Present membership totals eleven hundred. Currently it has sections to which scientists are assigned to deal with the following areas: Anthropology, Astronomy, Biochemistry, Biology, Chemistry, Engineering, Genetics, Geology, Geophysics, Mathematics, Microbiology, Physics, Physiology, Psychology, and Zoology. In 1916 the NAS formed an affiliate, the National Research Council (NRC), whose purpose was to involve a broader representation of the scientific community in the task of serving as the government's adviser on science and technology matters. Within itself the NRC created these divisions: Agriculture, Behavioral Sciences, Chemical Technology, Earth Sciences, Engineering, Mathematical Sciences, Medical Sciences, and Physical Sciences.

In 1964 the NAS created the National Academy of Engineering (NAE), which contained these committees: Aeronautics, Education, Medical Technology, Marine Board, Power Plant Siting, Public Engineering Policy, Telecommunications, and Transportation. It currently publishes a bimonthly

journal, *The Bridge*. The NAS further broadened its activities when it formed the Institute of Medicine (IOM) in 1970. Established originally as the
Board on Medicine of the NAS, its name was changed to IOM the same year
it was founded. The IOM conducts research and studies related to health
and medicine and disseminates information to governmental bodies and the
general public.

The functions of the affiliates are all directed by the present NAS. In 1916
President Woodrow Wilson asked the NAS to serve in an advisory capacity
relative to national preparedness. President Franklin D. Roosevelt made the
same request prior to World War II, although the work of the NAS was
subordinated to that of the Office of Scientific Research and Development.
Through its participation, the NAS helped contribute to the development of
many scientific inventions and discoveries that helped the war effort.

During the 1950s the NAS further expanded its activities under the leadership of Dr. Detlev W. Bronk, who headed medical research for the U.S. Air
Force during World War II, served for a time as president of Johns
Hopkins University, was chairman of the NRC, and was elected president
of NAS in 1950. Under his guidance the NAS initiated the International
Geophysical Year, created the Space Sciences Board, and prompted the formation of the American Institute of Biological Sciences. In 1967 NAS
established within itself the Environmental Studies Board and the Committee
on Science and Public Policy, the latter created to assess NAS's perfor-
mance because of criticism, such as that of former Secretary of the Interior
Stewart L. Udall, that NAS was a mere "puppet of government."

The NAS has contributed much toward the formation of government
policy as it relates to applied science and technology. Its research and investigations have been valuable to members of Congress and the general
public. The national headquarters of NAS is located in Washington, D.C.
Current president is Dr. Philip B. Handler, a biochemist from Duke University, with John S. Coleman serving as executive director. Members of the
NAS constitute the elite in science and are elected in accordance with their
record of achievement. NAS issues special reports and publishes a monthly,
*Proceedings of the National Academy of Science*, a *News Report*, and an
annual, *Organization and Members Directory*.

For more information, see Claude E. Barfield, "National Academy of
Sciences Tackles Sensitive Policy Questions," *National Journal*, January
30, 1971, pp. 101–112.

**NATIONAL AFRO-AMERICAN COUNCIL.** See National Afro-
American League.

**NATIONAL AFRO-AMERICAN LEAGUE (NAAL).** Founded in 1890 at
Chicago by a group of white and black delegates from twenty-three states

and the District of Columbia for the purpose of promoting civil rights for Negroes. Prime movers in the formation of NAAL were T. Thomas Fortune, editor of the *New York World*, and W. A. Pleger, a black editor from Georgia who edited the *Athens' Blade*. The NAAL's constitution called for full citizenship for blacks; protection of their civil rights; an end to discrimination; police action to prevent lynchings; and the removal of all obstacles that prevented blacks from exercising their right to vote.

The NAAL proposed the use of legal and political action to attain its goals. It was committed to peaceful means and hoped to influence public opinion by publicizing the plight of blacks. It tried to create state and local affiliates but met with little success. Whites in the North were generally apathetic to the organization, but those in the South were hostile. Within a few years after its formation, the NAAL was almost defunct.

In 1898 the NAAL merged with the National Association of Colored People to become the National Afro-American Council (NAAC). In its revived state, the NAAC became more militant in its demands for civil rights and government action to end lynching. The NAAC sought to dramatize its appeal for an end to oppression by calling for fasts and prayer vigils sponsored by Negro churches, particularly in the South. A letter of protest was also sent to President William McKinley denouncing his inaction in the field of civil rights and condemning U.S. imperialism in Cuba. McKinley ignored the protest, and the white public at large remained uninterested, by and large, about the issue of civil rights. This was an era of strong racial prejudice coupled with the Jim Crow system of segregation in the South. Although the NAAC survived until 1908, it had become moribund by the turn of the century.

For more information, see Emma Lou Thornbrough, "The National Afro-American League, 1887-1908," *Journal of Southern History* 24 (November 1961): 498, and Hanes Walton, Jr., *Black Political Parties: An Historical and Political Analysis* (1972).

**NATIONAL ALLIANCE OF BUSINESSMEN (NAB).** Founded in 1969 at Washington, D.C., by Henry Ford II for the purpose of creating jobs for the hard-core unemployed. One of the prime movers in the formation of NAB was President Lyndon B. Johnson, who urged businessmen to cooperate with the federal government in establishing job-training programs so that the number of chronic unemployed might be reduced. The NAB recruited business executives in over 150 major U.S. cities to form teams. Emphasis was placed on finding employment for minority groups, the disadvantaged, Vietnam veterans, young people, and ex-convicts. Through this cooperative venture, which involved the Department of Labor and organized labor, the NAB created over a million jobs between 1968 and 1972. Three-fourths of the funding for job training and vocational-education projects came from participating corporations, and the rest was supplied by the federal government. Between 1968 and 1979, NAB has spent nearly $60 million to create 6 million new jobs.

In addition to its job-training projects throughout the nation, the NAB operates the Summer Youth Program, the College-Industry Relations Program, and the College Cluster Program for minorities. It also bestows annually the National Commander's Distinguished Service Award for the best project that trains veterans for jobs in business or industry. Emphasis has been placed on involving more small businesses in NAB's overall program. Currently top business executives in NAB's programs include Thomas Murphy of General Motors, J. Paul Austin of Coca-Cola, and A. Dean Swift of Sears, Roebuck and Company. NBA did sponsor the training of five hundred thousand previously unemployed workers during fiscal year 1979. NAB participants demonstrated that by cooperating with government the business community can help reduce federal expenditures and lessen unemployment.

National headquarters of NAB is located in Washington, D.C. Current president is Ruben F. Mettler, chairman of the board of directors of the Cleveland-based TRW, Inc. NAB publishes two monthly magazines, *News Summary* and *Onboard*.

**NATIONAL AMERICAN WOMAN SUFFRAGE ASSOCIATION (NAWSA).** Founded in 1890 at New York City by the merger of two previously formed organizations, the National Woman Suffrage Association* and the American Woman Suffrage Association,* for the purpose of uniting the woman suffrage movement. The three most notable women among NAWSA's founders included Elizabeth Cady Stanton, its first president; Susan B. Anthony, vice-president; and Lucy Stone, chairwoman of the executive committee. Subsequent presidents were Carrie Chapman Catt, (1900-1904 and 1915-1920), and Dr. Anna Howard Shaw (1904-1915).

The NAWSA constituted one of the most powerful suffrage organizations ever formed, with chapters all over the country. It attracted not only suffragists but also feminists and men working for equal rights for women. The NAWSA was very active politically on both the state and federal levels. Its members lobbied, conducted parades, and publicized the suffrage movement with an intensity that could not be ignored. Commitments were sought from the major parties, with political endorsement going only to those candidates pledging support for woman suffrage. By 1912 NAWSA had secured woman suffrage in nine states and was successful in attaining a woman suffrage plank in the platform of the Progressive (Bull Moose) Party.*

World War I presented NAWSA with a prime opportunity. Since President Woodrow Wilson dedicated himself to make the "world safe for democracy," suffragists demanded that the wartime chief executive start the process at home by supporting woman suffrage. Wilson, who had opposed the vote for women, finally succumbed to daily demonstrations in front of the White House and political pressure to change his stance. In 1917 New York State approved woman suffrage after the incessant lobbying of the NAWSA. The makeup of Congress following the mid-term elections of 1918 was in part determined by the efforts of NAWSA to elect pro-woman-suffrage candidates and defeat those opposing it.

In 1920 the Nineteenth Amendment to the U.S. Constitution was ratified, giving women the franchise on an equal basis with men. Having attained its primary objective, NAWSA disbanded, with most of its membership being absorbed by the newly formed League of Women Voters of the United States.* NAWSA achievements were a result of its unification of the woman suffrage movement, the skillful manner in which it pursued its goals, and a persistence that overcame great obstacles.

For more information, see Aileen S. Kraditor, *Ideas of the Woman Suffrage Movement, 1890-1920* (1965), and June Sochen, *Herstory: A Woman's View of American History* (1974).


**NATIONAL ASSOCIATION FOR THE ADVANCEMENT OF COLORED PEOPLE (NAACP).** Founded in 1909 at New York City by a group of civil-rights activists who included W. E. B. Du Bois, black intellectual and militant leader of the Niagara Movement*; Mary White Ovington, who later wrote *Half a Man: Status of the Negro in New York* (1911); Henry Moskowitz, a social worker among Jewish immigrants; William English Walling, a socialist and author of *Russia's Message* (1908); and Oswald Garrison Villard, publisher of the *New York Evening Post* and editor of the *Nation*. Villard was conscience stricken by the treatment accorded blacks in the Springfield (Illinois) race riot of 1908 and decided something had to be done to advance the cause of civil rights for Negroes. He issued (and publicized) a "Lincoln Day Call" (on the one hundredth anniversary of Lincoln's birthday), which proclaimed, "We call all believers in democracy to join in a National Conference for the discussion of present evils, the voicing of protests, and the renewal of the struggle for civil and political liberty."

The result of this conference was the formation of the NAACP, whose objectives were "to promote equality of rights and eradicate caste or race prejudice among the citizens of the United States, to advance the interest of colored citizens; to secure for them impartial suffrage; and to increase their opportunities for securing justice in the courts, education for their children, employment according to their ability, and complete equality before the law."

The NAACP's first officers were Moorfield Storey, a noted lawyer, president; Frances Blascoer, executive secretary; and W. E. B. DuBois, director of publicity and research. Du Bois was also editor of the organization's official journal, the *Crisis*. Subsequent executive secretaries have included such distinguished individuals as James Weldon Johnson, author, songwriter, lawyer, and professor of creative writing at Fisk University; Walter F. White, novelist, holder of a Guggenheim Fellowship, and author of the study, *Rope and Fagot: The Biography of Judge Lynch* (1929); Roy Wilkins, reporter for the *Kansas City Call*, a superb organizer and lobbyist and recipient of the Presidential Medal of Freedom; and, currently, Benjamin Lawson Hooks, minister, lawyer, businessman, former judge, and past federal communications commissioner.

Membership in the NAACP today totals nearly five hundred thousand, with local chapters in cities throughout the nation. Currently Kivie Kaplan is president. National headquarters of the NAACP remains in New York City with a legislative bureau in Washington, D.C., and regional offices located in Atlanta, Chicago, Dallas, Philadelphia, San Francisco, and St. Louis.

Developing a reputation for its legal approach and moderate stance, the NAACP has attained a list of accomplishments topping that of any other civil rights organization. From the *Buchanan* v. *Warley* case (1917), which ruled city segregation ordinances unconstitutional, to the *Brown* v. *Board of Education of Topeka* decision (1954), ruling all school segregation unconstitutional, the Legal Department of the NAACP has achieved a brilliant record of Supreme Court victories. One of its best lawyers, Thurgood Marshall, who often argued cases before the U.S. Supreme Court, became the first black appointed to that high tribunal.

The NAACP played a significant role in gaining passage of such laws as the Civil Rights Acts of 1957, 1960, 1965, and 1968. It has worked relentlessly to stop all lynchings, end job discrimination, eliminate de facto school segregation, and secure justice for black soldiers in the armed forces. The NAACP has succeeded in securing affirmative-action laws, enabling eligible blacks to register and vote, and motivating blacks to seek political office on the local, state, or national level. It also continues to focus public attention on police brutality in black communities, prison reform, unemployment, and the need for eradicating institutional racism in America.

NAACP activists participated in sit-ins and peaceful demonstrations during the 1960s but denounced those youthful militants who resorted to violence. Aptly dubbed the "long-distance runner," the NAACP has made remarkable contributions over the years to the civil rights movement and toward making democracy a workable system.

For further information, see Robert L. Jack, *History of the National Association for the Advancement of Colored People* (1943); Langston Hughes, *Fight for Freedom: The Story of the NAACP* (1962); and Charles F. Kellogg, *History of the National Association for the Advancement of Colored People, 1909-1929* (1967).

**NATIONAL ASSOCIATION KNIGHTS OF THE KU KLUX KLAN.** See Ku Klux Klan.

**NATIONAL ASSOCIATION OF BROADCASTERS (NAB).** Founded in 1922 at Washington, D.C., by Eugene F. McDonald, who served as president until 1925, and a group of radio broadcasters, for the purpose of promoting better broadcasting. Originally known as the National Association of Radio Broadcasters, it changed its name in 1951 to the National Association of Radio and Television Broadcasters. In 1957 it became the NAB.

One of the first pieces of federal legislation the NAB lobbied for was the passage of the Radio Act of 1927. It initiated the policy of assigned frequencies with private ownership of broadcasting stations. Over the years it has fought against federal censorship. It initiated voluntary regulation by first establishing the Radio Code Board and then the Television Code Review Board. Code authority offices are located in Washington, D.C., Hollywood, and New York City.

The NAB represents the radio and television industry before congressional committees, lobbies for or against legislation related to its interests, seeks to prevent limitations on television advertising, and opposes cable or pay television. The NAB established the Radio Advertising Bureau and the Television Advertising Bureau to promote the commercial use of its media. It also seeks to improve industry standards relative to the technical aspects of broadcasting and to broaden coverage of public events. It has proposed televising sessions of Congress and criminal trials. NAB attempts to force local and state governments and agencies to be open to radio or television coverage. To serve the general interest, the NAB encourages free public-service announcements on radio and television. It opposes groups such as Morality in Media* that try to impose censorship, control media content, or modify advertising.

National headquarters is located in Washington, D.C. The NAB has over five thousand members who represent radio and television stations of every network. Current president is Vincent T. Wasilewski. NAB publishes a weekly, *NAB Hotline*, and a monthly, *Code News.*

For more information, see Erik Barnow, *A History of Broadcasting in the United States*, 3 vols. (1970).

**NATIONAL ASSOCIATION OF MANUFACTURERS (NAM).** Founded in 1895 at Cincinnati, Ohio, by 583 small businessmen for the purpose of promoting domestic commerce and international trade. During its early existence the NAM almost became defunct. It began to expand when it took a stand against recognizing labor unions. Under the leadership of David Parry and T. W. Van Cleave, the NAM strongly opposed the concept of collective bargaining as undue interference with the private ownership of business and industry. In lieu of recognizing labor unions as collective-bargaining agents for workers, it proposed the American plan, which advocated company unions and an open shop.

During the 1920s the membership in the NAM tended to reflect the views of big business rather than those of the small businessman, an orientation that has continued. For a long time the NAM championed high protective tariffs. Even after lessening its opposition to reciprocal trade, it has insisted on a peril point protective device for American producers (that point at which the volume of imports imperil domestic producers). The NAM supports research activities; monitors federal legislation; keeps members informed on relevant court decisions; represents business at congressional hearings; disseminates information to influence public opinion; and lobbies with members of Congress to persuade them to vote for or against legislation as determined from a pro-business viewpoint.

The NAM challenged the constitutionality of the Lobbying Act of 1946, which would have required it to register as a lobbying organization. It won in the lower court, but the decision was later reversed by the U.S. Supreme Court. It still did not register and in 1963 formed the Business-Industry Political Action Committee* to strengthen its activities related to congressional elections. The NAM was forced to comply with the Lobbying Act in 1975 following a court suit initiated by Common Cause.* It now has thirteen full-time lobbyists on its staff and a budget of over $8 million.

The NAM opposed most of the New Deal legislation during the presidency of Franklin D. Roosevelt. It also fought most of the Fair Deal programs proposed by President Harry S. Truman. It has consistently championed free enterprise with little or no regulation by government. It opposes federal involvement in business, such as public power or government ownership, and seeks to diminish the power of federal regulatory agencies. It fought unsuccessfully to defeat the Clean Air Act of 1970, as it did relative to the Clean Air Amendments Act of 1977. In 1971 the NAM successfully opposed the legislative activities disclosures bill proposed by the House Committee on Standards of Conduct. In 1977 the NAM was instrumental in engineering a defeat in Congress of the common-situs picketing bill.

In 1973 the NAM's national headquarters was moved from New York City to Washington, D.C. Membership currently totals a little over thirty-one thousand and primarily represents the economic and political outlook of those who own or operate larger business firms. It sponsors the Institute on Industrial Relations and has conducted negotiations with the Chamber of Commerce of the United States* about a possible merger. Current NAM president is W. P. Gullander. NAM publications include a weekly, *NAM Reports*, and a quarterly, *Action Report*.

For more information, see Albert K. Steigerwalt, *The National Association of Manufacturers* (1964).

**NATIONAL ASSOCIATION OF PROBATION OFFICERS.** See National Council on Crime and Delinquency.

**NATIONAL ASSOCIATION ON INDIAN AFFAIRS.** See Association on American Indian Affairs.

**NATIONAL BLACK POLITICAL ASSEMBLY (NBPA).** Founded in 1972 at Gary, Indiana, by the Black Congressional Caucus* for the purpose of promoting the participation of blacks in the political process. Prime movers in the formation of the NBPA were Congressman Charles Diggs, Jr. (D-Mich.), Mayor Richard Hatcher of Gary, and Imamu Admiri Baraka (formerly Leroi Jones), a poet and black nationalist who presided as temporary chairman. An assemblage of thirty-five hundred black delegates approved the Gary Declaration, which called upon all blacks to cease their "political dependence on white men and their systems." Other resolutions opposed busing to achieve racial integration or enforced mergers of black and white colleges in the South. No presidential candidate was nominated or endorsed, but a set of demands was forwarded to both major parties.

A permanent 427-member coordinating committee was created to write a platform. This so-called black agenda contained the following proposals: a call for an "independent black political movement"; payment of government "reparations" to the black community; enactment of an urban homestead act; establishment of a $5 billion developmental fund for blacks; an amendment to the U.S. Constitution guaranteeing proportional representation for blacks in Congress; protection of the civil liberties of black prisoners; cessation of harassment by the Federal Bureau of Investigation; an immediate end to police brutality; a reorientation of U.S. foreign policy relative to South Africa and Rhodesia; and condemnation of Israel's role in relation to the Arab nations (this modified an earlier stand in favor of Israel's destruction as a nation). Because of its disagreement over the ideological tone of the NBPA's pronouncements, representatives of the National Association for the Advancement of Colored People* withdrew prior to the issuance of the final document.

Another meeting of the NBPA took place at Cincinnati in 1976. Leaders of the convention included Congressman Ronald V. Dellums (D-Calif.), Dick Gregory, and Julian Bond. Delegates voted to offer Dellums the presidential nomination, but he refused it, saying he would rather stay in Congress as a member of the Democratic Party.* The platform stressed the need to eliminate racism; called for aid to the poor; demanded assistance to the Third World; and insisted on a foreign policy that would support the black nations of Africa against both South Africa and Rhodesia.

Plans were made for a future conference either to nominate a presidential candidate or endorse the nominee of another party, but no specific date was set. Some black leaders and politicians refused to participate in the proceedings of the NBPA on the basis that it was divisive and ineffectual as a political party. When most leaders in the black community publicly endorsed Democrat Jimmy Carter in 1976, the NBPA did not convene a special convention. The future impact of the NBPA on the black voters and the two major political parties will be determined by its ideological orientation. Moderate blacks are often alienated by the radical nature of its platforms and therefore are not influenced by its stand. The other factor working against the NBPA is that many black politicians belong to the Democratic Party and see it as the vehicle to promote benefits for the black community.

**NATIONAL CENTER FOR VOLUNTARY ACTION (NCVA).** Founded in 1970 at Washington, D.C., by George W. Romney, former governor of Michigan and NCVA's first president, for the purpose of promoting volunteerism and problem solving by local action organizations. The NCVA regards volunteer service not only as a means to develop human resources and better community life but as a means of enriching one's personal life and renewing the essential aspects of democracy. Its goals are to include as many people as possible in volunteer programs, coordinate them, and maximize their effectiveness.

The initial funding for NCVA's activities came from a W. K. Kellogg Foundation grant, which permitted it to conduct institutes to train volunteers and to serve local groups. The NCVA also received federal funds under provisions of the Housing and Community Development Act of 1974 and the Highway Safety Act of 1975. Projects initiated and carried out by NCVA include Meals on Wheels, to provide nutritional meals for needy senior citizens; finding homes for Vietnam refugees; the Alcohol Safety Countermeasure Program; Volunteers in Probation, where first offenders are permitted to render service to the community rather than to serve jail sentences; and such programs as VISTA and Foster Grandparents.

The NCVA is seeking an amendment to the Comprehensive Employment and Training Act of 1973 to permit the use of volunteers and nonprofit agencies to conduct job-training and rehabilitation programs. It also supports a bill introduced by Congressman Barber B. Conable (R-N.Y.) that would amend the Internal Revenue Code to permit nonprofit, tax-exempt civic-action groups or charitable organizations to lobby in order to influence legislation related to its activities.

In 1976 the NCVA sponsored the first National Congress on Volunteerism and Citizenship. Some three hundred participants from thirty-three states met and formed committees dealing with Volunteerism and Voluntary Action; Community and Family Services; Health Care; Criminal Justice System; Citizen-Government Relations; Education; and Senior Citizen Concerns. The meeting was held in Washington, D.C., and co-chaired by Mary Ripley and Joyce Black. It was decided to hold an annual congress, sponsor the National Student Volunteer Program, and establish a permanent Volunteer Advisory Council for the President. Other decisions related to the establishment of advisory groups for governors and local municipalities; promotion of citizen self-help groups in an effort to deter crime; development of preretirement programs in volunteerism; and sponsorship of a White House Conference on Volunteerism.

The NCVA disseminates information to the general public to encourage individuals to volunteer their services and assists local communities in utilizing volunteers. The NCVA sponsors an annual National Volunteer Week, April 22–28, to promote the formation of local volunteer organizations. Such groups are provided with model programs so that they may contribute to the betterment of their local community. Thousands of people have benefited from the work of these volunteer groups.

Present national headquarters is located in Washington, D.C. Membership consists of hundreds of local volunteer groups. Current president is Douglas K. Kinsey, with Kerry Kenn Allen serving as executive director. The NCVA publishes a monthly, *Voluntary Action News*, and a quarterly, *Voluntary Action Leadership*.

For more information, see Marlene Wilson, *The Effective Management of Volunteer Programs* (1976), and Gordon Manser and Rosemary Cass, *Volunteerism at the Crossroads* (1976).

**NATIONAL CHRISTIAN ASSOCIATION (NCA).** Founded in 1867 at Aurora, Illinois, by Jonathan Blanchard, president of Wheaton College, for the purpose of promoting a campaign against secret societies. It was formed into a national organization that same year at a convention held in Pittsburgh, Pennsylvania. Prime movers, in addition to Blanchard, were C. H. Underwood and N. D. Fanning, both Methodist clergymen. With permanent headquarters located at Chicago, the NCA began publishing a magazine, the *Christian Banner*, whose name was altered that same year to *Christian Cynosure*.

The NCA constituted a throwback to the ideals and objectives of the Anti-Masonic Party.* NCA members, which at NCA's height in 1876 reached nearly five thousand, feared that the freemasons and other secret lodges posed a threat to both Christianity and democracy. In 1876 the NCA formed the American National Party.* It censured all secret organizations regardless of their objectives; among those condemned were Knights of Columbus*; American Protective Association*; Order of the Knights of Pythias*; Ku Klux Klan*; Knights of the Golden Circle*; and even the Grand Army of the Republic* for its secret initiation ritual. The NCA did influence the Christian laity not to become involved with secret societies, but its impact upon the general public was minimal. The NCA became moribund in 1969 when Thomas P. Kellog, its president, died. Kellog was the grandson of the founder and had continued to publish the *Christian Cynosure*, but without his guidance, the NCA died and the magazine ceased publication.

For more information, see Clarence N. Roberts, "The Crusade Against Secret Societies and the National Christian Association," *Journal of the Illinois State Historical Society* 64 (Winter 1971): 382–400.

**NATIONAL CHRISTIAN DEMOCRATIC PARTY (NCDP).** Founded in 1979 at Marion, Illinois, by Garrett Brock Trapnell for the purpose of conducting a presidential campaign from within a federal penitentiary. The national headquarters of the NCDP is Trapnell's cell in the prison where he is an inmate. Trapnell, forty-one years of age and from Los Angeles, is serving a life sentence, convicted in 1973 for hijacking a commercial airline. In 1978 Barbara Oswald commandeered a helicopter and ordered the pilot to land in Marion prison to free Trapnell. She was shot and killed by the pilot. Later in the year, Oswald's daughter hijacked a commercial airliner in another unsuccessful attempt to free Trapnell.

Officials of the Bureau of Federal Prisons are investigating the legality of the NCDP and the feasibility of permitting Trapnell to run for the presidency. In 1929 Eugene V. Debs ran for the presidency as the nominee of the Socialist Party of America* while serving a ten-year sentence in the federal prison at Atlanta. Trapnell claims that he has a legal right to seek the presidency from prison. Officials declined to allow Trapnell out of prison for the purpose of campaigning even though he claimed to be a bonafide candidate. Officials viewed it as a subterfuge to escape, since the NCDP has no other followers and Trapnell's name does not appear on the ballot of any state.

**NATIONAL CITIZENS POLITICAL ACTION COMMITTEE (NC-PAC).** Founded in 1944 at New York City by the executive board of the Congress of Industrial Organizations (CIO) for the purpose of promoting both the reelection of President Franklin D. Roosevelt and the election to Congress of pro-labor, liberal, left-wing Democrats.* Initially formed as an adjunct of the CIO's Political Action Committee,* the NC-PAC soon broadened its membership base and became an independent entity. Honorary chairman was ex-Senator George Norris of Nebraska, with Clark Foreman serving as director. In 1945 Foreman was replaced by Calvin B. Baldwin. That same year former Governor Elmer Benson of Minnesota was named chairman and Dr. Frank Kingdon the vice-chairman.

Among the ten thousand members of NC-PAC were such prominent individuals as Gifford Pinchot, former chief of the Forestry Bureau and ex-governor of Pennsylvania; James Patton, president of the National Farmers

Union*; Alexander F. Whitney, president of the Brotherhood of Railroad Trainmen; Bishop R. R. Wright of the African Methodist Church; Dr. Robert C. Weaver, a prominent black leader; Dorothy Parker, a well-known novelist; Freda Kirchwey, editor of the *Nation*; and Elinor Gimbel, wealthy heir to the Gimbel department store fortune.

Politically the NC-PAC represented the more radical element of liberalism. It was useful to Franklin D. Roosevelt, since it attracted votes for him from socialists, quasi-socialists, and even communists. Although most of the members of NC-PAC were New Deal liberals, it included enough radicals to make its campaign rhetoric appealing to the left-wing groups. The NC-PAC was highly effective in New York City. It no doubt contributed to F.D.R.'s 316,591 plurality in the Empire State over New York's Governor Thomas E. Dewey, the 1944 presidential nominee of the Republican Party.* In 1946 the NC-PAC merged with the Independent Citizens Committee for the Arts, Sciences and Professions* to form the Progressive Citizens of America.*

For more information, see Curtis D. MacDougall, *Gideon's Army*, 3 vols. (1976), and Norman D. Markowitz, *The Rise and Fall of the People's Century* (1973).

**NATIONAL CIVIC FEDERATION (NCF).** Founded in 1893 at Chicago by civic activist Ralph M. Easley to promote the World's Columbian Exposition. President Grover Cleveland was present at the opening-day ceremonies. During the course of the festivities to honor the four hundredth anniversary of the discovery of America, a young professor of history from the University of Wisconsin, Frederick Jackson Turner, presented his famous paper, "The Significance of the Frontier in American History."

Having gotten the cooperation of business and labor leaders for the promotion of such an enterprise as the Columbian Exposition, the NCF sought to expand its role as peacemaker between labor and capital. In 1901 Senator Marcus "Mark" Hanna (R-Ohio), a former businessman and adviser to President William McKinley, became president. Another important leader in the NCF was Samuel Gompers, president of the American Federation of Labor, who became NCF's vice-president. Frequently working with the NCF was George Perkins, an insurance executive, member of the House of Morgan, and an adviser to President Theodore Roosevelt.

In 1902 Mark Hanna utilized his role as head of the NCF to help bring about an end to the strike led by John Mitchell, president of the United Mine Workers, against the anthracite coal industry. The industry was led by George F. Baer, legal counsel to J. P. Morgan and noted for his statement that the coal miners should entrust their fate in the hands of "the Christian men to whom God, in his infinite wisdom, has given control of the prosperity interests of the country." Hanna used his contacts with both President

Theodore Roosevelt and J. P. Morgan to obtain a fair settlement for the UMW.

In an era of ruthless competition between businessmen and violent labor disputes caused by anti-union activity on behalf of industry, the NCF sought to promote industrial harmony and amicable relations with trade unions. With foresight, the NCF looked toward the day when corporations would act responsibly in their relationship with unions. In taking this moderate position, the NCF was attacked both by the National Association of Manufacturers* for ostensibly selling out to the unions and by reformers for being allegedly pro-business.

The NCF gave its full support to World War I and worked to preserve labor-management cooperation as part of the war effort. Its distaste for radicalism became evident when it supported the arrest of anti-war agitators and defended the activities of Attorney General A. Mitchell Palmer during the red hysteria of the 1920s. The failure of unions to hold wartime gains and the death of Samuel Gompers in 1924 caused labor to spurn the mediation efforts of the NCF. This dealt a severe blow to the NCF, and it disbanded in 1925.

For further information, see Marguerite Green, *National Civic Federation and Labor Movement, 1900-1925* (1956), and Bruno Ramirez, *When Workers Fight: The Politics of Industrial Relations in the Progressive Era, 1898-1916* (1977).


**NATIONAL CIVIL SERVICE LEAGUE (NCSL).** Founded in 1881 at Washington, D.C., by George W. Curtis, publisher of the *Tribune and Farmer* and NCSL's first president, and a group of reformers, for the purpose of promoting civil service based on merit so as to end the spoils system in government. Formed originally as the National Civil Service Reform League, it changed its name to NCSL in 1945. The NCSL was headed by a succession of prominent individuals, among them Carl Schurz, who as interior secretary in the administration of President Rutherford B. Hayes had initiated the merit system; Richard Henry Dana, lawyer and famous for his novel *Two Years Before the Mast* (1840); and William Dudley Foulke, president of the American Woman Suffrage Association* (1885-1890) and later author of *Fighting the Spoilsman* (1919).

The primary objective of the NCSL was to end the practice of using patronage as part of the spoils of political victory without any regard to qualifications in fulfilling the duties of an appointed office. Appointees of defeated parties were often discharged without regard to merit for the reason of freeing the position for a party faithful of the winning party. Not only were party hacks appointed to fill jobs needing expertise, they were frequently expected to kick back a portion of their salaries for a campaign slush fund. This practice often resulted in corrupting appointees, who sought to enrich themselves by graft and selling influence.

In 1883 the NCSL was instrumental in getting Congress to enact the Pendleton Act, which established the Civil Service Commission. This legislation implemented a merit system for federal employees, initially covering only 10 percent of them, and prevented their dismissal for purely political reasons. Eventually the number of federal employees covered was extended to almost all who held positions below the highest levels. Continued lobbying and public agitation pressured state and local governments to implement civil-service systems also, a move that helped to create a higher degree of professionalism among civil servants who, prior to this time, were subject to the whims of political bosses.

In 1940 the NCSL helped gain passage of the Hatch Act, which forbade political contributions to political parties or candidates by federal office-holders. This protected civil servants, since pressure was often put on them by the party in power to contribute money for political campaigns. The NCSL supported the recommendations made by the Hoover Commission (headed by ex-President Herbert C. Hoover) to reorganize the executive branch of the government. Some of the recommendations, made in 1949 and again in 1955, were implemented. One of these was the establishment of a General Services Administration.

Most of the ten million government workers (local, state, and federal) are now covered by some type of civil service. Due to the efforts of the NCSL, 90 percent of the federal government's three million employees are so covered. One problem the NCSL now faces is that of appointees regarding their tenure in office as a sinecure. Agencies have become lax in enforcing merit and often refuse to discharge bureaucrats who do not perform their duties according to the prescribed rules.

Present national headquarters of NCSL is located in Washington, D.C. Current executive director is Jean J. Couturier. The NCSL has a membership of about twenty-five hundred and operates the National Program Center for Public Personnel Management. NCSL publications include a monthly, *NCSL Exchange Newsletter*, and a quarterly, *Good Government*.

For further information, see William D. Foulke, *A Hoosier Autobiography* (1922), and Claude M. Fuess, *Carl Schurz, Reformer* (1932).


**NATIONAL CIVIL SERVICE REFORM LEAGUE.** See National Civil Service League.


**NATIONAL COMMITTEE FOR A SANE NUCLEAR POLICY, THE.** See SANE: A Citizen's Organization for a Sane World.

**NATIONAL COMMITTEE FOR AN EFFECTIVE CONGRESS (NC-FEC).** Founded in 1947 at New York City by a concerned group of citizens for the purpose of promoting the election of members of Congress committed to civil rights and a bipartisan foreign policy. Candidates were endorsed on a nonpartisan basis solely on where they stood on issues supported by the NC-FEC. In the 1948 congressional elections and during the 1950s and 1960s, the NC-FEC backed candidates pledged to vote for civil-rights legislation and then raised campaign funds to help elect these candidates. This type of action eventually helped elect sufficient members to Congress to enact long-needed civil rights legislation.

In the 1970 congressional elections, the NC-FEC supported candidates favoring U.S. withdrawal from the war in Vietnam. It has since endorsed candidates of both parties pledged to reduce military expenditures so that needed domestic programs would not be hampered because of lack of funds. In 1971 it led the fight to update the Corrupt Practices Act of 1925 pertaining to campaign expenditures. Serving as a coordinating organization for other lobbying groups (including Common Cause,* Americans for Democratic Action,* and the Twentieth Century Fund,*) the NC-FEC was successful in getting Congress to enact the Federal Election Campaign Act of 1971, a measure that established limits on the amount of money that could be spent by any one candidate and requried an accurate reporting of campaign contributions.

Present national headquarters of the NC-FEC is located in Washington, D.C. Current national director is Russell D. Hemenway. Membership totals about twenty-five thousand. The NC-FEC periodically publishes *Congressional Report*.

**NATIONAL COMMITTEE FOR CITIZENS IN EDUCATION (NCCE).** Founded in 1962 at Washington, D.C., by journalist-lecturer Agnes E. Meyer, who served as its president until her death in 1971, for the purpose of promoting greater financial support for education. Formed originally as the National Committee for Support of the Public Schools, it was renamed NCCE in 1974 and at the same time its national headquarters was moved to Columbia, Maryland. Although membership has never exceeded more than several thousand, it has included some prominent individuals, such as ex-President Harry S. Truman; Dr. James D. Conant of Harvard University; and former head of the Joint Chiefs of Staff, General Omar Bradley.

The membership of NCCE represents agriculture, business, civic groups, organized labor, and the professions. Through seminars, discussion groups, and conferences, the NCCE disseminates information and statistical data to influence public opinion. It works with local community organizations to promote bond issues or tax increases needed to fund public schools. NCCE has also sought to obtain more state and federal aid for local school districts. With funding from the Ford Foundation, the NCCE conducts research and has published its results in two studies, *Fits and Misfits: What You Should Know About Your Child's Learning Materials* (1972) and *Children, Parents and School Records* (1973). The latter was influential in gaining congressional passage of the Elementary and Secondary Act of 1974, which established safeguards for the privacy of school records.

Leadership of NCCE now resides with three senior associates: Carl L. Marburger, former commissioner of education in New Jersey; J. William Rioux, former president of Merrill Palmer Institute in Detroit; and Stanley Aslett, former assistant commissioner of education in New Jersey. Donald Rappaport currently serves as chairman of the governing board. NCCE publications include special reports, proceedings, and a quarterly, *Fact Sheet*.

**NATIONAL COMMITTEE FOR SUPPORT OF THE PUBLIC SCHOOLS.** See National Committee for Citizens in Education.

**NATIONAL COMMITTEE OF INQUIRY (NCI).** Founded in 1968 at Washington, D.C., by a group of black leaders for the purpose of uniting black voters behind one presidential candidate in the 1968 national election. Prime movers in the formation of NCI were Bayard Rustin, Congressman John Conyers, Jr. (D-Mich.), and Mayor Richard Hatcher of Gary, Indiana. In order to form a bloc of black votes for bargaining purposes before endorsing one of the presidential candidates of the Democratic* or Republican* Parties, the NCI nominated its own presidential ticket. Chosen as its presidential nominee was the Reverend Channing Philip of the District of Columbia and Julian Bond of Georgia as his vice-presidential running mate. Bond declined since he was running for office in Georgia as a candidate of the Democratic Party.*

The NCI decided it would seek commitments from Democratic presidential aspirants before endorsing any one of them for the nomination. It particularly wanted assurances that civil-rights legislation would be enforced and that the economic welfare of the black community would be furthered. It also supported all challenges by blacks seeking to gain their seats in various state delegations. In particular, the NCI helped the Loyal Democrats of Mississippi* to be seated instead of the all-white regular Democratic delegation.

When Vice-President Hubert H. Humphrey, who had a strong civil rights record, pledged his support for NCI objectives, the organization endorsed him for the presidency. Its own presidential candidate withdrew, and the NCI worked for the election of Humphrey, who nevertheless lost in a close election to Richard M. Nixon. Following the 1968 presidential election, the

NCI disbanded. The NCI was instrumental in gaining black votes for Humphrey, but his link with President Lyndon B. Johnson and the war in Vietnam were too much to overcome.

For more information, see P. W. Romero, ed., *In Black America* (1969).

## NATIONAL COMMITTEE ON THE CAUSE AND CURE OF WAR
(NCCCW). Founded in 1925 at Washington, D.C., by Carrie Chapman Catt, renowned suffragist and one of the founders of the Woman's Peace Party,* for the purpose of furthering world peace. Catt served as NCCCW's chairperson from its inception until 1932.

The NCCCW advocated disarmament and international cooperation through both the League of Nations and the World Court. Its membership was always small, drawing upon pacifist groups and women's organizations for support. It did contribute to the postwar belief that U.S. entry into World War I had been a tragic mistake.

During the 1930s, NCCCW supported the neutrality acts, opposed rearmament, and fought against U.S. involvement in the conflicts that were taking place. When Germany invaded Poland and it appeared that Hitler was truly a menace to the world, disagreement erupted over whether the NCCCW should endorse the concept of collective security. That issue could not be resolved, and the split brought about the demise of the NCCCW. As was the case with many other peace groups, it could not be decided whether aggression was an evil greater than war itself. This in turn posed the moral question as to whether the specific victims of aggressors, such as Poland, Czechoslovakia, and Ethiopia, should be helped or sacrificed. The NCCCW could not bring itself to decide that force must be used if the aggression of dictators was to be stopped. Its abstract opposition to war thus had no effect upon the power realities of World War II.

For further information, see Mary Gray Peck, *Carrie Chapman Catt* (1944).

## NATIONAL COMMITTEE TO FREE AMERICA FROM JEWISH DOMINATION. See National Socialist White People's Party.

## NATIONAL CONFERENCE FOR A NEW POLITICS (NCNP). Founded in 1965 at Chicago as a broad coalition for the purpose of electing anti-Vietnam war candidates in the upcoming mid-term elections. Prime movers in the formation of this informal organization included such leaders of the Students for a Democratic Society* (SDS) as Paul Booth, Tom Hayden, Clark Kissinger, Arthur Waskow, and Lee Webb. The NCNP cooperated with the Committee for Independent Political Action in Chicago and the Detroit Committee to End the War in Vietnam to elect peace candidates to Congress.

In preparation for the presidential election of 1968, a formal convention was called to make NCNP a national organization. Some twenty-one hundred delegates, representing the SDS, radical groups, black militants, and anti-war coalitions, met at Chicago in 1967 to work for the defeat of President Lyndon B. Johnson (who had not yet announced he would withdraw from the presidential race) and to support candidates committed to ending U.S. participation in the Vietnam war. Simon Cassady was chosen chairperson. Selected to the steering committee were such leaders as Carlos Russell of the black caucus; Donna Allen of the Washington chapter of the Mobilization Committee to End the War in Vietnam*; James Foreman, Student Non-violent Coordinating Committee*; and Floyd McKissick, Congress of Racial Equality.* Other civil rights and anti-war activists who played a key role were Roy Innis, Bertram Garskoff, Arthur Waskow, and Peter Weiss.

Soon after the NCNP convened at Chicago in 1967, the 180 blacks in attendance formed a black caucus and made two demands: that they be given 50 percent of the votes and that the entire convention approve a platform committed to black power. Included in the caucus's thirteen-plank resolution was a proposal condemning the "imperialist Zionist war" being conducted by Israel against the Arab nations. After a heated debate and an attempt by white Jewish delegates to get the anti-Israel plank deleted (including appeals to do so by Dr. Martin Luther King, Jr., and Dr. Benjamin Spock), the thirteen-point resolution was adopted by a three-to-one margin. Because of this action, many pro-Israel whites walked out of the convention.

This anti-Israel stand and the radical nature of the platform alienated many anti-war and civil rights activists. As a consequence, the NCNP collapsed in 1968 and played no role in influencing the course of national elections. Former members of NCNP drifted into other organizations, with some ultimately joining the People's Party (1971)*. The demise of the NCNP was caused by the inability of radicals and militant activists to compromise or work together in harmony for common goals.

For further information, see Michael Brown, *The Politics and Anti-Politics of the Young* (1969).

**NATIONAL CONFERENCE OF ALTERNATIVE STATE AND LOCAL PUBLIC POLICIES (NCA-SLPP).** Founded in 1975 at Madison, Wisconsin, by the Institute for Policy Studies (IPS) for the purpose of developing lines of communication among the academic community, the citizenry, and political adherents to the New Left movement. Richard J. Barnet and Marcus G. Raskip, codirectors of the IPS (which had formerly been the Peace Research Institute) were prime movers in the formation of the NCA-SLPP.

The NCA-SLPP holds four regional meetings yearly to bring together New Left radicals who have been elected to state and local offices. They discuss common problems and exchange views. Also invited to attend are representatives of the general public and academic community. In this way, a dialogue takes place and better understanding is promoted. Under the leadership of Mayor Jeffrey Friedman of Austin, Texas, and Mayor Paul Soglin of Madison, both thirty-three years old and both former adherents of the New Left, the NCA-SLPP seeks recruits from the radical Left to run for political office on both the state and local level. The broad objectives of the NCA-SLPP are to democratize politics, humanize laws, meet the needs of the people, and reform society from the vantage point of local communities rather than the federal level.

Specific goals include working for the enactment of equal opportunity and open-housing ordinances, establishing day care centers for working parents, constructing inexpensive housing for the elderly, and revitalizing mass transit. The NCA-SLPP seeks to promote participatory democracy by pragmatic politics as practiced by local units of government. Success at the polls for NCA-SLPP-backed candidates has been most noticeable in communities in which colleges or universities are located—partly because of the student vote and partly because of the liberalization of voter registration.

**NATIONAL CONFERENCE OF CHRISTIANS AND JEWS (NCCJ).** Founded in 1928 at New York City by a distinguished group of Christians and Jews for the purpose of promoting brotherhood. Prime movers in the formation of the NCCJ were Newton D. Baker, S. Parkes Cadman, Everett R. Clinchy (its first president), Carlton J. H. Hayes, and Roger W. Straus. The objectives of the organization as stated in its by-laws were "To promote justice, amity, understanding, and cooperation among Christians and Jews, and to analyze, moderate, and strive to eliminate intergroup prejudices which disfigure and distort religious, business, social, and political relations, with a view to maintaining at all times a society in which the religious ideals of brotherhood and justice shall become the standards of human relationships."

The NCCJ has committees that develop programs for young people, local communities, those suffering from job discrimination, parent groups, education, equal administration of justice, and intercreedal relations. It disseminates educational materials in an attempt to influence public thinking; operates a religious news service; conducts seminars and training programs; and sponsors Brotherhood Commitment Week. One of its most notable projects has been to initiate the formation of human-relations councils in local communities to prevent bigotry and racial prejudice from poisoning relations between Christians and Jews, as well as between whites and blacks.

NCCJ national headquarters is located in New York City, with seventy regional offices in cities throughout the United States. The NCCJ has a three-hundred-member board of trustees representing a diversity of Christian denominations and Jewish groups. Current president is Dr. David Hyatt. It issues a quarterly publication, *NCCJ Newsletter.*

**NATIONAL CONFERENCE OF CONCERNED DEMOCRATS (NCCD).** Founded in 1967 at New York City by Allard K. Lowenstein and other Democratic doves for the purpose of promoting a "dump Johnson" movement. President Lyndon B. Johnson's continuation of the war in Vietnam had spawned protest marches and militant demonstrations by anti-war doves. Some of the liberal and left-wing Democrats began to agitate within the Democratic Party* for U.S. withdrawal from Vietnam. The doves considered President Johnson an irreconcilable hawk and therefore formed the NCCD to prevent his renomination as the 1968 presidential nominee of the Democratic Party.

In attempting to find an alternative presidential candidate pledged to halt the war, representatives of the NCCD, whose membership at this time was relatively small, approached Senator Robert F. Kennedy (D-N.Y.), but Kennedy refused to consider challenging LBJ for the nomination. Members of the NCCD then persuaded Senator Eugene McCarthy (D-Minn.) to enter the Democratic primary in New Hampshire in opposition to LBJ. In the final returns of the New Hampshire primary, Johnson received 29,021 to McCarthy's 28,791 votes. The slim 230-vote victory provided the NCCD with political ammunition to call upon Democrats everywhere to join the anti-Johnson bandwagon. A poll by *Newsweek* magazine indicated that the New Hampshire vote was more anti-Johnson than anti-war. The campaign conducted for Johnson had done much to alienate Democrats who believed that allegations made against McCarthy were unfair. The poor showing in the primary, the Tet offensive in Vietnam, and military requests for two hundred thousand more soldiers served to enhance NCCD's anti-Johnson campaign.

After the New Hampshire primary, President Johnson began a peace initiative in Vietnam and subsequently withdrew from the presidential race. At this time Senator Robert Kennedy decided to become a candidate. His announcement created dissension within the ranks of the NCCD, since many felt they now owed their allegiance to McCarthy for having the courage to challenge LBJ in the primaries. Lowenstein and others, however, joined the Kennedy campaign. When Kennedy was assassinated after winning the California primary, NCCD members again had to make a choice. Some continued to support McCarthy, but others supported the eventual Democratic presidential nominee, Hubert H. Humphrey. When the election was over, in which Humphrey lost to Republican* Richard M. Nixon in a close contest, the NCCD disbanded.

**NATIONAL CONFERENCE OF STATE LEGISLATIVE LEADERS (NCSLL).** Founded in 1959 at Milwaukee, Wisconsin, by a group of state legislative leaders for the purpose of promoting better state government. Membership in the organization was made up of legislators holding leadership positions, such as speakers, minority leaders, and party whips. Its purpose was to permit such leaders to meet and share experiences, as well as to discuss common problems. In 1966 the NCSLL, in conjunction with the Eagleton Institute of Politics at Rutgers University, established the Center for Legislative Services. Membership in the NCSLL was never more than fifty, but it included the top leadership of the state legislatures represented. The official publications of the NCSLL were an annual, *State Legislative Leader*, and the *NCSLL Yearbook*. Many legislators benefited from their connection with the NCSLL. To make itself a more effective organization, the NCSLL entered into a merger in 1975 in which it joined with the National Society of State Legislators* and the National Legislative Conference* to form a new organization, the National Conference of State Legislatures.*

**NATIONAL CONFERENCE OF STATE LEGISLATURES (NCSL).** Founded in 1974 at Albuquerque, New Mexico, as a result of a merger of the National Legislative Conference,* National Conference of State Legislative Leaders,* and the National Society of State Legislators* for the purpose of improving the quality and effectiveness of state legislatures. The first president was Kevin Harrington, a state senator from Massachusetts. Membership in the organization was made up of the country's 7,500 legislators and their staffs. It is funded through state appropriations and is governed by a forty-three member executive committee which includes twenty-nine legislators and fourteen legislative staff members.

In the by-laws of the NCSL the purposes and objectives are stated as follows:

To advance the effectiveness, independence and integrity of the several legislatures as equal coordinate branches of government in the several states, territories, and commonwealths of the United States; to seek to foster interstate cooperation; to vigorously represent the states and their legislatures in the American federal system of government; and to work for the improvement of the organization, processes, and operations of the state legislatures, and the knowledge and effectiveness of individual legislators and staff, and to encourage the practice of high standards of personal and professional conduct by legislators and staff.

To guide its lobbying efforts before the federal government, the NCSL has established a State-Federal Assembly, composed of 800 legislators from throughout the country. It meets three times each year, at which time nine standing committees work out recommendations on issues affecting relationships between the states and the federal government. The current committees are education, energy, government operations, human resources, law and justice, natural resources, rural development, and transportation and urban development. Once policy recommendations are adopted by the State-Federal Assembly, they must be approved at the annual meeting of the NCSL.

A similar structure, the Assembly on the Legislature, has been created to provide guidance on issues internal to state legislatures. It meets quarterly in state capitals to prepare model legislation and conduct studies of problems facing state legislatures. Its work is done by the six following standing committees: ethics, elections and reapportionment, fiscal affairs and oversight, legislative information needs, legislative management, and science and technology. Appointments to the Assembly on the Legislature and the State-Federal Assembly are made by the legislative leadership in each state.

The permanent headquarters of the NCSL is located at Denver, Colorado, with an office of state-federal relations in Washington, D.C. The latter serves as the lobbying arm of the nation's state legislatures. Its professional staff promotes NCSL policy positions, meets regularly with members of Congress and representatives of the executive department, arranges meetings between legislators and federal officials, monitors federal agencies, provides information and analysis for legislatures on state-federal issues, and coordinates the appearance of legislators before congressional committees.

The NCSL conducts a yearly series of national and regional seminars dealing with substantive issues and professional development. It also develops special projects in response to research requests, need for technical assistance, and calls for specialized data. Specialized newsletters are issued in the following areas: *Energy Report*, issued irregularly on timely energy topics; *The Fiscal Letter*, a bimonthly report on government finance issues in the states; *Criminal Justice Monitor*, a monthly report on state and federal trends in criminal justice; *Leaders' Letter*, a biweekly report to legislative leaders on state-federal issues; *Science and Technology for the Legislatures*, a monthly report on state and federal actions and other information on scientific and technical issues; and *State Legislative Report*, an irregular series dealing with substantive and procedural issues relating to state legislatures.

Current president of the NCSL is Representative George B. Roberts, Jr., the Speaker of the House of the New Hampshire state legislature. NCSL's official magazine, issued ten times a year, is *State Legislatures*.

## NATIONAL CONGRESS OF PARENTS AND TEACHERS (PTA).
Founded in 1897 at Washington, D.C., by a "Mother's Congress" for the

purpose of promoting education through better relations between parents and teachers. The prime mover for this meeting was Alice McLellan Birney, the PTA's first president, who had urged the formation of such an organization in 1895 while addressing the Chautauqua forum in New York. When first formed, the original name was the National Congress of Parents. In 1908 it was changed to the National Congress of Mother and Parent-Teachers and, finally, in 1924 the National Congress of Parents and Teachers.

At its birth, two notable vice-presidents were elected: philanthropist Phoebe Apperson Hearst, who financed the PTA's activities in its earliest years, and Letitia Green Stevenson, the wife of Vice-President Adlai Ewing Stevenson. The PTA had an auspicious beginning when Frances Folsom Cleveland, the president's wife, gave a reception for its members at the White House.

The basic goal of the PTA was to foster better education by promoting cooperation between teachers and parents. In bringing the school and home closer together, coordinated efforts could be initiated to further the welfare of the nation's children. During the 1900s the PTA agitated for nurseries, kindergartens, juvenile courts, and protective child-labor laws. In the 1920s the PTA, in conjunction with the World Federation of Education Associations, conducted a crusade to eliminate illiteracy. It was instrumental in securing state laws for mandatory school attendance. In coping with the depression-ridden 1930s, the PTA fought for adequate financial support for schools and decent teachers' salaries. During the post-World War II population explosion, the PTA championed more state and federal aid to local school districts, supported increases in real estate taxes, and helped campaign for bond issues to enlarge school facilities.

During the 1950s special campaigns were undertaken to educate parents on the need for their children to receive Salk vaccine shots as an anti-polio preventative. With the advent of mass television viewing, the PTA sought to influence the content of television programming so as to eliminate excessive violence. During the decade of the 1950s certain right-wing extremist groups attempted to infiltrate and take over local PTAs. A program of the 1970s, Every Child Needs You, focused on preventing child abuse. Efforts were made to protect children's rights while promoting a healthy environment conducive to the normal rearing of children. While supporting the general concept of racial integration in the public schools, the PTA took an anti-busing stand, asserting, "We support a constitutional amendment opposing the involuntary assignment of students to achieve racial balance."

The PTA has commissions dealing with Education; Health and Welfare; Individual Development; Leadership Development; Organization Extension; and Program Services. The PTA was honored in 1972 with a commemorative U.S. postage stamp in honor of its seventy-fifth anniversary. National headquarters is located in Chicago. Membership totals nearly nine million in over thirty thousand local PTA chapters. Currently Lillie E. Herndon is president, with J. Robert Merrill serving as managing director. Prior to 1961 the PTA's official publication was *National Congress of Mothers Magazine*. Since that time it has issued the *National PTA Bulletin* and *PTA Magazine*.

For more information, see A. S. Auerback, *Trends and Techniques in Parent Education* (1961).

**NATIONAL CONSTITUTIONAL PARTY.** See Constitutional Union Party.

**NATIONAL COUNCIL FOR HISTORIC SITE AND BUILDINGS.** See National Trust for Historic Preservation.

**NATIONAL COUNCIL FOR INDUSTRIAL SAFETY.** See National Safety Council.

**NATIONAL COUNCIL FOR PREVENTION OF WAR (NCPW).** Founded in 1921 at Washington, D.C., by Frederick J. Libby, a leader in the disarmament movement and head of the Arms Limitation Council, for the purpose of promoting reductions in naval and armed forces on an international scale. Formed originally as the National Council for the Limitation of Armaments, the NCPW, with Libby as executive secretary, lobbied incessantly for the United States to set a moral example by taking the lead in arms reduction.

The NCPW sought to influence the U.S. delegation at the Washington Naval Disarmament Conference being held in the nation's capital from December 1921 to January 1922. It urged Charles Evans Hughes, secretary of state and head of the U.S. delegation, to initiate proposals to reduce drastically the naval strength of all the major maritime nations.

This pressure and that of other peace groups, including those advocating the outlawry of war, did have an effect on public opinion. Secretary Hughes, reacting to this sentiment (and to the fact that Congress desired to reduce the costs of naval appropriations), did present a set of proposals that resulted in a curtailment of the naval race. A tonnage limit was set based on the ratio of 5-5-3-1.75-1.75 (five hundred thousand, three hundred thousand, and one hundred seventy-five thousand) for the United States, Great Britain, Japan, France, and Italy. This tonnage ratio in the construction of naval vessels gave the United States and Great Britain parity in the size of their fleets. It allowed Japan to be second in the world in terms of the size of its navy while making France and Italy equal as the third place naval power. Obviously it was devised to give overall ocean supremacy to the United States and Great Britain.

During the 1930s the NCPW supported the neutrality acts, constantly advocated reductions in military appropriations, fought against Lend Lease, and opposed the draft law. Its actions contributed to the noninterventionist sentiment and to the lack of military preparation at the time the United States was plunged into World War II. Soon after the attack on Pearl Harbor, the NCPW ceased to function.

For further information, see Elton Atwater, *Organized Efforts in the United States towards Peace* (1963).

**NATIONAL COUNCIL FOR THE LIMITATION OF ARMAMENTS.** See National Council for Prevention of War.

**NATIONAL COUNCIL OF SENIOR CITIZENS (NCSC).** Founded in 1961 at Detroit, Michigan, by former U.S. Congressman Aime J. Forand (D-R.I.) and a group of leaders of senior citizens' organizations for the purpose of uniting to secure congressional enactment of a federal health-benefits program. Originally called the National Council of Senior Citizens for Health Care under Social Security, and subsequently shortened to NCSC, this coordinating association now represents three thousand affiliated clubs with a total membership of over three million. Forand, who served as NCSC's first president (holding office until 1963), had sponsored a medicare bill in 1957 and did much to secure congressional support for this legislation.

The NCSC endorsed Lyndon B. Johnson (D-Tex.) for the presidency in 1964 and in 1965 was instrumental in gaining passage of the federal Medicare Act. Also enacted was the Older Americans Act, which authorized the establishment of the Administration of Aging. In 1965 NCSC, in conjunction with other organizations, set up the Direct Drug Service to save money for its members. Legal Research and Services was established by NCSC in 1968. In 1972 they initiated the Senior AIDES program whereby funds provided by the government were utilized for the purpose of finding jobs for able and needy senior citizens. Recent programs implemented by NCSC include supplementary health insurance, noncancellable life insurance (with no physical examination required up to eighty-five years of age), and a Nursing Home Ombudsman Program. The group continues to try to secure increases in Social Security payments, funding for research in geriatrics, and added provisions for Medicare. In a display of "senior power" the NCSC once picketed the offices of *Reader's Digest* for printing an article indicating that the Social Security program was not adequately funded for future needs. The NSSC had been reassured repeatedly by Social Security officials that rumors to the effect the program was insolvent were false and that there was no need for concern. The NSSC therefore interpreted any criticism of the system as an attack on the program itself.

The NCSC is active politically on the local, state, and national levels. In recent years it has lobbied and agitated for health insurance; recreational facilities; low-cost housing or rental units; educational programs for older people; and sale of prescription drugs by generic names to reduce prices. The NCSC sponsors political rallies, disseminates information to influence public opinion, distributes films, and utilizes all forms of media to further its cause. Although it does not specifically endorse candidates, those who subscribe to its program receive campaign assistance and many senior citizen votes.

Present national headquarters is located in Washington, D.C. Current president is Nelson H. Cruikshank with William R. Hutton serving as executive vice-president. The NCSC publishes a monthly, *Senior Citizen News*.

For more information, see Henry J. Pratt, *The Gray Lobby* (1977).

**NATIONAL COUNCIL OF SENIOR CITIZENS FOR HEALTH CARE UNDER SOCIAL SECURITY.** See National Council of Senior Citizens.

**NATIONAL COUNCIL OF WOMEN OF THE UNITED STATES (NCW-US).** Founded in 1888 at Washington, D.C., by the leaders of twenty-nine women's organizations for the purpose of promoting unity among groups working to advance the status of women. The conference was called to commemorate the fortieth anniversary of the famous Seneca Falls Convention of 1848. Simultaneously with the founding of the NCW-US, the International Council of Women (ICW) was formed. Among the founders of these organizations were such prominent leaders of the women's movement as Susan B. Anthony, Clara Barton, Julia Ward Howe, Elizabeth Cady Stanton, Lucy Stone, and Frances E. Willard. Willard was chosen as the NCW-US's first president.

Although the NCW-US led to some cooperation among the various women's organizations, it did not bring about the desired unity. Most women's groups agreed on the necessity of agitating for woman's suffrage, equal rights, control of prostitution, and use of women as police matrons. But they disagreed on such issues as liberalization of divorce laws, social welfare, pacifism, and prohibition, and some women objected to the formation of specific women's parties, preferring to work within the Democratic* or Republican* parties. Overall the NCW-US did aid the women's movement in an era when progress was slow.

In more modern times, the NCW-US has worked for congressional approval of the equal rights amendment to the U.S. constitution and for its subsequent ratification by the states. It also champions human rights, universal education, equal job opportunities for women, and appointment of women to high governmental positions. The NCW-US has an observer status at the United Nations and has standing committees related to Arts;

Child and Family; Community Relations; Education; Health; Home Economics; Housing; Human Relations; International Relations and Peace; Laws; Legislation; Social Welfare; Radio, Television, and Movies; and Trades and Professions.

Since 1962 the NCW-US has given a Woman of Conscience award to those who speak and act fearlessly for the betterment of women and all humanity. Recipients of this honor have included Rachel Carson, author of *Silent Spring* (1962) and the first to receive the award; Hazel Brannon Smith, whose advocacy of voting rights for blacks prompted white racists to destroy her printing plant; Judge Florence M. Kelley for her humane treatment of juvenile offenders; Ellen Jackson, the prime mover of the program for busing Boston's inner-city black children to other schools for the purpose of achieving racial integration; Sister Ruth Dowd, for her work with school dropouts in Harlem; and Virginia Senders, author of the Minnesota plan for educating and retraining adult women who must assume the role of a wage earner.

In 1975 the NCW-US sent a delegation to Paris to participate in the observance of International Women's Year. In 1976 the NCW-US prepared a special bicentennial film for general distribution, *The Bicentennial: Beyond the Birthday*. In contemporary times the NCW-US serves to keep affiliates informed on issues affecting women and to coordinate activities to promote the advancement of women.

NCW-US national headquarters is located in New York City. It has some thirty affiliates throughout the United States, with a total membership of nearly twenty-five million. Current president is Mildred Talbot. The NCW-US publishes a monthly, *Bulletin*.

Headquarters of the International Council of Women (ICW) is located in Paris, France. It works on the international level for the advancement of women in all countries. It has consultative status with the United Nations and provides international agencies with the results of its own studies. It has standing committees dealing with all aspects of domestic and international affairs concerning women and the improvement of their status. Current president of the ICW is Jean Raguideau. The ICW issues periodic reports and bimonthly publishes *ICW Newsletter*.

For more information, see Mary Earhart, *Frances Willard: From Prayers to Politics* (1944), and Eleanor Flexner, *Century of Struggle: The Woman's Rights Movement in the U.S.* (1959).

**NATIONAL COUNCIL ON CRIME AND DELINQUENCY (NCCD).** Founded in 1907 at Minneapolis by T. D. Hurley and thirteen other probation officers for the purpose of promoting greater professionalism among those who deal with delinquents and criminals. By resolution it was declared that the organization should "offer a broader medium for the exchange of ideas, methods, reports, and questions; [and] to secure a working acquaintance between Probation Officers from different sections of the country." While attending the annual National Conference of Charities and Corrections, Hurley (of Chicago) called for the formation of the NCCD, which originally was named the National Association of Probation Officers. He was chosen its first president. The organization's name was changed shortly thereafter to the National Probation Association and in 1947, after absorbing the American Parole Association, it was renamed the National Probation and Parole Association. In 1960 it became the NCCD.

From its inception the NCCD has sought to initiate reforms in the penal and corrections system and establish the concept of reforming criminals instead of merely subjecting them to harsh punishment. The NCCD worked for more humane treatment of prisoners; indeterminate sentences; eligibility for parole after serving a minimum portion of a prison term; creation of prison farms; separation of lesser offenders from hardened criminals; juvenile and family courts; psychiatric treatment; and counseling for ex-convicts. It sponsors research, develops model legislation, initiates experimental projects, and disseminates information to the general public on problems related to penology and criminal justice. It has the following special standing committees: Citizens Action Program; Correctional Council; Council of Judges; Law Enforcement Council; and Research.

The NCCD maintains a library and operates special training programs. It cosponsors the annual National Institute on Crime and Delinquency. In conjunction with the President's Crime Commission, the NCCD set up the Youth Service Bureau in 1967 to assist in the establishment of community referral centers for young offenders. NCCD also organized the National Center for Youth Development to help train teachers, psychologists, and specialists in juvenile justice. It has always championed programs for crime prevention. In 1974 the NCCD was instrumental in securing congressional enactment of the Juvenile Justice and Delinquency Prevention Act. It has also prepared a model sentencing act, which seeks to incarcerate only incorrigibles, not imprisoning first (or noncriminal) offenders. The NCCD has been successful in getting some states to repeal laws that treat drunks as criminals. It now seeks to eliminate impositions of jail sentences on victimless crimes.

Present national headquarters of the NCCD is located in Hackensack, New Jersey. Membership is approximately sixty thousand and includes welfare workers, parole officers, penal administrators, juvenile officers, and the judiciary. Currently Milton G. Rector is serving as president. NCCD publications include *NCCD Newsletter, Crime and Delinquency* (quarterly), *Journal of Research in Crime and Delinquency* (semiannual), *Probation and Parole Directory of the United States and Canada* (periodic), and *Directory of Detention Institutions* (annual).

**NATIONAL DEMOCRATIC PARTY (NDP) [1860].** Founded in 1860 at Baltimore, Maryland, by dissident southern Democrats and anti-Douglas delegates for the purpose of forming a pro-slavery political party. The disagreement between Northern and Southern Democrats over the slavery issue had erupted six weeks earlier at the regular national nominating convention of the Democratic Party* at Charleston, South Carolina. Southern Democrats wanted a plank that specifically declared that no government—local, state, or federal—could make it illegal to own slaves in the territories. Northern Democrats rejected this position and approved a plank indicating that the question should be settled by the U.S. Supreme Court, and that all citizens should abide by that decision. Southern delegates by and large opposed front-runner Stephen A. Douglas of Illinois because of his Freeport doctrine pronouncement during the Lincoln-Douglas debates. His solution was based on popular sovereignty, letting the people of a territory decide the slavery issue when they applied for statehood. When they could not get their way on the platform, the majority of six southern delegations bolted the convention. Six weeks later, after the convention reconvened at Baltimore, the same squabble over the slavery plank prompted a similar walkout by another southern and anti-Douglas faction.

These dissenting Democrats met and held their own convention at another hall in Baltimore, where they nominated their own ticket. For the presidency, the NDP nominated John C. Breckinridge of Kentucky. He was the vice-president of the United States, and contended that the Union could be preserved only if Congress did not try to exclude slavery from the territories. For the vice-presidential candidates, the NDP delegates chose Joseph Lane of Oregon. The delegates who had originally bolted the Charleston convention had assembled at Richmond, Virginia, where they awaited the results at Baltimore. When a group of dissenters walked out, they were joined by the Charleston bolters at Baltimore to nominate a southern ticket.

The NDP, or Breckinridge Democrats, endorsed the 1856 Cincinnati platform of the Democratic Party with the following additional planks: all territories must be open to slavery; slaves, as property, were to be protected everywhere in the United States; neither a state constitution nor federal laws could prohibit slavery; the Fugitive Slave Law must be enforced; Cuba was to be acquired as an American possession; naturalized citizens should have the same protection under the law as native-born citizens; and legislation was to be enacted as quickly as possible for the construction of a transcontinental railroad from the Mississippi River to the Pacific Ocean. It was in the final paragraph of their short platform that the Breckinridge faction identified themselves as the NDP.

The 1860 presidential election was a four-way contest in which Abraham Lincoln represented the Republican Party,* John Bell the Constitutional Union Party,* Stephen A. Douglas the regular Democratic Party, and John

C. Breckinridge the NDP. Breckinridge polled the third highest total, with 843,356 popular and 72 electoral votes. All of his electoral votes were from eleven southern states, indicating the purely sectional appeal of the NDP. By splitting the Democratic Party, Breckinridge and his faction ensured the defeat of Stephen A. Douglas. The fissure within the ranks of the Democrats was but one of the many steps toward secession and the Civil War. Once the election was over, the NDP disbanded. Vice-President Breckinridge finished out his term trying to work out a compromise to save the Union. When the Confederacy was formed, he eventually left Kentucky to fight on the side of the South.

For more information, see Ollinger Crenshaw, *Slave States in the Presidential Election of 1860* (1945); Roy F. Nichols, *The Disruption of American Democracy* (1948); Avery Craven, *The Coming of the Civil War* (1957); and Norman A. Graebner, ed., *The Politics and Crisis of 1860* (1961).

**NATIONAL DEMOCRATIC PARTY (NDP) [1896].** Founded in 1896 at Indianapolis, Indiana, by the pro-gold standard faction of the Democratic Party* for the purpose of opposing the coinage of silver and the election of William Jennings Bryan as president. When Bryan received the presidential nomination of both the Populist Party* and the regular Democratic Party, the gold Democrats and Clevelandites refused to accept Bryan or his silver platform. Although President Grover Cleveland did not sanction the formation of the NDP, he opposed Bryan's nomination.

When the NDP convention met at Indianapolis in 1896, delegates from forty-one states and three territories convened to choose John M. Palmer of Illinois as their presidential nominee. Simon P. Buckner of Kentucky was selected as the vice-presidential candidate. The NDP platform praised the administration of Grover Cleveland for "its wisdom and energy in the maintenance of civil order and the enforcement of the laws, its equal regard for the rights of every class and every section, its firm and dignified conduct of foreign affairs, and its sturdy persistence in upholding the credit and honor of the nation." It denounced free coinage of silver; condemned the Populist Party; called for a tariff for revenue only; upheld the independence of the U.S. Supreme Court; demanded strict economy in government; favored arbitration for settlement of international disputes; and supported a "liberal policy of pensions to deserving soldiers and sailors of the United States."

In a close election that saw Republican* William McKinley defeat William Jennings Bryan by a popular vote of 7,218,039 to 6,511, 495, John M. Palmer's total of 133,435 (0.96 percent) seemed insignificantly small. But the defection of the NDP ruined any chances that Bryan, a fusion candidate, might have had in winning the presidency. The fact that a segment of the Democratic Party and the incumbent president would not support him doomed whatever chances he had for a victory at the polls. When Bryan once more won the presidential nomination of the Democratic Party and Populist Party in 1900 and would not publicly disavow his stand on silver, the members of the NDP continued to criticize him. Although they did not go so far as to convene a national convention, the Cleveland gold Democrats nevertheless refused to endorse or campaign for Bryan. Following the presidential election of 1900, with Bryan suffering another defeat by McKinley, the NDP disbanded.

For more information, see Stanley L. Jones, *The Presidential Election of 1896* (1964); Paola E. Coletta, *William Jennings Bryan: Political Evangelist, 1860-1908* (1964); and Horace S. Merrill, *Bourbon Leader: Grover Cleveland and the Democratic Party* (1957).

**NATIONAL DEMOCRATIC PARTY OF ALABAMA (NDPA).** Founded in 1968 at Birmingham, Alabama, by the Alabama Democratic Conference (ADC) for the purpose of promoting participation by blacks in politics. The ADC was a black organization involved in black voter registration. Prime movers in the formation of the NDPA were Dr. John Cashin, a black dentist, and Charles Morgan, Jr., a white lawyer working for the American Civil Liberties Union.* NDPA came into existence as a result of the failure of the regular state Democratic Party* to permit blacks to participate in primaries or to seek seats on the delegation to the national convention.

At the first convention of the NDPA in 1968, Cashin was chosen as party chairman, Joe Gannon as treasurer, and F. Jackson Zylman as executive director. The delegates in attendance adopted a constitution, wrote a platform, and selected a delegation to challenge the regular Democrats at the national nominating convention. In its constitution the NDPA complied with the loyalty pledge required by the 1964 national convention by stating, "No person shall serve as a Delegate to The Democratic National Convention from Alabama who does not fully support the Nominees of that Convention at its conclusion." In NDPA's platform the planks pledged tax reform; aid to small industries in rural areas; stricter controls over pollution; an end to racial discrimination in employment, education, and housing; protection during peaceful protests; termination of the draft; abolition of capital punishment; provision of free legal services for the poor; abolition of the position of justice of the peace; establishment of racial balance on all juries; reorganization of the prison system; a guarantee of free education for every Alabamian; inclusion of black history in the school curriculum; assistance to small farmer cooperatives; the right of collective bargaining for farm workers; restructuring of the welfare programs; raising the minimum wage; immediate withdrawal of U.S. troops from Vietnam; abolition of the State Sovereignty Commission and replacement of it by a state commission on human relations; and liquidation of the state monopoly on liquor.

The NDPA sent its delegation to the Chicago Democratic National Convention to challenge the regular state delegation, which was pledged to support George C. Wallace for president. NDPA leaders argued that this stance violated the loyalty pledge, since Governor Wallace intended to run for the presidency as the self-proclaimed nominee of the American Independent Party.* The credentials committee rejected the NDPA delegation, but Senator Eugene McCarthy (D-Minn.) introduced a minority report to the convention at large. On a vote by all convention delegates, the NDPA delegation was rejected by a tally of 1,607 to 880¾. Although the NDPA lost its fight to be seated, it received national coverage and thus gave wide publicity to the situation in the South relative to the exclusion of blacks in state party matters.

Returning to Alabama, NDPA leaders decided to run a full slate of candidates in the 1970 election. Nominated to run for governor was Dr. Cashin, and Isaiah Hayes was slated for lieutenant-governor. Candidates were also selected for all state and congressional offices, as well as those in counties and local communities. Of the 176 candidates nominated by the NDPA, twenty-one won election. Cashin lost in his bid for the governor's office but polled 106,000 (16 percent) votes. The impact of the black vote had been demonstrated by establishing a rival party to the regular Democrats, thus forcing the state and national leaders of the Democratic Party to take steps to bring blacks into full participation at the local level. Therefore NDPA's actions had national significance. Much like the activities of the Loyal Democrats of Mississippi,* the Lowndes County Freedom Organization,* and the Mississippi Freedom Democratic Party,* the NDPA laid the foundation for both its own demise and the full integration of blacks into southern politics.

For more information, see Hanes Walton, Jr., *Black Political Parties: An Historical and Political Analysis* (1972).

**NATIONAL EDUCATION ASSOCIATION.** See National Education Association-Political Action Committee.

**NATIONAL EDUCATION ASSOCIATION-POLITICAL ACTION COMMITTEE (NEA-PAC).** Founded in 1972 at Washington, D.C. by the National Education Association (NEA) for the purpose of promoting political activity among teachers and school administrators. The parent organization, the NEA, was founded in 1857 at Philadelphia by forty-three educators from twelve states as an organization for classroom teachers. Originally named the National Teachers' Association (NTA), it sought to achieve "educational brotherhood" by organizing "all the teachers of our whole country."

In 1866 the NTA admitted women for membership and in 1867 was instrumental in getting Congress to establish the U.S. Office of Education. A merger in 1870 of the NTA, the American Normal School Association, and the National Association of School Superintendents gave birth to the NEA. It was subsequently chartered by Congress in 1906 as a tax-exempt educational organization. Within NEA, in 1880, the National Council of Education was established to formulate curriculum principles and courses of study. One of its significant contributions was the 1894 report of the Committee of Ten on Secondary Schools chaired by Charles W. Eliot, president of Harvard University. In many ways, this was the last time that representatives of institutions of higher learning controlled educational policy as it pertained to secondary schools. The election of Ella Flagg Young, Chicago's first woman superintendent of schools, as president of the NEA in 1910 served as an indication of the organization's future course. In 1918 the NEA Commission on Education and Reorganization issued its "Seven Cardinal Principles," which indicated a break with the traditional college preparatory, subject-matter-oriented curriculum.

In 1920 the NEA-sponsored Commission on the Emergency in Education recommended that all teachers of elementary and secondary schools have four years of college training. This initiated a move for professional standards and official state certification. Success in this objective ultimately was achieved in all of the fifty states. The NEA charter was amended in 1920 to place final policy decisions into the hands of a representative assembly of delegates from state and local affiliates. In cooperation with the American Legion,* American Education Week was inaugurated in 1921. That same year the NEA began publishing a monthly magazine, *NEA Journal* (later renamed *Today's Education*).

Membership in NEA is nearly two million, representing two-thirds of the nation's teachers. Members are drawn from the ranks of classroom teachers (both elementary and secondary), school administrators, and college professors (both four-year and community colleges). Members must belong to the local and state affiliate to be eligible for NEA membership. National NEA headquarters is located in Washington, D.C. Current president is John Ryor, with Terry Herndon serving as executive director. The NEA operates with a staff of six hundred, including eleven registered lobbyists.

In 1970 the NEA voluntarily changed its tax-exempt status so that it could become politically active in seeking to gain benefits for its members. For a time it even contemplated a merger with the American Federation of Teachers. In the last decade the NEA has supported strikes by teachers and has become much more aggressive politically. The formation of the NEA-PAC in 1972 was the culmination of a trend that was set in motion during the 1960s. During the administrations of Lyndon B. Johnson and Richard M. Nixon, federal funding of education was substantially reduced. Much of this was due to heavy costs of the Vietnam War, but it came at a time when there was an oversupply of teachers. Hence the NEA sought to gain economic benefits for its members by becoming much more active in politics.

The NEA-PAC controlling body is composed of the NEA president, the president-elect, the immediate past president, the NEA board of directors, and a representative from each state affiliate. Stanley J. McFarland, who serves as NEA's director of government relations, is the executive director of NEA-PAC. Its headquarters is located in the nation's capital in the same building as the NEA. Currently the NEA operates on an annual budget of over $35 million. In the 1978 elections, the NEA-PAC spent $331,127 for campaign contributions for candidates whom the NEA had endorsed.

NEA-endorsed candidates receive money and campaign assistance from the NEA-PAC. Of the 165 candidates running for the House of Representatives in 1972, who were endorsed by the NEA and assisted by the NEA-PAC, 128 won election. In the U.S. Senate, the record was twelve of nineteen. Elections directly attributed to the efforts of the NEA-PAC were the reelection of Senator Claiborne Pell (D-R.I.), chairman of the Senate Labor and Public Welfare Education Subcommittee, and Senator William D. Hathaway's (D-Maine) victory over incumbent Senator Margaret Chase Smith (R-Maine). The endorsement of candidates by the NEA is bipartisan, based solely on the candidate's commitment to NEA's political program, but in fact, most are Democrats.

At its 1974 national convention, the NEA decided to ask its members for a one-dollar annual contribution to fund the activities of the NEA-PAC. It also agreed, for the first time, to endorse one of the 1976 presidential candidates when and if one of the contenders received at least 58 percent of the members' votes (as polled by mail). At the 1976 convention, the NEA membership decided to endorse Jimmy Carter, the presidential nominee of the Democratic Party.* Candidates receiving NEA-PAC endorsement won in 197 of 247 races for the House of Representatives and in thirteen of twenty-four contests for the U.S. Senate, for a victory average of 77 percent. NEA endorsement and NEA-PAC assistance thus have a significant political impact on the make-up of Congress.

NEA's current legislative goals are to achieve one-third federal funding for education; an amendment to the National Labor Relations Act to legalize collective bargaining for teachers; mobile teacher retirement funded by the federal government; and federal funding of the Education for All Handicapped Children Act. Laws that the NEA wants continued and/or expanded include the Community Service and Continuing Education Act; Public Health Service Act; Improvement of Undergraduate Instruction Act; Graduate Program Act; College Library Assistance Act; Community Colleges Act; and the Vocational Education Act. Programs the NEA seeks to extend are Teacher Corps, Teacher Centers, and the National Institute of Education.

To increase its lobbying power in Congress, the NEA has helped to create two coalition groups. One is the Legislative Conference of National Organizations. Besides the NEA it includes the American Association of School Administrators, Council of Chief State School Officers, National Association of State Boards of Education, National School Boards Association, and National Congress of Parents and Teachers.* The second is the Coalition of American Public Employees. In addition to the NEA, it includes the American Federation of State, County, and Municipal Employees and the Independent National Treasury Employees. Through the Future Teachers of America, founded by the NEA in 1938, some six thousand high school clubs and one thousand college chapters are kept abreast of new trends in education and issues confronting teachers. The NEA publishes research findings and special reports and issues *NEA Reporter, NEA Higher Education*, and an annual, *NEA Handbook*.

The NEA-PAC has many successes to its credit. In the mid-term elections of 1978 of the 271 candidates it endorsed 211 were victorious. From the Carter administration it won a 25 percent increase in federal aid to state and local schools, totaling fifteen billion dollars annually. In 1980 a cabinet-level Department of Education was created. That same year the NEA-PAC once again endorsed Jimmy Carter for reelection as president.

For more information, see Edgar B. Wesley, *NEA: The First Hundred Years* (1957).

**NATIONAL EMERGENCY COMMITTEE (NEC).** Founded in 1940 at New York City by Grenville Clark, a prominent attorney who served as its chairman, for the purpose of promoting the enactment of military conscription. Membership, which never exceeded one hundred, included General John J. Pershing; Dr. James Conant, president of Harvard University; Colonel William "Wild Bill" Donovan, who would head the Office of Strategic Services during World War II; Senator Edward A. Burke (R-Nebr.); Senator Henry Cabot Lodge (R-Mass.); and Congressman James W. Wadsworth (R-N.Y.).

The NEC was formed to combat the isolationists who opposed a draft bill, military appropriations, and any involvement in the war in Europe. Members of the NEC viewed Hitler's Germany as a threat to the security of the United States and feared that, if Great Britain were defeated, America's future would be threatened. The initial objective of the NEC was to influence public opinion and to lobby in Congress for enactment of the Burke-Wadsworth bill to inaugurate military conscription. The U.S. army was quite small, seventeenth in the world (tied with Portugal). The NEC was instrumental in securing passage of the Selective Service Act of 1940, which raised the strength of the U.S. Army to one hundred thousand.

Following this success, the NEC agitated for having the U.S. Navy convoy British merchant vessels to prevent them from being torpedoed by German submarines. It supported the Lend-Lease Act and the Destroyer Deal, whereby fifty U.S. destroyers were exchanged for ninety-nine year leases of British bases, and it defended President Franklin D. Roosevelt's undeclared war against Germany. Members of the NEC suggested that Henry L. Stimson, Herbert Hoover's secretary of war, be brought into the Roosevelt cabinet as secretary of war. FDR did appoint Stimson to this cabinet post, as well as Frank Knox, Alfred M. Landon's 1936 vice-presidential running mate, as secretary of the navy. The NEC worked with the Committee to Defend America by Aiding the Allies* to give much-needed support to Roosevelt's foreign policy at a time when isolationist sentiment was high in Congress. The NEC disbanded after the attack on Pearl Harbor, when Japan and subsequently Germany declared war on the United States.

**NATIONAL EQUAL RIGHTS LEAGUE (NERL).** Founded in 1864 at Syracuse, New York, by 140 delegates of the National Convention of Colored Citizens for the purpose of promoting civil rights for blacks. Frederick Douglass was chosen as president. The objectives of the NERL were to secure Negro suffrage; personal liberty; the right to testify in courts and serve on juries; to be able to buy and sell property; and to gain all of the privileges associated with American citizenship. The NERL utilized lobbying, informed whites of the abridgement of the liberties of blacks to create a more receptive public opinion, organized peaceful protests, wrote memorials, and sent petitions to Congress to gain its goals.

Immediately after being formed, the NERL sought to establish affiliates in all states with heavy black populations. A few came into existence, notably in New York, Ohio, and Pennsylvania. At its national convention at Cleveland, Ohio, in 1865, the NERL petitioned Congress requesting suffrage for blacks. In 1866 Frederick Douglass led an NERL delegation to the White House for a conference with President Andrew Johnson. The president maintained that the suffrage question was up to the various states, since the federal government had no constitutional power in this area. Johnson, whose states' rights political philosophy was very strong, even argued that insistence on voting would provoke race riots.

Disappointed by President Johnson's negative attitude, Douglass and the other NERL members approached the Radical Republicans.* Seeing an opportunity to bring voting blacks into the Republican Party,* the Radical Republicans, such as Congressman Thaddeus Stevens (R-Mass.) and Senator Charles Sumner (R-Mass.), reacted positively to NERL's plea for the franchise. Congress first expanded the Freedmen's Bureau and in 1869 passed the Fifteenth Amendment to the U.S. Constitution whereby "the right of citizens of the United States to vote shall not be denied or abridged by the United States or by any State on account of race, color, or previous condition of servitude." The amendment was ratified by the states in 1870.

In 1866 in an effort to influence Congress, a group of women suffragists joined with the NERL to form the American Equal Rights Association* (AERA). Since women were not given the vote in the Fifteenth Amendment as passed by Congress, the AERA disbanded in 1869. One year later, after the Fifteenth Amendment was ratified, the NERL disbanded. Blacks presumed they had won a great victory in getting the vote, but following the Radical Reconstruction the former states of the Confederacy began to impose so many obstacles (the poll tax was the major one) that most blacks were virtually disfranchised by the 1890s. It was not until modern times that blacks regained the unimpaired right to vote in the South.

For more information, see W. E. Brinkley, *American Political Parties* (1944).

**NATIONAL FARM WOMEN'S FORUM.** See American Agri-Women.

**NATIONAL FARMERS ORGANIZATION (NFO).** Founded in 1955 at Corning, Iowa, by Oren Lee Staley, its first and until recently its only president, to promote the economic welfare of farmers. The NFO sought to initiate a type of collective bargaining for farmers whereby higher prices could be obtained for agricultural commodities. Farmers would sign exclusive contracts with the NFO, thereby becoming members, and would be represented much as a labor union represents workers. The NFO acted as bargaining agent and seller in contracts negotiated with processors, meatpackers, and wholesalers. The NFO's goal was to control a sufficient part of the supplies to be able to dictate market prices. This objective has not been fully achieved.

To stimulate artificially an increase in farm commodity prices, the NFO initiated a policy of induced scarcity. In a series of withholding actions, crops were stored and deliberately held off the market. On some occasions hogs and cattle were killed, and milk was dumped to lessen supplies available to the public. When non-NFO members refused to participate in these withholding actions, some violence did erupt. Shots were fired into milk trucks and protest demonstrations were organized. By and large, these tactics by activists failed because they resembled strikes, and farmers have not been sympathetic to them.

In the early 1970s the NFO tried another tactic, publicly killing and burying calves in protest over excessively low farm prices. It wanted to attract the attention of the news media, but often the ensuing publicity caused a negative reaction on the part of the general public. Seeking to win over public opinion, the NFO inaugurated another plan of action in 1975: a program of selling directly to the consumer. Utilizing fairgrounds or supermarket parking lots (when permission was granted), beef and cheese were sold to consumers at a lower cost than in retail stores. This practice netted more profit to the farmer by bypassing the middlemen and garnered goodwill on the part of the buying public.

When the NFO was formed, it vigorously opposed the flexible price support farm policy of the Eisenhower administration as implemented by Secretary of Agriculture Ezra Taft Benson. Politically the NFO has tended to support the Democrats and their policy of high, rigid price supports. Its members, representing smaller or marginal farmers, have overwhelmingly endorsed all presidential nominees of the Democratic Party* since 1960.

Present national headquarters is located at Corning. Membership has declined in recent years but still remains near twenty-five thousand. Through Operation 30, NFO seeks to attract enough new members to gain control of 30 percent of the market. Thus far it has contracts with producers of less than 5 percent of the commodity market. In 1975 opposition arose within the NFO over the administrative policies of its president. At one time the NFO faced bankruptcy. But at its last convention in Kansas City, Oren Lee Staley was again reelected to another four-year term as president. In 1978 Staley resigned and was replaced by DeVon Woodland of Blackfoot, Idaho, the previous vice-president.

The NFO maintains lobbyists in the nation's capital to agitate for increased federal subsidies to farmers. Its influence has been greater when the Democrats have controlled the White House and legislative machinery. The NFO believes the government should guarantee farmers a fair price and that a primary objective of the nation's agricultural policy should be the preservation of small, family-owned farms. The militancy of the NFO makes it a propagator of the same type of agrarian radicalism as the old-time Populists. It holds an annual convention and issues a monthly publication, *NFO Reporter*.

For further information, see George Brandsberg, *The Two Sides in NFO's Battle* (1964).

**NATIONAL FARMERS UNION (NFU).** Founded in 1902 in Texas by Isaac Newton Gresham for the purpose of bettering economic conditions for farmers. Starting as a series of local units, it gradually formed into an organization known as the Farmers' Educational and Cooperative Union of America. As rural membership expanded to all parts of the country, it came to be known as the NFU but is usually referred to by an abbreviated version, Farmers Union.

Under the leadership of Charles S. Barrett, its first national president, the NFU sponsored cooperatives, constructed warehouses, operated grain elevators, sold insurance, and provided various types of services for its members. During the farm depression of the 1920s, it agitated for federal assistance and supported political candidates in agreement with its position.

During the Great Depression, its national president, John Simpson, represented the most radical element of farm leadership. Reminiscent of the Populists of the 1890s, Simpson championed cheap money and inflation as a means of returning to prosperity. He also demanded that the federal government guarantee farmers the cost of production, which, if implemented, would have meant total government management of agriculture. Milo Reno, president of the Iowa Farmers Union, organized the Farmers Holiday Association* in an attempt to force farm prices up by tactics resembling a strike (or withholding action).

In the 1940s and 1950s, with James G. Patton as national president, the NFU allied closely with the Democratic Party.* It supported high, rigid price supports (at 90 percent of parity) so that farmers would receive maximum subsidies from the government. When President Truman's agriculture secretary, Charles F. Brannan, proposed widening price supports to cover nonstorable perishables, the NFU supported this measure. The NFU lobbied incessantly for passage of the Brannan plan, but it was never enacted into law.

When Ezra Taft Benson, secretary of agriculture during the Eisenhower administration, sought to implement flexible price supports, the NFU opposed his efforts. By supporting congressional candidates opposed to Benson's farm policy, the NFU contributed to the defeat of many Republicans* in the Midwest and Far West. It endorsed John F. Kennedy in 1960 and was instrumental in winning rural votes for the Democratic presidential nominee. The NFU was a strong supporter of Orville Freeman, secretary of agriculture in the Kennedy and Johnson administrations.

In the 1960s and 1970s the NFU strongly opposed the agricultural policies of the Nixon and Ford administrations. Its support for Jimmy Carter in 1976 contributed to his margin of victory in certain rural areas. The NFU desired a return to high price supports, which would reverse the trend of the previous two administrations.

Present national headquarters is located in Denver, Colorado, with Tony T. Dechant currently serving as national president. Current membership stands at about 230,000. The NFU has incorporated the following subsidiaries: National Farmers Union Property and Casualty Company, National Farmers Union Service Corporation, National Farmers Union Life Insurance Company, and the Farmers Union Standard Insurance Company. It maintains a staff of lobbyists in the nation's capital to influence the course of agricultural legislation. Its general posture has been to support farm programs favorable to small family-type farms and oppose those favorable to large commercial farms or agribusiness. The NFU issues special bulletins and publishes the *Washington Newsletter*.

For further information, see William P. Tucker, "Populism Up-to-Date: The Story of the Farmers Union," *Agricultural History* 21 (1947): 198–208.

**NATIONAL FEDERATION OF BUSINESS AND PROFESSIONAL WOMEN'S CLUBS (NFBPWC).** Founded in 1919 at Washington, D.C., as an outgrowth of the War Work Council of the Young Women's Christian

Association of the United States. The NFBPWC was incorporated in 1921, with permanent national headquarters located in the nation's capital. Its basic objective was to "elevate the standards for women in business and in the professions." In 1934 during the depths of the Great Depression, its goals were broadened to include a "demand for women employment, appointment, salary, and promotion on equal terms with men."

Over the years NFBPWC has played a leading role in working to secure equal pay for women when they do the same work as men. In 1923 it was instrumental in getting uniform civil service classifications for all jobs without regard to sex. A significant achievement came in 1963 when NFBPWC lobbied successfully for passage of the Equal Pay Act as an amendment to the Fair Labor Standards Act of 1938. This law specifically prohibited discrimination in the payment of wages relative to women when the latter performed the same work as men. The NFBPWC agitated for congressional approval of the equal rights amendment (ERA) to the U.S. Constitution. When enactment was realized, it then raised a campaign fund of $250,000 to secure ratification by the legislatures of the various states. Securing ratification of ERA is the organization's top priority. It has lobbied, with other women's groups, to attain an extension from Congress of the time needed for ratification by the states (from seven to ten years and including the provision that no state could rescind its approval).

The 140,000 members of NFBPWC, with 3,750 local clubs and fifty-three federations in all fifty states (plus the District of Columbia, Puerto Rico, and the Virgin Islands), represent over seven hundred occupations. Its emblem is the Nike of Samothrace, the Winged Victory statue now located in the Louvre in Paris. Selected in 1921, it symbolizes progress and eventual success in NFBPWC's objectives. Nike Clubs are sponsored for high school girls and Samothrace Clubs for college women. Biennial legislative conferences are held for members, and a national convention is held annually. The NFBPWC supports the Professional Women's Foundation to fund research activities. In 1930 the NFBPWC helped form the International Federation of Business and Professional Women at Geneva, Switzerland. The Hemispheric Friendship Committee was established in 1958 to promote cultural exchanges with women living in Latin American countries.

Throughout its existence, the NFBPWC has offered financial support to women students of superior talent through the Lena Lake Forrest Fellowship (1923), United Nations Fellowship (1961), Sally Butler International Scholarship (1962), and the Medical College of Pennsylvania Fund (1966). In 1970 it established the Talent Bank; when high-level government positions became available, files of qualified women were forwarded to federal officials. The NFBPWC urged the administrations of Gerald Ford and Jimmy Carter to appoint more women to government posts and judgeships. It also encourages women to seek advancement in business and the professions. The NFBPWC endorses the principle of affirmative action as it pertains to women and invites females to initiate federal action when discriminated against relative to salary or promotion.

Currently Maxine Hays is president of the NFBPWC and Lucile H. Shriver serves as executive director. From its headquarters in the nation's capital, NFBPWC publishes *National Business Woman* each month.

**NATIONAL FEDERATION OF REPUBLICAN WOMEN (NFRW).** Founded in 1937 at Washington, D.C., by the Women's Division of the Republican National Committee* for the purpose of promoting greater participation in politics by women. Formed originally as the National Federation of Women's Republican Clubs, it changed its name to NFRW in 1938 when eleven state local affiliates met in convention at Chicago. Its first president was Marion Martin. The prime purpose of the NFRW was to get more women into the Republican Party.*

The impetus for the formation of the NFRW came after Franklin D. Roosevelt's overwhelming defeat of Republican Alfred M. Landon in the 1936 presidential election. Subsequent to its formation, the NFRW established permanent committees to deal with Americanism; Minorities; Nationalities; Research; and the United Nations. It functions during both mid-term congressional elections and presidential elections to elect Republican candidates. Members of the NFRW volunteer to help campaign by distributing brochures, giving speeches, soliciting campaign contributions, holding meetings, and conducting political rallies. In the 1976 presidential election, its members contributed over sixteen million hours of work and raised nearly $3 million in campaign funds. NFRW's motto is "In politics, influence is earned on the basis of today's results and tomorrow's performance."

The NFRW maintains a speakers' bureau, recruits women for government positions, and distributes literature to the general public to promote Republican policies and candidates. To aid in the saving of the nation's energy supplies, it issued *The NFRW Energy-Saving Cookbook*. Membership in the NFRW totals nearly five hundred thousand. The expertise and resources they make available to political candidates have been invaluable and have no doubt resulted in victory for some Republicans because of their assistance. Present national headquarters is located in Washington, D.C. Current president is Mrs. Norman C. Armitage, who is automatically a member of the Republican National Committee, with Dorothy Goodknight serving as executive director. The NFRW publishes a monthly magazine, *Challenge*.

**NATIONAL FEDERATION OF THE BLIND (NFB).** Founded in 1940 at Wilkes-Barre, Pennsylvania, by Dr. Jacobus tenBroek, a lawyer and political scientist who became its first president, and fifteen other delegates representing local groups in seven states, for the purpose of promoting the interests of the blind and those with poor eyesight. The NFB motto is "Security, Opportunity, Equality." Its objectives were to have blind people integrated into society and to work for the improvement of social and economic conditions as they pertain to the blind.

The NFB lobbies for government benefits to the blind and disseminates information to the public to educate people with normal eyesight relative to the special problems of the blind. The NFB was instrumental in obtaining revisions of the Social Security Act so that the blind were given increased benefits commensurate with the increase in the cost of living, exemption of income earned from benefit payments as an incentive for rehabilitation, and an end to the discrimination against the blind relative to federal civil service jobs.

In 1964 the NFB prevailed upon President Lyndon B. Johnson to declare October 15 of each year as White Cane Safety Day. The white cane is NFB's symbol of equality, mobility, and integration. Dr. tenBroek was the prime mover in 1964 for the formation of the World Council for the Welfare of the Blind at New York City (of which he became the first president). The NFB established the Jacobus tenBroek Endowment Fund in 1968 and awards the Howard Rickard Brown Scholarship for blind students seeking education in a profession. The NFB testifies before congressional committees and monitors federal legislation. It provides employment for members and raises revenue for its projects by operating the Fedco Corporation (a chain of discount stores) and a plastics company.

Present national headquarters is located in Des Moines, Iowa. Membership totals some fifty thousand in 350 locals and forty-seven state chapters. Current president is Kenneth Jemigan, director of the Iowa Commission for the Blind. The NFB issues two monthly publications, *Legislative Bulletins* (ink-print and braille) and *Braille Monitor* (also in inkprint and on talking records).

**NATIONAL GOVERNORS' CONFERENCE (NGC).** Founded in 1908 at Washington, D.C., by President Theodore Roosevelt and the governors of thirty-four states (and of the territories of Alaska, Arizona, Hawaii, New Mexico, and Puerto Rico) for the purpose of promoting federal-state cooperation relative to conservation. Formed originally as the Governors' Conference, the name was changed to NGC in 1965. As an outgrowth of the first conference, annual meetings were instituted commencing in 1910 and have been held every year since with the exception of 1917. Bipartisanship is ensured because NCG's Articles of Organization permits no more than five of any one party on the nine-person executive committee and calls for a rotating chairpersonship so that neither a Democrat* nor a Republican* can dominate its leadership.

Initial meetings of the NGC centered on discussions of common problems and the fostering of cooperation among the states. Following World War I, meetings focused on problems stemming from the postwar depression in agriculture and the enforcement of prohibition. During the 1930s the NGC concerned itself with issues related to mass unemployment, mortgage foreclosures, bank failures, municipal bankruptcies, relief, public works, and the need for federal assistance. Conferences during the New Deal era centered on federal-state relations and how best to implement programs authorized by the National Industrial Recovery Act, Agricultural Adjustment Act, and Social Security Act. Meetings often reflected competition among the states for projects carried out by the Public Works Administration, Works Progress Administration, Civilian Conservation Corps, National Youth Agency, Soil Conservation Agency, Rural Electrification Administration, and the Farm Security Administration.

During World War II, problems arose relative to mobilization, manpower shortages, implementing the draft, location of federally funded war plants, rationing, and civil defense. Following the war, many states decided to give veterans a bonus based on time and type of service in the armed forces. Other postwar questions revolved around reconversion, such as veterans being reinstated in their jobs, rent control, housing shortages, and conversion of war plants for peacetime production. In the 1950s the NGC pressed the federal government for assistance in expanding educational institutions, constructing airports, building roads and highways, and implementing public power and flood-control projects. The cold war also heightened concerns about loyalty programs and anti-Communist oaths for teachers. The 1960s brought a host of new problems with which the NGC had to be concerned. These involved the use of the National Guard in controlling civil rights demonstrations and anti-Vietnam war protests, crime, and enforcement of drug laws. In the 1970s the NGC considered issues related to administrative reform; decisions made by the U.S. Supreme Court affecting the states; reapportionment; matching funds for constructing interstate highways; transportation (mass transit); revenue sharing for local communities; new taxes; mental health, assistance to senior citizens; welfare; and anti-pollution programs.

In recent years the competition among the various states for federal aid has prompted the formation of factions within the NGC. In 1977 when the NCG met at Detroit, two groups were formed. The Great Lakes Caucus, representing the governors of Illinois, Indiana, Minnesota, Ohio, and Wisconsin, formed to seek more federal benefits for their respective states. These governors complained that the South and West were getting a disproportionately large share of federal money. They were also concerned about reductions in government programs dealing with welfare and big city populations. In 1977 the governors of seventeen western states also met separately (and again in 1978 at Vail, Colorado) to discuss how they might secure restoration of federal funds for water projects cut by President Jimmy Carter. They made it known that government compensation was needed for growing urban areas and locations where the development of oil, gas, and minerals have caused a negative impact. The governors of the West also opposed rapid exploitation of natural resources, were critical of environmental regulations, and were opposed to sending western oil and coal to other parts of the country.

The 1978 meeting of the NCG took place at Boston, Massachusetts, with Governor William G. Milliken (R-Mich.) presiding as chairman. Three-fourths of the governors were members of the Democratic Party. The two main speakers who addressed the conference were Governor Jerry Brown (D-Calif.) and Senator Edward M. Kennedy (D-Mass.). Governor Brown discussed the impact of proposition 13 and the repercussions on state government of the loss of $8 billion in real estate property taxes. Senator Kennedy discussed the need for national health insurance, but the NGC voted not to endorse the measure.

The highlight of the 1980 meeting in Denver was the maneuvering by pro-Kennedy and pro-Carter forces at the caucus of Democratic governors. Governor Hugh Carey of New York and Patrick Lucey, former governor of Wisconsin, sought to persuade the Democratic governors to endorse the idea of an open convention. Lobbying against this proposal was Robert Straus, Carter's campaign manager, who claimed such a rule change would be unfair. Carter had won his delegates by winning primaries and they were committed to him by the rules laid down by the last Democratic nominating convention. After a heated session, the Democratic governors decided not to endorse a rule change.

Present national headquarters of the NGC is located in Lexington, Kentucky. Membership includes the governors of the fifty states plus those of American Samoa, Guam, Puerto Rico, and the Virgin Islands. There are six standing committees: Executive Management and Fiscal Affairs; Crime Reduction and Public Safety; Natural Resources and Environmental Management; Rural and Urban Development; Transportation, Commerce, and Technology; and Human Resources. The Council of State Governments* acts as a coordinating agency for the NGC. Currently Charles Byrley serves as executive director. The NGC publishes its *Proceedings* annually.

For more information, see Glenn E. Brooks, *When Governors Convene: The Governors' Conference and National Politics* (1964).

**NATIONAL GRANGE (NG).** Founded in 1867 at Washington, D.C., by Oliver Hudson Kelley, a Department of Agriculture employee, for the purpose of promoting social and educational activities for farmers. Formed originally as the Patrons of Husbandry, with local chapters called granges, the organization grew rapidly in rural regions of the United States. By 1875 there were over nineteen thousand granges in existence, with a membership of some 1.5 million (an all-time high).

The operation of the NG as a secret, fraternal organization dedicated to social and educational activities changed dramatically after the panic of 1873. Members of granges began to discuss politics and decide on ways to better their economic status. Their political activity at first centered on lobbying with state legislatures to secure regulatory legislation relative to railroads and grain elevators. They also sought to elect pro-grange legislators and members of Congress. Many states where the NG was strong did enact so-called granger laws that regulated rates and storage fees charged by railroads and grain elevators. In the case of *Munn* v. *Illinois* (1877), the U.S. Supreme Court upheld the constitutionality of this type of state regulation on the basis that it was in the public interest. Later the high tribunal reversed itself in *Wabash* v. *Illinois* (1886), when it ruled that no state could regulate freight rates because in so doing it infringed upon federal prerogatives relative to interstate commerce. Grangers then lobbied in Congress to secure passage of the Interstate Commerce Act of 1887.

During the 1890s the Grange agitated for rural free delivery (initiated in 1896); antitrust legislation, improved farm-to-market roads, easy credit, better rural schools, and vocational education for farm youth. In the early 1900s, the NG strove to secure federal assistance to farmers in times of economic duress, a system of rural credit banks, parcel post, regulation of the stockyards and commodity exchanges, exemption of cooperatives from antitrust prosecution, and postal savings. During the New Deal era the NG supported the Agricultural Adjustment Act and other measures aimed at helping to raise farm income. Following World War II it supported flexible price supports and during the Truman administration opposed the Brannan plan. During the Eisenhower administration the NG supported Agriculture Secretary Ezra Taft Benson in his efforts to lessen government management of agriculture. During the 1950s and 1960s the NG took a middle position between the conservative American Farm Bureau Federation* and the more liberal National Farmers Union.* Since the 1970s the Grange has been much less influential on the political scene than in previous times.

Present national headquarters is located at Washington, D.C. Current grand master is John W. Scott. Membership in six thousand granges totals nearly six hundred thousand. The NG is strongest in New England, the North Central states, and the Northwest. It operates cooperatives; lobbies for legislation beneficial to farmers; runs a credit union; provides insurance to members; sponsors activities for women and youth; presents community service awards; conducts educational and social programs; and disseminates information to influence public opinion. Grange publications include a biweekly, *View from the Hill*, a monthly, *Grange Newsletter*, and an annual, *Official Roster*.

For more information, see Solon J. Buck, *The Granger Movement* (1963); George H. Miller, *Railroads and the Granger Laws* (1971); and Dennis S. Nordin, *The Rich Harvest: Mainstreams of Granger History, 1867-1900* (1974).

**NATIONAL (GREENBACK) PARTY.** See Greenback Party.

**NATIONAL GREENBACK-LABOR PARTY.** See Greenback Party.

**NATIONAL GUN CONTROL CENTER (NGCC).** Founded in 1976 at Washington, D.C., by a group of concerned citizens for the purpose of promoting gun control legislation. Prime movers in the formation of the NGCC were Mayor Maynard Jackson of Atlanta, who was selected national chairperson, and Morriss Dees, chief trial lawyer for the Southern Poverty Law Center, who was chosen vice-chairperson. Members of the national committee included Archibald Cox, professor at Harvard Law School and a special Watergate prosecutor; Theodore Sorensen, a presidential aide to John F. Kennedy; Andrew Young, U.S. ambassador to the United Nations; and Marjorie Benton, head of the Chicago Better Government Association.

Although its membership is small, the NGCC lobbies in Congress and seeks to influence public opinion in order to obtain stringent gun-control legislation. The NGCC believes that the only way to control crime in urban areas is to reduce the supply of guns available to criminals. It especially would like to see a prohibition on the manufacture and sale of the "Saturday night special," a type of handgun made cheaply and widely possessed by criminals. One of the objectives of the NGCC is to counter the propaganda of the National Rifle Association of America.* It hopes to mobilize public opinion so as to exert pressure on Congress to enact a law that would severely restrict the indiscriminate sale of guns.

National headquarters of the NGCC is located in Washington, D.C. Current national chairperson is Mayor Maynard Jackson of Atlanta, Georgia. The NGCC publishes a bimonthly, *Gun Control News.*

**NATIONAL HAMILTONIAN PARTY (NHP).** Founded in 1966 at Flint, Michigan, by Eric Sebastian, Adrian Tilt, Lindsay Williams, Maxwell Byrnes, J. Thomas Aldrich, and Claiborne Case for the purpose of promoting Hamiltonian principles in government. The NHP was named after Alexander Hamilton, a founder of the Federalist Party* and treasury secretary in the administration of George Washington. Its main purpose is to propagate Hamilton's political philosophy as it relates to government operated by a truly independent electoral college; election of U.S. senators by state legislatures; substitution of a uniform percentage rate for the present graduated income tax; establishment of minimal voter qualifications;

elimination of all welfare programs; and the election to high government offices of educated and qualified candidates.

In both 1968 and 1972 Eric Sebastian was the NHP's presidential nominee, with Adrian Tilt as his vice-presidential running mate. Having little or no following throughout the nation, the NHP candidates drew a handful of write-in votes in several states. The NHP does endorse both Democrats* and Republicans* who agree with their platform. Attempts have been made to organize minor parties into a United Front Fusion Party, but little success has been achieved along these lines. The NHP sponsors the following organizations: League of Voluntary Disenfranchisement, National Hamiltonian Women, and the Student League for Dignity. It maintains a collection of Hamiltonian memorabilia and bestows the Gaius Petronius Award for excellence in public service.

Current national headquarters of the NHP is located in Flint, Michigan. Present national chairman is Alec Sebastian. On an irregular basis, the NHP publishes the *Hamiltonian*.

**NATIONAL HOUSING CONFERENCE (NHC).** Founded in 1931 at Washington, D.C., by a group of concerned businessmen, public figures, and professional people for the purpose of promoting federal assistance in the field of public housing. Originally formed as the National Public Housing Conference, it was organized as an outgrowth of the President's Conference on Home Building and Home Ownership. This 1931 meeting, called by President Herbert C. Hoover, was cochaired by Commerce Secretary Robert P. Lamont and Secretary of the Interior Ray Lyman Wilbur.

Little in the way of government-funded public housing was achieved during the presidency of Herbert Hoover, since the Iowan was opposed to federal involvement in such projects. The NHC was much more successful during the New Deal era of Franklin D. Roosevelt. It was instrumental in securing congressional passage of the National Housing Act of 1934, which created the Federal Housing Administration (FHA). It was also successful in getting enactment of the United States Housing Act of 1937, which established the initial precedent for federal subsidies to promote construction of housing projects for people in the lower-income levels.

More success came in 1949, as part of President Harry S. Truman's Fair Deal, when the Housing Act of that year formally set as a national goal the elimination of slums and the attainment of suitable housing for all Americans. The preamble to this law, which is NHC's official slogan, read, "A decent home in a suitable environment for every American is still a vital and valid goal." The NHC continued to lobby and exert influence to secure congressional appropriations for urban renewal, slum clearance, and FHA programs. It has also striven to assure veterans of federal assistance in the purchase of homes.

Through lobbing and by influencing public opinion, the NHC has helped gain passage of the following measures: the Housing Acts of 1954, 1956, 1961; Economic Opportunity Act of 1964; creation of the Department of Housing and Urban Development as a cabinet position during the administration of Lyndon B. Johnson; Housing and Urban Act of 1964 (which implemented the rent supplement program for the poor); Housing and Urban Development Act of 1965; Demonstration Cities and Metropolitan Act of 1966 (implementing the Model Cities program); Housing and Urban Development Act of 1968 and 1969; Emergency Home Finance Act of 1970; and the Housing and Urban Development Act of 1970. During the administrations of Richard M. Nixon and Gerald R. Ford, the NHC opposed special revenue sharing on the basis that it would not contribute to better housing. Because of the anti-inflation program initiated by President Jimmy Carter, which resulted in a reduction in federal spending, the NHC has been less successful in its lobbying activities in recent years.

Present national headquarters of the NHC is located in Washington, D.C. Membership totals about thirty-five hundred. Current president is James H. Scheur, with Bessie C. Economou serving as executive vice-president. The NHC issues special reports, bulletins, and informational pamphlets. It also publishes a *Newsletter* each month and an annual, *Housing Yearbook*.

**NATIONAL LABOR REFORM PARTY (NLRP).** Founded in 1872 at Columbus, Ohio, by Richard Trevellick, president of the National Labor Union, and members of his labor organization for the purpose of nominating pro-labor candidates for that year's presidential election.

This labor-oriented political party nominated Judge David Davis of Illinois for the presidency and Joel Parker of New Jersey as his vice-presidential running mate. Its platform called for an inflationary monetary policy (greenbacks); exclusion of Chinese; an eight-hour workday; abolition of contract (convict) labor; low tariff; federal regulation of railroad and telegraph; civil service reform; restriction of public-land sales to actual settlers; and limitation of the presidency to one four-year term.

When Davis declined to run on their ticket, the party suffered a blow from which it never recovered. Nevertheless, the presidential nominee of the NLRP received one electoral vote when an elector pledged to the Democratic* candidate, Horace Greeley, cast his ballot for David Davis.

The American public consistently has not been attracted to labor parties as in Great Britain, and the NLRP failure is typical of all such attempts to organize one.

For further information, see Norman J. Ware, *The Labor Movement in the United States, 1860-1895* (1929).

**NATIONAL LEAGUE OF CITIES (NLC).** Founded in 1924 at Washington, D.C., by a group of mayors for the purpose of promoting the solution of problems common to cities in America. Known originally as the American Municipal Association, the NLC exists today as a federation of state leagues and represents cities in all fifty states and Puerto Rico. Permanent committees exist relative to: Community Development; Environmental Quality; Human Resources; Municipal Government and Administration; Public Safety; Revenue and Finance; and Transportation.

The NLC lobbies in Congress; represents cities before congressional committees and federal agencies; monitors federally funded programs for urban areas; and operates an information bureau for city officials. The NLC maintains a library, initiates research, and disseminates information in order to influence public opinion. It was instrumental in securing passage of a $30 billion revenue-sharing program in 1971 so that tax money would be returned to the local communities for use as they desired. At its 1976 national convention in Miami, Florida, attended by some three thousand city officials from all over the United States, the NLC strongly urged President Gerald R. Ford and members of Congress to renew such a program. The same request was made to President Jimmy Carter. The NLC also urged President Carter not to curtail other urban programs as part of his anti-inflation program. The NLC maintains that the big cities of the nation are facing a crisis, and any reduction in governmental expenditures will have an adverse effect on urban areas. The NLC cooperates with the United States Conference of Mayors* in lobbying for increased federal assistance to the nation's cities.

Present national headquarters of the NLC is located in Washington, D.C. Mayor Carlos Romero of San Juan, Puerto Rico, currently holds the office of president, with Allen E. Pritchard, Jr., serving as executive vice-president. The NLC represents some twenty thousand cities and municipalities. NLC publications include: *Urban Affairs Abstracts* (weekly); *Index to Municipal League Publications* (monthly); *Nation's Cities* (monthly); *Congress of Cities Proceedings* (annual); and *National Municipal Policy* (annual).

**NATIONAL LEGISLATIVE CONFERENCE (NLC).** Founded in 1948 at Washington, D.C., by a group of state legislators for the purpose of promoting better government at the state level. Known originally as the Legislative Service Conference, its name was changed in 1954 to the National Association of Legislative Service Agencies. In 1955 it was renamed the NLC. In 1975 the NLC merged with the National Conference of State Legislative Leaders* and the National Conference of State Legislators to form a new organization, the National Conference of State Legislatures (NCSL).

During its existence the NLC maintained committees dealing with: Inter-governmental Relations; Legislative Improvements and Modernization; Legislative Security; Science and Technology; and Training and Development. It promoted better state-federal relations; sponsored training programs; conducted research; provided legislators with technical information; and assisted with agencies in serving members of state legislatures. It also provided assistance in the drafting of bills and code revisions, as well as information relative to auditing and fiscal matters. Studies were conducted to implement legislative reform, reapportionment, and uniformity of state laws.

The national headquarters of the NLC until its merger was located at Washington, D.C. At the time it became part of the NCSL, Congressman Charles F. Kurfess, house minority leader from Ohio, was president. It had local chapters in all fifty states, representing some two thousand members. NLC publications included *Dateline Washington for State Legislators* (biweekly); *NLC Washington* (monthly); *American Legislator* (quarterly); and *Washington Report for State Legislators* (quarterly).

**NATIONAL LIBERTY PARTY (NLP).** Founded in 1904 at St. Louis, Missouri, by a group of black delegates from thirty-six states for the purpose of promoting the civil rights of Negroes. George Edwin Taylor, former president of the Negro National Democratic League, was chosen as its presidential nominee. No vice-presidential or other candidates were nominated. The NLP platform demanded the right to vote in any state in the nation, complete civil rights as guaranteed by the U.S. Constitution, desegreation of public facilities and transportation, and an end to racial discrimination.

In an era when racism was rampant, the NLP found it impossible even to get on the ballot in any state. Its presidential nominee received a few write-in votes but no appreciable support from either black or white voters. Its attempt to inform whites failed because of lack of funds and disinterest on the part of the general public. Its significance lies in the fact that this party represented a protest in an era when blacks were presumed to be docile and compliant with the Jim Crow system of white supremacy. Because of its poor showing and difficulties in organizing blacks, the NLP was defunct by 1908.

For more information, see Hanes Walton, Jr., *Black Political Parties: An Historical and Political Analysis* (1972).

**NATIONAL MUNICIPAL LEAGUE (NML).** Founded in 1894 at Philadelphia by 147 distinguished citizens from twenty-seven different cities for the purpose of promoting better city government. The NML was formed as the outgrowth of the National Conference for Good City Government, which was sponsored by the City Club of New York and the Municipal League of Philadelphia. Clinton Rogers, a lawyer and member of the latter organization, was the moving force in the formation of the NML. He served as NML's executive director for twenty-five years.

Other notable personages at the founding convention included Theodore Roosevelt, then a member of the U.S. Civil Service Commission and soon to become police commissioner of New York City; Woodrow Wilson, then president of the Short Ballot Organization and a professor of jurisprudence and political economy at Princeton University; Charles W. Eliot, president of Harvard University; Charles Evans Hughes, lawyer and later governor of New York; Carl Schurz, president of the National Civil Service League* and editorialist for *Harper's Weekly*; Marshall Field, Chicago merchant; Richard T. Ely, economist from the University of Wisconsin; Louis D. Brandeis, lawyer and later an associate justice of the U.S. Supreme Court; and James G. Carter, a leading lawyer and NML's first president.

To achieve its major objective, improving the quality of municipal government, the NML utilized four techniques: to hold an annual conference to focus public attention on the problems confronting local government; to publish the monthly *National Municipal Review* (renamed the *National Civic Review* in 1959); to establish the Municipal Administration Service (later renamed the Consultant Service); and to conduct intensive research into the theory of municipal government for the purpose of developing models.

During the Progressive era the NML concentrated upon ridding city government of bosses and corruption. Working under the auspices of the NML, Richard S. Childs, who was president of the NML from 1927 to 1931 (and is currently honorary chairman of the executive committee), developed the model for the city-manager type of municipal government. It became the most used form of municipal government in the nation.

Under the leadership of Alfred Willoughby, who served as executive director from 1948 to 1969, the NML focused its efforts on the reform of state governments. It pioneered in developing model state constitutions based upon a more equitable representation between rural and urban areas. Helping to bring about the "one man, one vote" edict of the U.S. Supreme Court in the 1962 *Baker* v. *Carr* decision, the NML became a major source of information relative to revising state constitutions in accordance with this decree. The NML received grants from the Ford Foundation in 1962 and 1965 to assist in implementing the "reapportionment revolution."

Other significant research carried out by the NML related to voter registration, municipal bond laws, taxes on real estate, and model budgeting procedures. The NML has these permanent committees: Election Systems; Executive Organization; Model Fiscal Program; Representation; and State Constitutional Revision. It disseminates information to local governments relative to city and county charters, federal legislation, and problems common to municipalities. It also sponsors the annual All-American Cities Competition.

The national headquarters of the NML was moved from Philadelphia to New York City in 1921, where it is now located. Present membership nears seven thousand, with William N. Casella, Jr., serving as executive director. The current president is Wilson W. Wyatt, former mayor of Louisville and a charter member of the Americans for Democratic Action.* He replaced William W. Scranton, former GOP* governor of Pennsylvania and presidential aspirant in 1964. The spirit of nonpartisanship is also exemplified by the fact that the executive council has had such contrasting political figures as the late Senator Hubert H. Humphrey (D-Minn.), once mayor of Minneapolis and the Democratic* presidential nominee in 1968, and Senator Barry M. Goldwater (R-Ariz.), a former city councilman in Phoenix and the Republican presidential nominee in 1964.

For more information, see Frank M. Stewart, *A Half Century of Municipal Reform: The History of the National Municipal League* (1950).

**NATIONAL NEGRO CONGRESS (NNC).** Founded in 1936 at Chicago by some eight hundred delegates representing over five hundred organizations for the purpose of promoting civil rights and a better life for Negroes. The NNC was formed as an outgrowth of the Conference on Economic Conditions of the Negro held at Washington, D.C., in 1935. A prime mover in the formation of the NNC was John P. Davis, who became the organization's executive secretary. At its first meeting the delegates of the NNC elected A. Philip Randolph as president (he was also president of the Brotherhood of Sleeping Car Porters). Once founded, the NNC moved its national headquarters to Washington, D.C., and began to organize local councils. It was funded by contributions from individuals and affiliated organizations. The NNC hoped to become an umbrella organization that would coordinate activites aimed at bettering the lives of blacks all over the United States.

When the NNC convened at Washington, D.C., in 1937, over eleven hundred delegates, both black and white and representing all political viewpoints, were present. Included were New Deal Democrats,* conservative Republicans,* black nationalists, Socialists, and Communists. Resolutions were passed calling for full civil rights for blacks and an end to job discrimination. There was considerable internal dissension over what role the NNC should play and how its activities were to be financed. When, for instance, John P. Davis endorsed the Steel Workers Organizing Committee of the Congress of Industrial Organizations, A. Philip Randolph, whose union was affiliated with the American Federation of Labor, was not even informed. Likewise Davis started lobbying for an anti-lynching bill in Congress without seeking the counsel of the National Association for the Advancement of Colored People,* an affiliate that contributed much to the NNC's finances.

In 1940 the NNC held its last national convention at Washington, D.C. By this time the Communists had infiltrated to the extent they controlled the NNC and were also secretly funding its activities. When A. Philip Randolph, as president, denounced the Communists, some two-thirds of the delegates staged a walkout. Not wanting to preside over a Communist-front organization, Randolph resigned, a move that proved to be the death knell of the NNC. At its last convention resolutions were passed defending the Nazi-Soviet Pact of 1939, indicating to non-Communists that the NNC was now a pawn to promote Stalin's foreign policy. The NNC continued to exist for a time, but by 1945 it was defunct. During its existence the NNC was not an effective organization. Its significance lies in the fact that once it became a known tool of the Communists, affiliated black groups pulled out. Blacks would not permit Communists to exploit them, and the death of the NNC was such an example.

For more information, see Lester B. Granger, "The National Negro Congress: An Interpretation," *Opportunity* (May 1936): 151–153, and Gunnar Myrdal, *An American Dilemma* 2 vols. (1944).

**NATIONAL ORDER OF WOMEN LEGISLATORS (NOWL).** Founded in 1938 at Washington, D.C., by Julia M. Emery, a member of the Connecticut state legislature and NOWL's first president, for the purpose of fostering greater participation by women in state government. NOWL's constitution set forth the following major goals: "To kindle and promote a spirit of helpfulness among present and former women state legislators; to encourage greater participation of competent women in public affairs; . . . and to act as a clearing house for information for the members of the Order."

NOWL restricts membership to women who are now serving or have served in one of the state legislatures of the United States. Its efforts have encouraged many more women to run not only for seats in the various state legislatures but also for municipal and other local offices. NOWL also promotes the appointment of women to high-level state positions, including judgeships. The organization supports ratification of the equal rights amendment and backs state legislation beneficial to women. It has two permanent committees: Achievement Awards and Past Presidents. At its annual convention, a yearly certificate of achievement is awarded to an outstanding woman legislator. Present membership totals 455, with Nancy Brown Burkheimer currently serving as president. National headquarters is located at Colora, Maryland, from where it issues the quarterly publication *NOWLETTER*.

**NATIONAL ORGANIZATION FOR THE REFORM OF MARIJUANA LAWS (NORML).** Founded in 1970 at Washington, D.C., by R. Keith Stroup for the purpose of reforming laws dealing with the possession and use of marijuana. Stroup, NORML's first head, received financial assistance from the Playboy Foundation to start his organization. The primary objective of NORML is to decriminalize the possession or use of marijuana everywhere in the United States. To achieve this, NORML lobbies in Congress and at state legislatures to obtain the revocation of laws that impose strict penalties for being caught with marijuana.

NORML has achieved some success in its efforts to decriminalize marijuana. It has been instrumental in having such laws passed in Alaska, California, Colorado, Maine, Minnesota, Ohio, and South Dakota. In these states, possession of small amounts of marijuana for personal use is no longer considered a crime. NORML spokespersons argue that the use of marijuana is so widespread that making it a criminal offense to possess it is unrealistic. It contends that possession of one ounce or less should no longer be penalized with prison sentences as it has been in the past. NORML advocates that a nonprofit organization should be allowed to raise and sell it, with the profits going into drug rehabilitation programs. It asserts that this legalization would drive the illicit traffic out and ensure that the final product is pure and safe to use. In 1978 when a batch of marijuana from Mexico had been sprayed with paraquat, NORML published the names of laboratories that would test samples sent in to see if it was safe to use. NORML contends that this type of contaminated marijuana would not exist if it were legally grown and sold. Opponents to NORML argue that such legalization would result in very young children having access to marijuana, much in the manner in which cigarettes can be acquired from vending machines. Opponents also maintain not enough is known as to how marijuana affects the nervous system and what its long-term effects are on the human body.

NORML lobbies, monitors state and national laws, testifies before legislative and congressional committees, sponsors research, collects data, provides speakers, and disseminates information to the public. It also maintains a library related to marijuana. Present national headquarters is located in Washington, D.C. Current director is R. Keith Stroud. NORML claims to represent thirteen million smokers of marijuana. Most of its enthusiastic supporters are young people of college age. NORML publishes *NORML Newsletter* every other month and *Marijuana Penalty Pamphlet* annually.

**NATIONAL ORGANIZATION FOR WOMEN (NOW).** Founded in 1966 at Washington, D.C., by Betty Friedan and a group of feminists for the purpose of achieving equality for women. Friedan, author of *The Feminine Mystique* (1966), served as NOW's president from 1966 to 1970. Included among its founders were Ada Allness, Mary Benbow, Analoyce Clapp, Kathryn Clarenbach, Catherine Conroy, Caroline Davis, Mary Eastwood, Edith Finlayson, Dorothy Haener, Anna Roosevelt Halstead, Lorene Harrington, Mary Lou Hill, Esther Johnson, Nancy Knaak, Min L. Matheson, Helen Moreland, Pauli Murray, Ruth Murray, Inka O'Hanrahan, Pauline Parish, Eve P. Purvis, Edna Schwartz, Gretchen Squires, Mary Jane Snyder, Betty Talkington, and Caroline Ware. At its first meeting NOW resolved to take all necessary "action to bring women into full participation in the mainstream of American society *now*, assuming all the privileges and responsibilities thereof in fully equal participation with men."

Present national headquarters of NOW is located in Chicago, with a National Action Center in operation at Washington, D.C. Current president is Eleanor Smeal, a housewife from Pittsburgh. She succeeded Karen DeCrow, a lawyer from Syracuse and the author of *Sexist Justice* (1975). Smeal seeks to gain more members from the ranks of homemakers by stressing programs that would give this group of women more independence and economic security. Total membership of NOW is in excess of fifty thousand and is distributed among eight hundred local chapters throughout the United States.

To combat what it describes as sexism—discrimination against women solely because of their sex—NOW has action-oriented task forces working to achieve the following objectives: ratification of the equal rights amendment (ERA) to the U.S. Constitution (which would guarantee that the "equality of rights under the law shall not be abridged . . . on account of sex"); enforcement of those titles of the Civil Rights Act of 1964 that apply to women; elimination of sexist materials in textbooks; modification of marriage and divorce laws; legalization of abortion; and ending the practice of women volunteering without pay for charity work or community service. NOW also seeks revision of income tax and Social Security laws; repeal of state work laws for females; establishment of a national network of child-care centers; paid maternity leaves for women workers; and freedom for women to choose their own lifestyle (including lesbianism).

In 1975 NOW designated October 29 as Alice Doesn't Day (a reference to a movie titled *Alice Doesn't Live Here Anymore*), a national day of protest for women. Organized demonstrations included such activities as work stoppages, demands for pay increases, picketing, refusal to babysit, not spending money, donating no free service to volunteer organizations, and participating in consciousness-raising workshops. At its 1975 national convention in Philadelphia, NOW delegates decided either to endorse or oppose political candidates on both the national and local levels. Special effort was made to elect state legislators in favor of ERA and to defeat those opposed to its ratification. NOW unsuccessfully sought to prevent the Senate confirmation of Judge John Paul Stevens as an associate justice of the U.S.

Supreme Court. It was charged that Stevens had a "deplorable record on women's rights."

A minority caucus was formed within NOW to push for more militant action, particularly in securing funding for implementation of a lesbians' rights program. Opponents of this faction, led by Mary Lynn Myers of Pierre, South Dakota, alleged that the caucus represented only the eastern radicals whose anti-housewife prejudice and anti-male bias were unrelated to the general quest for equal rights for women. Another faction came into existence, called Womansurge, because it believed that NOW's activities were not radical enough. This turn of events prompted the creation of a countergroup, Eagle Forum, to oppose all forms of radicalism and broaden the membership base of NOW to include women from the ranks of the lower class as well as from racial minority groups.

NOW exerted sufficient pressure on Congress to secure $5 million to fund the International Women's Year Conference in 1977. More than fourteen hundred delegates were selected at regional meetings and four hundred were appointed by the International Women's Year Commission. The conference took place at Houston, Texas, where debates occurred between the various factions of NOW. Abortion, lesbianism, and ratification of ERA were the main issues in dispute.

In 1978 NOW declared a state of emergency relative to ERA and made a final push to secure its ratification before the time limit expired. When ratification seemed doomed, NOW was successful in pressuring Congress to extend the time limit (from seven to ten years while at the same time preventing states that had already ratified it from rescinding their action.) That same year it also initiated its Project on Equal Education Rights to pressure the Department of Health, Education and Welfare to enforce those provisions of the Civil Rights Act of 1964 relative to education. Other goals included elimination of job discrimination, equal pay for equal work, revision of rape laws to prevent cross-examination of the victim as an enticer, greater political representation and making women eligible for such awards as the Rhodes scholarship. In 1976 thirteen women of thirty-two Americans were named Rhodes scholars, while in 1977 twelve women of thirty-two Americans were selected.

Since its founding in 1966, NOW has emerged as a powerful spokesperson for women's rights. Through its leadership, it has expressed criticism of President Jimmy Carter for not appointing more women to important positions within his administration. It has been highly successful in its congressional lobbying but less so on the state and local levels. Some members believe that NOW represents the views of professional women more than it does the average housewife. A few think men should be allowed to join. NOW publishes *Do it Now* monthly and *NOW Acts* quarterly.

For further information, see June Sochen, *Herstory, A Woman's View of American History* (1974).

**NATIONAL PARTY (NP).** Founded in 1896 at Pittsburgh by a seceding faction of the Prohibition Party* (PP) that desired a broader platform rather than one limited solely to the single issue of prohibition. Led by John Pierce St. John, the former governor of Kansas and a previous presidential nominee of the PP, the delegates of the NP adopted a platform advocating prohibition; free and unlimited coinage of silver; government ownership of railroad and telegraph systems; land grants only to actual settlers; free trade; income tax; abolition of contract labor; initiative, referendum, and proportional representation; woman suffrage; direct election of president, vice-president, and senators; liberal veterans' pensions; English-language public school and no tax support for sectarian institutions; revision of immigrant laws; and international arbitration.

The Reverend Charles E. Bentley of Nebraska was nominated for president and James H. Southgate for vice-president. This ticket received 14,003 popular votes in eighteen states (0.1 percent of the total cast). No doubt many who might have supported the NP ticket decided to vote for William Jennings Bryan. As the fusion candidate of both the Populist Party* and the Democratic Party,* Bryan not only championed most of the causes endorsed by the NP but had a better chance of winning. Following the election of 1896 the NP began to disintegrate. In 1900 the NP nominated Donelson Caffrey of Louisiana for the presidency and Archibald M. Howe of Massachusetts for the vice-presidency. When these designated candidates refused to accept the nomination, the NP disbanded.

For further information, see Jack S. Blocker, Jr., *Retreat from Reform* (1976).

**NATIONAL PLANNING ASSOCIATION (NPA).** Founded in 1934 at Washington, D.C., by a group of private citizens representing agriculture, business, labor, and the professions for the purpose of promoting rational planning and cooperation among the various sectors of the economy. Formed originally as the National Economic and Social Planning Association, it changed its name to NPA in 1941. In a 1948 statement on "Principles and Objectives" the NPA declared "We, as Americans, reject a planned society in which plans are imposed from above or from abroad. We reject a planless society where everybody grabs for what he can get without regard for the common good. We believe in cooperative planning in all activities and at all levels of enterprise, private and public."

Members of the board of trustees of NPA have included Beardsley Ruml, economist; Donald R. Murphy, editor of *Wallaces' Farmer and Iowa Homestead*; Walter Reuther, president of the Congress of Industrial Organizations (CIO); James B. Carey, secretary-treasurer of the CIO; Leonard Woodstock, president of the United Automobile Workers; Leon Henderson, economist; Eric Johnston, president of the Motion Picture Association of America; Allan B. Kline, president of the American Farm

Bureau Federation*; James G. Patton, president of the National Farmers Union*; Robert C. Tait, president of Stromberg-Carlson Company; and J. D. Zellerbach, president of Crown Zellerbach Corporation.

Policy is established by the board of trustees, with implementation through a steering committee and four standing committees: Agriculture, Business, Labor, and International Relations. The National Council, consisting of 750 members, was also established to serve as a sounding board of opinion. The NPA is funded by contributions from some two thousand citizen members, various organizations, foundation grants, contracted research for federal, state, and local agencies, and the sale of publications.

The NPA endorsed such New Deal measures as the National Industrial Recovery Act and the Agricultural Adjustment Act. It also supported the work of the National Resources Planning Board, which had been created in 1934 by President Franklin D. Roosevelt. During World War II the NPA helped prepare both congressional and public opinion on the need for postwar planning. To enlighten members of Congress and the public at large, the NPA issued three significant reports: *When Demobilization Comes* (1943), *Reconversion of Industry* (1943), and *National Budget for Full Employment* (1945). The last helped gain the enactment of the Full Employment Act of 1946, which established the Council of Economic Advisers, a joint House-Senate economic committee, and required the president to present a special address to Congress, the State of the Economy message. It usually is televised nationally for the edification of the public as well as Congress.

The results of NPA-sponsored research were published in *Strengthening the Congress* (1945) and prepared the way for passage of the Legislative Reorganization Act of 1946. The food stamp program and other anti-poverty programs were given strong support by such studies as *Food for the Hungry: Direct Distribution and Food Stamp Programs for Low-Income Families* (1969) and *A Balanced National Program to Attack the Conditions of Poverty in America* (1970).

With a professional staff of more than seventy, the NPA recently has been engaged in technical research related to demographic projections; environmental protection; energy needs; social problems; vocational education; future food requirements of the United States and the world; and economic problems related to international trade. Based on the premise that "planning rests on respect for facts," NPA seeks realistic solutions to emerging problems that confront the nation and the world. Research studies published in serial form include "National Economic Projection Series," "National Technical Information Service Reports," and the "Advisory Commission and Council Reports."

National headquarters of the NPA is located in Washington, D.C. Currently John Miller is president, with Everard Munsey serving as executive director. Ten issues per year are published of *Looking Ahead* and *Projection Highlights*.

For more information, see J. D. Millett, *The Process and Organization of Government Planning* (1947).

**NATIONAL PROBATION ASSOCIATION.** See National Council on Crime and Delinquency.

**NATIONAL PROGRESSIVE REPUBLICAN LEAGUE (NPRL).** Founded in 1911 at Washington, D.C., by Senator Robert M. La Follette (R-Wis.) and other Progressive Republicans to promote opposition to the renomination of President William Howard Taft as the 1912 presidential nominee of the Republican Party.* At a NPRL convention in the fall of 1911, held at Chicago, delegates formed the Progressive Republican Party and designated Senator La Follette as its presidential nominee. Its platform called for vigorous prosecution of trusts; regulation of big business; low tariff; federal assistance to farmers; direct election of senators; direct primaries; conservation of natural resources; woman suffrage; and the initiative, referendum, and recall.

With the Progressive movement gaining momentum, it appeared that La Follette would be able to mount a strong challenge to incumbent President Taft. Many of the Progressive principles of popular government had been implemented by La Follette while he was governor of Wisconsin. His "Wisconsin idea" became a model for other states to emulate. The state was a pacesetter in establishing regulatory commissions, pensions, operating a non-commercial radio station, and in using experts from the University of Wisconsin to advise the governor and members of the state legislature. Insurgent Republicans who represented the Progressive viewpoint within the GOP backed La Follette until an incident at Philadelphia in 1912 where he delivered an intemperate harangue and seemed to collapse both physically and psychologically.

Following La Follette's illness, which seemed to have taken him out of the presidential race, ex-President Theodore Roosevelt entered Republican primaries in six states to contest Taft. Roosevelt won over Taft in all six primaries plus gaining endorsements from four other state delegations. When TR lost the nomination to Taft at the Republican national convention, Roosevelt and other insurgents formed the Progressive Party.* When the party nominated Roosevelt as its presidential nominee, La Follette refused to support the new party or its ticket. Following the presidential election of 1912, La Follette cooperated with Woodrow Wilson, who emerged the victor over both Taft and Roosevelt. In 1924 La Follette helped create another Progressive Party,* which nominated him for the presidency.

For more information, see Robert M. La Follette, *Autobiography, A*

*Personal Narrative of Political Experiences* (1913 [1960]); E. N. Doan, *The La Follettes and the Wisconsin Idea* (1947); and Robert S. Maxwell, *La Follette and the Rise of Progressives in Wisconsin* (1956).

**NATIONAL PROGRESSIVES OF AMERICA (NPA).** Founded in 1938 at Madison, Wisconsin, by Governor Philip F. La Follette and Senator Robert M. La Follette, Jr. (R-Wis.), for the purpose of promoting economic recovery from the Great Depression and raising the living standards of the general public. The La Follette brothers viewed the NPA as a left-of-center political party that would unite Progressives, liberals, and radicals to advance economic and social reforms that were not being implemented by the New Deal of President Franklin D. Roosevelt.

The impetus for the formation of the NPA came in 1937 when President Roosevelt initiated cuts in appropriations for public works. This reduced the roles of the Works Progress Administration and made many jobless. Also an economic recession set in and wiped out some of the recovery gains made since 1933. Furthermore since the La Follette brothers were isolationists (as were some other leading liberals), they opposed FDR's interventionist foreign policy and national defense program. The nucleus of the NPA was the Wisconsin Progressive Party,* which Philip La Follette formed in 1935 to run for the governorship.

The platform of the NPA, as enunciated by Governor La Follette, called for a massive program of public works to eliminate unemployment; national planning and development of the nation's natural resources; low-cost federal housing; elimination of trusts; minimum wages; government assistance to farmers; cessation of a naval expansion program; reduction in military expenditures; and no international involvement or commitments that could embroil the United States in a foreign war.

Formation of the NPA was given much publicity in the newspapers of the day. Governor La Follette received over twenty-five thousand inquiries about the party within its first month of existence. Interest in the NPA was voiced by Norman Thomas, the 1936 presidential nominee of the Socialist Party of America,* and William Lemke, the previous presidential nominee of the Union Party.* Many New Deal liberals did not look favorably upon the NPA, which they regarded as disruptive of unity among pro-Roosevelt supporters. This view prompted Senator George Norris (R-Neb.) and Mayor Fiorello La Guardia of New York City to stand aloof from the NPA, lest it split the ranks of liberals who were supporting the New Deal.

Several factors caused the quick demise of the NPA. At President Roosevelt's urging in 1938, Congress enacted the Agricultural Adjustment Act and the Fair Labor Standards Act, pleasing farmers and organized labor. Also he secured greater appropriations for the WPA and other public works programs. The result was a reduction in unemployment. But it was the outcome of the 1938 election that destroyed the NPA. Governor Philip La Follette lost his bid for reelection in 1938. Republican* Julius P. Heil, who was also endorsed by the Democrats,* defeated La Follette by a popular vote of 543,675 to 353,381. Criticism of La Follette over his strong-arm tactics in dealing with the state legislature caused an erosion of his backing among Progressives. The NPA emblem was a cross and circle, which was supposed to depict the power of the ballot combined with the power of the people. It gave some people the impression that it was a manifestation of a symbolic swastika for a strong-man type of organization similar to that of Huey Long of Louisiana.

State affiliates of the NPA fared even worse than the Wisconsin slate did in the 1938 mid-term elections. Raymond Haight, running as the NPA candidate for governor in California, drew only 64,418 out of a total of over 2.6 million votes cast. In Iowa the NPA candidates polled less than 2 percent of the total vote. In other states, NPA tickets did not even equal that percentage. These losses, plus the fact that Philip La Follette, the party's leader, was no longer in office, caused the NPA to become defunct by 1940. President Roosevelt had defused the thrust of the NPA in 1938 by continuing to construct a welfare state. By 1940 the attention of many voters was on the war in Europe and the need for the United States to mobilize. When Roosevelt ran for a third term in 1940, he regained the support of most liberals and thus signaled the death knell of the NPA.

For more information, see Donald R. McCoy, *Angry Voices, Left-of-Center Politics in the New Deal Era* (1958), and Donald Young, ed., *Adventures in Politics: The Memoirs of Philip La Follette* (1970).

## NATIONAL REPUBLICAN CONGRESSIONAL COMMITTEE (NRCC).

Founded in 1866 at Washington, D.C., by Congressman Thaddeus Stevens (R-Mass.) and a group of Radical Republicans* to promote the election to Congress of those supporting their program for Reconstruction of the South. The Radicals had opposed President Abraham Lincoln's lenient program for reuniting the nation and were seeking to thwart President Andrew Johnson's policies. By securing the election of many members of Congress, the Radicals gained control of Reconstruction and initiated impeachment proceedings against President Johnson.

The NRCC evolved into a permanent adjunct of the Republican Party.* Its membership includes one representative from each state having elected Republicans to the House of Representatives. The designated member is elected by fellow members of the House from his or her respective state. A new NRCC is selected every two years, following the congressional elections. Its prime purpose is to assist in the reelection of GOP incumbents and to aid Republicans challenging seats in the House held by Democrats.* This assistance may come in the form of financial aid, advertising material, publicity, or by supplying radio and television time. The amount of support given to candidates sometimes depends upon which faction, conservative or liberal, controls the NRCC. From the standpoint of a Republican running for the House of Representatives, assistance from the NRCC often can mean the difference between victory or defeat.

Present national headquarters of the NRCC is located in Washington, D.C. Current chairman is Congressman Robert H. Michel (R-Ill.). Monthly meetings are held in which strategy and policy are agreed upon to enhance the chances of electing Republicans to Congress. The NRCC publishes a weekly, *Republican Congressional Newsletter*.

For more information, see Hugh A. Bone, *Party Committeess and National Politics* (1958).

**NATIONAL REPUBLICAN HERITAGE GROUPS COUNCIL (NRHGC).** Founded in 1971 at Washington, D.C., by the Republican National Committee* (RNC) for the purpose of promoting the Republican Party* among ethnic groups. One of the prime movers in the formation of the NRHGC was Congressman Edward J. Derwinski (R-Ill.), whose own district is multiethnic: Polish, 23 percent; black, 4 percent; German, 3 percent; Italian, 3 percent; Spanish, 2 percent; British, 1 percent; Irish, 1 percent; and Canadian, 1 percent. Derwinski was aware that the Democratic Central Committee of Cook County* utilized the ethnic and hyphenate vote in Cook County to deliver huge majorities for Democratic candidates. The basic objective was to emulate the Democrats and court this vote in an attempt to win them over the GOP.

The NRHGC conducts voter registration drives; researches ethnic opinion on various issues; advises candidates of the needs or desires of the various nationalities; identifies foreign policy issues of interest to hyphenate voters; maintains liaison with ethnic communities; sponsors ethnic folk festivals; and supports ethnic-oriented legislation. The NRHGC also seeks to attract candidates from among ethnic groups to enhance the GOP's chances of winning a larger share of the hyphenate vote. There has been some success in this effort, but most of the ethnic vote still goes to the Democratic Party.*

The national headquarters of the NFHGC is located in Washington, D.C., with regional offices in Chicago and Palos Hill, Illinois, home of the current chairperson, Congressman Derwinski. Anna Chennault serves as co-chairperson. Membership totals over fifty thousand, with local chapters in twenty-four states. The NRGHC publishes a monthly, *GOP Nationalities News*.

**NATIONAL REPUBLICAN PARTY (NRP).** Founded in 1824 at Washington, D.C., by John Quincy Adams and Henry Clay for the purpose of opposing the election of Andrew Jackson as president and to promote a domestic program of internal improvements. The Adams-Clay forces represented business leaders, farmers, industrialists, laborers, and mechanics. The political philosophy of the National Republicans, as contrasted to that of the Democratic-Republican Party,* advocated a strong national government. The platform of the NRP included federally funded internal improvements; a Bank of the United States; protective tariff; expenditures for national defense; canals; national road; and a sound currency. When the election of 1824 was thrown into the House of Representatives, Henry Clay, the Speaker, helped promote the election of John Quincy Adams over Andrew Jackson. Later, President John Quincy Adams appointed Henry Clay to his cabinet as secretary of state. President Adams not only advocated a program of internal improvements, but asked Congress to found a national university and provide funds for the support of the arts and sciences.

In 1828 President John Quincy Adams sought reelection as the nominee of the National Republicans with Richard Rush of Pennsylvania as his vice-presidential running mate. Andrew Jackson headed the presidential ticket of the Democratic Republicans, with John C. Calhoun of South Carolina as the vice-presidential candidate. The Jackson supporters in Congress had engineered a high tariff bill, dubbed by southern foes the tariff of abominations, and this helped defeat John Quincy Adams. Jackson's followers also spread the rumor that Clay had conspired with Adams to deny Jackson the presidency in 1824. Jackson had more popular votes than Adams, though lacking a majority, thus allowing his supporters to make the charge of a stolen election. The Adams-Rush ticket drew 508,064 popular and 83 electoral votes to the Jackson-Calhoun total of 648,286 popular and 178 electoral votes.

In 1831 the NRP held its first and only national nominating convention at Baltimore, Maryland. One hundred sixty-eight delegates from eighteen states were in attendance. Henry Clay of Kentucky was the unanimous choice for the presidency and John Sargeant of Pennsylvania had no opposition when he was selected as the vice-presidential nominee. No formal platform was adopted by the convention. In the spring of 1832 a convention of young National Republicans met at Washington, D.C. They passed a series of resolutions, which in fact served as a party platform, calling for immediate rechartering of the national bank; a protective tariff, and federal funding of internal improvements; this in essence was Clay's American system. The resolutions criticized President Jackson's disregard of the U.S. Supreme Court decision regarding the Cherokee Indians and the chief executive's blatant use of the spoils system. Henry Clay lost to President Andrew Jackson, the nominee of the Democratic Party,* by a popular vote of 687,502 to 530,189. The electoral vote was 219 to 49 in favor of Jackson.

Following the election of 1832, the anti-Jackson coalition that constituted the NRP began to crumble. This short-lived party disappeared by 1836 when many of its adherents gravitated into the newly formed Whig Party.* John Quincy Adams and Henry Clay were true statesmen, but neither could overcome the political magnetism of Andrew Jackson.

For more information, see Samuel R. Gammon, Jr., *The Presidential Campaign of 1832* (1922); Glyndon G. Van Deusen, *The Life of Henry Clay* (1937); and Samuel Flagg Bemis, *John Quincy Adams*, 2 vols. (1956).

**NATIONAL RESEARCH COUNCIL.** See National Academy of Sciences.

**NATIONAL RIFLE ASSOCIATION.** See National Rifle Association of America.

**NATIONAL RIFLE ASSOCIATION OF AMERICA (NRA).** Founded in 1871 at New York City by Colonel William C. Church, editor of *United States Army and Naval Journal*, Captain George Wood Wingate of the New York National Guard, and other officers of the Empire State militia for the purpose of promoting the "improvement of its members in marksmanship." Modeled after a similar organization in Great Britain, it was originally called the National Rifle Association. Its current name was adopted in 1877 when it obtained a charter from the state of New York. Civil War general Ambrose M. Burnside was its first president. Colonel Church served as vice-president and Captain Wingate as secretary; both later served terms as president of the NRA.

National headquarters was moved from New York City to Washington, D.C. in 1908. At that time, its goals were expanded. Its constitution set forth the following objectives:

To promote social welfare and public safety, conservation of natural resources, law and order, and the national defense; to sponsor the formation and affiliation of state and local organizations, and educate and train citizens of good repute in the safe and efficient handling of small arms, and in the techniques of design, production, and group instruction; to promote good sportsmanship, and increase the knowledge of small arms and efficiency in their use on the part of members of law enforcement agencies, the armed forces, and citizens who would be subject to serving in the event of war; and generally to encourage the lawful ownership and use of small arms by citizens of good repute.

The NRA maintains a number of permanent committees: Competition Rules and Firearms Legislation; Gun Collectors; High Power Rifles; Home Firearms Safety; Hunting and Game Conservation; Junior and College; National Match Policy; Pistol and Revolver; Shotgun Committee; and Small Bore Rifle. The NRA sponsors Olympic teams; operates a museum; maintains a library; publishes rifle manuals and rule books; promotes competition in marksmanship; conducts training courses; devised qualifications tests for shooting competition; officiates contests; collects information on hunting casualties; operates target ranges; conducts research; and carries out testing procedures on firearms. Membership is drawn from the ranks of hunters, police officers, gun collectors, target shooters, gunsmiths, and those desiring to preserve the right of citizens to bear arms.

The NRA has been a controversial organization, primarily because of its historic stand against gun-control legislation. Former NRA president Robert J. Kukla stated this position in his book *Gun Control* (1973): "Gun permits, registration, and confiscation are anathema to freedom and should be resisted by every citizen at every level of government through every available legal means. There is no rational justification in a republic for the imposition of restraints on gun ownership among responsible, law-abiding citizens regardless of race, color, or social class."

From the time the Sullivan Act of 1911 was enacted in New York State, the NRA has consistently opposed licensing, registration, and any other type of control legislation. In 1934 the NRA lobbied successfully to gain modification of the National Firearms Act so that its restrictions applied only to machine guns, submachine guns, sawed-off rifles or shotguns, gadget guns (disguised weapons), and gun silencers. Under this law rifles and revolvers were exempt from a special tax levied by the federal government to stop their sale or transfer. NRA was also successful in obtaining modifications of the Federal Firearms Act of 1938 so that the illegality of possessing a rifle or handgun applied only to a convicted felon or one who was under indictment for such a crime.

After the assassination of President John F. Kennedy in 1963, Senator Thomas J. Dodd (D-Conn.) tried to secure passage of S.1592, which would have prohibited the mail-order sale of firearms to private citizens; made it illegal to sell pistols to individuals under twenty-one years of age and rifles to those under eighteen years of age; made it mandatory that gun sellers obtain a federal license; prohibited the importation of surplus military weapons; established federal regulation on such devices as bazookas, grenades, anti-tank guns, bombs, missiles, and rockets; and increased license fees for dealers in guns and ammunition from one dollar to one hundred dollars. In opposing this legislation, a spokesperson for the NRA claimed that "responsible citizens have the right to possess firearms for purposes of self-protection, security of the nation, hunting, and recognized sporting activities."

The NRA, pointing to its research, denied that gun registration served as a deterrent to crime by noting the ineffectiveness of the Sullivan Act in New York. When charged with preventing right-wing groups who are capable of violence from being deterred in their acquisition and use of weapons, the NRA cited the Voorhis Act of 1941, which already required that "every organization, the purpose or aim of which, . . . is the establishment, control, conduct seizure or overthrow of a government . . . by use of force, violence, military measures, or threats'' must file a registration statement providing a detailed ''description of all firearms or other weapons owned by the organization.''

Again in 1970 the NRA opposed a bill introduced by Congressman Abner J. Mikva (D-Ill.), which called for a prohibition on the manufacture or sale of all handguns (particularly the so-called Saturday night special) except for police and security personnel. It was argued that criminals who used such guns should be punished severely, but no infringement should be made on the constitutional right of private, law-abiding citizens to own and bear arms. This ideological stance of the NRA is uncompromising and garners support from conservative and right-wing organizations. The NRA has been a successful lobby and has prevented strict gun regulation in the United States.

The national headquarters of the NRA is located in Washington, D.C. Membership totals over one million in local chapters all over the country. Current president is G. E. Gutermuth, with General Maxwell Rich serving as executive vice-president. NRA publications include two monthlies *Tournament News* and the *American Rifleman*, and a semiannual, *Uniform Hunter Casualty Report*.

For more information, see James E. Serven, ed., *Americans and Their Guns: The National Rifle Association Story Through Nearly a Century of Service to the Nation* (1967).

**NATIONAL RIGHT TO LIFE COMMITTEE (NRLC).** Founded in 1971 at Washington, D.C., by a group of physicians and lay citizens for the purpose of opposing the legalization of abortion. Prime movers in the formation of NRLC were Dr. J. C. Willke, M.D., Kenneth van Derhoff, Robert F. Greene, and Dr. Mildred F. Jefferson, M.D. Jefferson, a black woman, the daughter of a Methodist minister and a graduate of Harvard Medical School, was selected as president.

According to NRLC's articles of incorporation, its objectives are as follows: ''In order to guarantee the right to life of all people of the United States of America, the purposes of the National Right to Life Committee, Inc., are to engage in educational, charitable, scientific, and political activities, projects, or purposes, including specifically . . . to promote respect for the worth and dignity of all human life, including the life of an unborn child from the moment of conception; to promote, encourage, and provide protection for human life before and after birth, particularly for the defenseless, the incompetent, the impaired, and the incapacitated.''

In order to overturn a 1973 seven-to-two ruling by the U.S. Supreme Court that abortions can be performed legally prior to the first trimester of pregnancy, the NRLC seeks passage by Congress of a human rights amendment to the U.S. Constitution. The NRLC wants to reduce the one million abortions now performed every year in the United States. Section two of this proposed constitutional amendment states: "No unborn person shall be deprived of life by any person, provided, however, that nothing in this article shall prohibit a law permitting only those medical procedures required to prevent the death of the mother." Fourteen state legislatures have thus far adopted resolutions calling for a constitutional convention for the purpose of adopting an anti-abortion amendment.

In 1976 the NRLC initiated a class action suit (*Macrae* v. *Califano*) to prevent abortions from being paid for by Medicaid funds. When it lost this case, the NRLC focused on implementation of the so-called Hyde amendment. It was an amendment to an appropriations bill sponsored by Congressman Henry J. Hyde (R-Ill.) that prohibits the use of federal funds for abortions unless they are part of a medical procedure to save the life of the mother. It was passed in 1976 but the Health, Education and Welfare Department did little to implement it until the Supreme Court upheld the validity of the law. While the NRLC does not officially endorse presidential candidates, most of its members supported Ronald Reagan's candidacy in 1980 because the Republican platform contained a strong anti-abortion plank.

The NRLC lobbies on both the state and national levels, disseminates educational materials to influence public opinion, and supports the election of political candidates favorable to its viewpoint. The NRLC cooperates with the Committee for Pro-Life Activities, the National Committee for a Human Life Amendment of the Bishop's Conference (representing the Roman Catholic church), and the Americans United for Life. It opposes such organizations as the Association for the Study of Abortion,* American Civil Liberties Union,* National Organization for Women,* and the Planned Parenthood Federation of America.

The NRLC has formed a separate organization, Alternatives to Abortion International (AAI). With its national headquarters located at Toledo, Ohio, the AAI operates over eight thousand Pregnancy Service Centers throughout the United States. It offers counseling, courses in parental skills, childbirth education, employment referrals, and other services to pregnant women. The NRLC sponsors research, monitors the activities of government agencies, and prepares model legislation. Its work is funded by contributions and sale of circle-of-life bracelets. The symbol of the NRLC is a flag with a red flame within intertwining blue circles, indicating the interrelationship of the sanctity-of-life ethic as part of the Judeo-Christian heritage. The influence of the NRLC has been significant relative to Congress, with membership or support from affiliated groups growing over the years. In 1977 its annual convention was aired on national television. Although she was not officially endorsed by the NRLC, many Right-to-

Lifers supported Ellen McCormick's entry into the Democratic* presidential primary in 1976. Running in the Massachusetts primary, McCormick drew 4 percent of the total vote running on a platform that included making abortions illegal. In New York the Right to Life Party was formed to elect its own candidates to office. In the 1978 election it polled some 127,000 votes, 7,000 more than the Liberal Party* received. Members of the NRLC also claimed credit in 1978 for the defeat of Senator Dick Clark (D-Iowa). Although a one-issue organization, the NRLC has become a formidable political power to be reckoned with by pro-abortion advocates.

National headquarters of the NRLC is located in Washington, D.C. Current president is Dr. Mildred F. Jefferson, M.D., with Dr. Carolyn F. Gerster, M.D., serving as chairperson of the board of directors. Membership totals some eleven million in over fifteen hundred chapters throughout the United States. The NRLC operates with an annual budget of 1.3 million. NRLC publications include the *National Right to Life News* and the *National Right to Life Report*.

**NATIONAL RIGHT TO WORK COMMITTEE (NRWC).** Founded in 1955 at Washington, D.C., by a group of workers, religious leaders, and small businessmen for the purpose of promoting voluntary unionism. Impetus for its formation came when organized labor initiated a campaign to repeal section 14-b of the Taft-Hartley Act of 1948, which permitted states to enact "right-to-work" laws. Spurred by revelations of infiltration into labor unions by racketeers and Communists and the use of union dues for political activity not condoned by individual union members, the NRWC sought to get many states to pass legislation making mandatory membership in unions illegal. It believes in the open shop, which makes membership in a union voluntary, rather than the closed shop, in which workers are required to join to hold their jobs and automatically dues are deducted from wages ("check off").

The NRWC does not oppose trade unionism but opposes mandatory membership, which it believes violates the civil liberties of workers who, for religious or reasons of conscience, do not want to belong to a labor union. The NRWC regards forced membership in a union to acquire or hold a job as unfair and unjust. Since the Taft-Hartley Act of 1948 (which modified the Wagner Act of 1935) permitted states to adopt laws barring the union (or closed) shop, the NRWC has lobbied in state legislatures ever since for passage of such measures. To date, twenty-two states have passed such laws.

The NRWC also lobbied in Congress for legislation to prevent corruption and dictatorial bossism in labor unions. It was instrumental in securing enactment of the Labor-Management Reporting and Disclosure Act of 1959. Popularly known as the Landrum-Griffin Act, it provided for secret elections; provided criminal penalties for bribery, extortion, or misappropriation of union funds; established a bill of rights for union members; and set restrictions on convicted felons and Communists in terms of holding offices in a union. The NRWC monitors activities of the National Labor Relations Board, continues to lobby for right-to-work laws, and agitates for congressional legislation to curtail the power of unions to coerce its members or employers.

In 1975 the NRWC initiated a massive campaign to prevent Congress from passing legislation that would have permitted common-situs picketing by labor unions. Such common-site picketing was regarded by the NRWC as an infringement of freedom and rights of the companies not actually involved in a labor dispute and would prove ruinous to the construction industry. The construction industry is unique in that more than one company is involved in a building project; hence many are bystanders in a specific labor dispute involving only one company with a union. In its campaign, NRWC sent out from twelve to fifteen million pieces of literature, costing $750,000, and purchased full-page advertisements in fifty newspapers in seventeen states where the votes of thirty-four senators were regarded as vital. The efforts of the NRWC were instrumental in causing this measure to be defeated.

National headquarters of the NRWC is located in Washington, D.C. Current executive director is Reed E. Larson, with Andrew Hare serving as chief lobbyist. Membership totals over 1.3 million, representing all parts of the country. The NRWC disseminates information to the public and publishes the *National Newsletter* and *Free Choice* monthly.

For more information, see Edward A. Keller, *The Case for Right to Work Laws: A Defense of Voluntary Unionism* (1956), and Norman J. Ornstein and Shirley Elder, *Interest Groups, Lobbying and Policymaking* (1978).

**NATIONAL RIVERS AND HARBORS CONGRESS.** See Water Resources Congress.

**NATIONAL SAFETY COUNCIL (NSC).** Founded in 1912 at Milwaukee, Wisconsin, by Lew R. Palmer and Ralph Richards for the purpose of promoting greater safety in industry. Palmer, who issued the call for the First Cooperative Safety Congress (FCSC), was safety director for Jones and Laughlin Steel Company and chairman of the Association of Iron and Steel Electrical Engineers. Richards was a safety engineer for the Chicago and Northwestern Railroad. In 1913 the National Council for Industrial Safety (NCIS) evolved from the FCSC, and in 1914 the latter became the NSC.

The NSC first concerned itself primarily with prevention of industrial accidents. It lobbied for protective legislation on the state and federal level to upgrade safety regulations covering workers. It also initiated a campaign to secure enclosure of dangerous machinery; greater use of safety equipment; wearing safety clothing (shoes with steel toes, goggles, or special gloves); and formation of plant safety committees. By 1920 industrial accidents had been reduced substantially because of its efforts.

Subsequent safety campaigns featured a motto printed within a green circle: "Safety First, Individual-Public-Industrial." The current motto (and symbol) is "Green Cross for Safety." Individuals, industries, labor unions, insurance companies, schools, civic groups, and government agencies are NSC members. The NSC concerns itself with promoting safety not only in industry but also in the home, farm, school, highway and streets. Accidents related to drug abuse is another area of concern. Members and the general public are provided with statistics, research data, and information for prevention of accidents. The NSC was instrumental in securing congressional passage of the Occupational Safety and Health Act of 1970. It also inaugurated a home safety program for the careful use of power tools, lawn mowers, and flammable fabrics; operates a Safety Training Institute; promotes driver-training programs; and initiated a Highway Safety Program Services to provide professional assistance (by workshops and conferences) relative to traffic engineering. It maintains a library and disseminates information in an effort to make the general public safety conscious.

National headquarters of the NSC is located in Chicago, Illinois. Current president is Howard Pyle. Membership currently totals nearly twelve thousand, with over four hundred local councils located throughout the United States. Monthly publications of the NSC include *National Safety News, Traffic Safety, Industrial Supervisor, Safe Worker*, and *Safe Driver*. Other publications are *Farm Safety Review* (bimonthly), *Family Safety* (quarterly), *Journal of Safety Research* (quarterly), *National Safety Congress Transactions* (annual), and *Accident Facts* (annual).


**NATIONAL SECURITY LEAGUE (NSL).** Founded in 1914 at New York City by a group of leading public figures for the purpose of promoting national preparedness. Leaders in the NSL included ex-President Theodore Roosevelt; General Leonard Wood of Spanish-American War fame; Henry L. Stimson, former secretary of war in the cabinet of President William Howard Taft; and Senator Henry Cabot Lodge (R-Mass.). Formation of the NSL was prompted by the quick collapse of unprepared Belgium and its subsequent occupation by German troops.

Many of the members of the NSL, which was relatively small in numbers but important in influence, were displeased with President Woodrow Wilson's call that all Americans be neutral "in thought as well as action." Most within the NSL were pro-Allies and were interventionists rather than believing the United States should be impartially neutral. The NSL's major criticism of President Wilson was that his anti-war sentiment prevented him from mobilizing the nation so that it could protect its national self-interest relative to interference by Germany. The NSL regarded Germany as a threat to U.S. security and argued that even America's rights as a neutral would not be respected unless its military strength served as a deterrent.

Because Woodrow Wilson ran for reelection on the campaign slogan, "He kept us out of the war," most Republicans* in the NSL supported the GOP nominee, Governor Charles Evans Hughes. Once Wilson was reelected, he did gradually shift his position to one of offering to mediate between Germany and the Allies. When the German use of submarine warfare incensed President Wilson, he became a champion of intervention. The NSL did influence public opinion via public rallies, and once Wilson decided upon a declaration of war against Germany, the NSL backed this decision. When the United States actually became a belligerent in the war, the NSL disbanded. Many NSL members were also participants in the League to Enforce Peace.*

For more information, see William H. Harbaugh, *Power and Responsibility: The Life and Times of Theodore Roosevelt* (1961).

**NATIONAL SILVER PARTY.** See Silver Republican Party.

**NATIONAL SILVER REPUBLICAN PARTY.** See Silver Republican Party.

**NATIONAL SILVER REPUBLICANS.** See Silver Republican Party.

**NATIONAL SMALL BUSINESS ASSOCIATION (NSBA).** Founded in 1937 at Washington, D.C., by Daniel C. Roper, the secretary of commerce in the cabinet of President Franklin D. Roosevelt, for the purpose of promoting the prosperous growth of independently owned small businesses. The National Small Business Men's Association (NSBMA), its original name, was formed as an outgrowth of a Small Business Conference sponsored by the U.S. Department of Commerce. In 1962 the NSBMA merged with the Association of Small Business to become the NSBA.

The objectives of the NSBA were to serve as the collective voice of small business; to be advised of services available from the federal government; to lobby for favorable legislation; and to promote foreign trade in products produced by small business firms. During World War II it was instrumental in securing war contracts for smaller businesses. Members were drawn from the ranks of manufacturers, retailers, wholesalers, and service companies. The NSBA has standing committees dealing with Education; Foreign Trade; Labor; and Taxes. It has agitated for access to government research and statistical information, tax legislation to induce growth among small businesses, and right-to-work laws to prevent labor unions from pressuring their employees.

National headquarters is located at Washington, D.C. Current executive director is John E. Lewis. Present membership is in excess of forty thousand and represents all sectors of the small business community. The NSBA publishes a monthly magazine, *Voice of Small Business*.

For more information, see Daniel C. Roper, *Fifty Years of Public Life* (1942), and Harmon Zeigler, *The Politics of Small Business* (1961).

**NATIONAL SOCIALIST WHITE PEOPLE'S PARTY (NSWPP).** Founded in 1959 at Arlington, Virginia, by George Lincoln Rockwell for the purpose of promoting naziism in the United States. Rockwell, the self-appointed commander of the NSWPP, was a former naval officer. He began to associate with extremist right-wing groups while working as a cartoonist. After reading *Mein Kampf* he became converted to naziism and thereafter idolized Adolf Hitler. He first formed the Committee to Free America from Jewish Domination. In 1958 this evolved into the American Nazi Party and in 1959 it became the NSWPP.

The NSWPP operated as a paramilitary organization. Members wore army-style uniforms (usually brown or black) with swastika arm bands. They engaged in militant demonstrations against Jews, blacks, or any movement they designated as being Communist. Members revealed their racism by such activities as driving a "Hate Bus" through the South with slogans on its sides reading, "We Do Hate Race-Mixing" and "We Hate Jew-Communism." Parades were conducted, with members carrying placards with such slogans as "Dump Israel Now," "White Power," and "Hitler Lives." Giving vent to his racism and anti-democratic ideas, Rockwell set forth his views in such pamphlets as *The Rockwell Report* and *The Stormtroopers*. In 1963 he issued a privately printed book, *This Time the World*. His writings were filled with racial slurs as well as vicious attacks against those supporting integration, civil rights legislation, and the United Nations.

The NSWPP propagated its viewpoint with a bumper sticker with the inscription, "Hitler Was Right," and a comic book, the *Diary of Anne Fink* (Anne Frank was a Dutch teenage girl killed by the Nazis because she was a Jew). The book contained pictures of Jews in concentration camps with supposedly humorous captions beneath grotesque scenes of horror.

In 1962 Rockwell sought an alliance with the Nation of Islam, headed by Elijah Muhammad, for the advancement of the segregation of the races. No agreement was reached when Rockwell refused to condone a separate black nation within the United States. In 1962 Rockwell also established the World Union of National Socialists at London, England with himself as "World Leader." This self-styled fuehrer not only preached overt racism but boldly advocated violence. His plan was to gain notoriety by instigating riots, convince Americans of the correctness of his philosophy, gain power by running for the presidency, set up a fascist state, and then dispose of un-wanted minorities. Although creating considerable disturbance wherever he and his followers went, the NSWPP under his leadership never had more than twenty-five to fifty members.

Another neo-Nazi group, under the leadership of John Patler (whose real last name was Patsalos), was formed in 1962. Named the American Na-tional Party (ANP), it published a magazine, *Kill*. In 1963 the ANP merged with the NSWPP and Patler became Rockwell's right-hand man. After Patler was expelled over a disagreement with Rockwell, he shot and killed the latter in a supermarket parking lot at Arlington in 1967. Patler was con-victed of murder and was sentenced to twenty years in prison for his crime. After the assassination of Rockwell, Matt Koehl became NSWPP's national commander. Commencing in 1977, members of the NSWPP (usually a handful in number) make a pilgrimage to Bloomington, Illinois, on each March 9 to commemorate Rockwell's birthday at the place of his birth. They lay a wreath on the steps and chant, "White Power."

A rival group of Nazis was formed by Frank Collin at Chicago after he was expelled from the NSWPP for being part Jewish. Collin called his organization the National Socialist Party of America (NSPA). His group gained national attention in 1978 when it attempted to demonstrate on Hitler's birthday in Skokie, Illinois, where many of the Jewish residents are survivors of the Holocaust. When the city council of Skokie refused to issue a permit, the American Civil Liberties Union* took the matter to court and won the legal right for the NSPA to conduct a march. Threat of a counter-demonstration by the Jewish Defense League* prompted a shift by the NSPA to a park in Chicago. The NSPA and the NSWPP were investigated in 1977 about a possible plot to assassinate prominent Jews in America after a known Nazi sympathizer committed suicide with cyanide after being ac-cused of poisoning a Jewish businessman.

Since the media have tended to give the NSPA and NSWPP much publicity, their strength has been grossly overestimated. Actually their ranks contain misfits and racists, but total strength is extremely small. Whenever they demonstrate publicly, most bystanders reflect total repugnance at their words and behavior.

For more information, see "The Deadly Friendship: George Lincoln Rockwell and John Patler," *New Republic*, September 23, 1967, pp. 13–15, and Milton Ellerin, *American Nazis—Myth or Menace* (1978).

**NATIONAL SOCIETY OF STATE LEGISLATORS (NSSL).** Founded in 1965 at Washington, D.C., by a group of state legislators for the purpose of improving the quality of state government. As a bipartisan organization it promoted an exchange of information and ideas among legislators of the various states; served as a national forum; disseminated information to educate the general public on problems facing state legislatures; provided training facilities; and initiated studies to upgrade state government.

Projects inaugurated by the NSSL included seminars on these topics: modernization of the criminal justice system; public health; reapportionment of state legislative districts; revision of state constitutions; federalism versus local control; reform of the electoral college; new sources for tax revenue; aid to private and parochial schools; ratification of the equal rights amendment; welfare; and standardization of licenses and professional credentials. The NSSL established the Legislative Information Service and the Public Affairs Committee.

National headquarters was located at Chicago, Illinois. Membership totaled nearly two thousand, representing legislators from all fifty states. State Senator Ralph C. Dills of California was its last president. Its regular publication was *Quorum*. In 1975 the NSSL merged with the National Conference of State Legislative Leaders* to form a new organization, the National Conference of State Legislatures* (NCSL). With the formation of the NCSL, the NSSL ceased to exist as a separate organization.

**NATIONAL SOCIETY OF THE ARMY OF THE PHILIPPINES.** See Veterans of Foreign Wars of the United States.

**NATIONAL STATES' RIGHTS PARTY (NSRP).** Founded in 1958 at Atlanta, Georgia, by a group of white supremacists who were irreconcilably opposed to racial integration in the South. Prime movers in the formation of the NSRP were Dr. Edward R. Fields, a chiropractor and its permanent national secretary, and Jesse B. Stoner, an attorney. Stoner was convicted by a federal court in 1977 for masterminding the bombing of a black church during the civil rights turmoil of the 1960s.

The platform of the NSRP called for permanent segregation of blacks and whites; encouragement of black resettlement in Africa; prohibition of intermarriage of whites with black, yellow, Jewish, or other so-called mongrel peoples; restriction of immigration to Caucasians; impeachment of public officials seeking to implement racial integration; withdrawal of the United States from the United Nations; uncompromising opposition to communism at home and abroad; and the "strengthening of cultural and moral ties among all White nations, in view of the world-wide survival crisis which the White Man faces." Other planks endorsed the Tennessee Valley Authority, Rural Electrification Administration, Medicare, and Social Security (with substantial increases in old-age pensions for senior citizens).

Symbolic of its militancy, the NSRP had a flag, consisting of a Confederate battle flag upon which was superimposed a white disk circumscribing a red bolt of lightning, and arm bands depicting the bolt of lightning symbol that were worn at public rallies and demonstrations. Other protest activities included picketing local headquarters of the Southern Christian Leadership Conference,* sponsoring boycotts of integrated places of business, and promoting a program of inducing black migration by deliberately refusing to employ blacks. Civil rights leaders accused NSRP members of engaging in illegal acts of violence, but party officials denied both knowledge of and responsibility for such incidents.

In 1960 the NSRP nominated Governor Orval Faubus of Arkansas as its presidential candidate. Admiral John G. Crommelin, a retired naval officer and once head of the Blue Angels, the U.S. Navy's stunt-flying team, was selected as the vice-presidential nominee. The party's platform, though not formally written as a document, represented a racist position relative to domestic and foreign policy. On the ballot in six states (five southern and one border), the Faubus-Crommelin ticket drew 227,881 popular votes (0 3 percent). The largest vote came in Louisiana with 169,572, which constituted 21 percent of that state's total tally.

When Senator Lister Hill (D-Ala.) came up for reelection in 1962, he was challenged unsuccessfully by John G. Crommelin. A national ticket was again selected by the NSRP in 1964. This time John Kasper was nominated for the presidency, with Jesse B. Stoner chosen as his vice-presidential running mate. On the ballot in only three states (Arkansas, Kentucky, and Montana), the Kasper-Stoner ticket attracted 6,953 votes. In 1972 the NSRP did not nominate a presidential slate but instead endorsed Governor George C. Wallace of Alabama, who was seeking the Democratic Party's* nomination.

Because of its adamant position on white supremacy, the NSRP was never large and tended to attract only fanatic racists on the extremist fringe of the political spectrum. It failed to win a mass following and did not have a major impact on public opinion in the South. From its high tide in 1960, membership gradually decreased as racial integration became a fact of life throughout the nation. Until 1974, the NSRP maintained a national headquarters at Marietta, Georgia, where it published a monthly newspaper, the *Thunderbolt*.

For further information, see James Graham Cook, *The Segregationists* (1962).

**NATIONAL STUDENT ASSOCIATION (NSA).** Founded in 1947 at Madison, Wisconsin, by Bill Welsh, its first president, and a group of student activists for the purpose of promoting greater student interest in domestic and international affairs. Known originally as the United States National Student Association, its formation stemmed from conferences of students at London in 1945 and Prague in 1946, and as an immediate outgrowth of the International Union of Students, started in 1946. NSA's original purpose was to foster goodwill among American and foreign students.

Soon after its formation, the NSA became politically active. Its orientation on the political spectrum was liberal to left wing, including some radical elements. In 1948 the NSA supported the presidential candidacy of Henry A. Wallace and the Progressive Party.* During the 1950s it opposed the anti-Communist crusade of Senator Joseph McCarthy (R-Wis.) and advocated an end to the cold war stance of the United States. In the 1960s its members participated both in the civil rights and anti-Vietnam war movements. In efforts to promote peace, NSA leaders made an illegal visit to North Vietnam in 1968 and 1970. This activity culminated in the signing of a so-called People's Peace Treaty. Because of this action, President Richard M. Nixon placed the NSA on his "enemies list," had the Internal Revenue Service review its tax-exempt status, and ordered surveillance by the Federal Bureau of Investigation. This harassment ceased after President Nixon resigned in 1973.

During the early 1970s the NSA sponsored such projects as the operation of a Tutorial Assistance Center; a Center for the Study of Democracy in Greece; the Women's Center (to eradicate sexism in American society); Labor-University Alliance (to get workers in the liberation movement); Center for Educational Reform; Education Liberation Front; Gay Liberation Center; Student Unionization Center; Center for the Study of Student Legal Rights; the holding of an annual National Student Congress (NSC); and affiliation with the National Third World Student Organization. Much of this activity reflected the militant radicalism of the New Left, of which many of the NSA leaders were a part.

At its 1975 NSC, the NSA decided to reorient its political activism. Moving away from broad domestic and international issues, it focused instead on student consumer issues such as a rollback on college tuitions, seeking an open-admission policy; increasing vocational and continuing-education programs, and increased student participation in university governance. It was also decided to establish the National Student Foundation, which would be tax exempt and would permit the NSA to lobby and engage in activities hitherto illegal. The NSC instructed the officers of the NSA to discuss merger with the National Student Lobby* and to cooperate with other organizations seeking benefits for students. The NSA was publicly embarassed in 1975 when it was revealed through a congressional investigation that the Central Intelligence Agency had at one time channeled funds to the organization (although it had not sought to control its policies).

In 1976 the NSC moved even further away from ideological questions. It decided to press for a guaranteed minimum wage for students; seek legislation that would make students eligible for food stamps and unemployment benefits; acquire collective bargaining for graduate students who were teaching assistants and force colleges and universities to grant them full employee status; get a cost-of-living escalator attached to financial-aid formulas; obtain more state and federal scholarships; and seek federally funded day-care centers for students with children.

National headquarters of the NSA is located in Washington, D.C. Current president is Clarissa Gilbert, with Drew Olim serving as executive director. The student bodies of about five hundred colleges and universities are represented as members. The NSA provides member affiliates with information, book club discounts, inexpensive student insurance, and speakers for college programs. In 1979 the NSA and the National Student Lobby merged to become the United States Student Association (USSA). The NSA published the *USNSA Newsletter, College Law Bulletin, EdCentric*, and *Interchange*.

**NATIONAL STUDENT LOBBY (NSL).** Founded in 1971 at Washington, D.C., by a group of student activists for the purpose of promoting opposition among college students against the war in Vietnam. The immediate impetus for its formation was the incursion of Cambodia order by President Richard M. Nixon. The NSL was formed by a steering committee of students based upon the model of two California state student lobbies started in 1969. Early in its existence the NSL was led by radicals and those oriented toward the New Left. Once the United States withdrew from Vietnam, the NSL reoriented itself toward issues of immediate economic concern to college students.

In order to further the interests of students and gain benefits for them, the NSL utilized a professional staff, student interns, and registered lobbyists. It worked for reduction of tuition rates; amnesty for draft dodgers and deserters; establishment of campus child-care centers for students with children; enactment of environmental-control legislation; and laws to end sex discrimination. Student consensus was ascertained through an annual referendum.

By concentrating its efforts on obtaining increased financial aid from the federal government for college students, the NSL was instrumental in securing legislation that increased appropriations for basic grants to needy students and for funding guaranteed student loans. It also helped to gain benefits for veterans who were students; passage of legislation to ensure student privacy relative to school records and the right to see them on request; implementation of a college work-study program; and restoration of an air fare discount for students. It also agitated for an increase in the minimum wage; voter registration by mail; student representation on college or university boards of trustees; and student representation in collective bargaining between faculty and administration.

With national headquarters in Washington, D.C., the NSL solicits individual memberships from students (dues are six dollars per year) and service memberships from student government or college newspapers ranging from seventy-five to one thousand dollars (depending upon the size of the institution and the services to be obtained). NSL claims to represent one million college and university students. In 1979 the NSL and the National Student Association* merged to become the United States Student Association (USSA).

**NATIONAL TAXPAYERS UNION (NTU).** Founded in 1969 at Washington, D.C., by Wainright Dawson, its first and current president, and James Dale Davidson, its first executive director and now chairman of the executive committee, for the purpose of lowering taxes and reducing governmental expenditures. Members of the executive committee include Scott Burns, financial editor of the *Boston Herald-American*; Mark Frazier, director of the Local Government Center; Robert D. Kephart, publisher of the *Inflation Survival Letter*; Charles G. Koch, chairman of Koch Industries; and Murray Rothbard, an economist. Included on the board of advisers are Harber Hall, former Illinois state senator; C. Lowell Harriss, professor of economics at Columbia University; Henry Hazlitt, economist; Louis Jenkins, member of the Louisiana state legislature; Charles Peters, editor-in-chief of the *Washington Monthly*; Robert S. Sherrill, author; John Sonneland, chairman of We the People; and actress Elizabeth Ashley.

The primary goal of the NTU is to cut taxes and reduce government spending, especially at the federal level. The NTU monitors government agencies, conducts fiscal-impact studies, seeks to eliminate waste, and lobbies for a balanced budget. It works with some five hundred other groups in all fifty states to eliminate waste and reduce taxes on the local level. Members of the NTU supported proposition 13 (the Jarvis-Gann amendment), passed by the voters of California in 1978, which imposes stringent tax ceilings on real estate that cannot be exceeded by municipal taxing bodies. The NTU is now working for passage by Congress of a balanced-budget amendment to the U.S. Constitution, which would require the federal government to keep annual expenditures in line with revenue.

NTU membership is about one hundred thousand. National headquarters is located in Washington, D.C., with William Bonner serving as executive director. The NTU has published the following booklets: *Taxpayer Alerts* and *How to Fight Property Taxes*. It also issues a monthly newsletter, *Dollars & Sense*, and *Annual Report*.

**NATIONAL TEACHERS' ASSOCIATION.** See National Education Association–Political Action Committee.

**NATIONAL TENANTS ORGANIZATION (NTO).** Founded in 1969 at Washington, D.C., by a concerned group of citizens for the purpose of promoting the interests of low-income tenants. The primary objectives of the

NTO are to upgrade the quality of housing; prevent the economic exploitation of the poor through high and exorbitant rents; protect the legal rights of those who rent; improve the social environment of slum areas; and involve tenants in political action to secure federal benefits.

The impetus to form the NTO came when the cost of the war in Vietnam tended to prevent the adequate funding of Great Society programs enacted during the administration of President Lyndon B. Johnson. Among these anti-poverty programs were low-cost housing projects and the upgrading of the inner core of major cities in the United States. The NTO lobbied for complete funding and expansion of programs aimed at helping the poor and low-income sectors of the population. It was instrumental in getting passage of a rent-subsidy program and federal funding of home improvements in run-down areas. It has also taken legal action to secure compliance with open housing laws and to prevent banks and insurance companies from applying discriminatory rates to slum areas.

The NTO has been very effective in protecting the rights of tenants against slum landlords who seek to exploit the poor. Some of its affiliates are student organizations that have banded together to secure just rental rates and fair lease arrangements relative to off-campus student housing. National headquarters of the NTO is located in Washington, D.C. Membership totals some two hundred thousand, representing local affiliates in forty states. Present director is Jesse Gray. The NTO publishes a monthly, *Tenants Outlook*.

**NATIONAL TRUST FOR HISTORIC PRESERVATION (NTHP).** Founded in 1947 at Washington, D.C., by David E. Finley, director of the National Gallery of Art, in conjunction with forty other directors of museums, libraries, archives, and civic associations, for the purpose of creating a nongovernmental organization to promote the preservation of significant structures or sites. General U. S. Grant III, head of the National Capital Park and Planning Commission, was elected its first president. The NTHP was granted a charter by Congress in 1949, and in 1954 it absorbed the National Council for Historic Sites and Buildings.

The NTHP has agitated for congressional legislation to establish the American Folklore Center in the Library of Congress; supports an amendment to the Land and Water Conservation Act of 1966 to permit preservation of areas of historical importance; seeks establishment of a national trust for the preservation of historic ships; desires tax credit for maintaining historic barns; wants a law making unused railroad passenger depots available for cultural activities; urges passage of an amendment to the Emergency Home Purchase Assistance Act of 1974 to provide funds for the restoration of historic homes; and has requested a presidential proclamation for the observance of a national preservation week.

The NTHP serves local communities by providing expert counsel, conducting seminars, maintaining a library, disseminating information, and operating a summer intern program. It seeks to generate enthusiasm among the general public relative to the need for enhancing national culture by preserving significant sites, buildings, structures, and objects of historical significance. It also promotes programs on how to raise funds, restore historic architecture, and protect monuments threatened by destruction. Permanent NTHP committees are: Education and Training Services; Field Services; Finance and Investment; Historical Properties; International Relations; and Professional Consultants.

To ensure preservation, the NTHP owns and administers the following historical properties: Belle Grove in Middleburg, Virginia; Casa Amesti in Monterey, California; Cleveden in Philadelphia: Cooper Adobe in Monterey; Chesterwood in Stockbridge, Massachusetts; Decatur House in Washington, D.C.; Lyndhurst in Tarrytown, New York; Oatlands in Leesburg, Virginia; Pope-Leighey House in Mount Vernon, Virginia; Shadows-on-the-Teche in New Iberia, New York; Woodlawn Plantation in Mount Vernon, Virginia; and the Woodrow Wilson House in Washington, D.C. In 1975 it secured a nine-month option on the Wainright Building in St. Louis, Missouri, in order to find time to secure a sympathetic buyer who would preserve this 1892 structure (one of the first steel-frame skyscrapers). The NTHP bestows annual awards for outstanding achievement in support of historic preservation.

National headquarters for the NTHP is located in Washington, D.C. Present membership totals nearly twenty thousand. Current president is James Biddle. NTHP publications include a monthly, *Preservation News*, and a quarterly, *Historic Preservation*.

**NATIONAL UNION FOR SOCIAL JUSTICE (NUSJ).** Founded in 1934 at Royal Oak, Michigan, by Father Charles E. Coughlin for the purpose of promoting social and economic reforms for the benefit of the poor masses. As a Roman Catholic priest and pastor of the Shrine of the Little Flower, he preached his message over the radio to weekly audiences of millions. The "radio priest" criticized the New Deal as being far too conservative either to alleviate or remedy the hardships of the Great Depression.

From the radio pulpit and through his magazine, *Social Justice*, Father Coughlin called for massive domestic reforms, an inflationary monetary policy, redistribution of the national wealth, and enactment of widespread welfare measures. Congressional districts all over the country were organized into political action cells. At its peak in 1936, the NUSJ attracted over five hundred thousand members and became the nucleus for the Union Party.*

Coughlin allied with Senator Huey P. Long (D-La.) and his Share Our Wealth Movement* in 1935 and proposed him as a presidential candidate for the Union Party* in 1936. When Long was assassinated, Coughlin turned to Congressman William Lemke of North Dakota as his chosen presidential candidate. "Liberty Bell Lemke," as he was dubbed by the press, was a member of a rural Socialist party, the Nonpartisan League,* and polled 892,492 votes (1.96 percent of the total vote) but gained no electoral votes for the Union Party.

President Franklin D. Roosevelt's so-called second New Deal, which moved markedly to the left, did much to deflate what was remaining of the NUSJ. Its further decline in popularity was prompted by Father Coughlin's increasingly extreme and controversial views. After 1936 he championed isolationism, defended Mussolini, appeared to be anti-Semitic, and was accused of being pro-Nazi. In 1941 Edward Cardinal Mooney intervened to stop his radio broadcast, and in 1942 *Social Justice* was barred from the U.S. mails as seditious literature.

After Pearl Harbor the NUSJ began to collapse, and in 1944 it disbanded. Father Coughlin and the NUSJ no doubt contributed to the leftward movement of the New Deal. By backing Social Security, increasing public works, putting more on relief, raising taxes on the rich, and providing more assistance to farmers, President Roosevelt blunted the political impact of the NUSJ and even won over many of its members.

The writings of Father Coughlin include *Christ or the Red Serpent* (1930), *By the Sweat of Thy Brow* (1931), *The New Deal in Money* (1934), and *Am I Anti-Semitic?* (1939).

For further information, see Charles J. Tull, *Father Coughlin and the New Deal* (1965).

**NATIONAL UNION PARTY (NUP).** Founded in 1864 at Baltimore, Maryland, by President Abraham Lincoln and leaders of the Republican Party* to provide a vehicle for attracting votes of pro-Union Democrats in that year's presidential election. By temporarily altering the name of the Republican Party, it was hoped that the preservation of the Union, not partisan differences over party labels, would be the primary issue.

To increase President Lincoln's chances for reelection, the NUP dropped Vice-President Hannibal Hamlin and replaced him with Andrew Johnson of Tennessee. Johnson would appeal to War Democrats, since he was a Southern Democrat who had remained loyal to the U.S. government. The Lincoln-Johnson ticket defeated the nominees of the Democratic Party* in 1864 by a popular vote of 2,219,362 to 1,805,063 and an electoral count of 212 to 21. In a relatively close election, the margin of victory came as a result of some Union Army triumphs on the battlefield and the tactic of renaming the Republican Party as a means of winning broad support at the polls.

After Abraham Lincoln was assassinated and Andrew Johnson ascended to the presidency, he too sought renomination in 1868 by convening an

NUP convention in Philadelphia. Since the Radical Republicans* repudiated him, he failed to be nominated. At the regular Republican convention in Chicago, which used the name National Union Republican Party (this was the last time the GOP ever used the National Union label), General Ulysses S. Grant was nominated for the presidency, with Schuyler Colfax of Indiana chosen as his vice-presidential running mate. The team of Grant and Colfax won over the Democratic opposition, Horatio Seymour and Francis P. Blair, by a popular vote of 3,013,421 to 2,076,829. In the electoral college the NUP candidates drew 214 votes to 80 for the Democrats. Because of the Reconstruction policy set by Congress, the former Confederate states of Mississippi, Texas, and Virginia were not permitted to cast their twenty-three electoral votes.

For further information, see Edward C. Kirkland, *Peacemakers of 1864* (1927); William F. Zornow, *Lincoln and the Party Divided* (1954); and Charles H. Coleman, *The Election of 1868* (1933).

**NATIONAL UNION REPUBLICAN PARTY.** See National Union Party.

**NATIONAL WOMAN SUFFRAGE ASSOCIATION (NWSA).** Founded in 1869 at New York City by Elizabeth Cady Stanton (its first president), Susan B. Anthony (chairwoman of its executive committee), and other suffragists to promote the adoption of an amendment to the U.S. Constitution giving women the right of franchise. Stanton, along with Anthony, previously had formed the New York State Suffrage Society in 1854, and they were instrumental in gaining passage of a state law giving women equal property rights. In 1868 Stanton started the *Revolution*, a weekly periodical championing women suffrage; wrote *Woman's Bible* (1898); published her memoirs, *Eighty Years and More* (1898); and with Anthony and Matilda Gage compiled a four-volume work, *The History of Woman Suffrage* (1902).

Stanton and Anthony constituted a two-woman team that dominated the NWSA and provided brilliant leadership to the suffrage movement in general. In 1863 they founded the Women's National Loyal League to support the Union and emancipation of slaves. They supported amendments giving citizenship and the right to vote to blacks. When the Fifteenth Amendment to the U.S. Constitution was passed by Congress, they fought to include women along with freedmen as having the right of franchise. When women were left out, they formed the NWSA. Their aim was to secure congressional approval and state ratification of a woman suffrage amendment. To achieve this goal the NWSA, with Stanton and Anthony as its prime spokeswomen, dedicated all of its efforts to sending out speakers, issuing publications, and lobbying continuously for congressional action.

To advance the cause of woman suffrage, Stanton and Anthony launched the International Council of Women in 1888 with offices in both London and Washington, D.C. In order to unite all women involved in the suffrage movement, the NWSA merged with the National American Woman Suffrage Association* (NAWSA). Elizabeth Cady Stanton was elected NAWSA's first president and held that office until 1892. Susan B. Anthony served as NAWSA's first vice-president until she succeeded Stanton as president in 1892. As pioneers in the suffrage movement, these two women and the organizations they headed did much to lay the groundwork for the success that would come with the enactment and final ratification of the Nineteenth Amendment in 1920.

For further information, see Selma Lutz, *Created Equal: A Biography of Elizabeth Cady Stanton* (1940); Katherine Anthony, *Susan B. Anthony: Her Personal History and Her Era* (1954); and Eleanor Flexner, *Century of Struggle: The Woman Rights Movement in the United States* (1959).

**NATIONAL WOMAN'S CHRISTIAN TEMPERANCE UNION.** See Woman's Christian Temperance Union.

**NATIONAL WOMAN'S PARTY (NWP).** Founded in 1917 at Washington, D.C., by feminist Alice Paul to promote woman suffrage. The NWP evolved from the Congressional Union for Woman Suffrage, an organization formed by Alice Paul and Crystal Eastman in 1912. Under Alice Paul's leadership, the NWP used militant tactics to secure passage of the Nineteenth (woman suffrage) Amendment. The NWP took the position that because the Democratic Party* controlled the Congress and White House, it must be held responsible for preventing women from attaining universal suffrage. This differed from the nonpartisan stance of the National American Woman Suffrage Association* (NAWSA), to which Paul had once belonged.

Since President Woodrow Wilson opposed woman suffrage, he was made the special target of many NWP activities. Marches, demonstrations, and picketing the White House became daily occurrences. Messages on banners and posters condemned the president for waging a war to make the "world safe for democracy" while at the same time refusing to give women the right to vote. NWP's severe criticism of the president was construed by some as constituting opposition to World War I. As a result, its members were frequently harassed by hostile crowds and unsympathetic policemen. Even the NAWSA disapproved of NWP's partisan approach as harming, not helping, the cause of woman suffrage.

In the mid-term election of 1918 the NWP exerted all of its influence to defeat Democrats. This strategy proved effective in those states where women had the right to vote. NWP's efforts helped the Republican Party* gain control over the U.S. Senate. Success came in 1920 when the Nineteenth Amendment was passed by Congress and ratified by the necessary states in time for women to vote in the presidential election. It was noteworthy that the Democratic platform of 1920 endorsed its ratification, although too late to win the plaudits of the NWP.

In 1923 Paul secured the introduction in Congress of the first equal rights amendment (ERA) to the U.S. Constitution. It was dubbed the "Lucretia Mott Amendment." The NWP never succeeded in gaining its approval by Congress. Peak membership in the NWP was about fifty thousand in 1920. Its activities and effectiveness declined steadily in the post-World War II era as Paul became less and less active as its leader. At one time Pearl Mesta, Ambassador to Luxembourg, and Pearl Buck, a noted author, were prominent members.

Although supporting legislation giving women equal rights relative to employment (as part of the civil rights movement of the 1960s), the NWP played but a small role in securing enactment of such laws. By the time ERA was approved by Congress in 1970, the NWP was considered old-fashioned and genteel by modern activists in the women's movement. Although never really existing as a political party, the NWP as an organization has lost its militancy and effectiveness. Currently the NWP works for ratification of ERA, encourages women to seek political office, and makes recommendations of women for appointment to government positions. National headquarters is still located in the nation's capital, but membership is relatively small. Currently Elizabeth L. Chittick serves as president.

For more information, see Inez Haynes Irwin, *Up the Hill with Banners Flying* (1964).

**NATIONAL WOMEN'S POLITICAL CAUCUS (NWPC).** Founded in 1971 at Washington, D.C., by a group of activists for the purpose of promoting women's rights. Prime movers in NWPC's formation included Congresswoman Bella S. Abzug (D-N.Y.), who was also an organizer of the Women's Strike for Peace in 1961 and a cofounder of the New Democratic Coalition; Congresswoman Shirley Chisholm, who in 1972 was the first black woman to seek the presidency; Betty Friedan, a founder and past president of the National Organization for Women*; Gloria Steinem, a feminist and leader in the women's movement; and Sissy Farenthold, a one-time gubernatorial candidate in Texas who in 1972 vied for the vice-presidenial nomination of the Democratic Party.*

The platform of the NWPC set objectives in the categories of civil rights, human rights, economic rights, and national commitment to women. In the realm of civil rights, top priority was given to the ratification of the equal rights amendment (ERA) to the U.S. Constitution. Other goals included amendments to existing federal legislation to prohibit any discrimination on the basis of sex and to extend the jurisdiction of the Civil Rights Commission to cover such cases. Relative to human rights, the NWPC sought passage of comprehensive legislation to legalize abortion; establish child-care centers; provide maternity care and birth control aid; ensure fair treatment of families headed by women; and reform the criminal justice system to eliminate sexism.

Concerning economic rights, the NWPC advocated elimination of tax inequities affecting women; amendment of the Social Security Act to provide equitable retirement benefits for working wives, widows, and women heads of households (and their children); amendment of the Internal Revenue Code to permit deductions for expenses related to care for children or disabled dependents; disability payments during pregnancy, childbirth, and recovery (including miscarriage and abortion); equal pay and unemployment insurance for women; and a guaranteed minimum income for all Americans.

Pertaining to a national commitment to women, the NWPC urged additional appointment of women to top government positions; inclusion of women on all federal commissions; passage of the Women's Equality Act to implement recommendations made by the President's Task Force on Women's Rights and Responsibilities; enactment of the Women's Education Act; and federal financing of state commissions on the status of women.

The "Win with Women '74" project conducted by the NWPC was responsible for getting more women to run for local, state, and national political offices. Women were also encouraged to seek positions in all of the professions. NWPC claims much of the credit for increasing the number of women appointed to the federal court system from five in 1977 to forty-two in 1980. Working with women delegates to the Democratic national convention, it succeeded in getting a plank that would deprive candidates from receiving party funds if they opposed ratification of ERA. Claimed also as one of its victories was the rule that 50 percent of the delegates at the 1980 Democratic convention be female.

With over forty-five thousand members, the NWPC maintains lobbyists in the nation's capital to agitate for legislation beneficial to women. Current chair (her official title) is Iris F. Mitang, an attorney from Orinda, California. The NWPC holds an annual convention, sponsors regional meetings, and publishes a monthly *Newsletter*.

For more information, see June Sochen, *Herstory, A Woman's View of American History* (1974).

**NATIONAL YOUTH ALLIANCE (NYA).** Founded in 1969 at Washington, D.C., by Louis T. Byers, a supporter of Governor George C. Wallace of Alabama for president, for the purpose of attracting young people to the banner of the American Independent Party.* The NYA grew out of an organization called Youth for Wallace, which had been formed during the presidential election of 1968.

Reflecting a conservative and right-wing stance, the NYA supported the concept of law and order; opposed the use or sale of narcotics (including marijuana); condemned efforts to involve the United States in any further foreign wars; and announced its intention of combating black power. It attempted to organize local chapters on college campuses but had relatively little success.

Permanent headquarters was established in the nation's capital with Carey J. Winters serving as national secretary (its last one). The NYA organized "Right Power" rallies and issued two monthly publications, *Action* and *Attack!* At the outset, NYA membership totaled some three thousand, but as Governor Wallace's political fortunes waned, so did the organization. It continued to decline during the 1970s, and by the presidential election of 1976 the NYA was defunct.

For further information, see Dennis C. McMahon, "The National Youth Alliance," *American Mercury* 105 (Spring 1972): 61ff

**NATIONALIST PARTY OF PUERTO RICO.** See Fuerzas Armádas de Liberacion Nacíonal Puertorriqueña.

**NATIONALITIES DIVISION OF THE DEMOCRATIC NATIONAL COMMITTEE.** See All American Council.

**NATION-WIDE COMMITTEE ON IMPORT-EXPORT POLICY (NWC-IEP).** Founded in 1953 at Washington, D.C., by O. R. Strackbein and a group of businessmen representing agriculture, labor, and industry for the purpose of promoting tariff protectionism. The NWC-IEP was formed as an outgrowth of the Nation-Wide Committee of Industry, Agriculture, and Labor in Import-Export Policy. The former, founded by Strackbein in 1950, first evolved into the National Labor-Management Council on Foreign Trade Policy and then in 1968 became the NWC-IEP.

The NWC-IEP was organized specifically to promote protectionism at a time when the General Agreement on Tariffs and Trade (GATT) was up for renewal. It desired continuation of escape clauses, which had been inserted in the 1951 renewal, so that tariff duties might be raised on certain products when their importation imperiled the economic position of American producers. Whereas the extension of GATT for two more years continued the trend toward free trade, initiated first by the Reciprocal Tariff Agreement Act of 1934, the "peril point" concept was also extended. This authorized the president to modify tariff concessions when domestic industries were suffering economic duress.

When GATT was before Congress in 1955, the NWC-IEP lobbied for greater protection. The renewal authorized the president, at his discretion, to reduce tariffs no more than 5 percent per year in return for foreign concessions. In 1958 the NWC-IEP was instrumental in getting GATT amended so that quota restrictions could be imposed by the president when certain domestic industries were being hurt by imports. In this manner, quotas were established on the importation of oils, lead, and zinc. Japan was induced to impose voluntary quotas on exports to the United States that were underselling comparable American products.

Although the Trade Expansion Act of 1962 set as a goal the reduction of tariffs by 50 percent in five years, the NWC-IEP was instrumental in securing a provision that injured industries in the United States would be eligible for federal assistance. This government aid was available in the form of low-interest loans, tax adjustments, technical assistance, allowances for unemployment, and funding for the retraining or relocation of workers. During the 1970s the trend toward lowering of tariffs continued. The United States, as a large producer of agricultural and industrial goods, profited overall by this free trade policy by gaining a larger share of foreign markets. At times, reciprocity caused dislocations in the United States relative to certain producers. These producers through the NWC-IEP could not reverse the trend but did force Congress to take certain remedial action. Japan was again induced to restrict its exports of steel and textiles into the United States. Quotas were also made operative relative to the importation of dairy products (particularly cheese), meat (particularly New Zealand beef), and sugar (to protect the beet sugar industry).

The NWC-IEP has supported government efforts to stimulate U.S. exports. It endorsed the Agricultural Trade Development and Assistance Act of 1954, which promoted the sale of surplus farm commodities by barter, dollars, or foreign currency. It has encouraged East-West trade, extension of credits to foreign countries, deferred taxes for exporters, and devaluation of the dollar to make U.S. products more competitive abroad. The deficits in trade balance incurred by the United States seem to indicate that protectionism cannot be adopted completely, yet unemployment caused by distressed industries has given the NWC-IEP a basis for gaining limited success by import quotas.

National headquarters for the NWC-IEP is located in Washington, D.C. Membership includes some 150 affiliated groups representing certain sectors in agriculture, industry, and organized labor. Current president is O. R. Strackbein. The NWC-IEP disseminates information to the general public and monitors imports. It continues to lobby for tariff revision when a member affiliate believes that imports are a detriment to its economic prosperity.

For more information, see Raymond A. Bauer et al., *American Business and Public Policy: The Politics of Foreign Trade* (1967).

**NATIVE AMERICAN PARTY.** See Know-Nothing Party.

**NAVY LEAGUE OF THE UNITED STATES (NLUS).** Founded in 1902 at New York City by a group of advocates for a large navy for the purpose of promoting U.S. naval superiority. The motto of the NLUS claims, "Control of the seas is essential to the life of the nation." Benjamin F. Tracy, who served as secretary of the navy in the administration of President Benjamin Harrison, was chosen its first president. Ardent supporters of the NLUS included Senator Henry Cabot Lodge (R-Mass.); President Theodore Roosevelt, who later contributed part of his Nobel Peace Prize money for its activities; and Captain Alfred Thayer Mahan, who wrote such influential books as *The Influence of Sea Power upon History, 1660-1783* (1890) and *The Interest of America in Sea Power* (1897).

Spokespeople for the NLUS argued that since the power of the U.S. Navy gave it victory in the Spanish-American War in 1898, the United States should sustain or even expand its sea power. It lauded President Theodore Roosevelt for sending the "Great White Fleet" on a world cruise in 1907 and for his advocacy of naval superiority. Prior to World War I, the NLUS warned of Germany's rising naval power and agitated for greater expansion of the U.S. Navy. Following World War I, it pointed to the fact that the British Navy, not the U.S. Navy, had played a central role in the Allied victory over the Central Powers. During the 1920s the NLUS opposed naval reduction on the part of the United States. It maintained that the United States should increase the size of its navy and keep it modern. It also argued for enlarging the U.S. Merchant Marine, keeping the Coast Guard strong, and keeping the U.S. Marines at top strength.

During the 1930s the influence of the NLUS was at its lowest. The isolationism of the 1930s, coupled with the Great Depression and the need to cut miliary expenditures, was too strong for the NLUS to overcome. It warned that American national survival might be imperiled unless the nation initiated a naval-building program, particularly because of Japan's new navy. President Franklin D. Roosevelt, who had been the assistant secretary of the navy during World War I, agreed with the NLUS. Following World War II, the NLUS agitated for keeping the naval superiority gained during the war. It believed that the cold war could be won by sea power.

In more recent times the NLUS has concentrated its efforts on warning Americans of the dangers of an increasing Soviet sea power. Through "seapower seminars" and the dissemination of information, it has sought to enlighten the public on the fact that the Soviet Union has a large surface fleet, many nuclear-powered submarines, considerable expertise in oceanography, a big merchant marine, and a vast fishing fleet.

Since 1922 the NLUS has sponsored Navy Day. Until 1972 it was held on Theodore Roosevelt's birthday (October 27). Now it is observed on October 13, the day that the Continental Congress authorized the building of the first navy. Through its Active Duty Assistance Program Team, the NLUS, as a civilian organization, provides legal service to seamen and assists them in gaining benefits from the Soldiers and Sailors Civil Relief Act. The NLUS also conducts Operation Highline to aid ex-sailors in adjusting to civilian life.

National headquarters of the NLUS is located in Washington, D.C. Membership totals nearly fifty thousand, representing some 350 local councils in all parts of the United States. Current president is Ernest A. Carrere, Jr., with Vincent C. Thomas serving as executive director. The NLUS maintains a library and publishes *Now Hear This* (monthly), *Sea Power* (monthly), and *National Directory* (annual).

**NAZI PARTY.** See National Socialist White People's Party.

**NEW AMERICAN PARTY.** See People's Party (1971).

**NEW PARTY.** See People's Party (1971).

**NIAGARA MOVEMENT (NM).** Founded in 1905 at Niagara Falls, Ontario (Canada), by Dr. W. E. B. Du Bois of Atlanta University and twenty-eight other black intellectuals for the purpose of promoting civil rights for blacks in America. In a "Declaration of Principles," the NM set forth the following objectives: "We want full manhood suffrage and we want it now. . . . We want discrimination in public accommodations to cease. . . . We want the Constitution of the country enforced. . . . We want our children educated. . . . We are men. We will be treated as men. And we shall win!"

The NM represented the educated element of the black community of its day and resented the apparent capitulation of Booker T. Washington to the Jim Crow system of the South. The NM militantly denounced white supremacy, disenfranchisement, discrimination, institutional racism, segregation, and the failure of the federal government to enforce the Fourteenth and Fifteenth amendments to the U.S. Constitution. Members of the NM, who were a tiny majority of the blacks in America, denounced Booker T. Washington, the founder of Tuskegee Institute and the chief spokesman for blacks in that era, for his strategy of accommodation as set forth in his Atlanta Compromise enunciated in 1895 at the Atlanta Exposition.

Most whites regarded Du Bois and the NM as radical militants seeking to promote racial disturbances. The demands of the NM were regarded as dangerous in the South and generally ignored by the North. Because of the elitism of Du Bois, with his doctrine of the "talented tenth," the Negro masses failed to rally to the banners of the NM. Some local chapters were formed in various parts of the United States, but NM's influence on either whites or blacks was minimal. The NM did advance the cause of civil rights, however, by keeping alive the hopes of educated blacks, a legacy that did much to inspire black civil rights leaders of the 1950s and 1960s. In 1909 the NM merged with the National Association for the Advancement of Colored People* (NAACP). Du Bois then became editor of the NAACP's journal, *Crisis*.

For more information, see Francis L. Broderick and August Meier, *Negro Protest Thought in the Twentieth Century* (1965), and Julius Lester, ed., *The Seventh Son: The Thought and Writings of W.E.B. Du Bois*, 2 vols. (1971).

**NO PARTY.** See People's Party (1971).

**NON-PARTISAN COMMITTEE FOR PEACE THROUGH REVISION OF THE NEUTRALITY ACT (NPCP-TRNA).** Founded in 1938 at Washington, D.C., by Clark Eichelberger, who at the time was director of the American Union for Concerted Peace Efforts, for the purpose of promoting revisions in the Neutrality Act of 1937. William Allen White, editor of the *Emporia* (Kansas) *Gazette* and later head of the Committee to Defend America by Aiding the Allies,* served as chairman. Although relatively small in numbers, the NPCP-TRNA proved useful to President Franklin D. Roosevelt in seeking to overcome the isolationist orientation of U.S. foreign policy.

The original Neutrality Act of 1935 represented the isolationist viewpoint. Enacted by Congress following Italy's invasion of Ethiopia, it required the president, once acknowledging that a war existed, to prohibit the sale or shipment of all arms, munitions, and other war material to either belligerent. President Roosevelt signed the measure, although he disapproved of it. It, in effect, hurt the victim of aggression, Ethiopia, while having little or no impact on Mussolini's war effort. In 1937 after the Spanish Civil War started, the Neutrality Act was revised. F.D.R. sought more flexibility, but the provisions were still too rigid. It continued the embargo on munitions but did authorize the sale of nonmilitary commodities on the basis that they be paid for in cash and be carried by foreign ships. It also gave the government power to license and control the export of all munitions and specifically prohibited the arming of American merchant vessels.

The ineffectiveness of this revised version of the Neutrality Act was demonstrated when Japan launched an attack on China in 1937. Again the victim, China, could not be aided, while Japan was not affected by any embargo. Also that year the Japanese attacked and sank an American gunboat, the *Panay*, while it was on patrol in China. Following the Munich Conference in 1938, the Sudetenland was detached from Czechoslovakia and given to Germany. At this point the NPCP-TRNA was formed. It was obvious to interventionists that greater assistance had to be given to the victims of aggression or Germany, Italy, and Japan would continue their conquests unhindered.

The fight for revision in Congress was a fierce contest. Isolationists did not want to make the law more flexible, reasoning that any intervention by the United States would eventually embroil it in a war. Those seeking more realistic provisions contended that without rendering aid to victims of aggression, the nation would soon be isolated, with no friends or allies. During the debate in Congress over revision, Italy invaded Albania and Germany invaded Poland. Proponents of revision, such as the NPCP-TRNA, now got the upper hand. On November 2, 1939, a new Neutrality Act was passed. It permitted the president to issue a proclamation of neutrality without implementing an embargo on military equipment and munitions. It also contained a cash-and-carry provision, which allowed friendly belligerents to buy munitions provided that they paid cash in the United States and carried the cargo in their own vessels. Not satisfied with the revisions, although they permitted some U.S. aid to victims of aggression, the NPCP-TRNA lobbied for still more flexibility. It was instrumental in obtaining congressional approval of the Pittman Resolution, which permitted sale of munitions to Latin American nations.

After Germany defeated France in 1940 and began its air assault on Great Britain (Battle of Britain), the Committee to Defend America by Aiding the Allies (William Allen White Committee) was formed. At this time the NPCP-TRNA dissolved, with most of its members becoming active in the new committee. Their goal now was total repeal of the Neutrality Act and all-out assistance to Britain. The work of the NPCP-TRNA helped influence public opinion toward accepting the realities of foreign policy, but the isolationist sentiment was so strong that the revisions of the Neutrality Act often came too late to help the victims of aggression either in Europe or Asia.

After the 1940 election, President Roosevelt procured the enactment of the Lend Lease Act, which, though not repealing the Neutrality Act, simply replaced it with a massive aid program to Britain and the Soviet Union so they would not succumb to Germany. Britain's prime minister, Winston Churchill, called this the "most unsordid act in history."

For more information, see John E. Wiltz, *From Isolation to War, 1931-1941* (1968).

**NONPARTISAN LEAGUE (NL).** Founded in 1915 at Bismarck, North Dakota, by Arthur C. Townley (its first chairperson), A. F. Bowen, and Fred B. Wood for the purpose of organizing the farm vote as a bloc in a state that had been dominated by the Republican Party.* Their aim was to capture primaries and elect government officials sympathetic to the economic demands of farmers. Socialist in orientation, the NL's platform called for state ownership of grain elevators, processing mills, storage facilities, and meat-packing companies; hail insurance; easy rural credit through state-operated banks; and tax exemptions for farm improvements.

The NL won a major victory in 1916 when it elected Lynn J. Frazier as governor of North Dakota (receiving 79 percent of the total vote). NL candidates also won 81 of the 113 house seats in the legislature and 19 of 49 in the Senate. This period constituted the high tide of the NL when membership totaled over 188,000. Most of the members resided in Minnesota (where it helped give birth to that state's Farmer-Labor Party*), Montana, North Dakota, and South Dakota. Scattered membership existed in nine other states, primarily Idaho and Washington.

Growth of the NL was hampered during World War I because many of its leaders were against U.S. participation in the overseas conflict. This seemingly pro-German stance, although it was not an official party position, did hurt its reputation. The NL's advocacy of socialistic measures was not popular during the "normalcy" of the 1920s. It made somewhat of a comeback during the Great Depression of the 1930s because of its strong advocacy of federal assistance to farmers. Agrarian radicalism was evident when NL Governor William Langer used North Dakota's National Guard to prevent farms from being sold at auction when owners defaulted on mortgages.

In the U.S. Congress Senator Lynn Frazier and Congressman William Lemke sponsored the Farm Bankruptcy Act in 1934, permitting a moratorium on mortgage foreclosures. Lemke went on to become the presidential nominee of the Union Party* in 1936. During the 1930s many NL leaders again were identified with isolationism and noninterventionist positions relative to World War II.

In 1956 the remnant of the NL still active in North Dakota voted to affiliate with the Democratic Party.* It was instrumental in electing Quentin N. Burdick to the U.S. Senate in 1960, but its endorsement no longer wields the power of former days.

For further information, see Theodore Saloutos, "Rise of the Non-Partisan League in North Dakota," *Agricultural History* 20 (1946): 43–52; Andrew Bruce, *Non-Partisan League* (1921); Robert L. Morlan, *Political Prairie Fire: Nonpartisan League, 1915-1922* (1955); and Charles E. Russell, *The Story of the Nonpartisan League: A Chapter in American Evolution* (1974).

**NONVIOLENT ACTION AGAINST NUCLEAR WEAPONS.** See Committee for Nonviolent Action.

**NORTHERN IRISH AID COMMITTEE (NIAC).** Founded in 1970 at New York City by Matt Higgins, a former member of the Irish Republican Army

(IRA), and a group of Irish-Americans for the purpose of promoting U.S. assistance in achieving the unification of Ireland. Other prime movers in NIAC's formation were Joe Cahill, an active Irish participant in the IRA, and John Morrison, a Chicago carpenter. Local chapters were organized in Baltimore, Chicago, Los Angeles, Philadelphia, and San Francisco.

The NIAC's objective is to assist the IRA in driving the British out of Ulster so as to bring all of Ireland under one government. It seeks donations from Irish-Americans to finance the war against England. Funds were ostensibly to be used for nonmilitary equipment or medical purposes, but the British government has charged that some $2 million raised by the NIAC have been used to purchase arms and ammunition. Since this would be an illegal activity in the United States, the NIAC operates covertly and does not specify what its collected funds are to be used for. Even its membership rolls are kept secret.

The NIAC has been highly successful in raising money from the Irish community in large U.S. cities. It has even gotten prominent political leaders to defend the IRA and its activities. Two such individuals making pro-IRA statements were Senator Edward Kennedy (D-Mass.) and Mayor Richard Daley of Chicago. A significant aspect of NIAC's activity may be that it helps to prevent a peaceful settlement of the England-Ireland controversy. With financial aid from Irish-Americans, the IRA has continued its terrorist activities and refuses to seek a negotiated peace.

For more information, see Dennis J. Clark, *Irish Blood: Northern Ireland and the American Conscience* (1977).

# O

**OLD AGE REVOLVING PENSIONS, LTD.** See Townsend Plan National Lobby.

**ORDER OF THE STAR-SPANGLED BANNER.** See Know-Nothing Party.

**ORDER OF UNITED AMERICANS.** See Know-Nothing Party.

**ORGANIZATION OF AFRO-AMERICAN UNITY (OAAU).** Founded in 1962 at New York City by Malcolm X, whose original name was Malcolm Little and who was also known as el-Hajj Malik El-Shabazz, for the purpose of promoting black nationalism. Malcolm X became a Black Muslim while in prison and in 1952, when he was released, became a minister of the Nation of Islam (NOI). He was suspended from the NOI in 1964 for speaking in derogatory terms about the assassination of President John F. Kennedy. Malcolm X then founded his own organization, Muslim Mosque, Inc. Because of his charismatic personality, he began to attract a considerable following of his own. His teachings stressed black nationalism and separation from whites and reflected a hatred of white culture and society.

In 1964 Malcolm X made a pilgrimage to Mecca and as a result became converted to the Sunni Muslim faith of orthodox Islam. On his return to the United States that same year, he founded the OAAU. Malcolm X now promulgated a black nationalism that emphasized pride in race rather than separatism or hatred of whites. He stressed the doctrine of brotherhood and taught that blacks and whites could live together amicably. He also was influenced by the socialism of the Third World and promoted pan-

Africanism. Malcolm X attracted a large following among the black masses and was influential as a civil rights leader. In 1965 he was assassinated by a black gunman, presumed to be a Black Muslim wanting to terminate his role as a rival to Elijah Muhammad, the head of the NOI. With Malcolm X gone, the OAAU soon became moribund.

For more information, see J. H. Clark, ed., *Malcolm X* (1969), and Peter Goldman, *Malcolm X* (1972).

**OTHER AMERICANS, INC.** See Society of Separationists.

# _P_

**PACIFICA FOUNDATION.** See War Resisters League.


**PARALYZED VETERANS OF AMERICA (PVA).** Founded in 1945 at Washington, D.C., by a group of World War II veterans who were paralyzed because of spinal injuries incurred while in the U.S. armed forces for the purpose of promoting government benefits for those so injured. Current membership also includes veterans who are paraplegics from wounds caused or diseases caught while serving in one of the branches of the armed services during the Korean and Vietnam wars.

The PVA has been instrumental in securing special federal benefits for paraplegic veterans and their families. It continues to lobby for greater assistance and monitors the activities and policies of the Veterans Administration and other government agencies dealing with crippled veterans. It disseminates information to the general public and seeks to enlighten government bodies on the need for constructing buildings for easy access for people in wheelchairs. It sponsors programs involving wheelchair sports and activities for the handicapped. It also attempts to enlist not only the help of the general public but to generate sympathy and understanding of the plight of those confined to wheelchairs. The PVA assists in raising funds for medical research; promotes vocational training; sponsors special driver training courses for the handicapped; and assists members in finding suitable employment. In 1947 it founded the National Paraplegic Foundation. Other projects include agitating for job preference for all veterans, pensions when necessary, and housing geared for paraplegics.

National headquarters of PVA is located in Washington, D.C. Membership totals some eight thousand in thirty local chapters located all over the United States. Current executive director is James A. Maye. The PVA publishes a monthly, *Paraplegia News*.

**PATRIOTIC PARTY (PP).** Founded in 1966 at Norborne, Missouri, by Robert Bolivar DePugh for the purpose of promoting patriotism and protection of the United States from both its internal and external enemies. The PP was formed as an outgrowth of a paramilitary organization, the Minutemen, started by DePugh in 1960 as a body of "crack shock troops" to protect the United States from either invasion or infiltration by Communists. As a militant right-wing organization, the PP proclaimed its intention of engaging in what it called "counterassassination" and "counterterror."

The platform (or program) of the Radical Right PP was in part a reaction to the civil rights and anti-war protest activity of the New Left, as well as the fear that these radical left wingers were part of the Communist conspiracy to gain control over the U.S. government. With a secret membership list, estimated at one time to be from four hundred to one thousand, DePugh as national coordinator organized the PP into state units, which in turn were subdivided into local teams. The PP publication, *On Target*, advised members to purchase arms and weapons of all types for the day when it would be necessary to conduct a counterrevolution.

Secretly the underground forces of the PP held maneuvers and field exercises, even though they were illegal. Similar groups came into existence, some affiliated with the PP and others as independent organizations. These included the Loyal Order of Mountain Men; Minute Women; Minutemen for Christ; Sons of Liberty; Brothers of the Iron Cross; Paul Revere Associated Yeoman; U.S. Rangers; Counter-Insurgency Council; and Soldiers of the Cross. Although these groups were relatively small in numbers, they constituted a menace due to their proclivity for using violence as a political weapon.

The PP claimed that a "pro-American government could no longer be established by normal political means." Thus a PP directive indicated that the "objectives of the Minutemen are to abandon wasteful, useless efforts and begin immediately to prepare for the day when Americans will once again fight in the streets for their lives and their liberty." It claimed that certain powerful minorities and corrupt political machines had gained control of the United States and that the fight against communism was being lost by "bunglers or traitors within our own government." Some of these charges resembled those enunciated by the John Birch Society.* PP manuals published for training Minutemen included *Realistic Combat Training*, *Assault Battle Drill*, *Combat Intelligence*, and *On War and Guerrillas*.

In 1967 DePugh and several associates were arrested, tried, and convicted for violations of the Federal Firearms Act. Before serving his four-year jail sentence DePugh resigned his position as PP's leader and appointed a secret executive committee to run the movement. With his absence and due to the decline of cold war tensions, the PP and similar paramilitary groups have tended to disband. Following U.S. withdrawal from Vietnam and the cessation of protest marches and civil rights demonstrations, almost all of these groups became moribund by 1970.

For more information, see "The Armed Superpatriots," *Nation,* November 11, 1961, pp. 12-13, and J. Harry Jones, Jr., *The Minutemen* (1968).

**PATRONS OF HUSBANDRY.** See National Grange.

**PEACE AND FREEDOM PARTY (PFP).** Founded in 1968 at Ann Arbor, Michigan, by a biracial coalition representing the Black Panther Party* (BPP) and white radicals for the purpose of promoting revolutionary changes in American society. The assembled delegates selected Eldrige Cleaver, minister of education for the BPP, as its presidential nominee. He won the nomination over comedian Dick Gregory, who was subsequently chosen as the presidential candidate of the Freedom and Peace Party.* Dr. Douglas F. Dowd, professor of economics at Cornell University, was chosen as the PFP's vice-presidential nominee.

The platform adopted by the PFP called for a social revolution; liberation of blacks; black nationalism; redistribution of the nation's wealth; an end to American imperialism in Vietnam; and the "right to defend ourselves against the Pig Cops." While campaigning, Cleaver denounced Congressman Adam Clayton Powell (D-N.Y.) for being an "Uncle Tom" and demanded that the United Nations recognize the Black Panthers as an independent organization representing an oppressed minority. He also asked for U.N. observers to be placed in cities with large black populations so that they might report on police brutality. On the ballot in nineteen states, the Cleaver-Dowd ticket drew 136,385 popular and no electoral votes.

In 1970 the PFP ran a slate of twelve candidates in California, including nominees for governor and various state offices (including seats in the legislature). All were defeated soundly. Following this poor showing, the remnants of the PFP affiliated with the new People's Party* in 1971. During its brief existence the PFP represented an episode where black militants and New Left whites sought to form a revolutionary coalition. Its rhetoric was too extremist and radical to attract a large following of either blacks or whites. It did give militants a chance to participate legitimately in the political process and in this sense served a useful purpose.

For more information, see J. Erroll Miller, "The Negro in National Politics in 1968," in P. W. Romeo, ed., *In Black America* (1969); Robert Scheer, ed., *Eldrige Cleaver: Post-Prison Writings and Speeches* (1969); and Hanes Walton, Jr., *The Negro in Third Party Politics* (1969).

**PENDERGAST MACHINE (PM).** Founded in 1892 at Kansas City, Missouri, by Jim Pendergast for the purpose of gaining political control of the municipal government. In that same year Pendergast won a seat as an alderman on the city council of Kansas City. In order to gain control of the Democratic Party* in Kansas City, he started the Jackson County Democratic Club so that he could acquire votes from the rural environs of Kansas City. During his reign as party boss, Pendergast had to share power with another Democratic chieftain, Joseph Shannon. Shannon eventually was elected to Congress and thus was removed from the scene.

Pendergast's political power grew to the extent that in 1900 his handpicked candidate for mayor, James A. Reed, was an easy victor. Mayor Reed, in turn, appointed Thomas "Tom" Joseph Pendergast, Jim's younger brother, to the post of superintendent of streets. In 1910 Tom Pendergast was elected to the city council, where he would remain for six years, and in 1910 Tom became the boss of the machine when his brother Jim died. By 1916 Tom was in total control of the Democratic Party in Kansas City and Jackson County.

In 1920, when prohibition went into effect, Tom Pendergast closed his saloons and got out of the wholesale liquor business and started the Eureka Petroleum Company and the Ready-Mixed Concrete Company. Both firms received many city and county contracts and soon made him a millionaire. In 1925 Pendergast forced the city council to appoint his crony, Henry F. McElroy, as city manager. From then until 1939 corruption became commonplace. In that year Pendergast was tried for income tax evasion and sentenced to fifteen months in Leavenworth prison. McElroy was about to be indicted by a federal grand jury when he died of a heart attack. Investigations indicated that $10 million had been extracted from city employees in kickbacks, an $11 million water bond fund had been diverted for other uses, and some three thousand ward heelers were on the city payroll without performing any work for the city.

In 1922 a Pendergast candidate for county judge, Harry S. Truman, was elected to his first term. A county judge levied taxes and supervised the construction of roads. Truman lost his bid for reelection, but won again in 1926 and held that office until 1932. In 1929 when Mike Pendergast (Tom's brother) died, County Judge Truman became a powerful figure in rural Jackson County. By 1932 Pendergast's machine not only controlled Kansas City and Jackson County but most state offices, and it dictated who would be elected to Congress.

In 1932 Tom Pendergast was able to dominate the selection of Missouri's delegation to the Democratic National Convention. Pendergast backed Senator James A. Reed (D-Mo.), whom his machine had elected to office, for the presidential nomination. When it became apparent that Governor Franklin D. Roosevelt of New York would get the Democratic presidential nomination on the fourth ballot, Pendergast jumped on the bandwagon and shifted Missouri's votes to FDR. The New Deal era was to be the height of

Pendergast's power. He had his own newspaper, the *Missouri Democrat* (which he started in 1925), and utilized federal patronage to enhance his political control over Missouri. Pendergast made use of the Civil Works Administration and the Works Progress Administration to provide jobs for ward heelers and precinct captains. Workers who got jobs on federally funded public works were reminded to vote for Pendergast-endorsed candidates. In 1934 Pendergast chose Harry S. Truman to be the Democratic candidate for the U.S. Senate. Truman defeated Republican* Senator Roscoe Conkling Patterson by some 262,000 votes. This was the pinnacle of power for the Pendergast machine.

Complaints began to be heard about the Pendergast regime in Kansas City when big-time criminals began to operate freely. Not only did a red-light district operate, so did big-time gambling and bootlegging. When prohibition was repealed, Tom Pendergast immediately reestablished the Pendergast Wholesale Liquor Company to make up for the huge amounts he lost at gambling, his real weakness (throughout his life he no doubt lost millions on horse races).

The rise of organized vice eventually prompted reform groups to oppose Pendergast. Tom's own demise came in 1939 when he was convicted of income tax evasion. When he was in prison the Pendergast machine was run by Tom, Jr., his son, but the machine was doomed. Its last victory, and it only contributed a small part at that, was to reelect Harry S. Truman to the Senate in 1940. That same election witnessed the loss of Pendergast's control of Kansas City. Tom's nephew, Jim, had taken over from his son, but a nonpartisan Citizens Reform Organization won an overwhelming victory in the city election. When Tom Pendergast got out of prison, he could not regain control of the Democratic Party in Kansas City or Jackson County. When he died in 1945, the Pendergast machine was also dead. Although Harry S. Truman owed his rise in politics to the Pendergast machine, there is no evidence that he personally was involved in wrongdoing or corruption. Later investigations proved that Tom Pendergast utilized vote fraud, intimidation, and contact with organized crime to maintain political control over Kansas City. Controlling Kansas City and its environs also permitted him to be highly influential in state and national politics. The demise of the Pendergast machine was a positive victory for good government and the democratic process.

For more information, see Alfred Steinberg, *The Bosses* (1972), and Lyle W. Dorsett, *Franklin D. Roosevelt and the City Bosses* (1977).

**PEOPLE UNITED TO SAVE HUMANITY (PUSH).** Founded in 1971 at Chicago, Illinois, by the Reverend Jesse Jackson for the purpose of promoting civil rights and the betterment of the black community. The formation of PUSH was an outgrowth of Operation Breadbasket, a project that Jackson had started while active in the Southern Christian Leadership Conference.* PUSH seeks to better the lives of blacks who live in urban areas by promoting slum clearance, equal job opportunities, adequate nutrition, medical care, good education, and solutions to other ghetto-related problems.

The Reverend Jackson has thousands of followers and has gained national stature as a civil rights leader. He not only conducts fund-raising activities for PUSH but serves as a spokesperson for the black community on national and international issues. Jackson counsels blacks to be active politically and to better their own lives by taking advantage of available opportunities. He particularly stresses the value of education as a means for young blacks to rise in their social and economic status. While he seeks federal and states' assistance for blacks, Jackson has continually emphasized the need for self-help.

In 1972 Jackson joined with Chicago Alderman William Singer to challenge the political power of Mayor Richard M. Daley within the Democratic Central Committee of Cook County.* The Jackson-Singer coalition sent a rival delegation to the Democratic National Convention to contest the seats of those handpicked by Mayor Daley. The credentials committee unseated fifty-nine delegates selected by the Daley machine (including Mayor Daley himself) and replaced them with members of the rival delegation headed by Jackson and Singer who, as part of the 170-member Illinois delegation, supported the presidential nomination of Senator George M. McGovern (D-S.D.). On election day the Daley machine gave only lukewarm support to McGovern, as the Democratic presidential candidate, who lost Illinois to Republican Richard M. Nixon by a margin of over 874,000 votes. By 1976 Mayor Daley had regained control of the Democratic Party* in Chicago and Cook County and personally headed the delegation to the Democratic National Convention.

Although Jackson lost his political power within the Daley machine, he still wielded great influence among black voters. His political endorsement was sought by candidates who wanted to attract a large segment of the black vote. Jackson's independence and articulate advocacy of equality for blacks has made him an important national political figure.

For more information, see Barbara Reynolds, *Jesse Jackson: The Man, the Movement, the Myth* (1975).

**PEOPLE'S PARTY (PP) [1823].** Founded in 1823 at Albany, New York, by political opponents of the Bucktail Republicans (a faction of the Democratic-Republican Party* supporting Andrew Jackson for president) for the purpose of securing electoral reform and electing John Quincy Adams as president. Prime movers in the formation of the PP were two members of the New York state legislature, Henry Wheaton of New York City and Isaac Ogden of Walton (both Clintonians). Membership was also drawn from the ranks of anti-Clintonians, anti-Bucktails, and the virtually defunct Federalist Party.* Prominent political personages joining the PP included David B. Ogden, Jonas Platt, Peter A. Jay, Jacob R. Van Rensselaer, and Abraham Van Vechten.

At the PP state convention at Utica in 1824, former Governor DeWitt Clinton was nominated as the party's gubernatorial candidate, with General James Tallmadge as the nominee for lieutenant governor. The PP platform supported popular election of presidential electors and urged the election of John Quincy Adams as president. The "People's Ticket" (sometimes referred to as the "People's Men") defeated their Empire State rivals to win control of Albany and in so doing helped carry New York for John Quincy Adams. The PP dissolved by 1826 when the popularity of Andrew Jackson began to obliterate political divisions among rival factions of what would become the Democratic Party.*

For further information, see Dixon Ryan Fox, *The Decline of Aristocracy in the Politics of New York* (1919 [1965]).

**PEOPLE'S PARTY (1891).** See Populist Party.

**PEOPLE'S PARTY (PP) [1971].** Founded in 1971 at Dallas, Texas, by a group of radical and anti-war activists for the purpose of selecting a slate of candidates opposed to the war in Vietnam. Some two hundred delegates were in attendance, representing such organizations as the National Conference for a New Politics (NCNP), Peace and Freedom Party* (PFP), and the New Party (which had already merged with the PFP). Selected on a provisional basis for the presidential nomination was Dr. Benjamin M. Spock, the noted pediatrician, with Julius Hobson, a black educator, being chosen as his vice-presidential running mate. This ticket was reaffirmed in 1972 by 250 delegates meeting at a St. Louis nominating convention.

Dr. Spock, a former chairperson of both the NCNP and the National Committee for a Sane Nuclear Policy,* was a militant anti-war protester who had been convicted of conspiring to aid draft dodgers (the conviction was subsequently overturned by an appeals court). Spock campaigned primarily on the peace issue, calling for an immediate end to U.S. involvement in Vietnam. He also espoused a "democratic and decentralized socialism." The PP platform demanded withdrawal from Vietnam; cutting the military budget by half; reduction of the federal bureaucracy; enactment of a steeply progressive income tax with a $50,000 limit on personal income; abolition of both the property and sales tax; a federally guaranteed minimum income of $6,500 for every American family; affirmative action to place workers on the boards of directors of major industries and businesses; legalization of abortion and marijuana; establishment of health-care agencies; and neighborhood control of police and schools.

The Spock-Hobson ticket was on the ballot in ten states for the presidential election of 1972. It polled 78,801 popular and no electoral votes. Supporters of Senator George S. McGovern (D-S.D.), the presidential nominee of the Democratic Party,* claimed that the PP candidates siphoned away votes that made it possible for President Richard M. Nixon to be reelected more easily.

Following the election, the PP sought to make itself into a permanent party. National headquarters was established in Washington, D.C. It evolved into a coalition of autonomous state parties. Typical of these affiliates are the following: Commongood Party (N.Y.), Country People's Caucus (N.J.), Country People's Party (Mo.), Human Rights Party (Mich.), New American Party (Pa.), New Party (Ariz.), No Party (Mass.), Peace and Freedom Party (Calif.), and the Liberal Union (Vt.).

At its 1974 national convention in Indianapolis, Indiana, the PP adopted the following resolution: "We demand the nationalization by the people of the means of production, distribution, and communication." The platform included planks condemning imperialism, colonialism, sexism, racism, and discrimination on the basis of age. Supported were student rights; statehood for the District of Columbia; free medical care for everyone; independent sovereignty for Indian nations; election of judges; a prisoner's bill of rights; amnesty for Vietnam draft dodgers and deserters; the right of Chicanos to move freely across the U.S. border; decriminalization of drug usage; withdrawal of all U.S. troops from overseas military bases; community control over educational policy and schools; busing to achieve racial balance; abolition of compulsory education; free education at all levels for those desiring it; land reform; planned use of land on a national scale; restructuring of the economy for attainment of a balanced ecosystem; the right of workers to control their labor unions democratically; establishment of a new department at cabinet rank, to be called the Department of Culture and Arts; and a constitutional amendment to abolish the electoral college.

With Chuck Avery serving as national executive, the PP provided speakers through an educational and fund-raising service called Spokespeople. It issued the following publications: *Grass Roots, Our Newsletter*, and *Party Line*. The PP did not nominate a national ticket in the presidential election of 1976. Currently membership in the various local affiliates has eroded to the point where most are moribund or even defunct.

The PP, which was never connected in any way with the old Populist Party* (also called the People's Party), had very little impact on the American electorate. PP's formation came out of the anti-war protest movement and its subsequent domestic program was far too radical to win wide popular support. In many ways it was a phenomenon of an era of protest when activists sought political vehicles to vent their personal feelings and frustrations.

For more information, see Andrew H. Malcolm, "Spock Nominated by People's Party," *New York Times*, July 30, 1972, p. 27.

**PEOPLE'S PEACE PROSPERITY PARTY (PPPP).** Founded in 1970 at Modesto, California, by the Reverend Kirby James Hensley for the purpose of providing voters with an alternative to the two-party system. According to its platform (founding principles) the PPPP's main purpose was to "organize independent thinking people into a strong third political party devoted solely to the task of returning government control to the people and reestablishing a true democratic form of government in the United States of America." Claiming to be the true "voice of the people," the PPPP regarded itself as the most appropriate vehicle for democratizing the U.S. government and making it respond to the will of the people.

The Reverend Hensley was the bishop and founder of the Universal Life Church, Inc., and had been the presidential nominee in 1964 and 1968 of the Universal Party.* In 1970 he ran for the governorship of California but attracted only a token vote. Running as presidential nominee of the PPPP in 1972, Hensley received a minuscule write-in vote. The lack of popular support for the PPPP brought about the quick demise of this short-lived political party. Its significance lies in the fact that it represented the political aspirations of a tiny minority group without a broad base.

**POLISH NATIONAL ALLIANCE (PNA).** Founded in 1880 at Chicago, Illinois, by a group of Polish-Americans for the purpose of promoting social and cultural unity among Poles who had emigrated from Poland to the United States. Membership was open not only to Polish immigrants but Lithuanians, Ruthenians, and those of Slovak descent. Members of the PNA found that by organizing, they could wield political power and aid each other in adapting to the new way of life in America.

The formation of the PNA coincided with the high tide of immigration from Southern and Eastern Europe. Since Poles and affiliated ethnic groups spoke an entirely different foreign language, were generally Roman Catholic in religion, and had customs and traditions entirely different from native-born Americans, the PNA served as an organization to help immigrants both to adjust to a new way of life and to preserve their Old World culture. Newly arrived immigrants and those who lived in the United States for a time could speak their native tongue, read foreign-language newspapers, socialize with fellow countrymen, and participate in folk festivals. They also were introduced to potential employers and met political leaders.

When World War I started in Europe in 1914, members of the PNA were divided in their attitude toward the Central Powers and the Allies. Polish nationals were fighting with Germany against Russia in an attempt to liberate lands controlled by the czar. In 1916 Germany and Austria proclaimed independence for Poland, but Prussian troops continued to occupy it. After U.S. entry into World War I and eventual victory for the Allies, Poland regained its independence. The PNA applauded President

Woodrow Wilson's advocacy of self-determination and supported ratification of the Treaty of Versailles, which forced Germany to return Prussian Poland to Poland and gave the latter access to the Baltic Sea by the Polish corridor.

In 1939 when Germany invaded Poland, the PNA agitated for U.S. intervention into World War II. After the United States became a belligerent, PNA officials sought assurances from President Franklin D. Roosevelt that after their homeland was liberated, Polish independence would be restored. This would mean the Soviet Union would withdraw from portions it had occupied in agreement with Nazi Germany in 1939. The PNA supported the Polish government in exile and presumed that the Yalta Agreement of 1945 would restore Poland as a truly independent nation. When the Soviet Union installed a Communist regime (the so-called Lublin government), the PNA became strongly anti-Communist in its political orientation and continually called for liberation of Poland. The PNA endorsed such varied political figures as Senator Paul H. Douglas (D-Ill.) and Secretary of State John Foster Dulles, who served in the cabinet of President Dwight D. Eisenhower, for their stands in opposition to recognition of the Soviet satellite system that held Eastern Europe behind the Iron Curtain. In 1976 many members of the PNA opposed the reelection of President Gerald R. Ford for his agreeing to the Helsinki Agreement, which accepted as fact that Eastern Europe (including Poland) was permanently in the Soviet sphere of influence. Members of the PNA tended to support President Jimmy Carter for his human-rights stand, believing it meant that one day the people of Poland will have the same democratic rights as Americans enjoy.

The PNA agitates for inclusion in school textbooks of information about Polish-American patriots, criticizes the media for propagating derogatory jokes about Poles, and promotes cultural exchange programs between the United States and Poland. The PNA viewed with pride the coronation of Pope John Paul II because of his Polish origin. The PNA sponsors educational programs, festivals, and charity drives and provides life insurance for members.

National headquarters of PNA is located in Chicago. Current president is Aloysius A. Mazewski. Membership totals over three hundred thousand in some fourteen hundred local chapters. The PNA maintains a library and supports Alliance College in Cambridge Springs, Pennsylvania. The PNA publishes the *Polish Daily Zgoda*, a semimonthly, *Zgoda*, and a quarterly, *Promien Youth Magazine*.

**POLITICAL ACTION COMMITTEE (PAC).** Founded in 1943 at Washington, D.C., by the executive board of the Congress of Industrial Organizations (CIO) for the purpose of electing pro-labor candidates in the presidential election of 1944. The PAC was formed as a result of the recommendations made by a group of CIO officials appointed by Philip Murray, national president, to consider ways of replacing labor's Nonpartisan League (which had been incorporated by ex-CIO President John L. Lewis into the United Mine Workers of America). Members of the committee were Nathan Cowan, chief congressional lobbyist; John Brophy, director of state councils; and J. Raymond Walsh, head of the research department.

At the time the PAC was formed, Sidney Hillman, president of the Amalgamated Clothing Workers of America (ACWA), was designated its first director. He held that post until his death in 1946, when his assistant Jack Kroll, also of the ACWA, was appointed director. Kroll held the position until the CIO's merger with the American Federation of Labor (AFL). In 1955 the PAC was incorporated into the newly formed Commit.  .e on Political Education* (COPE).

The primary objectives of the PAC in 1944 were to reelect President Franklin D. Roosevelt (to whom organized labor owed much), elect as many New Dealers to Congress as possible, and defeat anti-labor candidates (members of Congress who had voted to override FDR's veto of the Smith-Connally measure, the War Labor Disputes Act) whenever possible.

The PAC raised money from CIO members to finance a massive campaign in 1944. It contributed much to FDR's triumph at the polls by turning out a huge labor vote. The PAC publicized the president's "Four Freedoms," supported the formation of the United Nations, and championed Roosevelt's economic bill of rights (which included low-cost housing, medical care, old-age security, and full employment) as the foundation for postwar prosperity.

Added recognition for the PAC's power was gained when in 1944 it was instrumental in preventing war mobilizer James F. Byrnes of South Carolina from being considered seriously as the Democratic vice-presidential candidate; in helping to elect Hubert H. Humphrey mayor of Minneapolis; and in causing the defeat of Congressman Martin Dies, Jr., of Texas (the ultraconservative and controversial chairman of the House Un-American Activities Committee).

Severe reverses befell the PAC in 1945 and 1946. Even with four hundred thousand CIO members in the city of Detroit, it failed to ensure the election of Richard T. Frankensteen, vice-president of the United Automobile, Aerospace and Agricultural Implement Workers of America, as mayor. In preparation for the congressional elections of 1946 the PAC sponsored the Chicago Conference of Progressives, at which time it joined ranks with the National Citizens Political Action Committee* and the Independent Citizens Committee for the Arts, Sciences and Professions.* Since these two organizations were left wing in nature (both had been infiltrated by Communists), they further identified the PAC (its parent the CIO was also having problems with Communist-controlled unions) in the eyes of voters with radicalism and a pro-Russian outlook just when the cold war was intensifying. PAC-backed candidates lost heavily in the mid-term elections, which saw the Republican Party* gain control of both houses of Congress. Subsequently the GOP-controlled Eightieth Congress passed the Taft-Hartley Act over President Truman's veto. Labeled the "slave labor act" by labor leaders, it sought to regulate unions far more than did the lenient Wagner Act.

Philip Murray took firm action to sever the PAC's relationship with the radical Left. He also initiated a purge of Communists within the CIO. Murray aligned the PAC with the AFL's newly formed Labor's League for Political Education* and the liberal, non-Communist Americans for Democratic Action.* This reorganized PAC endorsed Harry S. Truman in 1948 and contributed heavily to his surprising upset victory over Republican Thomas E. Dewey.

In 1950 many PAC-backed candidates lost congressional races in the mid-term elections. Notably the PAC failed to unseat Senator Robert A. Taft (R-Ohio), one of the cosponsors of the Taft-Hartley Act. Another PAC-supported candidate, Congresswoman Helen Gahagan Douglas (D-Calif.), was also beaten by the GOP candidate for the U.S. Senate, Congressman Richard M. Nixon (R-Calif.).

The election of 1952 proved equally disastrous for the PAC. It endorsed and worked for Governor Adlai E. Stevenson II (D-Ill.), only to have him lose the presidency to General Dwight D. Eisenhower. The PAC failed to defeat three senators whom it considered anti-labor: John Bricker (R-Ohio), William Knowland (R-Calif.), and Joseph McCarthy (R-Wis.). It also could not prevent the election of Senator Barry Goldwater (R-Ariz.). The PAC did, however, contribute to the election of Congressman John F. Kennedy (D-Mass.) to the U.S. Senate.

In 1954 the PAC conducted its last and most successful campaign. It employed its own news commentator on radio, John W. Vandercook, and organzied "family conferences" to win the votes of housewives. It also used dollar drives (for a campaign fund), encouraged the registration of voters, and waged a massive get-out-the-vote campaign. Of 256 PAC-endorsed candidates for the House of Representatives, 126 were elected, and of the twenty-four people backed for the U.S. Senate, fifteen were victorious, among them Hubert H. Humphrey (D-Minn.), Paul H. Douglas (D-Ill.), Estes Kefauver (D-Tenn.), Richard Neuberger (D-Oregon), and Patrick McNamara (D-Mich.). McNamara was an AFL union official who defeated the Republican incumbent, Homer Ferguson.

The twelve-year existence of the PAC dramatically changed organized labor's traditional nonpartisan approach to politics, initiated by Samuel Gompers. Although the PAC became a virtual adjunct to the Democratic Party,* none of its members was ever given a seat on the Democratic National Committee.* It nevertheless helped to create a liberal-labor bloc within the Democratic Party, which in turn produced legislation of benefit to the rank-and-file membership of the CIO.

For further information, see Joseph Gaer, *The First Round, The Story of the CIO Political Action Committee* (1944), and James Caldwell Foster, *The Union Politic: The CIO Political Action Committee* (1975).

**POLITICAL RIGHTS DEFENSE FUND.** See Young Socialist Alliance.

**POOR MAN'S PARTY (PMP).** Founded in 1952 at Newark, New Jersey, by Henry Krajewski for the purpose of providing an alternative to the platform and candidates of the two major political parties. In 1952 Krajewski, a swine producer, designated himself as the presidential nominee of the PMP. Frank Jenkins, also of the Garden State, was named as his vice-presidential running mate. The PMP's platform contained the following planks: reduction of taxes; nonrecognition of the People's Republic of China; annexation of Canada; maintenance of a strong national defense; continuation of the Korean War until victory was achieved; resistance to communism everywhere in the world; and a mandatory year of work on a farm for every youth in the nation. On the ballot only in the state of New Jersey, the PMP ticket drew only 4,203 popular votes (0.2 percent).

In 1956 Krajewski ran for the U.S. Senate on the PMP ticket. By polling a little over 35,000 votes Krajewski may have contributed to the victory of the Republican Party* nominee, Clifford P. Case, over Democrat Charles Howell in an extremely close contest. Krajewski may well have attracted votes that might normally have gone to the Democratic candidate. Krajewski planned to run for the presidency in 1960, but his death that year caused the demise of the PMP. During its short-lived existence, the PMP served as an outlet for protest but attracted no following to sustain its life beyond that of its founder.

**POOR PEOPLE'S CAMPAIGN (PPC).** Founded in 1967 at Atlanta, Georgia, by the Reverend Dr. Martin Luther King, Jr., for the purpose of promoting civil rights and economic benefits for Negroes. Dr. King planned the PPC as a means to apply pressure on Congress and the White House. After Dr. King's assassination in spring 1968, his successor as head of the Southern Christian Leadership Conference* (SCLC), the Reverend David Abernathy, and the Reverend Walter E. Fauntroy, SCLC's Washington, D.C., bureau director, implemented a protest march on the nation's capital.

Thousands of poor blacks descended upon Washington, D.C., and from May 11 to June 23, 1968, camped out on the grounds between the White House and the capitol. A "Resurrection City" was constructed out of tents, boxes, and other makeshift quarters. President Lyndon B. Johnson pleaded with the demonstrators to leave peacefully, but many refused to do so. Some protesters, including Abernathy, were arrested, but finally the squatters agreed to leave. Congressional leaders promised them that consideration would be given to the increased funding of the Great Society's anti-poverty programs. Leaders of the PPC also demanded an end to the war in Vietnam, since its costs were depriving poor people of needed government assistance. Once the massive encampment disbanded, it cost the National Park Service $71,795 to dismantle Resurrection City and clean up the grounds. The overall effect of the PPC on public opinion cannot be fully assessed, but it did focus national attention upon the plight of the poor blacks. No doubt it contributed to President Johnson's decision to seek an end to the Vietnam war.

**POPULAR FRONT.** See Communist Party of the United States of America.

**POPULIST PARTY (PP).** Founded in 1891 at Cincinnati, Ohio, by leaders of the Farmers' Alliance to nominate and elect candidates sympathetic to the economic needs of rural America. Originally named the People's Party, it soon became known as the PP.

At a nominating convention held in Omaha, Nebraska, in 1892, the Populists selected General James B. Weaver as their presidential standard-bearer (he had been the presidential nominee of the Greenback Party* in 1880). Paired with Weaver was James G. Field of Virginia as his vice-presidential running mate. The PP's platform called for free and unlimited coinage of silver; graduated income tax; postal savings banks; government ownership of railroads, telegraph, and telephone; prohibition of alien ownership of land; placement of all federal employees under civil service; and implementation of the subtreasury plan, which would establish government-sponsored facilities where farmers could store agricultural commodities, on which they would receive federal loans, until they could be sold in the commercial market.

The PP's proposals seemed radical at the time because they involved considerable intervention on the part of the federal government. The PP was far too rural oriented and overly class conscious to have widespread appeal for urban voters. Despite these handicaps, the Weaver-Field ticket polled 1,041,028 popular and 22 electoral votes (four states). This constituted 8.63 percent of the total vote cast. (See table 7.)

Because the panic of 1893 increased the economic woes of farmers and workers, the various local PP candidates in the mid-term election of 1894 drew well. The PP elected six senators and seven congressmen to the U.S. Congress. The high tide of the so-called Populist revolt came in the presidential election of 1896, when it appeared the PP might have a chance to capture the White House.

**TABLE 7 Populist Party Presidential Candidates and Votes, 1892-1908**

| YEAR | CANDIDATE | TOTAL POPULAR VOTE |
|---|---|---|
| 1892 | James B. Weaver | 1,041,028 |
| 1896 | William Jennings Bryan | 6,502,925 |
| 1900 | Wharton Barker | 50,605 |
| 1904 | Thomas E. Watson | 117,183 |
| 1908 | Thomas E. Watson | 29,147 |

At their 1896 national convention in St. Louis, Missouri, the delegates of the PP selected William Jennings Bryan for the presidency. The Nebraskan had already won the presidential nomination of the Democratic Party.* Paired with Bryan was Thomas E. Watson of Georgia as his vice-presidential running mate. The Democrats previously had named Arthur Sewall of Maine as their vice-presidential candidate.

The 1896 platform of the PP repeated most of the planks of four years before and also included additional demands: free homes for bona-fide settlers on all public lands; direct election of the president, vice-president, and U.S. senators; initiative and referendum; federal legislation to abolish labor injunctions; public works to provide jobs for the unemployed; home rule for territories; and total independence for Cuba. In a hard-fought campaign, the PP-Democratic candidates drew 6,502,925 popular votes in a losing cause. William McKinley and Garret A. Hobart, the presidential and vice-presidential nominees of the Republican Party,* polled 7,104,779 to win the election. The GOP won 271 electoral votes to 176 for the Populist-Democratic fusion ticket.

The defeat of William Jennings Bryan in 1896 was the climax of populism, but the PP continued to survive as a weak and insignificant entity. In 1900 the PP nominating convention met at Cincinnati, Ohio. A so-called middle-of-the-road faction or anti-fusion group, which refused to be absorbed into the Democratic Party, nominated Wharton Barker of Pennsylvania as their presidential candidate, with Ignatius Donnelly of Minnesota as his vice-presidential running mate. The platform reiterated its support of the 1892 Omaha document, adding several planks relating to the direct election of judges and calling for public ownership of all public utilities. The Barker-Donnelly ticket drew only 50,605 popular and no electoral votes.

An even smaller faction of Populists, known as the Fusion Party, nominated William Jennings Bryan (also renominated for the presidency by the Democrats) as their 1900 presidential candidate. Charles A. Towne of Minnesota was designated as Bryan's running mate. The votes of this group, which ceased to exist after 1900, contributed little to Bryan's losing effort to unseat President McKinley.

Meeting in Springfield, Illinois, the 1904 nominating convention of the PP selected Thomas E. Watson of Georgia as their presidential nominee and Thomas H. Tibbles of Nebraska for the vice-presidency. Their platform once more reaffirmed adherence to the planks in the Omaha document of 1892 but added support for the eight-hour workday, right of recall, abolition of child labor, prohibition of convict labor, and exclusion from the United States of foreign pauper labor. Watson and Tibbles polled 117,183 popular and no electoral votes.

The last national convention of the PP was held at St. Louis in 1908. Thomas E. Watson was once again nominated for the presidency, with Samuel W. Williams of Indiana as his vice-presidential running mate. Again the Omaha platform was reaffirmed, with additional planks calling for proportional representation, regulation of commodity futures to prevent speculation, and federal legislation to enforce industrial safety and make employers liable for accidents. The Watson-Williams ticket garnered 29,147 popular votes.

Some local candidates ran on the PP ticket in 1912 but none were elected. Populism as a political force for reform had already been replaced by the Progressive movement, and after 1912 the PP ceased to exist.

The legacy of agrarian radicalism still survives under the name of neo-populism. Contemporary southern politicians appealing to rural voters are in this mold. Senator Fred Harris of Oklahoma ran for the 1972 Democratic presidential nomination as a neo-Populist, as did Governor George Wallace of Alabama. Hence the Populist tradition has survived as a permanent element of the American political system.

For further information, see John D. Hicks, *Populist Revolt* (1931); Norman Pollack, *The Populist Response to Industrial America* (1962); and Robert F. Durden, *Climax of Populism: The Election of 1896* (1965).

**PROGRESSIVE ALLIANCE (PA).** Founded in 1979 at Washington, D.C., by Douglas Fraser, president of the United Automobile, Aerospace and Agricultural Implement Workers of America (UAW), for the purpose of promoting social reform. Fraser, a former member of the Labor-Management Advisory Group, seeks to revive the liberal-labor coalition of the New Deal era, as well as to revitalize trade unionism. The major objectives of the PA are to restore organized labor's ties with liberal organizations; increase labor's influence within the Democratic Party*; work with minorities and underprivileged groups; and make labor more effective in politics at the grass-roots level.

Charter members in the PA included Benjamin Hooks, president of the National Association for the Advancement of Colored People*; Rafe Pomperance, legislative director of Friends of the Earth*; Ellie Smeal, president of the National Organization for Women*; Cesar Chavez, president of the United Farm Workers' Union; and Bella Abzug, liberal feminist and a former member of the House of Representatives. Thus far some twenty labor unions have affiliated with the PA, with others indicating interest.

The PA seeks to broaden organized labor's political horizons by going beyond the traditional goals of trade unionism. The PA supports reciprocal trade, affirmative action, welfare programs, and environmental protection. It opposes transfer of industry from unionized states to those with right-to-work laws, has protested budget cuts in welfare programs made by President Jimmy Carter, and proposes more national planning to ensure full employment. The PA is critical of the stance taken by George Meany, former president of the American Federation of Labor-Congress of Industrial Organizations, for his narrow stance and obstructionism. Fraser, who is the PA's chairman, has patterned his political outlook after that of the late Walter Reuther, a UAW president for whom Fraser served as administrative assistant.

For more information, see Ron Chermow, "Douglas Fraser: Labor's Courtly Rebel," *Saturday Review* (April 1979): 17–20.

**PROGRESSIVE CITIZENS OF AMERICA (PCA).** Founded in 1946 at a joint convention of the National Citizens Political Action Committee* and the Independent Citizens Committee for the Arts, Sciences and Professions* for the purpose of effecting a merger of the two organizations. Featured speakers at this founding session were Mayor Fiorello La Guardia of New York, site of the conference, and former Vice-President Henry A. Wallace. Dr. Frank Kingdon, a radio newscaster, and Jo Davidson, a renowned sculptor, were named co-chairpersons. Calvin B. "Beanie" Baldwin, former assistant director of the Farm Security Administration, was selected to serve as executive secretary.

The constitution of the PCA stated its objectives as follows: "To promote and support legislation which will serve the economic and social needs of the people. . . . To strive for a just and enduring peace throughout the world. . . . To eliminate from our national life all discrimination based on race, color, creed or national origin. . . . To work for the realization of the Four Freedoms."

The PCA took a stand in favor of retaining rent controls; endorsed the Wagner-Ellender-Taft Housing Bill; called for tax relief for lower-income groups; defended David E. Lilienthal's appointment as chairman of the Atomic Energy Commission (his confirmation was being opposed by some conservatives); and demanded an end to President Harry S. Truman's loyalty program because of its alleged purge of liberal-left-wing government employees.

By 1948 membership in PCA totaled nearly one hundred thousand. Its members represented the left of center, including ex-New Dealers, radicals, and Communists. Because of the undue influence of the Communists, many liberals who were members quit and others were reluctant to join. The extreme pro-Soviet stance of the PCA also deterred many liberals from affiliating with an organization that saw many evils in American foreign policy but recognized none in that of the Soviet Union.

Critical of both President Truman's domestic and foreign policy, the PCA met in Chicago in 1948 to organize a third party. At this meeting the Progressive Party* was formed. Thus transformed into a political party, the PCA ceased to exist as a separate entity.

For further information, see Curtis D. MacDougall, *Gideon's army*, 3 vols. (1965).

**PROGRESSIVE LABOR PARTY (PLP).** Founded in 1964 at New York City by a small group of Communists for the purpose of promoting the Communist doctrines of Mao Tse-tung on the American political scene. The PLP stemmed from the Progressive Labor Movement (PLM) and was given impetus by the May 2nd Movement (M2M). The PLM was founded in 1962 by Milton Rosen, who became PLP's national chairman, after he had been expelled from the Communist Party of the United States of America* (CPUSA) for being a Maoist revisionist. The M2M condemned U.S. participation in the Vietnam war as being a manifestation of American imperialism. Other leaders in the PLP were Bill Epton, who had organized the Harlem Defense Council and was vice-chairman of PLP, Fred Jerome, and Mortimer Scheer. Within a year the PLP had about six hundred members. Its two official publications were *Progressive Labor* and a newspaper, *Challenge*.

According to the PLP's constitution, the prime objective of the organization was to "build a revolutionary movement with the participation and support of millions of working men and women as well as those students, artists, and intellectuals who will join with the working class to end the profit system." Dedicated to the Marxist-Leninist-Maoist ideology, the PLP accepted party discipline by the "scientific principles of democratic centralism," which meant that the members were to submit to authoritarian leadership. It viewed its first task as one of radicalizing the working class.

From the outset, the PLP revealed itself as a militant organization that advocated the violent overthrow of the U.S. government. While organizing blacks in Harlem, Bill Epton used such inflammatory language to incite violence that he was indicted, tried, and sent to prison for "criminal anarchy" and advocating the "overthrow of the government of the state of New York by force and violence." The PLP kept up its anti-Vietnam war demonstrations by controlling the M2M and sought to enlist students as members through its Student Committee for Travel in Cuba.

At its 1965 convention, the delegates of the PLP reaffirmed by resolution that the American "war of aggression in Vietnam was part of a world-wide counterrevolution strategy of the U.S." Opposing both capitalism and the democratic system, it labeled "liberalism as the main ideological danger to the developing radical movements." It was also decided to make the PLP into a working-class party despite the fact that of the some two hundred delegates present, only four were actually workers.

When the Students for a Democratic Society* (SDS) met for its 1966 convention at Clear Lake, Iowa, a contingent of PLP members attended. Some SDS members disliked the disciplined democratic centralism of the PLP and wanted to bar them from attending, but this was not done. The PLP sought to infiltrate and ultimately control the SDS in support of its ideological position of forging a worker-student alliance to serve as a vanguard of the revolution. In 1966 the National Committee of the PLP issued a statement of party principles, "Road to Revolution II," that reiterated its criticism of the Soviet Union and the CPUSA for its revisionism and also attacked North Vietnam for accepting aid from the Soviets. To those members of the SDS who disdained the idea of a worker-student alliance it asserted, "Revisionism is fundamentally the substitution of individual bourgeois interests for the interests of the working class, and that is precisely what happens when members refuse to join the people."

In 1967 the PLP initiated a summer program, Vietnam Work-In, that sought to get students to take jobs in factories in order to radicalize workers. In the main this project failed because blue-collar Americans generally despised both campus radicals and Vietnam war protesters. Furthermore the PLP's criticism of Hanoi alienated many radicals. Some PLP members quit and others were expelled for not accepting the party line relative to Maoist dogma. In an effort to stem defections, the PLP redoubled its efforts at base building, a policy of getting students to desist from creating more campus confrontations related to student power and instead to become more involved in forging the student-worker alliance. The PLP still played an influential role in the SDS but could not gain control of the organization.

At the SDS convention in 1968 on the campus of Michigan State University at East Lansing, several factions made a concerted effort to expel the PLP members for their criticism of North Vietnam. This attempt failed, just as it did in 1969, when adherents to the Black Panther Party* tried again to dislodge the PLP. The PLP not only restated its criticism of the Soviet Union and North Vietnam but added Cuba to its list because of Fidel Castro's verbal attack on the People's Republic of China. Members of the PLP also began to oppose black nationalism and black studies programs on college campuses as constituting racism and anti-working-class black power. In order to make the PLP more palatable to workers, the supposed vanguard of the capitalist revolution, the PLP now stood in opposition to Castro, Ché Guevara, campus riots, drugs, long hair, and bourgeois student activity.

When the Weatherman* faction developed within the SDS, the PLP found itself on the defensive once more. In 1969 the attempt to purge the PLP from the SDS failed, but the latter was torn asunder in the struggle. With the majority leaving under the leadership of Bernadine Dorhn, the remnant of the SDS now became the PLP-SDS. The Weatherman condemned the PLP-SDS for its attack on the Black Panthers, Ho Chi Minh and North Vietnam, and Cuba's Fidel Castro. Isolated and small in number, the PLP-SDS chose Alan Spector, a twenty-four-year-old University of Wisconsin graduate, as its new national secretary. The Weatherman, meantime, selected Mark Rudd to be national secretary. By 1970 the PLP-SDS membership had dwindled to several thousand in a dozen or so chapters, primarily in New York and California. Throughout 1972 more chapters became defunct. The final blow came in 1972 when President Richard M. Nixon visited the People's Republic of China and was greeted personally by Mao Tse-tung. Mao was the PLP's revolutionary hero, and his gesture to the United States seemed to be a repudiation of world revolution for national self-interest.

With its ideological foundation destroyed and student interest dissipating, the PLP disintegrated and then went defunct. It had capitalized on the anti-Vietnam war sentiment but made practically no real political inroads on either students or workers. Its ideological rigidity made it impossible for it to work with other radical groups and soon disillusioned students who displayed some interest in Mao's doctrines. Once the war in Vietnam was being terminated, the PLP, as part of the New Left movement, dissipated. The vast majority of Americans were never interested in revolution, and without the anti-Vietnam sentiment it is doubtful that the PLP would have attracted more than a handful of followers on college campuses. Certainly its greatest obstacle to success was the refusal of laborers to support it, for according to its own doctrines the working class was to precipitate the revolution. In America, however, this has never been the case. The working class has generally supported the Democratic Party* rather than revolutionary parties. Their aspirations are basically sympathetic to traditional democratic and middle-class values.

For more information, see John P. Diggins, *The American Left in the Twentieth Century* (1973), and Kirkpatrick Sale, *SDS* (1973).

**PROGRESSIVE PARTY (PP) [1912].** Founded in 1912 at Albany, New York, by a group of Progressive insurgents within the Republican Party* for the purpose of promoting opposition to the renomination of President William Howard Taft at the upcoming GOP national convention in Chicago. The PP was an outgrowth of the National Progressive Republican League,* which had been formed in 1911 by Senator Robert M. La Follette (R-Wis.). La Follette considered himself the chief opponent to Taft, but when ex-President Theodore Roosevelt decided to contest the renomination of the incumbent president, the man he had handpicked to be his successor, most of the liberal Progressives within the GOP considered Roosevelt to be the best challenger.

Although Theodore Roosevelt had demonstrated his popularity with the voters by defeating Taft in a series of Republican primaries, the conservatives in the GOP controlled the party machinery; consequently Taft won renomination. This action so incensed Roosevelt that he and his followers bolted and met at their own convention in Chicago. Senator La Follette was hoping to get the PP presidential nomination, but it went to Roosevelt on the first ballot by acclamation. Senator Hiram W. Johnson (R-Calif.) was named as his vice-presidential running mate. The decision of the delegates to place Roosevelt at the head of the PP's presidential ticket so alienated La Follette that he withheld his support and did not participate in the fall campaign.

Theodore Roosevelt had once boasted, "I am as strong as a bull moose." From this statement the PP got its nickname and symbol, Bull Moose. The platform of the Bull Moose or PP included the following planks: woman suffrage; direct primaries; short ballot; initiative, referendum, and recall; abolition of child labor; protective legislation for women; registration of lobbyists; limitations on campaign contributions; legal and judicial reform; outlawing labor injunctions so as to protect the right of collective bargaining; a minimum wage; accident and unemployment insurance; eight-hour workday; establishment of a cabinet-level department of labor; creation of a national health service; federal regulation of corporations to prevent monopolies; conservation of natural resources; construction of national highways; a graduated income tax; parcel post; and implementation of better methods for assimilating foreign immigrants into American society.

During the presidential campaign Roosevelt called his program the New Nationalism. Its political philosophy was based on that enunciated by Herbert Croly in his book, *The Promise of American Life* (1909). Croly argued, and Roosevelt agreed, that liberalism should jettison Thomas Jefferson's belief that the least government is the best and adopt Alexander Hamilton's concept of positive government. The Jeffersonian tenets of states' rights, laissez-faire economics, and small government contributed to the rise of trusts. Only by the actions of a strong federal government could big business be brought under control. The New Nationalism was but a more formalized statement of Roosevelt's Square Deal program that was carried out previously while he was serving as president.

The 1912 presidential contest was a four-way race among Roosevelt, Taft, Democrat Woodrow Wilson, and Socialist Eugene V. Debs. Roosevelt came in second, outpolling Taft by 4,127,788 to 3,485,831 (88 electoral votes to 8), but lost the presidency to Wilson, who drew 6,301,254 popular and 435 electoral votes. The Democratic Party's* Woodrow Wilson thus won the White House with only 41.8 percent of the popular vote. By running on the PP ticket and thus splitting the GOP, Roosevelt ensured Taft's defeat at the polls and also contributed to Wilson's triumph.

A recurring problem in politics is that of party loyalty. When a contender for the presidential nomination of his party loses, he must decide whether to support the eventual nominee. If each contender took the attitude that if he did not win no support for the winner would be forthcoming, the party could never be victorious in an election. This is, in effect, what Theodore Roosevelt did. Had he gained the GOP nomination in 1912, he would have wanted Taft's support. Also, by taking the Progressives with him, Roosevelt branded the liberal Republicans as traitors to the Republican Party. The conservatives never again fully trusted the liberal wing of the GOP because of its disloyalty. When Progressives wanted to make the PP permanent, Roosevelt discouraged them in 1916 by endorsing GOP nominee Governor Charles Evans Hughes of New York for the presidency. Most Republican Progressives followed Theodore Roosevelt back into the GOP, with a few giving their support to incumbent President Wilson. Eight years later, in 1924, Senator La Follette would try to reconstruct a liberal coalition by forming a new Progressive Party.*

For more information, see George E. Mowry, *Theodore Roosevelt and the Progressive Movement* (1946 [1968]); Spencer C. Olin, Jr., *California's Prodigal Sons: Hiram Johnson and the Progressives, 1911-1917* (1968); and John Allen Gable, *The Bull Moose Years: Theodore Roosevelt and the Progressive Party* (1978).

**PROGRESSIVE PARTY (PP) [1924].** Founded in 1924 at Cleveland, Ohio, by a coalition of liberal left-of-center groups and members of labor unions for the purpose of nominating Senator Robert M. La Follette (R-Wis.) for the presidency. Delegates present at the founding convention included representatives from the following organizations: Conference for Progressive Political Action,* Nonpartisan League,* Socialist Party of America,* and the Minnesota Farmer-Labor Party. La Follette and his vice-presidential running mate, Senator Burton K. Wheeler (D-Mont.), were also supported by leaders of the American Federation of Labor.

The PP platform that was adopted called for public control over all natural resources; the elimination of all monopolies; increased taxes on incomes of the wealthy; legal protection for the right of collective bargaining; public works to eliminate unemployment; prohibition of child labor; repeal of the Transportation Act of 1920; establishment of a government marketing corporation; abrogation of the appellate jurisdiction of the U.S. Supreme Court; forbidding courts to use labor injunctions; election of all federal judges; protective legislation for women workers in industry; revision of the Treaty of Versailles; reduction of armaments; outlawry of war; a public referendum on a declaration of war; and the guarantee of civil liberties for all Americans.

Considered by many to be an agrarian radical and a pro-German isolationist, La Follette nevertheless polled 4,832,532 popular votes but won only the electoral vote of Wisconsin. In relation to the total vote, La Follette pulled 16.6 percent; John W. Davis, the Democrat,* 28.8 percent; and President Calvin Coolidge, the Republican* who was reelected, 54 percent.

Since La Follette was the moving force behind the PP, his death in 1925 doomed the party to an early demise. Robert M. La Follette, Jr., who won his father's seat in the Senate, tried to keep the PP alive, but with little success. In 1938 Governor Philip La Follette, another son, tried to resurrect the PP as the National Progressives of America.* This too proved abortive because most Progressives were won over to the New Deal of Franklin D. Roosevelt and eventually joined the Democratic Party.

For more information, see Kenneth C. Mackay, *The Progressive Movement of 1924* (1947); Belle Case and Fola La Follette, *Robert M. La Follette*, 2 vols. (1953); and Roger T. Johnson, *Robert M. La Follette, Jr., and the Decline of the Progressive Party in Wisconsin* (1964).

**PROGRESSIVE PARTY (PP) [1948].** Founded in 1948 at Philadelphia when 3,240 delegates and alternates met at a national nominating convention to approve Henry A. Wallace as their presidential nominee and Senator Glen Taylor (D-Idaho) as his vice-presidential running mate. The formation of the PP, later dubbed Gideon's Army by former Vice-President Wallace, actually stemmed from activities dating back to 1946. After Wallace had been discharged from his position as secretary of commerce by President Harry S. Truman for interfering in matters of foreign policy, the Progressive Citizens of America* initiated the move to form a third party. Subsequently a Wallace for President Committee was established on January 29, 1948, and Calvin B. Baldwin, a former assistant director of the Political Action Committee,* was designated campaign manager.

With the selection of its presidential ticket a foregone conclusion, the PP convention in 1948 drew up a platform that was extremely critical of U.S. foreign policy. It denounced the Marshall Plan, Truman Doctrine, stockpiling of atom bombs, establishment of military bases all over the world, universal military training, and military aid (given to Nationalist China, Greece, and Turkey). It also demanded immediate recognition of Israel as an independent nation; severance of diplomatic relations with Franco's Spain; "negotiation and discussion with the Soviet Union to find areas of agreement to win the peace"; action to transform the United Nations into a system of world government; and measures to be taken to ensure success of a world disarmament argreement. Support was also given to independence for Puerto Rico and the establishment of "unified homelands" for the Irish and Armenians.

Regarding domestic affairs, planks condemned racial segregation of blacks and job discrimination against women. Other demands included a one dollar an hour minimum wage, a five-year program of price supports for farmers at 90 percent of parity, a national old-age pension of one hundred dollars per month for all people over sixty years of age, national health insurance, and federal aid to education. It promised the creation of a department of education and a department of culture, both with cabinet-level status. The platform urged repeal of the Taft-Hartley Act, the Displaced Persons Act, and the National Security Act, plus the abolition of the House Committee on Un-American Activities, discontinuance of the president's loyalty program, and an end to attempts to outlaw the Communist Party of the United States of America* (CPUSA).

From the outset the PP acquired a reputation as being too pro-Soviet and therefore created an image of itself as being manipulated by Communists. Although Henry Wallace and Glen Taylor were not Communists, they acquired such a label when leadership of the PP seemed to gravitate toward known Communists. Public suspicions were confirmed at the convention by the rejection of the so-called Vermont resolution, proposed by James Hayford, chairperson of the three-person Vermont delegation: "Although we are critical of the present foreign policy of the United States, it is not our intention to give blanket endorsement to the foreign policy of any other nation." Because of its implied criticism of the Soviet Union, its defeat was engineered by PP leaders despite the adverse repercussion on public opinion.

Henry Wallace, who conducted a vigorous campaign under adverse circumstances (he was constantly heckled at rallies), compounded his own troubles by not clearly disavowing Communist support. This, he later admitted, should have been done when the CPUSA endorsed him instead of running its own presidential candidate. Wallace never realized until too late how great the Communist influence was in the PP. Wallace had been a former agriculture secretary (1933-1940), vice-president (1941-1945), secretary of commerce (1945-1946), and editor of the New Republic (1946-1948). He was basically a New Deal Democrat who championed a high parity farm program, pro-labor legislation, civil rights, low-cost housing, medical insurance, and equal rights for women. Regarding foreign policy he hoped for Soviet-American cooperation, disarmament, and greater reliance on the United Nations. His campaign oratory varied in tone from sounding like an apologia for Soviet imperialism to idealistic speeches advocating that the beatitudes of the Bible be applied as solutions to all international problems.

During the course of his campaign Wallace was pilloried by the the press and sometimes prohibited from speaking, especially in the South where he refused to address segregated audiences. Such international events as the Berlin blockade and the Communist coup d'état in Czechoslovakia made Wallace's efforts to defend Soviet actions appear treasonous at a time when cold war tensions were at their height. The formation of the PP may have actually helped President Truman win reelection because it allowed the Democrats to claim that left-wingers and Communists were supporting Wallace.

Falling far short of the popular vote expected, the PP ticket drew a national total of only 1,157,140 votes, most of them from just two states, California and New York. After the outbreak of the Korean War in 1950, Henry Wallace resigned from the PP and retired to his experimental farm in South Salem, New York.

Debilitated but not yet dead, the PP survived until 1952 when it nominated its last presidential ticket. Vincent Hallinan, an advocate of radical causes and a California lawyer, was selected as the PP's presidential candidate, with Charlotte Bass, a black woman and civil rights activist, chosen as his vice-presidential running mate. The ticket attracted a mere 140,023 votes, thus signaling the final demise of the PP.

For further information, see Curtis D. MacDougall, *Gideon's army*, 3 vols. (1965); Edward L. and Frederick H. Schapsmeier, *Prophet in Politics: Henry A. Wallace and the War Years, 1940-1965* (1970); and Allen Yarnell, *Democrats and Progressives: The 1948 Election as a Test of Postwar Liberalism* (1974).

**PROHIBITION PARTY (PP).** Founded in 1869 at Chicago when five hundred delegates from twenty states met at the call of the Independent Order of Good Templars to organize what has become the oldest of the minor (or third) parties. One impetus for the formation of a national PP came when the federal government legalized and taxed the interstate traffic of liquor during the Civil War. Prohibitionists considered such a move to be a form of special recognition and hence constituted federal protection of the liquor industry from state regulatory laws. More fundamental reasons for establishing a national PP at this time were a desire to revive the reform movement of the pre-Civil War era, which had been spearheaded by abolitionists, to focus the zeal for reform into temperance activity, and to unite local and state groups into a single party organization for more effective political action.

At its first nominating convention, held at Columbus, Ohio, in 1872, the PP chose James Black for president and the Reverend John Russell as his vice-presidential running mate. Russell, called by some the Father of the Prohibition Party, had started a state PP in Michigan in 1867. The platform asserted, "That the traffic in intoxicating beverages is a dishonor to Christian civilization, inimical to the best interests of society, a political wrong of unequalled enormity, subversive of the ordinary objects of government, not capable of being regulated or restrained by any system of license whatever, but imperatively demanding for its suppression effective legal Prohibition by both State and National legislation.'' The first PP ticket drew only 5,588 popular votes in six states. (See table 8.)

**TABLE 8 Prohibition Party Presidential Candidates and Votes, 1872-1980**

| YEAR | CANDIDATE | TOTAL POPULAR VOTE |
|---|---|---|
| 1872 | James Black | 5,588 |
| 1876 | Green Clay Smith | 9,630 |
| 1880 | Neal Dow | 10,364 |
| 1884 | John P. St. John | 150,957 |
| 1888 | Clinton B. Fisk | 250,122 |
| 1892 | John Bidwell | 271,111 |
| 1896 | Joshua Levering | 131,285 |
| 1900 | John G. Woolly | 210,200 |
| 1904 | Silas C. Swallow | 259,163 |
| 1908 | Eugene W. Chafin | 252,704 |
| 1912 | Eugene W. Chafin | 209,644 |
| 1916 | J. Frank Hanly | 220,505 |
| 1920 | Aaron S. Watkins | 189,467 |
| 1924 | Herman P. Faris | 57,551 |
| 1928 | William F. Varney | 20,106 |
| 1932 | William D. Upshaw | 81,869 |
| 1936 | D. Leigh Colvin | 37,661 |
| 1940 | Roger W. Babson | 58,725 |
| 1944 | Claude A. Watson | 74,761 |
| 1948 | Claude A. Watson | 103,343 |
| 1952 | Stuart Hamblen | 72,778 |
| 1956 | Enoch M. Holtwick | 41,397 |
| 1960 | Rutherford L. Decker | 46,220 |
| 1964 | E. Harold Munn, Sr. | 23,267 |
| 1968 | E. Harold Munn, Sr. | 15,121 |
| 1972 | E. Harold Munn, Sr. | 12,818 |
| 1976 | Benjamin C. Bubar | 15,898 |
| 1980 | Benjamin C. Bubar | 7,149 |

For the presidential elections of 1872, 1876, and 1880, the vote total of the PP never exceeded 0.1 percent of the total cast. The locus of party support during this period and throughout its first half-century was the northeast quadrant bounded by the Mason-Dixon line and the Ohio and Mississippi rivers. Commencing in 1884, after many voters became convinced that the Republican Party* was not interested in reform of any kind, the ranks of the PP suddenly increased. That year the party nominated John Pierce St. John for the presidency, paired with William Daniel as the vice-presidential nominee. St. John, a former Republican governor of Kansas, had gained national attention four years previously by sponsoring a successful prohibition amendment to the constitution of the Jayhawker state. The PP vote in 1884 increased fifteenfold to 150,957, 1.5 percent of the total cast in that election. Of significance nationally was the fact that St. John siphoned some 25,000 Republican votes from James G. Blaine in the key state of New York and thereby contributed to Grover Cleveland's narrow victory in the presidential race.

In 1888 the PP added another 100,000 votes nationally, winning 2.2 percent of the total. This was due to several factors. The previous year an affiliated Intercollegiate Prohibition Association had been formed, and the PP's platform was broadened to include other issues besides prohibition. Planks called for the "right of suffrage" without regard to "race, color, sex, or nationality"; strict enforcement of immigration laws; abolition of polygamy; observance of the "Sabbath as a civil institution"; equal pay for women; and arbitration of labor disputes. Campaigning on these issues the PP's presidential nominee, General Clinton Bowen Fisk (founder of Fisk University), and his vice-presidential running mate, the Reverend John Anderson Brooks, polled 250,122 votes.

The 1892 platform of the PP was its most radical ever adopted. While still considering "prohibition of the liquor traffic" as the "dominant issue," other planks demanded federal regulation of railroad, telegraph, and public corporations; restrictions on immigration; a wealth tax; limitations on grain speculation; a ban on ownership of land by nonresident aliens; sole government control over currency; woman suffrage; a six-day work week; and support for public schools rather than those of a sectarian nature. Championing these reforms were General John Bidwell, the PP's presidential nominee, and the Reverend James Britton Cranfill, who occupied second place on the ticket. They attracted 271,111 popular votes, the largest ever achieved by the PP.

An internal clash took place in 1896 when one faction, consisting of the southern and eastern wings, sought to return to the single-issue prohibition platform. The western wing, influenced by the radicalism of the Populist Party,* wanted to embrace a wide variety of reforms and finally seceded to form the short-lived National Party.*

From the turn of the century to World War I, the PP was influenced by the Progressive movement. In addition to insisting upon national prohibition, platforms during this period appealed for reform of divorce laws; direct election of U.S. senators; tariff revision; initiative and referendum; postal savings; inheritance tax; conservation; single presidential term of six years; government ownership of all public utilities, grain elevators, and terminals; federally operated warehouses for the storage of cotton; old-age pensions; unemployment insurance; and an item veto for the president on appropriation bills.

The 1916 platform not only contained many progressive planks but also spoke out vigorously on the anti-war issue. Munitions makers and the peacetime draft were condemned, as was President Woodrow Wilson's use of troops in Mexico. The PP appealed for a "compact among nations to dismantle navies and disband armies." Running on this highly progressive peace platform were former Indiana Governor J. Frank Hanly and Ira Landrith. On the ballot in forty-two states (the largest number ever), this ticket drew 220,505 (1.2 percent) votes.

PP's national convention in 1920 was a jubilant affair as reflected in the platform, which gave "thanks to Almightly God for the victory over the beverage liquor traffic which crowns fifty years of consecrated effort." Seemingly, however, the party's very reason for being established no longer existed. Its delegates decided to continue the party as the best vehicle for enforcing the Eighteenth (prohibition) Amendment and the Volstead Act. But the fortunes of the PP steadily declined as a result of the crime and social ills (such as bootlegging and speakeasies) accompanying the "Great Experiment" and then passage and ratification of the Twenty-first (repeal) Amendment in 1933. Prohibition on a national scale had been repudiated permanently because of the impossibility of enforcement, and therefore voters were no longer attracted to a party linked to this issue.

Great issues attending the Great Depression, World War II, and the cold war overrode any concern on the part of the public with reimposing prohibition. The PP became impotent in the 1930s and 1940s, never again polling as much as 1 percent of the popular vote. Despite occasional victories by local candidates, the PP has been hampered since 1948 by increasingly strict election laws that by 1976 had removed it from the ballot in all but fourteen states. In 1976 its presidential candidate, Benjamin C. Bubar, attracted only 15,898 popular votes.

In 1980 the PP changed its name to the Statesman Party as an experiment to see if would attract more voters. The change in name would ostensibly camouflage its basic one-issue image. Its presidential nominee was Benjamin C. Bubar and the vice-presidential candidate was Earl F. Dodge. The party was on the ballot in only eight states and received 7,149 votes.

Moribund but defying death, the PP still maintains a national headquarters in Denver, Colorado, and a historical collection at the University of Michigan. The PP issues a monthly publication, *National Statesman*. Current executive secretary is Earl F. Dodge.

For further information, see James R. Turner, "The American Prohibition Movement, 1865-1897" (Ph.D. dissertation, University of Wisconsin, 1972); D. Leigh Colvin, *Prohibition in the United States* (1926); Roger C. Storm, *Partisan Prophets* (1972); Jack S. Blocker, Jr., *Retreat from Reform: The Prohibition Movement in the United States, 1890-1913* (1976); and Norman H. Clark, *Deliver Us from Evil: An Interpretation of American Prohibition* (1976).

**PROTECT AMERICA'S CHILDREN (PAC).** Founded in 1977 at Miami, Florida, by Anita Bryant for the purpose of promoting restrictive legislation relative to homosexuals. Formed originally as Save Our Children, its name was changed to PAC in 1978. The impetus for the formation of PAC stemmed from Anita Bryant's successful crusade to secure repeal of an ordinance in Miami that had forbidden discrimination against homosexuals in housing and employment. Bryant, a noted singer and television personality, founded the PAC to expand her anti-homosexual campaign to other parts of the country.

The basic objective of PAC is to prevent homosexuality from attaining legal sanction or being protected by local, state, or national legislation. Bryant and members of the PAC contend that homosexuality is morally evil and constitutes an abnormality that should not be condoned by law. While not seeking punitive legislation against homosexuals, PAC does strive to prevent enactment of laws protecting them against discrimination. PAC believes that landlords should not be forced to permit homosexuals to live as "married" couples nor should school boards be forced to employ individual homosexuals as teachers, a practice that it believes has a detrimental influence upon children and should not be tolerated.

Most of the some fifty thousand members of PAC are religious fundamentalists convinced that homosexuality violates the moral code of the Judaic-Christian heritage and therefore should not be given legal protection. PAC joins with religious groups all over the nation to secure repeal of anti-discriminatory ordinances wherever they exist. Homosexuals, led by the National Gay Task Force, seek to prevent such repeal whenever PAC conducts such a campaign. This has resulted in some hotly contested elections in many localities. At times PAC convinces voters to repeal anti-discriminatory ordinances, but on other occasions it has lost its fight.

From its national headquarters in Washington, D.C., and with Anita Bryant as president, PAC plans greater involvement in politics to seek approval of its viewpoint from the general voting public.

**PTA.** See National Congress of Parents and Teachers.

**PUBLIC CITIZENS, INC.** See Public Interest Research Group.

**PUBLIC INTEREST RESEARCH GROUP (PIRG).** Founded in 1970 at Washington, D.C., by Ralph Nader for the purpose of promoting consumer protectionism. The formation of the PIRG came as an outgrowth of Nader's attack on the automobile industry in his book, *Unsafe at Any Speed* (1965), which resulted in the passage by Congress of the National Traffic and Motor Vehicle Safety Act of 1966, and his establishment of the Center for the Study of Responsive Law (CSRL) in 1969. With a grant from the Carnegie Foundation and the help of volunteer lawyers serving as summer interns, the CSRL investigated violations of public interest by business groups and government agencies. These investigatory teams, called Nader's Raiders, produced some significant reports: *Report of the Federal Trade Commission, Vanishing Air, Old Age: The Last Segregation, Water Wasteland, The Closed Enterprise System, Caution—This Job May Kill You, Tractor Safety, Crash Safety in General Aviation, The Chemical Feast, The Interstate Commerce Commission,* and *What to Do with Your Bad Car: An Action Manual for Lemon Owners.*

In 1971 Nader established the Corporate Accountability Research Groups, as well as Public Citizens, Inc., which served as an umbrella for the following organizations: Congress Watch, the lobbying arm; Critical Mass, environmental issues; Health Research Group, food, medicine, and drugs; Freedom of Information Act Clearinghouse, to secure information from government agencies; Tax Reform Research Group, for tax reform; and the Public Citizens Visitors Center. Other public-interest groups that were formed later include the Public Citizens Litigation Group; Citizens Action Group; Aviation Consumer Action Project; Retired Professionals Action Group; the Capitol Hill News Service; and Fight to Advance the Nation's Sports.

The public-interest conglomerate established by Ralph Nader serves to bring out the facts, rally public opinion, initiate class-action suits, and lobby for legislative action. Issues in which they have been involved include agitation for the creation of a federal consumer protection agency; safer automobiles; protection of the environment; occupational safety and health; women's rights; protection of the rights of mental health patients; truth in lending; banishment of harmful food additives; prevention of exposure to hazardous chemicals and drugs; an end to secrecy in government; less waste in government; closer congressional supervision of federal regulatory agencies; elimination of tax loopholes; an end to price gouging by oil companies; the prevention of accidents at nuclear power plants; compelling the Food and Drug Administration to issue warnings relative to the side effects caused by oral contraceptives; forcing the Federal Aviation Commission to set aside certain seats where no smoking would be permitted; and pressuring for stricter enforcement of antitrust laws.

Since the formation of PIRG, Ralph Nader has been highly successful in influencing public opinion and in lobbying for reform legislation. In his role as a national ombudsman, he has been dubbed a "public citizen." Nader does not involve himself in party politics nor does he profit from his public endeavors. Nader's objectives have been to make the system work rather than destroy it and stimulate civic action by an enlightened citizenry to attain remedial measures for protecting the public interest. Nader has sometimes been compared to the muckrakers in the Progressive era. Highly independent and prone to eschew compromise, Nader has nevertheless accomplished much that benefits the consuming public.

National headquarters of PIRG is located in Washington, D.C. Nader supervises the work of PIRG and other public-interest organizations he founded and has the services of both a professional staff and hundreds of volunteers. Support for these groups comes from hundreds of thousands of people, plus grants from various foundations. Recent PIRG publications have included *Who Runs Congress* and *Inside the Capitol.*

For more information, see Robert F. Buckhorn, *The People's Lawyer* (1972); Charles McCarrey, *Citizen Nader* (1972); Andrew S. McFarland, *Public Interest Lobbies: Decision Making on Energy* (1977); and Norman J. Ornstein and Shirley Elder, *Interest Groups, Lobbying and Policymaking* (1978).

**PUSH.** See People United to Save Humanity.

# — Q ————————————————

**QUAY MACHINE (QM).** Founded in 1885 at Philadelphia by Matthew Stanley Quay for the purpose of promoting the political fortunes of the Republican Party* in Pennsylvania. Quay, who at the time of the formation of the QM was state treasurer, wrested away control of the GOP from James McManes' Philadelphia Gas Ring, a municipal Republican machine so named because McManes served as a trustee of the Philadelphia Gas Works.

In 1887 Quay was elected by the state legislature to the U.S. Senate. He remained there, with a brief exception in 1900, until his death in 1904. During this time he was the undisputed boss of the GOP in Pennsylvania. Either as chairman of the Pennsylvania Republican Committee or by virtue of his political power, Quay controlled patronage, chose state candidates, raised campaign funds, and delivered his state's votes for GOP presidential candidates. The height of his influence and power was in 1888. Named national chairman of the Republican National Committee,* he masterminded the presidential election of Benjamin Harrison. During the course of Benjamin Harrison's administration, Quay broke with the president over the issue of civil service reform, opposing any measures that would limit patronage or hamper the spoils system. As a result of this disagreement, Quay refused to work for Harrison's reelection in 1892. This contributed to Harrison's defeat by the Democrat, former President Grover Cleveland.

In 1896 Quay worked for the election of William McKinley as president. In 1900 Quay maneuvered the nomination of Governor Theodore Roosevelt of New York, who was also a hero in the Spanish-American War, as the GOP vice-presidential nominee. The McKinley-Roosevelt ticket won handily, and after McKinley was assassinated in 1901, Roosevelt became president. Quay was a staunch supporter of TR and helped set the stage for Roosevelt's reelection in 1904. Before election day, however, Quay died. In addition to furthering the careers of Benjamin Harrison and Theodore Roosevelt, Quay was responsible for bringing businessman Mark Hanna into national politics as his close aide. As a political boss Quay was ruthless but brilliant in helping keep the Republican Party in power in his home state and on the national scene.

For more information, see Harry J. Sievers, *Benjamin Harrison*, 3 vols. (1968).

**RADICAL REPUBLICANS (RR).** Founded in 1860 at Washington, D.C., by Congressman Thaddeus Stevens (R-Mass.) for the purpose of promoting a militant stand against the extension of slavery and the use of force relative to the states that seceded from the Union. The formation of the RR faction stemmed from abolitionism and the influx of anti-slavery proponents into the Republican Party.* Once the Civil War began, the RR gradually assumed control of Congress. It sought to control the conduct of the war, abolish slavery, and initiate its own Reconstruction once the Confederacy collapsed. Leading members of the RR in the House included James M. Ashley, George S. Boutwell, Benjamin F. Butler, Henry W. Davis, Joshua R. Giddings, George W. Julian, and William D. Kelley. Radical leaders in the U.S. Senate included Zachariah Chandler, Oliver P. Morton, Charles Sumner, Benjamin F. Wade, and Henry Wilson.

During the Civil War the RR established the Committee on the Conduct of the War to ensure congressional control over the prosecution of the war effort. Through this committee, the Radicals often harassed President Abraham Lincoln and interfered with military strategy. In 1864 the RR was responsible for passage of the Wade-Davis bill, pocket vetoed by President Lincoln, which would have initiated a punitive Reconstruction policy upon the South. The Radicals opposed Lincoln's renomination for a second term but were not strong enough to prevent it. When Lincoln was assassinated in 1865 and Andrew Johnson ascended to the presidency, a bitter battle ensued when Johnson vetoed a civil rights bill.

In the mid-term elections of 1866, the RR captured Congress by an overwhelming majority. The Radicals proceeded to enact the Reconstruction Act of 1867—overriding President Johnson's veto—which divided the South into five military districts. In addition to military occupation, blacks were enfranchised while many ex-Confederates were disenfranchised. The RR tried to limit presidential power by the Tenure of Office Act of 1867. Congressman Thaddeus Stevens led the impeachment fight in the House.

Despite their great strength, the RR fell one short of the needed two-thirds vote in the Senate to remove Johnson from the presidency.

The RR picked General Ulysses S. Grant as their presidential candidate. After his victory, the Radicals controlled the course of Reconstruction (often called Radical Reconstruction) until the election of Rutherford B. Hayes as president in 1876. In 1877 President Hayes removed the federal troops from the South and ended Reconstruction. James G. Blaine and the Half-breed faction of the GOP then took over control of the Republican Party and focused national policy on the fostering of industrialization. The Half-breeds got their name from the RR as a term of derision for favoring a conciliatory policy toward the South. The Half-breeds also favored civil service, end of the spoils system, high tariff, and a political alliance with business interests. The RR should be given credit for the adoption of the Thirteenth, Fourteenth, and Fifteenth amendments to the U.S. Constitution. A negative aspect of the Reconstruction policy was the political exploitation of the blacks as part of the carpetbagger and scalawag governments imposed on southern states. The military occupation of the South also left a legacy of hatred that lasted for many decades.

For more information, see T. Harry Williams, *Lincoln and the Radicals* (1941); Fawn M. Brodie, *Thaddeus Stevens: Scourge of the South* (1959); Eric L. McKitrick, *Andrew Johnson and Reconstruction* (1960); Kenneth M. Stampp, *Era of Reconstruction* (1965); Avery O. Craven, *Reconstruction: Ending of the Civil War* (1969); and Harold M. Hyman, ed., *Radical Republicans and Reconstruction* (1967).

**REFERENDUM '70 (R-70).** Founded in 1970 at Washington, D.C., by Fred Dutton, Richard Goodwin, and Ted Van Dyck for the purpose of promoting the election of candidates pledged to end U.S. participation in the Vietnam war. Dr. John Kenneth Galbraith, Harvard University economist and a member of the Americans for Democratic Action,* served as honorary chairman. The advisory committee included Mayor Charles Evers of Fayette, Mississippi; Gloria Steinem, feminist leader and a member of the National Organization for Women*; Andrew Young, civil rights leader and vice-president of the Southern Christian Leadership Conference*; and Vernon Newton of New York.

The membership of R-70 was relatively small and represented the liberal-dove faction of the Democratic Party.* It was hoped to make the 1970 off-year election a referendum on whether the United States should withdraw from Vietnam. Although this was a primary issue during the campaign, the other main issue was that of law and order versus campus demonstrations and lawlessness in the streets. R-70 members were highly critical of both President Richard M. Nixon and Vice-President Spiro T. Agnew. While the Democrats won 52 percent of the popular votes in the 1970 election, they gained only nine seats in the House and lost two in the Senate. Congress was in the control of the Democrats, but those committed to a quick termination of the Vietnam war did not have sufficient votes to accomplish it either in 1971 or 1972. Endorsement by R-70 in no way assured victory and in some instances branded a candidate as a dove, thus contributing to defeat. Following the 1970 congressional election, the R-70 disbanded.

**REPUBLICAN CONGRESSIONAL COMMITTEE.** See National Republican Congressional Committee.

**REPUBLICAN GOVERNORS ASSOCIATION (RGA).** Founded in 1962 at Miami Beach, Florida, by Republican governors attending the National Governors' Conference* for the purpose of promoting political unity in the GOP. Governor Robert Smylie of Idaho was elected the first chairman of the RGA. It was funded by the Republican National Committee* and established three permanent committees: Executive, Policy, and Campaign. The decision was made to hold two meetings annually. Membership was to be open to any newly elected Republican governor.

The purpose of the RGA was to foster the exchange of ideas on mutual state problems, coordinate activity with the executive branch of the federal government, and plan campaign strategy. The RGA also served as a liaison between GOP governors and the national leaders of the Republican Party.* The governors wanted to help formulate GOP policy relative to issues affecting their respective states, to have more contact with Republicans in Congress, and to have some control over patronage. The RGA was instrumental in securing additional delegates to the national convention when a state elects a Republican governor.

National headquarters of the RGA is located in Washington, D.C. Current chairman is Governor Winfield Dunn of Tennessee, with James R. Galbraith serving as executive director.

**REPUBLICAN NATIONAL COMMITTEE (RNC).** Founded in 1856 at Pittsburgh, Pennsylvania, by group of former Whigs* and anti-Nebraska Democrats* for the purpose of making preparations for the calling of a national nominating convention of the newly formed Republican Party.* The first national chairman was Edwin D. Morgan of New York, who later served as the governor of the Empire State (1859-1863) and in the U.S. Senate (1863-1869). The first GOP national convention was held at Philadelphia and selected John C. Frémont as its presidential nominee. The convention delegates also chose the members of the RNC, who would serve for four years until the next convention convened, and adopted the rules under which they would operate.

Current membership of the RNC is made up of a national chairman; a co-chairman; a fifteen-member executive committee; three representatives from each state, the District of Columbia, Guam, Puerto Rico, and the Virgin Islands; and one representative from the U.S. Senate, House of Representatives, Republican Governors Association,* Republican National Finance Committee, National Federation of Republican Women,* Republican State Chairmen's Advisory Committee, Young Republican National Federation,* College Republican National Committee, National Republican Heritage Groups Council,* and National Black Republican Council.

The RNC conducts the affairs of the GOP between national conventions; keeps party officials informed on issues; issues public statements in the name of the party; maintains a speakers' bureau; maintains a library and newspaper file; issues biographical information on candidates and keeps election statistics; selects a convention site; certifies delegates; helps prepare the party platform; and sets the agenda for the convention. The RNC, in turn, is subject to the direction of the nominating convention and membership is again determined by the assembled delegates. Once a presidential ticket is nominated, the RNC plays a key role in conducting the national campaign. An important aspect of its work is to inform party workers on the issues; coordinate the activity of local and state organizations; solicit campaign contributions; prepare campaign materials for radio, television, billboards, newspapers, and other media; and plan speaking schedules for candidates.

In 1977 the RNC initiated Project Recovery. With a $7.5 million budget, it sought to recruit minorities into the GOP; revitalize local and state organizations; concentrate on electing Republicans to state legislatures; and cooperate with the National Republican Congressional Committee* to increase the number of Republicans in the House of Representatives. The RNC has endorsed the Kemp-Roth (tax-cut) bill and has issued statements criticizing President Carter's energy program. It also opposes elimination of the electoral college and modification of the Hatch Act.

In 1980 at Detroit when the Republican platform was being formulated, William Brock, national chairman of the RNC, sought to mediate between the ultra-conservatives and moderates over what planks should be accepted. Mary Crisp, co-chairman, was so incensed over the adoption of an anti-Equal Right Amendment that she resigned her position. She maintained it reversed a forty-year commitment in Republican platforms.

Present national headquarters is located in Washington, D.C. RNC publications include *Monday* (weekly), *First Monday* (monthly), *Women in Politics*, and *Convention Proceedings*.

**REPUBLICAN PARTY (RP).** Founded in 1854 at Ripon, Wisconsin, by a group of some fifty anti-slavery advocates for the purpose of promoting opposition to the Kansas-Nebraska Bill. Shortly after this meeting in a one-room schoolhouse in Ripon, state conventions were held at both Jackson, Michigan, and Bloomington, Illinois (with Abraham Lincoln in attendance), where the designation of RP was also adopted but in a more formal manner. The name of the new party is generally attributed to Joseph Medill, an abolitionist, who purchased the *Coshcocton* (Ohio) *Whig* in 1849 and immediately changed its name to the *Coshcocton Republican*.

After passage of the Kansas-Nebraska Act in 1854, which implemented the doctrine of popular sovereignty relative to western territories (thus allowing the people there to decide whether slavery would be permitted when they petitioned for statehood), the fledgling RP grew rapidly. It attracted followers who had previously been adherents to the Whig Party,* conscience (anti-slavery) Whigs, Democratic Party,* anti-Nebraska Democrats, Liberty Party,* Free Soil Party,* and the Know-Nothing Party.* Some who joined were merely opposed to the extension of slavery while others were confirmed abolitionists.

The first national convention of the RP was held in 1856 at Philadelphia. Colonel John C. Frémont, the noted western explorer and a former Democratic senator from California, was nominated for the presidency. William L. Dayton of New Jersey was named as his vice-presidential running mate. The platform demanded the admission of Kansas as a free state; opposed the repeal of the Missouri Compromise; condemned polygamy and slavery as the "twin relics of barbarism"; denounced the Ostend Manifesto; supported improvement of rivers and harbors; and called for the construction of an "emigrant road" to the Pacific and a transcontinental railroad. In a field of three, Frémont made a surprisingly strong showing. His 1,341,028 popular votes (33.3 percent) (see table 9) garnered 114 electoral votes (all from free states) and ranked him second only to Democrat James Buchanan. Millard Fillmore, the Know-Nothing nominee, ran last.

When the Republicans met at Chicago in 1860, Senator William H. Seward of New York, a former Whig, was the leading contender for the presidential nomination. On the third ballot, however, the delegates chose the prairie lawyer from Illinois, Abraham Lincoln (also an ex-Whig), as their standard-bearer. Hannibal Hamlin of Maine was selected as the vice-presidential candidate. The platform denounced the Democrats for their policy of extending slavery, reviving the slave trade, and issuing "threats of disunion." It called for Kansas to be admitted as a free state; cessation of the slave trade; implementation of a free-homestead policy; passage of a protective tariff; construction of a transcontinental railroad; appropriations by Congress for rivers and harbors; and full citizenship rights for immigrants who became naturalized citizens.

In one of the most crucial elections in American history, Abraham Lincoln emerged triumphant in a field of four. Lincoln polled 1,867,198 popular

### TABLE 9 Republican Party Presidential Candidates and Votes, 1856-1980

| YEAR | CANDIDATE | TOTAL POPULAR VOTE |
|---|---|---|
| 1856 | John C. Frémont | 1,341,028 |
| 1860 | Abraham Lincoln | 1,867,198 |
| 1864 | Abraham Lincoln | 2,219,362 |
| 1868 | Ulysses S. Grant | 3,013,421 |
| 1872 | Ulysses S. Grant | 3,597,375 |
| 1876 | Rutherford B. Hayes | 4,035,924 |
| 1880 | James A. Garfield | 4,454,433 |
| 1884 | James G. Blaine | 4,852,234 |
| 1888 | Benjamin Harrison | 5,445,269 |
| 1892 | Benjamin Harrison | 5,181,466 |
| 1896 | William McKinley | 7,113,734 |
| 1900 | William McKinley | 7,219,828 |
| 1904 | Theodore Roosevelt | 7,628,831 |
| 1908 | William Howard Taft | 7,679,114 |
| 1912 | William Howard Taft | 3,485,831 |
| 1916 | Charles Evans Hughes | 8,548,935 |
| 1920 | Warren G. Harding | 16,153,115 |
| 1924 | Calvin Coolidge | 15,719,921 |
| 1928 | Herbert C. Hoover | 22,829,501 |
| 1932 | Herbert C. Hoover | 15,760,684 |
| 1936 | Alfred M. Landon | 16,684,231 |
| 1940 | Wendell L. Willkie | 22,348,480 |
| 1944 | Thomas E. Dewey | 22,017,617 |
| 1948 | Thomas E. Dewey | 21,991,291 |
| 1952 | Dwight D. Eisenhower | 33,936,234 |
| 1956 | Dwight D. Eisenhower | 35,590,472 |
| 1960 | Richard M. Nixon | 34,108,157 |
| 1964 | Barry Goldwater | 27,178,188 |
| 1968 | Richard M. Nixon | 31,785,480 |
| 1972 | Richard M. Nixon | 47,167,319 |
| 1976 | Gerald R. Ford | 39,146,006 |
| 1980 | Ronald Reagan | 43,899,248 |

(39.8 percent) and 180 electoral votes; Stephen A. Douglas, the presidential candidate of the Democratic Party, drew 1,379,434 (29.4 percent) popular and 12 electoral votes; John C. Breckinridge pulled 854,248 (18.2 percent) popular and 72 electoral votes as the nominee of the National Democratic Party*; and John Bell of the Constitutional Union Party* attracted 591,658 (12.6 percent) and 39 electoral votes.

Within a month after Lincoln's election to the presidency, South Carolina seceded from the Union. By the time he was inaugurated president, the Confederate States of America had been formed. Once in office, the prairie statesman was confronted with the actual tragedy of Civil War. Despite the bloodshed incurred by this protracted struggle, Lincoln, as war president, vigorously set about to preserve the Union. He did not hesitate to use his executive powers as commander in chief and those bestowed by the U.S. Constitution during supreme emergencies to conduct the war in a vigorous manner. He issued the Emancipation Proclamation, imprisoned Copperheads, and prevented foreign intervention. His skills as a politician and national leader kept the support of such myriad groups as the Radical Republicans,* abolitionists, and border state Unionists. War weariness in the North made Lincoln's reelection in 1864 doubtful, particularly because General George B. McClellan, his Democratic challenger, called for an end to hostilities.

To broaden the base of his political support, President Lincoln and loyal Republicans created the National Union Party.* Meeting at Baltimore, this coalition party renominated President Lincoln and selected Governor Andrew Johnson of Tennessee, a former Democrat who opposed secession, as the vice-presidential candidate. The platform praised Lincoln's efforts to preserve the Union; demanded "unconditional surrender" of the "Rebels"; called for ratification of the Thirteenth Amendment to abolish slavery; supported construction of a transcontinental railroad; admonished the Confederacy relative to the maltreatment of captured black soldiers; encouraged immigration; and warned France about its attempt to establish a monarchy in Mexico. Lincoln's victory at the polls was helped enormously by such preelection military successes as Admiral David Farragut's capture of Mobile, Alabama; General William T. Sherman's occupation of Atlanta, Georgia; and General Philip H. Sheridan's defeat of Jubal Early's troops in the Shenandoah Valley of Virginia. Lincoln was reelected president by a popular vote of 2,219,362 (55.1 percent), which included 77.5 percent of the soldier vote, and an electoral count of 212.

The assassination of Abraham Lincoln in 1865 by John Wilkes Booth removed from the presidency the one man capable of reuniting the nation "with charity for all." The intense hatred exhibited by the Radical Republicans toward President Andrew Johnson culminated in their impeachment of him. Although Johnson was not removed from office, he became totally impotent as chief executive. When Republicans met in Chicago at their 1868 nominating convention, they chose as their presidential nominee the national war hero, General Ulysses S. Grant. Schuyler Colfax of Indiana was named the vice-presidential candidate. Now dubbing themselves the National Union Republican Party, but more often referred to in the post-Civil War era as the Grand Old Party (GOP), the party lauded the Reconstruction policy of Congress and the platform called for "radical reform" of the "corruptions which have been so shamefully nursed and fostered by Andrew Johnson." Other planks called for "equal suffrage" to all "loyal men" in the South; payment of the national debt; reduction of taxes; U.S. protection for naturalized citizens; promotion of immigration;

and pensions for Union veterans. Grant won easily over Governor Horatio Seymour of New York, the presidential candidate of the Democrats, by polling 3,013,421 (52.7 percent) of the popular and 214 electoral votes.

Despite a corrupt administration that did not reflect glory upon President Grant, he was renominated unanimously at Philadelphia in 1872. Senator Henry Wilson of Massachusetts replaced Schuyler Colfax as the vice-presidential nominee. Ignoring the fact that a reform-minded group of Liberal Republicans had bolted the GOP, the platform lauded the RR by claiming, "During eleven years of supremacy it has accepted with grand courage the solemn duties of the time." Various planks called for civil service reform; civil rights for blacks; "additional rights" for women; benefits for veterans and their dependents; setting aside lands in the public domain for "free homes for the people"; continuation of a hard-money policy; abolition of the franking privilege; a revenue-producing protective tariff; and payment of the national debt. With the help of the Grand Army of the Republic* and "waving the bloody shirt" campaign rhetoric, President Grant won easily over Democrat Horace Greeley, also the presidential nominee of the Liberal Republican Party,* by polling 3,597,375 (55.6 percent) of the popular vote and 286 electoral votes.

Notwithstanding a second mandate, President Grant's administration continued to be marred by widespread political corruption, blatant use of the spoils system, and exploitive carpetbag state government in the South. Grant would have liked a third term, but the Liberal Republicans, representing those wanting civil service reform, and the Half-breeds, wanting an alliance with the rising industrialists, opposed him. The Half-breed faction was led by James G. Blaine, the Speaker of the House and a leading contender for the presidential nomination. The eventual compromise nominee, however, was Governor Rutherford B. Hayes of Ohio. Second place on the presidential ticket went to Congressman William A. Wheeler of New York. The platform continued to wave the bloody shirt by charging the "Democratic Party with being the same in character and spirit when it sympathized with treason." Other planks asked voters to permit the GOP to complete the "permanent pacification of the Southern section of the Union"; continue to redeem greenbacks in gold; support women's rights; prohibit the use of public funds for sectarian schools; terminate railroad land grants; stop polygamy; investigate the ill effects of the "immigration and importation of Mongolians"; and provide federal benefits to veterans. In perhaps the most controversial election the nation ever witnessed, Hayes was declared the winner over Governor Samuel J. Tilden, the Democratic nominee, by a specially appointed election commission. Hayes had polled 4,035,924 popular votes (47.9 percent), which was over 250,000 fewer than Tilden received. It appeared initially that Hayes had lost, since his Democratic opponent had 184 electoral votes and needed only 1 of the disputed 20 in question. But Hayes was awarded all 20 and with 185 electoral votes was declared the winner. In acquiescing to this "stolen election," the Democrats extracted a set of promises known as the Compromise of 1877. Hayes agreed to terminate military occupation of the South, appoint a southerner to the cabinet, ensure that internal improvements were carried out in the South, and allow southerners to benefit by patronage. In ending Reconstruction, blacks were abandoned and left to the mercy of white supremacists in the South.

At the time of the 1880 Republican nominating convention, the rigidity of the gold standard had resulted in the formation of a third-party greenback movement. At the same time the solid South was evolving into a Jim Crow society, with rigid separation of the races. Senator Roscoe Conkling of New York led the Stalwart faction, which wanted to continue the corruption of the spoils system, in an attempt to gain the nomination for ex-President Grant. But the assembled delegates at Chicago gave the presidential nomination to Congressman James A. Garfield of Ohio, with second spot going to Chester A. Arthur of New York. This represented a victory for the pro-industrial or Half-breed faction of the RP, now the dominant group. Once again the platform prided itself on suppressing the rebellion, freeing the slaves, and reconstructing the Union. It emphasized that the U.S. Constitution is a "supreme law, and not a mere contract." It noted the successful construction of the nation's railroads, the sound money policy based on the gold standard, and the large amounts of benefits paid to Civil War veterans. Promised were the abolition of polygamy; protection against "secret sectarianism"; exclusion of Chinese; and civil service reform. Garfield emerged the winner when he drew 4,454,433 (48.3 percent) popular and 214 electoral votes to triumph over Democrat Winfield S. Hancock and James B. Weaver, the presidential nominee of the Greenback Party.*

Shortly after taking office in 1881, President Garfield was assassinated by a demented office seeker, Charles J. Guiteau, and this elevated Chester A. Arthur to the presidency. Surprisingly Arthur performed well as president despite the fact that he had belonged to the Stalwart faction. He surprised everyone by supporting the Pendleton Act of 1883, which established the Civil Service Commission in an effort to control the scandalous dispensation of patronage. The era of the corrupt spoils system was now over. Arthur did not seek renomination in 1884 by the Republican convention at Chicago due to illness, which caused his death a year later. The presidential nomination went to James G. Blaine of Maine, the leader of the Half-breed faction who had served as senator and secretary of state. Senator John A. Logan of Illinois was designated the vice-presidential nominee.

The GOP platform of 1884 denounced the importation of contract labor, polygamy, and the "fraud and violence practiced by the Democracy in Southern states by which the will of the voter is defeated." It pledged tariff protection for wool producers; restoration of the U.S. Navy to its "old-time strength"; reservation of public lands for actual settlers; public regulation of railroads; creation of a national bureau of labor; enforcement of the eight-hour workday; federal benefits for Union veterans and their dependents; reform of civil service; no entangling alliances relative to foreign policy; establishment of an international standard for the coinage of gold and silver; passage of such legislation "as will secure to every citizen, of whatever race and color, the full and complete recognition, possession, and exercise of all civil rights and political rights." The failure of dissident reform-minded Republicans, labeled Mugwumps,* to support Blaine's candidacy contributed to the Plumed Knight's defeat by Democrat Grover Cleveland. In a losing cause, Blaine gained a popular vote of 4,852,234 (48.3 percent) with an electoral count of 182. This was the first time the GOP had failed to control the White House since 1861.

Many contenders vied for the presidential nomination when the Republicans assembled at Chicago in 1888. Former Senator Benjamin Harrison of Indiana, the grandson of President William Henry Harrison, emerged as the GOP nominee, with Congressman Levi P. Morton of New York as his vice-presidential running mate. The platform was critical of the Democrats for not allowing blacks to vote freely in the South and for proposing a reduction in tariff rates. President Cleveland specifically was chastised for his many vetoes of private pension bills. Promised were support for a protective tariff; reduction of postage rates; the use of both gold and silver as money; benefits for veterans; repeal of taxes on tobacco and (industrial) alcohol, opposition to trusts; prohibition on the importation of contract labor; restoration of unearned railroad land grants to the public domain for use by actual settlers, not aliens; immediate statehood for the territories of Montana, North Dakota, and Washington; assertion of federal sovereignty over the "political power of the Mormon Church" in Utah and the abolition of polygamy; rehabilitation of the merchant marine; rebuilding of the navy; implementation of the Monroe Doctrine; construction of a Nicaraguan canal; civil service reform; and promotion of temperance and morality.

Benjamin Harrison eked out a slim victory over incumbent President Cleveland. Harrison actually lost the popular vote 5,445,269 (47.8 percent) to Cleveland's 5,540,365 (48.6 percent) but triumphed in the electoral college, 233 to 168, to win the presidency. During Harrison's administration, six new states were admitted to the Union. In 1890 Congress enacted both the Sherman Anti-Trust Act and the Sherman Silver Purchase Act. For the first time in the nation's history, Congress voted for appropriations that totaled over $1 billion. In 1892 the GOP national convention met at Minneapolis, Minnesota, to renominate President Harrison on the first ballot. Incumbent Vice-President Levi Morton was replaced by Whitelaw Reid, a former editor of the *New York Tribune*.

The GOP platform of 1892 reaffirmed its support for a protective tariff;

favored bimetallism; endorsed civil rights for blacks; called for extension of foreign commerce; promised free rural delivery; opposed "any union of Church and State"; upheld home rule for Ireland; pledged construction of the Nicaraguan canal; recommended that the states enact legislation to ensure the safety of workers; endorsed the cession of arid lands in the public domain to the various states; indicated support for federal funding of the World's Columbian Exposition; and voiced sympathy with "wise and legitimate" efforts to promote temperance. President Harrison lost to Cleveland, who as ex-president was the Democratic nominee, by polling only 43 percent of the popular vote. That total amounted to 5,181,466 and netted a mere 145 electoral votes.

When the Republicans convened at St. Louis in 1896, the silver issue was paramount. It would eventually divide both the GOP and the Democrats and spawn a fusion between the Silver Democrats and the Populist Party.* Standing firm on the gold standard, however, the delegates nominated Governor William McKinley of Ohio and named Garret A. Hobart of New Jersey for the vice-presidency. The platform blamed the Democrats for the economic ills stemming from the panic of 1893; denounced the Wilson-Gorman Tariff of 1894; condemned lynching and suppression of Negro civil rights; criticized reductions in veterans' pensions; and indicated indignation over the Turkish massacre of Armenians. It promised enactment of a protective tariff; construction of a Nicaraguan canal; acquisition of Hawaii; purchase of the Danish Islands; enlargement of the navy; creation of a national board of arbitration; legislation to restrict "criminal, pauper, and contract immigration"; admission of the remaining territories as states; congressional representation for Alaska; and implementation of the Monroe Doctrine. Sympathy was extended to Cuban revolutionaries and efforts to "prevent the evils of intemperance." When a silver plank was rejected and one supporting the gold standard adopted, Senator Henry M. Teller (R-Colo.) led a small contingent of silverites in a walkout. They subsequently formed the Silver Republican Party.* Despite this defection and the challenge of William Jennings Bryan as the fusion candidate of the Democrats and Populists, McKinley emerged triumphant with 7,113,734 (51 percent) popular and 271 electoral votes.

The major event of McKinley's first term was the Spanish-American War. Through military victory the United States ensured Cuban independence and acquired both the Philippines and Puerto Rico. Hawaii was also annexed in 1898. Passage of the Gold Standard Act of 1900 seemingly ended the controversy over the silver issue. Jubilant Republicans gathered at Philadelphia in 1900 to renominate President McKinley unanimously. McKinley was paired with Governor Theodore Roosevelt of New York, who had won national fame during the Spanish-American War as the leader of the Rough Riders. The platform applauded McKinley's leadership during the war and praised the Dingley Tariff of 1897 for protecting American industry and labor. Other planks favored restrictions on immigration; improvement of highways and roads; enforcement of the Fifteenth Amendment; reciprocal trade; expansion of foreign commerce; benefits for veterans; condemnation of monopolies; extension of rural free delivery; construction of an isthmian canal; early admission of statehood for the territories of Arizona, New Mexico, and Oklahoma; and expansion of the merchant marine. Turning aside the charges of imperialism made by the Democratic challenger, President McKinley once again defeated William Jennings Bryan with a total of 7,219,828 (51.7 percent) popular and 292 electoral votes.

When President McKinley was assassinated in 1901 by anarchist Leon Czolgosz, the forty-two-year-old Theodore Roosevelt was elevated to the presidency. As a Progressive Roosevelt provided dynamic leadership at home and relative to foreign policy. His domestic program of trust-busting reversed the pro-industrial laissez-faire policy of the post-Civil War era, and his balance-of-power foreign policy modified the traditional isolationism by making America a world power involved in both Asiatic and European affairs. At the 1904 national convention in Chicago President Roosevelt was unanimously renominated, with Senator Charles W. Fairbanks of Indiana chosen by acclaim to be his vice-presidential running mate. The platform lauded the record of the Republicans in suppressing the insurrection in the Philippines; acquiring the Panama Canal route; building up the navy; expanding foreign markets; upholding the gold standard; enlarging the merchant marine; providing pensions for veterans of the Spanish-American War; and protecting American citizens abroad. Other planks called for proportional reduction in the electoral college for southern states that disfranchised blacks, protection for combinations of capital and labor if neither infringed upon the rights and interests of the people, and settlement of international disputes by arbitration. Pitted against a hapless Democratic opponent, Alton B. Parker, Roosevelt prevailed easily by polling 7,628,831 (56.4 percent) of the popular vote and garnering 336 electoral tallies.

Through his Square Deal and diplomatic efforts, Theodore Roosevelt amassed an enviable record as president. To ensure continuation of what he had started, he handpicked William Howard Taft of Ohio as his successor. This choice was ratified in 1908 at Chicago by the GOP national convention on the first ballot. Congressman James S. Sherman of New York was selected for the vice-presidency. The platform heaped praise on Theodore Roosevelt's administration. It supported the establishment of a bureau of mines and mining; U.S. citizenship for Puerto Ricans; initiation of an eight-hour workday in the construction of all public works; enactment of an employers' liability law; establishment of postal savings; a more accurate definition of the federal court procedure in issuing writs of injunction; an increase in pension benefits; the defense of the principle of protectionism (but it also promised tariff revision); admission of the territories of Arizona and New Mexico as states; and the enforcement of the Thirteenth, Fourteenth, and Fifteenth amendments. Democrat William Jennings Bryan suffered his third defeat at the hands of Taft, who polled 7,679,114 (51.6 percent) popular votes and 321 electoral votes.

The disenchantment of Republican Progressives with President Taft's weak leadership caused a rift in the ranks of the GOP when delegates assembled at Chicago in 1912. Both Theodore Roosevelt and Senator Robert M. La Follette (R-Wis.) were challenging Taft, who by now had allied with the "Standpatters" or conservative wing of the RP. When Taft was renominated, the Roosevelt insurgents bolted the GOP, formed the Progressive Party,* and nominated Theodore Roosevelt as their presidential candidate. The RP platform championed a protective tariff; proposed legislation to "limit effectively the labor of women and children"; supported workmen's compensation; favored judicial reform but not the recall of judges; pledged supplementary legislation to existing antitrust laws; endorsed the creation of "financial machinery" for rural credit; supported an amendment to the Federal Employer's Liability Law to include all government workers; favored legislation relative to revelation of campaign contributions and outlawing such contributions by corporations; called for the establishment of parcel post for the benefit of rural communities; maintenance of an adequate navy; enlargement of the merchant marine; continuance of conservation and reclamation programs; federal assistance in the area of flood control; improvement of rivers and harbors; opening federal coal reserves for development; restriction on undesirable immigration; protective legislation for American seamen; vigorous enforcement of the Pure Foods and Drugs Act; and citizenship for the people of Puerto Rico. Midway during the campaign, Vice-President James S. Sherman died. He had been renominated with Taft. The Republican National Committee* replaced him with Nicholas Murray Butler, the president of Columbia University. Pitted against Democrat Woodrow Wilson and Progressive Theodore Roosevelt, Taft ran a poor third, with only 3,485,831 (23.1 percent) popular and a mere 8 electoral votes.

With World War I raging in Europe, the 1916 Republican National Convention met in Chicago to nominate Charles Evans Hughes, former Progressive governor of New York and an associate justice of the U.S. Supreme Court, as its presidential standard-bearer. Second place on the ticket was given to ex-Vice-President Charles W. Fairbanks of Indiana. The platform criticized the Wilson administration for its foreign-policy failures. It called for "strict and honest neutrality between belligerents" while insisting "upon all our rights as neutrals without fear or favor." Denounced were the outrages perpetrated by Mexican bandits and Wilson's "indefensible methods of interference in the internal affairs of Mexico." The Underwood-Simmons Tariff Act of 1913 was condemned outright, as was the Democratic proposal for government ownership of the merchant marine. Pledged were the strengthening of the army and navy; development of a federal system of interstate highways; rural credit; extension of rural free delivery; vocational education; a child labor law; workman's compensation; continuation of the "husbandry of all the natural resources"; and woman suffrage while recognizing the "right of each state to settle this question for itself." Due to the loss of the state of California by fewer than 3,000 votes, caused by a misunderstanding with Governor Hiram Johnson, Hughes failed to unseat incumbent President Wilson from the White House. Hughes lost while pulling 8,548,935 (46.1 percent) popular and 254 electoral votes.

The public mood in 1920 relfected its desire to return to "normalcy." The GOP nominating convention at Chicago could not break a deadlock among the three leading contenders: Major General Leonard Wood of New Hampshire, Senator Hiram Johnson of California, and Governor Frank Lowden of Illinois. The impasse was broken when GOP leaders backed Senator Warren G. Harding of Ohio. He had been identified with the conservative Standpatters and had placed Taft's name in nomination in 1912. Accompanying his nomination for the presidency was the choice by the delegates to award the vice-presidential nomination to Governor Calvin Coolidge of Massachusetts, who had gained national attention for his handling of a police strike in Boston. The GOP platform censured President Wilson for his "executive autocracy"; failure to prepare for either war or peace; despotic refusal to end the war or yield up emergency powers; uncompromising stance on the League of Nations; and attempt to acquire Armenia as a U.S. mandate. It promised reduction of taxes; readjustment of the economy to a peacetime basis; quotas on immigration; participation in an international association without compromising national independence; encouragement of agricultural cooperatives; expansion of export trade; denial of the right to strike against the government; liquidation of the national debt; a simplified form of income tax return; development of water transportation service; enactment of a protective tariff; free speech except for those who advocate the "violent overthrow of the government"; the deportation of aliens guilty of agitating against the U.S. government; an anti-lynching law; appropriations for highway construction; benefits for disabled veterans; support for the ratification of the Nineteenth (woman suffrage) Amendment; elimination of child labor; a limit on the hours of employment for women; and home rule for Hawaii. In a presidential election where women exercised the right of universal suffrage for the first time, Harding won a landslide victory over Democrat James M. Cox by procuring 60.3 percent of the popular vote (16,153,115 votes) and received an electoral count of 404.

While on a speaking tour in 1923 that carried him to Alaska, President Harding died. Soon after his death the Teapot Dome and other scandals were made public. These revelations seemd to have doomed the Republican Party in the upcoming national election, yet when Calvin Coolidge assumed the presidency, he quickly restored national confidence in the GOP. President Coolidge was nominated on the first ballot in 1924 at Cleveland, the first national convention to be broadcast by radio. Governor Frank O. Lowden of Illinois was chosen as the vice-presidential nominee, and when he refused to accept, the nod went to Charles G. Dawes of Illinois, a banker and Harding's budget director. When the "Wisconsin platform," sponsored by Senator Robert M. La Follette was rejected, the Wisconsinite bolted the GOP and accepted the presidential nomination of his own Progressive Party.* The Republican platform took cognizance of the Harding scandals by demanding "fearless and impartial prosecution of all wrong doers" but lauded the integrity of the late president. It took advantage of the Coolidge prosperity by taking credit for reduced taxes, full employment, economy in government, and the economic benefits resulting from the protective-oriented Fordney-McCumber Tariff. Various planks promised collection of war debts; reorganization of the executive department; classification of postmasters under civil service; no entry into the League of Nations but endorsement of the World Court; benefits for World War I veterans; contingency plans for future emergency mobilization; no entangling commitments to foreign countries; promotion of commercial aviation; enactment of a federal anti-lynching law; and improvement of naturalization laws. President Coolidge won with ease over John W. Davis, the Democrat, and Senator La Follette, the Progressive, by polling 15,719,921 (54 percent) popular and 382 electoral votes.

In 1928, at the peak of a phenomenally prosperous era, Republicans convened at Kansas City to make Secretary of Commerce Herbert C. Hoover their presidential nominee on the first ballot. Senator Charles Curtis of Kansas was named the vice-presidential candidate. The platform enthusiastically claimed for the GOP "a major share of the credit for the position which the United States occupies as the most favored nation on the globe." Deemed worthy of praise were such achievements as lowered taxes; reduction of the national debt; expanded trade; development of a Mississippi system of inland transportation; flood relief; subsidies for the merchant marine; leasing of public land for mining; initiation of airmail service; sound fiscal policies; enactment of the Fordney-McCumber Tariff and the Kellogg-Briand Pact; benefits to veterans; enfranchisement of American Indians; and restrictions on immigration. Pledged were creation of a federal farm board; construction of roads and trails in national forests; passage of an anti-lynching law; utilization of commercial radio for the benefit of all Americans; collection of foreign debt; refusal to join the League of Nations; restoration of order in Nicaragua; examination of prospective immigrants in their home countries; limitation on naturalization to those who "are in sympathy with our national traditions, ideals, and principles"; repealing of any laws inconsistent with Indian citizenship; and promotion of self-reliance by expecting municipal and state governments to solve their own problems. The "Great Engineer," as Hoover was dubbed, campaigned on the belief that the "American system" of free enterprise and rugged individualism could in fact eliminate poverty in America. Hoover overwhelmed Governor Alfred E. Smith of New York, the Democratic nominee, by a popular vote of 22,829,501 (57.4 percent) and an electoral count of 472.

Barely in office, President Hoover was confronted with the devastating crash of the stock market in 1929 and the economic repercussions of the Great Depression. For this reason a mood of pessimism pervaded in the 1932 Republican national convention in Chicago. The GOP delegates demonstrated little enthusiasm in renominating President Hoover. Vice-President Charles Curtis overcame stiff opposition to win the second spot on the ticket again. The platform, which was the longest in the GOP's history, vainly tried to give credit to Hoover for his valiant efforts to cope with the multitude of problems stemming from "an economic depression that has swept the world." Credit was given for the Agricultural Marketing Act, Reconstruction Finance Corporation, Railroad Credit Corporation, National Credit Corporation, and other positive steps designed to bolster the collapsing economy and arrest the depression. Commended also were such actions as initiating economy in government; enacting the Hawley-Smoot Tariff; defending the gold standard; reducing military expenditures; avoiding international entanglements; restoring order in Haiti; befriending the American Negro; protecting the property rights of the American Indians; and preserving "American principles and traditions." Democrats were castigated for proposing the issuance of fiat money, manipulating commodity prices, proposing federal guarantee of bank deposits, and unbalancing the budget through "pork-barrel appropriations." Pledged were continued reduction of expenditures; revision of banking laws; creation of a system of federally supervised home loan discount banks; promotion of cooperative marketing associations; control of acreage under cultivation and diversion of submarginal lands from farming; avoidance of entangling international commitments; participation in the World Court; development of the Great Lakes-St. Lawrence Seaway; federal cooperation with states to build roads; enactment of rigid penal laws to stamp out gangsters, kidnappers, and racketeers; enforcement of prohibition; reorganization of government bureaus; and the use of "all available means consistent with sound financial and economic principles to promote an expansion of credit to stimulate business and relieve unemployment." On election day Hoover attracted only 15,760,684 (39.6 percent) of the popular vote with a mere 59 electoral tallied. This was a massive repudiation of the RP and its pro-business political philosophy of fostering capitalism by maintaining a laissez-faire attitude on the part of the federal government.

To have dislodged Franklin D. Roosevelt from the White House in 1936 would have taken a political miracle. Meeting in Cleveland the Republican delegates at the national convention chose Governor Alfred M. Landon of Kansas as their presidential standard-bearer. He had been one of the few GOP governors to survive the Democratic landslides of 1932 and 1934. Since he had been a Bull Mooser in 1912, he was more amenable to an expanded role for government in stabilizing the economy. Landon was paired with Colonel Frank Knox, the publisher of the *Chicago Daily News* and an arch-conservative. The Republican platform reflected more of the views of ex-President Hoover than those of Alf Landon, who was a former Progressive. It began by stating, "America is in peril," and went on to condemn the New Deal of FDR for having "dishonored American traditions"; unbalancing the budget; permitting the president to usurp both the powers of Congress and the U.S. Supreme Court; engaging in "frightful waste"; using public works for partisan advantage; destroying the morale of Americans by making them dependent upon the federal government; creating a vast bureaucracy; initiating a policy of scarcity in agriculture; ruining civil service; and undermining the soundness of the currency. The GOP committed itself to reduce waste; preserve free enterprise; maintain the American system of constitutional and self-government; repeal the Reciprocal Trade Agreements Act; improve the Social Security Act; initiate a national land-use program; balance the budget; enforce laws against trusts and monopolies; not become a member of the League of Nations or "make any entangling alliances in foreign affairs"; protect the economic status and personal safety of "our colored citizens"; and collect the war debts. Landon suffered one of the most devastating political defeats in American history when he won only the 8 electoral votes of Maine and Vermont. His popular vote was 16,684,231 (36.5 percent of the total cast).

Europe was at war in 1940 when the Republicans gathered at Philadelphia to nominate their presidential candidate, Wendell L. Willkie of Indiana. He was a former Democrat, a defender of private utilities, and a man who had never before been in politics. His vice-presidential running mate was Senator Charles L. McNary of Oregon, the minority leader, who supported some New Deal measures. The platform scored the New Deal for its failure to promote recovery while instead encouraging regimentation, waste, corruption, and class hatred. Voters were assured that the GOP would end the confusion in government; strengthen national defense; avoid "involving this nation in a foreign war"; eliminate politics from relief; reduce the national debt; extend the unemployment compensation provisions of the Social Security Act; continue benefit payments to farmers while promoting a national land use program; repeal the Thomas Inflation Amendment of

1933 and the Silver Purchase Act of 1934; end deficit spending; pass an amendment to the U.S. Constitution "providing for equal rights for men and women"; end the practice of appointing to "high positions of trust" members of "un-American groups"; encourage small business; and prevent the entry into the United States of undesirable aliens. Willkie conducted a whirlwind campaign but went down to defeat with 44.8 percent of the popular vote. His popular vote was 22,348,480 and his electoral vote 82.

With World War II nearing its conclusion, the 1944 nominating convention at Chicago picked a young governor of New York, Thomas E. Dewey, for its standard-bearer. Matched with this liberal-internationalist Republican was conservative-isolationist Governor John W. Bricker of Ohio. The platform pledged prosecution of the war to "total victory"; participation in an international "cooperative organization" but not by joining a "World State"; abolition of the poll tax and enactment of an anti-lynching law; beneifts for veterans; unrestricted immigration by Jews into Palestine; removal of wartime controls; enactment of a "fair protective tariff"; elimination of overlapping bureaucracy; abrogation of farm subsidies; removal of government from competition with private industry; extension of old-age and unemployment insurance; return of the public-employment-office system to the states; provision of relief for the people of liberated countries; limiting the president to two terms by a constitutional amendment; passage of an equal right amendment for women; continuation of the oil depletion allowance; and initiation of home rule for Alaska and Hawaii. Stressing the need for new leadership, Governor Dewey waged a strong campaign, but on election day he became the fourth GOP candidate to go down to defeat at the hands of FDR. Dewey polled 22,017,617 (45.9 percent) popular votes, which netted only 99 electoral tallies.

Jubilant Republicans gathered at Philadelphia in 1948 to nominate what seemed to be a winning team. Roosevelt had died and his successor, Harry S. Truman, was struggling and appeared to have lost the confidence of the voting public. Governor Thomas E. Dewey was once again the GOP presidential nominee, this time paired with the equally liberal Governor Earl Warren of California. The platform reflected both a progressive and internationalistic outlook. It pledged support to the United Nations; endorsed collective security; favored foreign aid; embraced the concept of collective security; and accepted the system of reciprocal trade. Other promises included reduction of the cost of government; implementation of anti-inflation measures; rooting out communism wherever found; maintenance of adequate armed forces to ensure national security; enactment of an anti-lynching law and an end of racial segregation in the armed services; equal rights for women; statehood for Alaska, Hawaii, and Puerto Rico; restoration to the states of submerged tidelands; recognition of Israel as a nation; and continuation of a bipartisan foreign policy. Despite the headline in the morning edition of the *Chicago Tribune* the day after the election, which erroneously asserted "Dewey Defeats Truman," the reverse had happened. In his losing cause Dewey had polled 21,991,291 (45.1 percent) popular and 189 electoral votes. His defeat was accredited to overconfidence and conducting an apathetic campaign.

The Korean War was still in progress when the 1952 GOP national convention opened at Chicago. Squared off against each other were General Dwight D. Eisenhower and Senator Robert A. Taft of Ohio. Eisenhower was backed by the Dewey liberal wing, while Taft (called "Mr. Republican" in the Senate) represented the conservatives. The war hero from Kansas won the presidential nomination on the first ballot, with the vice-presidential nod going to young Senator Richard M. Nixon of California. The platform chastised the Truman administration for allegedly plunging the nation "into war in Korea without the consent of our citizens"; shielding "traitors"; fostering the "goal of Socialism"; corruption in government; "appeasement of Communism at home and abroad"; an ineffective loyalty program; and the "Brannan plan scheme." Planks outlining GOP goals included opposing rent control; balancing the budget; reducing the national debt; lowering taxes; revising the internal revenue code; providing commodity loans on nonperishable farm crops; modifying the Taft-Hartley Act "as time and experience show to be desirable"; granting benefits to Korean war veterans; enlarging the scope of Social Security; opposing compulsory federal health insurance; enacting legislation to end lynching, the poll tax, and segregation in the District of Columbia; implementing the Hoover Commission's recommendations on the reorganization of government; building a seventy-group air force; passing an equal rights amendment for women; and immediate statehood for Alaska and Hawaii. With the twin slogans of "Communism, Korea, and Corruption" and "I Like Ike," Eisenhower beat Democrat Adlai E. Stevenson II with a popular vote of 33,936,234 (55.1 percent), which netted an electoral vote of 442.

Despite some health problems, President Eisenhower inaugurated his program of "Modern Republicanism" with wide public support. He accepted the New Deal and welfare state but planned to operate it with "fiscal integrity," or balanced budgets. GOP delegates at the 1956 convention in San Francisco renominated Eisenhower by acclaim. A short-lived attempt by Harold Stassen to dump Vice-President Richard Nixon from the ticket failed, and Nixon too was renominated. The platform extolled the Eisenhower administration for ending the war in Korea, restoring integrity to government, being fiscally responsible, and expanding overseas markets. Noted also were the "Atoms for Peace" program; "Open Sky" proposal; extension of Social Security; creation of the Department of Health, Education and Welfare; the Soil Bank; and construction of the St. Lawrence Seaway. In a "Declaration of Determination" it was pledged to reduce government spending further; gradually reduce the national debt; lower taxes; expand the school milk program; promote rural development; build new post offices; support statehood for Alaska and Hawaii; recognize that the U.S. Constitution is the supreme law of the land concerning civil rights; support South Korea and Nationalist China; bolster collective defense systems; reunite Germany; liberate the Soviet satellites; strengthen civil defense; and provide pensions for disabled war veterans. With the slogan "Peace and Prosperity" Eisenhower again triumphed over Democrat Adlai E. Stevenson II. In the rematch Ike enlarged his margin of victory to 57.4 percent of the total vote cast, which amounted to 35,590,472 popular and 457 electoral votes.

When the Republicans met at Chicago in 1960 the conservatives, led by Senator Barry M. Goldwater (R-Ariz.), were angry over the "compact of Fifth Avenue," an agreement concluded by Vice-President Richard M. Nixon, the front-runner, and Governor Nelson Rockefeller, the leader of the liberals, to harmonize their respective positions. Nixon wanted Rockefeller to be his vice-presidential running mate, but the New Yorker declined. Nixon won the presidential nomination on the first ballot and picked U.N. Ambassador Henry Cabot Lodge to fill the second place on the ticket. The platform lauded the accomplishments of the Eisenhower-Nixon administration in foreign policy, civil rights, education, and agriculture. Pledged were continuation of the mutual security program; intensified development of civil defense; production of new strategic weapons; tax reform; abolition of featherbedding; expansion of the workmen's compensation coverage; intensification of the Food for Peace program; utilization of flexible price supports to increase farm income; a change in the electoral college system; implementation of the civil rights acts of 1957 and 1959; extension of the student loan program; expansion of Social Security coverage; continuation of slum clearance; establishment of a commission on equal job opportunity; a change of Senate rule 22; and affirmation of the right of "peaceable assembly to protest discrimination in private business establishments." Nixon's poor showing in his four televised debates with his Democratic opponent, John F. Kennedy, and his failure to make full use of President Eisenhower as a campaigner contributed to a narrow defeat. Only 0.2 percent separated Nixon and Kennedy in the total popular vote. In losing, Vice-President Nixon attracted 49.5 percent of the popular vote, which for him amounted to 34,108,157, and a total of 219 electoral votes.

The 1964 GOP national convention at San Francisco witnessed a sharp reversal of the party's orientation from the Willkie-Dewey-Eisenhower mold to one reflecting the leadership of the ultraconservative old guard. Senator Barry M. Goldwater, representing the Republican right wing, was nominated for the presidency, and he in turn chose Congressman William R. Miller of New York, also a conservative, to be his vice-presidential running mate. Bitter floor fights ensued over the issues of extremism, civil rights, and control of nuclear weapons. The Goldwaterites triumphed in all three. The platform called for military victory in Vietnam; balancing the budget; cutting taxes; reducing government's involvement in school financing; constitutional amendments to permit states to implement reapportionment other than on the "one man, one vote" principle enunciated by the U.S. Supreme Court and to permit prayer in the public schools; revitalizing the North Atlantic Treaty Organization; strengthening alliances; opposition to communism everywhere in the world; recognition of the Cuban government in exile; a demand that the Berlin wall be taken down; tax reform; anti-inflation measures; enforcement of the Civil Rights Act of 1964 with the recognition that "the elimination of any such discrimination is a matter of heart, conscience, and education, as well as of equal rights under the law"; enactment of legislation to prevent obscene materials from passing through the mail; and medical care for the elderly through a federal-state plan. The tone of Goldwater's campaign was set when, in his acceptance speech, he claimed "extremism in the defense of liberty is no vice." Although he drew the support of the John Birch Society* and other ideologically motivated right wingers, Goldwater could not attract the votes of moderates. His loss was a debacle, pulling only 38.5 percent of the popular vote. This amounted to 27,178,188 popular and 52 electoral votes.

The fortunes of the GOP looked better in 1968 when the national convention convened at Miami Beach, Florida. The Vietnam war was unpopular, anti-war demonstrations were erupting in violence, and the inner cores of cities were being burned by discontented blacks. Goldwater conservatives were backing Governor Ronald Reagan of California and liberals championed the nomination of Governor Nelson A. Rockefeller. The delegates, however, chose as a compromise candidate the former vice-president, Richard M. Nixon, as their presidential nominee. He, in turn, selected Governor Spiro T. Agnew of Maryland as his vice-presidential running mate. The platform sought to placate both conservatives and liberals, as well as "hawks" and "doves." It labeled the Vietnam policy of the Johnson administration a failure and promised a "strategy permitting a progressive de-Americanization of the war." Other planks pledged the development of a "clear and purposeful negotiating position"; support for Israel; removal of "frustrations that contribute to riots"; prosecution of subversives; initiation of an all-out federal-state-local "crusade against crime"; enactment of legislation to control firearms and lower taxes; passage of legislation to give eighteen-year-olds the right to vote; tax credits to induce businesses to stay in the inner cities; tax credits for training the disadvantaged; creation of a volunteer army; federal assistance for Indians and Eskimos; improvement in postal service; modernization of Congress; reform of the electoral college; improvement of military weapons; and opposition to seating the People's

Republic of China in the United Nations. Pitted against Democrat Hubert H. Humphrey and George C. Wallace, the presidential candidate of the American Independent Party,* Nixon won with 31,785,480 (43.4 percent) of the popular and 301 electoral votes.

Just prior to the 1972 Republican national convention at Miami Beach, President Nixon surprised the nation by visiting the People's Republic of China. Through his policy of Vietnamization, he sought an honorable withdrawal for the United States and by implementing a program of New Federalism, Nixon attempted to revive local government by revenue sharing. Both President Nixon and Vice-President Agnew were enthusiastically renominated. The platform commended the president for his effort "to negotiate honorable terms" while condemning the "New Democratic Left" for undercutting American defenses and having "America retreat into virtual isolation." Pledges were made to support self-determination for South Vietnam; oppose amnesty for draft dodgers or deserters; remove economic controls "once the economic distortions spawned in the late 1960s are repaired"; secure a return of American prisoners of war; support the equal rights amendment; create a department of natural resources; bolster Social Security; lower the voting age to eighteen; implement a health insurance program involving the government, employers, and employees; safeguard the right of responsible citizens to own firearms; oppose court-mandated busing or arbitrary quotas; support voluntary prayer in the public schools; oppose the legalization of marijuana; support passage of legislation permitting individuals to buy, hold, or sell gold; give federal support for family farms; support continued withdrawal of U.S. troops from Vietnam and implementation of the "Nixon doctrine." Nixon won reelection over his Democratic challenger, George McGovern, with a whopping 47,167,319 popular votes (60.7 percent) and a huge electoral count of 521.

In 1973 Vice-President Spiro Agnew resigned his office after pleading no contest to a charge of tax evasion. Congressman Gerald R. Ford (R-Mich.), the House minority leader, was approved by Congress as the new vice-president. One year later, President Richard M. Nixon resigned his office during the controversy over the cover-up of the Watergate break-in, thus elevating Ford to the presidency. Congress then approved Nelson A. Rockefeller to fill the vacant office of vice-president. When the Republicans gathered at their 1976 nominating convention in Kansas City, the stage was set for a bitter contest over the presidential nomination. Governor Ronald Reagan of California, leader of the right-wingers within the GOP, mounted a strong challenge. As a representative of the liberal Republicans, Nelson Rockefeller had already indicated that he would not seek the vice-presidential nomination. President Ford won the nomination on the first roll call, but by a slim margin of 117 votes. He chose Senator Robert Dole of Kansas as his vice-presidential running mate.

The 1976 GOP platform proposed an attack on inflation by cutting government spending. It opposed government-controlled grain reserves; a uniform national primary; federal postcard registration; court-mandated busing; compulsory national health insurance; federalizing the welfare system; guaranteed annual income; dependence on foreign oil; détente with the Soviet Union on a basis of U.S. inferiority in arms; and the Humphrey-Hawkins Bill. Pledged were welfare and tax reform; revenue sharing; legislation for public disclosure of financial interests by members of Congress; the right of citizens to keep and bear arms; the right of states to impose the death penalty; extension of catastrophic illness protection; ratification of the equal rights amendment; diversion of funds from the interstate highways to mass transit; elimination of price controls on oil and newly discovered natural gas; reduction of air pollution; deployment of B-1 bombers; keeping commitments to Taiwan; maintaining control over the Panama Canal; supporting self-determination for Africa; and maintaining military superiority over the Soviet Union. In a close election President Ford lost to Democrat Jimmy Carter, but in so doing polled 39,146,006 (48.0 percent) of the popular vote and 240 electoral votes.

By the time the Republican National Convention met at Detroit in 1980 the former governor of California, Ronald Reagan, had won sufficient primary delegates to lock up the GOP presidential nomination. Chosen as his vice-presidential running mate was Ambassador George Bush, a former head of the CIA. Another contender, Representative John Anderson (R-Ill.), decided to the bolt the Republican Party and conduct an independent campaign for the presidency.

The Republican platform was highly critical of the Carter administration. It maintained that "unless taxes are reduced and federal spending is restrained, our nation's economy faces continued inflation, recession, and economic stagnation." Criticism was leveled at the Democratic Congress for producing "a jumble of degrading, de-humanizing, wasteful, overlapping and inefficient programs that invite waste and fraud but inadequately assist the needy poor." Various planks called for reductions in the income tax; a balanced budget; welfare reform; rejection of a guaranteed annual income; economic expansion through regulatory reform and other incentives; the right of state legislatures to accept or reject the ERA "without federal interference or pressure"; reaffirmation of the traditional role and values of the family in our society; ratification of a right to life constitutional amendment and passage of legislation to restrict the use of taxpayer's dollars for abortion; decontrol of gas and oil prices at the well-head; support for voluntary prayer in the schools; condemnation of forced busing; tougher laws to prevent distribution of drug paraphernalia; opposition to protectionist tariffs; assurance to the states of the right to enact right-to-work laws; an increase in defense spending; early deployment of the MX missile and B-1 bomber; correction of the great inequities in pay and benefits of career military personnel; opposition to a peacetime draft; achievement of military and technological superiority over the Soviet Union; integration of Spain into NATO; holding Panama "to strict interpretation of the language of the treaties"; support for the "sovereignty, security, and integrity of the State of Israel"; friendship with "moderate Arab states"; strong ties with Japan; caution and prudence in dealing with the People's Republic of China; concern for the security of Taiwan; opposition to the federally imposed 55-mile speed limit; and appointment of judges at all levels "who respect traditional family values and the sanctity of innocent human life."

Pollsters predicted a close contest but when the election was over the Reagan-Bush ticket won in a massive landslide triumph over the Democratic Carter-Mondale slate. The GOP margin of victory was 43,899,248 to 35,481,435 in the popular total and 489 to 49 in the electoral vote. Republicans also won control of the U.S. Senate, picked up thirty-three seats in the House of Representatives, gained four governorships, enlarged their numbers in state legislatures, and elected many local candidates to office. On the national level the Republican Party had won a decisive mandate to solve the nation's domestic problems and rebuild its power relative to the international scene. The magnitude of Ronald Reagan's landslide was reflected in the fact he carried forty-four states and won 50.75 percent of the popular vote to Carter's 41.02 percent. It constituted one of the widest margins of victory for the Republican Party in modern times.

For more information, see Malcom C. Moos, *Republicans: A History of Their Party* (1956); George H. Mayer, *Republicvan Party, 1854-1966* (1967); and Kevin Phillips, *The Emerging Republican Majority* (1969).

**REPUBLICANS.** See Republican Party.

**REPUBLICANS FOR PROGRESS (RFP).** Founded in 1964 at Cincinnati, Ohio, by Charles P. Taft for the purpose of promoting the election of moderate members of the Republican Party.* Formed originally as the Committee to Support Moderate Republicans, its name was changed to RFP in 1965. Taft is the son of President William Howard Taft and was a leader in the National Council of the Churches of Christ. He also had held the following offices: mayor of Cincinnati; member of the Cincinnati City Council; director of Wartime Economic Affairs in the State Department during World War II; and chairman of the Fair Campaign Practices Committee.

With a membership never in excess of one hundred, the RFP advocated the Modern Republicanism of President Dwight D. Eisenhower and sought to promote the election of other GOP candidates who also embraced this political philosophy. It opposed the nomination of Senator Barry M.

Goldwater (R-Ariz.) as the GOP presidential candidate in 1964, believing that his right-wing stance would harm the positive image of the Republican Party developed during the Eisenhower years. Once Goldwater got the nomination, the RFP concentrated its efforts on supporting moderates running for Congress and state offices. It did succeed in helping some moderate-liberal Republicans to win, but the landslide defeat of Goldwater resulted in many losses for moderates who could not disassociate themselves from the national campaign.

In 1966 and 1968 the RFP agitated for a reorientation of GOP policy to a middle-of-the-road position. It provided research assistance and financial support for candidates who eschewed the right-wing stance of Goldwaterites. Through its *Newsletter* it promoted the candidacy of Richard M. Nixon as one representing ties with the Eisenhower administration. After Nixon was elected president, the RFP disbanded. During its existence it served as a moderating influence on the extreme conservatism of the right-wing faction of the GOP.

**RESURGENCE YOUTH MOVEMENT.** See Anarchist Federation.

**REVOLUTIONARY YOUTH MOVEMENT.** See Students for a Democratic Society.

**RIGHT TO LIFE COMMITTEE.** See National Right to Life Committee.

**RIGHT TO WORK COMMITTEE.** See National Right to Work Committee.

**RIPON SOCIETY (RS).** Founded in 1962 at Cambridge, Massachusetts, by a group of seventeen graduate students from Harvard University and the Massachusetts Institute of Technology (MIT) for the purpose of influencing the Republican Party* toward a more liberal orientation. Named after Ripon, Wisconsin, one of the several communities claiming to be the birth-place of the GOP, the RS's symbol is a profile of Abraham Lincoln's head.

The first president of the RS was John Saloma, a graduate student at MIT (now a member of the political science department at that institution). Current president is Josiah Lee Auspitz, a doctoral candidate at Harvard University. Present membership is about one thousand in eleven chapters drawn primarily from the ranks of business, professional, and academic communities. The greatest numbers of members are in the East where urban Republicans tend to be more liberal and internationalist in outlook than the Midwest or the Far West.

Relative to contemporary politics the RS reeks to remold the GOP into a dynamic, nonracist party that will offer the American electorate a viable alternative to the Democratic Party.* It sponsors conferences, formulates position papers, champions progressive causes, and backs candidates receptive to its point of view. Many RS members were active supporters of Governor Nelson A. Rockefeller (R-N.Y.) for the presidential nomination in 1964 and 1968. Although openly critical of Vice-President Spiro T. Agnew, five RS leaders (John R. Price, Christopher DeMuth, Barbara D. Greene, Lee W. Huebner, and Bruce Rabb) served in the Nixon administration.

In 1976 the RS supported the retention of Nelson Rockefeller as the vice-presidential nominee and opposed the presidential candidacy of Ronald Reagan, a former governor of California. Most RS members worked to reelect President Gerald R. Ford, whom, they believed, had served the nation well in the post-Watergate period.

In 1980 the RS opposed the nomination of Ronald Reagan. While it made no formal endorsement during the primaries, many in the organization favored Ambassador George Bush, whose record when a member of Congress was that of a moderate. Some also desired the nomination of ex-President Gerald R. Ford. During the campaign, after Reagan won the Republican presidential nomination, RS executive director Steve Livengood issued a statement critical of both Reagan and President Jimmy Carter. It called upon both candidates to abandon "negative campaigning" and "address the major issues of our time." Carter was attacked for avoiding economic issues and Reagan for claiming the president was courting the vote of the Ku Klux Klan.* The RS urged all the major candidates to "repudiate image-building, negative campaigning, sloganeering, rank appeal to special voting blocs, the use and promise of patronage and federal largesse to gain political advantage."

In 1975 the RS moved its national headquarters to Washington, D.C., where it publishes research studies, *National Journal* (quarterly), *Ripon Forum* (semimonthly), and *Annual Report*.

**RURAL AMERICAN WOMEN, INC. (RAW).** Founded in 1977 at Washington, D.C., by Jane R. Threat, executive director of the Association for the Development of Education (ADE) and RAW's first president, for the purpose of forming a national coalition to promote a better life for women living in rural areas. Included on the initial board of directors were Lupe Anguiano, president of the National Women's Program Development; Mildred Black, manager of a sewing cooperative for low-income blacks; Unita Blackwell, mayor of Mayersville, Mississippi; Lorna Bourg, administrator for the Southern Mutual Help Association, Inc.; Marguerite Chapman of the Arkansas Folklore Society; Marie Cirillo, organizer for Sharecroppers Fund; Dayle Deal, Illinois field supervisor for the National Farmers Union*; Agnes Dill, a Pueblo Indian leader; Dr. Betty Hamlin, representing the Oregon Women for Agriculture; Jeanne Hoffman, president of the Council on Appalachian Women; Stephenie Irvine, a member of

Maine's International Women's Year Commission; Dr. Carolyn Karr, professor of history at Marshall University; Brownie Ledbetter, activist in rural development in Arkansas; Pat Sacrey of Northampton, Massachusetts; and Dr. Shirley Hill Witt, executive director of the Mountain Regional Office (in Denver, Colorado) of the U.S. Civil Rights Commission.

The first action taken by the board of directors was to call a National Rural American Women Leadership Conference. It was convened February 21-25, 1978, at the Chevy Chase 4-H Center near the nation's capital. Speakers addressing the conference included Senator Muriel Humphrey (D-Minn.); Judy Carter, President Carter's daughter-in-law; Carol Tucker Foreman, assistant secretary of agriculture; and Alexis Herman, director of the National Women's Bureau.

At this First National Rural American Women Leadership Conference, officers were formally elected and a series of forum groups was set up to discuss issues confronting rural women. Following discussions the 350 delegates present at the conference passed a series of resolutions calling for ratification of the equal rights amendment to the U.S. Constitution; national health insurance; expansion of medical facilities in rural areas; more vocational programs for women; implementation of the Family Farm Act of 1978; increased appropriations by Congress for rural development programs; legislation to ensure that foreign agricultural products are inspected, identified, and accurately labeled; greater funding for the Home Economics Section of the U.S. Department of Agriculture Cooperative Extension Service; establishment of shelters for battered women in rural areas; enactment of a national plan for the rational development of energy resources; enforcement by the Civil Rights Commission of laws pertaining to women's rights; endorsement of the Humphrey-Hawkins full employment bill; increased employment opportunities for rural women; the addition of rural women to the Small Business Administration's list of minorities; opposition to the deportation of Mexicans who come to the United States as farm laborers; a guaranteed income and jobs for rural women who head families; protection of Indian women; expansion and upgrading of rural transportation systems; and federal funding of projects to expand cultural opportunities for rural Americans.

The RAW hopes to become a grass-roots organization with a nationwide membership. It plans to monitor state and federal legislation pertaining to rural women, serve as a clearinghouse for organizations dealing with rural problems, coordinate activities to achieve greater success, and inform the media or relevant agencies of the needs of rural America. Present national headquarters is located in Washington, D.C.

# _S_

## SANE: A CITIZENS' ORGANIZATION FOR A SANE WORLD

**(SANE).** Founded in 1957 at New York City by a conference of notable dignitaries for the purpose of promoting some form of international control over nuclear weapons. A meeting was called by Norman Cousins, editor of the _Saturday Review_, and Clarence Pickett, secretary emeritus of the American Friends Service Committee. The prime mover at the founding meeting was Norman Thomas, the titular leader of the Socialist Party of America.*

Known originally as the National Committee for Sane Nuclear Policy (until 1969), SANE attracted a peak membership of some twenty-five thousand in the 1960s. Among its members were such nationally known personalities as Steve Allen, television performer; Pablo Casals, musician and refugee from Franco's Spain; Leonard Bernstein, composer and director of the New York Philharmonic Orchestra; Dr. Benjamin Spock, pediatrician and later in 1972 presidential nominee of the People's Party*; H. Stuart Hughes, historian; James L. Wadsworth, former U.S. ambassador to the United Nations; James Baldwin, black writer; Stuart Chase, economist; Benjamin V. Cohen, former adviser to President Franklin D. Roosevelt; Jules Feiffer, newspaper cartoonist; Dr. David Riesman, sociologist; Dr. Erich Fromm, psychiatrist and the one who suggested the organization's name; and the Jewish scholar Rabbi Jacob Weinstein.

SANE's first project was to run a full-page advertisement in the _New York Times_ warning the American public, "We are facing a danger unlike any danger that has ever existed." In 1958 during the summit conference in Geneva between President Dwight D. Eisenhower and Soviet leader Nikita Khrushchev, SANE sponsored an "Appeal to the Men at Geneva." It was also endorsed by U.N. head Trygve Lie, humanitarian Albert Schweitzer, pacifist Bertrand Russell, and former first lady Eleanor Roosevelt. The appeal called for nuclear disarmament.

The goals of SANE were broadened in 1959 to include universal disarmament (including conventional weaponry), transition to a peace-based economy, and reliance upon the United Nations as the world's best peace-keeping institution. During the 1960 presidential election SANE inaugurated an intense disarmament campaign with a huge rally at the old Madison Square Garden in New York City. Highlighting the event were such speakers as Eleanor Roosevelt; Norman Thomas; Alfred M. Landon, the 1936 presidential nominee of the Republican Party*; Walter Reuther, president of the United Automobile Workers of America; and Governor G. Mennen Williams (D-Mich.).

During the Cuban missile crisis in 1962, SANE ran two appeals in the *New York Times* urging President John F. Kennedy to allow U.N. mediation to resolve the issue. SANE was also critical of Kennedy's decision to continue the atmospheric testing of nuclear devices simply because the Soviets were continuing to do so. SANE likewise criticized the inadequacy of America's civil defense program. Once the Soviet Union and the United States had negotiated a limited test ban treaty (1963) abolishing the atmospheric testing of atomic and hydrogen bombs, SANE conducted a massive campaign to secure Senate ratification.

SANE began opposing U.S. involvement in Vietnam in 1964 and was one of the first anti-war groups to organize protest demonstrations. It opposed the renomination of President Lyndon B. Johnson in 1968 and instead endorsed the presidential candidacy of Senator Eugene McCarthy (D-Minn.). Its anti-Vietnam war activities culminated in the formation of the Coalition on National Priorities and Military Policy. Pacifists and advocates of universal disarmament within SANE also agitated for an end to the MIRV (multiple independently targeted reentry vehicles) program, which was geared to enhance the destructive power of the intercontinental ballistic missiles.

During the 1970s SANE encouraged continuation of the SALT (Strategic Arms Limitation Treaty) talks, favored détente with the Soviet Union, and advocated dismantling of the so-called military-industrial complex. It was one of the first national organizations to endorse Senator George McGovern (D-S.D.) for the presidency because he promised an immediate end to U.S. participation in the Vietnam war. SANE also protested French hydrogen bomb tests in the South Pacific and more recently has been critical of the Soviet Union for its ill treatment of dissenters.

Membership in SANE, representative of the more intellectual and liberal-left-wing spectrum of American politics, has fallen off markedly since the end of the Vietnam war, the diminution of the cold war, and the signing of Strategic Arms Limitation Treaties. Current national headquarters is in Washington, D.C. (since 1960), with Sanford Gottlieb serving as executive director. SANE maintains a speakers' bureau, provides videotapes for television, and publishes a monthly magazine, *Sane World*.

**SAVE OUR CHILDREN.** See Protect America's Children.

**SENIOR CITIZENS.** See National Council of Senior Citizens.

**SHARE OUR WEALTH MOVEMENT (SOWM).** Founded in 1934 at Washington, D.C., by Senator Huey P. Long of Louisiana for the purpose of redistributing the nation's wealth. Dubbed the "Kingfish" for the dictatorial manner in which he ran Louisiana as governor, Long's political philosophy combined rural radicalism, neopopulism, and quasi-socialist ideas to propose simplistic solutions to alleviate the complex social and economic problems caused by the Great Depression.

Planning to run for the presidency in 1936, Long's political power was based on thousands of Share Our Wealth clubs. His platform called for guaranteed minimum incomes of five thousand dollars annually for each family; old-age pensions; public works to end unemployment; cash bonuses for veterans of World War I; a free homestead for those wishing to farm; and other social benefits to be provided by the federal government. He also proposed to confiscate all fortunes over $5 million and inaugurate a future tax rate that would prevent the accumulation of fortunes over $1 million thereafter. His slogan was "Everyman a King" (which also was the title of a book he wrote).

In reaction to Long's radical SOWM, President Franklin D. Roosevelt shifted to the left in 1935. The New Deal sought to undermine the movement by supporting such measures as Social Security, the National Labor Relations Act, providing more relief to the needy, enlarging the Works Progress Administration, and enacting a "soak the rich" tax act.

When it appeared that Senator Long might become the presidential nominee of the Union Party,* Democrats* were duly concerned lest the left-of-center voters be lost in 1936. Long, however, met a sudden death in 1935 at the hands of an assassin, Dr. Carl A. Weis, the son-in-law of a political foe seeking revenge. Senator Long, who had built a political empire by dubious, demagogic methods, wrote two books: *Everyman a King* (1933) and *My First Years in the White House* (1935). His controversial career prompted novelist Robert Penn Warren to fictionalize his life in *All the King's Men*, subsequently made into a widely viewed movie. Where some contemporary observers saw Long as a dangerous demagogue, others viewed him as a true Populist-type champion of the common people against the power of the plutocrats.

For more information, see Allan P. Sindler, *Huey Long's Louisiana* (1956); T. Harry Williams, *Huey Long* (1969); and Hugh D. Graham, ed., *Huey Long* (1970).

**SIERRA CLUB (SC).** Founded in 1892 at San Francisco by the renowned naturalist John Muir for the purpose of promoting the preservation of wilderness areas. Muir popularized the concept of preservation through such books as *The Mountains of California* (1894), *Our National Parks* (1901), *The Yosemite* (1912), and *A Thousand-Mile Walk to the Gulf* (1916). Muir influenced Theodore Roosevelt, who as president did much to foster conservation and the preservation of wilderness areas by creating national parks. The SC annually presents the John Muir Award to individuals who contribute to the preservation of wilderness areas.

From its original 182 charter members, all located in California, the SC today has forty-two regional chapters with an active membership of over 135,000. It has become the most respected and influential organization involved in the ecology movement. It concerns itself with problems related to forest management; energy; air and water pollution; mining; environmental controls; transportation; water resources; conservation; wildlife preservation; and the safeguarding of wilderness areas. The SC helped bring the National Park Service and the National Forest Service into existence. Through its efforts many national parks were created, including Kings Canyon, Olympic Redwoods, and North Cascades.

Currently the SC has permanent committees dealing with Economics; Energy; Environmental Education; Environmental Research; Forest Practices; International Environment; Mountaineering; National Land Use; National Water Resources; Native American Issues; Outings; Population; Wilderness; and Wildlife and Endangered Species. Through publications, films, and conferences, the SC seeks to inform the public on the need to conserve natural resources and preserve wilderness areas.

The SC is an effective lobby relative to Congress. It was instrumental in securing passage of such significant legislation as the Wilderness Act of 1964 and the Wild and Scenic Rivers Act of 1968. By helping to secure enactment of the Alaskan Native Claims Settlement Act of 1971, it ensured the establishment in that region of twelve national parks, including reserves, wilderness areas, and monuments. Through its Legal Defense Fund, the SC has initiated court suits to seek enforcement of or compliance with laws aimed at protecting the ecosystem. It has joined with other organizations having similar goals, such as the National Parks Association, Izaak Walton League, Wilderness Society, and the National Audubon Society, to form the Natural Resources Council of America. The council coordinates lobbying activities in promoting federal action in the fields of conservation or preservation. This type of concerted action has brought specific results with regard to laws protecting endangered species of wildlife.

National headquarters for the SC is located in San Francisco. Current executive director is J. Michael McClosky. The SC issues educational materials and since 1949 has held an annual Wilderness Conference. The SC also serves as a nongovernment organization cooperating with the United Nations. SC publications include *National News Report* (weekly), *Sierra Club Bulletin* (monthly), and *Ascent: Sierra Club Mountaineering* (annual).

For more information, see Holway R. Jones, *John Muir and the Sierra Club* (1964).

**SILVER REPUBLICAN PARTY (SRP).** Founded in 1896 at St. Louis, Missouri, by Senator Henry Moore Teller of Colorado and a group of Silver Republicans who bolted the national convention of the Republican Party* when it rejected a plank calling for free and unlimited coinage of silver. Sometimes called the National Silver Republican Party or the National Silver Party, it was made up of dissidents from the regular GOP who represented the silver interests of the West. In many ways it was the political arm of the American Bimetallic League* (ABL), which represented the western silver mine owners who provided SRP with funds for campaign purposes. The ABL had actually created the American Bimetallic Party early in 1896 at Washington, D.C., in case silverites had no candidates for whom to vote.

The SRP platform was a one-issue document demanding remonetization of silver while denouncing the gold standard. Meeting simultaneously with the nominating convention of the Populist Party* (also held in St. Louis), the SRP also nominated William Jennings Bryan for the presidency. Since Bryan previously had been chosen as the standard-bearer of the Democratic Party,* this action by the SRP created a Democratic-Populist-Silver Republican fusion ticket united in the cause of silver.

With no permanent state or local organizations, the SRP served primarily as a source of money and speakers during the course of the campaign. Following the defeat of William Jennings Bryan in 1896, the SRP disbanded. Senator Teller became a silver Democrat and supported Bryan for the presidency again in 1900. Most of the SRP's following, however, returned to the ranks of the GOP.

For more information, see Elmer Ellis, "Silver Republicans in 1896," *Mississippi Valley Historical Review* 18 (1932): 519; Elmer Ellis, *Henry Moore Teller* (1941); Stanley L. Jones, *The Presidential Election of 1896* (1964); and Lawrence Goodwyn, *Democratic Promise* (1976).

**SILVER REPUBLICANS.** See Silver Republican Party.

**SILVER SHIRTS.** See Christian Party.

**SINGLE TAX CLUBS.** See Single Tax Movement.

**SINGLE TAX MOVEMENT (STM).** Founded in 1879 at San Francisco by Henry George for the purpose of promoting his single tax plan. Frequently named Single Tax Clubs or Land Labor Clubs, the STM attracted thousands who had read George's *Progress and Poverty* (1879), in which he maintained that rising land values gave landlords an "unearned increment" that should be taxed. It was his contention that this single tax on land would provide sufficient revenue to run government so that no other taxes would be needed. George also opposed monopolies and advocated federal ownership of utilities.

The STM, though not effective in promoting George's single tax idea, did give impetus to economic reform. By calling attention to the gap between those who lived in poverty and the wealthy who contributed little in the way of taxes, the STM inspired social reformers to seek antitrust legislation and the redistribution of the national wealth by taxation. Significant individuals influenced by the STM included George Bernard Shaw, Sidney Webb, John Dewey, Clarence Darrow, Tom L. Johnson, Bolton Hall, Hazen S. Pingree, and Hamlin Garland. The STM was superseded by the formation of the Populist Party* in 1892, and by the time of George's death in 1897 the movement ceased to exist as a national political entity. Currently a few private Single Tax Clubs exist, mostly in the state of California.

For more information, see Steven B. Cord, *Henry George: Dreamer or Realist?* (1965).

**SOCIAL DEMOCRACY OF AMERICA.** See Social Democratic Party of America.

**SOCIAL DEMOCRATIC FEDERATION (SDF).** Founded in 1936 at New York City as a result of an ideological split and personality clashes within the Socialist Party of America* (SPA). A dissenting group led by Mayor Jasper McLevy of Bridgeport, Connecticut, and Algernon Lee, president of the Rand School of Social Science (and SDF's first chairperson), were prime movers in the withdrawal movement. The small McLevy-Lee faction regarded the leadership provided by Norman Thomas, SPA's presidential candidate, as ineffectual.

At its first convention at Pittsburgh in 1937 the SDF called upon all socialists, labor unions, and progressives to form a major third party. When this did not materialize, the SDF supported independent candidates. In New York they endorsed candidates of both the American Labor Party* and Liberal Party.*

Following World War II the SDF gradually disintegrated. Its membership, never large, had only a minor impact on the American political scene. With members of SDF gradually gravitating back to the parent SPA, by 1956 the two organizations merged. In 1972 the Union of Democratic Socialists-Jewish Socialist Verband merged with the SDF-SPA to form the Social Democrats U.S.A. The latter, with a token membership, maintains a headquarters in New York City, but its political activity (mainly educational) is rather limited in scope.

**SOCIAL DEMOCRATIC PARTY OF AMERICA (SDPA).** Founded in 1897 at Chicago by Eugene V. Debs at a convention of the American Railway Union, of which he was president. Originally called the Social Democracy of America, its name was changed to SDPA in 1898 following reorganization by Debs and Victor L. Berger, editor of the *Wisconsin Vorwärts*.

In 1900 the SDPA nominated Debs for the presidency (he was also endorsed by a dissident group called the Socialist Labor Party* [SLP]) with Job Harriman of California as his vice-presidential running mate. The SDPA platform called for an end to the "system of wage slavery"; public ownership of the means of production; federally financed public works for the jobless; unemployment, accident, and old-age insurance; equal rights for women; and "abolition of war and the introduction of international arbitration."

The Debs-Harriman ticket polled 87,814 popular and no electoral votes. This poor showing prompted Debs in 1901 to merge the SDPA with a faction of the SLP headed by Morris Hillquit (a Jewish intellectual and socialist theoretician) to form the Socialist Party of America.*

For further information, see Ira Kipnis, *The American Socialist Movement, 1897-1912* (1952), and Ray Ginger, *Eugene V. Debs: A Biography* (1962).

**SOCIAL DEMOCRATIC WORKINGMEN'S PARTY.** See Socialist Labor Party.

**SOCIALIST LABOR PARTY (SLP).** Founded in 1877 at Newark, New Jersey, by a group of delegates representing the Social Democratic Workingmen's Party. The latter organization, sometimes referred to as the Workingmen's Party of America, had been formed in 1874 at New York City by a conglomeration of small socialist (Marxian) groups. The SLP represents the first nationally organized Marxist party in America and the second oldest of the so-called third parties (the Prohibition Party* is the oldest).

The SLP's initial platform declared its prime purpose to be that of attaining the "industrial emancipation of labor, which must be achieved by the working classes themselves, independent of all other parties but their own." Philip Van Patten of the Knights of Labor was its first national secretary. Starting with fewer than three thousand members, the SLP always remained relatively small because of its doctrinaire stance and limited appeal to American workers.

From 1890 to his death in 1914, the fortunes of the SLP were controlled by the domineering Marxist theoretician Daniel DeLeon, a lawyer who had lectured on international law at the Columbia Law School and was editor of the *Daily People*. Sarcastically dubbed "the Pope" by his enemies within the socialist movement (and there were many), he pontificated on Marxian ideology (subsequently labeled "DeLeonism") in such works as *Socialist Reconstruction of Society* (1905) and *As to Politics* (1907).

Considered an original thinker by some and merely adept at synthesizing by others, DeLeon initially sought to interpret the teachings of Karl Marx so as to make them relevant to the American political system. Later he seemed to incorporate elements of both anarchism and syndicalism into his socialist theory. DeLeon himself ran unsuccessfully for governor of New York on the SLP ticket in 1890 and 1902. Thereafter he was more concerned with militant trade unionism as the revolutionary mechanism that would permit the proletariat to perform its supposed historic mission of transforming the capitalistic system into a classless society.

The SLP named its first presidential slate in 1892 with a ticket consisting of Simon Wing of Massachusetts for president and Charles H. Matchett of New York for vice-president. The platform called for the creation of a "cooperative commonwealth," control of the means of production by the people, and "abolition of the Presidency, Vice-Presidency, and Senate." Government was to consist of an "Executive Board" to be elected by the people, and "abolition of the Presidency, Vice-Presidency, and Senate." be the "only legislative body." Running on this unusual platform, the Wing-Matchett ticket attracted only 21,173 popular votes. (See table 10.)

**TABLE 10 Socialist Labor Party Presidential Candidates and Votes, 1892-1976**

| YEAR | CANDIDATE | TOTAL POPULAR VOTE |
| --- | --- | --- |
| 1892 | Simon Wing | 21,173 |
| 1896 | Charles H. Matchett | 36,356 |
| 1900 | Joseph F. Malloney | 40,900 |
| 1904 | Charles H. Corregan | 31,249 |
| 1908 | August Gillhaus | 14,021 |
| 1912 | Arthur E. Reimer | 29,374 |
| 1916 | Arthur E. Reimer | 15,284 |
| 1920 | William W. Cox | 30,418 |
| 1924 | Frank T. Johns | 28,368 |
| 1928 | Verne L. Reynolds | 21,608 |
| 1932 | Verne L. Reynolds | 34,028 |
| 1936 | John W. Aiken | 12,790 |
| 1940 | John W. Aiken | 14,883 |
| 1944 | Edward A. Teichert | 45,336 |
| 1948 | Edward A. Teichert | 29,038 |
| 1952 | Eric Hass | 30,250 |
| 1956 | Eric Hass | 44,300 |
| 1960 | Eric Hass | 47,521 |
| 1964 | Eric Hass | 44,697 |
| 1968 | Henning A. Blomen | 55,591 |
| 1972 | Louis Fischer | 53,811 |
| 1976 | Jules Levin | 9,616 |

In 1896, the high tide of populism (an indigenous American radicalism), the SLP nominee for the presidency was Charles H. Matchett, the previous vice-presidential candidate. Paired with him was Matthew Maguire of New Jersey as the choice for vice-president. The platform proposed the "abolition of classes, the restoration of the land and of all the means of production, transportation, and distribution to the people as a collective body." Also demanded were such reforms as a progressive income tax, compulsory education for children under fourteen years of age, public works for the unemployed, abolition of the veto power (for governors as well as the president), and universal suffrage (without regard to color, creed, or sex). The Matchett-Maguire team polled 36,356 popular votes.

The national ticket of 1900 consisted of Joseph F. Malloney of Massachusetts for president and Valentine Remmel of Pennsylvania for vice-president. The SLP's platform asserted that through the "natural course of social evolution" it was time for the workers to organize into a "class-conscious body" to ensure the establishment of a "cooperative commonwealth." It insisted that the "machinery of government must be owned and controlled by the whole people" so that capitalism might be destroyed and the workers liberated from wage slavery imposed by plutocratic capitalists. The Malloney-Remmell ticket drew 40,900 votes. This was an increase from the previous presidential election but still constituted only 0.29 percent of the popular vote cast in 1900.

SLP made few converts to its brand of socialism after the turn of the century. Its 1904 presidential ticket, made up of Charles H. Corregan of New York and William W. Cox of Illinois, polled a meager 31,249 votes. The SLP nominees in 1908, August Gillhaus of New York for president and Donald L. Munro of Virginia for vice-president, attracted a scant 14,021 votes. The short and relatively identical platforms of those two elections reiterated the need for workers to overthrow the capitalistic system, but it obviously appealed little to either organized or unorganized labor in America.

In 1912, during the peak of the Progressive movement, the SLP nominated Arthur E. Reimer of Massachusetts for president and August Gillhaus (the previous presidential candidate) for vice-president. The platform that year importuned that "to imply the Social Revolution with the ballot only, without the means to enforce the ballot's fiat, in case of Reaction's [capitalism's] attempt to override it, is to fire blank cartridges at a foe." It implored the working class, as the "historically revolutionary element," to initiate creation of the "Social or Industrial Commonwealth." Deaf to the SLP's plea, the electorate delivered the party 29,374 votes (0.2 percent of the total cast).

During the presidential election of 1916, when the major parties were concerned about such issues as preparedness and whether to intervene in

World War I on the side of the Allies, the SLP ignored the war and continued to sound its doctrinaire call for the working class to lead in the overthrow of capitalism. Its presidential ticket of Arthur E. Reimer of Massachusetts and Caleb Harrison of Illinois managed to draw but 15,284 votes. The 1920 platform blamed World War I on the capitalists and entreated workers to join the Worker's International Industrial Union to bring about the "social ownership of the means of production" so that it might be "industrially administered by the workers." The SLP's nominees in this election were William W. Cox of Missouri for president and August Gillhaus, once again, for vice-president. The Cox-Gillhaus team polled a disappointingly small vote of 30,418.

The vote tallies in 1924 and 1928 were equally insignificant. The 1924 platform insisted that the capitalist system had to be supplanted by a "Socialist Industrial Republic" if workers were to receive the full products of their labor. The SLP's nominees, Frank T. Johns of Oregon for president and Verne L. Reynolds of New York for vice-president, drew a slim 0.1 percent of the popular vote with their total of 28,368. The 1928 platform repeated its belief that true to "sociologic laws" the "proletariat is awakening to its consciousness of class, and thereby to the perception of its historic mission." Unaware of Marxian dialectics, the American worker ignored the fact that the "Socialist or Industrial Government" was "throbbing for birth." The SLP's standard-bearers that year were Verne L. Reynolds and Jeremiah D. Crawley of New York. Only 21,608 voters supported them at the polls.

With the nation in the throes of the Great Depression, the year 1932 seemed propitious for the SLP. Carrying the presidential banner once more was Verne L. Reynolds, with John W. Aiken of Massachusetts as his vice-presidential partner. The platform took note that a "crucial period of history is facing humanity today." Without a doubt, it went on, a "state of social dissolution is now upon us." The time was ripe for workers to perform their historic mission of initiating the advent of a "Socialist or Industrial Commonwealth of Emancipated Labor." Despite the economic crisis facing capitalism, the SLP national ticket polled a minute protest vote of 34,028 (0.09 percent).

According to the SLP platform of 1936, the New Deal policy of "creating artificial scarcity" was appalling. It announced once more that the "hour of Social Revolution has struck." Capitalism was depicted as a decaying system and all workers were invited to embrace the SLP with its "progressive and revolutionary program." Nominated for the presidency was John W. Aiken (the previous vice-presidential candidate) and for the vice-presidency, Emil F. Teichert of New York. As vote getters, their 12,790 total made them dismal failures.

Taking cognizance of the war overseas in 1940, the SLP advised

Americans that "capitalism means war." The platform stated its oft-announced belief that only through the creation of a socialist industrial union (to be run by an "Industrial Union Congress") would true peace and prosperity ensue. Other planks castigated the American Federation of Labor and the Congress of Industrial Organizations as "agencies of capitalism," and condemned New Dealers as "political henchmen of the capitalist class." Leading the SLP ticket once more was John W. Aiken, this time paired with Aaron M. Orange of New York. This team drew a weak 14,883 votes at the polls.

Undaunted by its dwindling numbers, the SLP offered voters a presidential slate in 1944 consisting of Edward A. Teichert of Pennsylvania and Arla A. Albaugh of Ohio. The platform attributed the cause of World War II to the "prewar struggle among the capitalist powers for the markets and resources of the world." It reproached the Roosevelt administration for ostensibly planning to "continue wartime controls into the postwar era, the establishment of permanent military conscription, the anti-strike laws, the creation of a huge State bureaucracy, and the spread of anti-Semitism and racism." Promising to initiate "revolutionary change," Americans were asked to join in the establishment of the "Socialist Brotherhood of Man, the Republic of Peace, Plenty, and International Fraternity." The Teichert-Albaugh duo won 45,336 popular votes.

Despite the small number of votes won four years before, Edward A. Teichert headed the SLP presidential ticket once more in 1948, paired this time with Stephen Emery of New York. The platform predicted the failure of the United Nations because it was "built on the foundation of capitalist dry rot." Americans were warned of imminent war with the Soviet Union due to the evil machinations of the capitalist-controlled press, radio, and motion pictures. The only way to avoid war, it claimed, was to embrace socialism, since "Socialism alone supplies a sound foundation for peace and for the free cultural and material intercourse among the peoples of the world." This proposed solution to the cold war netted Teichert and Emery 29,038 votes.

With Eric Hass of New York and Stephen Emery, a repeater from the previous election, as the SLP's presidential slate in 1952, the platform categorized the Korean war as "senseless war to all but the capitalists and Russian imperialist interests that profit from it." Other planks lambasted U.S. militarism; persecution of Communists; the "Bureaucratic despotism masquerading as 'Marxist' in the Soviet Union"; and the "reformist outfits, such as the British Labor Party, falsely claiming to be 'Socialist.' " Hass and Emery won 30,250 popular votes (0.05 percent).

Indefatigable in the cause of the SLP, Eric Hass again carried the presidential banner in 1956 but with a new running mate, Georgia Cozzini of Wisconsin. The platform decried the existence of the hydrogen bomb;

labeled détente between the United States and Soviet Union as an accommodation between "two rival imperialisms" and reminded voters that "socialism is the answer to all social problems." Workers were informed also that the socialism advocated by the SLP was not the type practiced in the Soviet Union. SLP's version was defined as being conceived by Karl Marx and "developed" by Daniel DeLeon, the "great American Marxist." The ticket polled only 44,300 popular votes.

In what seemed a hopeless attempt to win over the American electorate, Eric Hass and Georgia Cozzini as the presidential ticket in 1960 once again expounded the virtues of the SLP. In its platform, the SLP boldly claimed, "Socialism is the answer to all our grave and pressing social problems": economic depression, poverty, unemployment, racial prejudice, crime, juvenile delinquency, mental illness, alcoholism, dope addiction, and "other manifestations of capitalist decadence." The ticket won 47,521 votes.

Dedicated to the cause of socialism but nevertheless representing what amounted to a token presidential candidate, Eric Hass again placed the SLP standard on his shoulder in 1964. This time he was paired with Henning A. Blomen. Together they drew 44,697 votes. Blomen took a new partner in 1968, George S. Taylor, but the 55,591 popular votes received constituted a minute 0.07 percent of the total cast.

Reflecting very little growth, even during the radical, anti-Vietnam war era, the SLP continued to nominate candidates for the presidency and vice-presidency. In 1972 Louis Fischer headed the ticket with Genevieve Gunderson slated as the vice-presidential nominee. This team polled 53,811 (again 0.07 percent). The 1976 presidential slate consisted of Jules Levin for president and Constance Blomen for vice-president. Their popular vote was 9,616 (0.01 percent).

The SLP has attracted very few converts to its Marxist-DeLeon banner. In 1980 it nominated no presidential ticket. Present national headquarters is located in Palo Alto, California (having moved from Brooklyn, New York, in 1975). The current national secretary-treasurer, Nathan Karp, serves a dozen or so state chapters with fewer than three thousand permanent members. The SLP publishes a newspaper, *Weekly People*.

For more information, see Don K. McKee, "Daniel DeLeon: A Reappraisal," *Labor History* 1 (Fall 1960): 264–297, and Arnold Peterson, *Daniel DeLeon: Socialist Architect* (1941).

**SOCIALIST PARTY OF AMERICA (SPA).** Founded in 1901 at Indianapolis, Indiana, by a group of delegates representing the Social Democratic Party of America* and the anti-DeLeon faction of the Socialist Labor Party.* The prime mover in this fusion movement was Eugene V. Debs, former president of the American Railway Union. Important members included Victor L. Berger, editor of the *Social Democratic Herald*; George D. Herren, clergyman and Christian socialist; Morris Hillquit, a socialist theoretician and future author of *Socialism in Theory and Practice* (1912); and Upton Sinclair, muckraker and soon to become famous for his work *The Jungle* (1906).

In 1904 the SPA nominated a presidential ticket consisting of Eugene V. Debs for president and Benjamin Hanford of New York as his vice-presidential running mate. The platform promised that through its acceptance of socialism, the American people would be rescued from the "assault of capitalism upon the liberty of the individual." A host of planks called for such reforms as woman suffrage; old-age pensions; shorter workday and higher wages; accident, health, unemployment insurance; public ownership of the means of transportation, communication, and exchange; inheritance and graduated income taxes; abolition of child labor; prohibition on the use of force to break strikes; initiative, referendum, and recall; and municipal home rule. All of these were to be achieved with the establishment of a socialist "cooperative commonwealth." Under the SPA banner Debs and Hanford drew 402,489 (2.98 percent) of the popular and no electoral votes. (See table 11.)

**TABLE 11 Socialist Party of America Presidential Candidates and Votes, 1904-1980**

| YEAR | CANDIDATE | TOTAL POPULAR VOTE |
|------|-----------|--------------------|
| 1904 | Eugene V. Debs | 402,489 |
| 1908 | Eugene V. Debs | 420,390 |
| 1912 | Eugene V. Debs | 900,369 |
| 1916 | Allan L. Benson | 589,924 |
| 1920 | Eugene V. Debs | 913,664 |
| 1924 | Robert La Follette | 4,822,856 |
| 1928 | Norman Thomas | 266,453 |
| 1932 | Norman Thomas | 881,951 |
| 1936 | Norman Thomas | 187,785 |
| 1940 | Norman Thomas | 116,827 |
| 1944 | Norman Thomas | 80,518 |
| 1948 | Norman Thomas | 138,973 |
| 1952 | Darlington Hoopes | 20,065 |
| 1956 | Darlington Hoopes | 2,044 |
| 1980 | David McReynolds | 6,720 |

The same ticket carried the SPA's standard in 1908. The platform repeated much of the previous document but contained some added planks demanding public works for the jobless; election of judges; abolition of the U.S. Senate; elimination of the U.S. Supreme Court's power to nullify legislation enacted by Congress; and revision of the procedure to alter the

Constitution so that a majority of the states could ratify an amendment. Although attracting more votes than four years before, 420,390, the total was actually less in percentage (2.82 percent).

Becoming the perennial presidential nominee of the SPA, Debs was paired with Emil Seidel of Wisconsin in 1912. The platform reaffirmed the necessity for public ownership of the means of production, transportation, communication, and banking. It added planks relative to the need for conservation; federal loans (without interest) to states and municipalities for public works; a five and one-half day work week; abolition of the monopoly ownership of patents; elimination of the president's veto power; election of the president and vice-president by direct vote of the people; suffrage for the District of Columbia; extension of democratic government to all U.S. territories; creation of a bureau of health; the abolition of all federal district and circuit courts; curbing the power of courts to issue injunctions; free administration of the law; and the calling of a convention to revise the U.S. Constitution. Although Debs and his running mate polled 900,369 or 5.99 percent of the popular vote, this was the election that saw both Woodrow Wilson (who won the presidency) and Theodore Roosevelt, the nominee of the Progressive Party,* outdraw Republican* incumbent William Howard Taft. The results indicated the preference of American voters for Progressive-oriented candidates over both the conservative and radical alternatives.

The national election of 1916 revolved around key issues such as preparedness and possible entry into World War I on the side of the Allies. The SPA platform of that year claimed that all Americans should join with the Socialists in presenting a "united front in the fight against preparedness and militarism." It called for a referendum to declare war, proposed that the United States summon a "congress of neutral nations to mediate between the belligerent powers," and repeated demands for social and economic reforms. SPA's presidential nominee, Allan L. Benson of New York, was teamed with George R. Kirkpatrick of New Jersey. Their vote total dropped to 589,924 (3.18 percent) in the popular column and never again reached their high tide of 5.99 percent as they had done in 1912.

Although Eugene V. Debs was sentenced to the federal penitentiary at Atlanta for his anti-war activities, he nevertheless accepted the SPA presidential nomination in 1920. His vice-presidential running mate was Seymour Stedman of Illinois. The platform severely censured the Wilson administration for its suppression of civil liberties, censorship of the press, deportation of alien radicals (associated with the president's zeal in prosecution of the war), and the notorious Palmer raids. It demanded "full civil, political, industrial, and educational rights" for blacks; abrogation of the League of Nations (to be replaced with an international parliament democratically elected); full pardons for those jailed under the provisions of the Espionage Act; and recognition of the Irish Republic as an independent nation. Debs and Stedman polled a surprising 913,664 popular votes, but this constituted only 3.42 percent of the total cast in an election that saw women vote for the first time and allowed Warren G. Harding to win the presidency in a landslide.

When Senator Robert M. La Follette (R-Wis.) resurrected the Progressive Party in 1924 and ran for the presidency with Senator Burton K. Wheeler (D-Mont.), the SPA endorsed them, albeit in a losing cause. Eugene V. Debs might well have led the ticket again four years hence, but he died in 1926. The SPA's presidential nomination for 1928 thus fell to Norman M. Thomas, who then would become its perennial candidate every four years until 1952. Thomas was a former Presbyterian clergyman, a leader in the Fellowship of Reconciliation,* a founder of the American Civil Liberties Union,* a codirector of the League for Industrial Democracy,* for a time an associate editor of the *Nation* (1921-1922), and previously an SPA candidate for such offices as governor of New York and mayor of New York City.

At the helm of the SPA and as its presidential aspirant in 1928, Thomas was paired with James H. Maurer (president of the Pennsylvania Federation of Labor) as his vice-presidential running mate. In a campaign that heard GOP candidate Herbert C. Hoover promise to eradicate poverty, the SPA platform renewed its call for basic social and economic reforms; a broad program of nationalization; public electrical power; enactment of an anti-lynching law; encouragement of cooperatives; withdrawal of U.S. armed forces from Nicaragua; cancellation of all war debts; independence for the Philippines; diplomatic recognition of the Soviet Union; and negotiation of multilateral treaties outlawing war. Using radio for the first time, Thomas sought not only to revitalize the SPA but to reawaken public interest in socialism. Although commanding considerable respect among intellectuals, Thomas never attracted a mass following. He and Maurer received 266,453 (0.72 percent) popular votes in an election that witnessed the triumph of Iowa-born Herbert Hoover over Governor Al Smith of New York.

The combination of Thomas and Maurer again did battle for the SPA in the election of 1932. Depicting the Great Depression as the "breakdown of the capitalist system," the platform offered socialism to the American people as the way to save the nation from total economic collapse. It demanded federally sponsored relief; public works; unemployment, health, accident, and old-age insurance; protection of the rights of workers to bargain collectively; government aid to farmers and home owners; repeal of prohibition; U.S. entrance into the League of Nations and World Court; prohibition of the sales of munitions to foreign countries; and "reduction of armaments, leading to total disarmament." Despite a vigorous campaign in which the SPA ticket was predicted to pull over two million votes, Thomas and

Maurer actually polled 881,951 (a little over 2 percent of the total vote cast). It was obvious that if the SPA could not register a massive protest vote in the depths of the depression, it was never going to be a major third party in the United States.

After 1933 the SPA had internal squabbles resulting first from the death of Morris Hillquit, longtime national secretary, and second, from its decision to invite into its ranks Communists and radical left-wingers of all persuasions. Norman Thomas, however, denounced Father Charles Coughlin and Dr. Francis Townsend; refused to accept Earl Browder's invitation to run with Thomas on a fusion SPA and Communist Party of the United States of America* presidential ticket; and in 1937 led a move to expel disruptive Trotskyites from the SPA.

In 1934 Norman Thomas ran as the SPA candidate for the U.S. Senate and pulled a respectable 194,952 votes in a losing cause. This prompted him to accept again with optimism the SPA's presidential nomination in 1936. His vice-presidential running mate was George A. Nelson, head of the Wisconsin Farmers Union. The 1936 platform asserted that under the "capitalist New Deal America has drifted increasingly toward insecurity, suppression, and war." It described the Japanese seizure of Manchuria and Italy's invasion of Ethiopia as "examples of the forces at work under capitalism." Its anti-war plank declared vehemently, "Not a penny, not a man to the military arms of the Government." Other planks called for continuation of public works by the Works Progress Administration at union wage rates; passage of an American youth act (to provide for educational and economic needs); establishment of a thirty-hour work week; and guaranteed cost of production for farmers. In reacting to claims by pro-Roosevelt supporters that FDR's New Deal had already embraced much of the domestic program advocated by the SPA, Thomas retorted, "Roosevelt did not carry out the Socialist platform unless he carried it out on a stretcher." In a race that saw President Roosevelt overwhelm Republican Alfred M. Landon and William Lemke of the Union Party,* Thomas and Nelson ran far behind with 187,785 (0.41 percent) popular and no electoral votes. Again, the American public rejected a socialist alternative when offered the welfare state of the New Deal.

The 1940 platform of the SPA boasted that "the best of what goes by the New Deal name . . . were first demanded by the Socialist Party." While welcoming the "defeat of Hitler," the anti-war plank insisted in isolationist terms, "To drive war out of the world, we must first keep America out of war!" The day after the SPA national nominating convention, which once again selected Norman Thomas as its presidential nominee paired with Maynard C. Krueger (a professor of economics at the University of Chicago), Hitler's armies invaded Denmark and Norway. The national executive committee issued a denunciation of "Hitler's crime" but nevertheless called for U.S. neutrality. Thomas and Krueger drew 116,827 (0.23 percent) votes in an election that saw FDR reelected to a third term.

Pearl Harbor created a dilemma for the SPA, since the moral onus for starting the war was on the Japanese. At its 1942 mid-term convention, held at Milwaukee, Norman Thomas sponsored a resolution calling for "critical support" of the war effort by the Socialists. Although modified, this proposal was adopted. Harry Fleischman, editor of the *Socialist Call* and future author of *Norman Thomas, A Biography* (1964), emerged as the new national secretary. As Thomas's campaign manager in two previous elections, he set about preparing for the 1944 presidential election.

Norman Thomas kept in the public eye by criticizing the internment of Japanese-Americans in "relocation centers," publicizing the Katyn Forest massacre by the Soviets of Polish prisoners of war, and demanding that the U.S. amend its immigration law to permit the entry of Jewish refugees. Nominated for a fifth time for the presidency, Thomas ran with a new vice-presidential running mate, Darlington Hoopes, who had served three terms in the Pennsylvania state legislature. The SPA platform outlined the usual socialist proposals; opposed the policy of unconditional surrender; called for postwar aid to war-devastated countries; made an appeal for a permanent peace based upon disarmament of enemy nations, a United States of Europe, and world federation; demanded an end to colonialism, imperialism, and militarism; and supported civil rights for minorities and restoration of peacetime civil liberties. The 80,518 (0.16 percent) popular vote received by Thomas and Hoopes had little effect on the outcome of the presidential race in which FDR won reelection to a fourth term.

In 1948 it appeared that SPA votes might appreciably alter the outcome of the national election in which Harry S. Truman was seeking reelection. Because of the formation of the Progressive Party* and States' Rights Party* (Dixiecrats), it appeared that enough liberal left-of-center and right-wing votes might be drawn away from the Democrats to permit Governor Thomas E. Dewey of New York, the GOP nominee, to win the presidency.

Running for the last time as the SPA presidential candidate, Norman Thomas had yet another vice-presidential partner, Tucker P. Smith, head of the department of economics at Olivet College in Michigan. The platform denounced capitalism but also condemned communism, which it claimed "marches under masked banners." It pledged implementation of a vast program, including expansion of unemployment insurance and Social Security; raising the minimum wage level; a national system of health insurance; federal aid to education; legislation to end racial segregation; public housing; continuation of rent control; repeal of the Taft-Hartley Act; elimination of poll taxes; international control of atomic energy; transformation of the United Nations into a true world government; elimination of all trade barriers; continuation of the Marshall Plan; and assurance that the

Jewish community in Palestine would be given self-government. To the surprise of Thomas, his 138,973 popular votes (0.28 percent) did not prevent Harry Truman from pulling off a "miracle victory" to retain the presidency.

Some wanted Norman Thomas, who was revered as socialism's senior statesman, to run for the presidency once again in 1952. But instead the national convention selected Darlington Hoopes (a previous vice-presidential candidate) as the presidential standard-bearer and Samuel H. Friedman of New York, a longtime party faithful, as his vice-presidential running mate. Thomas, the real titular head of the SPA, did some campaigning but advised SPA to convert itself into an educational organization instead of continuing as an ineffective political party. The platform, written as if it were an apologia for socialism, asked, "What is this Socialism that the American people are asked to fear and reject? It is any form of enterprise where public service cuts out private profit." In a lengthy document the SPA program for domestic and world tranquility was rehearsed in detail, but to the average American voter it sounded far too utopian to be practical. The SPA ticket attracted a paltry 20,065 (0.03 percent) at the polls on election day.

There was debate within the ranks of the depleted SPA as to whether a presidential ticket should even be selected in 1956. It did so reluctantly when Hoopes and Friedman hit the campaign trail, hoping to win enough converts to socialism so as to preserve the life of the dying SPA. The platform pledged the party to build a "new, more democratic society in the United States; a society in which human rights come before property rights; a nation which can take its place in a World Federation of Cooperative Commonwealths which will eliminate war, racial antagonism, hunger, disease, poverty, and oppression." Its presidential slate received a scant 2,044 votes.

After its disastrous showing at the polls, the remaining handful of party faithful decided to fight for the socialist cause in a Fabian role as an educational organization rather than an electoral manner. In 1957 the SPA merged with the Social Democratic Federation* (SDF), and shortly thereafter the SDF absorbed the Independent Socialist League, a small group of ex-Trotskyites led by Max Shachtman. In 1972 the SDF was renamed Social Democrats USA (SD-USA).

When Norman Thomas, the party's grand old leader, died in 1968, leadership gravitated to younger socialists such as Michael Harrington. His *The Other America* (1962) influenced President John F. Kennedy to initiate an anti-poverty program, subsequently carried out by President Lyndon B. Johnson. Harrington worked within the Democratic Party* and in 1969 won a seat in Congress from the Sixth Congressional District in Massachusetts.

Those within the socialist movement who disagreed with the Shachtman-Harrington realignment strategy of working within the Democratic Party formed a Debs Caucus in 1972. Instead of supporting George McGovern for president, as did the Coalition Caucus formed by Harrington, they backed the presidential candidacy of Benjamin Spock of the People's Party.* In 1976 the Debs Caucus named old-time Socialist Frank P. Zeidler, who had been mayor of Milwaukee from 1948 to 1960, as its token presidential candidate instead of supporting Jimmy Carter.

In 1980 the Debs Caucus revived the moribund party founded by Eugene V. Debs and christened it the Socialist Party U.S.A. (SP-USA). Headquartered in Milwaukee, its members met to name a presidential ticket and to write a party platform. Chosen as its presidential nominee was David McReynolds, a pacifist and leader of the Debs Caucus. For its vice-presidential nominee, the SP-USA selected Sister Diane Drufenbrock of the School Sisters of St. Francis. Planks in the platform called for an immediate slash of the military budget of 25 percent with the ultimate goal of disarmament; rent control and price controls on food, housing, and transportation; health care for all citizens; "worker's control of industry"; public ownership of all natural energy resources; decommissioning of all nuclear plants; mass transit; public finance of neighborhood mutual aid societies; 100 percent parity for farm products; collective bargaining; abolition of the CIA; legal rights for lesbians and gays; support for affirmative action programs; ratification of ERA; legalization of victimless crimes; release of prisoners of conscience; an end to the death penalty; unconditional amnesty for all draft resisters and military deserters from the Vietnam period; destruction of all nuclear weapons; withdrawal of all U.S. troops from foreign bases; dissolution of NATO and all military alliances; 1 percent of the U.S. Gross National Product to be allocated to aid Third World development; reconstruction aid to and recognition of the Socialist Republic of Vietnam; opposition to military registration; and increased aid to Vietnam veterans.

On the ballot in eleven states the SP-USA's presidential ticket drew a total vote of 6,720.

Present SD-USA headquarters is located in New York City, with Joan Suall currently serving as national secretary. The organization, while small in number, continues its educational work and endorses candidates deemed worthy of political support. Its current role is that of being the avant-garde for the left wing of the Democratic Party.

For further information, see Morris Hillquit, *History of Socialism in the United States* (1910); Ray Ginger, *The Bending Cross: A Biography of Eugene V. Debs* (1949); Ira Kipnis, *The American Socialist Movement, 1897-1912* (1952); David A. Shannon, *The Socialist Party of America* (1955); Murray B. Seidler, *Norman Thomas, Respectable Radical* (1961); James Weinstein, *The Decline of Socialism in America, 1912-1925* (1967); and Bernard Johnpoll, *Pacifist's Progress* (1970).

**SOCIALIST PARTY-DEMOCRATIC SOCIALIST FEDERATION.** See Socialist Party of America.

**SOCIALIST WORKERS PARTY (SWP).** Founded in 1938 at Chicago by James P. Cannon and other American Trotskyites to promote Marxism as interpreted by the exiled Russian Communist Leon Trotsky (then living in Mexico). At the same time that Joseph Stalin drove Trotsky out of the Soviet Union, the Communist Party of the United States of America* (CPUSA) expelled Trotsky's followers from their organization. This ideological conflict stemmed from Trotsky's advocacy for world revolution and Stalin's insistence of "socialism for one country, viz. the Soviet Union, as the model for others." The SWP therefore was highly critical of Stalinism while strongly advocating the international revolutionary ideology of Marx, Lenin, and Trotsky. Its membership was never large, numbering at most several hundred, due to its rigidly doctrinaire and militant stance. Intraparty squabbles constantly dissipated its already thin ranks as in 1963, when Jim Robertson led a group of dissenters into what was called the Spartacists.

It was not until 1948 that the SWP ran a slate of presidential candidates. Its first presidential nominee was Farrell Dobbs of New York, who had been a resolute opponent of U.S. entry into World War II. Grace Carlson of Minnesota was selected as his vice-presidential running mate. Although the SWP had been placed on the attorney general's list of subversive organizations in 1947, this did not deter it from seeking approval from the American electorate. In Pennsylvania the SWP ticket was listed on the ballot as the Militant Workers Party.

The 1948 platform of the SWP announced boldly that it was flying the banner of "[Karl] Marx and [Friedrich] Engels, [Vladimir Ilyich] Lenin and [Leon] Trotsky, [Eugene V.] Debs and [William D.] Haywood." It denounced rivals such as the CPUSA (dubbed Stalinists); the Socialist Party of America* (from which its members had been expelled in 1937) for seeking to "reform and not to abolish capitalism"; and the Progressive Party,* labeled with disdain the "party of Henry Wallace." Planks called for a six-hour workday, thirty-hour work week; repeal of the Taft-Hartley Act and all other anti-labor legislation; an end to red baiting; civil rights for minorities; elimination of the sales tax; nationalization of all basic industries; substitution of a national referendum for Congress's power to declare war; withdrawal of U.S. troops from foreign soil; and a cessation of cooperation with the United Nations because that international organization was "dominated by despots of every variety and designed to spread the illusion that peace is possible under capitalism." The Dobbs-Carlson ticket drew only 13,614 (0.03 percent) popular votes. (See table 12.)

In 1952 Farrell Dobbs again headed the SWP ticket, this time paired with Myra Tanner Weiss of New York. The platform reacted to the Korean war then in progress by demanding that the United States "get out of Korea." It claimed, "It is not 'Communism' from afar, but reaction directed from Washington that threatens the precious liberties of the American people at home.'' The only hope for the nation, it asserted, was to ''reorganize the wealth of our country on a socialist basis.'' That appeal was rejected as Dobbs and Weiss polled only 10,312 (0.02 percent) votes.

**TABLE 12 Socialist Workers Party Presidential Candidates and Votes, 1948-1980**

| YEAR | CANDIDATE | TOTAL POPULAR VOTE |
|---|---|---|
| 1948 | Farrell Dobbs | 13,614 |
| 1952 | Farrell Dobbs | 10,312 |
| 1956 | Farrell Dobbs | 7,797 |
| 1960 | Farrell Dobbs | 60,166 |
| 1964 | Clifton DeBerry | 32,327 |
| 1968 | Fred Halstead | 41,390 |
| 1972 | Linda Jenness | 37,423 |
| 1976 | Peter Camejo | 91,310 |
| 1980 | Clifton DeBerry | 40,105 |

The same presidential team represented the SWP in 1956, with even less success. Reacting to the death of Joseph Stalin and his subsequent denunciation by Soviet leader Nikita Khrushchev, the platform predicted a ''new upsurge in the world socialist revolution.'' However, it went on to condemn the Soviet Union's new policy of ''peaceful coexistence'' as being harmful to the ''struggle against capitalism'' because it helped ''undermine the revolutionary process which stands as the only effective obstacle to imperialist war.'' This doctrinaire stance at a time when most Americans were happy to see cold war tensions eased netted Dobbs and Weiss only 7,797 votes (0.01 percent of the total cast).

Despite their previous poor showing, Dobbs and Weiss once more carried the standard for the SWP in 1960. The platform now pointed to the Soviet Union as a model for the United States to emulate. ''In less than forty years,'' it claimed, ''planned economy brought Russia from one of the weakest of powers to one of the mightiest.'' It also asserted, ''The demonstrated success of planned economy in underdeveloped countries shows what tremendous benefits it could bring to America.'' Foreign policy planks called for the diplomatic recognition of the People's Republic of China and support for Fidel Castro's Cuban revolution. In the last try by the Dobbs-Weiss slate, they polled 40,166 votes (0.06 percent of the popular vote).

The 1964 SWP national ticket consisted of two New Yorkers, Clifton DeBerry (a militant black) for the presidency and Edward Shaw for the vice-presidency. The platform was critical of American foreign policy insofar as John F. Kennedy sought to thwart Castro's Cuban revolution and Lyndon B. Johnson increased U.S. involvement in Vietnam. DeBerry and Shaw attracted 32,327 votes, a drop from the previous four years.

By 1968 the SWP was deeply involved in the anti-Vietnam war movement. Its platform and presidential candidate, Fred Halstead (who was paired with Paul Boutelle), were highly critical of U.S. involvement in Vietnam and called for immediate American withdrawal. At the polls the SWP slate garnered 41,390 popular votes (0.06 percent of the total cast).

SWP's national ticket in 1972 was headed by feminist Linda Jenness, with Andrew Pulley as her vice-presidential running mate. The platform took a strong stand against the Nixon administration and demanded immediate U.S. withdrawal from Vietnam, support for black nationalism, and "liberation of women, gays, and all oppressed minorities." Jenness and Pulley drew 37,423 votes (0.05 percent).

It was revealed in 1975 by the Rockefeller Commission, an executive commission headed by Vice-President Nelson Rockefeller to investigate the Central Intelligence Agency (CIA), that the CIA had monitored, infiltrated, and kept a file on the SWP as part of its surveillance of "domestic dissent activities" that might ostensibly be linked to attempts by a foreign power to undermine the U.S. war effort. The Political Rights Defense Fund, a New York-based organization established by the Young Socialist Alliance,* provided legal assistance to the SWP in order to expose the activities of the CIA fully. Through the Freedom of Information Act the CIA was forced to disclose the existence of a secret file, "Operation Chaos," which revealed that undercover activity had taken place. The SWP subsequently filed a damage suit against the CIA, which was litigated in the courts.

Believing itself to be a legitimate political party and not an agent of a foreign power or an illegal revolutionary cabal, the SWP ran a presidential ticket in 1976 consisting of two Californians, Peter Camejo and Willie Mae Reid. But its radical stance, evident throughout its existence, did not attract many voters. Only 91,310 (0.1 percent) were registered for the SWP slate.

In 1980 the SWP selected Andrew Pulley, a black steelworker and member of Local 1066 of the United Steelworkers of America, to be its presidential nominee. Matilde Zimmerman, an anti-Vietnam war activist, was chosen to be his vice-presidential running mate. Since Pulley was twenty-nine years old, thus making him ineligible under the Constitution to serve as president, legal technicalities prevented his name from being on the ballot in all the thirty-six states where the SWP ticket was qualified to be listed. In twenty-three states and the District of Columbia Clifton DeBerry was the stand-in for Pulley and in Ohio it was Rick Congress.

The SWP platform promised to abolish draft registration; eliminate the war budget; remove all U.S. planes and ships from the Persian Gulf region; attach cost-of-living escalator clauses to all wages, pensions, and welfare benefits; initiate a thirty-hour work-week for all workers; nationalize the automobile, steel, and oil industries; implement a massive public works program; ratify the Equal Rights Amendment; "jail racist killers" in Atlanta,

Buffalo, Greensboro, and Miami; abolish the Hyde amendment which prevents federal funding for abortions; and shut down all nuclear power plants immediately.

Pulley and Zimmerman canvassed actively for votes and the SWP publication, *The Militant*, was used to disseminate the party's views. Members of the Young Socialist Alliance* also campaigned for the SWP candidates. Final returns gave the SWP presidential tickets only 50,966 votes. (DeBerry 40,105; Pulley 6,032; and Congress 4,829)

Present national headquarters is located in New York City. The current national secretary is Jack Barners. Despite its lack of appeal to the American electorate, the SWP remains small but dedicated to its doctrinaire version of Marxism.

For more information, see James P. Cannon, *The History of American Trotskyism* (1944), and Constance Ashton Myers, *The Prophet's Army: Trotskyists in America, 1928-1941* (1976).

**SOCIETY FOR THE PREVENTION OF CRUELTY TO ANIMALS.** See American Society for the Prevention of Cruelty to Animals.

**SOCIETY OF CHRISTIAN SOCIALISTS (SCS).** Founded in 1889 at Boston by the Reverend W. D. P. Bliss, an Episcopalian clergyman and educator, for the purpose of promoting Christian socialism. Primarily educational in character, with but a very small membership (mostly in the East), the SCS published a journal, the *Dawn* (discontinued in 1900), and sought to propagate a belief in the moral superiority of socialism over that of capitalism.

Bliss, the son of a Christian missionary, was a tireless worker in seeking to equate socialistic reforms with the concept of establishing a Kingdom of God on earth. This so-called Christian Cooperative Commonwealth was to be a virtual utopia where universal affluence and brotherhood abounded. Bliss wrote *Handbook of Socialism* (1895) and *Encyclopedia of Social Reform* (1910). When he died in 1926, his organization became defunct.

**SOCIETY OF SAINT TAMMANY.** See Tammany Hall.

**SOCIETY OF SEPARATIONISTS (SOS).** Founded in 1963 at Austin, Texas, by Madalyn Murray O'Hair for the purpose of promoting atheism and the separation of church and state in the United States. Formed originally as Other Americans, Inc., its name was changed shortly thereafter to SOS. Madalyn Murray O'Hair, the author of *Freedom under Siege* (1974), is president of the SOS. She initiated the suit that culminated in the 1962 decision by the U.S. Supreme Court (*Engel* v. *Vitale*) banning official or required prayers in the public schools.

The SOS, a militant organization, actively seeks to promote total separation of church and state in the United States. Through agitation and court suits it has sought the prevention of astronauts from uttering prayers either in space or while on missions; the abolition of the tax exemption given to churches; the removal of the words "In God We Trust" from U.S. coins; the elimination of religious ceremonies from military activities; the modification of oaths or pledges by eliminating the references to a deity; and the cessation of using Christian symbols on Christmas trees in public buildings.

The SOS prepares programs for radio and television, operates a book club, maintains a library, and sponsors seminars. National headquarters is located in Austin, Texas. Membership totals some thirty thousand. The SOS publishes a monthly, *Poor Richard's Newsletter*, and a quarterly, *American Atheist Magazine*.

**SOCIETY OF TAMMANY.** See Tammany Hall.

**SONS OF LIBERTY (SOL).** Founded in 1765 at Boston, Massachusetts, by Samuel Adams for the purpose of promoting opposition to the Stamp Act enacted by the British Parliament. The name was taken from a phrase used by Isaac Barré, a member of Parliament, who stood in opposition to the Stamp Act and supported the American colonials. Leading American patriots belonging to the secret SOL included John Hancock, Paul Revere, Patrick Henry, John Lamb, Alexander McDougall, James Otis, and John Dickinson.

The SOL agitated for noncompliance to the Stamp Act and harassed those who did pay the taxes levied by this measure. Not averse to using violence, the SOL was responsible for burning the mansion of Governor Thomas Hutchinson of Massachusetts. The SOL helped form the Non-Importation Association in 1768 to oppose the Townshend Acts. Samuel Adams and other members of the SOL also were instrumental in establishing the Committees of Correspondence* to promote their revolutionary views. In 1773 they were participants in the Boston Tea Party and in the forefront of those calling for independence from Great Britain. The demonstrations, protests, and agitation by the SOL helped bring about the American Revolution. Many members of the SOL were instrumental in the calling of a Continental Congress in 1774. The SOL achieved its basic goal in 1776 when the Declaration of Independence was adopted. Adherents to the SOL then became either leaders in government or soldiers in the Continental Army.

For more information, see John C. Miller, *Sam Adams: Pioneer in Propaganda* (1936), and Pauline Maier, *From Resistance to Revolution, 1765-1776* (1972).

**SOUND MONEY DEMOCRATS.** See National Democratic Party (1896).

**SOUTH CAROLINA COLORED DEMOCRATIC PARTY.** See South Carolina Progressive Democratic Party.

**SOUTH CAROLINA PROGRESSIVE DEMOCRATIC PARTY (SCPDP).** Founded in 1944 at Columbia, South Carolina, by John H. McCray for the purpose of promoting civil rights for blacks. McCray was the head of the Negro Citizens Committee and publisher of the *Lighthouse and Informer*. The SCPDP grew out of the Fourth-Term-for-Roosevelt Clubs and was originally called the South Carolina Colored Democratic Party. The name was changed to SCPDP at its first convention.

At its first convention in 1944 at Columbia, South Carolina, 172 delegates voted to implement the decision by the U.S. Supreme Court in *Smith* v. *Allright* (1944), which ruled that white primaries were unconstitutional. A resolution was passed demanding proportionate representation in the regular Democratic Party.* Osceola McKaine, the keynote speaker, told the delegates, "It is to correct these unfair conditions, to give the disinherited men and women of both races in South Carolina some voice in their government, some control over their destinies, and some hope for reasonable security and happiness in the future that the Progressive Democratic Party has been founded." The convention closed by adopting as its official song, "Climbing Jacob's Ladder."

After the convention, an SCPDP delegation, consisting of John McCray, A. J. Clement, Jr., and Dr. Roscoe Wilson, went to Washington, D.C., to meet with Democratic national chairman Robert Hannagan. They received assurances that the Democratic National Committee* would assist them in getting delegate seats to the forthcoming national convention. When blacks were not included in the South Carolina delegation, the SCPDP sent a rival delegation to challenge the seats of the all-white delegation. The national convention refused to seat the SCPDP delegation.

Returning to South Carolina, the SCPDP nominated Osceola McKaine to run for the U.S. Senate in opposition to Governor Olin D. Johnston. McKaine received 4,500 votes in a losing cause. Following this defeat the SCPDP concentrated on getting more blacks registered so as to increase their voting power. Operating in forty-three of South Carolina's forty-six counties, black voter registration was raised from thirty-five hundred to over fifty thousand by 1946. In that year the SCPDP dissolved as an official political party but continued to exist as a black caucus group. This was done on the advice of Thurgood Marshall, then the leading attorney for the National Association for the Advancement of Colored People.* He was pursuing the illegality of all-white delegations in the courts and with national leaders of the Democratic Party.

In 1948 members of the SCPDP black caucus again challenged the regular, all-white South Carolina delegation at the Democratic National Convention. This time a minority report was read on the floor sympathizing with the SCPDP. This action and the adoption of a strong civil rights plank caused the South Carolina delegation to walk out. They later attended the convention of the States' Rights Party,* which nominated J. Strom Thurmond for the presidency. When blacks became part of the regular South Carolina delegation, the SCPDP dissolved as an entity. During its existence it promoted political integration at a time when blacks were all but excluded from the political process.

For more information, see Hanes Walton, Jr., *Black Political Parties: An Historical and Political Analysis* (1972).

**SOUTHEASTERN GOVERNORS' CONFERENCE.** See Southern Governors' Conference.

**SOUTHERN CHRISTIAN LEADERSHIP CONFERENCE (SCLC).** Founded in 1957 at Atlanta, Georgia, by the Reverend Dr. Martin Luther King, Jr., and a group of black clergymen to further the cause of civil rights in the South. Dr. King, a Baptist minister, became SCLC's first president and held that position until his assassination in 1968. Dr. King, who had gained national prominence as head of the Montgomery Improvement Association (a bus boycott to end segregated seating in Montgomery, Alabama), molded the SCLC into a powerful instrument for breaking down the southern Jim Crow system of segregation through nonviolent passive resistance.

To promote its peaceful program for social integration, the SCLC sponsored an Institute on Nonviolent Resistance to Segregation and held workshops to instruct blacks (primarily college students) on how to conduct sit-ins, whereby blacks sat on stools at lunch counters or in eating establishments where they were never before served. The SCLC sought federal implementation of the Civil Rights Act of 1957 and helped create a groundswell of public opinion for passage of the Civil Rights Act of 1960. In 1960 SCLC members were also instrumental in starting the Student Nonviolent Coordinating Committee* and the following year in initiating the "freedom riders" campaign to terminate racial segregation in all public transportation. Two additional projects were subsequently inaugurated in 1962. Operation Breadbasket concentrated on gaining new employment opportunities for blacks by boycotts, protest marches, and direct negotiations with community leaders, and the Citizenship Education Program focused on training black adults so they could pass voter qualification tests and become active in local politics.

Dr. King and other SCLC members were jailed in Birmingham,

Alabama, in 1963 for participating in a civil rights demonstration. King then wrote his famous "Letter from Birmingham Jail," which eloquently defended civil disobedience and appealed to white Christians and Jews for their assistance in combating the resistance of such groups as the Ku Klux Klan* and Citizens' Councils of America.* This call for justice and equality for blacks won widespread sympathy among white moderates in the South, as well as in other parts of the country.

Later in 1963 the SCLC and other black organizations sponsored a march on Washington. Standing in front of the Lincoln Monument and speaking to over two hundred thousand people, Dr. King gave his famous "I have a dream" speech. His moving rhetoric had a profound and positive effect on national public opinion. In 1964 Dr. King was awarded the Nobel Peace Prize. His dramatization of the evils of racism as manifested in segregation and discrimination and the overall efforts of the SCLC were instrumental in securing enactment of the Civil Rights Act of 1964.

The efforts of the SCLC were expanded on a national scale in the mid-1960s. It strove to secure federal protection for blacks in exercising their right of franchise; recruited and trained over a thousand black students for its Summer Community Organization and Political Education (SCOPE) project; encouraged blacks to seek political office in southern communities where they were actually in the majority; and worked to open job opportunities previously closed to blacks. The SCLC participated in the "March against Fear" in Mississippi after the black civil rights leader, James Meredith, was killed in 1966; organized open-housing marches in the suburbs of Chicago; took part in a strike of sanitation workers in Memphis, Tennessee; and with Dr. King as spokesman participated in anti-Vietnam war demonstrations. The SCLC sponsored mass demonstrations against de facto segregation in northern cities where schools serving black ghettoes where grossly inferior to those where white children attended.

After Dr. King's assassination in 1968 by James Earl Ray, the presidency of SLCL passed to the Reverend Dr. Ralph David Abernathy. His initial project, in cooperation with the Reverend Walter E. Fauntroy, the SCLC's Washington bureau director, was to carry out the previously planned Poor People's Campaign.* Thousands of blacks and members of other minority groups descended upon the nation's capital. In the area between the Capitol and the White House a Resurrection City was erected on federal property. From May 11 to June 23, 1968, the demonstrators lived in tents and other temporary quarters. Chanting "Freedom Now," protesters marched around the Capitol demanding enforcement of civil rights laws, open housing, greater appropriations for social welfare, and more jobs for unemployed blacks. When the hordes of squatters refused to leave their makeshift campsites, many, including Dr. Abernathy, were arrested. The Poor People's Campaign focused national attention upon a problem that was being exacerbated by the financial drain of the Vietnam war. President Lyndon B. Johnson's War on Poverty program, as part of the Great Society, was in effect nullified by the huge military expenditures in Vietnam. This SCLC campaign may have contributed to the growing anti-war sentiment among the general public, since it pointed out the dilemma of guns versus butter when it came to monetary priorities.

In 1970 the SCLC organized Politics '70 for Representative Government to help blacks seek political office in national, state, and local elections. It declared a "war against repression" in 1971 and joined with other organizations to protest curtailment of and reductions in welfare payments. Dr. Abernathy and other SCLC leaders protested peacefully at the 1972 national convention of the Democratic Party,* seeking platform commitments for more economic benefits to alleviate poverty conditions among blacks. Most of the SCLC leadership endorsed Senator George McGovern of South Dakota when he received the Democratic nomination for the presidency. Following the Nixon administration's cuts in the budget of the Office of Economic Opportunity, SCLC organized lobby-ins to protest this action. It also assisted other groups, among them Indians and Chicanos, that were seeking to gain further advancements in civil and economic rights. After U.S. involvement in Vietnam terminated, the SCLC supported national amnesty for those who resisted the war as deserters or draft dodgers. In preparation for the 1976 general election the SCLC inaugurated a Crusade for the Ballot. The objective was to increase registration and voting, which in turn would make black ballots more powerful at the polls if cast in large blocs.

Using the Gandhi-like technique of passive resistance initiated by Dr. Martin Luther King, Jr., the SCLC became a powerful factor in the civil rights struggles of the 1960s. It helped trigger a Negro revolution that ultimately culminated in a second reconstruction of the South. Dedicated to peaceful protest, Dr. King and his followers were subjected frequently to brutality and humiliation. At times King had difficulty controlling situations where the SCLC marches were met with violence and in controlling the actions of black militants who were not committed to either Christian forbearance or passive resistance. After Dr. King's death, the SCLC and the civil rights cause suffered from the loss of his charismatic leadership. Under the guidance of Dr. Abernathy, who resigned as president in 1977 to seek a congressional seat (one formerly held by U.N. ambassador Andrew Young), the SCLC could not maintain its key leadership role among black civil rights organizations.

Current national headquarters is located in Atlanta, Georgia, with Dr. Joseph E. Lowry serving as president. On May 27, 1979, an SCLC march in Decatur, Alabama, to protest the conviction of Tommy Lee Hines, a twenty-seven-year-old mentally retarded black man, met armed resistance from Ku Klux Klan* members. In the riot that ensued, four people were wounded by gunfire. Thus it appears that some racial unrest still exists and the SCLC's goal of social integration has not been achieved fully. Local SCLC chapters exist throughout the country, mostly in the South, but membership rolls are far less than at the height of the civil rights movement in the 1960s. A national convention is held annually and a monthly *SCLC Newsletter* is published.

For more information, see Martin Luther King, Jr., *Why We Can't Wait* (1964) and *Where Do We Go from Here: Chaos or Community* (1967); Leslie H. Fishel, Jr., and Benjamin Quarles, *The Black American* (1970); and J. C. Harvey, *Black Civil Rights during the Johnson Administration* (1973).

**SOUTHERN GOVERNORS' CONFERENCE (SGC).** Founded in 1934 at Warm Springs, Georgia, by a group of southern governors for the purpose of promoting the political and economic interests of the South. Among the founders of what was originally called the Southeastern Governors' Conference (its current name was adopted in 1939) were Governor Eugene Talmadge (D-Ga.), Governor Ibra C. Blackwood (D-S.C.); Governor-elect Olin D. Johnson (D-S.C.); Governor Dave Scholtz (D-Fla.); Governor-elect Bibb Graves (D-Ala.); and Lieutenant Governor A. H. Graham (D-N.C.), who was representing Governor J. C. B. Ehringhaus (D-N.C.).

The immediate cause for the formation of the SGC was a scheduled meeting at Warm Springs with President Franklin D. Roosevelt concerning the need to end discriminatory railroad freight rates then being levied on the South. This practice started after the Civil War and placed an undue economic burden on southern businessmen. Success was eventually achieved in 1945 when all freight rate disparities were terminated.

At a 1940 meeting of the SGC, a goal was agreed upon to seek a more balanced economy in the South so as to provide a stable prosperity for the entire region. This meant striving to enlarge the industrial base of the South. In 1941 the SGC pledged all-out support for the war effort but also called upon the federal government to distribute war production contracts on a regionally equitable basis.

By 1951 sixteen southern governors were members of SGC. They came from the states of Alabama, Arkansas, Delaware, Florida, Georgia, Kentucky, Louisiana, Maryland, Mississippi, North Carolina, Oklahoma, South Carolina, Tennessee, Texas, Virginia, and West Virginia. The SGC staunchly supported the Korean war but opposed the civil rights program of the Truman administration. During the Eisenhower administration the SGC went on record as favoring continued high price supports for southern farmers, especially those on cotton and tobacco. Following the 1954 *Brown* v. *Topeka Board of Education* decision by the U.S. Supreme Court, the SGC denounced the high tribunal and defended racial segregation in the schools. Opposition to desegregation continued during the 1960s but with resolutions calling for compliance with the laws of the land. By the 1970s its opposition to integration per se ceased, but it then leveled its criticism at court-mandated busing to achieve racial balance in the public schools.

During the 1970s, regional problems taken up by the SGC included those related to the environment, energy, urban crime, rural poverty, tourism, transportation, and agriculture. As the South industrialized and increased its urban centers, issues confronting governors became less regional in nature and more national in scope, a trend that prompted a slow but sure transition from thinking in terms of states' rights to thinking in terms of seeking federal assistance.

The SGC maintains a permanent headquarters in Atlanta, Georgia, with Herb Wiltsee serving as secretary. Current chairman is Governor Reubin Askew (D-Fla.). Special standing committees exist in the areas of Executive Management and Fiscal Affairs; Law Enforcement, Justice, and Public Safety; Natural Resources and Environmental Management; Rural and Urban Development; Transportation and Commerce; Freight Rates; Nuclear Energy, Space and Technology; Power and Energy; and Human Resources. Annual conventions are held on a rotation basis among the member states.

**SOUTHERN REGIONAL COUNCIL (SRC).** Founded in 1944 at Atlanta, Georgia, by a concerned group of blacks and whites as an interracial organization for the purpose of promoting racial harmony in the South. Among its founders were SRC's first president Dr. Howard W. Odum, a white sociologist at the University of North Carolina who was president of the antecedent organization (the Commission on Interracial Cooperation, which was started by Will W. Alexander in 1918); Dr. Gordon B. Hancock, a black educator from Virginia Union University; and Ralph McGill, editor of the *Atlanta Constitution*. The SRC policy is determined by a 120-member biracial governing board drawn from the eleven southern states.

Impetus for starting SRC came from World War II when the United States was engaged in a war with Hitler's Germany. The repugnant racial policies of the Third Reich made it seem imperative that racism in America also be terminated. Councils of Human Relations were established by the SRC in all of the southern states to promote racial harmony. Through rational discourse and moral suasion, it was hoped that such atrocities as lynchings would cease and gradually be replaced with understanding and goodwill between the races.

The SRC endorsed the civil rights program of the Truman administration in 1948 and opposed the stand of the States' Rights (Dixiecrat) Party.* It applauded and supported the 1954 *Brown* v. *Topeka Board of Education* decision by the U.S. Supreme Court outlawing racial segregation in schools. Much of its efforts during the 1950s and 1960s were directed at achieving a peaceful desegregation process. Playing the role of conciliator, the SRC sought to mediate between such organizations as the Southern Christian Leadership Conference* and heads of local communities.

Members of the SRC supported passage of the Civil Rights Acts of 1957, 1960, and 1964. In 1965 it sponsored the Crusade for the Ballot project designed to encourage black citizens to register and vote in national, state, and local elections. The SRC also called for federal programs to enlarge employment opportunities for blacks, eliminate job discrimination, and alleviate the conditions of poverty that were widespread in the South. Its most recent projects have included training seminars for blacks seeking political office or careers in public administration, monitoring affirmative-action programs, financing research, and issuing documents to enlighten public opinion. Recent studies have been made on ways and means to end institutional racism, eradicate poverty in the South, and make local government more responsive to the needs of the people.

In 1974 the SRC formed the Task Force on Southern Rural Development. Its chairman was Dr. Alexander Heard, chancellor of Vanderbilt University. Prominent members included Governor Jimmy Carter (D-Ga.), Ray Marshall (who served as secretary of labor in President Jimmy Carter's administration), and Juanita Kreps (who served as secretary of commerce in the Carter administration). The work of this group was published in 1977 as *Increasing the Options: A Report of the Task Force on Southern Rural Development.*

Present national headquarters is located in Atlanta. Currently Vivian W. Henderson is president and George H. Esser, Jr., serves as executive director. The SRC's research projects and programs are funded by grants and private contributions. The official publication of the SRC is a monthly, *Southern Voices.*

For further information, see Morton Sosna, *In Search of the Silent South: Southern Liberals and the Race Issue* (1977).

**STATES' RIGHTS PARTY (SRP).** Founded in 1948 at Birmingham, Alabama, by dissident Southern Democrats for the purpose of promoting segregation and states' rights. This founding convention was the result of opposition in the South toward the civil rights planks adopted previously by the Democratic National Convention at Philadelphia. The platform of the Democratic Party* called for enactment of a federal anti-lynching law, abolition of the poll tax, and the establishment of a permanent Fair Employment Practices Commission. Rather than endorse these planks or participate in the nomination of Harry S. Truman as the Democratic presidential nominee, a group of delegates from the South walked out of the national convention. This group, primarily from Alabama and Mississippi, became the nucleus for the SRP. Shortly after the Democratic National Convention adjourned, some five hundred southerners met at Birmingham in a rump convention to form the SRP.

The keynote speaker at the SRP convention was Governor Frank Dixon of Alabama. Dubbed Dixiecrats by the press, the delegates nominated Senator Richard Russell of Georgia for the presidency. When he declined, the choice went to Senator J. Strom Thurmond of South Carolina. Second place on the presidential ticket went to Governor Fielding Wright of Mississippi. The platform condemned the civil rights planks adopted by the Democrats at Philadelphia as being "infamous and iniquitous" and designed to "embarrass and humiliate the South." Included were planks upholding states' rights, segregation of the races, and opposition to "totalitarianism at home and abroad." It was hoped that the Thurmond-Wright ticket would demonstrate to the Democratic Party that it could not win a national election without the support of the solid South. This strategy failed when the SPR ticket polled only 1,169,121 popular and 39 electoral votes. The SRP won only in the four southern states of Alabama, Louisiana, Mississippi, and South Carolina. This defection was not large enough to defeat Harry Truman, who was reelected president in a narrow victory over Republican Thomas E. Dewey.

The SRP named no presidential ticket in 1952 because many Dixiecrats were supporting Republican Dwight D. Eisenhower for president. The U.S. Supreme Court decision in 1954, *Brown* v. *Topeka Board of Education*, and President Eisenhower's decision to enforce school desegregation with federal troops, caused southern segregationists to revive the SRP. In 1956 the SRP nominated T. Coleman Andrews of Virginia for the presidency and Thomas H. Werdel of California for the vice-presidency. The Andrews-Werdel ticket drew only 107,929 popular and no electoral votes. In Kentucky another party calling itself the SRP named Senator Harry Byrd (D-Va.) as its presidential nominee, with William E. Jenner of Indiana as his vice-presidential running mate. They received 2,657 votes.

Following the poor showing of the SRP in the national election of 1956, it disbanded. Some of its members joined the Republican Party,* as did J. Strom Thurmond; some returned to the Democratic Party; and others joined other parties such as the National States' Rights Party.* During its existence the SRP gave segregationists and states' righters a forum, but it could not prevent racial integration from taking place. Based on white supremacy, the racist attitudes of the SRP were too narrow to attract sufficient voters to make it a permanent fixture on the American political scene.

For more information, see V. O. Key, Jr., *Southern Politics* (1949), and Amile B. Ader, *The Dixiecrat Movement: Its Role in Third Party Politics* (1955).

**STATESMAN PARTY.** See Prohibition Party.

**STRAIGHT-OUT DEMOCRATIC PARTY.** Founded in 1872 at Louisville, Kentucky, by dissident Democrats* who disapproved of their party's nomination of Horace Greeley for president in conjunction with the Liberal Republican Party.* The Straight-Outs nominated Charles O'Conor of New York as their presidential candidate and John Quincy Adams II of Massachusetts as his vice-presidential running mate.

The platform emphasized states' rights and called for federal legislation beneficial to labor. Despite the fact that both O'Conor and Adams officially declined the nomination, the party's ticket drew 29,464 votes in twenty-three states. Following the 1872 national election, it disbanded.

For more information, see Fred E. Haynes, *Third Party Movements since the Civil War* (1916 [1966]).

**STUDENT COMMITTEE FOR THE LOYALTY OATH.** See Young Americans for Freedom.

**STUDENT COORDINATING COMMITTEE.** See Student Nonviolent Coordinating Committee.

**STUDENT LEAGUE FOR INDUSTRIAL DEMOCRACY.** See Students for a Democratic Society.

**STUDENT NONVIOLENT COORDINATING COMMITTEE (SNCC).** Founded in 1960 at Raleigh, North Carolina, by a group of sixteen black and white college students for the purpose of fostering racial desegregation in the South. Prime movers in the formation of SNCC were James Forman, a former Chicago teacher; Robert Moses, a graduate of Harvard University; Charles Sherrod, a divinity student from Virginia; and Mendy Samstein, a graduate student at the University of Chicago. Others involved in SNCC's founding included Sam Block, James Bond, MacArthur Cotton, Lawrence Guyot, John Lewis, Willie Peacock, and Lafayette Surney.

The motivating factor in SNCC's founding was a successful sit-in at Greensboro, North Carolina, in 1960. In this southern town, a group of college students forced desegregation by sitting at lunch counters and conducting demonstrations at previously segregated beaches, swimming pools, restaurants, business establishments, hotels, and other public accommodations. Success at Greensboro prompted the establishment of a permanent type of organization such as SNCC to carry on the work of forcing desegregation throughout all of the South.

Initially interracial, with a ratio of 80 percent black membership to 20 percent white, SNCC grew rapidly during the early years of its existence. Members were recruited from college campuses all over the country, and field offices were set up in key southern cities. Within three years it had over one hundred full-time field workers (paid subsistence wages) and an annual budget of $250,000. Funding came from gifts and contributions from individual donors, churches, and private foundations.

SNCC projects were oriented toward direct action but with nonviolence. Practicing civil disobedience, SNCC members deliberately violated segregation laws by sitting at restaurants until served; using drinking fountains and toilet facilities labeled "white only"; entering areas where Negros were prohibited; and conducting freedom rides to desegregate both local and interstate means of transportation. These confrontations frequently provoked violence on the part of white supremacists and often resulted in mass arrests of SNCC members. Decrying the caution of older black civil rights leaders, such as Roy Wilkins of the National Association for the Advancement of Colored People* and Dr. Martin Luther King, Jr., of the Southern Christian Leadership Conference,* SNCC became increasingly militant.

To attract the support of young blacks, SNCC published the *Student Voice*. It organized high school students, as well as those in colleges and universities. SNCC rallies and marches in the mid-1960s often ended in violence. This new orientation toward militant activism and the use of force gained momentum in 1966 when Stokely Carmichael became leader. Carmichael, born in Trinidad, was raised in the United States, graduated from Howard University, and represented a new type of black leader. He challenged the efficacy of the democratic system, claimed that U.S. involvement in Vietnam was a manifestation of American imperialism, and began advocating revolutionary violence. Influenced by black nationalist ideas, Carmichael initiated a policy of black power and expelled all white members.

SNCC's revolutionary tactics carried out by Carmichael and like-minded radical activists attracted more militants but alienated other civil rights followers, both black and white, who were committed to integration and the preservation of the democratic system. Black leaders such as Wilkins and Dr. King were dubbed "Uncle Toms" by SNCC's revolutionaries. Carmichael ultimately became a Black Panther,* while others in SNCC sought to promote black power through politics. SNCC was instrumental in organizing the Lowndes County Freedom Organization* and the Mississippi Freedom Democratic Party.* Both were attempts to establish black voter blocs in order to wrest power from the white political establishment of Mississippi.

With passage by Congress of a series of civil rights acts, implementation of desegregation under federal auspices, and government programs aimed at advancing the economic status of blacks, public opinion turned against the radical revolutionaries, both black and white. The termination of the war in Vietnam and the advances in civil rights caused the eventual demise of SNCC. Reorganized in 1970 as the Student Coordinating Committee

(SCC), the remnants of SNCC all but ceased to exist within the next four years.

For more information, see Howard Zinn, *SNCC: The New Abolitionists* (1964), and Stokely Carmichael and Charles V. Hamilton, *Black Power: The Politics of Liberation* (1967).

**STUDENTS FOR A DEMOCRATIC SOCIETY (SDS).** Founded in 1959 at New York City when the League for Industrial Democracy* (LID) reactivated a moribund affiliate, the Student League for Industrial Democracy (SLID), by renaming it SDS. Robert Alan "Al" Haber, a graduate student at the University of Michigan and a former leader of SLID, was designated field secretary.

Following an organizational meeting at Ann Arbor, Michigan, in 1960, the SDS received a grant of $10,000 from the CIO's United Automobile Workers (UAW), which enabled the fledgling organization to set up an independent headquarters in New York City. At its first national convention in that city the same year, twenty-nine members representing nine universities attended. They elected Al Haber as president, Jonathan Weiss of Antioch as vice-president, and Eric Walther of Yale as international vice-president. Chosen to be on the national executive committee were Eldon Clingan (Columbia University), Bob Craig (University of Wisconsin), Sharon Jeffrey (University of Michigan), Barbara Newman (Queens College), Michael Rosenbaum (Columbia University), Richard Weihart (Yale University), and Carol Weisbrod (Columbia University), who also held the post of national secretary.

For the next several years the SDS published the *SDS Bulletin*, organized local chapters on college campuses throughout the nation (its high point was in 1968 with some one hundred thousand members in five hundred chapters), and became active in the growing civil rights movement. Members participated in sit-ins, conducted boycotts, joined freedom marches, took part in strikes (walking with union pickets), and in general supported protests against racial segregation.

The social action program of SDS was broadened considerably in 1962 when fifty-nine delegates representing eleven colleges met in convention at Port Huron, Michigan. Authored chiefly by Tom Hayden, also an activist on the University of Michigan campus in a local group known as VOICE, the sixty-page Port Huron statement was approved by the delegates. It asserted, "We would replace power rooted in possession, privilege, or circumstances by power and uniqueness rooted in love, reflectiveness, reason, and creativity." The document called for "participatory democracy" as a means of achieving democratic self-regulation of all political, economic, and social institutions. With the slogan, "Let the people decide," SDS seemingly advocated a humanitarian, individualistic type of liberalism. It also condemned racism, an inhumane welfare state, the evils of technology, the futility of conducting a negative foreign policy based upon anti-communism, and irresponsible use of power by the so-called military-industrial complex.

Tom Hayden wrote to UAW's president, Walter Reuther, in 1963 asking for more money from the union. The response was a check for $5,000 to fund the Educational Research and Action Project (ERAP). Initially headed by Al Haber, ERAP's leadership was soon given to Rennie Davis, who had helped organize the Progressive Student League at Oberlin College. Davis solicited more money from unions and foundations and initiated a series of projects that took the SDS away from college campuses into the slums and ghettos. ERAP's aim was to initiate an interracial movement among the poor so as to aid them in improving their economic position. It failed in many of its objectives because the poor whites and blacks did not possess the same values or life-styles as college-educated SDS members, and thus they lacked rapport. By 1965 ERAP had dissolved.

When Charles Clark Kissinger, a graduate of the University of Wisconsin and a mathematics teacher at Mundelein College in Chicago, took over as national secretary in 1964, he renewed organizational activities on college campuses. An excellent administrator, he also strengthened SDS's ties with the LID to ensure continued financial support from its parent, which amounted to four hundred dollars a month. At this time, with President Lyndon B. Johnson increasing America's involvement in Vietnam, the SDS began organizing anti-war protest marches. As the war escalated, so did the militancy of the SDS. Soon Vietcong flags were in evidence, and protest demonstrations turned more and more to violence. As student bodies became radicalized, the cry "student power" became a rallying point for coercive tactics aimed at college administrations.

At its 1965 national convention at Kewadin, Michigan, the 450 delegates decided to decentralize and not focus their primary attention on anti-war demonstrations. All ties to LID were severed, and no national projects were planned. Instead local chapters were urged to form their own projects and goals, with no direct leadership from the national headquarters. When the National Coordinating Committee to End the War in Vietnam (and a host of other anti-war organizations) sprang up, many SDSers joined in and were often given credit (or blame) for demonstrations in which they merely participated but had not organized.

When General Lewis B. Hersey, director of the Selective Service System, announced in early February that draft deferments for students with low academic grades would be revoked, SDS reacted quickly. Anti-war marches resumed, demonstrations ensued, administration buildings on college campuses were occupied (the first being the University of Chicago), and pickets began demonstrating around local draft boards. Along with sit-ins and participation in teach-ins, students frequently held draft-card burnings to symbolize their opposition to conscription.

Parallel to the anti-draft movement, the SDS organized the Free University Committee in 1965. The emphasis was to be on open admission, relevant courses, curriculum innovation, and courses to aid radicalism. The first to be established was at Berkeley where courses were offered in revolution, Zen Buddhism, Marxism, Maoism, anarchism, and other subjects (some frivolous and some of substantive value). The lasting value was not in the "free university," which passed as a fad, but in curriculum changes that resulted in better teaching and offerings in black studies, black history, women's history, and other innovative courses.

Meeting at Clear Lake, Iowa, in 1966, the national convention of the SDS was attended by 350 delegates representing 140 local chapters. An anarchistic tone pervaded the meeting, dubbed "prairie power," which resulted in even more decentralization. It was decided to continue resistance to the draft, inaugurate a Radical Education Project, push for more student power on campuses, and to sabotage the bureaucratic establishment whenever possible. A move by Bettina Aptheker, active at Berkeley as a member of the Communist Party of the United States of America* (CPUSA), to have the SDS follow the leadership of the CPUSA was overwhelmingly rejected.

Over the next years the SDS became increasingly violent in its anti-war activities. Protests were frequently aimed at the draft and against campus recruiters for the armed forces, and even attempted to prevent representatives of large companies (if they were involved in the manufacture of munitions) from hiring college graduates. All too often demonstrations turned into riotous gatherings where police were taunted and destruction of property was commonplace. Protest gatherings on occasion became meaningless when too many participants had taken drugs. By this time many adults who considered themselves open-minded liberals were alarmed by the seemingly irrational rampages of students who made nonnegotiable demands that could not possibly be approved. Strikes closed down some colleges, and others became veritable battlegrounds. All the while the SDS fomented "revolutionary consciousness" and radicalized campuses, even on high schools.

Embracing ideas of Herbert Marcuse, Frantz Fannon, Ché Guevara, and Mao Tse-tung, SDS leaders synthesized Freudian and neo-Marxist concepts with the revolutionary thought of the Third World. This prompted an increasingly revolutionary tempo to SDS action on campuses. Amid chants of "stop the killing" (in Vietnam), bombs began to explode in college buildings. Records of draft boards were deliberately destroyed, and the flag of the National Liberation Front was carried to the Pentagon as protesters marched near wary guards. Confrontations were inevitable, in fact desired, so that fellow students would sympathize with SDS members who were hit by police clubs.

The "Ten Days of Resistance," in what amounted to a seizure of Columbia University in the spring of 1968, initiated another wave of campus violence that resulted in both arson and bombings. Books were ripped up in libraries, catalog cards destroyed, and classes disrupted by strikes as the SDS simultaneously waged all-out war against dozens of universities. Tom Hayden claimed that the Columbia rebellion was an instance where the student members of SDS were "taking an internationalist and revolutionary view of themselves in opposition to the imperialism of the very institutions in which they have been groomed and educated." When Bernadine Dohrn was chosen interorganizational secretary at the 1968 SDS national convention, she defiantly described herself as a "revolutionary Communist."

With the fusion of the Progressive Labor Party* (PLP) with the SDS in 1968 (until ideological differences drove them apart), outright revolution seemed to be the primary objective of militant locals. It appeared as if the SDS had forsworn activism and militant participation in democratic politics for violent overthrow of the American government. Pamphlets began to circulate on how to make bombs, set fires, and disrupt orderly processes of government. In the fall of 1968 SDS formed the Revolutionary Youth Movement (RYM), and this in turn led to the Weatherman* faction, which patterned itself after revolutionary guerrillas who resorted to terrorism and other tactics used by underground fighters. Other factions developed such as the Jesse James Gang; White Panthers; Up against the Wall, Motherfuckers; and Crazies.* The nihilistic antics of the last group alarmed even anarchists.

By 1969 college campuses increasingly became battlefields of confrontation. The SDS and members involved with other groups, both white and black, seized buildings, held large-scale demonstrations, and made nonnegotiable demands at Cornell University (where black students openly carried arms), San Francisco State, Stanford, University of Chicago, and at the University of California at Berkeley (which was in perpetual turmoil). With 304 local chapters, most on college campuses, it appeared for a time that the SDS would impede all higher education by its violent activity. Allied with Black Power groups and feminist radicals belonging to such groups as Bread and Roses, Redstockings, and WITCH, even high schools found themselves targets of guerrilla theater, demonstrations, and symbolic acts of defiance. "Death to the Pig" took on ominous tones as a slogan when protest marches turned into riotous mob scenes.

The capstone of this violent activism came in 1970 when several hundred demonstrators, including SDS members, confronted a National Guard contingent at Kent State University. Protesting President Richard M. Nixon's Cambodian incursion order, the student demonstrators interacted with a small unit of the Guard, which resulted in their firing into the crowd. Four people died. The SDS initiated widespread protests against this act of official violence. Such demonstrations on over seventy college campuses invariably led to more troops and more bloodshed before order was restored.

After this outburst of violence and counterviolence, a calm settled down on college campuses. The winding down of the war with Vietnam, declining draft calls, détente with the Soviet Union, and President Nixon's visit to the People's Republic of China removed many of the causes for protest. The SDS ranks subsequently became depleted as students lost interest and factionalism within led to total confusion. Many former members turned to regular politics again and joined the crusade to try and elect Senator George McGovern (D-S.D.) to the presidency. Tom Hayden ran in the Democratic primary for the U.S. Senate in the state of California. The public had become weary of the excesses of the SDS, and it began to demand strict enforcement of laws on campuses. A taxpayers' revolt also ensued, and many university administrations now found themselves penalized for what many citizens considered to be cowardly permissiveness.

By 1972 the SDS was all but defunct. What was left of the organization went underground, and those few fanatics who remained active operated out of secret revolutionary cells. Their terrorist activity soon made them fugitives from the law. After a few more years, most voluntarily surrendered or were arrested for their crimes. Never before in American history had such an organization existed as the SDS. Its actions, for ill or good, still have to be fully assessed in terms of their long-range effects upon education, youth, law, morality, and the democratic process.

The SDS did contribute to the anti-war sentiment, but it has left a legacy of direct action, violence, and interference in the normal proceedings of society that has been emulated by others. Farmers of the American Agriculture Movement* block the highways in protest of farm prices. Truckers stop highway travel, protesting the price of diesel fuel.

For further information, see George F. Kennan, *Democracy and the Student Left* (1968); Kirkpatrick Sale, *SDS* (1973); and G. Louis Heath, *Vandals in the Bomb Factory* (1976).

**SUPPORT YOUR LOCAL POLICE COMMITTEE.** See John Birch Society.

# T

**TAMMANY HALL (TH).** Founded in 1783 at New York City by a group of Federalists for the purpose of promoting the political fortunes of the Federalist Party.* Known originally as the Columbian Order, it soon became known as the Society of Tammany. Later it was dubbed Tammany Hall because of its place of meeting. The name Tammany was taken from a Delaware tribal chief, Tammanend. TH's early ritual was based on Indian traditions and the Indian word for chief, *sachem*, was used as a title for its leaders. In its early existence it was also referred to as Saint Tammany, since it was the practice of aristocratic societies to name themselves after a patron saint.

In 1800 TH came under the control of Aaron Burr and began to support the Democratic-Republican Party.* It later backed Andrew Jackson for president and thereafter became identified with the Democratic Party.* TH actually was synonymous with the New York County Democratic Committee. In 1835 the Locofoco* faction broke away from TH and formed the Equal Rights Party,* but this did little to weaken the organization. When William Marcy "Boss" Tweed became grand sachem in 1868, TH was turned into a corrupt political machine. Tweed and the Tammany Tiger, a name given to TH by cartoonist Thomas Nast of *Harper's Weekly*, were responsible for defrauding the city of New York of some $200 million. In 1871 Tweed was indicted, tried, and sent to prison.

The techniques devised by TH became the prototype of all big-city machines. The boroughs of New York were divided into wards, each having a captain, and then subdivided into precincts. Tammany workers were often put on the city payroll but their job was to get out votes at election time. Immigrants were courted by the machine and frequently were the recipients of what amounted to welfare. TH helped settle them, get them jobs, get them out of jail when they got arrested, provided food, and generally won the allegiance of newly arrived immigrants in order to get them to vote for TH candidates. This sometimes took the form of hauling carloads of immigrants to vote over and over again in different precincts. Along with this unsavory practice went ballot stuffing or undercounting the votes of opponents. Patronage was used to tie city workers to the machine and as a source for getting money to run campaigns. Other vote-getting practices included street rallies, door-to-door canvassing, posting campaign placards where they would be seen by passing crowds, and delivering campaign literature to residences. Like an army TH workers left nothing to chance. It was when TH resorted to the more odious practices of stealing votes that the machine gained a bad reputation or after its leaders indulged in stealing money from the city's taxpayers.

TH was revived by Richard Crocker in 1886, and by 1905 its boss was George Washington Plunkett. Plunkett, who became rich, defended "honest graft" by the celebrated remark, "I seen my opportunities and I took 'em." TH was reformed by Alfred E. Smith, who used it to propel himself into the governorship of New York. Al Smith's association with TH hurt his chances for the presidency in 1928 because many voters regarded this big-city political machine as having an unsavory reputation. Scandal again marred the reputation of TH, headed by John Curry, when Mayor James "Jimmy" Walker, a Tammany man, was investigated for graft and malfeasance in office.

In 1932 Tammany boss Charles F. Murphy backed Al Smith for the Democratic presidential nomination. After Franklin D. Roosevelt became president, TH consistently supported him and contributed greatly to winning New York for him at election time. Tammany wielded great influence in both New York and national politics during the 1930s and 1940s. In the 1950s the taint of corruption again hurt TH, especially during the mayoral administrations of William O'Dwyer and Carmine De Sapio. Attempts at reform during the mayoral administration of John W. Lindsey (1966-1973) failed, and the power of TH steadily declined. In recent years no real boss has existed, and the very term TH is seldom used to describe the New York County Democratic Committee. Historically TH was very successful in its efforts to integrate immigrants and their ethnic descendants into the political process. The cost for this service, however, was corruption, bossism, and extralegal political power.

For more information, see Gustavus Myers, *The History of Tammany Hall* (1917); M. R. Werner, *Tammany Hall* (1928); William L. Riordon, *Plunkett of Tammany Hall* (1963); and Jerome Mushkat, *Tammany* (1971).

**TAX CUT PARTY (TCP).** Founded in 1960 at Chicago by Lar Daly for the purpose of promoting his own presidential candidacy. Running on a platform promising drastic reductions in taxes, Daly sought publicity by appearing in public dressed in a red, white and blue Uncle Sam uniform. Because of his demands for television time as a bona-fide presidential candidate, Congress repealed the equal-time provision of the broadcasting code so that the Nixon-Kennedy television debates could take place. Daly was invited to appear on some late-evening television talk shows, but more as an entertainment novelty than a serious political candidate. Daly, paired with Merrit B. Curtis as his vice-presidential running mate, drew only 1,761 popular votes. The TCP dissolved after the 1960 national election.

**TELEVISION BROADCASTERS ASSOCIATION.** See National Association of Broadcasters.

**THEOCRATIC PARTY (TP).** Founded in 1960 at Queens Village, New York, by Homer A. Tomlinson, a bishop in the Church of God, for the purpose of promoting Christian principles in politics. Prior to the formation of the TP, Bishop Tomlinson had run for the presidency as a member of the Church of God Party. In 1952 he was paired with Isaac Bass of North Carolina as his vice-presidential running mate. In 1960 Tomlinson was teamed with Raymond L. Teague of Alaska and in 1964 with William R. Rogers of Missouri. In 1968 Rogers ran alone as the presidential nominee of the TP. The TP platform of "Righteousness" was actually a statement of the doctrines of the Church of God. Never on the ballot in any state, TP candidates received no recorded vote. After the TP dissolved following the 1968 national election, Bishop Tomlinson went on to declare himself the "King of all the Nations of Men." Calling himself King Home I, he planned to establish a new nation in the Middle East (northeast of Jerusalem) to be called Ecclesia.

**TOWNSEND CLUBS.** See Townsend Plan National Lobby.

**TOWNSEND CLUBS OF AMERICA.** See Townsend Plan National Lobby.

**TOWNSEND NATIONAL INSURANCE PLAN, INC.** See Townsend Plan National Lobby.

**TOWNSEND NATIONAL RECOVERY PLAN, INC.** See Townsend Plan National Lobby.

**TOWNSEND PLAN.** See Townsend Plan National Lobby.

**TOWNSEND PLAN, INC.** See Townsend Plan National Lobby.

**TOWNSEND PLAN NATIONAL LOBBY (TPNL).** Founded in 1933 at Long Beach, California, by Dr. Francis E. Townsend, a sixty-six-year-old physician, for the purpose of promoting federal pensions for citizens over sixty years of age. Originally chartered in California under the name Old Age Revolving Pensions, Ltd., with Dr. Townsend as president, it underwent a series of name changes: Townsend Clubs of America; Townsend National Recovery Plan, Inc.; Townsend National Insurance Plan, Inc.; and in 1938, after being incorporated in Chicago, it was called Townsend Plan, Inc. This name was changed to TPNL in 1966 when the national headquarters was moved to Hyattsville, Maryland.

Commencing in 1933, Dr. Townsend formulated an old-age pension plan whereby each citizen attaining the age of sixty years would automatically receive a monthly stipend from the government of two hundred dollars. Recipients would be required to spend their pension within thirty days. The plan was to be funded by a 2 percent national sales tax. Townsend argued that not only would senior citizens be taken care of in their old age, but his plan would promote prosperity. At the height of its strength in 1935, there were 11,496 Townsend Clubs in the then forty-eight states and the territory of Alaska, with nearly three million members. Acting as an attorney for the TPNL was Sheridan Downey, who would later be elected to the U.S. Senate from California as a Democrat.*

The lobbying and political agitiation of the TPNL was instrumental in prompting Congress to pass the Social Security Act of 1935. It was to be funded by contributions from the employer, employee, and the federal government. The size of the pension would be determined by how much was paid into the plan. A provision was made for payment of an old-age annuity to those who were already over sixty-five years of age or who would be able to pay in very little in their remaining working years. Overall the Social Security plan enacted by Congress was fiscally more practical than that proposed by Dr. Townsend. In 1936 Townsend backed the presidential nominee of the Union Party.* When Franklin D. Roosevelt was reelected in 1936 with a massive popular vote, the membership of the TPNL began to decline rapidly.

Early publications of the TPNL included the *Townsend Crusader* (1933) and starting in 1935 the newspaper *Townsend National Weekly*. The activities of the TPNL were funded by small dues from members and contributions. Contemporary lobbying efforts of the TPNL are concentrated on securing amendments to the Social Security Act of 1935 to provide for health insurance. This plan, called the "Pay-As-You-Go Social Security and Prosperity Insurance Act," calls for medical benefits to all who are over eighteen years of age when suffering from either physical or mental disability. Other features of the proposal include financial assistance to orphans and students and basing pensions for those age sixty and over on a cost-of-living index. Payroll deductions for Social Security and health insurance would start on incomes over five hundred dollars per month. This measure was introduced in the U.S. House of Representatives by John J.

McFall (D-Calif.). The TPNL also supports the national health insurance plan proposed by Senator Edward Kennedy (D-Mass.).

Present national headquarters of the TPNL is located in Hyattsville, Maryland. Membership is less than one thousand. Current president and chairman of the board of trustees is Robert C. Townsend, the son of the founder (the latter died in 1960). John Doyle Elliot serves as both secretary and chief lobbyist.

For more information, see Francis E. Townsend, *New Horizons, An Autobiography* (1943), and Abraham Holtzman, *The Townsend Movement* (1963).

**TRADE RELATIONS COUNCIL OF THE UNITED STATES (TRC-US).** Founded in 1885 at New York City by Henry S. Eckert, president of the Eastern Pig Iron Association, and W. P. Shinn, president of the American Protective Tariff Association, for the purpose of promoting high, protective tariffs. Originally formed as the American Protective Tariff League, its name was changed to TRC-US in 1959. Its first president was Edward H. Ammidown. From its inception the TRC-US tended to support the election of Republicans because of the traditional high tariff stand of the GOP.

The TRC-US supported congressional enactment of such high tariffs as McKinley Tariff of 1890; Dingley Tariff of 1894; Payne-Aldrich Tariff of 1909; Emergency Tariff of 1921; Fordney-McCumber Tariff of 1922; and the Hawley-Smoot Tariff of 1930. The last was the highest tariff the nation ever had and was the last of its kind. The TRC-US opposed attempts by the Democrats to lower tariff duties by the Wilson-Gorman Tariff of 1894, Underwood Tariff of 1913, and the Reciprocal Trade Agreements Act of 1934. In 1947 it sought modifications in the General Agreement on Tariffs and Trade and lobbied for protective devices in the Trade Expansion Act of 1962. During the administration of Richard M. Nixon, the TRC-US was instrumental in securing a 10 percent surtax on certain manufactured goods to cushion foreign competition.

The TRC-US supported the Mansfield-Hruska omnibus tariff bill, proposed by former Democratic Senate Majority Leader Mike Mansfield (D-Mont.) and Roman L. Hruska (R-Nebr.) during Lyndon B. Johnson's administration, which called for import quotas on Japanese goods and Asian textiles. The bill was defeated, and America continues to maintain a low tariff policy.

The TRC-US carries on research, conducts educational programs, disseminates information to the general public, monitors trade relations, and lobbies for higher tariffs.

Present national headquarters is located in Washington, D.C. Membership consists of 150 individuals or firms representing manufacturing, mining, or agribusiness. Current president is James A. Mogle, with Richard Rose serving as chairman of the board of directors. The TRC-US issues special reports and has published *Employment, Output and Foreign Trade of the U.S. Manufacturing Industries, 1967-73* (1974).

**TRILATERAL COMMISSION, THE (TTC).** Founded in 1973 at New York City by David Rockefeller, chairman of the board of directors of Chase Manhattan Bank, for the purpose of promoting world trade and international monetary stability. Professor Zbigniew K. Brzezinski of Columbia University, later to become special assistant for national security affairs to President Jimmy Carter, was appointed director. Brzezinski, whose book *Between Two Ages* (1970) advocated "a community of the developed nations," was asked to select two hundred people from Europe, Japan, and the United States who would constitute TTC's elite membership. George S. Franklin, executive director of the Council on Foreign Relations,* was named secretary.

Among the individuals chosen to be members of TTC were Georgia Governor Jimmy Carter; Senator Walter Mondale (D-Minn.); Hedley Donovan, editor-in-chief of *Time*; Arthur Taylor, president of the Columbia Broadcasting Company; J. Paul Austin, president of Coca-Cola; Arthur M. Wood, chairman of the board of directors of Sears, Roebuck and Company; I. W. Abel, president of the United Steelworkers of America; Leonard Woodcock, president of the United Automobile Workers; Lane Kirkland, secretary-treasurer of the American Federation of Labor-Congress of Industrial Organizations; Congressman Donald Fraser (D-Minn.), president of the Americans for Democratic Action*; and Congressman John Brademas (D-Ind.), Democratic majority whip. Current members who at one time served the Carter administration include Cyrus Vance, secretary of state; Andrew Young, ambassador to the United Nations; Harold Brown, secretary of defense; W. Michael Blumental, secretary of the treasury; Warren Christopher, deputy secretary of state; Richard N. Cooper, undersecretary of state-economic affairs; Lucy Wilson Benson, undersecretary of state-security affairs; Paul Warnke, director of the Arms Control and Disarmament Agency; Richard Holbrooke, assistant secretary of state-East Asia and public affairs; Sol Linowitz, co-negotiator of the Panama Canal treaty; Elliot Richardson, ambassador-at-large; and Richard Gardner, ambassador to Italy. Also included among the membership are the top executives of Bank of America, Wachovia Bank and Trust Company, Texas Instruments, Exxon, Caterpillar Tractor, Hewlett-Packard, Continental Illinois National Bank and Trust Company, Brown Brothers, Harriman and Company, Shell, Fiat, Barclays Bank, Bank of Tokyo, Seiko, Datsun, Hitachi, Sony, Toyota, *Chicago Sun-Times*, *Los Angeles Times*, *New York Times*, *Wall Street Journal*, *Newsweek*, and the *Christian Science Monitor*.

In 1977 TTC issued a report, *Collaboration with Communist Countries in Managing Global Problems: An Examination of the Options*, which proposed the creation of an international-type federal reserve system using a new currency to be called "Bancor" and the establishment of a world food reserve. Other proposals put forth by TTC included improvements and revisions in the General Agreement for Tariffs and Trade, the International Monetary Fund, and the World Bank. Recommendations relating to U.S. policies included raising prices on new natural gas, reorganizing the National Security Council to include a representative from the Treasury Department, eliminating import controls, promoting exports by expanding contributions to the World Bank, permitting the dollar to devalue against foreign currencies as a step toward using Bancor as a worldwide currency, relinquishing U.S. control over the Panama Canal, eliminating human rights as a test as to whether a foreign country received U.S. aid, and creating a common fund to assist underdeveloped nations.

Although relatively small in number of members, TTC constitutes a significant group of influential businessmen, political leaders, and opinion makers. Since Jimmy Carter was subsequently elected president and Zbigniew Brzezinski was appointed chairman of the National Security Council, some of the proposals made by TCC have been implemented. National headquarters of TTC is located in New York City. It publishes a quarterly magazine, *Trialogue*.

For more information, see Anthony Sutton and Patrick Wood, *Trilaterals over Washington* (1979).

**TWEED RING.** See Tammany Hall.

# U

**UNION LABOR PARTY (ULP).** Founded in 1887 at Cincinnati by a group of farm leaders and remnants of the Greenback Party* for the purpose of forging a voting coalition between farmers and trade unionists. Its membership, which was relatively small, tended to represent the rural debtor class, but it vainly sought to win political support from the Knights of Labor.

At its national nominating convention in 1888, also held in Cincinnati, the ULP selected Alson J. Streeter of Illinois as its presidential nominee, with Charles E. Cunningham of Arkansas as his vice-presidential running mate. Its platform declared, "Farmers are suffering from a poverty which has forced most of them to mortgage their estates" while "laborers are sinking into greater dependence." It denounced land monopoly and made an appeal for legislation enabling "all industrious persons to secure a home."

Additional planks called for homestead tax exemptions; public ownership of the means of communication and transportation; establishment of a national monetary system beneficial to the common people; free coinage of silver; postal savings banks; abolition of convict labor; arbitration to settle strikes; equal pay for women; enforcement of industrial safety; prohibition of child labor; graduated income tax; direct election of U.S. senators; cessation of the practice of importing foreign contract labor; Chinese exclusion; woman suffrage; and pensions for Civil War veterans.

There was an attempt to merge the ULP with the United Labor Party,* which was also holding its national convention in Cincinnati, but this failed to come about. Drawing its support primarily from rural areas of the South and West, the Streeter-Cunningham ticket drew 147,606 popular and no electoral votes. Its aggregate vote was a little over 1 percent of the total cast. This disappointing showing caused the ULP to disband. Most of its adherents later affiliated with the Populist Party.*

For further information, see John A. Garraty, *The New Commonwealth, 1877-1890* (1968).

**UNION LEAGUE (UL).** Founded in 1862 at Cleveland, Ohio, by pro-Unionists to further the war effort against the Confederate States of America. This Cleveland convention unified thousands of individual ULs into the Union League of America and established a national headquarters in Washington, D.C. A Grand Council was formed to act as the governing body, with James M. Edmunds serving as its president. President Abraham Lincoln was one of the prime movers for creation of a national UL so that its pro-war activities might be enhanced, thus giving support to his administration.

The many Union Leagues formed throughout the country, including the Confederacy, often had different names as local organizations. While UL was the most prevalent designation, many had such names as Union Clubs, Loyal Leagues, Strong Bands, National Leagues, and National Union Associations. The first Union Club to be formed was in Kentucky in 1861 for the express purpose of "vigorous prosecution of the war." Hundreds of ULs sprang up spontaneously in 1862, and when they banded together in a national organization that same year, their effectiveness increased enormously.

The UL in most localities was a secret organization that required a loyalty oath from each member. They were totally dedicated to the preservation of the Union by winning the Civil War, then in progress. Many ULs initially were formed to combat and counter the activities of such pro-southern organizations as the Knights of the Golden Circle,* Sons of Liberty, Order of American Knights, McClellan Guards, and Copperheads in general. The UL recruited both blacks and whites for the Union Army, supported conscription, distributed millions of pieces of pro-war literature, provided social services for soldiers, and campaigned politically for the election of candidates committed to victory over the South. The UL's endorsement of Abraham Lincoln for the presidency in 1864 not only assured him the presidential nomination of the Union Party* but aided greatly in his reelection. The UL, in conjunction with such groups as the New England Loyal Publication Society, spent much money and circulated millions of pieces of campaign literature to elect Lincoln and members of the Republican Party.*

The UL, acting as a nonpartisan organization (which it was not), sought to enlist the help of War Democrats and independent voters. Many local ULs were controlled by Radical Republicans* who wanted the South punished by having the federal government confiscate the property of all who fought in the Confederate Army. At times the UL took up arms to resist seditious acts of pro-Confederate sympathizers. Use of tar and feathers, intimidation, and force were all utilized to keep such states as Indiana, Missouri, and Kentucky in the Union camp. Governors—for example, Oliver P. Morton in Indiana and Richard Yates in Illinois—sometimes called upon the UL to act as a home militia. They were also used to guard polling stations, get out the soldier vote, and suppress anti-war demonstrations.

It has been estimated that by 1864 UL membership neared one million. They were largest and most effective in the East, what is now the Midwest, and the Far West. Prominent personages belonging to the UL included Oliver Wendell Holmes, J. B. Lippincott, George B. Loring, George Cadwalader, Andrew J. Antello, John F. Meigs, and George Bancroft. Abraham Lincoln had many friends in the UL, especially on the Grand Council. In terms of sustaining the general public's support for continuance of the war, the UL was highly successful. It did much to counter war weariness, the appeals of Peace Democrats, and the anti-war activities of the Copperheads.

The UL acquired an odious reputation during Radical Reconstruction. Serving as the arm of the Republican Party, it organized many local chapters in the South where it concentrated on gaining freed blacks as members so that they would use their newly acquired franchise to vote for Republicans. In doing so, the UL cooperated with the Freedman's Bureau, carpetbaggers, and scalawags. This made most southern whites regard the UL as part of the hateful Yankee occupation of their homeland. UL members were special targets of the Ku Klux Klan* and other extremist groups seeking to overthrow Republican rule. Ulysses S. Grant and Rutherford B. Hayes gained Republican votes in the South due to the UL's ability to deliver large blocs of black votes. When President Hayes withdrew federal troops from the South in 1877, all Republican regimes fell, and soon all ULs became moribund. The only surviving ULs were a few in such cities as Chicago, New York City, and Philadelphia, and they continued only as elite social clubs.

For further information, see Guy Gibson, "Lincoln's League: The Union League Movement during the Civil War" (Ph.D. dissertation, University of Illinois, 1957), and Clement M. Silvestro, "None But Patriots: Union League in Civil War and Reconstruction" (Ph.D. dissertation, University of Wisconsin, 1959).

**UNION PARTY (UP).** Founded in 1936 at Royal Oak, Michigan, by Father Charles Coughlin, William Lemke, and Thomas O'Brien for the purpose of challenging both the Democratic* and Republican* parties in the national election. The UP was an outgrowth of Father Coughlin's National Union for Social Justice.* Other radicals of the era supporting the UP included Dr. Francis E. Townsend, founder of the Townsend Plan National Lobby,* and Gerald L. K. Smith, head of the Share Our Wealth Movement.* A group of UP supporters met at Cleveland, Ohio, later in 1936 to ratify Father Coughlin's choice of the presidential ticket. Senator Huey Long (D-La.) had been the favorite, but he was assassinated in 1935, so the presidential nomination went to William "Liberty Bell" Lemke of North Dakota, a leader of the Nonpartisan League* and a member of the U.S.

House of Representatives. Second place on the ticket went to Thomas O'Brien of Massachusetts, a railroad union lawyer.

The UP platform called for a high, protective tariff; creation of a central bank under the control of Congress; refinancing of farm and home mortgages; placement of all federal jobs under civil service; enactment of legislation to place a limitation on net personal income; expansion of the amount of currency in circulation; greater federal assistance to the aged and retired; establishment of an adequate national defense; and "no foreign entanglements, be they political, economic, financial or military." Radical, but not to the point of advocating confiscation of wealth, the UP directed its appeal to the lower, debtor class. Because the rhetoric of Father Coughlin and the Reverend Gerald L. K. Smith tended to be anti-Semitic in tone, many voters came to regard the UP as representing political bigotry. William Lemke also proved to be a poor campaigner. His image as a rural bumpkin was hard to dispel when he used campaign rhetoric unsuited to urban audiences.

In the presidential election of 1936, President Franklin D. Roosevelt won reelection by a landslide popular vote. William Lemke polled only 892,267 popular (2.0 percent) and no electoral votes. This poor showing doomed the UP. It continued to exist on the local level until 1939, when it became defunct. Its radical left and anti-New Deal orientation made it unacceptable to most voters. Franklin D. Roosevelt's so-called second New Deal, participation in politics. The formation of the UCP stemmed from the South were passed, siphoned off much popular support the UP may have received. The demise of the UP attests to the fact that while Americans in 1936 desired social and economic reform, they did not want it in the radical form advocated by such demagogues as Father Coughlin.

For more information, see Donald R. McCoy, *Angry Voices: Left-of-Center Politics in the New Deal Era* (1958), and David H. Bennett, *Demagogues in the Depression: American Radicals and the Union Party* (1969).

**UNITED CITIZEN'S PARTY (UCP).** Founded in 1969 at Columbia, South Carolina, by John Roy Harper II, an attorney, and Victoria DeLee, a militant civil rights advocate, for the purpose of promoting greater black participation in politics. The formation of the UCP stemmed from the South Carolina Voter Education Project, whose goal was to increase black registration. It was decided to establish the UCP, since up to 1969 it had been impossible for any black to win nomination for any office when running in the primary of the Democratic Party.*

In 1970 the UCP obtained the signatures of ten thousand registered voters so that it was certified as a legal party. At a convention in Columbia that same year, Thomas D. Broadwater, an attorney, was nominated for the governorship and the Reverend Julius M. McTeer for the lieutenant governorship. Three black independents were endorsed for the state legislature, as well as numerous candidates for local offices. Broadwater and McTeer received fewer than a thousand votes each, but three UCP candidates were elected to the state legislature. James L. Felder, Herbert Fielding, and I. S. Levy Johnson were the first blacks elected to the South Carolina legislature since Reconstruction. Several UCP candidates also won local offices, such as city councilmen and members of school boards.

Because in many South Carolina counties the blacks outnumbered the whites, the Democrats were forced to take note of black candidates. Although the success at the polls was limited, the significance of the UCP was in forcing the Democrats and Republicans alike to nominate black candidates. This occurred in 1972 and 1976. Thus the UCP, while short-lived, did demonstrate the importance of the black vote and, in so doing, forced the major parties to open up their membership to blacks. Once this took place, blacks began to play a role in local, state, and national politics within the traditional two-party system.

For more information, see Hanes Walton, Jr., *Black Political Parties: An Historical and Political Analysis* (1972).

**UNITED COMMUNIST PARTY.** See Communist Party of the United States of America.

**UNITED FARMERS EDUCATIONAL LEAGUE (UFEL).** Founded in 1926 at Bismarck, North Dakota, by Alfred Knutson for the purpose of promoting communism among American farmers. Knutson was authorized by the Communist Party of the United States of America* (CPUSA), of which he was a member, to launch the UFEL as a branch of the *Krestintern* or Red Peasant International (RPI), known in the United States as the Farmers International. The RPI had been established previously in 1923 at Moscow at the direction of the Soviet Union's Vladimir Ilyich Lenin.

Knutson, who had earlier worked as an organizer for both the Nonpartisan League* and the Farmer-Labor Party,* designated himself as executive secretary of the UFEL and editor of its official organ, *United Farmer*. He also selected the following individuals to serve on the UFEL's national committee: fellow Communists A. C. Miller of North Dakota and Charles E. Taylor of Montana: R. H. Walker of the Nonpartisan League; E. R. Meitzen, former editor of the *Farm-Labor Union News*; and William Bouck, president of the Western Progressive Farmers (later to be expanded into a short-lived national organization, the Progressive Farmers of America). The UFEL, which at its peak membership never enrolled more than five thousand farmers, at first espoused a reformist rather than a revolutionary program. Initially it called for reduction of rural taxes, a mortgage moratorium, and formation of farmer cooperatives to promote collective action. Later it championed a farmer-worker alliance, nationalization of banks and railroads, and an end to U.S. imperialism. Its affiliation with the RPI was never admitted publicly.

Following the sixth world congress of the Communist International in 1928, which was dominated by Russia's new ruler, Joseph Stalin, the orders went out to cease cooperation with non-communist, radical groups. Thereafter the UFEL ceased its relatively mild educational program and shifted to a stance of militant leadership in the fight against capitalism.

Although Knutson was dubious of the party line as it pertained to the American scene, he nevertheless implemented it. The pages of the *United Farmer* now contained harsh criticism of other farm organizations relative to their failure to advance the class struggle. As a result of assuming an overt revolutionary stance, membership in the UFEL began to decline rapidly. Knutson's problems were further compounded when an ideological struggle within the CPUSA prompted a sudden change in leadership. Knutson himself was denounced and subsequently dismissed as head of the UFEL.

In 1930 Rudolph Jarju took over as the new executive secretary. In addition, the name of the UFEL was changed to the United Farmers League (UFL) and its national headquarters was shifted to New York Mills, Minnesota. Under orders from the CPUSA not to cooperate with other farm groups, no matter how radical they were, the UFL embarked upon a course that led to its extinction.

Despite the economic woes of the Great Depression, farmers in Minnesota and nearby Montana, Wisconsin, and the Dakotas, as well as other rural regions throughout most of the country, eschewed the communist cause. Since American farmers were interested in neither violent revolution nor state-owned collectives, the UFL had no appeal upon which to build revolutionary rural cadres. Not only did the UFL die by 1937, so did its parent organization, the Red Peasant International.

For further information, see Lowell K. Dyson, "The Red Peasant International in America," *Journal of American History* 58 (March 1972): 958-973, and Gunther Nollau, *International Communism and World Revolution: History and Methods* (1961).

**UNITED KLANS OF AMERICAN KNIGHTS OF THE KU KLUX KLAN.** See Ku Klux Klan.

**UNITED LABOR PARTY (ULP).** Founded in 1877 at Pittsburgh by a group of trade unionists for the purpose of promoting economic reform and bettering the working conditions for labor. The ULP supported national candidates selected by the Greenback Party* until the election of 1888, when it nominated its own presidential ticket. In 1886 the ULP backed

Henry George, author of *Progress and Poverty* (1879) and champion of the single tax, for mayor of New York City. George ran second in a field of three in an election that saw Democrat* Abram S. Hewitt win and Republican* Theodore Roosevelt come in last.

In 1888 the ULP met in Cincinnati to nominate Robert H. Cowdry of Illinois as its presidential candidate and William H. T. Wakefield of Kansas as his vice-presidential running mate. Its platform asserted, "We aim at the abolition of the system which compels men to pay their fellow-creatures for the use of the common bounties of nature, and permits monopolizers to deprive labor of natural opportunities for employment." In advocating the single tax, it proposed "taxation of land according to its value and not according to its area." Other planks called for monetary reform, public ownership of railroads and telegraph, prohibition of child labor, shortening of the workday, abolition of convict labor, legal assistance for the poor, and adoption of the Australian (secret) ballot.

An attempt was made to merge with the Union Labor Party,* but this failed. When Cowdry withdrew from the presidential race prior to election day, the ULP ticket (on the ballot in Illinois, New York, and Oregon) drew a mere 2,818 popular votes. The ULP disbanded soon thereafter.

For further information, see Charles A. Barker, *Henry George* (1955).

**UNITED NATIONS ASSOCIATION OF THE UNITED STATES OF AMERICA (UNA-USA).** Founded in 1964 at New York City as a merger of the American Association for the United Nations (1945) and the United States Committee for the United Nations (1948) for the purpose of more effectively promoting the United Nations and its activities. Eleanor Roosevelt was chairwoman of the former organization, which came into existence as an outgrowth of the League of Nations Association.* Robert Benjamin, who was chairman of the latter organization, became the first chairman of the board of governors of the newly formed UNA-USA. Eleanor Roosevelt and Adlai E. Stevenson II, who was the U.S. ambassador to the United Nations (U.N.), were prime movers in the merger movement.

In 1965 the UNA-USA also absorbed a number of minor groups to become the single most important organization devoted to the enlistment of public support for the U.N. According to UNA-USA's constitution, its purpose "is to study and promote the fundamental basis of peace with justice and the machinery necessary for its development." This was to be achieved through "educational and informational activities" to induce continued support by the United States for the U.N. and its affiliated agencies.

Significant personages on the board of governors included I. W. Abel, president of the United Steelworkers of America; James S. McDonnell, chairman of the board of McDonnell-Douglas Corporation; and G. William Miller, president of Textron, Inc. Honorary chairpersons have included Ralph Bunche, Dwight D. Eisenhower, Arthur J. Goldberg, Paul G. Hoffman, Henry Cabot Lodge, Anna Lord Strauss, and Harry S. Truman. Earl Warren once served as chairman.

The UNA-USA was instrumental in getting October 24 of each year to be observed as U.N. Day. It prepares thousands of informational kits for general distribution to schools and to the general public. Special reports are also issued on all aspects of the U.N.'s activities. Expert panels have been headed by such prominent individuals as Nicholas Katzenbach, John D. Rockefeller III, Kingman Brewster, Jr., Theodore Sorensen, and Robert R. Nathan. The UNA-USA has sponsored studies relating to foreign policy, nuclear energy, space communications, world population, controlling international conflicts, and how to make the U.N. more effective.

Present national headquarters of UNA-USA is located in New York City. Current chairman is Robert Benjamin, chairman of the board of directors of United Artists. Membership totals nearly fifty thousand. The UNA-USA publishes a newsletter, *Report from the UNA*, and *UISTA* bimonthly.

**UNITED STATES COMMITTEE FOR THE UNITED NATIONS.** See United Nations Association of the United States of America.

**UNITED STATES COMMITTEE TO AID THE NATIONAL LIBERATION FRONT OF SOUTH VIETNAM (USC-NLF).** Founded in 1965 at New York City by Walter Teague and group of anti-war advocates for the purpose of promoting U.S. withdrawal from the Vietnam war. Primarily a students' organization, its members were also frequently members of other groups, such as the Students for a Democratic Society.* In addition to claiming that the United States was an imperialist nation, the USC-NLF championed the cause of the National Liberation Front (Vietcong). It also denied that North Vietnam soldiers invaded South Vietnam but contended that the struggle in the latter was truly an internal revolution.

When members of the USC-NLF participated in anti-war demonstrations and protest marches, they openly displayed the Vietcong flag. To raise money for the Vietcong, they sold replicas of its flag on T-shirts, bumper stickers, and buttons. The USC-NLF was most active on college campuses. Its members conducted teach-ins, utilized guerrilla theaters, and organized protest marches (some of which ended in violence). Because of the radical nature of the USC-NLF, it also attracted Communists, Maoists, and other revolutionaries. Some anti-war organizations not ideologically oriented opposed the practice of displaying the Vietcong flag, disagreeing with the USC-NLF's support of an enemy that was involved in killing U.S. soldiers. For a time the USC-NLF published a *Newsletter*. Never very large in membership, probably never exceeding several hundred, the USC-NLF was nevertheless influential among campus radicals and in inciting student anti-war activity. When the United States withdrew from the war in Vietnam during the administration of President Gerald R. Ford, the USC-NLF disbanded. Some of its more militant adherents drifted into the Weatherman* to continue their revolutionary activity as underground terrorists. Since North Vietnam's victory over the South, the Vietcong has been suppressed and no longer exists.

**UNITED STATES CONFERENCE OF MAYORS (USCM).** Founded in 1932 at Washington, D.C., by a group of mayors for the purpose of promoting federal assistance to urban areas during the Great Depression. Big-city mayors, such as Anton J. Cermak of Chicago, took the lead in demanding that President Herbert C. Hoover support relief and public works in order to alleviate the problems caused by mass unemployment. One of the most vigorous spokesmen for big-city mayors was Fiorello H. La Guardia of New York, who served as president of the USCM from 1936 to 1945.

Following the election of Franklin D. Roosevelt to the presidency and the advent of the New Deal, members of the USCM found the White House more receptive. The USCM supported such public works programs as the Works Progress Administration and the Public Works Administration. It endorsed relief programs that provided food stamps and clothing for destitute city dwellers. It also endorsed other New Deal legislation, such as the Social Security Act of 1935 and the Wagner-Steagall Act of 1937, which created the U.S. Housing Authority for the financing of slum clearance and the construction of low-rent housing.

The USCM maintains committees on Community Development; Environment; Human Resources Development; and Legislative Action. It conducts research on municipal problems; seeks to promote cooperation among the local, state, and federal governments and their respective agencies; maintains a library on urban affairs and city codes; monitors federal legislation related to cities of over thirty thousand population; and awards the Distinguished Service Citation to citizens who make noteworthy contributions to improve municipal government.

The USCM endorsed President Lyndon B. Johnson's War on Poverty program, which produced the Model Cities Act of 1966. It was also a strong supporter of President Richard M. Nixon's revenue-sharing program. A contemporary concern of the USCM is the difficult task of providing services to citizens while not raising local taxes. Mayors increasingly look to the federal government for assistance. Immediate problems confronting cities are the increasing crime rate, deteriorating streets, rundown inner cores, unemployment, shortage of low-cost housing, and the rising costs of government. The USCM was critical of President Ronald Reagan for cutting funds for cities in an attempt to promote his anti-inflation program. Cooperating with the National League of Cities,* the USCM supports revenue sharing and seeks more appropriations from Congress to assist cities.

Present national headquarters is located in Washington, D.C. Membership totals nearly eight hundred, representing mayors of cities of over thirty thousand population in all parts of the country. Current president is Mayor Richard Carver of Peoria, Illinois. Within the USCM exists a Democratic* Mayors Caucus, headed by Mayor Henry Maier of Milwaukee, Wisconsin, and Republican* Mayors Caucus, presided over by Mayor Ralph Perk of Cleveland, Ohio. The USCM publishes a weekly, *Urban Affairs Abstracts*; a semimonthly, *Mayor*; a monthly, *Index to Municipal League Publications*; and an annual, *City Problems*.

**UNITED STATES NATIONAL STUDENT ASSOCIATION.** See National Student Association.

**UNIVERSAL NEGRO IMPROVEMENT ASSOCIATION (UNIA).** Founded in 1914 at Kingston, Jamaica, by Marcus M. Garvey for the purpose of promoting black nationalism. In 1916 Garvey moved to New York and established UNIA headquarters at Harlem. At an international convention of the UNIA held in Harlem in 1920, the Declaration of the Negro Peoples of the World made the following demands: an end to racial discrimination; termination of the Jim Crow system; federal legislation to prevent lynching; universal enfranchisement; integrated schools; and an end of colonialism. It also called for black control of institutions in their communities; equal job opportunities; better education; the teaching of black history; and the liberation of Africa. And it adopted the anthem, "Ethopia, Thou Land of Our Fathers," and a red, black and green flag.

Marcus Garvey initiated a back-to-Africa movement and designated himself provisional president of Africa. His negotiations with Liberia for the resettlement of American blacks failed to be satisfactory to that African country. Other ventures included the founding of the African Orthodox Church, Negro Political Union, Negro Factories Corporation, Black Star Steamship Line, and a newspaper, *Negro World*.

In 1934 Garvey met with the imperial grand wizard of the Ku Klux Klan,* Charles Simmons, to discuss the possibility of forming a segregated black community in the United States. This met with considerable criticism from W. E. B. Du Bois and the National Association for the Advancement of Colored People,* who were fighting for integration, not segregation. Black intellectuals and those representing the black middle class also did not like Garvey's uniforms and gaudy style. At its peak the UNIA had over one million members located in large cities with heavy black populations.

The UNIA began to disintegrate in 1923 after Garvey was convicted of fraud. He served time in a federal penitentiary at Atlanta until his sentence was commuted by President Calvin Coolidge. Garvey then sought to revive the UNIA. It held an international convention at Kingston in Jamaica in 1930, but the UNIA soon became moribund. Garvey moved to London, England, where he published a magazine, *Black Man*, until he died in 1934.

During its existence the UNIA did much to engender racial pride in blacks, particularly at a time when white supremacy was at its high tide. It left a legacy of black nationalism, black capitalism, pan-Africanism, anti-colonialism, and black religion. Some of those later involved in forming the Nation of Islam were part of the Garvey movement. Considered by some to be a black demagogue and by others as a farsighted leader, Garvey's UNIA was nevertheless an important organization in the history of the civil rights movement.

For more information, see E. David Cronon, *Black Moses: The Story of Marcus Garvey and the Universal Negro Improvement Association* (1955), and Amy Jacques Garvey, *Garvey and Garveyism* (1970).

**UNIVERSAL PARTY (UP).** Founded in 1963 at Berkeley, California, by the Reverend Kirby James Hensley for the purpose of promoting the principles in politics of the Universal Life church, which he had founded and led. Without benefit of a national nominating convention in 1964, Hensley named himself the UP's presidential nominee and chose John O. Hopkins of Iowa to be his vice-presidential running mate. The UP platform called for the elimination of all taxes, abolition of usury, federal legislation to prohibit lobbying, and the establishment of an educational system based upon the "science of man." On the ballot in the state of California, the UP ticket of Hensley and Hopkins drew only nineteen votes.

In 1968 Hensley again designated himself the UP presidential nominee and selected Roscoe B. McKenna of Iowa as his vice-presidential running mate. The platform was the same as in 1964. On the ballot in Iowa, the Hensley-McKenna ticket attracted a mere 142 popular votes. The 1972 presidential ticket of the UP consisted of Gabriel Green of Iowa for the presidency and Daniel W. Fry of California for the vice-presidency. Running on the same platform as their predecessors, the UP ticket received 21 votes in California and 199 in Iowa. Following these repeated poor showings, the UP became moribund.

**URBAN COALITION ACTION COUNCIL OF NEW YORK.** See Common Cause.

## V

**VETERANS OF FOREIGN WARS OF THE UNITED STATES (VFW).**
Founded in 1899 at Columbus, Ohio, by James Romanis and a group of
Spanish-American War veterans belonging to the U.S. Army Seventeenth
Infantry Regiment for the purpose of promoting benefits for ex-
servicemen. Romanis and his twelve comrades, who had all served in Cuba,
originally called their organization the American Veterans of Foreign Service
(AVFS). In 1903 the AVFS merged with the National Society of the Army
of the Philippines to form the Army Veterans of the Philippines, Cuba, and
Puerto Rico. In 1914 the group renamed itself the VFW.

The VFW supported U.S. entry into World War I. Following the war,
servicemen who had fought in Europe or had served overseas were eligible
for membership in the VFW. In 1936 the VFW was chartered by Congress
as a "fraternal, patriotic, historical, and educational" organization devoted
to the following goals: "To assist worthy comrades; to perpetuate their
memory . . . ; and to assist their widows and orphans; to maintain true
allegiance to the Government of the United States; to maintain and extend
the institutions of freedom; and to preserve and defend the United States
from all her enemies, whomsoever."

In 1920 VFW's commander, Robert G. Woodside, wrote the organization's motto, "Honor the Dead by Helping the Living." The VFW initiated
the sale of the buddy poppy, a red crepe-paper poppy, to finance its activities to aid veterans. It agitated for veterans' pensions after World War I,
and some of its members were involved in the famous bonus march of 1932.
Following World War II, the VFW lobbied for passage of the GI Bill of
Rights and for federal assistance for crippled veterans. It created a Service
Department within itself to assist veterans in their dealings with the U.S.
Veterans Administration (VA). Following the Korean and Vietnam wars,
veterans of these wars were also eligible for membership, and the VFW lobbied
to gain benefits for those who had served in the armed forces.

The VFW has consistently fought against all efforts to reduce expenditures for VA hospitals or to reduce their services. Through its Legislative Service Department, which employs a staff of lobbyists, the VFW has been instrumental in securing benefits for veterans relative to rehabiliation, education, and vocational training. The VFW has committees dealing with Americanism; Civil Service and Employment; Community Activities; Rehabilitation Service; Safety; Voice of Democracy; and Youth Activities. In 1961 the Women's Auxiliary was established. Its membership totals nearly nine thousand, with Odie Lee Gossett serving as president.

It was primarily due to the efforts of the VFW in 1931 that "The Star Spangled Banner" was adopted by Congress as the national anthem. The VFW offers scholarships as prizes for its Voice of Democracy script-writing contest. It operates a 640-acre National Home at Eaton Rapids, Michigan, as an orphanage for sons and daughters of deceased members. It also sponsors a Drive to Survive Course, carries out a Lite-a-Bike campaign relative to bicycle safety, and encourages local projects related to improving the environment. The VFW in recent years has opposed amnesty for draft dodgers or deserters, defends patriotism, and supports national preparedness.

The VFW has consistently defended veterans' preference in receiving government civil service jobs. Criticized by women's groups for denying women employment in government due to veterans' preference, it has successfully defended this position before the U.S. Supreme Court, which in a 1979 decision (*Personnel Administration of Massachusetts* v. *Feeney*), upheld a Massachusetts veterans' preference law.

Present national headquarters of the VFW is located in Kansas City, Missouri. Membership totals nearly 1.75 million, thus making it the second largest veterans organization (next to the American Legion*). Current commander in chief is John J. Stang, a lieutenant colonel in the U.S. Army Reserve and the first black man to hold that office. The VFW publishes a bimonthly, *Post Exchange*, and several monthly journals: *VFW Magazine, Legislative Newsletter*, and *American Security Reporter*.

**VFW.** See Veterans of Foreign Wars of the United States.

**VOTER EDUCATION PROJECT (VEP).** Founded in 1962 at Atlanta, Georgia, by the Southern Regional Council* (SRC) for the purpose of increasing voting among blacks and promoting their active participation in political affairs. In the wake of civil rights legislation and the abolition of the poll tax, the SRC sought to intensify voter registration by establishing the VEP as an arm of its own organization. In 1970 the VEP became an independent entity in order to continue the work of getting blacks registered, encouraging voting, and assisting blacks to become candidates for political office.

The VEP maintains regional offices in Arkansas, North Carolina, and

South Carolina. It operates in the eleven states in the South where blacks were unaccustomed either to voting or participating in the political process. Since its formation, the VEP has been responsible for getting over three million blacks registered in the South. It has also contributed to the election of many black officials in local, state, and national offices. The VEP sponsors research on elections, provides information to elected black officeholders, collects election statistics, monitors elections, and conducts classes on political participation. Its existence has contributed significantly to the increase in voting by blacks in all of the southern states.

Present national headquarters is located in Atlanta, Georgia. The VEP employs a professional staff and utilizes hundreds of volunteer workers. Current executive director is John Lewis. The VEP published *How to Conduct a Registration Campaign* (1970) and issues an annual, *National Roster of Black Elected Officials*.

## W

**WAR RESISTERS LEAGUE (WRL).** Founded in 1915 at Brooklyn, New York, by pacifists Jessie Wallace Hugham, Tracy D. Mygatt, Sarah Cleghorn, and Francis Witherspoon for the purpose of promoting opposition to U.S. intervention into World War I. Originally called the Anti-Enlistment League (AEL), it enrolled some four thousand young men as members in its first year of existence by having them sign pledges not to enlist in the armed forces or respond to military conscription. In 1921 the AEL became the WRL when it affiliated with the newly founded War Resisters International.

Besides being anti-militaristic, the WRL was anti-capitalist. It accepted the Marxian-Leninist ideology that capitalism creates the prime conditions for war. Thus the WRL contained not only pacifists as members but also socialists, communists, and radical revolutionaries. The WRL joined with other pacifist groups in the outlawry-of-war movement and championed the Kellogg-Briand Pact of 1928 as a major accomplishment for ensuring a warless world. During the 1930s the WRL supported the sit-in strikes of the Congress of Industrial Organizations. It also joined with isolationists in opposing the efforts of President Franklin D. Roosevelt to increase the military power of the United States prior to World War II. The WRL had opposed intervention into the war in Europe, but when Adolph Hitler ordered the German Wehrmacht into the Soviet Union in 1941 many members of the WRL desired that the United States assist the Soviet Union. This same ideological reversal was taken by the Communist Party of the United States of America* when the Soviet Union faced defeat by Germany. What had been a so-called imperialist war now suddenly became a war against fascism. Before the German invasion of the Soviet Union, the WRL had joined with other anti-war groups to form the National Service Board for Religious Objectors. Later it softened its opposition to the military draft.

During the administration of President Harry S. Truman, the WRL agitated against universal military training. It also opposed the Korean war as being a manifestation of U.S. imperialism. The WRL advocated the destruction of the atomic bomb, argued for total disarmament, and opposed the idea of the United States having overseas military bases. In 1950 WRL members founded the Pacifica Foundation in San Francisco to operate an FM radio station so as to reach a larger audience with its socialist-pacifist message.

WRL members cooperated with the Committee for Nonviolent Action* to prevent nuclear weapons from being tested in the Pacific Ocean. During the early 1960s the WRL participated in freedom rides in the South and was active in all phases of the civil rights movement. But as the Vietnam war continued, the efforts of the WRL increasingly concentrated on ending the war. It counseled potential draftees to burn their draft cards and, if conscripted, not to enter the armed forces. It also advised soldiers and sailors to desert. Although advocating nonviolent protest, some of the anti-war demonstrations it participated in did turn out to be violent in nature. In recent years the WRL has concentrated its attention on securing amnesty for draft dodgers and deserters.

Present national headquarters is located in New York City, with branch offices in Albuquerque, Atlanta, Kansas City, and San Francisco. The current national chairwoman is Irma Zigas. WRL publishes the biweekly *WIN Magazine* and the bimonthly *WRL News*.

For more information, see Igal Roodenko, *War Resisters League 1973 Peace Calendar: Fifty Years of Nonviolent Resistance* (1973).

**WATER RESOURCES ASSOCIATION.** See Water Resources Congress.

**WATER RESOURCES CONGRESS (WRC).** Founded in 1901 at Washington, D.C., by a group of private citizens and public officials for the purpose of promoting the development of ports and navigable waters. Originally organized as the National Rivers and Harbors Congress, it merged with the Water Resources Association in 1971 to form the WRC. President Theodore Roosevelt was a prime mover and a member of the WRC. Honorary memberships have been bestowed upon all members of Congress and service has been rendered to every president since Roosevelt.

One of the first objectives of the WRC was to convince members of Congress that water resources should not be handled as pork-barrel legislation. WRC promoted the idea of scientifically developing harbors, rivers, and navigable waterways in such a manner as to utilize water resources while taking into account environmental considerations. Much of its early efforts were aimed at overcoming the prevalent attitude that rivers and harbors appropriations were part of the spoils system to be exploited merely to obtain projects for various congressional districts.

As more scientific knowledge became available, the WRC broadened its outlook to embrace all aspects of ecology and environmental control. Special committees were established relative to domestic and foreign commerce; navigable waterways; harbors and terminals; river traffic and coastal transportation; environment; research and technology; public affairs; flood control; reclamation; irrigation; recreation; wildlife; soil and water conservation; and preventing water pollution. The WRC both monitors and maintains liaison with such government agencies and bureaus as the Office of Management and Budget; Water Resources Council; Environmental Protection Agency; Council on Environmental Quality; U.S. Army Corps of Engineers; Bureau of Reclamation; and Department of Agriculture.

Membership in the WRC is drawn from state, county, and local agencies, as well as commercial businesses and agricultural associations dealing in water transportation, irrigation, and reclamation. It continues to promote the development of all water resources, such as rivers, lakes, and harbors, but in such a manner as to protect the environment and provide recreational facilities for the general public. Recent concerns have focused on power generation, particularly the use of nuclear energy and controlling its polluting effect on water. The WRC serves as an intermediary between those needing to use or harness water resources and the governmental regulatory agencies concerned with environmental controls. The WRC presents a Distinguished Service Award to those who contribute to solutions relating to the utilization of water resources within established ecological guidelines.

Present national headquarters of the WRC is located in Washington, D.C. Membership totals nearly eight thousand, representing all fifty states. Current president is John Simmons, the head of the Sabine River Authority, with E. Michael Cassaday serving as executive vice-president. The WRC publishes a monthly, *Washington Report*, and an annual, *Platform*.

**WEATHER UNDERGROUND.** See Weatherman.

**WEATHERMAN.** Founded in 1969 at Chicago as a result of an ideological split within the Students for a Democratic Society* (SDS). A policy statement was prepared by an SDS faction, the Revolutionary Youth Movement (RYM), in opposition to the stand of the Progressive Labor Party* (PLP). The RYM statement was entitled, "You don't need a weatherman to know which way the wind blows." This line from Bob Dylan's song, "Subterranean Homesick Blues," provided the ultimate name for the group of SDSers, who would walk out and take the name Weatherman.

The Weatherman statement, prepared by these SDS members—Karen Ashley, Bill Ayers, Bernadine Dohrn, John Jacobs, Jeff Jones, Howie

Machtinger, Gerry Long, Jim Mellen, Terry Robbins, Mark Rudd, and Steve Tappis—boldly asserted, "The main struggle going on in the world today is between U.S. imperialism and the national liberation struggles against it." Also praised were the "black liberation struggles" then being conducted by the Black Panther Party.* The document called for the formation of a "revolutionary party" with a "cadre organization" to operate secretly to initiate the "armed struggle" against imperialism. The declaration concluded with the cry, "Long live the victory of people's war," a line taken from a slogan coined by Lin Piao of the People's Republic of China.

After Bernadine Dohrn led the Weatherman faction out of the SDS convention, it met later that same year in Cleveland to hold a "national war council." It then formally embarked upon a mission of underground guerrilla warfare to liberate the American people from its supposed imperialistic government. Amid pictures of its heroes, such as Castro, Ché Guevara, Ho Chi Minh, Mao Tse-tung, and Lenin, Mark Rudd exclaimed, "It must be a really wonderful feeling to hit [kill] a pig [policeman]."

Known also as Weatherpeople (less sexist than its original name), plus such other variants as Weatherfolk, Weatherbureau, and Weather Underground, the Weatherman embarked upon ventures of an increasingly violent nature. Initial projects included "jailbreaks" (radicalizing high school students); "kick-ass" (turning peaceful demonstrations into violent ones); "smashing monogamy" (collectives where marriage partners were exchanged); "trashing" (breaking windows); and using cans of spray paint to decorate public buildings with revolutionary slogans (often punctuated with vulgarity). During the "days of rage" at Chicago in 1969, Bernadine Dohrn led a "women's militia" in a rampage of riot and destruction.

When the Weatherman resorted to deliberate bombings that resulted in the deaths of bystanders, all but the hard-core militants dropped out of the organization. By 1970 the Weather Underground had become a tiny cadre of terrorists bent on overthrowing the government. Bernadine Dohrn, Billy Ayers, Jeff Jones, and Celia Sojourn issued a political statement from their secret cell, *Prairie Fire, The Politics of Revolutionary Anti-Imperialism*. This 152-page document (whose title stems from a quotation of Mao Tsetung, "A single spark can start a prairie fire"), announced, "We are a guerrilla organization. We are communist women and men, underground in the United States for more than four years. . . . Our intention is to engage the enemy . . . to wear away at him, to harass him, to isolate him, to expose every weakness, to pounce, to reveal his vulnerability." In February 1975 it published the first issue of *Groundswell*, a newsletter inviting participation in the task of developing "revolutionary consciousness" in America.

Grand jury indictments, arrests, and self-destruction (Ted Gold, Diana Oughton, and Terry Robbins were killed when their bomb factory exploded) depleted the ranks of the Weather Underground to a mere handful of fugitives. Threats on the life of President Gerald R. Ford were made by those identifying themselves as members of the Weather Underground, who have also claimed responsibility for scattered bombings over the years, but it is not known whether they were in fact responsible.

The resort to irrational violence and the use of terrorist tactics brought the Weatherman into total disrepute even among radicals. Its illegal activity and doctrinaire allegiance to unconstitutional principles ultimately took it beyond the point where it could operate within the democratic system. Its lawlessness contributed much to the demise of the entire New Left movement.

For further information, see Jack Weinberg and Jack Carson, *The Split in the SDS* (1969), and Harold Jacobs, ed., *Weatherman* (1970).

**WEATHERPEOPLE.** See Weatherman.

**W. E. B. DU BOIS CLUBS OF AMERICA.** Founded in 1964 at Berkeley, California, as an outgrowth of a Marxist study group formed on the University of California campus as early as 1961. It was also considered to be a successor to the Young Communist League.* The name honored the renowned black intellectual (one of the founders of the National Association for the Advancement of Colored People*) Dr. William Edward Burghardt Du Bois, who late in life embraced communism, left the United States, and died in 1963 in Ghana as a citizen of that country.

Leaders of the Du Bois Clubs included Bettina Aptheker, an active member of the Communist Party of the United States of America*; Carl Bloise, editor of *People's World*; Mike Ryerson, who had visited Hanoi in North Vietnam without a passport; Mortimer Daniel Rubin, who had previously run for state office in California as a Communist candidate; and the six sons of Vincent Hallinan, the last presidential candidate in 1952 of the 1948 Progressive Party* and a lawyer who championed left-wing causes.

In a 1964 statement presented to the platform committee of the Democratic Party,* the Du Bois Clubs identified themselves as a "youth organization committed to Socialism as the best and only effective solution to the social problems of our time." The document warned that they would have to "wrest concessions" because "in reality, we see no tradition of 'orderly' progress in America. Instead we see a history of militant struggle."

Organized on college campuses throughout the United States, Du Bois Clubs had relatively small memberships and operated as rather autonomous units. They frequently collaborated with other radical groups such as the Students for a Democratic Society* and the Progressive Labor Party.* They protested militantly against U.S. participation in the war in Vietnam, opposed the draft, and were involved in civil rights marches. Its members often displayed Vietcong flags and publicly announced that they would welcome a victory of the North over South Vietnam. Members were prone to use violence in protest demonstrations, and as a result many student members casually interested in Marxism dropped out. Internal disputes over ideological positions frequently erupted so that it was often fragmented. When the war in Vietnam ended, the Du Bois Clubs gradually went defunct.

For further information, see Paul Jacobs and Saul Landau, *The New Radicals* (1968).

**WESTERN GOVERNORS' CONFERENCE (WGC).** Founded in 1963 at Phoenix, Arizona, by the governors of thirteen western states for the purpose of the betterment of their respective states. The first chairman was Governor Edmund G. "Pat" Brown of California. Represented at the founding meeting were the territories of Guam and American Samoa, as well as the following states: Alaska, Arizona, California, Colorado, Hawaii, Idaho, Montana, Nevada, New Mexico, Oregon, Utah, Washington, and Wyoming.

The purpose of the WGC was to provide a medium for the "exchange of views and experiences on subjects of general importance . . . ; to foster interstate cooperation and regional development; to attain greater efficiency in state administration; and to facilitate and improve state-local and state-federal relationships." The WGC holds annual (and special) conferences, maintains a professional staff, sponsors research, monitors federal legislation and agencies dealing with the West, provides technical information, and disseminates information to the general public. The WGC was instrumental in establishing the Western Interstate Commission on Higher Education, the Western States Water Council, and the Western Interstate Nuclear Board. It is concerned with water resources, national parks, reclamation, irrigation, missile sites, and the development of rivers and harbors.

The WGC has been concerned with the large amount of public land controlled by the federal government in the West. It frequently lodges complaints about undue government control over lands within western state boundaries. It has consistently fought for greater federal appropriations for reclamation projects and the construction of dams. It has sought to ease federal restrictions relative to grazing in national forests and the use of water for irrigation. The WGC has been highly critical of President Jimmy Carter for cutting funds for water resource projects in the West. It has also striven to gain federal facilities for the West that might otherwise be located in the South and to maintain those already in the West.

Present national headquarters of the WGC is located in San Francisco. Membership totals fifteen. Current chairman is Governor Mike O'Callaghan of Nevada. The WGC periodically issues special reports.

**WHIG PARTY (WG).** Founded in 1833 at Washington, D.C., by a coalition of anti-Jackson political leaders for the purpose of promoting opposition to the policies of President Andrew Jackson. The impetus for the development of this coalition stemmed from the fact the National Republican Party* had been dealt a death blow when President Jackson was reelected in 1832. Jackson's political opponents dubbed him "King Andrew" and took the name "Whigs" from the British Whigs who opposed the absolute monarchy in a previous era. The designation of Whig or Democratic Whig came into usage by 1833 and by 1836 was generally used to describe a coalition of state parties constituting the WP.

The WP attracted not only former National Republicans, but prior adherents to the Anti-Masonic Party* and dissident Southern Democrats. Members of the WP included John Quincy Adams, Henry Clay, John C. Calhoun, Willie P. Mangum, Samuel Southard, Robert Toombs, Daniel Webster, Alexander Stephens, William Seward, Thurlow Weed, and Henry White. Since the Whigs were not yet cohesive enough nationally in 1836, they decided to nominate three regional presidential candidates. It was hoped that Whig electors could unite on one candidate after the popular election or, if that failed, to get the final selection of the president thrown into the House of Representatives. The three Whig presidential candidates were General William Henry Harrison of Ohio, to appeal to the West; Daniel Webster of Massachusetts, to appeal to New England; and Hugh L. White of Tennessee, to appeal to the South. Francis Granger was chosen as the vice-presidential running mate for Harrison and Webster, and John Tyler to run with White.

No platform was written in 1836, but the WP generally stood for national unity, a protective tariff, rechartering of the Bank of the United States, reform of the spoils system, and limitations on the power of the chief executive. Although Martin Van Buren, the presidential nominee of the Democratic Party,* won the election with 764,176 popular and 170 electoral votes, the combined Whig opposition amounted to 738,124 popular and 124 electoral votes. The breakdown of the Whig vote was as follows: Harrison, 550,816 (36.63 percent), winning the states of Ohio, Indiana, New Jersey, and Vermont; White, 146,107 (9.72 percent), carrying Georgia and Tennessee; and Webster, 41,201 (2.74 percent), sweeping Massachusetts. (See table 13.)

In 1839 the first nominating convention of the WP was held at Harrisburg, Pennsylvania. Initially Henry Clay was the front-runner, but the presidential nomination went to William Henry Harrison, the best Whig vote getter in the previous national election. Paired with Harrison was John Tyler of Virginia. Again no platform was adopted, but the economic repercussions of the panic of 1837 gave the Whigs an important issue to exploit. Running on the slogan of "Tippecanoe and Tyler Too," while portraying

Harrison as a military hero who was born in a log cabin and drank hard cider, the Whig ticket triumphed over the Democratic team of Van Buren and Johnson. The Whigs amassed 1,275,390 popular (52.88 percent) and 234 electoral votes. When President Harrison died within a month after taking office, the presidency went to John Tyler. He soon revealed his narrow states' rights position by vetoing legislation rechartering the national bank. The Whigs disowned Tyler, making him a president without a party.

**TABLE 13 Whig Party Presidential Candidates and Votes, 1836-1856**

| YEAR | CANDIDATE | TOTAL POPULAR VOTE |
|------|-----------|--------------------|
| 1836 | William Henry Harrison | 550,816 |
|      | Hugh L. White | 146,107 |
|      | Daniel Webster | 41,201 |
| 1840 | William Henry Harrison | 1,275,390 |
| 1844 | Henry Clay | 1,337,243 |
| 1848 | Zachary Taylor | 1,361,393 |
| 1852 | Winfield Scott | 1,386,984 |
| 1856 | Millard Fillmore | 873,053 |

At the 1844 Whig nominating convention at Baltimore, Maryland, the delegates unanimously selected Henry Clay of Kentucky as their presidential nominee. Chosen for the vice-presidency was Theodore Frelinghuysen of New Jersey. For the first time the WP adopted a platform. It called for "a well regulated currency; a tariff for revenue . . . with special reference to the protection of the domestic labor of the country; the distribution of the proceeds of the sales of the public lands; a single term for the Presidency; a reform of executive usurpations; and . . . administration of the affairs of the country . . . [with] efficiency, controlled by a well regulated and wise economy." No mention was made of the explosive Texas annexation question, although it became an important issue in the ensuing campaign. In losing to Democrat James K. Polk, Clay polled 1,337,243 (48.8 percent) popular and 105 electoral votes. It was the third time "Harry of the West" had lost a presidential election (twice as a National Republican and once as a Whig), and this time by a plurality of fewer than thirty-nine thousand votes.

The Mexican War, controversy over the Wilmot Proviso, and President Polk's decision not to seek a second term gave the Whigs an opportunity for a comeback in 1848. Meeting in Philadelphia, Whig delegates chose General Zachary Taylor of Virginia, a war hero and slaveholder, as its presidential nominee. Millard Fillmore of New York was chosen for the vice-presidency. No formal platform was adopted, since the free-soil versus extension of slavery issue was too explosive. "Cotton Whigs" supported expansion while "Conscience Whigs" opposed the spreading of slavery into the Mexican

Cession. Following the convention a series of resolutions was passed praising the military exploits of General Taylor and pledging an "administration of the Government as one conducive of Peace, Prosperity, and Union." In a three-sided race Taylor attracted 1,361,393 popular and 163 electoral votes to defeat Democrat Lewis Cass and Martin Van Buren, the nominee of the Free Soil Party.*

When a secessionist crisis arose over whether California should be a free or slave state, President Taylor supported the free-soil position. His sudden death in 1850, however, permitted Millard Fillmore to succeed to the presidency. President Fillmore approved the Compromise of 1850 as worked out by Henry Clay and Stephen A. Douglas. When the Whig convention met in 1852 at Baltimore, the delegates were divided over the Compromise of 1850. On the fifty-third ballot, General Winfield Scott took the presidential nomination away from incumbent President Fillmore. William A. Graham of North Carolina, who was secretary of the navy, was named the vice-presidential nominee. The platform approved the Compromise of 1850 as a "settlement in principle and substance" of the slave versus free-soil issue, called for strict construction of the U.S. Constitution, endorsed a tariff for revenue, approved of internal improvements, and promised a foreign policy "free from all entangling alliances with foreign countries." In another three-cornered race pitting Scott against Democrat Franklin Pierce, who won, and Free Soiler John P. Hale, the Whig candidate drew 1,386,984 popular (43.87 percent) and 42 electoral votes.

In 1856 the Whigs were near collapse as a political party. Disagreement over the Kansas-Nebraska Act of 1854 had split the Whigs and spawned the Republican Party.* In 1856 a group of "Old Whigs"—or, as they were referred to, "Silver Grays"—met in Baltimore to endorse ex-President Millard Fillmore for the presidency and Andrew Jackson Donelson of Tennessee for the vice-presidency. They had already been selected as the ticket of the Know-Nothing Party.* The Whigs adopted their own platform, which denounced the Democrats and Republicans for appealing to sectional passions, and affirmed "that the Whigs of the United States are assembled here by reverence for the Constitution, and unalterable attachment to the National Union, and a fixed determination to do all in their power to preserve it for posterity." As a fusion candidate Fillmore polled only 873,053 popular (21.53 percent) and 8 electoral votes, running third to Democrat James Buchanan, the winner, and Republican John C. Frémont.

Attempts were made to keep the WP alive, but by 1858 it was dead. Former Whigs such as Washington Hunt of New York, William C. Rives of Virginia, Robert C. Winthrop of Massachusetts, and John P. Kennedy of Maryland were instrumental in the formation of the Constitutional Union Party.* Other ex-Whigs, such as Abraham Lincoln of Illinois and William Seward of New York, joined the Republican Party. During its relatively brief existence, the WP contributed to the tradition of a two-party system, helped develop the convention system for selecting a presidential ticket, promoted national unity by compromising controversial conflicts, and kept alive the Hamiltonian concept of positive government and internal improvements. Most of its policies would come to fruition in the administration of President Abraham Lincoln, who, though elected as a Republican, was in actuality the last Whig president.

For more information, see E. Malcolm Carroll, *Origins of the Whig Party* (1925); George R. Poage, *Henry Clay and the Whig Party* (1936); Wilfred E. Binkley, *American Political Parties: Their Natural History* (1959); and Kinley J. Brauer, *Cotton Versus Conscience: Massachusetts Whig Politics and Southwestern Expansion* (1967).

**WHITE CITIZENS COUNCILS.** See Citizens' Councils of America.

**WILLIAM ALLEN WHITE COMMITTEE.** See Committee to Defend America by Aiding the Allies.

**WISCONSIN PROGRESSIVE PARTY (WPP).** Founded in 1934 at Fond du Lac, Wisconsin, by Senator Robert M. La Follette, Jr., and his brother, Philip, for the purpose of promoting the reelection of the former and the election of the latter as governor. Of the some three hundred delegates present at the formation of the WPP, other organizations represented included the Wisconsin State Labor Federation, Wisconsin Farm Holiday Association, Cooperative Milk Pool, and the socialist-oriented Farmer-Labor Political Federation,* which was headed by Thomas R. Amlie, subsequently elected to Congress on the WPP ticket, who hoped that the La Follette-led party would evolve into a national third-party movement.

In addition to nominating the two La Follettes, a complete state and congressional slate was chosen. The WPP platform declared that "progressives in Wisconsin, cutting loose from all connections with the two old reactionary parties [Democratic* and Republican* parties] in this crisis, have founded a new national party." It criticized the "cruelty and stupidity" of capitalism and though not calling specifically for a socialist economy, advocated building a "new order of security and plenty for America." Additional planks called for government refinancing of farm and home mortgages; federally financed public works; payment of a bonus to World War I veterans; higher taxes on the wealthy; old-age pensions; unemployment and accident insurance; nationalization of industries that were monopolies; minimum wages; shortening of the workday; formation of more cooperatives; soil conservation; higher education opportunities for the poor; initiative and referendum; and a congressional amendment subjecting a declaration of war to a direct vote of the people.

WPP candidates who won included Senator La Follette, seven (of ten) to Congress, a majority of the lower house in the Wisconsin legislature, and thirteen in the upper house (pitted against fourteen Democrats and six Republicans). President Franklin D. Roosevelt took note of the power of the WPP and sought its support for the New Deal by channeling patronage and federal funds (particularly for Works Progress Administration projects) through La Follette. FDR's alliance with Senator La Follette ceased in 1937 when the latter became a bitter foe of the president's foreign policy and national defense programs.

In 1938 Philip La Follette, then governor, transformed the WPP into the National Progressive's of America.* The absorption of the WPP into the NPA ended the life of the former. During its short existence it had played a role in forcing President Roosevelt to move to the left in 1936 in order to thwart the formation of a radical anti-New Deal coalition.

For further information, see Roger T. Johnson, *Robert M. La Follette, Jr., and the Decline of the Progressive Party in Wisconsin* (1964).

**WOBBLIES.** See Anarchist Federation.

**WOMAN'S CHRISTIAN TEMPERANCE UNION (WCTU).** Founded in 1874 at Cleveland, Ohio, by representatives of various women's temperance societies. The momentum for starting this organization stemmed from a nationwide series of nonviolent demonstrations against saloons and the initiation of the Woman's Temperance Crusade one year previously. The purpose of the WCTU was to channel the energies released through the crusade into a continuing drive for social reform. Members were pledged to personal abstinence and support for prohibitory legislation.

Under its first president, Annie Wittenmyer, the WCTU concentrated on organizing around the single issue of temperance. After the election of Frances E. Willard as its president in 1879, however, the WCTU began to attack a broad range of social ills. Separate departments were set up to deal with morals, temperance and labor, child welfare, and franchise, among others, in order to coordinate the efforts of the membership on each area of interest. By the mid-1880s the WCTU had become a broad-based women's rights and social reform organization enrolling about 250,000 members in all sections of the United States.

From 1884 until Frances Willard's death in 1898, the WCTU supported the Prohibition Party.* Thereafter her successors as presidents, Lillian M. N. Stevens (1898-1914) and Anna A. Gordon (1914-1925), aligned the WCTU with the Anti-Saloon League of America* in political campaigns and lobbying for prohibition legislation. In 1891 the WCTU was instrumental in launching the World's Woman's Christian Temperance Union.

The WCTU was particularly successful in getting state legislatures to require temperance instruction in schools and in raising the legal age of consent, in convincing municipal authorities to provide police matrons, and in persuading many evangelical Protestant churches to abandon the use of sacramental wine in favor of grape juice. In addition the WCTU contributed to successful campaigns against legalized prostitution and in eliminating white slavery with passage of such federal legislation as the Mann Act in 1910. It also helped gain enactment of child labor laws, national prohibition, and woman suffrage.

A major defeat was suffered by the WCTU in 1933 with the repeal of prohibition, but this only prompted the organization to renew its efforts on behalf of temperance. Currently there are over six thousand local unions in all fifty states, with a total membership of some 250,000 (including Puerto Rico and the District of Columbia). World unions also exist in seventy-two nations around the globe.

Members still pledge total abstinence and conduct community campaigns for local prohibition. Agitation is also carried on for restrictive legislation relative to the operation of drinking establishments and the sale of intoxicating beverages. The WCTU supports educational programs that point out the effects of alcohol, drugs, and use of tobacco. New departments have been established, including Christian Outreach, Citizenship, Home Protection, Legislation, Public Relations, and Social Service. Groups sponsored for young people include the Loyal Temperance Legion, ages six through twelve, and the Youth's Temperance Council, ages thirteen through twenty-nine.

At its 106th annual convention held at Wichita, Kansas, in 1980, the WCTU passed a resolution calling upon Congress to pass a law that would require alcoholic beverage containers to carry labels warning that the contents are hazardous to personal health. Edith Stanley, WCTU's tenth president, reiterated that the organization's "founding mothers" had as their prime objective to put an end to the liquor business. She claimed the consumption of liquor "was the number one problem in the home and it still is." The WCTU vowed to continue its lobbying to curtail the liquor traffic.

With national headquarters in Evanston, Illinois, the WCTU publishes Signal Press publications and two monthly magazines, *Young Crusader* and *Union Signal* (the latter has appeared under the same name since 1883). Current president is Edith Stanley.

For more information, see Mary Earhart, *Frances Willard: From Prayers to Politics* (1944); Joseph R. Gusfield, *Symbolic Crusade: Status Politics and the American Temperance Movement* (1963); and John Kobler, *Ardent Spirits: The Rise and Fall of Prohibition* (1973).

**WOMAN'S PEACE PARTY (WPP).** Founded in 1915 at New York City by Jane Addams and a group of women opposed to U.S. involvement in

World War I. Jane Addams of Hull House, a pacifist, was chosen president, and Crystal Eastman, a feminist-pacifist and sister of Max Eastman, served as chairwoman. The preamble to its anti-war resolution stated, "As women, we are especially the custodians of the life of the ages. . . . As women, we feel a peculiar moral passion of revolt against both the cruelty and waste of war."

The WPP had chapters in several cities, but the one in New York City remained the largest and most militant. It called for an immediate end to the fighting in Europe, opposed U.S. military intervention, and agitated against war preparedness. The WPP, which did not permit men to become members, did endorse Henry Ford's ill-fated "peace ship" venture. Members of the WPP lobbied in Congress against military appropriations and opposed conscription. Anti-war parades were held with banners and singing. The favorite song of the marchers was, "I Didn't Raise My Boy to Be a Soldier." The WPP published the magazine *Four Lights* until 1917, when it was seized by the U.S. Post Office as being subversive to the war effort.

When the United States entered the war in 1917, the WPP lost all but its hard-core pacifist membership. Crystal Eastman continued to denounce the war and refused to condone or help the American cause. Jane Addams, on the other hand, worked for the Food Administration (then headed by Herbert C. Hoover). During the war many members became active in organizations seeking to protect the civil liberties of war protesters. At the end of World War I the WPP was absorbed by the Women's International League for Peace and Freedom.*

Although the WPP was short-lived and had but a relatively small membership, it was very vocal in its opposition to military preparedness and U.S. intervention. Most of its members were articulate professional people. Its demise came when the United States entered the war. Public opinion and fear of ostracism forced most to support the war effort and to demonstrate their patriotism. Jane Addams received a belated reward for her efforts when in 1931 she was the recipient of the Nobel Peace Prize.

For further information, see Marie Louise Degen, *History of the Women's Peace Party* (1939), and John C. Farrell, *Beloved Lady: A History of Jane Addams' Ideas on Reform and Peace* (1967).

**WOMEN'S INTERNATIONAL LEAGUE FOR PEACE AND FREE-DOM (WILPF).** Founded in 1915 at The Hague by the International Congress of Women (ICOW) for the purpose of promoting neutral mediation to end the fighting in Europe during World War I. Known originally as the International Committee of Women for Permanent Peace, prime movers in the formation of the WILPF were Jane Addams, its first president and chairwoman of the Woman's Peace Party*; Rosika Schwimmer, a feminist and pacifist from Hungary who later resided in the United States; and Julia

Grace Wales, a Canadian who taught English at the University of Wisconsin. Some twenty-four hundred delegates at the ICOW, representing many nations, approved the plan for neutral intervention in an attempt to terminate World War I.

When delegations were sent to neutral and belligerent countries, they were met with a cool reception. Even President Woodrow Wilson, who would later seek to mediate a conclusion to the war, was noncommittal when approached by representatives of the WILPF. Leaders of the WILPF were instrumental in influencing Henry Ford to charter a "peace ship," *Oscar II*, in an unsuccessful mission to negotiate an end to the war in 1915.

The WILPF was in the forefront of the isolationist-pacifist movement in the 1930s. It opposed U.S. military involvement in World War II, Korea, and Vietnam. It has continually voiced opposition to military conscription, an arms buildup, and use of force to settle international disputes. In 1924 the WILPF warned Americans of the rising tide of anti-Semitism in Europe; in 1925 condemned U.S. imperialism in Latin America; supported the Kellogg-Briand Pact of 1928; backed the U.S. Senate investigation of the munitions industry conducted by isolationist Senator Gerald P. Nye (R-N.D.); took part in the civil rights demonstrations during the 1960s; censured the U.S. Army for its activity in the field of chemical and biological warfare in 1969; and opposed the development of nuclear weapons. In 1931 Jane Addams received the Nobel Peace Prize for her work in the WILPF and other peace groups.

Contemporary activities of the WILPF include agitation for universal disarmament, abolition of racism, achievement of equality of women, demilitarization of society, an end to police brutality, comprehensive medical care for all Americans, and a guaranteed annual income to eliminate poverty in the United States. Committees exist to deal with Childhood Education for Peace and Freedom, Education, Human Rights, Scientific Contacts, and the United Nations.

The WILPF has national sections in twenty-two countries with international headquarters located at Geneva, Switzerland. The U.S. section has its headquarters at Philadelphia, with over 150 local branches in all regions of the nation. Membership in the United States totals nearly five thousand. Current national president is Marii Hasegawa, with Dorothy R. Steffens serving as executive director. The WILPF maintains lobbyists in the nation's capital. It also awards the Jane Addams Children's Book Award on an annual basis for the best work fostering international brotherhood.

Prominent members of WILPF have included Congresswoman Bella S. Abzug (D-N.Y.); Helen Gahagan Douglas, former U.S. senator from California; Coretta Scott King, wife of the late Dr. Martin Luther King, Jr.; Eleanor McGovern, wife of Senator George McGovern (D-S.D.); Ava Helen Pauling, wife of the two-time Nobel Prize scientist, Linus Pauling;

and Gloria Steinem, noted feminist and one of the founders of the National Women's Political Caucus.* It has been one of the most venerable pacifist organizations in American history. The WILPF conducts regional meetings and holds biennial conventions. It issues the following publications: *Peace and Freedom, Legislative Bulletin*, and *Program and Action Newsletter.*

For further information, see Gertrude Bussey and Margaret Tims, *Women's International League for Peace and Freedom, 1915-1965* (1965).

**WOMEN'S MILITIA.** See Weatherman.

**WOMEN'S NATIONAL DEMOCRATIC CLUB (WNDC).** Founded in 1923 at Washington, D.C., by Pauline Morton Sabin and Mrs. J. Borden "Daisey" Harriman for the purpose of involving women in the affairs of the Democratic Party.* Sabin served as WNDC's first president and later founded the Women's Organization for National Prohibition Reform.* Prior to the ratification of the Nineteenth (woman suffrage) Amendment to the U.S. Constitution, women took little or no part in forming policy or selecting candidates. Formation of WNDC sought to remedy this by recruiting women to participate on a higher level than merely being a voter.

By inviting prominent political figures to its luncheons and dinners, WNDC members were given the opportunity to meet party leaders and keep informed on key issues of the day. They also could question these speakers and make known their own views. The opportunity to appear before the WNDC provided government officials with an important public forum and presidential aspirants with a place to seek the support of women. Among those addressing the WNDC were such notables as Dean Acheson, Alben W. Barkley, Charles Bohlen, Charles W. Bryan, John W. Davis, William O. Douglas, John Nance Garner, W. Averell Harriman (cousin of the founder), Hubert H. Humphrey, Lyndon B. Johnson, John F. Kennedy, George McGovern, Frances Perkins, Eleanor Roosevelt, Franklin D. Roosevelt, Alfred E. Smith, Adlai E. Stevenson II, Harry S. Truman, Henry A. Wallace, and Woodrow Wilson.

The WNDC has endorsed the equal rights amendment (ERA), encourages women to seek political office at all levels, and agitates for the appointment of women to high-level government offices. Present membership totals around two thousand, with Mrs. Bernard Koteen serving as current president. It presents an annual Democratic Woman of the Year award, maintains a reference library, monitors congressional legislation through the Political Action Committee, and publishes a monthly, *WNDC News.*

**WOMEN'S NATIONAL REPUBLICAN CLUB (WNRC).** Founded in 1921 at New York City by Henrietta Wells Livermore and a group of politically oriented women for the purpose of promoting more participation by females in the political affairs of the Republican Party.* Following ratification of the Nineteenth (woman suffrage) Amendment to the U.S. Constitution, Livermore and her cohorts thought it desirable to attract more women into the Republican Party. Their hope was to have women serve in the higher echelons of the party and to take part in policy-making decisions.

The WNRC's clubhouse in New York City serves not only as an adult education center but as a place for social activities. It maintains the Calvin Coolidge Memorial Library, operates the Henrietta Wells Livermore School of Politics to train women for active roles in campaigns, and works with women volunteers throughout the nation to elect Republican candidates in national elections. Committees exist to deal with domestic affairs and international relations. Honorary members have included Mamie Eisenhower, Pat Nixon, Happy Rockefeller, and Betty Ford.

Present membership totals over twenty-five hundred. The WNRC is seeking to rebuild the Republican Party after the negative effect of Watergate, especially in getting more women to seek political office under the banners of the GOP. Currently Mrs. Rudolph A. Bernatske serves as president. The WNRC holds an annual convention and publishes a *Newsletter* and a *Journal*.

**WOMEN'S ORGANIZATION FOR NATIONAL PROHIBITION REFORM (WONPR).** Founded in 1929 at Chicago by Pauline Morton Sabin, a prominent socialite and a founder of the Women's National Democratic Club* (1923), for the purpose of securing the repeal of the Eighteenth (prohibition) Amendment. Other prominent upper-class women involved in the formation of the WONPR included Mrs. Cortland Nicoll, Mrs. Coffin Van Rensselaer, Mrs. Caspar Whitney, Mrs. William Lowell Putnam, and Mrs. Pierre S. du Pont. Pauline Mortin Sabin was chosen chairwoman, and a national headquarters was established in New York City.

At its first national convention at Cleveland, Ohio, in 1930 a resolution was adopted that asserted, "We are convinced that National Prohibition is fundamentally wrong." It condemned the "great experiment" for limiting states' rights, interfering with local home rule, causing corruption, fostering disrespect for laws, being unenforceable, and promoting an increase in crime. Later as the economic repercussions of the Great Depression became evident, the WONPR also stressed the heavy cost of federal attempts to enforce prohibition ($40 million per year), the loss in tax revenue at all levels ($1 billion annually), and the lost jobs for workers in the liquor industry (and income to farmers on grain sales).

By 1932 membership in WONPR totaled nearly 1.5 million women, drawing heavily from the upper and middle classes. It ranked as one of the largest anti-prohibiton organizations. In 1932 the WONPR endorsed Franklin D. Roosevelt, the presidential nominee of the Democratic Party,* because he campaigned for repeal. Considering that Sabin had supported Herbert Hoover in 1928 and most of WONPR's membership were normally Republicans,* this organization no doubt contributed to FDR's election. Its existence demonstrated the importance of the prohibition issue and demolished the myth that most women overwhelmingly favored it as being morally good. Once prohibition was repealed in 1933, the WONPR dissolved itself after a short but fruitful existence.

For further information, see David E. Kyvig, "Women against Prohibition," *American Quarterly* 28 (1976): 465, and Grace C. Root, *Women and Repeal: The Story of the Women's Organization for National Prohibition Reform* (1934).

**WORKERS (COMMUNIST) PARTY OF AMERICA.** See Communist Party of the United States of America.

**WORKERS PARTY OF AMERICA.** See Communist Party of the United States of America.

**WORKINGMEN'S PARTY (WP).** Founded in 1828 at Philadelphia, Pennsylvania, by a leatherworker, William Heighton, to promote the political aims of the working class. Membership was drawn from throughout the Northeast and although the WP never developed a national organization, it was successful in local elections in such cities as Philadelphia, Albany, Boston, and New York City. Dubbed by its opponents as the Dirty Shirt Party or the Workies, the WP nevertheless regarded itself as a reform party at a time when Andrew Jackson was assuming the presidency. It advocated a ten-hour workday, a mechanic's lien law, an end to imprisonment for debt, free public education, abrogation of all monopolies, reform of the judicial system, and abolition of militia training.

The ranks of the WP were decimated by intraparty disputes prompted by the utopian ideas of Frances Wright and Robert Dale Owen. Never a large party due to its radical orientation, the WP dissolved by 1832 when most of its members either drifted away into other parties or simply gave up politics, concentrating instead upon building up the labor movement. In New York City many former WPs joined the Equal Rights (Locofoco) Party.* Although the "Workies" ceased to be a viable political force by 1832, they left behind a significant body of labor literature written by leaders Thomas Skidmore, George Henry Evans, Frances Wright, Robert Dale Owen, and Stephen Simpson.

For more information, see Walter E. Hugins, *Jacksonian Democracy and the Working Class* (1960), and Edward Pessen, *Most Uncommon Jacksonians* (1967).

**WORLD FEDERALISTS (WF).** Founded in 1947 at Washington, D.C., by Norman Cousins and a group of liberal-democratic internationalists for the purpose of promoting world government. Cousins, who is now honorary chairman, was the editor of the *Saturday Review* and author of *Modern Man Is Obsolete* (1945). The WF supported the United Nations (U.N.) and sought to make it the institutional mechanism for achieving a lasting peace for the world. It stressed the point that U.S. support for the U.N. is less than 1 percent of what is spent on the military budget.

In 1978 the WF promulgated a U.N. reform project that called for the following: to develop a permanent mediation service and a system of arbitration; enlarge the jurisdiction of the International Court of Justice as a part of the peacekeeping machinery of the U.N.; transfer legal disputes from the political forum to judicial and arbitral areas; maintain a permanent U.N. peacekeeping force; establish an independent source for funding the peacekeeping force; create an international criminal court for trying hijackers and terrorists; devise a more equitable voting system in the U.N.; initiate a universal disarmament agreement supervised by the U.N.; set up an international ocean authority; establish a global resources agency; strengthen the U.N. environmental program; increase the funding for the U.N. development program; create a more effective international monetary and banking system; and initiate a more equitable set of agreements on tariffs and international trade.

The WF sponsors research, conducts seminars, and disseminates information to the general public. It maintains an observer at the U.N. and presents the annual Grenville Clark Editorial Award for the best editorial or cartoon relative to international affairs. The WF has been instrumental in gaining and holding American support for the U.N. In recent years it has sought to counter the arguments by some anti-U.N. proponents, such as the John Birch Society,* that the United States should withdraw from this international organization. Some observers maintain that the WF is too idealistic and that world government is not practicable or desirable. However, some of the U.N. reforms recommended by the WF have been incorporated into legislative proposals by Senator Howard Baker (R-Tenn.) and Senator George S. McGovern (D-S.D.).

Present national headquarters of the WF is located in Washington, D.C. Membership totals nearly twenty thousand. Current national chairperson is Mary N. Temple. The WF is affiliated with the World Association of World Federalists, which is located in Ottawa, Canada. The WF publishes the *Federalist* and *New Federalist*.

For more information, see Norman Cousins, *Present Tense: An American Editor's Odyssey* (1968).

# Y

**YOUNG AMERICANS FOR FREEDOM (YAF).** Founded in 1960 at Sharon, Connecticut, by a group of young conservatives for the purpose of promoting conservatism as a political philosophy. The YAF was formed as an outgrowth of the Student Committee for the Loyalty Oath, organized in 1958 by David Franke and Douglas Caddy, and the Youth for Goldwater for Vice-President, formed earlier in 1960. A prime mover in the formation of the YAF was thirty-five-year-old William F. Buckley, Jr., who was the editor of the *National Review* and the author of such books as *God and Man at Yale: The Superstitions of Academic Freedom* (1951), *McCarthy and His Enemies* (1954), and *Up from Liberalism* (1959).

Meeting at the home of William Buckley, some ninety conservative activists created an organization for young people under forty years of age. Their platform, called the Sharon statement, enunciated a set of political priniciples that encompassed the championing of less federal government; laissez-faire economics; libertarianism; victory over international communism; and a foreign policy that served the "just interests of the United States." Permanent committees were established in the following areas: Student Committee for Free Enterprise; University Research; Youth for Voluntary Prayer; and Stop-NSA, which referred to a project to get students to withdraw from the National Student Association,* which the YAF considered to be a communist-dominated organization.

Although officially nonpartisan, most YAF members belong to the Republican Party.* In 1964 the YAF worked to get the GOP presidential nomination for Senator Barry M. Goldwater (R-Ariz.). When he was chosen as the nominee, the YAF campaigned for him. In 1968 the YAF endorsed Governor Ronald Reagan of California for the GOP presidential nomination and in 1970 contributed much to the election of James Buckley, William's younger brother, to the U.S. Senate as a candidate of the Conservative Party.* The YAF supported Congressman John M. Ashbrook for the 1972 GOP presidential nomination. During the 1972 presidential election the YAF initiated a Youth against McGovern campaign. During the 1970s the YAF distributed blue buttons as a symbol against campus riots, denounced violence, held counterdemonstrations in support of the war in Vietnam, and worked to get students to quit the Students for a Democratic Society.* The YAF has been instrumental in reinvigorating the right-wing of the Republican Party. In 1976 the YAF again supported Governor Ronald Reagan in his attempt to win the GOP nomination from President Gerald R. Ford. This internecine party fight, however, created party disunity and contributed to Ford's close loss to Jimmy Carter.

During the 1980 presidential primaries many within the YAF worked for Ronald Reagan in his fight to win the GOP nomination from either George Bush or John Anderson. Some YAFers supported Congressman Phillip M. Crane of Illinois, believing the Republicans needed a younger man as their candidate. But when Crane pulled out of the primaries and endorsed Reagan, the latter drew most YAF members to his campaign against President Jimmy Carter. A few extreme conservatives in the YAF supported Edward Clark, the presidential nominee of the Libertarian Party.*

Present national headquarters is located in Washington, D.C. Membership totals nearly sixty thousand in over 830 chapters located in forty-nine states. Current national chairman is Ronald F. Docksai, with Frank J. Donatelli serving as executive director. In 1964 the YAF absorbed the Society for Conservative Studies at the University of Pittsburgh. YAF publications include a monthly magazine, *New Guard*, and a quarterly journal, *Dialogue*.

For more information, see Lee Edwards and Anne Edwards, *You Can Make the Difference* (1968).

**YOUNG COMMUNIST LEAGUE (YCL).** Founded in 1930 at New York City by Earl Browder, head of the Communist Party of the United States of America* (CPUSA), and Max Wess, CPUSA's educational director, for the purpose of promoting communism among the nation's youth. Originally formed as the Young Workers League, its name was quickly changed to YCL so as to have a wider appeal. Seeking to implement Lenin's dictum, "He who has the youth has the future," the YCL sought to attract young people who were victims of the Great Depression. Gil Green served as YCL's general secretary.

The YCL was noted for espousing the same party line as the CPUSA. In adhering to the ideology of the Marxist-Leninist-Stalinist version of communism, the YCL advocated the overthrow of capitalism by a revolution of the proletariat. This revolutionary dogma attracted very few young people in the United States. In 1934 the YCL formed a front organization, the American Youth Congress (AYC), to attract young people who would not know it was controlled by communists. Prior to 1939 both the YCL and AYC advocated a common front against fascism. Members of both organizations were recruited for the Abraham Lincoln Brigade to fight on the side of the Spanish Republic in Spain's civil war. Slavishly following the party line from Moscow, the YCL and AYC suddenly began advocating isolationism, noninterventionism, and disarmament after Hitler and Stalin signed the Nazi-Soviet Pact of 1939. Then in 1941, when Hitler's Wehrmacht invaded the Soviet Union, the YCL and AYC quickly reversed their position and began to champion U.S. intervention to prevent the Soviet Union from being defeated by Germany. This type of about-face caused many members of the AYC who were not hard-core communists to leave the organization. It was evident that the AYC was more interested in the needs of the Soviet Union than those of the United States.

In 1943 to foster the war effort and promote cooperation between the United States and the Soviet Union, the YCL was dissolved. In its place the American Youth for Democracy (AYD) was formed. It too was controlled by the communists, but the revolutionary ideology associated with communism was played down. Rather, it stressed U.S.-Soviet friendship and wartime collaboration. Leaders of the AYD were Naomi Ellison, Vivian Liebman, and Jack McMichael. Donald Henderson was honorary president. The AYD was affiliated with the World Federation of Democratic Youth. AYD activities included the selling of war bonds, soliciting blood for the Red Cross, collecting scrap metal, and encouraging enlistment in the U.S. armed forces. The AYD also formed Sweethearts for Servicemen to attract volunteers to work at canteens operated by the United Service Organizations.

The demise of the AYD came after the conclusion of World War II. Many factors were involved: the cold war, the investigations by Senator Joseph McCarthy (R-Wis.), revelations of Soviet espionage, passage by Congress of the Internal Security Act of 1950 and the Communist Control Act of 1954, and the death of Joseph Stalin. When Nikita Khruschev denounced Stalin, his predecessor, and promulgated a new policy of coexistence with the capitalist West, many within the CPUSA and AYD were expelled for Stalinist deviationism. Included in the purge was Earl Browder, the long-time head of the CPUSA. The last major effort of the CPUSA to influence American politics came in 1948. Its members infiltrated the leadership ranks of the Progressive Party,* while AYD members worked their way into the Young Progressives of America.* When Henry A. Wallace denounced the communists and announced his support for the United States in the Korean War, the CPUSA went into a marked decline in membership, and the AYD became defunct.

During the 1960s the CPUSA utilized its Communist Youth Organizing Committee in an attempt to recruit young people. These efforts failed in the main because New Left organizations regarded the CPUSA as part of the stodgy Old Left. Young civil rights activists, anti-Vietnam protesters, and radicals tended to join such groups as the Students for a Democratic Society,* whose members also championed ideologies other than traditional Marxism, such as the dogmas of Mao Tse-tung, Leon Trotsky, or those from the Third World. The United States' withdrawal from the war in Vietnam caused the quick demise of most revolutionary groups. When divorced from the anti-war movement, young people quickly lost interest in communism and other revolutionary ideologies.

For more information, see Jacob Spolansky, *The Communist Trail in America* (1951); John Gates, *The Story of an American Communist* (1958); and David A. Shannon, *The Decline of American Communism* (1959).

**YOUNG DEMOCRATIC CLUBS OF AMERICA.** See Young Democrats of America.

**YOUNG DEMOCRATS OF AMERICA (YDA).** Founded in 1932 at Washington, D.C., by the Democratic National Committee* (DNC) for the purpose of promoting the entry of young people into the Democratic Party.* A prime mover in the formation of the YDA, which was called the Young Democratic Clubs of America until the name was changed in 1975, was James A. Farley. As the new chairman of the DNC, he sought to enlist the twenty-one- to thirty-five-year-olds in the campaign to elect Governor Franklin D. Roosevelt as president. The YDA attracted young people with the appeal that only a "new deal" would assure them a future with any meaning. The YDA was successful in winning the votes of many young people.

In 1936 the YDA endorsed President Roosevelt's reelection and set about to organize rallies, distribute campaign literature, organize students, register twenty-one-year-olds, and help solicit campaign contributions. YDA members could point to New Deal projects that assisted young people, such as the Civilian Conservation Corps and the National Youth Administration. Again the YDA was instrumental in getting out the young people's vote to secure an easy reelection for FDR.

Prior to President Harry S. Truman's renomination in 1948, many in the YDA were opposed to the man from Missouri. Some opposed his proposal for universal military training, but most thought him too conservative or unqualified. When President Truman championed civil rights and initiated his "Give 'em Hell" campaign, hitherto reluctant YDA members became enthusiastic campaigners. In 1960 many of them worked in the primaries for Senator John F. Kennedy (D-Mass.) because he presented such a youthful image. His choice as the presidential nominee of the Democratic Party in 1960 spurred an all-out campaign by the YDA. In 1964 the YDA enthusiastically worked for the reelection of President Lyndon B. Johnson in his campaign against the GOP* presidential nominee, Senator Barry M. Goldwater of Arizona. By 1968, however, many in the YDA were opposed to President Johnson because of the Vietnam war.

In the 1968 New Hampshire primaries, many YDA members worked for Senator Eugene McCarthy of Minnesota, who was challenging President Johnson. When Senator Robert F. Kennedy of New York decided to enter the presidential race, it posed a problem for the YDA. Many felt a sense of loyalty to Senator McCarthy for having the courage to be the first to challenge Johnson, but most believed that Kennedy was the better candidate. During the 1960s and 1970s many members of the YDA were in the forefront of the civil rights and anti-Vietnam war movements. Sometimes state YDA chapters, particularly in California, embarrassed older Democrats by championing gay rights, legalization of marijuana, and legal abortion. In 1972 the YDA played an important role in gaining the Democratic presidential nomination for Senator George M. McGovern of South Dakota. He called for an end to U.S. participation in the Vietnam war, reduction of the voting age to eighteen, and greater participation at national conventions by young people. In recent years the YDA has supported amnesty for draft dodgers and deserters, decriminalization of marijuana, and more federal assistance for students. It has and continues to play a significant role in organizing the eighteen- to thirty-five-year-old group as an important part of the Democratic Party's voting coalition.

Present national headquarters of the YDA is located in Washington, D.C. Membership totals over one hundred thousand in fourteen hundred clubs (many on college campuses) throughout the nation. Two members of the YDA hold permanent seats on the DNC. One-third of the members of Congress and over half of the DNC were former YDA members. Current president of the YDA is deLesseps S. Morrison, Jr., with Martha Sampson serving as executive secretary. YDA publications include a periodic *YDA Newsletter* and the bimonthly *Open Letter*.

**YOUNG PEOPLE'S SOCIALIST LEAGUE (YPSL).** Founded in 1931 at New York City by the Socialist Party of America* (SPA) for the purpose of promoting socialism among the nation's youth. Formed originally as the Young Socialist League, its name was changed to YPSL in 1960. A prime mover in the formation of the YPSL was Norman Thomas, head of the SPA and its presidential candidate from 1928 to 1948, who wanted to attract the votes of young people in the upcoming 1932 national election. He set forth his views on socialism in his book *As I See It* (1932).

One of the first members attracted to the YPSL was Harry Fleischman. After graduating from high school Fleischman could find no employment, and the Socialist platform appealed to him. He, like thousands of other young men, felt socialism was a better alternative than capitalism. Fleischman went on in future years to be a campaign manager for Norman Thomas in 1944 and 1948, editor of the *Socialist Call*, and author of *Norman Thomas: A Biography* (1964). The era of the Great Depression represented the high tide of membership in the YPSL, reaching a total of nearly ten thousand. The New Deal programs of President Franklin D. Roosevelt prevented the further growth of the YPSL because many proposals made by Norman Thomas were implemented as part of FDR's recovery program to alleviate the depression. Also New Deal programs such as the Civilian Conservation Corps and National Youth Administration were aimed at young people.

During the 1930s members of the YPSL supported strikes by the Congress of Industrial Organizations. Members also worked on projects in conjunction with the League for Industrial Democracy* and the Southern Tenant Farmers Union. The YPSL became part of the pacifist-isolationist movement of the 1930s in opposition to national preparedness or rendering aid to victims of aggression lest the United States become involved in a war. Opposition to interventionism abruptly ceased after the attack on Pearl Harbor when most YPSL members reversed themselves and supported the war effort (as did Norman Thomas).

Following World War II YPSL membership dropped off. Members had mixed feelings about the cold war. The YPSL had always striven to keep communists from infiltrating or controlling its own organization. There existed a skepticism about Joseph Stalin's motives, but the Socialists' traditional anti-war stance surfaced again during the Korean War. By the time of the civil rights movement of the 1960s, only a relatively few chapters of the YPSL were in existence. In California the YPSL supported the free speech movement, while other isolated groups participated in civil rights demonstrations. It was hoped that by participating in these movements, membership on college campuses would increase.

In 1962 Richard Roman, head of the YPSL, joined the Students for a Democratic Society* (SDS), as did other members. Within the SDS members of the YPSL fought a losing battle to keep communists out. In fact the SDS, part of the New Left, tended to regard the YPSL as Old Left and nonrevolutionary. Usually members of the YPSL within the SDS, or similar radical and militant organizations, either became radicalized or found themselves ideologically isolated. In any case, membership in the YPSL continued to decline while more violently anti-war organizations grew in size and number. Following the U.S. withdrawal from Vietnam, student interest in extremist groups fell abruptly, and membership in the YPSL declined dramatically. In recent years the YPSL has served as the liaison between young people and the Social Democrats USA (the new name of the SPA). Its efforts are aimed at influencing the policies and programs of the Democratic Party* toward socialist goals. Present national headquarters is located in New York City. Membership totals less than one thousand. Current national secretary is Max Green. The YPSL publishes the *Young Socialist Review*.

For more information, see David A. Shannon, *The Socialist Party of America* (1955).

**YOUNG PROGRESSIVES OF AMERICA (YPA).** Founded in 1948 at Philadelphia by the executive committee of the National Youth for Wallace (NYW) for the purpose of attracting young people to the Progressive Party* (PP). Some two thousand delegates, representing all parts of the country, met to elect a slate of officers, to endorse the presidential candidacy of Henry A. Wallace, and to adopt a platform. The NYW itself was an outgrowth of the Young Progressive Citizens of America (YPCA), the youth arm of the National Citizens Political Action Committee.* The YPCA had been formed in 1946 with actor-dancer Gene Kelly as honorary chairman.

At the founding convention twenty-four-year-old Christine Walker, president of the United Office and Professional Workers of America, and twenty-six-year-old Alvin Jones of Louisiana were elected co-chairpersons. Those who made appearances at the convention included Henry A. Wallace, former vice-president and then editor of the *New Republic*; Senator Glen Taylor (D-Idaho), Wallace's vice-presidential running mate on the PP ticket; Congressman Leo Isaacson of New York, representing the American Labor Party*; and Paul Robeson, the black singer and civil rights activist. Adopted were resolutions opposing President Harry S. Truman's proposal for universal military training and demanding an end to the Jim Crow system.

Membership in the YPA probably never exceeded five thousand, with most members coming from the ranks of college students. Members helped get signatures on petitions so that the PP could be on the ballot in various states, conducted rallies, solicited campaign contributions, distributed campaign literature, and worked to get the youth vote for Wallace. The YPA displayed militancy by demanding the vote for eighteen-year-olds, joining picket lines, seeking to desegregate whites-only facilities, and engaging in civil rights demonstrations. Other activities included organizing tenant strikes, participating in protest marches against high food prices, and demanding an end to red baiting. This last activity became an issue when communists infiltrated the ranks of the YPA and made the entire organization appear to be apologists for the Soviet Union. The entire PP also gained this reputation when communists within the party propagated the party line for ideological purposes. Following the presidential election, when the Wallace-Taylor ticket was soundly beaten, the YPA disbanded.

For more information, see Curtis D. MacDougall, *Gideon's army*, 3 vols., (1965).

**YOUNG REPUBLICAN NATIONAL FEDERATION (YRNF).** Founded in 1931 by Robert H. Lucas, executive director of the Republican National

Committee* (RNC), for the purpose of attracting young people into the Republican Party.* Its first chairman was George H. Olmstead. Originally open to men and women between the ages of twenty-one to thirty-six, the minimum age has now been lowered to eighteen. Members of the YRNF, usually called YRers, are most frequently drawn from college campuses. In 1934 the YRNF became officially affiliated with the RNC. In 1936 the YRNF adopted a constitution and a set of by-laws written by Governor Styles Bridges of New Hampshire, himself a former YRer who was later elected to the U.S. Senate. In electing officers under its new constitution, J. Kenneth Bradley defeated Harold Stassen for the position of chairman. Stassen later became the governor of Minnesota, ran for the presidency, and served in the Eisenhower administration.

The YRNF maintains committees dealing with college voters, teenagers, labor, agriculture, foreign affairs, veterans, and first voters. Its members work in the campaigns of local candidates, as well as for the national ticket. YRers not only perform campaign chores but receive training as future candidates. The YRNF presents every Republican member of Congress with a copy of the party's platform, sponsors forums to inform the public of positions on key issues taken by the GOP, and maintains a Hall of Fame.

Present national headquarters of the YRNF is located in the Dwight D. Eisenhower Republican Center in Washington, D.C. Membership totals nearly five hundred thousand in seventeen hundred local clubs in all states, Puerto Rico, and the District of Columbia. Many exist on college campuses. Current chairman is Dick Smith, with Glen R. Wilson, Jr., serving as executive director. The YRNF publishes *Youth Campaign Source Book, Legislative Manual*, and a monthly, *Newsletter*.

**YOUNG SOCIALIST ALLIANCE (YSA).** Founded in 1960 at New York City by James P. Cannon, a Trotskyite who had been expelled from the Socialist Party of America,* to promote Marxian principles (as interpreted by Lenin and Trotsky) and socialist activity among American youth. The YSA constitution asserted, "We believe that Socialism can be initiated only as a result of struggle of the working class and its allies against the capitalist exploiters, which culminates in the creation of a new type of state, a workers' state."

The YSA formed locals on college campuses, sponsored study groups, and sought to indoctrinate students with its version of socialism. It participated in civil rights demonstrations and formed an affiliate, the National Peace Action, to protest U.S. involvement in the Vietnam war, frequently in conjunction with other radical, anti-war groups, such as Students for a Democratic Society.* It was also an early and consistent champion of Cuba's Fidel Castro. Because of its Trotskyite orientation, however, the YSA criticized the internal bureaucracies of both the Soviet Union and the

People's Republic of China. It furthermore condemned Soviet suppression of literary freedom by writers in the Soviet Union, such as the exiling of Aleksandr Solzhenitsyn, the author who exposed the terror of Stalin's labor camps in Siberia through the novel *One Day in the Life of Ivan Denisovich* (1962).

Other concerns of YSA involved aid to Cesar Chavez's United Farm Workers' Union, support to Chicanos for their La Raza Unida Party,* and backing of the women's movement. The YSA urges its members to become involved in student government, both on the high school and university level. It regularly endorsed the presidential ticket and state candidates of the Socialist Workers Party* (SWP) and conducted campaigns locally to win voter support for them. In 1975 it participated in the establishment of the Political Rights Defense Fund to fight what it considered to be illegal government surveillance. This was done after it had been revealed, because of the Freedom of Information Act, that both the Federal Bureau of Investigation and the Central Intelligence Agency had monitored the activities of both the SWP and the YSA.

Membership in the YSA never exceeded three thousand on college campuses, even at the zenith of the New Left movement. Its doctrinaire stance prompted it to be critical even of fellow socialists, let alone other radical groups, so that cooperation and compromise on a political level were virtually impossible. Current national headquarters is in New York City, and the current national chairperson is Andrew Pulley. At its national headquarters the YSA published two monthlies, *Young Socialist* and *International Socialist Review*.

**YRers.** See Young Republican National Federation.

## _Z

**ZIONIST ORGANIZATION OF AMERICA (ZOA).** Founded in 1897 at
New York City by a group of Zionists for the purpose of promoting zionism
in the United States. Formed originally as the Federation of American
Zionists, the name was changed to ZOA in 1915. The inspiration for forming
the ZOA came from Theodore Herzl. His book, *Der Judenstaat* (1896), and
the first World Zionist Congress in 1897 at Basel, Switzerland, which he
called, were instrumental in prompting American Jews to form a Zionist
organization. The ZOA's first president was Professor Richard Gottheil.
Among its members were such prominent individuals as Louis D. Brandeis,
Dr. Harry Friedenwald, Felix Frankfurter, Jacob de Hass, Louis Lipsky,
Julien W. Mack, Dr. Emanuel Neumann, Dr. Abba Hillel Silver, and Dr.
Stephen S. Wise.

Immediately upon its founding, the ZOA agitated for the formation of a
Jewish state in Palestine. In 1922 it succeeded in securing passage of resolutions in support of this objective in both the U.S. House of Representatives
and the Senate. In 1947 the ZOA was instrumental in getting a resolution to
that effect by the United Nations. Success crowned the ZOA's efforts in
1948 when President Harry S. Truman extended formal diplomatic recognition
to the new nation of Israel. Since that time the ZOA has devoted its attention to the promotion of Israel's survivial as a nation-state.

Following the formation of the Oil Producing and Exporting Countries
(OPEC), the ZOA endeavors to counter Arab influence and sustain pro-
Israel sentiment among the general public and in Congress. The ZOA supports
sales of military arms to Israel; promotes sale of Israeli bonds in the United
States; fosters American emigration to Israel (through its Aliya Department); helps create a demand for Israel's products; agitates for enforcement
of the Helsinki Agreement to permit Jews to leave the Soviet Union; and
promotes tourism in Israel. The ZOA maintains House in Israel to
strengthen cultural ties, organizes Israel investment clubs to advance that
nation's economic development, and operates two secondary schools in

Israel so that American youth of Jewish ancestry can get acquainted with their counterparts in Israel. The ZOA has given cautious support to President Carter's negotiation of the Egyptian-Israeli treaty but has insisted that the United States maintain its military commitments for the continued security of Israel.

Present national headquarters for the ZOA is located in New York City. Membership totals over one hundred thousand. Current president is Dr. Joseph P. Sternstein, with Leon Ilutovich serving as executive director. The ZOA issues five publications: a monthly, *American Zionist*; a weekly, *Zins* (Zionist Information Service), which is printed in English, Yiddish, and Spanish editions; *Campus Zionist*, aimed at collegians and young adults; *Public Affairs Memorandum*, which monitors developments in the Middle East as they relate to Israel and U.S. foreign policy; and a bimonthly for district and regional leaders, *ZOA in Review*.

For more information, see Melvin I. Uroosky, *American Zionism from Herzl to the Holocaust* (1975).

# LISTING OF ORGANIZATIONS BY PRIMARY FUNCTION

## AGRICULTURAL AND RURAL ORGANIZATIONS

American Agriculture Movement
American Agri-Women
American Country Life Association
American Farm Bureau Federation
American Protective Association
Committee for Economic Development
Farmer-Labor Party
Farmers Holiday Association
Free Soil Party
Greenback Party
Ku Klux Klan
League of Conservation Voters
Midwestern Governors Conference
National Farmers Organization
National Farmers Union
National Grange
Nonpartisan League
Populist Party
Rural American Women, Inc.
Water Resources Congress

## ASSOCIATIONS AND SOCIETIES

American and Foreign Anti-Slavery Society
American Anti-Slavery Society
American Anti-Vivisection Society
American Association of Retired Persons
American Association of University Women
American Association on Indian Affairs
American Automobile Association
American Bar Association
American Coalition of Patriotic Societies
American Colonization Society

American Country Life Association
American Equal Rights Association
American Library Association
American Peace Society
American Protective Association
American Society for Public Administration
American Society for the Prevention of Cruelty to Animals
American Society of Sanitary Engineering
American Woman Suffrage Association
Association Against the Prohibition Amendment
Association for the Study of Abortion
Association on American Indian Affairs
Continental Association
Farmers Holiday Association
Filipino American Political Association
Foreign Policy Association
Indian Rights Association
International City Management Association
International Downtown Executives Association
John Birch Society
Mexican-American Political Association
National Association for the Advancement of Colored People
National Association of Broadcasters
National Association of Manufacturers
National Christian Association
National Education Association-Political Action Committee
National Planning Association
National Rifle Association
National Small Business Association
National Society of State Legislators
National Student Association
National Woman Suffrage Association
Republican Governors Association
Ripon Society
Society of Christian Socialists
Society of Separationists
United Nations Association of the United States of America

## BUSINESS GROUPS

American Conservative Union
Americans for Energy Independence
Business-Industry Political Action Committee
Chamber of Commerce of the United States
Committee for Economic Development
Committee for the Nation to Rebuild Prices and Purchasing Power
Consumer Federation of America
International Downtown Executives Association
National Alliance of Businessmen
National Association of Broadcasters

National Association of Manufacturers
National Civic Federation
National Federation of Business and Professional Women's Clubs
National Housing Conference
National Safety Council
National Small Business Association
Nation-Wide Committee on Import-Export Policy
Public Interest Research Group
Trade Relations Council of the United States

# CIVIC IMPROVEMENT ORGANIZATIONS

Alianza Hispano-Americano
American Society of Sanitary Engineering
Council on Population and Environment
International City Management Association
International Downtown Executives Association
National Civic Federation
National Conference of Alternative State and Local Public Policies
National Council on Crime and Delinquency
National Housing Conference
National League of Cities
National Municipal League
National Planning Association
National Tenants Organization
People United to Save Humanity
United States Conference of Mayors

# CIVIL RIGHTS GROUPS
Action Committee to Increase Opportunities for Negroes
Afro-American Party
Alianza Federal de Mercedes
Alianza Hispano-Americano
American and Foreign Anti-Slavery Society
American Anti-Slavery Society
American Civil Liberties Union
American Equal Rights Association
American Indian Movement
American Woman Suffrage Association
Americans for Constitutional Action
Americans for Democratic Action
Amnesty International
Anti-Defamation League of the B'nai B'rith
Association on American Indian Affairs
Black Congressional Caucus
Black Panther Party
Congress of Racial Equality
Equal Rights Party

Fellowship of Reconciliation
Filipino American Political Association
Freedom and Peace Party
Freedom Now Party
Indian Rights Association
Jewish Defense League
Join Hands
La Raza Unida Party
Libertarian Party
Liberty Lobby
Liberty Party
Lowndes County Freedom Organization
Mexican-American Political Association
Mississippi Freedom Democratic Party
National Afro-American Council
National American Woman Suffrage Association
National Association for the Advancement of Colored People
National Black Political Assembly
National Committee of Inquiry
National Conference for a New Politics
National Council of Women of the United States
National Equal Rights League
National Negro Congress
National Organization for Women
National Woman Suffrage Association
National Woman's Party
Niagara Movement
Organization of Afro-American Unity
Peace and Freedom Party
People United to Save Humanity
Polish National Alliance
Poor People's Campaign
Progressive Citizens of America
South Carolina Progressive Democratic Party
Southern Christian Leadership Conference
Southern Regional Council
Student Nonviolent Coordinating Committee
Students for a Democratic Society
Universal Negro Improvement Association
W. E. B. Du Bois Clubs of America

## COMMITTEES AND CONGRESSES

Action Committee to Increase Opportunities for Negroes
America First Committee
American Medical Political Action Committee
American Veterans Committee
Business-Industry Political Action Committee
Citizens Committee for the Right to Keep and Bear Arms
Committee for Economic Development

Committee for Fair Divorce and Alimony Laws
Committee for Nonviolent Action
Committee for the Nation to Rebuild Prices and Purchasing Power
Committee for the New Majority
Committee of Americans for the Canal Treaties
Committee of One Million
Committee on Militarism in Education
Committee on Political Education
Committee to Defend America by Aiding the Allies
Committees of Correspondence
Congress of Racial Equality
Democratic Central Committee of Cook County
Democratic National Committee
Fair Campaign Practices Committee
Fair Play for Cuba Committee
Friends Peace Committee
Independent Citizens Committee for the Arts, Sciences and Professions
Keep America Out of War Congress
Mobilization Committee to End the War in Vietnam
National Citizens Political Action Committee
National Committee for an Effective Congress
National Committee for Citizens in Education
National Committee of Inquiry
National Committee on the Cause and Cure of War
National Congress of Parents and Teachers
National Education Association-Political Action Committee
National Emergency Committee
National Negro Congress
National Republican Congressional Committee
National Right to Life Committee
National Right to Work Committee
Nation-Wide Committee on Import-Export Policy
Non-Partisan Committee for Peace through Revision of the Neutrality Act
Northern Irish Aid Committee
Political Action Committee
Republican National Committee
Student Nonviolent Coordinating Committee
United States Committee to Aid the National Liberation Front of South Vietnam
Water Resources Congress

## CONFERENCES AND CLUBS

Citizens Conference on State Legislatures
Conference for Progressive Political Action
Midwestern Governors' Conference
National Conference for a New Politics
National Conference of Alternative State and Local Public Policies
National Conference of Christians and Jews
National Conference of Concerned Democrats
National Conference of State Legislative Leaders

National Conference of State Legislatures
National Governors' Conference
National Housing Conference
National Legislative Conference
Sierra Club
Southern Christian Leadership Conference
Southern Governors' Conference
United States Conference of Mayors
W. E. B. Du Bois Clubs of America
Western Governors' Conference
Women's National Democratic Club
Women's National Republican Club

## COUNCILS, INSTITUTES, AND FOUNDATIONS

All American Council
American Assembly
American Council of Christian Churches
American Council of Young Political Leaders
American Council on Alcohol Problems
American Security Council
Brookings Institution
Carnegie Endowment for International Peace
Christian Freedom Foundation
Citizens' Councils of America
Council of Energy Resources Tribes
Council of State Governments
Council on Foreign Relations
Council on Population and Environment
Democratic Advisory Council
Education for Democracy
Foreign Policy Association
Freedom Center International
Freedoms Foundation at Valley Forge
National Afro-American Council
National Council for Prevention of War
National Council of Senior Citizens
National Council of Women of the United States
National Council on Crime and Delinquency
National Republican Heritage Groups Council
National Safety Council
National Trust for Historic Preservation
Pacifica Foundation
Southern Regional Council
Trade Relations Council of the United States

## EDUCATIONAL ORGANIZATIONS

Action on Smoking and Health
American Assembly

American Association of University Women
American Library Association
Association for the Study of Abortion
Brookings Institution
Committee on Political Education
Consumer Federation of America
Education for Democracy
Freedom Center International
National Academy of Sciences
National Center for Voluntary Action
National Committee for Citizens in Education
National Congress of Parents and Teachers
National Council on Crime and Delinquency
National Education Association-Political Action Committee
National Planning Association
National Safety Council
National Student Association
National Student Lobby
Public Interest Research Group
United Farmers Educational League
United Nations Association of the United States of America
Voter Education Project

# FEDERATIONS AND LEAGUES

American Bimetallic League
American Commonwealth Political Federation
American Farm Bureau Federation
American League against War and Fascism
American League to Abolish Capital Punishment
American Liberty League
Anarchist Federation
Anti-Defamation League of the B'nai B'rith
Anti-Imperialist League
Anti-Saloon League of America
Consumer Federation of America
Farmer-Labor Political Federation
Free Speech League
Immigration Restriction League
Jewish Defense League
Labor's League for Political Education
League for Independent Political Action
League for Industrial Democracy
League of Conservation Voters
League of United Southerners
League of Women Voters of the United States
League to Enforce Peace
Marine Corps League
National Afro-American League
National Civic Federation

National Civil Service League
National Equal Rights League
National Federation of Business and Professional Women's Clubs
National Federation of Republican Women
National Federation of the Blind
National League of Cities
National Municipal League
National Progressive Republican League
National Security League
Navy League of the United States
Nonpartisan League
Union League
War Resisters League
Women's International League for Peace and Freedom
Young Communist League
Young People's Socialist League
Young Republican National Federation

## FOREIGN AFFAIRS GROUPS

All American Council
America First Committee
American Colonization Society
American Security Council
Amnesty International
Anti-Imperialist League
Committee of Americans for the Canal Treaties
Committee of One Million
Committee to Defend America by Aiding the Allies
Council on Foreign Relations
Fair Play for Cuba Committee
Foreign Policy Association
Fuerzas Armádas de Liberacíon Nacional Puertorriqueña
German-American Bund
League to Enforce Peace
National Afro-American League
National Committee on the Cause and Cure of War
National Council for Prevention of War
National Emergency Committee
Nation-Wide Committee on Import-Export Policy
Non-Partisan Committee for Peace through Revision of the Neutrality Act
Northern Irish Aid Committee
Organization of Afro-American Unity
Polish National Alliance
SANE: A Citizens' Organization for a Sane World
Trade Relations Council of the United States
Veterans of Foreign Wars of the United States
Women's International League for Peace and Freedom

World Federalists
Zionist Organization of America

## GOOD GOVERNMENT GROUPS

American Bar Association
American Civil Liberties Union
American Society for Public Administration
Americans for Constitutional Action
Americans for Democratic Action
Black Congressional Caucus
Brookings Institution
Citizens Conference on State Legislatures
Council of State Governments
Fair Campaign Practices Committee
Freedoms Foundation at Valley Forge
International City Management Association
League of Women Voters of the United States
Midwestern Governors' Conference
National Black Political Assembly
National Center for Voluntary Action
National Citizens Political Action Committee
National Civic Federation
National Civil Service League
National Committee for an Effective Congress
National Conference of Alternative State and Local Public Policies
National Conference of State Legislative Leaders
National Conference of State Legislatures
National Council on Crime and Delinquency
National Governors' Conference
National League of Cities
National Legislative Conference
National Municipal League
National Order of Women Legislators
National Planning Association
National Progressive Republican League
National Society of State Legislators
People United to Save Humanity
Public Interest Research Group
Southern Governors' Conference
United States Conference of Mayors
Western Governors' Conference

## HUMANITARIAN ORGANIZATIONS

American Society for the Prevention of Cruelty to Animals
Friends Peace Committee
National Center for Voluntary Action
National Council of Women of the United States

# LABOR PARTIES AND ORGANIZATIONS

American Labor Party
American Society of Sanitary Engineering
Anarchist Federation
Catholic Workers Movement
Committee on Political Education
Coxey's Army
End Poverty in California
Farmer-Labor Party
Fraternal Order of Police
Greenback Party
International Working People's Association
Jobless Party
Labor's League for Political Education
League for Industrial Democracy
National Labor Reform Party
National Right to Work Committee
Political Action Committee
Progressive Labor Party
Socialist Labor Party
Socialist Workers Party
Union Labor Party
United Labor Party
Workingmen's Party

# LOBBIES

American Bar Association
American Bimetallic League
American Civil Liberties Union
American Commonwealth Political Federation
American Conservative Union
American Equal Rights Association
American Farm Bureau Federation
American Liberty League
American Medical Political Action Committee
American Protective Association
American Woman Suffrage Association
Americans for Constitutional Action
Americans for Democratic Action
Anti-Imperialist League
Anti-Saloon League
Association against the Prohibition Amendment
Bipartisan Congressional Clearinghouse
Bonus Army
Business-Industry Political Action Committee
Citizens Conference on State Legislatures
Citizens' Councils of America

Committee for the New Majority
Committee of Americans for the Canal Treaties
Committee on Political Education
Common Cause
Conference for Progressive Labor Action
Coxey's Army
Education for Democracy
Fair Play for Cuba Committee
Filipino American Political Association
Immigration Restriction League
Independent Citizens Committee for the Arts, Sciences and Professions
Jewish Socialist Verband of America
Labor's League for Political Education
League for Independent Political Action
League for Industrial Democracy
League of Conservation Voters
Liberty Lobby
Movement for a New Congress
National American Woman Suffrage Association
National Association for the Advancement of Colored People
National Association of Manufacturers
National Black Political Convention
National Christian Association
National Citizens Political Action Committee
National Civil Service League
National Committee for an Effective Congress
National Committee of Inquiry
National Conference for a New Politics
National Conference of Alternative State and Local Public Policies
National Council of Senior Citizens
National Council of Women of the United States
National Education Association-Political Action Committee
National Emergency Committee
National Equal Rights League
National Farmers Organization
National Farmers Union
National Federation of Business and Professional Women's Clubs
National Federation of the Blind
National Legislative Conference
National Organization for Women
National Planning Association
National Right to Life Committee
National Right to Work Committee
National Small Business Association
National Student Association
National Student Lobby
National Taxpayers Union
National Union for Social Justice
Political Action Committee
Poor People's Campaign
Public Interest Research Group

SANE: A Citizens' Organization for a Sane World
Share Our Wealth Movement
Sierra Club
Society of Christian Socialists
Society of Separationists
Southern Regional Council
Students for a Democratic Society
Townsend Plan National Lobby
Trade Relations Council of the United States
Women's Organization for National Prohibition Reform
Zionist Organization of America

# MINORITY PARTIES AND ORGANIZATIONS

Afro-American Party
Alianza Federal de Mercedes
Alianza Hispano-Americano
All American Council
Alliance for Displaced Homemakers
American Equal Rights Association
American Indian Defense Association
American Indian Movement
Anti-Defamation League of the B'nai B'rith
Association on American Indian Affairs
Black Congressional Caucus
Black Panther Party
Congress of Racial Equality
Council of Energy Resources Tribes
Filipino American Political Association
Freedom Now Party
Fuerzas Armádas de Liberacíon on Nacional Puertorriqueña
Gray Panthers
Indian Rights Association
Jewish Defense League
La Raza Unida Party
Mexican-American Political Association
National Afro-American Council
National Association for the Advancement of Colored People
National Black Political Assembly
National Equal Rights League
National Federation of the Blind
National Negro Congress
National Republican Heritage Groups Council
Niagara Movement
Protect America's Children
Southern Christian Leadership Conference
Student Nonviolent Coordinating Committee
Universal Negro Improvement Association

# PATRIOTIC PARTIES AND SOCIETIES

American Coalition of Patriotic Societies
American Legion
American Security Council
AMVETS
Catholic War Veterans of the United States of America
Christian Anti-Communism Crusade
Christian Crusade
Christian Nationalist Party
Disabled American Veterans
Freedom Center International
Freedoms Foundation at Valley Forge
Liberty Lobby
Marine Corps League
National Civic Federation
National Security League
National Trust for Historic Preservation
Navy League of the United States
Patriotic Party
Sons of Liberty
Veterans of Foreign Wars of the United States

# PEACE GROUPS

Alternative Candidate Task Force for 1968
America First Committee
American Beat Consensus
American Civil Liberties Union
American League against War and Fascism
American Peace Society
American Union against Militarism
Anti-Imperialist League
Bipartisan Congressional Clearinghouse
Carnegie Endowment for International Peace
Committee for Nonviolent Action
Committee on Militarism in Education
Emergency Peace Campaign
Fellowship of Reconciliation
Freedom and Peace Party
Friends Peace Committee
Keep America Out of War Congress
League of Nations Association
League to Enforce Peace
Mobilization Committee to End the War in Vietnam
Movement for a New Congress
National Committee on the Cause and Cure of War
National Conference of Concerned Democrats

National Council for Prevention of War
National Student Association
Non-Partisan Committee for Peace through Revision of the Neutrality Act
Pacifica Foundation
Peace and Freedom Party
People's Peace Prosperity Party
Progressive Citizens of America
Progressive Party (1948)
Referendum '70
SANE: A Citizens' Organization for a Sane World
Students for a Democratic Society
United States Committee to Aid the National Liberation Front of South Vietnam
War Resisters League
W. E. B. Du Bois Clubs of America
Woman's Peace Party
Women's International League for Peace and Freedom
World Federalists

# POLITICAL AND ORGANIZATIONAL MOVEMENTS

Alianza Federal de Mercedes
American Agriculture Movement
American and Foreign Anti-Slavery Society
American Anti-Slavery Society
American Beat Consensus
American Indian Movement
American League to Abolish Capital Punishment
Anti-Imperialist League
Anti-Masonic Party
Anti-Monopoly Party
Anti-Saloon League of America
Bonus Army
Catholic Workers Movement
Christian Anti-Communism Crusade
Christian Crusade
Coxey's Army
Crazies
End Poverty in California
Farmers Holiday Association
Mobilization Committee to End the War in Vietnam
Movement for a New Congress
National American Women Suffrage Association
National Center for Voluntary Action
National Union for Social Justice
Niagara Movement
Poor People's Campaign
Populist Party
Progressive Party (1912)
Progressive Party (1924)
Progressive Party (1948)

Share Our Wealth Movement
Single Tax Movement
Townsend Plan National Lobby
Weatherman
Woman's Christian Temperance Union
Zionist Organization of America

# POLITICAL MACHINES, CAUCUSES, AND COALITIONS

Albany Regency
All American Council
Black Congressional Caucus
Breckinridge Democrats
Bull Moosers
Byrd Machine
Coalition for a Democratic Majority
Coalition for Human Needs and Budget Priorities
Committee for the New Majority
Conservative Caucus, The
Cox Machine
Crump Machine
Democratic Advisory Council
Democratic Central Committee of Cook County
Democratic Study Group
Essex Junto
Lowndes County Freedom Organization
Loyal Democrats of Mississippi
Mississippi Freedom Democratic Party
Mugwumps
National Black Political Assembly
National Christian Democratic Party
National Conference of Concerned Democrats
National Democratic Party (1860)
National Democratic Party (1896)
National Democratic Party of Alabama
National Federation of Republican Women
National Progressive Republican League
National Republican Congressional Committee
National Republican Heritage Groups Council
National Silver Party
National Women's Political Caucus
Pendergast Machine
Progressive Citizens of America
Quay Machine
Radical Republicans
Republican Governors Association
Republicans for Progress
Ripon Society
South Carolina Progressive Democratic Party

Tammany Hall
Tweed Ring
Women's National Democratic Club
Women's National Republican Club
Young Americans for Freedom
Young Communist League
Young Democrats of America
Young People's Socialist League
Young Progressives of America
Young Republican National Federation
Young Socialist Alliance

# POLITICAL PARTIES

Afro-American Party
American Beat Consensus
American Commonwealth Political Federation
American Conservative Union
American Independent Party
American Labor Party
American National Party
American Party
American Vegetarian Party
Anarchist Federation
Anti-Federalist Party
Anti-Masonic Party
Anti-Monopoly Party
Black Panther Party
Christian Nationalist Party
Christian Party
Citizens' Party
Communist Party of the United States of America
Conservative Party
Constitution Party
Constitutional Union Party
Democratic Party
Democratic-Republican Party
Equal Rights (Locofoco) Party
Equal Rights Party (1872)
Equal Rights Party (1884)
Farmer-Labor Party
Federalist Party
Free Soil Party
Freedom and Peace Party
Freedom Now Party
Free-State Party
Fuerzas Armádas de Liberacíon Nacional Puertorriqueña
Greenback Party
Independence Party

Independent Progressive Party
Independent Republican Party
Jobless Party
Know-Nothing Party
La Raza Unida Party
Liberal Party
Liberal Republican Party
Libertarian Party
Liberty Party (1839)
Liberty Party (1932)
Lowndes County Freedom Organization
Loyal Democrats of Mississippi
Mississippi Freedom Democratic Party
National Christian Democratic Party
National Democratic Party (1860)
National Democratic Party (1896)
National Democratic Party of Alabama
National Hamiltonian Party
National Labor Reform Party
National Liberty Party
National Party
National Progressives of America
National Republican Party
National Silver Party
National Socialist White People's Party
National States' Rights Party
National Union Party
National Woman's Party
Nonpartisan League
Patriotic Party
Peace and Freedom Party
People's Party (1823)
People's Party (1971)
People's Peace Prosperity Party
Poor Man's Party
Populist Party
Progressive Labor Party
Progressive Party (1912)
Progressive Party (1924)
Progressive Party (1948)
Prohibition Party
Republican Party
Silver Republican Party
Social Democratic Party of America
Socialist Labor Party
Socialist Party of America
Socialist Workers Party
South Carolina Progressive Democratic Party
States' Rights Party
Statesman Party
Straight-Out Democratic Party

Tax Cut Party
Theocratic Party
Union Labor Party
Union Party
United Citizens' Party
United Labor Party
Universal Party
Whig Party
Wisconsin Progressive Party
Woman's Peace Party
Workingmen's Party

# PROFESSIONAL ORGANIZATIONS

American Association of University Women
American Bar Association
American Library Association
American Medical Political Action Committee
American Society for Public Administration
American Society of Sanitary Engineering
Council of State Governments
Fraternal Order of Police
International City Management Association
International Downtown Executives Association
National Academy of Sciences
National Alliance of Businessmen
National Association of Broadcasters
National Association of Manufacturers
National Conference of State Legislative Leaders
National Conference of State Legislators
National Council on Crime and Delinquency
National Education Association-Political Action Committee
National Federation of Business and Professional Women's Clubs
National Municipal League
National Order of Women Legislators
National Planning Association
National Society of State Legislators

# REFORM GROUPS

American and Foreign Anti-Slavery Society
American Anti-Slavery Society
American Anti-Vivisection Society
American Equal Rights Association
American League to Abolish Capital Punishment
American Society for the Prevention of Cruelty to Animals
American Veterans Committee

American Woman Suffrage Association
Americans for Energy Independence
Anti-Monopoly Party
Anti-Saloon League of America
Center for Community Change
Citizens Conference on State Legislatures
Committee for Fair Divorce and Alimony Laws
Common Cause
Conference for Progressive Political Action
Consumer Federation of America
Democratic Study Group
Equal Rights Party (1872)
Equal Rights Party (1884)
Gray Panthers
Greenback Party
League of Conservation Voters
Morality in Media
National American Woman Suffrage Association
National Association for the Advancement of Colored People
National Black Political Assembly
National Civil Service League
National Conference of Alternative State and Local Public Policies
National Conference of State Legislative Leaders
National Council of Senior Citizens
National Council of Women of the United States
National Council on Crime and Delinquency
National Gun Control Center
National Housing Conference
National Labor Reform Party
National Municipal League
National Planning Association
National Progressive Republican League
National Union for Social Justice
Niagara Movement
People United to Save Humanity
Poor People's Campaign
Populist Party
Progressive Citizens of America
Progressive Party (1912)
Public Interest Research Group
Share Our Wealth Movement
Southern Christian Leadership Conference
Townsend Plan National Lobby
Woman's Christian Temperance Union
Women's Organization for National Prohibition Reform
World Federalists

# RELIGIOUS GROUPS AND ASSOCIATIONS

American Council of Christian Churches
Anti-Defamation League of the B'nai B'rith

Catholic War Veterans of the United States of America
Catholic Workers Movement
Christian Anti-Communism Crusade
Christian Crusade
Christian Freedom Foundation
Christian Front
Christian Nationalist Party
Christian Party
Fellowship of Reconciliation
Friends Peace Committee
Jewish Socialist Verband of America
Knights of Columbus
Moral Majority
Morality in Media
National Christian Association
National Christian Democratic Party
National Conference of Christians and Jews
Society of Christian Socialists
Southern Christian Leadership Conference
Theocratic Party
Woman's Christian Temperance Society
Zionist Organization of America

## SPECIAL INTEREST GROUPS

Action on Smoking and Health
Alliance for Displaced Homemakers
America First Committee
American Anti-Vivisection Society
American Bimetallic League
American Indian Movement
American League to Abolish Capital Punishment
American Society for the Prevention of Cruelty to Animals
American Union Against Militarism
American Woman Suffrage Association
Association Against the Prohibition Amendment
Association for the Study of Abortion
Christian Anti-Communism Crusade
Citizens Committee for the Right to Keep and Bear Arms
Committee for Fair Divorce and Alimony Laws
Committee on Militarism in Education
Committee to Defend America by Aiding the Allies
Common Cause
Consumer Federation of America
Council of Energy Resources Tribes
Indian Rights Association
League of Conservation Voters
Liberty Lobby
Marine Corps League
Mobilization Committee to End the War in Vietnam

Morality in Media
Movement for a New Congress
National Alliance of Businessmen
National American Woman Suffrage Association
National Association for the Advancement of Colored People
National Association of Manufacturers
National Civil Service League
National Committee for Citizens in Education
National Committee on the Cause and Cure of War
National Council for the Prevention of War
National Council of Senior Citizens
National Council on Crime and Delinquency
National Federation of the Blind
National Gun Control Center
National Organization for the Reform of Marijuana Laws
National Organization for Women
National Rifle Association of America
National Right to Life Committee
National Right to Work Committee
National Safety Council
National Security League
National Small Business Association
National Student Association
National Student Lobby
National Tenants Organization
National Union for Social Justice
Nation-Wide Committee on Import-Export Policy
Navy League of the United States
Northern Irish Aid Committee
Polish National Alliance
Poor People's Campaign
Public Interest Research Group
SANE: A Citizens' Organization for a Sane World
Share Our Wealth Movement
Sierra Club
Single Tax Movement
Society of Separationists
Townsend Plan National Lobby
United Nations Association of the United States of America
War Resisters League
Water Resources Congress
Woman's Christian Temperance Union
Zionist Organization of America

# VETERANS' ORGANIZATIONS

American Indo-China Veterans Legion
American Legion
American Veterans Committee
AMVETS

Bonus Army
Catholic War Veterans of the United States of America
Disabled American Veterans
Grand Army of the Republic
Marine Corps League
Navy League of the United States
Paralyzed Veterans of America
Veterans of Foreign Wars of the United States

# WOMEN'S GROUPS

Alliance for Displaced Homemakers
American Agri-Women
American Association of University Women
American Woman Suffrage Association
Association for the Study of Abortion
League of Women Voters of the United States
National American Woman Suffrage Association
National Council of Women of the United States
National Federation of Business and Professional Women's Clubs
National Federation of Republican Women
National Order of Women Legislators
National Organization for Women
National Woman Suffrage Association
National Woman's Party
National Woman's Political Caucus
Rural American Women, Inc.
Woman's Christian Temperance Union
Woman's Peace Party
Women's International League for Peace and Freedom
Women's National Democratic Club
Women's National Republican Club
Women's Organization for National Prohibition Reform

# YOUTH GROUPS

American Beat Consensus
American Council of Young Political Leaders
Crazies
Mobilization Committee to End the War in Vietnam
National Organization for the Reform of Marijuana Laws
National Student Association
National Student Lobby
National Youth Alliance
Student Nonviolent Coordinating Committee
Students for a Democratic Society
United States Committee to Aid the National Liberation Front of South Vietnam
War Resisters League

Weatherman
W. E. B. Du Bois Clubs of America
Young Americans for Freedom
Young Communist League
Young Democrats of America
Young People's Socialist League
Young Progressives of America
Young Republican National Federation
Young Socialist Alliance

# CHRONOLOGY

In the listing that follows, the founding dates of the political parties and civic action groups included in this volume are arranged chronologically by year. This appendix not only reveals periods of proliferation of organizations but also indicates the types of groups spawned by the events of a given era. Wars and periods of economic depression are significant progenitors of collective political action as were the cold war, civil rights movement, anti-Vietnam movement, environmentalist movement, consumerism, and neo-isolationism.

*1765*

Sons of Liberty

*1772*

Committees of Correspondence

*1774*

Continental Association

*1778*

Essex Junto

*1783*

Tammany Hall

*1787*

Anti-Federalist Party
Federalist Party

*1792*

Democratic-Republican Party

*1816*

American Colonization Society

*1820*

Albany Regency

*1823*

People's Party

*1824*

National Republican Party

*1826*

Anti-Masonic Party

*1828*

American Peace Society

*1832*

Democratic Party

*1833*

American Anti-Slavery Society
Whig Party

*1836*

Equal Rights (Locofoco) Party

*1839*

Liberty Party

*1840*

American and Foreign Anti-Slavery Society

*1848*

Democratic National Committee
Free Soil Party

*1849*

Know-Nothing Party

*1854*

Knights of the Golden Circle
Republican Party

*1855*

Free-State Party

*1856*

Republican National Committee

*1858*

League of United Southerners

*1860*

Constitutional Union Party

National Democratic Party
Radical Republicans

*1862*

Union League

*1864*

Independent Republican Party
National Equal Rights League
National Union Party

*1865*

Grand Army of the Republic

*1866*

American Equal Rights Association
American Society for the Prevention of Cruelty to Animals
Ku Klux Klan
National Republican Congressional Committee

*1867*

Knights of the White Camelia
National Christian Association
National Grange

*1869*

American Woman Suffrage Association
National Woman Suffrage Association
Prohibition Party

*1871*

National Rifle Association of America

*1872*

Equal Rights Party
Liberal Republican Party
National Labor Reform Party
Straight-Out Democratic Party

*1874*

Greenback Party
Woman's Christian Temperance Union

*1876*

American Library Association
American National Party

*1877*

Socialist Labor Party
United Labor Party

*1878*

American Bar Association

*1879*

Single Tax Movement

*1880*

Polish National Alliance

*1881*

National Civil Service League

*1882*

American Association of University Women
Indian Rights Association

*1883*

American Anti-Vivisection Society
International Working People's Association

*1884*

Anti-Monopoly Party
Equal Rights Party
Mugwumps

*1885*

Quay Machine
Trade Relations Council of the United States

*1887*

American Protective Association
Union Labor Party

*1888*

Cox Machine
National Council of Women of the United States

*1889*

American Bimetallic League
Society of Christian Socialists
Veterans of Foreign Wars of the United States

*1890*

National Afro-American League
National American Woman Suffrage Association

*1891*

Populist Party

*1892*

Friends Peace Committee

Pendergast Machine
Sierra Club

*1893*

National Civic Federation

*1894*

Alianza Hispano-Americano
Coxey's Army
Immigration Restriction League
National Municipal League

*1895*

Anti-Saloon League of America
National Association of Manufacturers

*1896*

National Democratic Party
National Party
Silver Republican Party

*1897*

National Congress of Parents and Teachers
Social Democratic Party of America
Zionist Organization of America

*1898*

Anti-Imperialist League

*1901*

Socialist Party of America
Water Resources Congress

*1902*

American Automobile Association
Free Speech League
National Farmers Union
Navy League of the United States

*1904*

National Liberty Party

*1905*

League for Industrial Democracy
Niagara Movement

*1906*

American Society of Sanitary Engineering

*1907*

National Council on Crime and Delinquency

*1908*

Independence Party
National Governors' Conference

*1909*

Crump Machine
National Association for the Advancement of Colored People

*1910*

Carnegie Endowment for International Peace

*1911*

National Progressive Republican League

*1912*

Chamber of Commerce of the United States
National Safety Council
Progressive Party

*1913*

Anti-Defamation League of the B'nai B'rith

*1914*

American Union against Militarism
Council on Religion and International Affairs
Fellowship of Reconciliation
International City Management Association
National Security League
Universal Negro Improvement Association

*1915*

Fraternal Order of Police
League to Enforce Peace
Nonpartisan League
War Resisters League
Woman's Peace Party
Women's International League for Peace and Freedom

*1916*

Brookings Institution

*1917*

National Woman's Party

*1918*

Foreign Policy Association

*1919*

American Country Life Association
American Legion
Communist Party of the United States of America

Farmer-Labor Party
National Federation of Business and Professional Women's Clubs

### 1920

American Civil Liberties Union
American Farm Bureau Federation
Association Against the Prohibition Amendment
League of Women Voters of the United States

### 1921

Council on Foreign Relations
Disabled American Veterans
Jewish Socialist Verband of America
National Council for Prevention of War
Women's National Republican Club

### 1922

Conference for Progressive Political Action
National Association of Broadcasters

### 1923

Marine Corps League
Women's National Democratic Club

### 1924

National League of Cities
Progressive Party

### 1925

Committee on Militarism in Education
Council of State Governments
National Committee on the Cause and Cure of War

### 1926

Byrd Machine
United Farmers Educational League

### 1927

American League to Abolish Capital Punishment

### 1928

National Conference of Christians and Jews
Workingmen's Party

### 1929

American Coalition of Patriotic Societies
Conference for Progressive Labor Action

League for Independent Political Action
Women's Organization for National Prohibition Reform

*1930*

Democratic Central Committee of Cook County
Young Communist League

*1931*

National Housing Conference
Young People's Socialist League
Young Republican National Federation

*1932*

All American Council
Bonus Army
Farmers Holiday Association
Jobless Party
Liberty Party
United States Conference of Mayors
Young Democrats of America

*1933*

American League against War and Fascism
Catholic Workers Movement
Committee for the Nation to Rebuild Prices and Purchasing Power
End Poverty in California
Farmer-Labor Political Federation
Townsend Plan National Lobby

*1934*

American Liberty League
American Society of Planning Officials
National Planning Association
National Union for Social Justice
Share Our Wealth Movement
Southern Governors' Conference
Wisconsin Progressive Party

*1935*

American Commonwealth Political Federation
Catholic War Veterans of the United States of America
Emergency Peace Campaign

*1936*

American Labor Party
Association on American Indian Affairs
Christian Party
German-American Bund
National Negro Congress
Social Democratic Federation
Union Party

*1937*

  National Federation of Republican Women
  National Small Business Association

*1938*

  Keep America Out of War Congress
  National Order of Women Legislators
  National Progressives of America
  Non-Partisan Committee for Peace through Revision of the Neutrality Act
  Socialist Workers Party

*1939*

  American Society for Public Administration
  Christian Front

*1940*

  America First Committee
  Committee to Defend America by Aiding the Allies
  National Emergency Committee
  National Federation of the Blind

*1941*

  American Council of Christian Churches
  Fight for Freedom

*1942*

  Committee for Economic Development
  Congress of Racial Equality

*1943*

  American Veterans Committee
  Political Action Committee

*1944*

  AMVETS
  Independent Citizens Committee for the Arts, Sciences and Professions
  Liberal Party
  National Citizens Political Action Committee
  South Carolina Progressive Democratic Party
  Southern Regional Conference

*1945*

  Paralyzed Veterans of America

*1946*

  Progressive Citizens of America

*1947*

  Americans for Democratic Action
  Christian Nationalist Party
  Independent Progressive Party

Labor's League for Political Education
National Committee for an Effective Congress
National Student Association
National Trust for Historic Preservation
World Federalists

*1948*

American Vegetarian Party
National Legislative Conference
Progressive Party
States' Rights Party
Young Progressives of America

*1949*

Freedoms Foundation at Valley Forge

*1950*

American Assembly
Christian Crusade
Christian Freedom Foundation
Fuerzas Armádas de Liberacíon Nacional Puertorriqueña

*1952*

Constitution Party
Poor Man's Party

*1953*

Christian Anti-Communism Crusade
Committee of One Million
International Downtown Executives Association
Nation-Wide Committee on Import-Export Policy

*1954*

Citizens' Councils of America
Fair Campaign Practices Committee

*1955*

American Security Council
Committee on Political Education
Liberty Lobby
National Farmers Organization
National Right to Work Committee

*1956*

People-to-People International

*1957*

Committee for Nonviolent Action
Democratic Advisory Council
SANE: A Citizens' Organization for a Sane World
Southern Christian Leadership Conference

*1958*

American Association of Retired Persons
Americans for Constitutional Action
Freedom Center International
National States' Rights Party

*1959*

John Birch Society
Mexican-American Political Association
National Conference of State Legislative Leaders
National Socialist White People's Party
Students for a Democratic Society

*1960*

Afro-American Party
American Beat Consensus
Anarchist Federation
Fair Play for Cuba Committee
Student Nonviolent Coordinating Committee
Tax Cut Party
Theocratic Party
Young Americans for Freedom
Young Socialist Alliance

*1961*

American Medical Political Action Committee
Amnesty International
National Council of Senior Citizens

*1962*

Conservative Party
Midwestern Governors Conference
Morality in Media
National Committee for Citizens in Education
Organization of Afro-American Unity
Republican Governors Association
Ripon Society
Voter Education Project

*1963*

Business-Industry Political Action Committee
Freedom Now Party
National Academy of Sciences
Society of Separationists
Universal Party
Western Governors' Conference

*1964*

Action Committee to Increase Opportunities for Negroes
Alianza Federal de Mercedes
American Conservative Union

Mississippi Freedom Democratic Party
Progressive Labor Party
Republicans for Progress
United National Association of the United States of America
W. E. B. Du Bois Clubs of America

## 1965

Association for the Study of Abortion
Citizens Conference on State Legislatures
Committee for Fair Divorce and Alimony Laws
Filipino American Political Association
National Conference for a New Politics
National Society of State Legislators
United States Committee to Aid the National Liberation Front of South Vietnam

## 1966

American Council of Young Political Leaders
Black Panther Party
Lowndes County Freedom Organization
Mobilization Committee to End the War in Vietnam
National Hamiltonian Party
National Organization for Women
Patriotic Party

## 1967

Action on Smoking and Health
Consumer Federation of America
National Conference of Concerned Democrats
Poor People's Campaign

## 1968

Alternative Candidate Task Force for 1968
American Independent Party
American Indian Movement
Center for Community Change
Crazies
Freedom and Peace Party
Jewish Defense League
Join Hands
Loyal Democrats of Mississippi
National Committee of Inquiry
National Democratic Party of Alabama
Peace and Freedom Party

## 1969

Council on Population and Environment
League of Conservation Voters
National Alliance of Businessmen
National Taxpayers Union
National Tenants Organization
National Youth Alliance

United Citizens' Party
Weatherman

*1970*

Americans for Indian Opportunity
Bipartisan Congressional Clearinghouse
Common Cause
Gray Panthers
La Raza Unida Party
Movement for a New Congress
National Center for Voluntary Action
National Organization for the Reform of Marijuana Laws
Northern Irish Aid Committee
People's Peace Prosperity Party
Public Interest Research Group
Referendum '70

*1971*

American Indo-China Veterans Legion
Black Congressional Caucus
Citizens Committee for the Right to Keep and Bear Arms
Education for Democracy
Libertarian Party
National Republican Heritage Groups Council
National Right to Life Committee
National Student Lobby
National Women's Political Caucus
People's Party
People United to Save Humanity

*1972*

National Black Political Assembly
National Education Association-Political Action Committee

*1973*

Coalition for a Democratic Majority
Coalition for Human Needs and Budget Priorities
Trilateral Commission, the

*1974*

American Agri-Women
Conservative Caucuses, The

*1975*

Alliance for Displaced Homemakers
Americans for Energy Independence
Committee for a New Majority
Democratic Study Group
National Conference of Alternative State and Local Policies

*1976*

National Gun Control Center

*1977*

American Agriculture Movement
Protect America's Children
Rural American Women, Inc.

*1978*

Committee of Americans for the Canal Treaties
Council of Energy Resources Tribes

*1979*

Moral Majority
National Christian Democratic Party
Progressive Alliance
United States Student Association

# GLOSSARY

*ABOLITIONIST.*  One who opposed slavery and assumed a militant stance in advocating its abolition.

*AFFIRMATIVE ACTION.*  A policy of giving special consideration to minorities and women relative to hiring, promotion, admittance, or wages.

*AGRARIANISM.*  A belief that agriculture is the fundamental industry, that rural life is superior to urban existence, that farm life makes for virtue, and that the farm population serves as a moral leavening agent in society.

*AMERICAN DEMOCRACY.*  A name for the Democratic Party no longer in use.

*AMERICAN SYSTEM.*  A program proposed by Henry Clay, and associated with the Whig Party in the 1840s and 1850s, consisting of internal improvements, rechartering the Bank of the United States, protective tariff, and returning to the states revenues received from the sale of public land.

*AMERICANISM.*  A belief in absolute loyalty to the United States and its political and economic system.

*ANARCHISM.*  A belief or political theory that all government should be abolished.

*ANTI-LECOMPTON DEMOCRAT.*  A member of the Democratic Party who opposed admission of Kansas as a slave state according to the constitution drafted at Lecompton, Kansas, in 1857.

*ANTI-MASONS.*  Those who opposed the Masons as a secret society and/or were members of the Anti-Mason Party.

*ANTI-NEBRASKA DEMOCRATS.*  Members of the Democratic Party who opposed the Kansas-Nebraska Act of 1854, many of whom eventually joined the Republican Party.

*ANTI-NEW DEALERS.*  Those conservatives within both the Republican Party and Democratic Party who opposed the New Deal of President Franklin D. Roosevelt.

*ANTI-QUIDS.*  Thos who opposed the Tertium Quids.

*ARBITRATION.*  The resolution of a dispute or controversy by a third party whose decision the principals involved have agreed in advance to abide by.

*AUSTRALIAN BALLOT.*  Secret ballot.

*BARNBURNERS.*  Radical Democrats who between 1843 and 1848 condemned internal improvements and banks and opposed the Albany Regency.

*BIMETALLISM.*  The use of both gold and silver as a basis for the issuance of money.

*BIPARTISAN.* An issue upon which the two major parties, Democratic and Republican, agree to deal cooperatively instead of on a partisan basis.

*BIRCHITE.* A member of the John Birch Society.

*BLACK AND TANS.* A reference to black and white Republicans in the South during Radical Reconstruction.

*BLACK MUSLIM.* A member of the Nation of Islam.

*BLACK POWER.* The advocacy of increased political involvement and control over all aspects of black life.

*BLACK REPUBLICANS.* A term of derogation given to members of the Republican Party for opposing slavery or advocating civil rights for freedmen.

*BOSS.* The leader of a political machine.

*BOURBON DEMOCRATS.* A term of derogation applied to Southern Democrats, who as the planter, ruling class, acted as if the Civil War had done nothing to lessen their power; usually indicating a reactionary Democrat.

*BRAIN TRUST.* The name given to a group who advised Franklin D. Roosevelt in the 1932 campaign and while he served as president.

*BRANNAN PLAN.* A farm program proposed by Secretary of Agriculture Charles F. Brannan in 1949 designed to reorient the acreage allotment system along the lines of an income support standard; provide direct subsidy payments; use units of production; base parity on a moving ten-year average of gross farm income; and make a maximum production payment of $26,000 to any one farmer.

*BRINK OF WAR.* A phrase used by John Foster Dulles while serving as secretary of state in the Eisenhower cabinet to indicate that a tough stand had to be taken against the Soviet Union; this policy, called brinksmanship, was criticized by some as being reckless rhetoric and overly bellicose.

*BRYANITES.* Followers of William Jennings Bryan.

*BUCKTAILS.* A faction of the New York Democratic-Republican Party that opposed the Clintonians and helped set the stage for the election of Andrew Jackson as president in 1828.

*BULL MOOSERS.* Members of the Progressive Party of 1912.

*CARPETBAGGER.* A northern politician who went to the South during Reconstruction to exploit blacks and take advantage of military occupation by Union troops.

*CHICANO.* One of Mexican heritage.

*CIVIL LIBERTARIAN.* One who advocates absolute free speech with no restrictions.

*CIVIL SERVICE REFORM.* Initiated in 1883 by passage of the Pendleton Act to begin the practice of selecting civil servants by examination and promotion by merit rather than have appointments made as part of the spoils system.

*CLINTONIANS.* Followers of Governor DeWitt Clinton of New York.

*COLD WAR.* The military and diplomatic confrontation between the Soviet Union and the United States (and Western Europe) since the end of World War II, when the Soviet Union refused to withdraw from Eastern Europe until Communist regimes were established; in more recent times the tensions have relaxed due to a policy of détente by the United States and of coexistence by the Soviet Union.

*COMMUNIST.* One who advocates Marxism or a variation of its revolutionary dogma; a member of the Communist Party of the United States of America.

*COMMUNIST FRONT.* An organization that is formed by communists or is infiltrated by them so that it may appear to be noncommunist while in fact it is dominated by them for political purposes.

*CONSCIENCE WHIGS.* Members of the Whig Party who opposed slavery.

*CONSERVATIVE.* At the time of Alexander Hamilton, this label applied to one who stood for centralized government, internal improvements, and positive federal management; but in modern times it applies to one who stands for limited government, reduced spending, states' rights, and less federal regulation.

*CONTINENTAL CONGRESS.* A de facto government established by the thirteen colonies in 1774; in 1776 the second Continental Congress adopted the Declaration of Independence and conducted the Revolutionary War until the Articles of Confederation were ratified in 1781.

*COPPERHEAD.* A derogatory term used to designate a member of the Democratic Party in the North or border states who supported the Confederacy.

*COTTON WHIGS.* Members of the Whig Party from the South who supported slavery.

*COUNTERCULTURE.* An anti-establishment lifestyle characterized by sexual freedom, long hair, freaky clothes, rock music, drugs, and rebellion against convention; stemmed from the beat generation of the 1950s and reached its height in the late 1960s.

*DARK HORSE.* A candidate who appears not to be in the running and is unexpectedly nominated.

*DEMAGOGUE.* One who resorts to appeals to emotion or prejudice in order to attract a following.

*DEMOCRATIC CENTRALISM.* Wherein the members of an ideologically oriented organization are bound to follow the decisions made by the leaders.

*DIXIECRATS.* Members of the States' Rights Party of 1948.

*DOUGHFACE.* A designation given to a northern politician who supported the southern position prior to the Civil War.

*DOVE.* One who opposes war.

*DRY.* One who supported prohibition.

*ELECTORAL COLLEGE.* A body of electors in each state equal in number to its total representation in Congress, who cast their ballots for president and vice-president on the basis of which candidates won the state's popular vote; sometimes electors have voted independent of the election results.

*ESTABLISHMENT.* Having reference to the groups, standards, traditions, and politico-economic system that make for a societal power structure and generally accepted guides for social behavior.

FAIR DEAL. The name President Harry S. Truman gave to his political proposals in 1949 to continue and expand upon the New Deal policies.

*FARM BLOC.* A bipartisan coalition in Congress during the 1920s of those representing rural constituencies.

*FAVORITE SON.* A presidential aspirant who has the support of his state delegation at a national nominating convention.

*FEMINIST.* A woman who advocates equality for women and an end to sexism.

*FIREATERS.* Those southerners calling for secession prior to the Civil War.

*FREE-SOILER.* One who opposed the extension of slavery into the territories and/or a member of the Free Soil Party.

*FREE SPEECH MOVEMENT.* Initiated at the University of California at Berkeley in 1964 to protest limitations on political activity on campus.

*FREEDOM RIDER.* One who sought to desegregate public transportation in the South during the 1960s.

*FREEMASON.* One who belongs to a secret society with rituals and accepts the principles of charity, brotherhood, and mutual aid.

*FUSION CANDIDATE.* A candidate who is nominated or supported by two political parties.

*GOLD BUGS.* The name given to those in the 1890s who advocated only gold money and opposed the issuance of silver money.

*GOLD DEMOCRATS.* Democrats in the 1890s who favored the gold standard and opposed the monetization of silver and/or were adherents to the National Democratic Party, which opposed William Jennings Bryan as the fusion candidate of the Democratic and Populist parties.

*GOLDWATERITES.* Followers of Senator Barry M. Goldwater (R-Ariz.).

*GOP.* Abbreviation for Grand Old Party, a name given to the Republican Party in the post-Civil War era.

*GRASS ROOTS.* Having popular appeal or acceptance at the local level in politics.

*GREAT COMMONER.* An appellation given to William Jennings Bryan.

*GREAT DEPRESSION.* That period of economic collapse and high unemployment from 1929 to 1939.

*GREAT EXPERIMENT.* A reference to prohibition.

*GREAT SOCIETY.* The designation given by President Lyndon B. Johnson to his massive legislative program designed to extend, expand, and update New Deal policies in the 1960s, and to eradicate poverty, racial discrimination, and environmental pollution.

*GREENBACKER.* One who advocated the issuance of greenbacks by the government and/or a member of the Greenback Party.

*GREENBACKS.* Fiat paper currency issued during the Civil War.

*HALF-BREEDS.* A faction of the Republican Party that opposed a third term for President Ulysses S. Grant and supported the termination of Radical Reconstruction.

*HARD MONEY.* Gold coins or specie.

*HAWK.* One who favors going to war.

*HONEST MONEY.* Gold coins or specie.

*HOOVER DEPRESSION.* A designation made by Democrats of the period from 1929 to 1932 when Herbert C. Hoover was president and the nation was in the throes of the Great Depression.

*HOOVERCRAT.* A Southern Democrat who supported Herbert C. Hoover for President in 1928 because of the fact that Governor Alfred E. Smith of New York was a Roman Catholic.

*HUNKERS.* Conservative Democrats who cooperated with slaveholders, 1845-1852, for the sole purpose of winning election to office.

*HYPHENATE VOTER.* A voter who represents a particular foreign-born group, such as German-American.
his or her party's nominees because of political principles.

*IMPERIAL PRESIDENCY.* A description given by historian, Arthur M. Schlesinger, Jr., to those presidents who asserted great power and thus made the office of president one with imperial prerogatives.

*INITIATIVE.* A process whereby the electorate, by petition, may initiate a referendum on specific legislation that a state legislature has refused to enact.

*INSURGENT.* A member of a political party who asserts independence and refuses to support the party on some issues or a particular issue; one who also refuses to support his or her party's nominees because of political principles.

*INTEREST GROUP.* An organized group seeking to pressure Congress or influence public opinion in order to obtain certain political objectives.

*INTERNAL IMPROVEMENTS.* A program funded by the federal government to construct interstate roads and canals and to improve rivers and harbors so as to promote economic prosperity and national unity.

*INTERVENTIONIST.* One who advocates that the United States utilize its military power, in a war if necessary, to protect the national self-interest.

*INVISIBLE EMPIRE.* Referring to the secret and clandestine activities of the Ku Klux Klan.

*ISOLATIONIST.* One who advocates that the United States make no foreign commitments that might entangle the nation in a war.

*JACKSONIAN DEMOCRACY.* Egalitarianism during the administration of President Andrew Jackson that reflected itself in the advocacy of states' rights, rotation in office or spoils system, universal manhood suffrage, destruction of the Bank of the United States, and the exaggerated virtue and intelligence of the common man.

*JEFFERSONIAN REPUBLICANS.* Followers of Thomas Jefferson who adhered to a political philosophy advocating limited government, laissez-faire economics, low tariff, narrow construction of the U.S. Constitution, and a minimal military establishment.

*JIM CROW.* A racist system based on white supremacy, segregation, and disfranchisement of blacks; prevalent in the South until the civil rights movement of the 1960s.

*JINGOISM.* A bellicose patriotism calling for the use of military might to uphold the national honor or the nation's self-interest.

*LAW AND ORDER.* A phrase connoting a desire for an end to violent demonstrations and termination of crime in the streets; interpreted by critics as implying a justification for police brutality.

*LEFT WING.* Those in a political party or a faction representing the more radical position on the political spectrum; usually advocating enlargement of the welfare state, increased federal expenditures to help the poor, and a dovish position relative to foreign policy.

*LIBERAL.* At one time the label for one who stood for states' rights, laissez-faire economics, low tariff, and limited government; but these Jeffersonian principles in modern times have yielded to the Progressive concept of positive government and support for the welfare state.

*LILY-WHITES.* Those in the South who opposed having blacks participate in political activity or vote in primaries.

*LOBBY.* An individual or group who seeks to influence a legislative body so as to acquire legislation or favorable treatment from a governmental agency.

*LOG-ROLLING.* The practice of supporting legislation or appropriations for other legislators or members of Congress in return for their votes on projects of interest to a particular district; particularly suited for pork barrel legislation.

*McCARTHYISM.* Named after Senator Joseph McCarthy (R.-Wis.) for his ruthless tactics of making reckless charges and presuming guilt by association while seeking to ferret out Communists from the government.

*McGOVERNITES.* Followers of Senator George M. McGovern (D-S.D.).

*MANIFEST DESTINY.* A commonly accepted rationale during and after the Mexican War to justify territorial expansion as if it were a predestined extension of democracy.

*MARSHALL PLAN.* A massive economic program initiated in 1948 for the rehabilitation of Western Europe to prevent it from going Communist.

*MARTLING MEN.* A faction of the Democratic-Republican Party in New York led by Aaron Burr against the followers of Thomas Jefferson; the name was acquired from the room where the faction met.

*MARXIST.* One who adheres to or advocates the economic and political philosophy of Karl Marx.

*MASON.* One who is a Freemason and accepts the principles of Freemasonry.

*MIDWEST REPUBLICANS.* Members of the Republican Party living in or representing constituencies in mid-America; sometimes characterized by conservatism, isolationism, and opposition to the welfare state.

*MILITANT.* One who adopts a defiant stance relative to a position or proposal.

*MISSILE GAP.* A phrase used by John F. Kennedy in 1960 during his campaign for the presidency to exploit politically the fact the Soviet Union had launched a sputnik into orbit before the United States could launch a satellite; actually the United States had missile superiority and no gap really existed.

*MODERN REPUBLICANISM.* A phrase describing the policies and programs of the Eisenhower administration from 1953 to 1961.

*MONROE DOCTRINE.* A message to Congress in 1823 by President James Monroe setting forth the doctrine that the United States would not tolerate interference by European countries in Latin America and implying that the United States considered this region to be its sphere of influence; this was elaborated upon by subsequent presidents and has become a traditional aspect of American foreign policy.

*NATIVIST.* One who regards native-born citizens as superior to immigrants or naturalized citizens.

*NATURALIZATION.* The procedure by which an immigrant becomes an American citizen.

*NEW DEAL.* The political program implemented by President Franklin D. Roosevelt from 1933 to 1939 for the purpose of initiating relief, recovery, and reform, and in so doing bring about the creation of the welfare state.

*NEW FREEDOM.* The name of the liberal-reform program advocated by Woodrow Wilson when running for the presidency as a Democrat in 1912.

*NEW FRONTIER.* A liberal political program championed by President John F. Kennedy from 1961 to 1963 that sought to extend, expand, or update New Deal policies.

*NEW LEFT.* A political movement starting in the late 1950s and culminating in the early 1970s that was characterized by the following: anti-establishment; ideologically oriented; rebelled against capitalism, colonialism, corporate liberalism, imperialism, materialism, and racism; advocated counterculture; opposed the war in Vietnam; sought student power; and was prone to use violence when protesting or staging demonstrations.

*NEW NATIONALISM.* The name Theodore Roosevelt gave to his liberal-reform program while running as a presidential candidate in 1912 on the Progressive party ticket.

*NEW POLITICS.* Political activity characterized by the following: appeal to the young; championing of women's and gay rights; legalization of abortion; opposition to war; decriminalization of marijuana; participatory democracy; support of the welfare state; ideological commitment; and concern for ecology.

*NOBLE EXPERIMENT.* A reference to prohibition.

*NORMALCY.* Referring to the era of Warren G. Harding and the nation's desire to return to the normality of pre-World War I times.

*OHIO GANG.*   A corrupt group of politicians from Ohio associated with the administration of President Warren G. Harding.

*OLD GUARD.*   A designation for the more conservative or reactionary faction of the Republican Party.

*OLD LEFT.*   Liberal and left-wing political activity prior to 1960 that was characterized by nonviolent participation in the democratic process, attempts to reform capitalism, compromise and consensus, and respect for the majority will.

*OLD REPUBLICANS.*   A designation for those within the Democratic-Republican Party who remained loyal to the principles of Jeffersonian Republicanism.

*OMBUDSMAN.*   One who receives complaints, investigates, and seeks remedies for private citizens relative to the conduct of a public official.

*OSTEND MANIFESTO.*   A statement in 1854 by several American ministers in Europe indicating it would be wise for Spain to sell Cuba to the United States lest the latter take it by force.

*OUTLAWRY OF WAR.*   A movement in the 1920s, culminating in the Kellogg-Briand Pact of 1928, to have nations renounce war as a means of settling international disputes.

*PACIFIST.*   One opposed to war for any reason.

*PARTY LINE.*   Rigid adherence to ideological dogma promulgated by a leader or organization; often associated with the Communist Party of the United States of America in its parroting of the party line from Moscow.

*PEACE DEMOCRATS.*   Members of the Democratic Party during the Civil War who wished to terminate the conflict by permitting the Confederacy to exist as a separate nation.

*PEOPLE'S LOBBY.*   A lobby formed ostensibly to serve the best interests of the public at large.

*PLATFORM.*   A statement adopted by a political party in which, by a series of planks or assertions, the position of the party on the issues of the day is enunciated.

*PLUTOCRAT.*   One who wishes to have a major voice in ruling a country because of great wealth.

*POLITICAL MACHINE.*   A political organization controlled by one party and usually run by a boss.

*POLL TAX.*   Prior to the ratification of the Twenty-fourth Amendment to the U.S. Constitution, a tax could be levied as a prerequisite to voting.

*POPULAR FRONT.*   A policy initiated by the Communists in 1935 to collaborate with liberals, trade unionists, and socialists to stop the advance of fascism; this continued until 1939 when the Nazi-Soviet Pact prompted the Communists to support isolationism, disarmament, and noninterventionism until 1941, at which time Adolf Hitler ordered the invasion of the Soviet Union by the German army.

*POPULAR SOVEREIGNTY.*   A doctrine set forth by Stephen A. Douglas in justifying the Kansas-Nebraska Act of 1854 on the basis that the peoples of the respective territory in question should have the right to determine whether slavery should exist in the newly formed state.

*PORK BARREL LEGISLATION.*   Usually having reference to appropriations for local projects, such as post offices and rivers and harbors improvement, which lends itself to *log-rolling* and extravagant expenditures.

*PRECINCT CAPTAIN.*   The designation given to a party worker or machine politician who organizes voters in a precinct.

*PRESIDENTIAL TIMBER.*   One who is considered a prospect as a presidential candidate.

*PRIMARY.* An election where members of one party vote to nominate candidates.

*PROGRESSIVES.* Those who accepted the concept of positive government, redistribution of wealth, and federal regulation of big business; sometimes referring to those members of the Progressive Party of 1912 but more often to those accepting the Hamiltonian ideas of government, whether in the Democratic or Republican Party.

*PROHIBITION.* The manufacture, distribution, or sale of alcoholic beverages was prohibited by the Volstead Act of 1919 and by ratification in 1920 of the Eighteenth (prohibition) Amendment to the U.S. Constitution.

*PROLETARIAT.* According to Marxist dogma, this is the exploited working class.

*PROPOSITION 13.* A 1978 initiative proposal approved by the voters in the state of California to place severe limitations on real estate taxes.

*PROTECTIONISM.* A belief that high tariffs are beneficial for the nation.

*QUIDS.* Same as *Tertium Quids.*

*RABBLE-ROUSER.* A demagogue, or one who appeals to the baser instincts of voters.

*RACISM.* A belief, whether covert or overt, that some race or races are innately inferior to others.

*RADICAL.* An extremist who advocates policies and programs considered too advanced by the moderate or middle-of-the-roader.

*RADICAL RECONSTRUCTION.* The policy of military occupation of the South, establishment of carpetbag state governments, and civil rights for blacks.

*REACTIONARY.* A modern conservative seeking to retain political principles and programs of a previous era.

*RECALL.* A process whereby the electorate, by petition, may remove a public official from office.

*RECESSION.* A decline in the economy not warranted severe enough to be considered a depression.

*RED BAITING.* Detraction of an opponent or organization by claiming it is communist or communist dominated.

*REFERENDUM.* A process whereby the electorate may nullify a law enacted by the state legislature.

*REPEAL.* Usual reference is to the repeal of prohibition by adoption of the Twenty-first Amendment to the U.S. Constitution in 1933.

*RIGHT TO LIFE.* In opposition to abortion other than for medical reasons in order to save the life of the mother.

*RIGHT TO WORK.* Open shop where workers may be employed without joining a labor union.

*RIGHT WING.* Members of a party or a faction representing the ultraconservative position on the political spectrum; usually advocating reduction in taxes, limited government, resistance to communism, and a hawkish position relative to foreign policy.

*SENIOR CITIZEN.* A private citizen who is sixty-five years old or older and is retired.

*SEPARATION OF CHURCH AND STATE.* A provision of the First Amendment to the U.S. Constitution forbidding public support for any religion or religious organization.

*SEXISM.* Discrimination against women purely on the basis of sex and an attitude reflected in societal institutions indicating a belief that women are innately inferior to men.

*SILVER REPUBLICANS.* Those Republicans in the 1890s who supported monetization of silver.

*SILVERITES.* Those in the 1890s who advocated the unlimited issuance by the government of silver money at a ratio of sixteen to one with gold.

*SOCIALIST.* One who advocates nationalization or state ownership of industry.

*SOFT MONEY.* Greenbacks or paper money.

*SOFT-SHELLS.* An anti-slavery and reform faction within the *Hunkers.*

*SONS OF THE SOUTH.* Organizations formed after congressional passage of the Kansas-Nebraska Act in 1854 to make Kansas a slave state.

*SOUTHERN DEMOCRATS.* Members of the Democratic Party in Congress representing the eleven former states of the Confederacy.

*SPOILS SYSTEM.* The blatant use of patronage to appoint members of a particular political party to public offices without regard for qualifications or merit.

*SQUARE DEAL.* Used to designate the presidential administration of Theodore Roosevelt.

*STALWARTS.* The spoilsmen or machine faction of the Republican Party, 1869-1880, who opposed reform and supported Ulysses S. Grant for a third term.

*STANDPAT REPUBLICAN.* Denoting Republicans at the turn of the century who refused to accept progressivism and held to their reactionary views.

*STUMP SPEAKER.* Originally referring to the use of a tree stump as a place to speak during a political rally, especially in rural areas; meaning one who is effective in addressing large crowds when campaigning.

*SUFFRAGIST.* A woman prior to 1920 who advocated and worked for getting the right to vote for all qualified (according to age) females.

*TAFT REPUBLICANS.* Members of the GOP in 1912 who remained loyal to President William Howard Taft or that faction of the Republican Party in the 1940s and 1950s who supported Senator Robert A. Taft of Ohio for the presidency.

*TERTIUM QUIDS.* A designation given in 1806 to John Randolph of Roanoke by those Jeffersonian Republicans who deviated from the principles of states' rights, limited government, and no internal improvements; the Latin phrase having reference to being "that third something."

*THIRD WORLD.* Those nations of Africa and Asia not aligned with the Communist bloc or the free world.

*TROTSKYITES.* Advocates of the revolutionary ideology of Leon Trotsky.

*TRUMAN DOCTRINE.* An aspect of foreign policy initiated by President Harry S. Truman in 1947 to contain communism and prevent its spread in Greece, Turkey, and Western Europe.

*TWO-THIRDS RULE.* Adopted by the Democratic Party in 1832 so as to require a two-thirds vote of a nominating convention to nominate a presidential and vice-presidential candidate; the rule was rescinded in 1936.

*UPPER CHAMBER.* The U.S. Senate.

*URBAN RENEWAL.* Slum clearance and rebuilding the inner core of cities.

*VIRGINIA DYNASTY.* Thomas Jefferson, James Madison, and James Monroe were all from Virginia and served successfully as presidents from 1801 to 1825.

*VISTA.* A domestic peace corps made up of volunteers.

*WAR DEMOCRATS.* Usually associated with those members of the Democratic Party who supported the Union during the Civil War.

*WAR HORSE.* A veteran politician who has served the party long and faithfully.

*WAR ON POVERTY.* Part of the Great Society program of President Lyndon B. Johnson to eradicate or alleviate the problems caused by poverty.

*WARD HEELER.*   A minor politician who serves a political machine on the local level.

*WAVING THE BLOODY SHIRT.*   A campaign tactic used by the Republican Party after the Civil War to remind voters that the Democratic Party was responsible for the deaths of Union soldiers and was the party of treason.

*WELFARE STATE.*   Stemming from the New Deal, where the federal government involves itself with the economic welfare of the citizenry as manifest in Social Security, Medicare, minimum wages, low-cost housing, welfare assistance to the poor, unemployment insurance, food stamps, and aid to education.

*WET.*   One who opposed prohibition.

*WHIP.*   A designated member of a party who seeks to keep members disciplined when voting on partisan issues.

*YIPPIE.*   A member of the Youth International Party formed in 1967 to protest against the war in Vietnam. Its members, sometimes called Yippies, were known for their advocacy of the counterculture and for their militant anti-war demonstrations.

*YOUNG AMERICA.*   A term used to denote a faction within the Democratic Party in the 1840s favoring expansionism and the acquisition of more territory by the United States on the American continent; Stephen A. Douglas was an eloquent spokesman for this group.

*ZIONISM.*   A movement initiated by Theodore Herzl in 1896, when he published *Der Judenstaat*, to establish an independent Jewish nation in Palestine; a goal that came to fruition in 1948 with the existence of Israel.

# INDEX

Page numbers in **boldface** indicate the location of the main entry.

Abernathy, Ralph David, 354, 428, 429
abolitionists, 233, 379
abortion, 71, 211, 312, 331
Abzug, Bella S., 330, 358, 475
Action Committee to Increase Opportunities
    for Negroes, **3**
Action on Smoking and Health, **3**
Adams, Charles Francis, 178, 229
Adams, John, 159, 171
Adams, John Quincy, 308, 347, 348, 468
Adams, Samuel, 108, 425
Addams, Jane, 473, 474, 475
affirmative action, 3
AFL-CIO Committee on Political Education.
    *See* Committee on Political Education
AFL's Labor's League for Political Educa-
    tion. *See* Labor's League for Political
    Education
Afro-American, 4, 247, 340
Afro-American Party, **4**
Agnew, Spiro T., 163, 395, 396, 400
agriculture, 11
Albany Regency, **4**
Alianza Federal de Mercedes, **5**
Alianza Hispano-Americano, **6**
alimony, 100
Alimony Unlimited. *See* Committee for Fair
    Divorce and Alimony Laws
All American Council, **7**
Allen, Charles, 214
Alliance for Displaced Homemakers, **8**
Alternative Candidate Task Force for 1968, **9**

America First Committee, **10**
America First Party. *See* Constitution Party
American Agriculture Movement, **11**
American Agri-Women, **13**
American and Foreign Anti-Slavery Society,
    **13**
American Anti-Slavery Society, **14**
American Anti-Vivisection Society, **15**
American Assembly, **16**
American Association for the United
    Nations. *See* United Nations Association
    of the United States of America
American Association of Retired Persons, **16**
American Association of University Women,
    **17**
American Association on Indian Affairs. *See*
    Association on American Indian Affairs
American Automobile Association, **18**
American Bar Association, **19**
American Beat Consensus, **20**
American Bimetallic League, **21**
American Civil Liberties Union, **21**
American Coalition of Patriotic Societies, **23**
American Colonization Society, **24**
American Commonwealth Political
    Federation, **25**
American Conservative Union, **26**
American Council of Christian Churches, **27**
American Council of Young Political
    Leaders, **28**
American Council on Alcohol Problems.
    *See* Anti-Saloon League of America

American Country Life Association, 28
American Equal Rights Association, 30
American Farm Bureau Federation, 30
American Federation of Labor Committee on
    Political Education. *See* Committee on
    Political Education
American Federation of Labor-Congress of
    Industrial Organization Political Action
    Committee. *See* Political Action
    Committee
American First Party. *See* Christian
    Nationalist Party
American Independent Party, 32
American Indian Defense Association. *See*
    Association on American Indian Affairs
American Indian Movement, 36
American Indo-China Veterans Legion, 37
American Institute of International Affairs.
    *See* Council on Foreign Relations
American Labor Party, 38
American League against War and Fascism,
    39
American League for Peace and Democracy.
    *See* American League against War and
    Fascism
American League to Abolish Capital
    Punishment, 40
American Legion, 41
American Legislators Association. *See*
    Council of State Governments
American Liberty League, 43
American Library Association, 44
American Medical Political Action
    Committee, 45
American Municipal Association. *See*
    National League of Cities
American National Party, 46
American Nazi Party. *See* National Socialist
    White People's Party
American Negro Labor Congress. *See*
    National Negro Congress
American Parole Association. *See* National
    Council on Crime and Delinquency
American Party (1856). *See* Know-Nothing
    Party
American Party (1968). *See* American
    Independent Party
American Peace Society, 47
American Protective Association, 48
American Protective Tariff League. *See*
    Trade Relations Council of the United
    States

American Republican Party. *See* American
    Independent Party
American Security Council, 49
American Society for Public Administration,
    50
American Society for the Prevention of
    Cruelty to Animals, 51
American Society of Sanitary Engineering, 51
American Union against Militarism, 52
American Vegetarian Party, 53
American Veterans Committee, 54
American Veterans of Foreign Service. *See*
    Veterans of Foreign Wars of the United
    States
American Veterans of World War II-Korea-
    Vietnam. *See* AMVETS
American Woman Suffrage Association, 54
American Workers Party. *See* Conference
    for Progressive Labor Action
Americans for Constitutional Action, 55
Americans for Democratic Action, 56
Americans for Energy Independence, 58
Americans for Indian Opportunity, 59
Amlie, Thomas, 25
amnesty, 60, 323, 460
Amnesty International, 60
AMVETS, 61
anarchism, 62, 201, 230, 409, 438
Anarchist Federation, 62
Anderson, John, 57, 227, 229, 397
animals, 51, 115
Anthony, Susan B., 249, 272, 328
anti-busing, 269
anti-Communist, 87, 88, 232, 351
Anti-Defamation League of the B'nai B'rith,
    63
Anti-Enlistment League. *See* War Resisters
    League
Anti-Federalist Party, 64
Anti-Imperialist League, 65
Anti-Masonic Party, 66
Anti-Monopoly Party, 67
Anti-Saloon League of America, 67
anti-Semitism, 63, 90, 91, 203, 475
anti-slavery, 14, 178, 183, 233, 378
anti-vivisection, 15
Armed Forces of Puerto Rican National
    Liberation. *See* Fuerzas Armádas de
    Liberacíon Nacional Puertorriqueña
arms. *See* firearms
Army of the Philippines, Cuba, and

Puerto Rico. *See* Veterans of Foreign
Wars of the United States
Arthur, Chester A., 383
Arvey, Jacob, 135
Association against the Prohibition Amend-
ment, **69**
Association for Humane Abortion. *See*
Association for the Study of Abortion
Association for the Study of Abortion, **71**
Association on American Indian Affairs, **72**
atheism, 424

Baldwin, Calvin B., 257, 358, 364
Baldwin, Roger, 21, 53, 60
Banks, Nathaniel P., 215
Barker, Wharton, 356
Barton, Clara, 272
beatniks, 20
Beecher, Henry Ward, 55
Bell, John, 123, 380
Benson, Ezra Taft, 31, 184, 185, 291
Bickley, George W. L., 211
bigotry, 211, 219, 265
Bill of Rights, 23
bimetallism, 21
Bipartisan Congressional Clearinghouse, **73**
Birch, John Morrison, 206
Birch Society, John. *See* John Birch Society
Birney, James G., 13, 233, 234
black caucus, 73, 254, 427
Black Congressional Caucus, **73**
black militants, 344
black nationalism, 117, 254, 298, 340, 435,
457, 458
Black Panther Party, **74**
Black Panthers. *See* Black Panther Party
Black Political Convention. *See* National
Black Political Assembly
black power, 117
black voters, 262, 277
Bland, Richard "Silver Dick," 21
blind, 287, 288
Blind Federation. *See* National Federation
of the Blind
B'nai B'rith, 63, 205
Bonus Army, **76**
Bonus Expeditionary Force. *See* Bonus Army
Bonus Marchers. *See* Bonus Army
bossism, 345, 374, 442
Bowers, Henry F., 48
boycott, 124, 125
Brandeis, Louis D., 297, 489

Brannan, Charles F., 285
Breckinridge, John C., 140, 275
Breckinridge Democrats. *See* National
Democratic Party
Brookings, Robert, 77
Brookings Institution, **77**
brotherhood, 265
Browder, Earl R., 39, 112, 113, 481
Brown, Edmund G. "Pat," 467
Bryan, Charles W., 148
Bryan, William Jennings, 65, 144, 146, 148,
276, 356, 406
Bryant, Anita, 370
Brzezinski, Zbigniew, 446, 447
Buchanan, James, 139, 140
Buckley, James, 26, 121, 480
Buckley, William F., Jr., 121, 207, 480
budget, 98
Bull Moose Party. *See* Progressive Party
[1912]
Bull Moosers. *See* Progressive Party [1912]
Burke-Wadsworth Act, 105, 108
Burr, Aaron, 159, 166, 441
Bush, George, 397, 398, 400
business, 317
Business and Professional Women's Clubs,
Inc., The Federation of. *See* National
Federation of Business and Professional
Women's Clubs
business community, 84, 99, 249, 318
Business-Industry Political Action
Committee, **79**
businessmen, 79, 252, 332, 430
Butler, Benjamin F., 191, 375
Butler, Nicholas Murray, 81
Byrd, Harry F., Jr., 80
Byrd, Harry F., Sr., 79, 122, 433
Byrd Machine, **79**
Byrne, Jane, 136, 352

Calhoun, John C., 309, 433
campaign, election, 168
Cannon, James P., 68, 421, 487
capital punishment, 40, 41
capitalism, 411, 412, 462, 471, 481
Carmichael, Stokely, 235, 435
Carnegie, Andrew, 65, 81
Carnegie Endowment for International
Peace, **81**
Carson, Rachel, 273
Carter, Jimmy, 155, 156, 157, 158, 281, 285,
302, 400, 432, 446, 447, 456, 467, 490

Catholic War Veterans of the United States of America, **82**
Catholic Workers Movement, **82**
Catholicism, 82, 148, 210
Catt, Carrie Chapman, 226, 249, 263
censorship, 244, 252
Center for Community Change, **84**
Center for the Study of Responsive Law. *See* Public Interest Research Group
*Century of Dishonor*, 198
Cermak, Anton J. "Tony," 134, 456
Cermak Machine. *See* Democratic Central Committee of Cook County
Chamber of Commerce of the United States
Chicago Boss System. *See* Democratic Central Committee of Cook County
Chicanos, 5, 6, 220, 238, 488
Chisholm, Shirley, 73, 330
Christensen, Parley P., 169
Christian American Patriots. *See* Christian Party
Christian Anti-Communism Crusade, **86**
Christian Crusade, **88**
Christian Freedom Foundation, **89**
Christian Front, **89**
Christian Nationalist Crusade. *See* Christian Nationalist Party
Christian Nationalist Party, **90**
Christian Party, **91**
Christians, 256, 265
Church of God Party. *See* Theocratic Party
Church Peace Union. *See* Council on Religion and International Affairs
CIO-Political Action Committee. *See* Political Action Committee
Citizens Committee for the Right to Keep and Bear Arms, **92**
Citizens Conference on State Legislatures, **93**
Citizens' Councils of America, **94**
Citizen's Party, **96**
city manager, 199, 200
City Managers' Association. *See* International City Management Association
civil disobedience, 101, 173, 184, 428, 435
civil liberties, 21, 60, 179, 254, 474
civil rights, 30, 117, 165, 174, 179, 180, 208, 248, 251, 261, 282, 296, 322, 330, 335, 431, 435, 436, 458, 463, 466, 485
civil service, 166, 259, 286
Civil War, 188, 276, 366, 375, 380
Clark, Edward, 232
Clay, Henry, 308, 468-70

Cleaver, Eldridge, 75, 344
Cleveland, Frederick A., 77
Cleveland, Grover, 143, 245, 258, 276
Clinton, DeWitt, 159, 172, 348
Clinton, George, 65, 159
Coalition for a Democratic Majority, **97**
Coalition for Human Needs and Budget Priorities, **98**
cold war, 89, 180, 210, 289, 322, 403, 482, 485
colonialism, 65, 457
colonization, 24, 212
commerce, 84
Commission on Interracial Cooperation. *See* Southern Regional Council
Committee for a Free China. *See* Committee of One Million
Committee for Economic Development, **99**
Committee for Fair Divorce and Alimony Laws, **100**
Committee for Nonviolent Action, **100**
Committee for the Nation to Rebuild Prices and Purchasing Power, **101**
Committee for the New Majority, **102**
Committee of Americans for the Canal Treaties, **102**
Committee of One Million, **103**
Committee on Conservative Alternatives. *See* American Conservative Union
Committee on Militarism in Education, **105**
Committee on Political Education, **105**
Committee to Defend America by Aiding the Allies, **107**
Committee to Support Moderate Republicans. *See* Republicans for Progress
Committees of Correspondence, **108**
Committees of Safety. *See* Committees of Correspondence
Common Cause, **108**
Commoner, Barry, 96
Commongood Party. *See* People's Party [1971]
Commonwealth of Christ. *See* Coxey's Army
communism, 87, 88, 90, 91, 112, 343, 421, 452, 466, 481
Communist, 39, 90, 298, 358, 359, 365, 455, 466, 482, 486
Communist Labor Party. *See* Communist Party of the United States of America
Communist Party of America. *See* Communist Party of the United States of America

Communist Party of the United States (Marxist-Leninist). *See* Communist Party of the United States of America

Communist Party of the United States of America, **110**

Communist Party, U.S.A. *See* Communist Party of the United States of America

Communist Political Association. *See* Communist Party of the United States of America

community, local, 84

Conference for Progressive Political Action, **116**

Congress of Industrial Organization-Political Action Committee. *See* Political Action Committee

Congress of Racial Equality, **117**

Congress on Population and Environment. *See* Council on Population and Environment

conscription, 281

conservation, 225, 288, 305, 405, 464

conservatism, 26, 56, 118, 232, 480

Conservative Caucus, The, **118**

Conservative Party, **120**

Conservative Party of New York. *See* Conservative Party

Conservative Union. *See* American Conservative Union

conservatives, 102, 118, 120

Constitution, U.S., 14, 19, 41, 56, 64, 166, 167, 170, 172, 182, 244, 324, 328, 476

Constitution Parties of the United States. *See* Constitution Party

Constitution Party, **121**

Constitutional Union Party, **123**

Consumer Federation of America, **124**

consumer protection, 124, 370

Continental Association, **124**

Cook County Machine. *See* Democratic Central Committee of Cook County

Coolidge, Calvin, 11, 29, 31, 85, 175, 195, 388, 389, 458

Copperheads, 213, 381, 450

CORE. *See* Congress of Racial Equality

Coughlin, Charles E., 89, 326, 327, 417, 450, 451

Council of Energy Resources Tribes, **125**

Council of State Governments, **125**

Council on Foreign Relations, **126**

Council on Population and Environment, **127**

country life, 28

Country Life Association. *See* American Country Life Association

Country's People's Caucus. *See* People's Party [1971]

Country People's Party. *See* People's Party [1971]

Counts, George S., 38, 228

Counsins, Norman, 402, 479

Cox, George Barnsdale, 128

Cox, James M., 147, 388

Cox, James R., 205, 206

Cox Machine, **128**

Coxey, Jacob S., 128, 129

Coxey's Army, **128**

Crazies, **129**

crime, 273

Croly, Herbert, 362

Crump, Edward H. "Boss," 130, 131

Crump Machine, **130**

Cuba, 168

Curtis, Carl, 26, 104

Daley, Richard J., 135, 137, 339, 347

Daley Machine. *See* Democratic Central Committee of Cook County

Darrow, Clarence, 41, 223, 407

Davis, Angela, 115

Davis, David, 294

Davis, John W., 44, 147, 148, 364, 389

Dawes, Henry Lauren, 198

Day, Dorothy, 82

Debs, Eugene V., 408, 413-16, 420, 421

DeLeon, Daniel, 408, 409, 413

Democratic Advisory Council, **133**

Democratic (Breckinridge Faction) Party. *See* National Democratic Party

Democratic Central Committee of Cook County, **134**

Democratic National Committee, **136**

Democratic Party, **137**

Democratic-Republican Party, **157**

Democratic Study Group, **160**

Democrats. *See* Democratic Party

Deutschamerikanische Volksbund. *See* German-American Bund

Dewey, John, 21, 174, 222, 224, 407

Dewey, Thomas E., 221, 392, 393, 418

Dirksen, Everett M., 135

Dirty Shirt Party. *See* Workingmen's Party

Disabled American Veterans, **161**

Disabled Veterans of the World War. *See* Disabled American Veterans
Dixiecrat Party. *See* States' Rights Party
Dixiecrats, 433
Dole, Robert, 26, 396
Dorhn, Bernadine, 361, 439, 464, 465
Douglas, Paul A., 104, 107, 174, 222, 351, 353
Douglas, Stephen A., 140, 141, 175
Douglass, Frederick, 165, 282
draft dodgers, 238, 348, 460, 463
Dubinsky, David, 38, 57
Du Bois, W. E. B., 222, 228, 250, 335, 457, 466
Du Bois Clubs of America. *See* W. E. B. Du Bois Clubs of America
Duke, David, 218
Dulles, John Foster, 351

Eastman, Crystal, 329, 474
ecology, 127, 405, 464
education, 261, 268
Education for Democracy, **163**
Eisenhower, Dwight D., 16, 206, 393, 394, 398, 455
Emergency Peace Campaign, **163**
End Poverty in California, **164**
energy, 58, 125, 304, 431
engineers, sanitary, 51
environment, 127
Equal Rights Amendment (ERA), 109, 227, 272, 286, 299, 301, 302, 330, 401, 476
Equal Rights Democrats. *See* Equal Rights (Locofoco) Party
Equal Rights (Locofoco) Party, **164**
Equal Rights Party [1872], **165**
Equal Rights Party [1884], **165**
Essex Junto, **166**

Fair Campaign Practices Committee, **168**
Fair Deal, 8, 58, 80, 151, 293
Fair Play for Cuba Committee, **168**
Falwell, Jerry, 241, 243
Farm Bureau. *See* American Farm Bureau Federation
Farmer, James, 117, 172, 224
Farmer-Labor Party, **169**
farmers, 11, 13, 29, 30, 44, 169, 170, 190, 283, 291, 448, 452
Farmer's Educational and Cooperative Union of America. *See* National Farmers Union

Farmers Holiday Association, **170**
Farmers Union. *See* National Farmers Union
fascism, 39, 57, 462, 481
Faubus, Orville, 321
Federalist Party, **170**
Federalist. *See* Federalist Party
Federation of American Zionists. *See* Zionist Organization of America
Fellowship of Reconciliation, **172**
feminists, 300, 329, 474
Fight for Freedom, **173**
Filipino-American, 173
Filipino American Political Association, **173**
Fillmore, Millard, 215, 469, 470
firearms, 93
Ford, Gerald R., 177, 205, 295, 396, 397, 400, 466
Ford, Henry, 474, 475
Ford, Henry II, 64, 248
Foreign Policy Association, **174**
Foreman, James, 264, 434
Forrest, Nathan Bedford, 216
Foster, William Z., 111, 113
Frankfurter, Felix, 21, 489
Fraser, Douglas, 357
Fraternal Order of Police, **175**
Free Democracy of the United States. *See* Free Soil Party
Free Democratic Party. *See* Free Soil Party
free enterprise, 84
Free Libertarian Party. *See* Libertarian Party
Freeman, Orville, 285
Free Soil Party, **178**
free speech, 179
Free Speech League, **179**
Freedom and Peace Party, **179**
Freedom Center International, **180**
Freedom Democrats. *See* Mississippi Freedom Democratic Party
Freedom Now Party, **180**
Freedoms Foundation at Valley Forge, **180**
Free-State Party, **183**
Frémont, John C., 198, 216, 377, 379
Friedan, Betty, 300, 330
Friends of the Earth. *See* League of Conservation Voters
Friends Peace Committee, **184**
Fuerzas Armádas de Liberacíon Nacional Puertorriqueña, **184**
fundamentalism, 27, 88, 207, 242, 370

Gardner, John W., 108
Garfield, James A., 143, 383
Garner, John N., 108, 149, 150
Garrison, William Lloyd, 14, 233
Garvey, Marcus M., 457, 458
gay. *See* homosexuals
George, Henry, 406, 407, 454
geriatrics, 271
German-American Bund, **187**
German-Americans, 188
gold, 276
Gold Bugs. *See* National Democratic Party
Gold Democrats. *See* National Democratic
    Party
Goldman, Emma, 179, 201
Goldwater, Barry M., 26, 207, 298, 353, 394,
    395, 480
Gompers, Samuel, 258, 353
GOP. *See* Republican Party
governors, 293, 288, 305, 377, 430, 467
Governors' Conference. *See* National
    Governors' Conference
Grand Army of the Republic, **188**
Grand Old Party. *See* Republican Party
Grange. *See* National Grange
Grant, Ulysses S., 216, 229, 328, 376, 381,
    382, 450
Grant, Ulysses S. III, 325
Gray Panthers, **189**
Great Depression, 101, 164, 205, 222, 234,
    286, 390, 404, 453, 477, 481
Great Society, 8, 58, 84, 325, 429
Greeley, Horace, 142, 229, 434
Green Cross. *See* National Safety Council
Greenback Independent Party. *See* Green-
    back Party
Greenback Nationalist Party. *See* Green-
    back Party
Greenback Party, **190**
Greenback-Labor and National Party. *See*
    Greenback Party
Greenback-Labor Party. *See* Greenback
    Party
greenbacks, 190, 294
Gregory, Richard "Dick," 179, 254, 344
gun-control legislation, 93, 292, 311


Haight, Raymond, 164, 307
Hale, John P., 178, 470
Hall, Gus, 114, 115
Hallinan, Vincent W., 39, 197, 366, 466

Hamilton, Alexander, 65, 157, 159, 166, 171,
    292
Hancock, Winfield Scott, 141, 142, 143
Hanna, Marcus "Mark," 258, 373
Harding, Warren G., 85, 129, 388, 389
Hargus, Billy James, 88
Harriman, Averell, 103, 228
Harrison, Benjamin, 373, 384, 385
Harrison, William Henry, 67, 384, 468
Hartford Convention. *See* Essex Junto
Hayden, Tom, 241, 263, 436, 437, 440
Hayes, Rutherford B., 213, 216, 382, 450
Haywood, William "Big Bill," 62, 421
Hearst, William Randolph, 195
Helms, Jesse, 102, 104, 118
Helsinki Agreement, 351, 489
Henry, Patrick, 65, 108, 425
Hensley, Kirby James, 350
Herzl, Theodore, 489
Hesburgh, Theodore M., 59, 103
Hillman, Sidney, 38, 352
Hillquit, Morris, 224, 408, 414, 417
historic preservation, 325, 326
Hobson, Henry W., 173
holding action, 12, 170, 283
Home Prohibition Party. *See* Prohibition
    Party
homemaker, 8
homosexuals, 120, 154, 370
Hooks, Benjamin Lawson, 251, 357
Hoover, Herbert C., 293, 389, 390, 456
Hoover, J. Edgar, 62, 175
Howe, Julia Ward, 54, 272
Hughes, Charles Evans, 270, 297, 317, 363,
    387, 388
Hughes, Langston, 39, 251
Human Rights Party. *See* People's Party
    [1971]
Humphrey Hubert H., 57, 170, 236, 298,
    352, 353, 396
Hutton, E. F., 180
hyphenate Americans, 7, 308

immigration, 23, 174, 194, 196, 442
Immigration Restriction League, **194**
imperialism, 65, 179, 248, 359, 365, 435,
    453, 455, 463, 465, 475
Independence League. *See* Independence
    Party
Independence Party, **195**
Independent Citizens Committee for the
    Arts, Sciences and Professions, **196**

Independent (Greenback) Party. *See* Greenback Party
Independent National Party. *See* Greenback Party
Independent Party. *See* Greenback Party
Independent Progressive Party, **197**
Independent Republican Party, **198**
Independent Republicans. *See* Mugwumps
Indian Rights Association, **198**
Indians, 36, 59, 72, 125, 198, 309
Industrial Workers of the World. *See* Anarchist Federation
Innis, Roy, 117
Institute for Democratic Education. *See* Anti-Defamation League of the B'nai B'rith
Institute for Government Research. *See* Brookings Institution
Institute for Policy Studies. *See* National Conference of Alternative State and Local Public Policies
Institue of Medicine. *See* National Academy of Sciences
integration, 117, 208, 254, 278
Intercollegiate Socialist Society of America. *See* League for Industrial Democracy
International City Management Association, **199**
International City Managers' Association. *See* International City Management Association
International Congress of Women. *See* Women's International League for Peace and Freedom
International Downtown Executives Association, **200**
International Working People's Association, **201**
internationalism, 56
internationalists, 173, 228, 316
Invisible Empire of the Knights of the Ku Klux Klan. *See* Ku Klux Klan
Irish-Americans, 339
Irish Republican Army, 338
isolationism, 327, 334, 482
isolationists, 10, 42, 105, 282, 337, 462, 485
IWW. *See* Anarchist Federation

Jackson, Andrew, 137, 138, 156, 159, 160, 309, 347, 468
Jackson, Helen Hunt, 198
Jackson, Jesse, 346, 347

Javits, Jacob K., 104, 120, 229
Jay, John, 65, 171
Jefferson, Thomas, 157, 159, 166
Jeffersonian Democrats. *See* Democratic-Republican Party
Jeffersonian Republicans. *See* Democratic-Republican Party
Jewish Defense League, **203**
Jewish Socialist Verband of America, **205**
Jews, 265
Jobless Party, **205**
John Birch Society, **206**
Johnson, Andrew, 282, 327, 381
Johnson, Hiram W., 362, 387
Johnson, Lyndon B., 8, 9, 29, 153, 219, 240, 241, 248, 264, 266, 271, 294, 403, 456, 483
Join Hands, **208**

Kahane, Meier, 203
Keep America Out of War Congress, **210**
Kelley, Florence, 53, 224
Kelley, Oliver Hudson, 290
Kelly, Edward J., 134, 135
Kelly-Nash machine, 134
Kelly-Nash Machine. *See* Democratic Central Committee of Cook County
Kennedy, Edward M. "Ted," 36, 56, 57, 74, 136, 137, 156, 290, 339, 445
Kennedy, John F., 8, 31, 57, 152, 153, 228, 238, 285, 353, 403, 483
Kennedy, Robert F. "Bobby," 177, 266
King, Martin Luther, Jr., 208, 264, 354, 427, 429, 435
King, Rufus, 172
Kirkland, Lane, 446
Kissinger, Henry, 103, 204
Knights of Columbis, **210**
Knights of the Golden Circle, **211**
Knights of the White Camelia, **213**
Know-Nothing Party, **214**
Korean War, 28, 463, 475
Kuhn, Fritz Julius, 187, 188
Ku Klux Klan, **216**

La Follette, Philip F., 306, 307, 364, 471, 472
La Follette, Robert M., Jr., 306, 364, 471, 472
La Follette, Robert M., Sr., 116, 169, 305, 361, 363, 364, 387, 416
La Follette, Suzanne, 120, 210

La Guardia, Fiorello H., 38, 306, 358, 456
La Raza Unida Party, 220
labor, organized, 38, 105, 314, 358, 453
Labor Party. *See* Farmer-Labor Party
Labor Reform Party. *See* National Labor
    Reform Party
Labor's League for Political Education, 221
Land Labor Clubs. *See* Single Tax Movement
Landon, Alfred M., 391, 403
Latinos, 5, 220, 238
lawyers, 19, 20
League for Independent Political Action, 222
League for Industrial Democracy, 223
League of Conservation Voters, 225
League of Nations, 174, 263
League of Nations Association. *See* Foreign
    Policy Association
League of United Southerners, 226
League of Women Voters of the United
    States, 226
League to Enforce Peace, 227
legislator, state. *See* state, legislators
legislature, state. *See* state, legislature
Lehman, Herbert, 38, 228
Lemke, William, 306, 327, 450
lesbianism, 302
Libby, Frederick J., 270
Liberal Party, 228
Liberal Republican Party, 229
Liberal Union, The. *See* People's Party
    [1971]
liberalism, 56, 436
liberals, 228, 258, 306, 399
Libertarian League. *See* Anarchist Federation
Libertarian Party, 230
libertarianism, 230, 480
Liberty League. *See* American Liberty
    League
Liberty Lobby, 232
Liberty Party [1839], 233
Liberty Party [1932], 234
Liberty Union. *See* People's Party [1971]
libraries, 44, 45, 325
Lincoln, Abraham, 198, 214, 307, 327, 379,
    449, 450, 470, 471
Lindbergh, Charles A., 10, 11, 173
Lippmann, Walter, 107, 224
Lockwood, Belva A. Bennett, 165
Locofoco Party. *See* Equal Rights
    (Locofoco) Party
Lodge, Henry Cabot (1850-1924), 194, 245,
    334

Lodge, Henry Cabot (1902-    ), 227, 281,
    394, 455
London, Jack, 223
Long, Huey P., 326, 404, 450
Lowenstein, Allard K., 58, 266
Lowndes County Freedom Organization, 235
Lowry, Joseph E., 429
Loyal Democrats of Mississippi, 235
Lucey, Patrick, 229, 290

MacArthur, Douglas, 56, 77
McCarthy, Eugene, 9, 240, 241, 266, 278, 403,
    484
McCarthy, Joseph R., 207, 322, 353, 482
McClellan, George B., 141, 381
McCormick, Ellen, 314
McGovern, George S., 97, 154, 155, 240,
    243, 347, 440, 484
McKinley, William, 248, 373, 385, 386
McKissick, Floyd, 117, 264
McReynolds, David, 420
Maddox, Lester, 35, 95
Madison, James, 157, 171
Mahan, Alfred Thayer, 334
Malcolm X, 340, 341
Marcantonio, Vito, 38, 228
marijuana, 34, 242, 300
Marine Corps League, 237
Marines, U.S., 237
Marshall, Thurgood, 251, 426
Marxism, 424, 467
masonry, 66
mayors, 295, 456
Mayors Conference. *See* United States
    Conference of Mayors
Mexican-American, 5, 6, 220, 238
Mexican-American Political Association, 238
Midwestern Governors Conference, 239
militarism, 52, 105, 415
Mills, C. Wright, 168
Minutemen. *See* Patriotic Party
Mississippi Freedom Democratic Party, 239
Mississippi Valley Association. *See* Water
    Resources Congress
Mobilization Committee to End the War in
    Vietnam, 240
Mondale, Walter, 155, 156, 157, 446
monopoly, 67
Monroe, James, 24, 159, 172
Moral Majority, 241
Morality in Media, 243
Most, Johann, 201

motion pictures. *See* movies
Mott, Lucretia, 30, 330
Movement for a New Congress, **244**
movies, 183, 243
Mugwumps, **245**
Muir, John, 404
Mundt, Karl, 55
Muste, Abraham, 172

Nader, Ralph, 190, 370, 371
Nader's Raiders. *See* Public Interest Research
    Group
Nash, Patrick, 134
National Academy of Sciences, **246**
National Afro-American Council. *See*
    National Afro-American League
National Afro-American League, **247**
National Alliance of Businessmen, **248**
National American Woman Suffrage
    Association, **249**
National Association for the Advancement of
    Colored People, **250**
National Association Knights of the Ku
    Klux Klan. *See* Ku Klux Klan
National Association of Broadcasters, **252**
National Association of Manufacturers, **252**
National Association of Probation Officers.
    *See* National Council on Crime and
    Delinquency
National Association on Indian Affairs. *See*
    Association on American Indian Affairs
National Black Political Assembly, **254**
National Center for Voluntary Action, **255**
National Christian Association, **256**
National Christian Democratic Party, **257**
National Citizens Political Action Committee
    **257**
National Civic Federation, **258**
National Civil Service League, **259**
National Civil Service Reform League. *See*
    National Civil Service League
National Committee for a Sane Nuclear
    Policy, The. *See* SANE: A Citizens'
    Organization for a Sane World
National Committee for an Effective
    Congress, **261**
National Committee for Citizens in Educa-
    tion, **261**
National Committee for Support of the
    Public Schools. *See* National Com-
    mittee for Citizens in Education
National Committee of Inquiry, **262**

National Committee on the Cause and Cure
    of War, **263**
National Committee to Free America from
    Jewish Domination. *See* National
    Socialist White People's Party
National Conference for a New Politics, **263**
National Conference of Alternative State and
    Local Public Policies, **264**
National Conference of Christians and Jews,
    **265**
National Conference of Concerned
    Democrats, **266**
National Conference of State Legislative
    Leaders, **267**
National Conference of State Legislatures,
    **267**
National Congress of Parents and Teachers,
    **268**
National Constitutional Party. *See* Con-
    stitutional Union Party
National Council for Historic Site and
    Buildings. *See* National Trust for
    Historic Preservation
National Council for Industrial Safety. *See*
    National Safety Council
National Council for Prevention of War,
    **270**
National Council for the Limitation of
    Armaments. *See* National Council for
    Prevention of War
National Council of Senior Citizens, **271**
National Council of Senior Citizens for
    Health Care under Social Security. *See*
    National Council of Senior Citizens
National Council of Women of the United
    States, **272**
National Council on Crime and Delinquency,
    **273**
National Democratic Party [1860], **275**
National Democratic Party [1896], **276**
National Democratic Party of Alabama, **277**
National Education Association. *See*
    National Education Association-Political
    Action Committee
National Education Association-Political
    Action Committee, **278**
National Emergency Committee, **281**
National Equal Rights League, **282**
National Farm Women's Forum. *See*
    American Agri-Women
National Farmers Organization, **283**
National Farmers Union, **284**

National Federation of Business and Professional Women's Clubs, **285**
National Federation of Republican Women, **287**
National Federation of the Blind, **287**
National Governors' Conference, **288**
National Grange, **289**
National Greenback-Labor Party. *See* Greenback Party
National (Greenback) Party. *See* Greenback Party
National Gun Control Center, **292**
National Hamiltonian Party, **292**
National Housing Conference, **293**
National Labor Reform Party, **294**
National League of Cities, **295**
National Legislative Conference, **295**
National Liberty Party, **296**
National Municipal League, **296**
National Negro Congress, **298**
National Order of Women Legislators, **299**
National Organization for the Reform of Marijuana Laws, **300**
National Organization for Women, **300**
National Party, **303**
National Planning Association, **303**
National Probation Association. *See* National Council on Crime and Delinquency
National Progressive Republican League, **305**
National Progressives of America, **306**
National Republican Congressional Committee, **307**
National Republican Heritage Groups Council, **308**
National Republican Party, **308**
National Research Council. *See* National Academy of Sciences
National Rifle Association. *See* National Rifle Association of America
National Rifle Association of America, **310**
National Right to Life Committee, **312**
National Right to Work Committee, **314**
National Rivers and Harbors Congress. *See* Water Resources Congress
National Safety Council, **315**
National Security League, **316**
National Silver Party. *See* Silver Republican Party
National Silver Republican Party: *See* Silver Republican Party

National Small Business Association, **317**
National Socialist White People's Party, **318**
National Society of State Legislators, **319**
National Society of the Army of the Philippines. *See* Veterans of Foreign Wars of the United States
National States' Rights Party, **320**
National Student Association, **320**
National Student Lobby, **323**
National Taxpayers Union, **324**
National Teachers' Association, **324**
National Tenants Organization, **324**
National Trust for Historic Preservation, **325**
National Union for Social Justice, **326**
National Union Party, **327**
National Union Republican Party. *See* National Union Party
National Woman Suffrage Association, **328**
National Woman's Christian Temperance Union. *See* Woman's Christian Temperance Union
National Woman's Party, **329**
National Women's Political Caucus, **330**
National Youth Alliance, **331**
Nationalist Party of Puerto Rico. *See* Fuerzas Armádas de Liberacion Nacional Puertorriqueña
Nationalities Division of the Democratic National Committee. *See* All American Council
National-Wide Committee on Import-Export Policy, **332**
Native American Party. *See* Know-Nothing Party
nativists, 48, 194, 214
Navy, U.S., 334
Navy League of the United States, **334**
Naziism, 188, 318, 319, 327
Nazi Party. *See* National Socialist White People's Party
neutrality acts, 11, 149, 163, 210, 263, 270, 336
New American Party. *See* People's Party [1971]
New Deal, 43, 57, 149, 164, 170, 293, 304, 306, 326, 327, 345, 391, 404, 451, 456, 472, 483, 484
New Frontier, 8, 58, 80, 152
New Left, 97, 154, 265, 322, 323, 344, 361, 466, 488

New Nationalism, 362
New Party. *See* People's Party [1971]
New Politics, 97, 106
Newton, Huey P., 74, 224
Niagara Movement, **335**
Niebuhr, Reinhold, 57, 222, 228
Nixon, Richard M., 98, 204, 393-96, 399, 439, 456
No Party. *See* People's Party [1971]
Non-Partisan Committee for Peace through Revision of the Neutrality Act, **336**
Nonpartisan League, **337**
Nonviolent Action against Nuclear Weapons. *See* Committee for Nonviolent Action
Norris, George W., 257, 306
Northern Irish Aid Committee, **338**
nuclear weapons, 184, 402, 463
Nye, Gerald P., 10, 173, 475

O'Hair, Madalyn Murray, 424
Old Age Revolving Pensions, Ltd. *See* Townsend Plan National Lobby
Order of the Star-Spangled Banner. *See* Know-Nothing Party
Order of United Americans. *See* Know-Nothing Party
Organization of Afro-American Unity, **340**
organized labor. *See* labor, organized
Other Americans, Inc. *See* Society of Separationists
outlawry-of-war, 81, 105, 270, 462

Pacifica Foundation. *See* War Resisters League
pacifists, 48, 83, 101, 105, 163, 172, 184, 403, 462, 474, 476, 485
Palmer, A. Mitchell, 259, 415
Palmer, John M., 276
Panama Canal, 103, 119, 447
Paralyzed Veterans of America, **342**
paraplegics, 342
parents, 269
Parker, Alton B., 145, 386
Patriotic Party, **343**
patriotism, 181, 207, 211, 238, 343, 425
Patrons of Husbandry. *See* National Grange
Patton, James G., 257, 285, 304
Paul, Alice, 329, 330
peace, 47, 184, 263
Peace and Freedom Party, **344**
Pelley, William Dudley, 91

Pendergast, James "Jim," 344, 345
Pendergast, Thomas J. "Tom," 345, 346
Pendergast Machine, **344**
People United to Save Humanity, **346**
People's Party [1823], **347**
People's Party [1891]. *See* Populist Party
People's Party [1971], **348**
People's Peace Prosperity Party, **350**
Pershing, John J., 107, 281
physicians, 46
Pierce, Franklin, 140, 178, 470
Pinchot, Gifford, 28, 257
Pinckney, Charles C., 172
planning, 303, 304
police, 175
Polish National Alliance, **350**
Polish-Americans, 350, 351
Political Action Committee, **351**
political machine, 128, 134, 345, 373, 441
Political Rights Defense Fund. *See* Young Socialist Alliance
Polk, James K., 14, 139, 234, 469
Poor Man's Party, **354**
Poor People's Campaign, **354**
Popular Front. *See* Communist Party of the United States of America
Populist Party, **355**
poverty, 164
preservation, 325, 405
*Progress and Poverty*, 406
Progressive Alliance, **357**
Progressive Citizens of America, **358**
Progressive Labor Party, **359**
Progressive Party [1912], **361**
Progressive Party [1924], **363**
Progressive Party [1948], **364**
Progressives, 116, 197, 305, 357, 361, 363, 407, 471, 486
prohibition, 69, 366, 473, 477
Prohibition Party, **366**
*Promise of American Life, The*, 362
Protect America's Children, **370**
protectionism, 332
PTA. *See* National Congress of Parents and Teachers
public administration, 50
Public Citizens, Inc. *See* Public Interest Research Group
public housing, 293
Public Interest Research Group, **370**
public works, 25, 129, 346

Puerto Rico, 184, 185
PUSH. *See* People United to Save Humanity

Quakers, 172, 184, 198
Quay, Matthew Stanley, 373, 374
Quay Machine, **373**

racism, 179, 219, 251, 254, 296, 318, 319,
    321, 335, 428, 432, 437
Radical Republicans, **375**
radicalism, 130, 302, 322, 438
radicals, 179, 264, 306, 344, 348, 455, 466
radio, 88, 221, 252, 308, 389, 463
Randolph, A. Philip. 298
Randolph, John, 24
Rascob, John Jacob, 43, 70
Reagan, Ronald, 26, 102, 243, 395, 397, 400,
    480, 481
Referendum '70, **376**
Reno, Milo, 170, 285
Republican Congressional Committee. *See*
    National Republican Congressional
    Committee
Republican Governors Association, **377**
Republican National Committee, **377**
Republican Party, **378**
Republicans. *See* Republican Party
Republicans for Progress, **398**
Resurgence Youth Movement. *See* Anarchist
    Federation
Reuther, Walter, 57, 224, 303, 437
Revolutionary Youth Movement. *See*
    Students for a Democratic Society
Ribicoff, Abraham A., 56, 104
rifle, 310, 311
right to life, 312, 313
Right to Life Committee. *See* National Right
    to Life Committee
Right to Work Committee. *See* National
    Right to Life Committee
right-to-work laws, 314, 317
Ripon Society, **399**
rivers, 463, 464
Rockefeller, David, 127, 446
Rockefeller, Nelson A., 26, 120, 394, 395,
    400
Rockwell, George Lincoln, 318, 319
Roman Catholic. *See* Catholicism
Romney, George, 255
Roosevelt, Eleanor (Mrs. Franklin D.), 57,
    224, 403, 454

Roosevelt, Franklin D., 149, 150, 173, 196
    206, 210, 228, 247, 257, 282, 293, 304,
    306, 334, 336, 345, 351, 352, 404, 430,
    451, 456, 462, 472, 477, 483, 485
Roosevelt, Franklin D., Jr., 57, 103, 121
Roosevelt, Theodore, 28, 195, 227, 245, 288,
    297, 316, 361, 373, 386, 463
Roosevelt, Theodore, Jr., 41
Roper, Daniel C., 317
Rowe, H. Edward, 89
Rural American Women, Inc., **400**
rural life, 12, 28

Sabin, Pauline Morton, 476, 477
safety, 315, 316
St. John, John Pierce, 303, 368
saloon, 67
SALT. *See* Strategic Arms Limitation Treaty
SANE: A Citizens' Organization for a
    Sane World, **402**
sanitary engineers. *See* engineers, sanitary
Save Our Children. *See* Protect America's
    Children
Schlafly, Phyllis, 26
Schlesinger, Arthur M., Jr., 57, 103, 133
Schurz, Carl, 229, 245, 259
scientists, 246
Scott, Winfield, 178, 470
Seale, Bobby, 74
Sebastian, Eric, 292, 293
sectionalism, 123
segregation, racial, 32, 92, 213, 217, 248,
    251, 335, 427, 431, 432, 433, 436
senior citizens, 16, 189, 201, 271
Senior Citizens. *See* National Council of
    Senior Citizens
Seward, William H., 379, 468, 470
sexism, 301, 322, 331
Seymour, Horatio, 141, 328, 382
Share Our Wealth Movement, **404**
Shotwell, James T., 81
Sierra Club, **404**
Silver Republican Party, **406**
Silver Republicans. *See* Silver Republican
    Party
Silver Shirts. *See* Christian Party
Simmons, William Joseph, 217
Sinclair, Upton, 164, 223, 414
Single Tax Clubs. *See* Single Tax Movement
Single Tax Movement, **406**
slavery, 13, 14, 226, 234, 275, 379

Smith, Alfred E. "Al," 44, 147, 148, 217, 442
Smith, Gerald L. K., 90, 450, 451
smoking, 3, 4
Social Democracy of America. *See* Social Democratic Party of America
Social Democratic Federation, **407**
Social Democratic Party of America, **408**
Social Democratic Workingmen's Party. *See* Socialist Labor Party
*Social Justice*, 326, 327
Social security, 190, 271, 444
socialism, 205, 223, 348, 466, 484, 487
Socialist Labor Party, **408**
Socialist Party of America, **413**
Socialist Party-Democratic Socialist Federation. *See* Socialist Party of America
Socialists Workers Party, **421**
socialists, 222, 223, 234, 298, 337, 407, 471, 484, 487
Society for the Prevention of Cruelty to Animals. *See* American Society for the Prevention of Cruelty to Animals
Society of Christian Socialists, **424**
Society of Friends. *See* Quakers
Society of Saint Tammany. *See* Tammany Hall
Society of Separationists, **424**
Society of Tammany. *See* Tammany Hall
Sons of Liberty, **425**
Sound Money Democrats. *See* National Democratic Party
South Carolina Colored Democratic Party. *See* South Carolina Progressive Democratic Party
South Carolina Progressive Democratic Party, **426**
Southeastern Governors' Conference. *See* Southern Governors' Conference
Southern Christian Leadership Conference, **427**
Southern Governors' Conference, **430**
Southern Regional Council, **431**
Spock, Benjamin M., 264, 348, 402, 420
spoils system, 5, 245, 259, 309, 383
Staley, Oren Lee, 283
Stanton, Elizabeth Cady, 249, 272, 328
state: government, 125; legislators, 267, 295, 299, 319; legislature, 93, 267, 305, 320, 452

states' rights, 95, 121, 432, 433, 434
States' Rights Party, **432**
Statesman Party. *See* Prohibition Party
Stayton, William H., 69, 70
Steffens, Lincoln, 179
Steinem, Gloria, 330, 376, 476
Stevens, Thaddeus, 282, 307, 375
Stevenson, Adlai E., 143, 144
Stevenson, Adlai E., II, 57, 106, 133, 151, 152, 221, 353, 454
Stevenson, Adlai E., III, 93, 244
Stone, Lucy, 54, 249, 272
Straight-Out Democratic Party, **434**
Strategic Arms Limitation Treaty (SALT), 50, 156, 242, 403
Streeter, Alson J., 448
Student Committee for the Loyalty Oath. *See* Young Americans for Freedom
Student Coordinating Committee. *See* Student Nonviolent Coordinating Committee
Student League for Industrial Democracy. *See* Students for a Democratic Society
Student Nonviolent Coordinating Committee, **434**
student, 321, 323, 360, 436, 455
Students for a Democratic Society, **436**
Sumner, Charles, 229, 282, 375
Support Your Local Police Committee. *See* John Birch Society
Supreme Court, U.S., 218, 289, 424, 426, 430, 433, 460

Taft, Charles P., 398
Taft, Robert A., 353, 393
Taft, William Howard, 195, 227, 386, 387
Taft-Hartley Act, 107, 221, 314, 353
Tammy Hall, **441**
tariff, 332, 445
Taylor, Glen, 197, 364
Taylor, Zachary, 469, 470
Tax Cut Party, **442**
taxpayers, 324, 442
teachers, 268, 269, 278
television, 88, 183, 190, 221, 252, 308, 443
Television Broadcasters Association. *See* National Association of Broadcasters
Teller, Henry Moore, 21, 385, 406
temperance, 68, 366, 472
tenants, 324, 325

terrorism, 63, 185, 439, 440, 456, 466, 479
Theocratic Party, **443**
Thomas, Norman, 172, 210, 222, 224, 306, 403, 407, 416, 418, 419, 484, 485
Thurmond, J. Strom, 104, 151, 427, 433
Tijerina, Reis López, 5, 6
Tilden, Samual J., 142, 382
Tower, John G., 56, 207
Townley, Arthur C., 337
Townsend, Francis E., 443, 450
Townsend Clubs. *See* Townsend Plan National Lobby
Townsend Clubs of America. *See* Townsend Plan National Lobby
Townsend National Insurance Plan, Inc. *See* Townsend Plan National Lobby
Townsend National Recovery Plan, Inc. *See* Townsend Plan National Lobby
Townsend Plan. *See* Townsend Plan National Lobby
Townsend Plan, Inc. *See* Townsend Plan National Lobby
Townsend Plan National Lobby, **443**
tractorcade, 12
Tracy, Benjamin F., 334
trade, 445, 446
Trade Relations Council of the United States, **445**
Trevellick, Richard, 294
Trilateral Commission, The, **446**
Trotskyites, 417, 421, 487
Truman, Harry S., 141, 228, 261, 293, 345, 353, 359, 430, 432, 431, 455, 462, 483, 489
Tweed, William Marcy "Boss," 441
Tweed Ring. *See* Tammany Hall
Tyler, John, 468, 469

Union Labor Party, **448**
Union League, **449**
Union Party, **450**
United Citizen's Party, **451**
United Communist Party. *See* Communist Party of the United States of America
United Farmers Educational League, **452**
United Klans of American Knights of the Ku Klux Klan. *See* Ku Klux Klan
United Labor Party, **453**
United Nations (UN), 454, 479, 489
United Nations Association of the United States of America, **454**

United States Committee for the United Nations. *See* United Nations Association of the United States of America
United States Committee to Aid the National Liberation Front of South Vietnam, **455**
United States Conference of Mayors, **456**
United States National Student Association. *See* National Student Association
Universal Negro Improvement Association, **457**
Universal Party, **458**
Urban Coalition Action Council of New York. *See* Common Cause
urban-renewal, 200

Vallandigham, Clement L., 212
Van Buren, Martin, 4, 138, 165, 178
vegetarianism, 53
veterans, 37, 41, 54, 61, 76, 82, 161, 188, 237, 248, 342
Veterans of Foreign Wars of the United States, **459**
VFW. *See* Veterans of Foreign Wars of the United States
Vietcong, 455, 456, 466
Vietnam War, 37, 204, 241, 244, 261, 266, 323, 344, 348, 355, 349, 376, 403, 435, 455, 459, 466, 475, 483, 487
Villard, Oswald Garrison, 22, 210, 222, 250
volunteerism, 255, 301, 372
Voter Education Project, **460**

Wadsworth, James W., 227, 281
Wadsworth, James W., Jr., 44, 402
Wallace, George C., 32, 278, 321, 331
Wallace Henry, 29
Wallace, Henry A., 29, 38, 113, 150, 151, 197, 228, 322, 358, 364, 421, 486
Wallace, Henry C., 29, 30
Warren, Earl, 206, 392, 455
War Resisters League, **462**
Washington, Booker T., 334
Washington, George, 157, 171
Water resources, 463, 467
Water Resources Association. *See* Water Resources Congress
Water Resources Congress, **463**
Watergate, 396, 477
Waters, Walter E., 76
waterways, navigable, 463
Watson, Thomas E. "Tom," 356, 357

Wattenberg, Ben, 97
Weather Underground. *See* Weatherman
Weatherman, **464**
Weatherpeople. *See* Weatherman
Weaver, James G., 143, 191, 355
W. E. B. Du Bois Clubs of America, **466**
Weed, Thurlow, 66, 468
Welch, Robert H., Jr., 206, 207
Western Governors' Conference, **467**
Wheeler, Burton K., 10, 116, 363, 416
Whig Party, **468**
White, Walter F., 251
White, William Allen, 107, 336
White Citizens Councils. *See* Citizens'
    Councils of America
white supremacy, 216, 296, 320
Wilkins, Roy, 251, 435
Willard, Frances E., 272, 472
William Allen White Committee. *See* Com-
    mittee to Defend America by Aiding the
    Allies
Willkie, Wendell L., 391, 392
Wilson, Woodrow, 146, 147, 195, 247, 249,
    297, 329, 351
Wisconsin Progressive Party, **471**
Wobblies. *See* Anarchist Federation
woman suffrage, 54, 165, 226, 249, 272, 305,
    328, 329
Woman's Christian Temperance Union, **472**
Woman's Peace Party, **473**
women: Democratic Club, 476; legislators,
    299; political party, 329; prohibitionists,
    477; rural, 400; university, 17
Women's International League for Peace and
    Freedom, **474**
Women's Militia. *See* Weatherman
Women's National Democratic Club, **476**

Women's National Republican Club, **476**
Women's Organization for National
    Prohibition Reform, **477**
Wood, Leonard, 316
Wood, Robert E., 10, 101
Woodhull, Victoria Claffin, 165
workers, 190, 206, 322, 360
Workers (Communist) Party of America.
    *See* Communist Party of the United
    States of America
Workers Party of America. *See* Communist
    Party of the United States of America
Workingmen's Party, **478**
World Federalists, **479**
World War I, 263, 334, 338, 350, 387, 462,
    474, 475
World War II, 263, 289, 304, 351, 475
Wright, Fielding, 433

Yancy, William Lowndes, 226
Young, Andrew, 292, 376, 446
Young Americans for Freedom, **480**
Young Communist League, **481**
Young Democratic Clubs of America. *See*
    Young Democrats of America
Young Democrats of America, **483**
Young People's Socialist League, **484**
Young Progressives of America, **486**
Young Republican National Federation, **486**
Young Socialist Alliance, **487**
YRers. *See* Young Republican National
    Federation

Ziedler, Frank P., 420
zionism, 203, 205, 489
Zionist Organization of America, **489**
Zumwalt, Elmo R., 58, 97, 103

## ABOUT THE AUTHORS

EDWARD L. SCHAPSMEIER is Professor of History at Illinois State University in Normal, Illinois.

FREDERICK H. SCHAPSMEIER is John McN Rosebush University Professor of History at the University of Wisconsin in Oshkosh. Together the Schapsmeiers have written such books as *Henry A. Wallace of Iowa* (chosen recently for inclusion in the new library of the Vice President's House), *Walter Lippmann: Philosopher Journalist*, and the *Encyclopedia of American Agricultural History* (Greenwood Press, 1975).